Architecture
in Uniform

Jean-Louis Cohen

Architecture in Uniform

Designing and Building for the Second World War

CCΛ

Canadian Centre for Architecture

Distributed by Yale University Press, New Haven and London

Contents

Foreword
Mirko Zardini

Greater production is the key to prosperity and peace. And the key to greater production is a wider and more vigorous application of modern scientific and technical knowledge.
Harry S. Truman, inaugural address, 20 January 1949

Harry S. Truman's inaugural address, in 1949, prefaced one of the twentieth century's major transformations: the world's shift from a system of production to an infinite system of global consumption. As Truman foresaw, after half a century of wars, the world was ready to be 'liberated' through the production – and implicit consumption – of 'more food, more clothing, more materials for housing and more mechanical power'.[1] Modern society, exemplified first and foremost by the middle-class consumer, was clearly grounded on ideas sponsored by post-war goods and their manufacturers. Simultaneously and without opposition, modern architecture followed the manufacturing industry's switchover from provisioning, producing and distributing the means of warfare to offering peace-time commodities. Truman's campaign for progress and scientific and technical knowledge captivated the public's attention and pocketbooks, while shifting their aesthetic sensibilities to fully engage in the upcoming 'good life'.

But architecture's prominent role in the post-war reconstruction owes much to the active and exceptional tasks it fulfilled during the war years. In fact, as Jean-Louis Cohen clearly explains in his introductory text to this catalogue, the competence of architects during the conflict 'proved to be as strategically indispensable as did the scientists and engineers'. The two clashing visions of the belligerents, those of the Axis and the Allies, managed to redefine architecture, 'whose primary methods were to be employed to new ends'. These 'new ends', significantly supported by architects'

technological knowledge and their cooperation with overall military efforts, bear great responsibility for the destruction and annihilation that took place during the war. On the one hand, the Axis quest for subordination and occupation was translated into urban renovations and projects that 'traced out the outlines of a future based on oppression and sometimes extermination'. On the other hand, the apparent 'reconstruction' efforts by the Allies were actually 'part of a process of modernisation intended to be both technological and social'.[2]

Architects and designers, like most citizens of warring nations, 'did not escape mobilisation and conscription to the fighting forces or to the direct support of the war;' in Cohen's view, 'even in uniform, they did not interrupt their own thinking processes'. This militarised organisation of society forced the design fields to address the emergence of new 'forms of conflict', including new territories, new construction methods and new materials – all yet to be designed.[3]

Architecture's 'new' tasks were driven by economy and imagination. The development of new technologies and materials forced designers not only to 'design' the objects, but also to 'design' the manufacturing processes and construction methods that would bring them to life. As Cohen's texts illustrate, laminated wood, plywood, aluminium, plastics, reinforced concrete, Plexiglas, vinyl, new types of rubber, along with every other innovation of this period, can be considered the 'best residuum of wars'.[4]

'Architecture in Uniform: Designing and Building for the Second World War' is part of a continuing effort of the Canadian Centre for Architecture to critically investigate the premises that lie at the heart of contemporary life, culture, society and architecture. Through the production of thematic research, exhibitions, books and digital means, we have set out to question the assumptions on which design fields operate today and investigate the fundamental relationship they have with the natural and built environment. The thorough study of these themes has expanded our field of vision and supports our effort to work within the usually neglected 'grey zones' of our discipline. Ideas on perception, energy, activism, ecology, time, the future and cultures have all found their way into the CCA's exhibitions 'Sense of the City' (2005–2006), '1973: Sorry, Out of Gas' (2007–2008), 'Actions: What You Can Do With the City' (2008–2009), 'Speed Limits' (2009) and 'Journeys: How travelling fruit, ideas and buildings rearrange our environment' (2010–2011). On this occasion, 'Architecture in Uniform' draws on the curatorial proficiency of Jean-Louis Cohen to investigate the consequences of the Second World War on the built environment and to unveil the immense development and responsibility that architecture carried during these years.

Today, wars have taken on a new form. They are more difficult to describe or predict in terms of a specific space or time frame. As a result, we have slowly moved towards a culture of control and subtle militarisation. Terrorism – a phenomenon that amplifies and accelerates this process – happens anytime and anywhere. New obsessions with intimidation and inspection trigger the development of new technologies, laws and mechanisms that slowly make their way into civilian life and public spaces. Surveillance and video equipment, security checkpoints, material tests and restrictions, prevention protocols and heavily armed security guards now adorn our city streets, building lobbies, airports, train and bus stations – even our homes. Unlike that of the Second World War, the current so-called adversary 'is not a territorial state or nation or government. There is no opposite number to negotiate with. There is no one on the other side to call a truce or declare a cease fire, no one among the enemy authorized to surrender.'[5] Today, sixty years after Truman's speech, his convictions resonate with astonishing appropriateness: 'If we can make it sufficiently clear, in advance, that any armed attack affecting our national security would be met with overwhelming force, the armed attack might never occur.'[6] Space, regardless of geography, has the latent possibility of becoming a war zone.

Since 2004, nearly forty-five wars have been fought and twelve are still taking place, mostly in countries in Africa and the Middle East.[7]

Contemporary environments are still largely governed, despite global efforts, by war and violent conflict. Whether low-tech or high-tech, warfare continuously redefines the conception and production of space and the way it is inhabited – and architecture remains partly responsible for the reconstruction ahead as well as the destruction behind.

1. Harry S. Truman, inaugural address, 20 January 1949, in *My Fellow Americans: Presidential Inaugural Addresses, from George Washington to Barack Obama* (Florida: Red and Black, 2009), 296.
2. See 'The Interplay of Institutions' and 'Troubled Futures', chapter 1.
3. See 'Professions and States' and 'Figures and Forms', chapter 1.
4. Richard Neutra's expression as quoted by Jean-Louis Cohen in 'Recycling, Recalling, Forgetting', chapter 12.
5. David Luban, 'The War on Terrorism and the End of Human Rights', in Larry May, Eric Rovie and Steve Viner, *The Morality of War: Classical and Contemporary Readings* (New Jersey: Pearson, 2006), 419.
6. Harry S. Truman, inaugural address, 20 January 1949, in op. cit. note 1, 296.
7. See article and illustrations in *L'Atlas Histoire: Histoire critique du XX siècle* (Paris: Le Monde diplomatique, 2010), 12–13.

Preface
Jean-Louis Cohen

Some books are born out of a flash of inspiration. Others take shape gradually and ineluctably over the years, to the point where they seem obvious. The unfolding of this book belongs to the latter category. If its writing required justification, I could enlist unimpeachable academic arguments in its support, such as the need to compensate for the omission of what remains the most deadly and extensive conflict in human history from most histories of architecture. And yet one of the reasons that led me to examine the years of the Second World War cannot remain unacknowledged: I was born in Paris four years after the surrender of Japan. My childhood was experienced in the shadow of a still recent conflict, to such an extent that the *maquisards* of the Resistance and the SS took the place of cowboys and Indians in the playground of my school in Paris.

More than three decades were to pass, during which I became an architect and historian, before I returned to these events, in response to several of those commissions for a piece of writing that, as Roland Barthes so clearly demonstrated, can sometimes serve a liberating role, forcing one into an excursus from otherwise working according to plan, and sometimes opening the way to new and extensive projects. In 1985, I was asked to contribute to a collection of essays edited by Hartmut Frank on fascist architecture in Europe, for which I wrote a brief study of 'French architectural culture between authoritarianism and technocracy' during the four years of the Vichy regime. Ten years later, in 1995, responding to François Bédarida's invitation, my piece on the architecture of the concentration camps was published in conjunction with an exhibition at the Musée d'Histoire Contemporaine de Paris

on deportation and the system of the Nazi camps. My contribution to a conference entitled 'Tra guerra e pace', organised in Turin in 1997 by the young scholars of the Politecnico around Carlo Olmo, provided me with the opportunity for a first attempt at setting up the analytic framework of this volume. It was then that I began to be amazed at the number of scholarly projects that were focusing on the years after 1945 in North America and Europe, while the war years remained in general obscurity and were mostly examined only in terms of the reconstruction programmes.

In the interim, a number of long-term projects had led me to consider some of the episodes that unfolded between 1939 and 1945 from different angles. I had been interested in André Lurçat, devoting both my doctoral thesis and a subsequent book to the twists and turns of this architect's career. My accounts of his activity in the Vichy reconstruction, which was followed by an interior exile that he would break by joining the Resistance, led me to become interested in the experiences of other architects during those dark years. In the course of a study in collaboration with André Lortie on the transformations of the former fortified ring around Paris, we later became aware of the extent to which these had been accelerated by the changes in ownership and morphology of plots in that zone as a result of measures taken during the occupation. This provided a first intuitive sense of the importance of these years for changes in territories, even those far from the fronts. More extensive studies, some in fact so lengthy as to not be completed to date, included research conducted between 1986 and 1989 with Hartmut Frank on the architecture of German and French occupations, which confirmed the importance of several lines of enquiry pursued below.

Finally, I cannot pass over that fact that another source for this venture can be traced back to the École Spéciale d'Architecture, when it was self-managed by its students in the aftermath of the upheavals of May and June 1968, which had led to the removal of its administration. Paul Virilio's seminars at that time, along with the publication of his first articles on the Atlantic Wall in *Architecture Principe*, came as a shock to me, for they proposed to raise the bunkers and military buildings of Nazi Germany, which I considered to be utterly excluded from the field of architecture, into objects of technical and aesthetic analysis.

But the specific origin of the present work and the accompanying exhibition is to be found in the conversations that started in 1995 with Nicholas Olsberg, who was at that time the chief curator of the Canadian Centre for Architecture, and which would lead by 1996 to a first and as yet unfocused project for an exhibition. Since that date, I have pursued research in North American and European archives, including materials in Russia, as well as in the field, through visits to sites and buildings. My own research has been extended through collaborative work with several groups of students in conjunction with a series of graduate seminars. The first of these was conducted in the spring semester of 2005 at the Institute of Fine Arts of New York University, my home port in the academic world since 1993; the second, in the spring semester of 2008, at Princeton University's School of Architecture; and the third in the spring trimester of 2009, at the Department of Architecture and Urban Design at the University of California, Los Angeles. These were followed by a brief course given at the faculty of planning and development at the Université de Montréal in the autumn semester of 2009. These seminars, together with contacts made in Europe, led to two scholarly conferences:

'Front to Rear', in New York, in March 2009, under the auspices of the Institute of Fine Arts and Princeton University, with the participation of the CCA, and made possible by the energetic assistance of Anna Jozefacka and Susan Schafer; and 'War Perspectives' at the Politecnico in Milan in January 2010, organised by Patrizia Bonifazio. Over the course of these two events, a dialogue between student research and contributions by scholars operating in an essentially new field of investigation was set in motion. Some of these are cited in the chapters of this work, and all the participants and students from the four seminars are listed at the end of the book.

The following analyses, assembled on the occasion of the exhibition held by the Canadian Centre for Architecture in the spring of 2011, were developed in part through dialogue with European and North American colleagues and students. In their initial form, these observations and interpretations seem already to have given rise to numerous undertakings, whose further development is being pursued through thesis work or various personal projects, ranging in scale from the essay to the book. In their current provisional form, the analyses presented here remain in many ways the product of a collective enterprise that is sure to find other outlets.

1/ Overture: The Test of War

I had participated in a war which, as we of the intimate circle should never have doubted, was aimed at world dominion. What is more, by my abilities and my energies I had prolonged that war by many months. I had assented to having the globe of the world crown that domed hall which was to be the symbol of new Berlin. Nor was it only symbolically that Hitler dreamed of possessing the globe. It was part of his dream to subjugate the other nations. France, I had heard him say many times, was to be reduced to the status of a small nation. Belgium, Holland, even Burgundy, were to be incorporated into his Reich. The national life of the Poles and the Soviet Russians was to be extinguished; they were to be made into helot peoples. Nor, for one who wanted to listen, had Hitler ever concealed his intention to exterminate the Jewish people. [. . .] Although I never actually agreed with Hitler on these questions, I had nevertheless designed the buildings and produced the weapons which served his ends.
Albert Speer, *Inside the Third Reich*, 1970[1]

It was indeed no accident that one of the war criminals judged at Nuremberg in 1945 was an architect. And the fact that he too, along with the judges, the lawyers and the spectators, was accommodated on seating designed by Dan Kiley, who would later become the most influential landscape architect in post-war America, was no

From left to right and top to bottom:
Albert Speer at the Nuremberg trial, 1945. Office of the United States Chief of Counsel, courtesy of the Harry S. Truman Library and Museum **Myron Goldsmith** in US Army uniform, c. 1944. Photograph by Naiman's Studio

Myron Goldsmith fonds, CCA Collection **Dan Kiley** in the uniform of the US Army Corps of Engineers, 1943. Frances Loeb Library, Harvard Graduate School of Design **Bruno Zevi** in the uniform of the British Army, 1944, in *Tutto Zevi*, 1934–2000, 2001 CCA Collection.

accident either. Bookended between these two figures – one a successful professional who had become a man of state, the other a young professional drafted into the secret service – were tens of thousands of cases in which architecture and architects were caught up in the war. For six years architecture was *put to the test*, so to speak, by this war, with its ideals, its procedures, its fundamental structures called into question. It was both actively drawn on, becoming a protagonist, and passively mobilised. There is in truth nothing new about the relationship between architecture and armed conflict. We have only to recall that Vitruvius was a military engineer who was part of Augustus' legions. But something else altogether was at stake at this particular time in the history of architecture, which prior to 1939 had been characterised by an interaction between the languages of modernity and the social transformations resulting from modernisation.

With the 'total' mobilisation, to borrow the term used by the warrior/writer Ernst Jünger in his 1930 analysis of the 'rational structure and mercilessness' of the First World War, 'there is no longer any movement whatsoever – be it that of the homeworker at her sewing machine – without at least indirect use for the battlefield.'[2] The tensions internal to practices and professions became visibly evident, and it would be a simple thing for Paul Virilio to extend this idea one step further and invoke the 'machine of social mobilisation', to claim in turn that: 'Everything is mobilised; not only men at work or at war, in every enterprise, but also, I would say, the very dynamic of their relations, the very dynamic of communication.'[3]

A Blank Space in Historical Accounts

My involvement in this set of questions is not merely the result of a kind of scopic pulsion stemming from my childhood,[4] for my desire to undertake this research arose from my profound frustration with histories of twentieth-century architecture.[5] Without exception, they all omit the war years, or consider them only in the light of the reconstruction of destroyed cities, as Anthony Vidler has correctly pointed out.[6] Nonetheless, there has been research on these subjects, and numerous studies have been devoted to biographical issues, such as Le Corbusier's extended sojourn in Vichy, or to specific urban situations, such as Warsaw and Dresden – to mention only two examples – or to the various modalities of professional life, such as those of Soviet architects. Even before his memorable presentation of Bunker Archaeology from 1975, Paul Virilio's entire work has been framed by a repeatedly reworked interpretation of the experiences of war. More recently, when most attention seemed to focus on post-war developments, a new generation of scholars, freed from any personal involvement in the events, has undertaken unprecedented investigations, ones that have sometimes been more limited, but have also been more methodical.[7] Since that time, there

have been numerous scholarly meetings to address the intersections of different disciplines in relation to the London Blitz, the construction of the Atlantic Wall, even the Nazi policies for the protection of artworks.

How should one define the *chronotope*, or rather the *chronotopes*, of the Second World War, if one deems this concept put forward by Mikhail Bakhtin to be relevant here?[8] To limit oneself to the narrow period of the conflict itself, from the invasion of Poland to the surrender of Japan, would not enable one to grasp the conditions during the preparations for war, or to take into account those experimental field conditions constituted by the wars of Ethiopia and Spain, the Japanese invasions of Manchuria and China, or the unprecedented migrations that followed them. Furthermore, historians today seem to hold the view that there was simply one long conflict from 1914 to 1945. This is the underlying thesis of Niall Ferguson in *The War of the World* and of Andrea Graziosi in *Guerra e rivoluzione in Europa*.[9] We will encounter many examples of this sort of continuity between human engagement and programmatic definitions in the sectoral politics studied below.

In geographical terms, even more than the First World War, the Second had a global dimension. Whilst many territorial areas remained outside the combat zones themselves, no continent escaped the conditions of the war altogether, not even South America. It was during the war that Brazil under Getúlio Vargas started up steelworks in Volta Redonda, in order to contribute to the Allied effort and began producing airplane engines in the Cidade dos Motores, a new town located in the state of Rio. The European colonies, protectorates and dominions were pressed into service, as well: the industrialisation of India, whose textile manufacturers would clothe the British forces and where aircraft manufacture started up, and the creation at the same time of the first airplane factories in South Africa, were a direct result of their inclusion into the British military production system. Canadian industry experienced a growth similar to that of its larger neighbour to the south. But the geography of nations and states was hardly a stable condition. From annexations to occupations, from temporary partitions to the erection of permanent borders resulting from those divisions and the creation of new nations after 1945, political boundaries were ceaselessly changing until the Yalta agreements finally settled them. These constant changes affected the warn-torn territories, with the creation of the Free Zone in France, for example, after the armistice of 1940, and the formation of the Republic of Salò in Italy after 1943.

Professions and States

Like the other citizens of the warring nations, the architects, landscape architects, engineers and designers discussed in this volume did not escape mobilisation and conscription to the fighting forces or to the direct support of the war. But even in uniform, they did not interrupt their own thinking processes. They observed the front and the territories they covered in their campaigns with their own codes, leaving us sketches and notebooks that are as informative as they are moving. Yet the architectural experience of the war was not merely a sum of individual

ones. It affected broad forms of human association, whole generations, professions and local communities.

Even more than the former conflict, the Second World War was made possible only through the militarised organisation of the entire society, at the cost of the extreme bureaucratisation that resulted from the many forms of state intervention. State control was required at every level of production and distribution, as the industrialist Walther Rathenau had fully realised in 1914–1918, as he moved on from the directorship of AEG to the management of the entire German war effort.[10]

The historian and political scientist Élie Halévy saw here the beginnings of the 'age of tyrannies', which he defined as '(1) In the economic sphere, the nationalisation, on a vast scale, of all the means of production, distribution and exchange; . . . (2) In the intellectual sphere, the "nationalisation of ideas" in two different forms, one negative, that is to say the suppression of all expressions of opinion that were thought to be opposed to the national interest, and the other positive. I shall call the positive aspect "the organisation of enthusiasm".'[11]

All of the belligerent powers set up national systems for the importing, the provisioning, and the distribution of raw materials, for the production of metals, of fuel, and of mechanical parts such as ball bearings, and of course, for the production of arms and equipment. Coming on top of the systematic changes that had been made between 1914 and 1918, an important threshold was everywhere crossed in the organisation of industry, transformed even as far afield as Japan by a second wave of Taylorism.[12]

Figures and Forms

Sustained by industrial economies whose power continued to increase despite all the bombardments, the war was measured in numbers: thousand of kilometres of fortifications and strategic roads, tons of steel and explosives, millions of men and women in uniform, populations driven from their homes or held in camps, not to mention the obscene and unimaginable numbers of victims of combat, bombardment or extermination programmes. In its numerical forms, the war came to occupy the visual realm and the field of representation. Aerial observation and radar multiplied the capacities of the belligerents to see, practically in real time, the movements of their adversaries, and to gauge the effects of their actions, to associate, as Paul Virilio puts it, 'transparency, ubiquity, [and] total and instantaneous knowledge'.[13] The photographic record of every episode was fed into gigantic archives, while the creation of consensus and production of propaganda consumed posters, illustrations and films.

   This tendency towards uniformity corresponded to Lewis Mumford's vision of warfare as the 'hygiene of the state'.[14] But it was also a conflict of forms: territories, constructions and naval, aerial and land equipment were all *designed* – into shapes that combined criteria that were universally valid for anything mechanical, ballistic, aerodynamic or optical, into particular concepts and interpretations that also resulted from firmly held aesthetic positions. It would be too simplistic to immediately define national 'styles' in this matter, to explain the differences between the angular stabilisers of the Messerschmitt Bf 109

fighter plane, as opposed to its rival, the Supermarine Spitfire, or the boxy form of the Willys Jeep in relation to the more tapered curves of the Kübelwagen, the military version of the Volkswagen. The clear contrasts between the fluid fortifications of the Maginot Line and the prismatic bunkers of the Atlantic Wall are doubtlessly better explained by looking to the kinds of combat that their designs anticipated rather than some Germanic predilection for sharp silhouettes as opposed to a French sense of flush contours.

The Interplay of Institutions

A temporary configuration of institutions was set in place. They actively reflected upon their function, at least in the democracies such as Great Britain and the United States. Normal education and training courses were interrupted in most of the belligerent nations, and schools were sometimes evacuated – as in the case of the Architectural Association in London, which was relocated to Hadley Common in 1939, and the École des Beaux-Arts in Paris, which was pulled back to Marseille. The pedagogy developed under these conditions led to a redefinition of architecture, whose primary methods were to be employed to new ends.

   Other institutions such as journals were also brought into play. As both indicators and active agents, they were suspended, reconfigured or mobilised, and they became important sources of information – especially in countries where the administration of the economy did not put an end to the workings of the market, as in the United States, in Great Britain and, to a lesser extent, in Italy. They also played a role in the recruitment of architects to the war effort. For example, in the days immediately following Pearl Harbor, the publisher of *Pencil Points* proposed to create a special office in Washington whose purpose would be to find ways of putting architects to work.[15] But publications were also subject to censorship, which somewhat limited them as sources of information. Their opportunism could be amusing, as for example when Hadrian's Wall was presented to readers of *The Architectural Review*, in January 1940, as 'the Maginot Line of the second century AD', even as the *Review* for many months ostensibly took no account of the war.[16]

Institutions also needed to reconsider their policies in terms of gender. Although dominated by men, they had no choice but to significantly open up to women. A distinctive feature of the times was the mobilisation of women to the front, where they did more than drive ambulances – in Russia they flew combat aircraft – as well as on the home front, where they worked in factories and occupied administrative positions. No longer restricted to family life and the home, women thus enjoyed a certain form of emancipation and cosmopolitanism. These changes affected architecture as well, through the promotion of women to positions in firms that were now left vacant by men, leading to new projects for post-war housing that addressed the requirements of newly demobilised but permanently transformed women.

A Narrative of Themes and Geographies

This account is not chronological in structure, even though the conflict can be broken up into distinct stages: the preparatory episodes, the 'Phoney War' of 1939–1940, the French campaign and the Battle of Britain from May to the end of 1940, the invasion of Russia and the raid on Pearl Harbor in 1941, the opening of a second front in Africa then in Italy in 1942–1943, the Battle of Stalingrad, the Normandy landings, and the allied invasion of Europe in 1944, the conquest of Berlin, and finally the victory in the Pacific in 1945. This study is deliberately thematic and comparative, even though it necessarily includes diachronic moments that connect episodes in question to both their antecedents and to subsequent developments after the war. To employ an architectural metaphor, the discourse is structured more as a series of cross-sections through the various theatres of the war than a longitudinal section through its main sequences.

These cross-sections shed light on the policies undertaken in parallel by the belligerents, such as the fortification of territories, anti-aircraft defences, and the transformation of the infrastructures of production. These programmes were planned for specific locations and created a kind of leopard-skin pattern of intense areas of direct or indirect impact from the war. Most importantly, these endeavours were marked by the presence of men and women whose experiences constitute the true framework of the account. It was obviously impossible to treat every territory affected by the war in one way or another in a strictly homologous manner, according to some principle that would have been both encyclopaedic and egalitarian. So the focus of the book jumps from one significant place to another in keeping with the intensity of the military, industrial or architectural events that took place there – from Los Angeles to London, from Auschwitz to Moscow, places that were made accessible to my work by the existence of historical material and useful interpretations. The case of Japan remains a special one, less because of the lack of archival material, even though most of it was destroyed or is difficult to access, but more because of my own ignorance of the language of the archipelago.

So the glimpses that follow are constructed around *theatres*, to use a metaphor often employed in strategic thinking, in which one theme or another reveals itself as particularly worthy of notice in some specific moment of the war. Some of them may seem to loom too large; others are seen from some distance. The importance of each of the various situations under examination is not proportional to the amount of text devoted to it. The analysis does not claim to provide a homogenous description, and the picture that it produces is more like a mosaic than a fresco, or even like some anamorphosis of the various situations whose assemblage makes up this fragment of history, a deformed reflection whose meanings take on more sense as one adopts some particular point of view – in this case the outlook of a professional culture that was first mobilised and then transformed over the course of six decisive years. The quotes, many of them extensive, which

appear throughout the text are also subject to these deformations, and are for the most part expressions of the apologetic or critical rhetoric of the protagonists.

Troubled Futures

Since the 1970s, the reconstruction of destroyed cities and territories has been the object of innumerable studies, ranging from monographs on particular cities to analyses of national politics and enterprises. This has become a quasi-autonomous domain of the history of architecture and town planning, whose development is due in part to the inclusion of post-war buildings into the architectural heritage. The phenomenal growth of studies about post-war architectural culture is no less spectacular.[17] These works provide an indispensable backdrop to the present study, but I will limit the scope of this work to an examination of projections for the future of cities and regions affected by destruction and occupation. The abundance of published works and the limits of this volume require that it remain strictly confined to activity during the war itself, prior to the surrender of Japan. Indeed, two visions of the future were then in conflict: for the Axis, the annexation or subordination of conquered territories translated into projects for urban transformations developed by architects absorbed into paramilitary teams. These projects traced out the outlines of a future

Cover of **Metron**, no. 31–32, 1949. Clockwise from upper left: Erich Mendelsohn, Alvar Aalto, Frank Lloyd Wright, Erik Gunnar Asplund, Richard Neutra, Ludwig Mies van der Rohe, Walter Gropius, Le Corbusier; centre: Sven Markelius. CCA Collection

metron 31·32
architettura urbanistica

based on oppression and sometimes extermination, and architecture was intended to make its own contributions to the definition of that future. For the Allies, reconstruction was not intended simply as 'reconstitution' – a term employed in France after 1918 – but was part of a process of modernisation intended to be both technological and social.

The work of architects during the war cast its own shadows on the post-war period. The reconstructions and urban extensions that were subsequently undertaken, depending on the nature of the briefs, sometimes extended associations and friendships established while in uniform. Although a few German architects were affected by the post-war purges, suffered indignities, or were barred from the profession, such as Hermann Giesler, who had developed plans for Linz in close contact with Hitler and run the Organisation Todt, first in the northern Russia and subsequently in Bavaria, others who held positions of responsibility under the Nazis, such as Friedrich Tamms, Herbert Rimpl and Ernst Neufert, were to enjoy considerable success in the Federal Republic. The Allies did not dispute their competence, and they proved to be as strategically indispensable as did the scientists and engineers working around Wernher von Braun on the production of rockets.

A Just War?

Finally, let us address an ambiguity that may hover over an account punctuated by destruction and massacre, in which the actions of the Allies could appear to be placed on the same plane as the actions of the Axis: the generalised and comparative approach taken here is in no way based on some idea that the war was simply the tragic confrontation of two blocks of nations of equal political or ethical footing. Although my approach may consider certain episodes in new ways that differ from existing accounts, my thesis is in no way revisionist. The second world conflict, unleashed unilaterally by Adolf Hitler, who had made no secret of his intentions, was a just war and remains so, one that the forces of democracy and humanity were obligated to wage against the forces of oppression and barbarity, even at the price of the destruction of German and Japanese cities, events whose uncontested horror in no way erases the crimes of the Axis forces.[18] Nor do I absolve, it must be said, the crimes of Stalin, which added to those committed by the Nazis, to the misfortune of the peoples of the USSR who were deported or repressed between 1941 and 1945 and of those prisoners who were released from the Nazi camps only to be transferred to the Gulag.

In a letter to Richard Neutra, sent from London in April 1940, Maxwell Fry expressed his pessimism as to the possibilities of architectural activity during wartime: 'I felt quite certain on the outbreak of war that architecture in England would be entirely eclipsed, and despite some slight resuscitation of interest in the idea of research, events have fulfilled my gloomiest prognostication. It is as difficult to develop the idea of architecture without building as it would be to develop music without instrumentation. And the loss is severe.'[19] The intensity of the episodes portrayed below contradicts this vision: far from being a dark and empty hole in the history of architecture in the twentieth century, the war was in fact a complex process of transformation, involving all the components of architecture in its total mobilisation. Its interpretation requires uncovering a dense network of episodes that might sometimes seem to have little to do with each other except for their proximity in time.

1. Albert Speer, *Inside the Third Reich*, translated by Richard and Clara Winston (New York and Toronto: Macmillan, 1970), 523.
2. Ernst Jünger, 'Total Mobilization', in *The Heidegger Controversy: A Critical Reader*, edited by Richard Wolin (Cambridge, Mass.: MIT Press, 1993), 126. Originally published as 'Die totale Mobilmachung' in Ernst Jünger, *Krieg und Krieger* (Berlin: Junker und Dünnhaupt, 1930), 11–30.
3. Paul Virilio and Marianne Brausch, *Voyage d'hiver, entretiens* (Marseille: Parenthèses, 1997), 9.
4. This pulsion was nourished by the series *Jeunesse héroïque* (n.p.: Éditions France d'abord, 1945–46), a collection published with support from the Association Nationale des Anciens Francs-Tireurs et Partisans Français, and the comic strip by Edmond-François Calvo, *La Bête est morte! – La Guerre mondiale chez les animaux*, story by Jacques Zimmermann and Victor Dancette (Paris: Gallimard, 1945).
5. A first formulation of this enquiry can be found in Jean-Louis Cohen, 'Prima del dopoguerra: Secondo conflitto mondiale et internazionalizzazione della condizione progettuale', in *Tra guerra e pace, società, cultura e architettura nel secondo dopoguerra,* edited by Patrizia Bonifazio and Sergio Pace (Milan: Franco Angeli, 1998), 111–17.
6. Anthony Vidler, 'Air War and Architecture', in *Ruins of Modernity*, edited by Julia Hell and Andreas Schönle (Durham: Duke University Press, 2010), 30.

7. I am referring primarily to the work of Andrew Shanken, Lucia Allais and Enrique Ramirez cited elsewhere in this volume.
8. Mikhail Bakhtin, 'Forms of Time and Chronotope in the Novel', in *The Dialogic Imagination Four Essays*, edited by Michael Holquist; translated by Caryl Emerson and Michael Holquist (Austin: University of Texas Press, 1981).
9. Niall Ferguson, *The War of the World: History's Age of Hatred* (London and New York: Allen Lane, 2006). Andrea Graziosi, *Guerra e rivoluzione in Europa, 1905–1956* (Bologna: Il Mulino, 2001). See also Martin Motte and Frédéric Thebault, *Guerre, idéologie, populations, 1911–1946* (Paris: L'Harmattan, 2005).
10. Walther Rathenau, *Die neue Wirtschaft* (Berlin: Fischer, 1918). See also *Great War, Total War, Combat and Mobilization on the Western Front, 1914–1918,* edited by Roger Chickering and Stig Förster (Cambridge, Mass., and New York: Cambridge University Press, 2000).
11. Élie Halévy, 'The Age of Tyrannies', translated by May Wallas, *Economica*, new series, vol. 8, no. 29 (February 1941), 78. Originally published as Élie Halévy, *L'ère des tyrannies. Études sur le socialisme et la guerre* (Paris: Gallimard, 1938), 214.
12. Satoshi Sasaki, 'The Rationalization of Production Management Systems in Japan during World War II', in *World War II and the Transformation of Business Systems: the International Conference on Business History 20: Proceedings of the Fuji Conference,* edited by Jun Sakudo and Takao Shiba (Tokyo: University of Tokyo Press, 1994), 30–54.
13. Paul Virilio, *Bunker Archaeology* (New York: Princeton Architectural Press, 1994), 32.
14. Lewis Mumford, 'Warfare and Invention', in *Technics and Civilization* (New York: Harcourt, Brace & Co., 1934), 85.
15. 'Jobs for Trained Men', *Pencil Points*, vol. 23, no. 2 (February 1942), 60–61.
16. Nigel Nicolson, 'Hadrian's Wall Today', *The Architectural Review*, vol. 87, no. 518 (January 1940), 1–6.
17. I am referring in particular to works as diverse as Werner Durth and Niels Gutschow, *Träume in Trümmern: Planungen zum Wiederaufbau zerstörter Städte im Westen Deutschlands, 1940–1950* (Braunschweig and Wiesbaden: Friedr. Vieweg & Sohn, 1988) and Beatriz Colomina, *Domesticity at War* (Barcelona: Actar, 2006).
18. Andreas Huyssen, 'War Burnout: Memories of the Air War', in *At War*, edited by Antonio Monegal and Francesc Torres (Barcelona: Centre de Cultura Contemporània, 2004), 339–45.
19. Maxwell Fry, letter to Richard Neutra, 9 April 1940, Thomas Hines collection, Los Angeles.

Unless otherwise mentioned, all translations are by the author.

8. ET LA GUERRE AÉRIENNE ?

TOC-TOC — N'entrez pas !

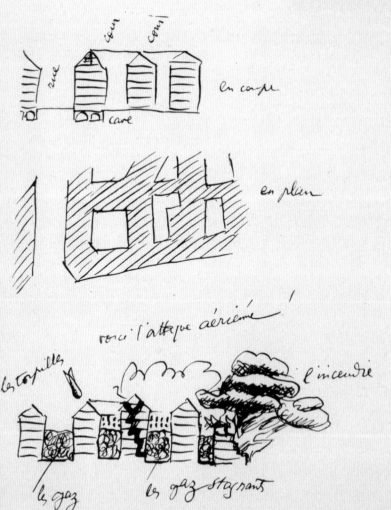

en coupe

en plan

voici l'attaque aérienne !

les torpilles

l'incendie

le gaz

les gaz stagnants

2/ Architects and Cities Go Off to War

War is declared, and oh macabre irony, the whole world suddenly has so much on its plate. Capital, labour, raw materials, transport, discipline are all in abundance. An immense and fantastic production. A superhuman leap. Five years of sustained effort, ever-growing, titanic. It is a miracle; a thing of beauty worthy of the gods. But no, you fools, it is **GOLD** which is dancing like a madman possessed! It is **DESTRUCTION** . . .
Le Corbusier, *Plans*, June 1931[1]

We must make it absolutely clear, to ourselves no less than to others, that first class architecture is necessary in war, not just for our fun or to line our pockets, but because good buildings can help to win the war.
RIBA Journal, October 1939[2]

It is something in war time to have the machines of civil defence neatly designed. This neatness is a sign of order and of something clean and good which survives the inevitable disorder and mess of war.
E. J. Carter, *Britain at War*, 1941[3]

The invasion of Poland by the Wehrmacht, on the first day of September 1939, was anything but a surprise. Few wars have been as widely expected as the one that set the planet awash in blood and fire for six years. Some nationalist forces, especially in the defeated powers of 1918, expected to obtain revenge for what they held up as

Le Corbusier
'What About Air War?',
in *La Ville radieuse*, 1935.
CCA Collection

the national humiliation in defeat. Intellectuals had early on taken measure of the threat of a new war, as the June 1931 issue of the Parisian journal *Plans* clearly indicated, with its contributions from writers, architects and technocrats, as well as texts solicited from Heinrich Mann and Thomas Mann, all preaching for the 'construction of Europe' rather than war.[4]

Preludes and Announcements

It seems to be generally accepted that a clear and perceptible continuity ties the two world conflicts to each other. They are tightly linked by causal relations, by the German frustrations exploited by the Nazis in their march to power, and in the construction of a consensus leading to the Second World War that fed upon the resentment against the Treaty of Versailles, signed in the aftermath of the First. In this perspective, the interwar period appears at most as a hiatus, during which the initial conflict continued to be pursued, for example through the military and technological alliance that existed between the USSR and Weimar Germany during the years from 1922 to 1933.

In a general way, the interwar period was only a parenthesis during which preparations for war would continue. As Lewis Mumford noted in 1938, 'The war capital, through its organs of indoctrination,

makes every subordinate province war-minded. The actual conflict, when it finally takes place, is a mere bursting of a vast pus-bag of vulgar pretense and power. But the intervening period, although sometimes fantastically referred to as "peace", is equally a state of war: the passive war of war-propaganda, war indoctrination, war-rehearsal: a preliminary maneuvering for position.'[5]

During this period of partial suspension of hostilities, which was nonetheless punctuated by smaller conflicts, an expectation of new forms of beauty emerged. As early and eager supporters of Italy's entry into the war in 1915, the Futurists insisted upon glorifying the spectacles promised by the future war. In his *Poema africano della divisione '28 ottobre'*, the founder of Futurism, Filippo Tommaso Marinetti wrote: 'War is beautiful because it creates new architecture [and new plastic compositions], like that of the big tanks, the geometrical formation flights, the smoke spirals from burning villages, and many others'.[6] Walter Benjamin made this passage famous through his slightly abbreviated quotation, in 'The Work of Art in the Age of Mechanical Reproduction' with its evocation of the threat of war to come. One might link this aesthetic evocation with Le Corbusier's enthusiastic reproductions of planes flying in formation and their condensation trails in his book *Aircraft* of 1935, when he wrote that 'the airplane might have written the word HOPE in the sky'.[7] One can see the convergence between the totalising ambitions of modernity and the total character of the war to come, whose inevitability was of little doubt to anyone.

Le Corbusier
'The airplane might have written the word "HOPE" in the sky', in *Aircraft*, 1935.
CCA Collection

COLLECTION DE L'ÉQUIPEMENT DE LA CIVILISATION MACHINISTE

DES CANONS, DES MUNITIONS?

LE CORBUSIER

MERCI! DES LOGIS... S.V.P.

ÉDITIONS DE L'ARCHITECTURE D'AUJOURD'HUI, 5, RUE BARTHOLDI, BOULOGNE (SEINE)

The ambiguity of Le Corbusier's position is emblematic and is worth examining. After justifying his 'Plan Voisin' of 1925 for Paris on the grounds of its hygienic benefits, he invoked 'the terrible menace which weighs down on every city, no matter how far from the borders . . . aerial warfare' in his presentation to his Soviet contacts of his proposals for the Moscow plan, mentioning bombs, gas and incendiaries: 'For ten years I have developed plans for urbanisation and habitation that respond to most of the requirements of anti-aircraft defence . . . A recent military report that examined the various urban solutions proposed for the development of Paris showed that mine were the only ones to respond to the requirements of anti-aircraft defence.'[8] The 'report' in question was none other than Paul Vauthier's book *La Guerre*

aérienne et l'avenir du pays, which will be the object of close attention below. In 1938, in a typical tactical manoeuvre, Le Corbusier did not hesitate to employ pacifist arguments in his book, *Des canons, des munitions? Merci! Des Logis . . . S.V.P.* The title can be compared to a passage in *Journey to the End of Night* by the pacifist Louis-Ferdinand Céline, in which he wrote 'The patriots kept clamouring: "Guns! Men! Ammunition!" They never seemed to get tired.'[9] This time, Le Corbusier assumes a posture hostile to rearmament as part of an argument in favour of a programme for building inexpensive housing.

Le Corbusier
Cover of ***Des canons, des munitions? Merci! Des logis . . . S.V.P.***, 1938.
CCA Collection

Cover of **'Problemes de la revolució'**, *A.C.* [*Documentos de arquitectura contemporánea*], no. 25, 1937. CCA Collection

Pacifists and Opportunists

The pacifism to which Le Corbusier subscribed was widespread in Europe and did not entail a refusal to consider the threat of a new war, as is evident in the issues published by periodicals in the second part of the 1930s. Only a few rejected outright the idea of a war with Germany, Frank Lloyd Wright being one of them. A confirmed isolationist, he rejected any armed intervention by the United States far from its homeland, which led to a vitriolic disagreement with Lewis Mumford, a committed antifascist, resulting in a rift between the two friends.[10] In France, Auguste Perret's flirtations with Italy and Germany were only harmless expressions of a diffuse form of pacifism that was quickly dissipated in 1939.

Many architects who were active on the left in Europe and North America were already aware of the threat of a new war by the mid-1930s, and made other connections between civil and military programmes. The Danish architect Knud Lonberg-Holm, who had emigrated to the United States, affirmed in 1936, using vaguely Marxist terminology, 'Technical development becomes increasingly the design of instruments of military aggression. In housing, technical advances are expressed in the production of gas-proof and bomb-proof "shelters". Liquidation becomes the planned destruction of new productive forces instead of the elimination of obsolete restrictive forces.'[11]

The events immediately preceding the invasion of Poland were not without their effects on the world of architecture. Even though Italy's aggression in Ethiopia between October 1935 and May 1936 did not appear to mobilise the architects directly, it nonetheless soon led some of them to develop a built environment for the Italian occupation. Between 1936 and 1939, Ignazio Guidi and Cesare Valle worked on the plan of Addis Ababa, whose town hall and cathedral were the focus of projects by Plinio Marconi and Cesare Bazzani.[12] In Spain, the involvement of architects was primarily political, especially in Catalonia, where the GATCPAC (Grup d'Arquitectes i Tècnics Catalans per al Progrés de l'Arquitectura Contemporània) was active in the Republican camp. The war coincided with the revolution in Barcelona, which José Luis Sert and Josep Torres-Clavé would take part in.[13] For his part, Luis Lacasa was involved in Madrid. Torres-Clavé died at the front in January 1939, and his colleagues were forced into exile, like dozens of architects. During the three years of the war, they worked on the protection of civilians and the cultural patrimony from air raids, on the one hand, and on propaganda and the mobilisation of the Republican forces, on the other.

The Second World War started with the mobilisation of all the belligerent forces,

Louis Leygues
'The master builder',
illustration in *L'Architecture
française*, November 1940.
CCA Collection

LE MAITRE D'ŒUVRE
Dessin de Louis Leygue

and constituted an experiment that each
profession contributed to using its own
specific resources. Writers and artists
were engaged both as combatants – at
the risk of their lives – and as members of
organisations called upon to construct a
national consensus.[14] Symptomatic of this,
for example, was the appointment in 1939,
in Paris, of writer Jean Giraudoux to the
Secrétariat d'État à l'Information. Within
this generally rigorous exploitation of
qualifications, architects found themselves
responsible for a wide array of missions.
When mobilised, deployed on the fronts,
killed or wounded, as prisoners or refugees,
they shared the fate of all citizens in time
of war. But they were not simple citizens
in uniform. They also participated in it
professionally. And yet no one has attempted
an appraisal of this multiplicity of figures,
even though such studies have been
made of other cultural fields.[15]

In the Mirror of the Journals

Professional practice was directly
affected by the establishment of the war
economy. 'Civil' production was stopped
by decree in all countries at varying times.
Unemployment followed quickly upon the
cessation of activity. Many educational
establishments were closed for the duration
of the conflict. Their teachers and students
were called to the colours or put to work
on civil defence. The oldest architects
returned to their villages of origin in
order to escape the urban shortages,
while the professional institutions made
do in more frugal conditions, which
slowed down their output and reduced
the frequency of cultural events: the
eighth Milan Triennale, scheduled for 1943,
did not take place. In certain countries,
periodicals were either suspended or
significantly reduced in number of pages
because of paper rationing. The Soviet
monthly *Arkhitektura SSSR* became a
mimeographed and sporadic journal, which
was published eighteen times between the
summer of 1943 and 1947. The *RIBA Journal*,
the publication of the Royal Institute of British
Architects, became significantly thinner.

The course of the war had a direct
impact on some publications. The Berlin
Monatshefte für Baukunst ceased publication
in December 1942. *L'Architecture d'aujourd'hui*
was closed down by its owner, André Bloc,
who was under threat from the racial
laws of Vichy. After the failure of Pierre
Vago's attempts to relaunch it, the journal
was replaced in 1941 by *Techniques et
architecture*, the functionalist counterpart
to *L'Architecture française* (founded that

same year by Michel Roux-Spitz) that supported the conservative positions of the Pétain regime. In Italy, in December 1943, after censoring several texts, the Fascist regime interrupted the publication of *Costruzioni* (previously known as *Casabella*, but renamed by editor Giuseppe Pagano). Nonetheless, the clearest expressions of the tasks of architects in times of war are to be found in periodicals. Every one of them called for a mobilisation of professional energies, but with a focus on a wide range of different priorities for architects. Some stressed a concern for quality, while many drew attention to the technical and economic issues at stake.

In autumn 1939, *L'Architecture d'aujourd'hui* addressed those architects 'who by reason of their age or responsibilities have remained at their post at the rear', to inform them 'of new programmes born of the necessities of the war: temporary constructions of all sorts for administrative functions, public or private, for factories, for the housing of evacuated populations, the construction of passive defence shelters, construction for military purposes, barracks and hospitals.[16] A few weeks earlier, the editors had observed that 'the state of war, while it has slowed some construction activities to the point of near standstill, has accelerated others in a similar measure. Among French architects who have been mobilised, many have been called to fulfil functions barely dissimilar from their civil profession. Among those not called up by the mobilisation, some see their normal activity continuing in part or moving in new directions; others take advantage of the waiting time to prepare for new work.'[17]

The *RIBA Journal*, which appeared less frequently after September 1939, asked in October 'what architecture can do'. The forecast was pessimistic: 'There is a risk that unless the profession corporatively succeeds in making the full value of its services known architects will be used too often merely in supervisory capacities, to place dreary unarchitectural huts on site and arrange drainage and services; that they will be used only as clerks-of-works or as engineers and not as architects.' The stakes were simple: 'To fight as *architects* in the fullest sense of the word', and the key word was 'planning', in order to ensure the best use value of all the programmes linked to the war effort, including new building types that were expected to appear. 'Standardisation or prefabricating systems which do not take a close account of plan needs are at fault. . . . If it is a system designed by an architect it will probably allow adequately for the plan-function factor, if by an engineer for structural factors only.'[18] Here war appears as clearly and as explicitly as possible as a new episode in the competition between design professions.

Even before the expected entry of the United States into the war, still coming to terms with the Japanese attack on Pearl Harbor, *Pencil Points* saw the design of constructions for industry as architects' first contribution to defence. 'In the forced expansion of the nation's industrial plants to provide space for more men and more machines to work in defense of America, architects have had a share. New industrial forms expressive of the steel, glass, brick and fabricated units utilized in this accelerating program begin to stand forth.'[19]

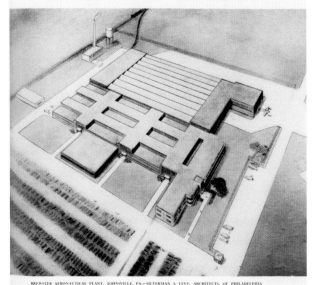

ARCHITECTS AND DEFENSE

IN THE FORCED EXPANSION OF THE NATION'S INDUSTRIAL PLANT TO PROVIDE SPACE FOR MORE MEN AND MORE MACHINES TO WORK IN DEFENSE OF AMERICA, ARCHITECTS HAVE HAD A SHARE. NEW INDUSTRIAL FORMS EXPRESSIVE OF THE STEEL, GLASS, BRICK, AND FABRICATED UNITS UTILIZED IN THIS ACCELERATING PROGRAM BEGIN TO STAND FORTH. IN THIS PORTFOLIO OF DRAWINGS AND PHOTOGRAPHS THE EDITORS HAVE SOUGHT TO INDICATE SOME OF THE NEW TRENDS AS WELL AS TO REFLECT THE EVIDENCES OF THE ARCHITECTS' INFLUENCE IN A FIELD OF DESIGN THAT CAME WITHIN PURVIEW OF THE PROFESSION LESS THAN FORTY YEARS AGO. YET THIS IS A PROGRAM HARDLY BEGUN, IF WE ARE TO DECENTRALIZE AND REBUILD OUR PRINCIPAL INDUSTRIES; IF ARCHITECTS ARE TO PLAY THEIR RIGHTFUL PART IN BUILDING AMERICA

BREWSTER AERONAUTICAL PLANT, JOHNSVILLE, PA.—SILVERMAN & LEVY, ARCHITECTS, OF PHILADELPHIA

OCTOBER 1941   657

'**Architects and Defense**',
in *Pencil Points*,
October 1941.
CCA Collection

In the summer of 1941, immediately after the German invasion, the Architects' Union of the USSR started the periodic publication *Stroitelstvo voennogo vremeni* (Construction in Time of War) in Moscow. After deploring the breakdown of the non-aggression pact with Germany, the first issue, under the editorship of Karo Alabian – leader of the young Stalinists in the profession – proceeded to outline the main features of the 'war missions of Soviet architects': 'In general, the war inevitably puts a large mass of people into movement. The normal development of cities cannot of course enable the creation and setting aside of reserve dwellings at a corresponding scale, so the question of projects and constructions

for the evacuated inhabitants is a pressing one. These types of constructions require the maximum use of local construction materials and unskilled labour . . . We should establish for ourselves the goal of completely freeing the transport system from dealing with the movement of construction materials, of using local resources as much as possible, and of designing types of construction that can rely for the most part on labour from the populace.'[20] The programmes that were highlighted as requiring the attention of Russian architects included factories related to defence and their associated housing, for which dry construction methods were recommended, and camouflage projects. The development of prefabrication and the use of substitute materials were also recommended.

On the Axis side, in October 1939, a month after the invasion of Poland, the editorialist of the *Deutsche Bauzeitung*, H. F. Geiler, already openly predicted a shortage of skilled workers and without any qualms anticipated the use of prisoners, indicating that 'most construction companies have already submitted requests to the labour bureau for the assignment of Polish construction workers'. He listed the programmes that architects would be called upon to deal with in a context of shortage of materials. These would require the development of *Werkstoffsynthese*, that is to say the production of substitute materials, such as Buna, the artificial rubber. In addition to purely military programmes, the main priority would be the completion of structures providing anti-aircraft protection, while 'the brakes should be applied' to housing programmes.[21] *Kenchiku zasshi*, the journal of the Academy of Architecture in Japan, which in the 1930s began preparing architects in the archipelago for war, devoted much attention to following German politics. In 1938, the important figure of Chûta Itô, professor at Tokyo Imperial University and at the University of Waseda, presented 'Japan and the new German culture' to the Academy. As he bluntly put it, 'World war is a great tragedy, but by divine grace, it is a way of renewing the World.'[22]

Wartime Jobs by the Thousands

The war put architecture in a state, so to speak, or rather it put architecture in all its phase states, to use a metaphor drawn from physics: in turn a solid, liquid or gas. More specifically, architects' paths during this period could be defined using three coordinate axes, one serving as a measure of the nature of their work, another their place in the war society, and the third one a measure of time, for the chronicle of these years sees them constantly changing location. Architects were engaged in activities ranging from planning and logistics to building projects, from camouflage to graphic design, from interior design to the protection of historic monuments, even to the most classical decorative work. These tasks put their specific expertise to use, which included their spatial, visual, technological, organisational, territorial and psychological expertise.

Recourse to civilian experts was an essential feature of the Second World War. Intellectuals in all disciplines, especially the scientific ones, were widely called upon. The victory of the Allies was largely due to the level of trust they accorded to physicists, mathematicians and chemists

THE SEABEES

for the development of offensive and defensive systems: this trust was at its highest in Great Britain and the United States, whereas the expulsion of the Jews and the Nazification of science proved to be a handicap to German research.[23] The British created a series of committees to respond to the requirements of the different services, with the support of the physician Frederick A. Lindemann, the advisor to Churchill (and future Viscount Cherwell): the Admiralty would mobilise more than

e Navy's fighting Builders

In peacetime these U. S. builders changed the face of a country. Today the bases they erect in obscure corners of the globe are changing the face of the world.

THE official motto of the Seabees, the Navy's two year old fighting construction battalions is: "Construimus Batuimus"—"We Build, We Fight." Aside from the motto, there is nothing classical about the Seabees. The newest branch of the Navy, the Seabees 262,000 strong are the toughest, most resourceful and energetic bunch of builders, dockwallopers, repair men and antibooby-trap operators this war has seen. As such they are something of an anomaly in the ceremonious and gentlemanly tradition of the Navy. But old traditions mean little to this outfit of horny-handed, cussing, gun-toting construction workers. Not young themselves—their average age is the middle thirties—the Seabees have built a lusty new tradition of their own. "Can Do" is the Seabee watch word from the Arctic wastes of the Aleutians to the dank jungles of the Southwest Pacific, from the Cen-

tral Pacific to the Atlantic, Africa, and Italy. Drawn from the ranks of the construction industry, the Seabees and their achievements in every corner of the globe are the industry's significant contribution toward victory.

In all of the last war, the Navy spent only $189 million on its shore installations. In this war $7.5 billion has already been spent since July, 1940. Before this war, the Navy never had to fight from bases that were under fire, never had to scramble from island to island to set up advance base after advance base with which to attack the enemy. World War II's two ocean Navy and its air arm are impotent without their global girdle of bases, and an island remains useless until the Seabees have transformed it into a base. Without the backbreaking backbone work of the Seabees, there would be no Major Foss, no Major Boyington, no front page stories of

49

'The Seabees: the Navy's fighting Builders', in *The Architectural Forum*, February 1944. CCA Collection

for weaponry such as aviation. Kurt Lewin, a behavioural psychologist of German origin, would observe that 'by providing unprecedented facilities and by demanding realistic and workable solutions to scientific problems, the war has accelerated greatly the changes of social sciences to a new developmental level.'[25]

As for the rank and role of architects, they ranged from enrolment as officer, non-commissioned officer or soldier to captivity, clandestine activity or exile – often as a result of racial or political persecution. Sometimes this exile occurred repeatedly. For example, Erich Mendelsohn passed from England to Palestine, and then to the United States. It is very difficult to assess these positions quantitatively, because the posts they occupied were rarely identified as architectural ones. One of the few revealing figures is the number of architects working with the Seabees (CBs, or Construction Battalions) of the US Navy. They were one thousand in number in the spring of 1945, at a time when the Corps of Engineers included five hundred thousand men, representing 8% of the total American armed forces.[26] But we have no idea how many architects were directly employed in the secret programmes of the time, many of them keeping their work quiet, like Wells Coates who had been involved, as he would later confess to his daughter, in the development of the de Havilland Vampire jet fighter for the RAF.[27]

A few revealing cases can be singled out, which enable one to gauge the diversity and breadth of the experiences. Within the mass of soldiers, some architects remained with their sketchbook in hand, but others saw combat and sometimes

four thousand researchers. In 1940, the Americans created the National Defense Research Committee, led by Vannevar Bush, and in 1941, the Soviets set up the Scientific and Technical Council, led by Sergei Kaftanov. Anthropologists and historians were recruited for the war in the Pacific. Ruth Benedict wrote her legendary book *The Chrysanthemum and the Sword*[24] to prepare American troops for the occupation of Japan. There was a massive mobilisation of the social sciences

lost their lives, such as the young British modern architect Valentine Harding, who fell at Dunkirk in 1950.[28] Arkady Mordvinov documented the condition of Stalingrad after the battle in his drawings.[29] The German Norman Braun drew scenes of the same front, but from the Nazi side.[30] Some of the men mobilised were overwhelmed by their discovery of military equipment, such as the Italian Marco Zanuso, a naval officer. Engineering research offices sometimes provided a somewhat calmer and more removed framework for thinking about projects. Bruce Goff spent eighteen months in the Aleutian Islands, attached to a Seabee battalion, rethinking his relationship to architecture in a landscape 'not spoiled by civilization', and learning to build with 'found' materials.[31] And many mysteries remain: will we ever know if the Roman architect Luigi Moretti

fought against the Allies in the forces of the Repubblica Sociale Italiana?

The forced idleness of many architects might be used to justify the hypothesis that the war was a vacuum, an 'empty' time. Some architects made every effort to find useful employment in the armed forces. From his rural retreat, Berthold Lubetkin sent flurries of messages to the Royal Air Force from 1941 to 1943, in a vain effort to be assigned as a contact to the Soviet ally. He stressed his language skills and youthful travels in central Asia in order to be recruited by the intelligence agencies. 'I should like to get a job with one of the Services if possible where either my

Arkady Mordvinov
The architect drawing in the ruins of Stalingrad, 1943.
Shchusev State Museum of Architecture

architectural and general organisational qualifications could be made use of, or my linguistic qualifications, and the knowledge I have of Southern Russia and my native Caucasus.'[32] Also in England, Jacqueline Tyrwhitt worked from 1939 to 1941 for the Women's Land Army, created during the First World War, whose purpose it was to replace farmers called to the colours with women by giving them a grounding in agricultural techniques.[33]

The production of armaments required the construction of numerous factories in every country, which enabled the youngest architects to escape being conscripted: after rebuilding farm buildings in Polish Wartheland, Hermann Henselmann became the head of Godber Nissen for the construction of a factory for Avia aircraft engines at Letňany, near Prague, from 1942 to 1944.[34] Many of the more established architects used these programmes to expand their offices. Kunio Maekawa, for example, opened an office in occupied Shanghai to build housing for the employees of the Kako bank.[35] As the landscape architect James Rose put it, referring to his work during the first years of the war in the offices of Antonin Raymond: 'The game had simply changed from gardens to anti-aircraft, and was played on a larger field.'[36]

Architects would also be called on to be 'painters to the army', in order to contribute to the production of artistic images commemorating the war or serving as propaganda. The Australian Raymond McGrath, who was working in London and had become interested in the threat from the air as early as 1934, painted watercolours of aircraft factories.[37] His compatriot Hugh Casson showed his impressions of airbases

featuring his designs for camouflage in various galleries. Another kind of witness, Philip Johnson, who would soon go to Harvard to study architecture, employed a pen and a notebook to document his discovery of Poland after the German conquest and did not hesitate to use outright anti-Semitic clichés in his chronicles for Father Conklin's pro-Nazi review, *Social Justice*.[38]

Prisoners and Resistance Fighters

After being mobilised in 1940, many French architects found themselves in Oflags (*Offizierlagern*, or officers' camps) located in the eastern part of Germany, where, like Henry Bernard, they organised workshops, put together libraries, and engaged in 'concours d'émulation', recreating the rituals of the École des Beaux-Arts. Some of their English colleagues pursued their studies in the hopes of passing their professional examinations upon their return. And the experience of deportation was one shared by many European Jewish architects, as well as by resistance fighters, or by both in one: Simone Guilissen-Hoa,[39] Alexandre Persitz (prisoner of war, escapee, deported to Auschwitz) and André Bloch-Bruyère (deported as a resistance fighter). There were many victims in Czechoslovakia and Hungary, where Farkas Molnár died in the battle for the liberation of Budapest. Some deported resistance fighters died, such as Gian Luigi Banfi and Giuseppe Pagano. Some were able to leave us with drawings of their experiences, such as Lodovico Belgiojoso, whose companion in Mauthausen and Gusen in 1944–45, the graphic designer Germano Facetti, brought out striking views drawn surreptitiously.[40]

The most astonishing case is of deported architects who were incorporated into groups that built and enlarged their own prison camps, such as Szymon Syrkus in Auschwitz.[41] His wife Helena Syrkus, who remained underground, directed the work of the architecture and urbanism studio (Pracownia Architektoniczno-Urbanistyczna), which operated out of a secret apartment in occupied Warsaw (see page 368).[42] Among those who chose to fight in the shadow army in France, several did at the peril of their lives, such as Jacques Woog, sentenced by the Vichy state tribunal and guillotined on 14 September 1941, and Fernand Fenzy, shot for passing information to London. André Lurçat was held in the Santé prison in Paris in 1943, before eventually being freed. His comrade Pierre Villon, alias Roger Ginsburger, escaped arrest and became the first president of the Front National, which combined the resistance organisations of the left, and Frantz-Philippe Jourdain set up a network in Marseille. In Italy, the very young Carlo Melograni and Giuseppe Campos Venuti participated in the Roman

Architecture studio in the prisoner-of-war camp at Stablack, East Prussia, c. 1944. Académie d'Architecture, Cité de l'Architecture et du Patrimoine, Archives d'Architecture du xxe Siècle, Fonds Henry Bernard

resistance fighting against the Nazis, and in Austria Margarete Schütte-Lihotzky joined the Viennese resistance before being arrested and barely escaping execution.[43]

Exiles at Home and Abroad

Of the architects who had to go into exile or move far from the cities, some worked on large-scale projects. This was the case of Ernst May in Kenya and Rhodesia. But nothing of the sort was true of Ernesto Nathan Roger's exile in Switzerland. His voice had already been silenced by the racial laws of 1938, after which he

André Lurçat
Map of Sicily, sketched during his detention in the Santé prison,

Paris, 1943.
Institut Français d'Architecture, Archives Nationales, fonds André Lurçat

Top: Germano Facetti
View of the camp at Gusen, December 1944.
Fondo Germano Facetti, Archivio Istituto

Piemontese per la Storia della Resistenza e della Società Contemporanea, Turin

published the unsigned 'Confessioni di un anonimo del XX secolo' in *Domus*.[44] Many architects read widely as a result of their enforced idleness. They corresponded with their peers and their friends, and devoted themselves to writing. Their written output was intense, ranging from the personal reminiscences of William Lescaze and the architectural treatises of André Lurçat to the reflections on the profession penned by many Italians and anonymous pamphlets. Hans Scharoun turned to paper architecture and to fantasies that he would turn into buildings after the war.[45] The émigrés arrived in the United States with claims of useful skills for the circumstances of war: in 1939 Charles Siclis presented himself as an expert in camouflage, and in 1941 Serge Chermayeff recounted his experiences during the Blitz in Britain.

Nor should we forget all those who continued their civilian work as if nothing else mattered. Eugène Beaudouin pursued his work on a plan for the development of Marseille, to the point of participating in the German army's destruction of the area around the Vieux-port. Between 1943 and 1945, Auguste Perret worked on a 'National Olympic Park' for the Vichy government's General Commission for National Education and Sport. As usual, it was Le Corbusier who most sharply perceived the opportunities at hand, as his text 'L'architecture et la guerre' makes clear. In the last issue of the *Gazette Dunlop* published before the German invasion, he wrote: 'The war has set off the new era of movement, an end to stagnation, new undertakings so vast as to encompass architecture and urbanism. What is the architecture of war? The withdrawal of factories far from places of vulnerability. The evacuation of civilian populations far from the military zones. The problem has two faces: the urgency of doing "whatever", so long as it is done – those are the instructions coming from our leaders, and they are right to do so. The other is the "WAY OF DOING IT", the art if you will – in this case the architecture. . . . Through these laboratory tests, to be able to finally show the leaders the tangible proof, the valuable contributions of technical realisations which point out the path towards the legitimate forms of development which will frame the country in peacetime.'[46] In short, Le Corbusier adopts a posture that is both opportunistic in the face of new programmes and experimental in its approach to the 'great laboratory'. Many of his colleagues took the same approach while pursuing their own activities during the years of combat.

Ernesto Nathan Rogers
'Confessions of an Anonymous Man of the Twentieth Century', unsigned article in *Domus*, February 1941.
CCA Collection

CONFESSIONI DI UN ANONIMO DEL XX SECOLO

1° Presentazione dell'Anonimo

The modern movement meant to most people sweeping bands of windows, vast areas of glass for shops, whole glass fronts for factories. Now we are forced into an extreme reaction against all that. The curious thing about this reversal of what appeared one of the essentials of modern design is that a public building with a plain brick front, and no windows except for small honeycombed areas wholly bricked up, looks just as strikingly contemporary. What is it that gives it this contriving appearance? What is it that introduced, the moment its windows were filled in by uncompromisingly flat and brick rectangles, such a convincing twentieth century rhythm into the vaguely Italianate façade of the Westminster Town Hall? What makes the dully traditional police box in the street suddenly look so up-to-date behind its new square brick screen?

Believers in modern design have for years pleaded for the abstract beauty of sheer surfaces. Now at last—and thanks only to the abnormal needs of the besieged fortress in which we live—these exceedingly blank surfaces have come. Authorities that had refused to consider the advantages, let alone the aesthetic qualities, of simplicity, cannot now help admitting the one, if not the other. Will they put the clock back after the war? Or will their tastes and those of all the people whom these new monuments of architectural culture now surround, insist on the abnormalism of the Victorian street surrounded them, have got used to the purer and healthier food they now enjoy? One should certainly not be over-optimistic. Shopkeepers, and what they have done to protect their windows, prove that by no means everybody is aware of the new requirements and their onus. Very few owners of shops have so far learnt the lesson of the day. They had to put up some shuttering. But what have they done? About 50 per cent of them seem to be satisfied with some utility boarding of no reasonably whatsoever—quite useful, no doubt, but an ever-whelming confutation of the old doctrine that fitness alone constitutes beauty. And the more ambitious have not been induced even by the war to give up their love of florid unrestrained decoration. The windows of Troughton and Young's (designed by A. B. Read) and of the Orient Line (designed by Brian O'Rorke) are rare exceptions indeed.

10, 11 and 12. THE IMPORTANCE OF UNBROKEN SUR-FACES. Emergency treatment of a police station and a police post in London, both useful against blast and, the latter in its bold bareness, providing an instructive contrast to the conventionally adorned wood and glass box of the original post. Similarly the bricking up of the windows of Westminster Town Hall has drawn as magnificent Victorian building into the more concrete rhythm of the twentieth century.

13 and 14. SHOP WINDOWS. Shop-owners have acted much against the laws that must govern emergency design. Only very few of them were as sensible and as successful as Troughton & Young's and the Orient Line.

15, 16 and 17. EXEGI MONUMENTUM. The monuments of London protested in different ways. A corrugated shed housed Le Sueur's statue of Charles I (until it was removed to the country), a cone of sandbags houses the Piccadilly Circos Eros, and concrete blocks transform the Artillery Memorial at Hyde Park Corner into a Dudok-looking configuration.

3. A New Pattern Emerges

Why is it that Cubism was conceived about 1909 and the abstract art about 1920 or 1925? Because artists had seen through the weariness of the subtle differentiations of impressionism and had got tired of so much delicacy, sensibility and nuance. They were pining for something strong and elementary and found it in the geometrical configurations which they worked out.

Concurrently, architects began to realise the possibilities of steel and concrete and be ashamed of the academical aloofness of their nineteenth century predecessors. They now took to the problems of industrial architecture and industrial production and found out that to work for such purposes satisfactorily they had to go back to fundamentals both of function and of manufacturing technique. This Back-to-Fundamentals attitude was reflected in the appearance of their work too—and it is in this that they found themselves unexpectedly at one with the Cubists and the abstract painters and sculptors.

However, to overcome the prejudices of patrons proved very hard indeed. They were in fact not overcome until the war started and suddenly drew the country with a multitude of Ben Nicholson forms. Huge loops in the fields, 19, humps and dents across the roads, and black and white, black and white, never ending along the kerbs of the streets, up the stairs, on posts, on the lamp standards, everywhere 18, 20, 21 and 22.

The new pattern that began to emerge is elementary and geometrical and it has all the convincing directness that it is so difficult to achieve in a painting. The traffic lights under their numbness hoods are reduced to tiny crosses, and

18 and 19. NEW MOTIFS. The snake-like effect of a street kerb in war attire ; and a modern Stonehenge—concrete pipes against invasion, a pattern as elementary and imposing as any abstract artist could dream of.

20, 21 and 22. BLACK AND WHITE. Black and white everywhere. And where that is not enough for safety illuminated crosses of equally convincing pattern value.

172   173

The City as Target and Battlefield

The Second World War was an urban war in more ways than one. It affected architects both as urban dwellers and as the protagonists of the production and transformation of cities. The cities were mobilised into the economy of a war that starved their inhabitants, that used them as theatres for great battles on the ground, and that, in a crucial new development, struck at them day and night with long-range aviation and, in the last months of the conflict, with missiles. This innovation was not lost, for example, on the editors of *The Architectural Forum*, who introduced in January 1942 a special issue on 'Civilian Defense', hurriedly put together after Pearl Harbor – unless it had been a prudent preparation for war made beforehand – by observing that 'for the first time, the US is in a world war where the non-combatant is not in the completely safe role of the man behind the man behind the gun. There is no assurance that anyone is far enough back of the lines to avoid all danger.'[47]

Even more than during the years of conflict of 1914–1918, and even before air raids had affected them directly, the war transformed everyday life in the affected cities.[48] Civilian construction came to a sudden standstill, mass transport and cars became scarce, lacking fuel and replacement tyres. Commerce dried up because of rationing and generated long queues in front of shop windows, which were either empty or filled with fake foodstuffs. Aerial defences filled up historic squares with sandbags in the most unexpected formations: pyramids piled up around fountains or statues,

'Protecting Buildings and Monuments',
in *The Architectural Review*, December 1941.
CCA Collection

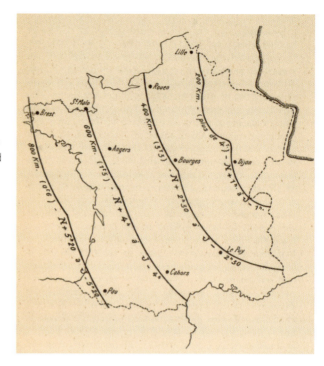

or with a layer of cylinders or ramparts to give added protective girth to monuments. And at the same time, anti-aircraft batteries with their listening posts and lights occupied the highest points. Night after night, the populations took refuge in shelters that sometimes afforded only an illusion of protection. From this point of view, architects shared the fate of all civilians.

Aerial Warfare According to Douhet

Strikes against cities punctuated the entire course of the war, from the Italian attacks on Addis Ababa to the Japanese raids in China, from the battles of the Spanish Civil War to the conquest of Berlin, and ultimately to the bombing of Hiroshima and Nagasaki. The aerial bombardment of cities had started during the First World War, but had only occasionally touched Paris, London, Karlsruhe and Cologne. Under Hugh Trenchard, the British had undertaken raids against German industrial and railway centres between 1914 and 1918, in the first aerial attacks on economic targets. Shortly thereafter, in 1921, the Italian general Giulio Douhet described the scope of the new weapons for the conduct of future wars in *Il dominio dell'aria, saggio sull'arte della guerra aerea*, a reflection on the consequences of aerial warfare since its beginnings in 1909.[49] Drawing lessons from the First World War, and especially from the aerial bombardments of Treviso by Austrian forces, Douhet saw the airplane as 'the offensive weapon par excellence' and called for the creation of independent air forces, capable of operating *en masse*. He developed

the theory of strategic bombing, that would target the rear, the centres of industrial production, and also civilian populations: 'In general, aerial offensives will be directed against such targets as peacetime industrial and commercial establishments; important buildings, private and public; transportation arteries and centres; and certain designated areas of civilian population as well.'[50] Douhet considered that 'No longer can areas exist in which life can be lived in safety and tranquillity, nor can the battlefield any longer be limited to actual combatants. On the contrary, the battlefield will be limited only by the boundaries of the nations at war, and all of their citizens will become combatants, since all of them will be exposed to the aerial offensives of the enemy.' He foresaw 'a complete breakdown of the social structure in a country subject to merciless pounding from the air'.[51] In an article that appeared just before his death, 'The war of 19 . . .', he presented an apocalyptic vision of a war

between the French and Germans, won by the latter in the air.[52] The prospects Douhet put forward attracted the attention of his French and American colleagues – including Paul Vauthier among the former and William Mitchell among the latter – as well as others in Germany and in the Soviet Union. His theories were widely translated and were discussed in every country. They raised alarmist visions of the almost instantaneous destruction of great cities by a handful of carefully used airplanes.[53]

As early as 1930, the main powers prepared themselves for a war dominated by aviation, and the role of the form of cities in protecting civilians became a subject for debate. In Great Britain, J. M. Spaight discussed the options and their consequences, while in France Lieutenant-Colonel Paul Vauthier, an eloquent proponent of Douhet's theories, elaborated his own reflections on aerial warfare in his 1930 publication, *Le Danger aérien et l'avenir du pays*. Vauthier's contribution to the discussion is interesting for many reasons, especially as in his book he takes very seriously the effects of the development of cities on their capacity to withstand aerial attacks, and endorses the approaches formulated by Le Corbusier at the beginning of the 1920s. The thinking of the naval engineer Camille Rougeron followed similar lines, when he underscored the weakness of the fleets in relation to aviation.[54]

Oceans of Fire

Military thinkers were far from being the only ones to make such sombre predictions. The novelist Paul Morand reacted to the bombardment of Barcelona in 1938 and drew

his own alarming conclusions: 'Like Saint Sebastian tied to his stake and defenceless against the rain of arrows, last September the urban populations awaited their demise. Never before had they felt the weight bearing down on their heads of an armed sky above, full of high menace, open traps, falling propellers and trajectories in flame.[55] As we shall see, a profusion of publications appeared in reaction to the war in Spain that sought to increase public awareness of future risks, based on the initiatives of a wide range of authors, ranging from inventive and critical military thinkers such as Rougeron to architects.[56] The sociologist and critic Lewis Mumford went so far as to see defence exercises as 'the materialization of a skillfully invoked nightmare'.[57]

After the Japanese raids in China (Chongqing, Shanghai) and the German and Italian raids in Spain (Madrid, Alicante, Barcelona, Guernica), the war after 1939 was punctuated by urban bombardment, first by

View of the ruins
of **Guernica** after
the Nazi bombardment
of 26 April 1937.
Mary Evans Picture Library

pages 40–41
**Aerial views of Hiroshima
before and after the
dropping of the atomic
bomb**, 6 August 1945,
in Albert Garcia Espuche,
*Ciudades del globo
al satélite*, 1994.
CCA Collection

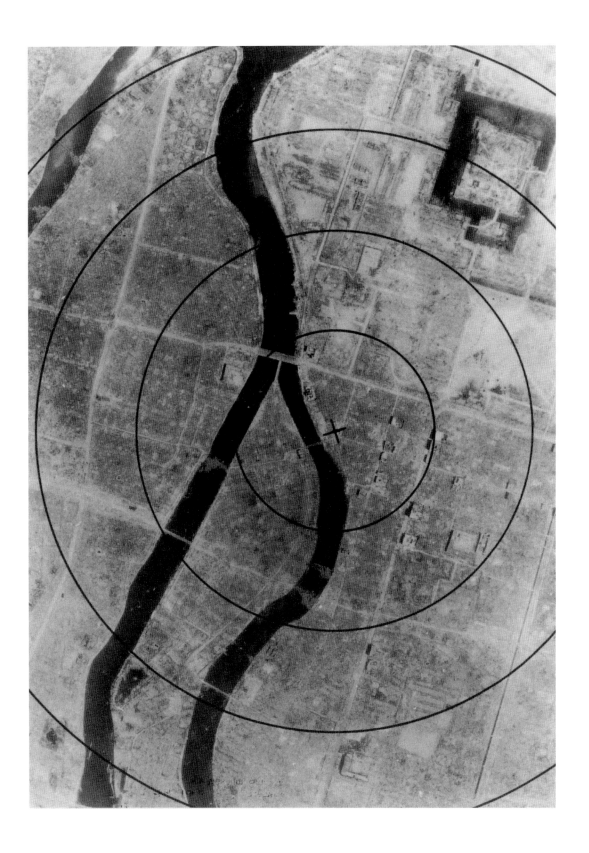

the Axis, as in Warsaw and Rotterdam, whose city centre was flattened by the Luftwaffe on 10 May 1940, as a prelude to the Blitzkrieg in the west. But the Allied raids on Germany, such as Operation Gomorrah on Hamburg, starting on 24 July 1943 and lasting for seven days, or the destruction of Dresden between 13 and 15 February 1945 as part of Operation Thunderclap, would take on completely new dimensions. They have taken their place in literature, with the eyewitness account by Kurt Vonnegut in *Slaughterhouse-Five* and Jörg Friedrich's *The Fire*.[58] Painstaking research in the German, British and American archives has documented the systematic preparation and execution of these raids, and their effects on the targeted cities.[59]

The Allied offensives against Germany and Japan, with their devastating consequences,[60] should not obscure the fact that it was only because they lacked sufficient means that the Nazis did not flatten London. As W. G. Sebald points out in his masterly essay *On the Natural History of Destruction*, 'Scarcely anyone can now doubt that Air Marshal Göring would have wiped out London if his technical resources had allowed him to do so.' Sebald observes that 'the real pioneering achievements in bomb warfare – Guernica, Warsaw, Belgrade, Rotterdam – were the work of the Germans. And when we think of the nights when the fires raged in Cologne and Hamburg and Dresden, we ought also to remember that as early as August 1942 the city of Stalingrad, then swollen (like Dresden later) by an influx of refugees, was under assault from twelve

Yakov Rubanchik
**Anti-aircraft balloons in
the streets of Leningrad,**
20 September 1942.
State Museum of the
History of Saint Petersburg

hundred bombers, and that during this raid alone, which caused elation among the German troops stationed on the opposite bank, forty thousand people lost their lives.'[61] These ordeals inflicted by distant enemies upon cities whose populations were primarily civilians shattered any illusion that cities would be places of refuge. They substantiated the most pessimistic claims made by the authors of the interwar period, except for one important point: aside from Italy in Ethiopia and Japan in China, no belligerent country used toxic gas, no doubt out of fear of reprisal.

Not only were cities the targets of long-range bombing and artillery, but they also became battlefields. They were theatres of fierce combat, sometimes for long years, or simply at the moment of a violent invasion: the Japanese massacres in Nanjing were carried out in seven weeks at the end of 1937. In some cases, a city was affected several times over the course of the conflict. Kharkov, the industrial capital of the Ukraine, was devastated four times by German and Russian forces. Blockades and shortages had a profound effect on daily life in the cities, where hunger and thirst added their own victims to those killed by the bombs. The siege of Madrid by the Nationalists lasted from October 1937 to March 1939, and Leningrad was under siege by German troops for a total of thirty-one months from September 1941 to January 1944.[62] During those years of danger and misery, architects participated in neighbourhood defences and documented in their drawings the anti-aircraft balloons, the monuments buried in sandbags and the buildings in ruin.[63]

Street fighting of unprecedented ferocity took place in the cities. The battle for Stalingrad, which was fought from house to house, as Konstantin Simonov and Vasily Grossman have related,[64] lasted more than six months, from August 1942 to February 1943, and decided the outcome of the war on the Eastern Front, while the final battle of Berlin lasted ten days or so in the spring of 1945. The most spectacular of these battles were only the extreme version of urban combat, which took many other forms, from occasional resistance to full-blown insurrection. In fact, the civilian populations that were the targets of the bombs and victims of shortages were the milieu in which clandestine organisations could develop and become the starting points for urban insurrection, such as in the ghetto and city of Warsaw in April 1943 and from August to October 1944, or in Paris during the uprising of August 1944.

Fragmented Cities

Daily life in cities was transformed by the invasions, bombardments, occupations, insurrections and liberations. A new geography appeared, whose focal points were the headquarters, the compounds and all places directly administered by the military, while the railway stations and factories constituted the poles of attraction for the influx of people and the rain of bombs. Closely monitored by the grids of passive defence, cities were cut up into new pieces, even when they were not occupied by an invader. In the case of conquered cities, the occupying forces established partitions between sectors, isolating whole segments of the population, as was the case in the ghettos of occupied Poland, whose largest, the Warsaw ghetto, was in turn bisected by a 'normal' city route. Bombardments

delineated new boundaries between the zones of burned ruins and the blocks that remained standing, as in Rotterdam, where the *brandgrens* (the edge of the burned zone) remains visible today, and has been the object of a landscape architecture project.[65]

Another division separated the daytime city, which did its best to carry on above ground, and the night-time city of basements, shelters, places of refuge and underground railway tunnels inhabited by city dwellers fleeing the bombs. A new set of movement patterns was added to the usual flows between home and work – the often-hurried movements towards the shelters and the rush to fresh air when a siren announced the end of the alert. The evacuations and exoduses that resulted from the raids and the arrival of hostile forces also punctuated the chronicles of the cities that were emptied of their permanent inhabitants only to overflow with arriving refugees.

Another subdivision would occur as well, but in time rather than space. Against a backdrop of ruins, temporary structures that were not meant to outlive the conflict became a welcome simulacrum of normal life. After the devastation of Rotterdam, the emergency stores built by Jan Brinkman and Jo van den Broek, and the shops built by Hugh Maaskant in 1941 on the cleared Nieuwe Binnenweg restored a vanished

Kogels · Heinemann Ostwald · Schürmann
Plan noodwinkels Dijkzicht
gevelschets.

ARCHITECTENBUREAU BRINKMAN & VAN DEN BROEK · ROTTERDAM

10071

Jan Brinkman
Jo van den Broek
**Project for a temporary
shop for Heineman &
Ostwald, Kogels and**

**Schürmann,
Dijkzicht,** Rotterdam,
elevation, December 1940.
Nederlands
Architectuurinstitut

The Significance of Planning

If there was a field in which the culture of
architects and town planners converged
with that of the civil and military powers
in wartime, it was that of planning. The
notion of the plan, which appeared during
the First World War to account for both
offensive projects at the front and industrial
mobilisation, and which was reflected
politically by the first economic measures
taken by Bolshevik Russia in 1920, was of
course familiar to architects, for whom it
denoted both a geometric mode of projection
and a form of organisation of buildings.[67]

   The projects undertaken during the conflict
itself to prepare for post-war society would
take up these planning intentions whose
means and ends differed from those of
architects, but it is useful to compare them,
if only to gauge their differences. One of the
features they shared was the mobilisation
in force of architects, town planners and
landscape architects in the service of these
visions. One can well imagine that many
of the architects working on the German
Generalplan Ost preferred the comfort of
a heated office to the rigours of the front,
but some of them were true ideologues,
arguing for plans that entailed the agrarian
colonisation and ethnic cleansing of the
eastern territories. Thousands of kilometres
to the west, the planning culture in the United
States, crystallised in the National Resources
Planning Board, aimed at a very different
kind of 'Fordist' society based on mobility
and the response to market forces, but one
whose definition and elaboration required
a comparable mobilisation of architects.

urbanity to the point of serving as an
example for the United States as early
as 1942.[66] And finally, the cities were also
theatres for the mass spectacles that were
interspersed among the main episodes
of the conflict, inscribed in the collective
memory as powerfully as the specifically
military episodes: parades of troops 'going
up' to the front and of prisoners coming
back down, spontaneous expressions of
popular enthusiasm and great orchestrated
celebrations of victories. Even nocturnal
fireworks were part of these spectacles,
their coloured explosions exorcising the
dangerous demons of the bombs and
the shells of the anti-aircraft defences.

1. Le Corbusier, 'La Guerre? Mieux vaut construire', *Plans*, vol. 2, no. 6 (June 1931), 66.
2. 'What Architecture Can Do', *RIBA Journal*, vol. 46, no. 30 (16 October 1939), 996.
3. Monroe Wheeler, ed., *Britain at War*, texts by T. S. Eliot, Herbert Read, E. J. Carter and Carlos Dyer (New York: The Museum of Modern Art, 1941), 74.
4. Heinrich Mann, 'Depuis que les derniers sont tombés . . .' and Thomas Mann, 'La Guerre', *Plans*, vol. 2, no. 6 (June 1931), 7–10.
5. Lewis Mumford, 'A Brief Outline of Hell', in *The Culture of Cities* (New York: Harcourt Brace & Company, 1938), 275.
6. Filippo Tommaso Marinetti, *Poema africano della divisione '28 ottobre'* (Milan: Mondadori, 1937), 28. The original does not include any punctuation. Partial translation by Walter Benjamin in 'The Work of Art in the Age of Mechanical Reproduction', in *Illuminations*, edited by Hannah Arendt (New York: Schocken Books, 1969), 241–42. The phrase missing from Benjamin's translation is in square brackets.
7. Le Corbusier, *Aircraft* (London: Faber & Faber, 1935), 83.
8. Le Corbusier, 'Commentaires relatifs à Moscou et à la Ville Verte', Moscow, 12 March 1930. Typescript, Fondation Le Corbusier A3(1)65, 10–11.
9. Louis-Ferdinand Céline, *Journey to the End of the Night*, translated by Ralph Mannheim (New York: New Directions Books, 1983), 70. Originally published in *Voyage au bout de la nuit* (Paris: Gallimard, 1952 [Denöel, 1932]), 84.
10. Bruce Brooks Pfeiffer and Robert Wojtowitz, eds. *Frank Lloyd Wright + Lewis Mumford: Thirty Years of Correspondence* (New York: Princeton Architecture Press, 2001), 22.
11. Knud Lonberg-Holm and C. Theodore Larson, 'The Technician on the Cultural Front', *The Architectural Record*, vol. 80, no. 12 (December 1936), 472; cited by Marc Dessauce in 'L'*Environmental Control* aux États-Unis et la poursuite du bonheur', in *Les Années 30. L'architecture et les arts de l'espace entre industrie et nostalgie*, edited by Jean-Louis Cohen (Paris: Éditions du Patrimoine, 1997), 161. See also: Knud Lonberg-Holm, 'The Political Aspects of City Planning and Housing (Part I)' and 'City Planning and Housing under Fascism (Part II)',

in *The Monthly Review*, vol. 1, no. 2 (September 1934) and no. 4 (November 1934), quoted in Dessauce, ibid.
12. Dario Matteoni, ed., 'Architecture in the Italian Colonies in Africa', *Rassegna*, no. 51 (September 1992). Giuliano Gresleri, Pier Giorgio Massaretti and Stefano Zagnoni, eds., *Architettura italiana d'oltremare: 1870–1940* (Venice: Marsilio, 1993).
13. *Problemas de la revolución, A.C.*, no. 25, 1937. See Enrique Granell, Antonio Pizza, Josep Maria Rovira and José Angel Sanz Esquide, eds., *A.C. La Revista del GATEPAC 1931–1937* (Madrid: Museo Nacional Centro de Arte Reina Sofiá, 2008).
14. *Écrivains dans la guerre, Revue des sciences humaines* [Université de Lille III], no. 204, 1986. Jean-Paul Ameline, ed., *Face à l'histoire, 1933–1996: l'artiste moderne devant l'événement historique* (Paris: Flammarion and Éditions du Centre Pompidou, 1996).
15. One notable exception is Giorgio Ciucci's analysis 'Gli architetti e la guerra', in *Storia dell'architettura italiana. Il primo Novecento*, edited by Giorgio Ciucci and Giorgio Muratore (Milan: Electa, 2004), 476 and 478.
16. Untitled editorial, *L'Architecture d'aujourd'hui*, vol. 10, no. 9–10 (1939), 9.
17. 'À nos abonnés, à nos amis', *L'Architecture d'aujourd'hui*, vol. 10, no. 8 (1939), 3.
18. 'What Architecture Can Do', *RIBA Journal*, vol. 46, no. 30 (16 October 1939), 995–96.
19. 'Architects and Defense', *Pencil Points*, vol. 22, no. 10 (October 1941), 657.
20. 'Boevye zadatchi sovetskogo arkhitektora', in *Stroitelstvo voennogo vremeni*, vol. 1, Moscow, Soyouz Sovetskikh Arkhitektorov (1941), 2–3.
21. H. F. Geiler, 'Das Bauprogram der Kriegswirtschaft', *Deutsche Bauzeitung*, vol. 73, no. 40 (4 October 1939), 785.
22. Chûta Itô, 'Shin doitsu bunka to Nihon' (The New German Culture and Japan) *Kenchiku zasshi*, vol. 53, no. 647 (February 1939), 191–96. My thanks to Benoît Jacquet for this information.
23. Guy Hartcup, *The Effect of Science on the Second World War* (London: Macmillan, 2000).
24. Ruth Benedict, *The Chrysanthemum and the Sword: Patterns of Japanese Culture* (Boston: Houghton Mifflin, 1946). The study was originally prepared for the army in 1944.

25. Kurt Lewin quoted by Branden Hookway, 'Cockpit', in *Cold War Hothouses. Inventing Postwar Culture, from Cockpit to Playboy*, edited by Beatriz Colomina, Annmarie Brennan and Jeannie Kim (New York: Princeton Architectural Press, 2004), 25.
26. 'The Seabees: The Navy's Fighting Builders', *The Architectural Forum*, vol. 80, no. 2 (February 1944), 48–58.
27. Wells Coates, letter to his daughter Laura, 17 September 1945. CCA, Wells Coates Papers.
28. He had designed one of the best modern houses of the interwar period in Britain: Six Pillars at Dulwich.
29. Alessandro de Magistris, ed., *URSS anni '30-50. Paesaggi dell'utopia staliniana* (Milan: Mazzotta, 1997), 216–17.
30. See the drawings at the Berlin Akademie der Künste, folder 1.77.
31. Bruce Goff, in Paul Heyer, *Architects of Architecture; New Directions in America* (New York: Walker & Co, 1968), 68. See also Philip B. Welch, ed., *Goff on Goff: Conversations and Lectures* (Norman: University of Oklahoma Press, 1996), 28.
32. Berthold Lubetkin to an unidentified correspondent, 7 January 1943. RIBA, Berthold Lubetkin Papers, series 10, box 11, LUB/11/2/28. The material includes numerous exchanges beween Lubetkin, the RAF, and Wells Coates.
33. RIBA, Jacqueline Tyrwhitt Papers, Box 1, TYJ/1/5.
34. Hartmut Frank and Ullrich Schwarz, *Godber Nissen. Ein Meister der Nachkriegsmoderne* (Hamburg: Dölling und Galitz Verlag, 1995).
35. Jonathan M. Reynolds, *Maekawa Kunio and the Emergence of Japanese Modernist Architecture* (Berkeley: University of California Press, 2001), 119–21.
36. James Rose, quoted by Marc Snow, *Modern American Gardens: Designed by James Rose* (New York: Reinhold Publishing Corporation, 1967), 95, in *Crafting a Modern World: the Architecture and Design of Antonin and Noémi Raymond*, edited by Kurt G. F. Helfrich and William Whitaker (New York: Princeton Architectural Press, 2006), 53.
37. They are conserved at the Imperial War Museum. See also his amusing project for a house designed to withstand aerial attacks in Raymond

McGrath, *Twentieth Century Houses* (London: Faber & Faber, 1934), 211.

38. Franz Schulze, *Philip Johnson: Life and Work* (New York: Knopf, 1996), 137–39.

39. Born in Beijing in 1916, died in Brussels in 1996. While awaiting completion of Christophe Pourtois's research, see Pierre-Louis Flouquet, 'La maison aujourd'hui. Interview de l'architecte Simone Guilissen-Hoa', *La Maison*, no. 6 (1967), 177–79.

40. Lodovico Barbiano di Belgiojoso, *Non mi avrete* (Venice: Edizioni del Leone, 1986). Massimo Simini, ed., *Dal lager. Disegni di Lodovico Belgiojoso* (Milan: Edizioni delle Raccolte storiche del commune di Milano, 2008).

41. Robert Jan van Pelt and Deborah Dwork, *Auschwitz: 1270 to the Present* (New Haven and London: Yale University Press, 1996), 192.

42. The plan of the studio, from the archives of Helena Syrkus in Wroclaw, is published in Niels Gutschow and Barbara Klain, *Vernichtung und Utopie: Stadtplanung Warschau 1939–1945* (Hamburg: Junius, 1994), 57.

43. Margarete Schütte-Lihotzky, *Erinnerungen aus dem Widerstand 1938–1945*, edited by Chup Friemert (Hamburg: Konkret Literatur Verlag, 1985).

44. [Ernesto N. Rogers], 'Confessioni di un anonimo del XX secolo', *Domus*, no. 158 (1941), 45. This was the first of nine unsigned articles, the last of which was published in no. 176 (1942), 333.

45. Achim Wendschuh, *Hans Scharoun: Zeichnungen, Aquarelle, Texte* (Berlin: Akademie der Künste, 1993).

46. Le Corbusier, 'L'architecture et la guerre', *Gazette Dunlop*, vol. 19, no. 232 (May 1940), 10–13. Typescript, FLC B3(5)204–206.

47. 'Civilian Defense Reference Number', *The Architectural Forum*, vol. 76, no. 1 (January 1942), 1.

48. Marlene P. Hillier, Eberhard Jäckel and Jürgen Rohwer, *Städte im Zweiten Weltkrieg, Ein internationaler Vergleich* (Essen: Klartext Verlag, 1991). Philippe Chassaigne and Jean-Marc Largeaud, eds., *Villes en guerre* (Paris: Armand Colin, 2004).

49. General Giulio Douhet, *Il dominio dell'aria, saggio sull'arte della guerra aerea* (Rome: Stabilmento poligrafico per l'amministrazione della guerra, 1921). In French: *La Guerre de l'air*, translated by Jean Romeyer (Paris:

Les Ailes, 1932) and *La Maîtrise de l'air*, translated by Benoît Smith and Jean Romeyer (Paris: Economica, 2007). In German: *Luftherrschaft*, translated by Roland E. Strunk (Berlin: Drei Masken Verlag, 1935). In English: *The Command of the Air*, edited by J. P. Harahan and R. H. Kohn, translated by Dino Ferrari (New York: Coward-McCann, 1942). In Russian: *Gospodstvo v vozdukhe*, translated by V. A. Vinograd (Moscow: Voenizdat, 1936).

50. General Giulio Douhet, *The Command of the Air*, 20.

51. Ibid., 9–10 and 58.

52. General Giulio Douhet, 'La Guerra del 19 . . .', *Rivista aeronautica*, vol. 6, no. 3 (March 1930), 409–502.

53. Karl Köhler, 'Douhet und Douhetismus', in *Wehrwissenschaftliche Rundschau*, vol. 14 (1964), 88–91. Edward Warner, 'Douhet, Mitchell, Seversky: Theories of Air Warfare', in *Makers of Modern Strategy*, edited by Edward Mead Earle (Princeton: Princeton University Press, 1948), 487–97. For an overview, see Lee Kennett, *A History of Strategic Bombing. From the First Hot-Air Balloons to Hiroshima and Nagasaki* (New York: Scribner's, 1980) and Sven Lindqvist, *A History of Bombing*, translated by Linda Haverty Rugg (New York: W. W. Norton & Co., 2001).

54. Camille Rougeron, 'La guerre totale et l'aviation', *L'Illustration* (2 September 1931), 382. See also Efi Markou, 'Les Villes des militaires: danger aérien et (pro)positions sociales durant les années trente', in *Villes, espaces et territoires: travaux de l'EHESS 1999* (Paris: EHESS, 1999), 142–53. See also Claude d'Abzac-Epezy, 'La pensée militaire de Camille Rougeron: innovations et marginalité', *Revue française de science politique*, vol. 54, no. 5 (2004), 761–79.

55. Paul Morand, 'Les villes-cibles', *Le Figaro*, 21 November 1938, 1.

56. Camille Rougeron, *Les Enseignements aériens de la guerre d'Espagne* (Paris: Berger-Levrault, 1939).

57. Lewis Mumford, 'A Brief Outline of Hell', in *The Culture of Cities*, note 5, 275.

58. Kurt Vonnegut, *Slaughterhouse-Five, or the Children's Crusade: a Duty-Dance with Death* (New York: Dell, 1968). Jörg Friedrich, *Der Brand: Deutschland im Bombenkrieg 1940–1945* (Munich: Propyläen, 2002);

English edition: *The Fire: The Bombing of Germany, 1940–1945*, translated by Allison Brown (New York: Columbia University Press, 2006).

59. On Hamburg, see Jörn Düwel and Niels Gutschow, *Fortgewischt sind alle überflüssigen Zutaten. Hamburg 1943: Zerstörung und Städtebau* (Berlin: Lukas Verlag, 2008). On Dresden, Oliver Reinhard, Matthias Neutzner and Wolfgang Hesse, eds., *Das rote Leuchten. Dresden und der Bombenkrieg* (Dresden: Edition Sächsische Zeitung, 2005); Paul Addison and Jeremy A. Crang, eds., *Firestorm. The Bombing of Dresden, 1945* (London: Pimlico, 2006).

60. For Japan, see Max Hastings, 'The Bombs', in *Retribution. The Battle for Japan 1944–1945* (New York: Alfred A. Knopf, 2008), 444–81.

61. Winfried Georg Sebald, *On the Natural History of Destruction*, translated by Anthea Bell (New York: Random House, 2004), 103–04.

62. Eva-Maria Stolberg, 'The Leningrad Blockade, 1941–1944: Life in the Fortress of the Rear', in *Endangered Cities: Military Power and Urban Societies in the Era of the World Wars*, edited by Marcus Funck and Roger Chickering (Boston: Brill Academic Publishers, 2004), 95–107.

63. Yu. Yu. Bakhareva, T. V. Kovaleva and T. G. Shishkina, *Arkhitektory blokadnogo Leningrada* (Saint Petersburg: Gosudarstvenny Muzei Istorii Sankt-Peterburga, 2005).

64. Konstantin Simonov, *Days and Nights*, translated by Joseph Barnes (New York: Simon and Schuster, 1945); Vasily Grossman, *Life and Fate*, translated by Robert Chandler (New York: New York Review of Books, 1985).

65. Paul van de Laar and Koos Hage, eds., *Brandgrens Rotterdam 1930 / 2010* (Bussum: Uitgeverij Thoth, 2010).

66. Talbot F. Hamlin, 'Design Standards in War Time', *Pencil Points*, vol. 23, no. 2 (February 1942), 76–71.

67. Le Corbusier, 'Reminder to Architects III. Plan,' in *Towards an Architecture*, translated by John Goodman, introduction by Jean-Louis Cohen (Los Angeles: Getty Research Institute, 2007), 119. Originally published as 'Rappel à Messieurs les architectes, III. le plan', in *Vers une architecture* (Paris: G. Crès & Cie, 1924 [1923]), 31.

August Sander
Aerial view of the centre of Cologne and the banks of the Rhine,
plate from the portfolio
Köln nach der Zerstörung
[Cologne after the destruction], 1945.
CCA Collection

August Sander
View of the Hohenzollern bridge in Cologne (top), and **view of the market and the Sankt Aposteln church in Cologne** (bottom), plates from the portfolio *Köln nach der Zerstörung* [Cologne after the destruction], 1945. CCA Collection

August Sander
Untitled [**view of the Sankt Maria im Kapitol church in Cologne**] (top), and **view of the Elendskirche in Cologne** (bottom), plates from the portfolio *Köln nach der Zerstörung* [Cologne after the destruction], 1945. CCA Collection

August Sander
View of the Sankt Gereon church in Cologne,
plate from the portfolio
Köln nach der Zerstörung
[Cologne after the
destruction], 1945.
CCA Collection

August Sander
**View of the arsenal
of Cologne,** plate from
the portfolio *Köln nach der
Zerstörung* [Cologne after
the destruction], 1945.
CCA Collection

HOMEMAKER'S WAR GUIDE

PLAN

Plan wisely, shop carefully. Look for ceiling prices, pay no more. Watch weights and measures. Carry your own bundles. Save money to pay taxes and BUY WAR BONDS.

MEALS

Guard your health. The Government food guide recommends these essential foods for everyone every day:

MILK & MILK PRODUCTS: At least a pint a day (more for children), or cheese or canned milk.

FRUITS & VEGETABLES: In season when possible. At least one a day: oranges, tomatoes, grapefruit, raw cabbage, salad greens, green or yellow vegetables, some raw, some cooked.

BUTTER & SPREADS are rich in vitamins and should be served at every meal.

EGGS: 3 or 4 weekly per person.

WATER: At least 6 glasses every day.

MEAT, poultry or fish: Only one serving a day.

RATIONING

MEAT. The fighting forces need meat. Make yours go further. Write to U.S. Dep't of Agriculture, Wash., D.C., for free booklet "99 Ways to Share the Meat."

SUGAR makes gunpowder. Get free booklet "Recipes to Match Your Sugar Ration" from your Regional or State Office of Price Administration.

SPARE TIME WAR ACTIVITIES

 Enroll at your Civilian Defense Volunteer Office.
ADDRESS................... TEL..................
Many women are now working in war plants. Take their places by helping all you can in

day nurseries   diet kitchens   clinics

CONSERVE

Buy only what you need. Make what you have last longer. Keep everything in good repair. Hoarding is unpatriotic.

FOOD

 When you shop, ask for "Victory Food Specials" recommended by the U.S. Dep't of Agriculture. You will help save foods for our fighting forces.
Look for this sign.

RUBBER: Rubber will last longer if washed frequently.

wash in warm water and mild soap / dry and store in cool, dark place / don't store in hot, light place

POTS & PANS

leave black on bottoms of pots / don't scrub until shiny / heat takes longer through shiny surface

FUEL

put in storm windows / weather-stripping / close off unused rooms

wear warm clothes / use less hot water / get along with fewer lights

CLOTHING

keep clean and mothproof / mend and repair / make over and refashion

SALVAGE

FATS

All types are needed: animal, poultry, vegetable fats make explosives.

Strain through fine mesh into metal container. / Keep in cool place. Rancid fat makes fewer bullets. / Sell to butcher when you have 1 pound or more.

DON'T waste a bit of fat or sell kitchen fats normally used for cooking.

RUBBER scrap of all kinds such as:

| MATS | HEELS | OVERSHOES | WATER BAGS | TENNIS SHOES |
| HOSE | BATHING CAPS | RUBBER BANDS | BATHING SHOES | RAINCOATS |

METALS, worn out objects like these:

| TUBES | STOVES | RADIATORS | PLUMBING | TOYS |
| BEDS | ELECTRIC CORD | BATTERIES | FLAT IRONS | PANS |

Tin cans are collected only in certain cities. Before saving them, check with your local Salvage Committee.

RAGS, cast-off things like:

| WOOLEN CLIPPINGS | TROUSER CUFFS | CAST-OFF CLOTHING | UNDERWEAR | DRAPERIES |
| MATTRESSES | CARPETS | PILLOWS | OLD STOCKINGS | MANILA ROPE |

HOW TO GET RID OF JUNK

1. DONATE to community scrap collection

2. SELL to junk dealer

3. BOY SCOUTS and other organizations will help

4. DEPT. OF AGRICULTURE, local branch, will advise you in farm areas

★ If in doubt about any point, call your local Salvage Committee ★ Scrap is bought by dealers, who are the only qualified agents to grade, sort, process and return it into war production channels.

★ Don't call for a collector until you have at least 100 pounds of salvage material. Try to take your own scrap to local dealer or collection center. Get the children to work for Victory.

AIR RAID PROTECTION

AIR RAID WARDEN: Name.............. Address.............. Tel..............

BLOCK LEADER: Name.............. Address.............. Tel..............

PREPARE

Safety in air raids depends on what you do beforehand.

 Choose a shelter room with least outer wall space and few windows.

Know your local air raid alarm signals.

 Assign every member of the family a specific job.

STAY HOME

The safest place in an air raid is at home.

Stay off the streets and away from all glass.

 If driving, park car by curb, turn off lights, take keys, but leave doors unlocked so car can be moved. Seek shelter.

Do not telephone—you may block calls for aid.

BLACKOUT

A quick and complete blackout will help fool the enemy.

 A candle light may be seen for miles from the air.

See that your shelter room can be blacked out efficiently so you may have light and be comfortable during alarms.

BOMBS

The enemy now uses more dangerous fire bombs.

 If bomb is in your home, flood the room with a jet of water. Keep behind heavy wall, only exposing hand holding hose. Crouch down as low as possible.

 Keep at least 10 gallons of water on hand. Sand is no longer recommended.

BLOCK PLAN

Your block is part of the war plan for the home front.

 Your Block Leader can tell you about civilian war services. In other lands, war is being fought block by block. You can fight it that way here. Help your Block Leader's campaigns which speed our victory.

VICTORY BEGINS AT HOME ★ DO YOUR PART

OWI Poster No. 20. Additional copies may be obtained upon request from the Division of Public Inquiries, Office of War Information, Washington, D.C.

U.S. GOVERNMENT PRINTING OFFICE 1942—O—498205

3/ Total Mobilisation, from the Factory to the Kitchen

It is obvious that we shall have to revise our system of individual specialisation and return to something like the self-reliant competence of our pioneer forefathers. We shall have to make more things for ourselves, and fix more things for ourselves – or do without. And to do without is not the American way of life.
The War-Time Guide Book for the Home, 1942[1]

Unusual materials, designs and methods of fabrication not used in normal times are entirely justified under prevailing conditions.
Herbert L. Whittemore, *Engineering News-Record*, 1942[2]

From the moment that governments found themselves at the centre of a panoptic wartime organisation, no private sphere remained untouched, no space remained unaffected. Mobilisation into the armed forces or into the factories resulted de facto in the requisition of housing. At a broader scale, all raw materials, mineral or agricultural, along with every industrial material, were placed in the service of the national effort. The exclusive concentration on war production and the disruption of some traditional transportation routes stimulated scientific research and the invention of new processes and forms. There was a significant

Ralph Illigan
'**Homemaker's War Guide**:
Plan, Conserve, Salvage,
Air Raid Protection.
Victory Begins at Home,
Do Your Part', poster, 1942.
Harry Ransom Humanities
Research Center, The University
of Texas at Austin

increase in the number of synthetic materials, ranging from elastomers and fuels to vast assortments of products. Several new approaches emerged as a result: the substitution of other materials for steel or concrete; the employment of new substances such as plastics; but also the ingenious and economic utilisation of existing materials such as wood and cardboard, especially as a result of advances in adhesives. These developments are easier to follow in the United States, especially through the abundant advertising for new materials in professional journals and magazines for the general public, but they were equally present in Great Britain, Germany and Italy, which had embarked on a policy of autarchy in 1936, after the League of Nations imposed sanctions in response to the aggression upon Ethiopia.

War Materials

In September 1944, *The Architectural Review* started publication of the 'Design Review', a monthly column devoted to new materials and their future uses. The column was edited by Sadie Speight, a member of the Design Research Unit, a group founded in 1943 by the art historian Herbert Read, under the watchful eye of Nikolaus Pevsner – the editor-in-chief's assistant on paper, but far more influential in actual fact on the content of the journal. The column was meant to

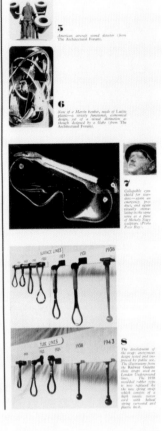

enable 'a discussion of new designs, new materials and new processes . . . as a reminder of the specific visual qualities of our age which war necessities are bringing out in their purest form, and which a more carefree and fanciful post-war world should not forget'.[3] In the first instalment, quasi-abstract images of insulating materials such as Rosiltex and Isoflex, panels of artificial expanded rubber such as Onazote, and of fibreglass were presented like novel ideas for Christmas presents. Later instalments presented consumer products that were more deliberately frivolous.[4]

The first stage consisted more in economising than in innovating.

The preoccupation with conserving material led to a new ethic of the project, based on economy. The issue of *The Architectural Record* that followed the attack on Pearl Harbor could not have been more explicit, when it affirmed that 'Total war means all-out conservation' and applied this slogan to all elements of building, including structural materials and plumbing.[5] The War Production Board, created in Washington in 1942, issued more than three hundred

'Design Review',
article in *The Architectural Review*, June 1944.
CCA Collection

orders of 'limitation' or 'economy of materials' in the first six months of its operation. It immediately called for 'American ingenuity' from the country's architects and engineers: 'The basic rule of conservation . . . is to eliminate the use of critical materials or to substitute materials that are less critical for the more critical ordinarily used; or through the use of materials that are entirely non-critical. To do this, changes in design and type or method of construction are usually necessary – the abandoning of the usual or "latest" forms is often essential in order that the goal may be attained. The answer is often found in "reverting to type", or those forms previously used and until recently superseded by more advanced methods.'[6] Another response lay in the simplification of production processes. Thus the American Portland Cement Association claimed in its advertisements

that using 'architectural' concrete, that is to say raw concrete showing traces of its formwork, would save in 'critical materials, transportation, equipment, construction time'.[7] For his part, the modern architect Howard Robertson called for 'structural economy' in Great Britain, motivated by concern for conserving resources, as shown in a wide variety of examples in 1940.[8]

Wood Reinvented

Innovation became an official policy in all the nations at war. One of the most remarkable examples of this direction was the discovery of the potential of wood. Even if torrential 'storms of steel' were falling that were even heavier than those Ernst Jünger had described in 1914–1918, I would venture the hypothesis that one of the most significant materials developed during the war was wood. The kind of wood in question did not come directly from sawmills, even if the Chicago School of Design under László Moholy-Nagy worked on furniture springs and mattresses from wood strips in order to replace metal wire, a programme undertaken in another form in Great Britain as well.[9] Instead, it was a reinvented wood, widely used as a substitute material, for example to take the place of steel in the truss work for the large shelters for the US Navy. In 1944, *The Architectural Forum* noted that 'With the suddenness of Pearl Harbor, steel virtually disappeared

War Speeds Concrete Progress

Drawn by Clestre B. Price for Lone Star Cement Corporation

'War Speeds Concrete Progress', advertisement in *The New Pencil Points*, June 1943.
CCA Collection

With metal springs out for the duration, wooden springs are being called on to provide comfort in upholstered furniture and bedding. A variety of types have been designed, all based on the natural resiliency of wood, and a few of these are now in production. In addition to individual spring designs, numerous ideas are being tried out by bed spring manufacturers, involving the use of wood slats, crossed webbing, cantilever construction, etc.

Most publicized of the new wooden springs is the Victory or "V" Spring developed by the School of Design in

"SLEEP LIKE A LOG"
On New Wood Springs

Chicago and pictured on this page. L. Moholy-Nagy, Director of the school, claims that his wooden springs can simulate any metal spring of any compression weight. Tests, intended to equal ten years' wear, indicate them to be fully as durable as metal springs and equally satisfactory in performance. Like metal springs they lose some of their flexibility from fatigue, but unlike metal springs they recover it.

The photographs on this page show the experimental work of wood springs at the Chicago School of Design made by Charles W. Niedringhaus, Martha Mc-Cown, Jack Waldheim, Kalman Toman, and L. Moholy-Nagy.

Jack Waldheim, student at the Chicago School of Design, measures the compression weight of a "Z" (double "V") spring. The school started these experiments in 1937.

Examples above and at top by Strand Ski Company

Source: IIT Archives (Chicago)

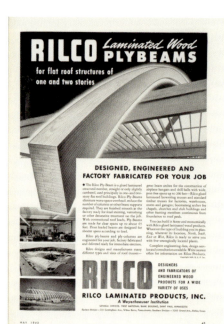

as a structural material for building frames. Wood, however, in replacing it, has proven so good a substitute that it is undoubtedly slated for a peacetime popularity it has not known since the introduction of steel construction. With war, long span trusses . . . in turn made the rapid erection of hangars and shops possible. The wartime use of laminated wood arches and plywood girders

Top: '"Sleep like a Log" on New Wood Springs', advertisement for mattress springs designed by László Moholy-Nagy at the School of Design, Chicago, in *Bruce Magazine*, May–June 1943. Illinois Institute of Technology Archives

Bottom: **Advertisement for 'RILCO laminated wood plybeams**, for flat roof structures of one and two stories', in *The Architectural Forum*, May 1943. CCA Collection

are developments which designers are eager to adopt for 194X buildings.'[10]

Indeed, progress in the chemistry of resins and adhesives permitted the use of small pieces of wood, assembled to form beams, trusses and arches, whose strength was comparable to similar elements in metal. This recourse to smaller pieces of wood was all the more crucial as the consumption of wood became all-devouring. Glued up laminates became available in a variety of structural pieces and enabled the construction of dirigible hangars or large sheds like the 2-million-square-foot Douglas Aircraft factory erected by the Austin Company at Orchard Place in Chicago – now the location of O'Hare Airport. The difference between these

Charles Eames
Ray Eames
Prototype for a glider nose piece of moulded glued-up wood laminate, in Anthony Denzer, *The Modern Home as Social Commentary*, 1943. CCA Collection

American solutions and those imagined without recourse to phenolic resins can be gauged by reading the issue that the French periodical *Techniques et architecture* devoted to wood in 1942. While the patriotic precedents of the curved girders invented by Philibert de l'Orme are justifiably invoked, the assemblages built up by using dowels, braces and bolting were far from performing at the level of those made of glued-up wood laminates.[11] In Italy, large three-hinged arches made of smaller elements of wood woven into lattices were also fabricated for factories and for the army.[12] By combining small pieces of wood and the techniques of moulding, Charles and Ray Eames designed nose pieces for transport gliders in 1943 that were made from moulded glued-up wood laminate. And Jean Prouvé, for his part, temporarily abandoned his research into steel furniture to design a chair in 1942 that was 'entirely in wood'.[13]

The use of plywood, a material invented in the 19th century, as Nikolaus Pevsner recounted in great detail in 1938 and 1939 in the pages of *The Architectural Review*,[14] became widespread due to its qualities, if not its price. As the same magazine affirmed: 'In plywood the composite construction serves to tame the wood to such a degree that it is in effect an entirely different material; one about which there has been a good deal of misunderstanding, and which in the minds of many is still a cheap substitute for something better. This is a double fallacy because, in addition to being fundamentally different from solid wood, it is not in fact a particularly cheap material.'[15] But this was not the problem, and its uses proliferated because powerful presses and casts were able to give it complex concave shapes, but most of all because of the new phenolic glues. Some airplanes, like the de Havilland Mosquito, had frames made of plywood impregnated with resin; this modern material was limited to military use in Great Britain. In the United States, where it became commercially available under different labels, such as Plymold, the 'wood that bends',[16] was used by László Moholy-Nagy at the Chicago School of Design to make moulded chairs. Between 1943 and 1945, Charles and Ray Eames employed it to make tailpieces for airplanes, and also for splints and litters in moulded plywood that seem to belong as much to the field of sculpture as to that of paramedical equipment. In the densely wooded country of Finland, the architect Karl Stigzelius worked on polygonal-shaped plywood tents in 1941 and 1941 with the manufacturer Parviainen.[17] As wood became increasingly rare due to the extent of its use, smaller and smaller pieces were recycled, for example in Homasote panels, consisting of wood pulp and bits of newspaper. In Great Britain, the use of wood in aviation led to its rationing in other industries.[18]

Alongside these technical and plastic advances, trees continued to be used in much less sophisticated ways. Le Corbusier, the champion of reinforced concrete, resorted to very primitive techniques in his designs for the 'Maisons Murondins', in the context of the 'return to the land' called for by the Maréchal Pétain after the French surrender. Given the lack of shelters produced in the workshop, 'The solution appeared like the egg of Columbus: the shelter must be built in situ, with unworked (or scarcely worked) materials found on-site, with earth, sand, wood from the forest, branches, bundles of sticks, and clumps of grass.'[19] The wood was to consist of unsquared logs set by volunteers with help from the qualified craftsmen of the Compagnons de France. This project for 'provisional rural villages' was part of a series of ventures using traditional techniques for wood. The same applied to construction in Finland with trunks or logs from birch trees during the Continuation War with the Soviet Union. Conceived by the designer Ilmari Tapiovaara, among others, they are of astounding plastic quality.[20] On the other side of the front, the Russians would have massive recourse to the simplest wood constructions for the needs of both the front and the rear.

Le Corbusier
Cover of *Les Constructions 'Murondins'*, 1942.
CCA Collection

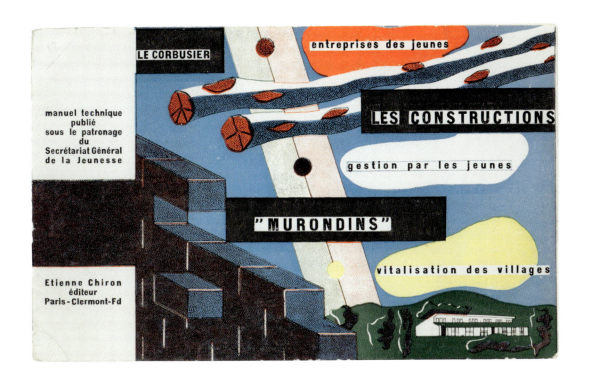

In his entry for a competition organised by Gio Ponti, the director of *Stile*, Carlo Mollino developed furniture derived from wooden airplane propellers, whose characteristic features, notably their continuity, absence of visible joints and resistance to torsion were 'the modern criteria that determined the form of aircraft construction when it was based on wooden structures, and where durability, reliability and ability to resist warping are indispensable. So it is in the construction of propellers and skis, where the use of plywood is now common, due to its advantages of reliability and cost.'[21]

Synthetic Products

The shortage of steel led to innovative solutions, the first of which were developed in Italy, starting in 1936, where reinforced concrete was recommended as a fundamental building material, to be dressed in marble or ceramic tiles for public buildings. Lightweight reinforced concretes, as well as concrete reinforced with bamboo, were also developed.[22] Several modern architects, such as Giuseppe Pagano, tended to resist the excesses of these campaigns and took positions against the 'mystique of autarchy' that was a point of pride for the publications of the regime.[23] At the same time, industry was finding its own solutions and developed innovative uses for aluminium, which Italy produced in quantity. Carlo Emilio Gadda, a writer trained as an engineer, had already devoted a hymn to aluminium in 1931.[24] Artificial rubber, asbestos, wood particle boards – Populit – and fibreglass were all widely distributed. The leading figures

of the profession discussed the issues of autarchy in 1938 in the columns of the *Popolo d'Italia*.[25] After studying a construction system of concrete reinforced with wood, the engineer Pier Luigi Nervi developed the technique of 'ferrocemento', using steel mesh.[26]

Le Corbusier
Maisons 'Murondins',
plan and section, 1940.
Fondation Le Corbusier

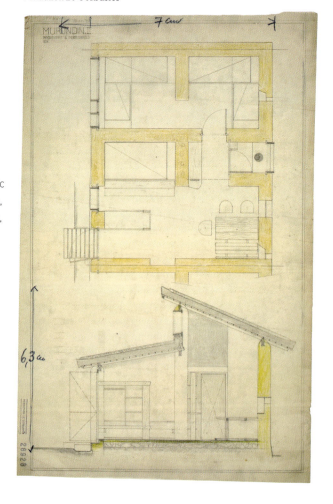

The directives applying to construction ranged from encouragement to constraint, and in some cases, to the complete banning of civil construction. The passage occurred smoothly in Germany, where the spectre of the restrictions of the First World War, which had led to a fateful demoralisation of the population, was still present. On the other hand, British industries strongly protested in 1940 against the curtailment of non-priority programmes, and they continued the debate thereafter[27] – which shows in passing that democratic life continued in wartime Great Britain. In the United States, the regulation of civil production was not achieved by interdiction, but by drawing up lists of priority materials that private builders could not obtain.[28] The sheer volume of construction in the United States required the invention or dissemination of new types of basic building materials, associated with the development of prefabrication. The plaster panels of the United Gypsum Company were used to build houses. One of the most successful materials in this connection was Cemesto, a construction panel of asbestos cement with a core of sugar cane fibres developed by Celotex.

But the most important changes in materials brought on by the war were

Advertisement for 'Populit', in *Costruzioni Casabella*, February–March 1942. CCA Collection

'Glass Fibres and their Use in Construction', article in *Costruzioni Casabella*, February–March 1942. CCA Collection

in the field of plastics. Although Bakelite, which had been invented in 1909, had been in widespread use before the war, an important threshold was crossed with the development of petroleum-based synthetic materials and the injection-moulding process. Metal pieces such as valves or faucets could be successfully replaced by identical fittings in polyvinyl chloride. And invention did not stop there, leading to new uses for compounds produced in the laboratory and the search for raw materials aside from the strategic ones, such as farm products, from milk to nuts.[29] Among the greatest technological successes was polymethyl methacrylate, or Plexiglas, invented in 1936 by a company of German origin, Rohm & Haas, which found its first uses in airplane canopies. Another was vinyl, which was widely

used by the US Navy as an insulating material. The Navy was also the first to use melamine formaldehyde for dishes.[30] Another area of technical invention was the combination of new materials with existing ones, such as the development of sandwich panels. *The Architectural Record* observed in 1943 that 'men who know plastics think of them as materials which, instead of replacing standard materials, often can serve to heighten their usefulness. Plastics and wood together, for instance, can be employed where neither material would do by itself. Resin bonded plywood is an illustration. There are many others:

'Celotex Cemesto Homes', in *Techniques et architecture*, November 1945. CCA Collection

The new world of plastics

by Raymond R. Dickey,
Editor, "Modern Plastics"

The future of plastics is exciting because of two things—availability and physical properties. They are made from everything. Wood waste, coal tar chemicals, petroleum gases, brine, limestone, air, cotton, natural gas, skim milk, fat products and wastes, and plant oils. They will be cheap in the world of tomorrow. They will have unusual and wonderful properties. Bright, water repellent, hard to break, warm, color-fast, glossy—all these properties are possible. In plastics, industry has magic things which can be altered to any need that the builders of the future may require. They can be transparent for windows that pass the ultraviolet light of the sun, or opaque, as you choose. They can be gaudy or somber, sound deadening or brassy loud, strong or fragile, smooth or rough, rigid or flexible—if you don't see what you want, ask. The only thing we haven't got is what hasn't been thought of yet.

Plastics, to any one outside the industry, present a somewhat bewildering array of chemical names and engineering properties. There are cellulose plastics, casein plastics, vinyls, phenolics, ureas, on through such tongue twisters as phenol-furfural, methyl methacrylate, and phenol-formaldehyde.

Plastics must be considered in the same light as metals. We have many metals for many jobs and the properties and engineering characteristics of each are well known to architects, designers, and engineers.

The new techniques in plastic-bonded plywood offer a type of home to the middle- and low-income groups that could have only come about with the use of synthetics derived through extensive chemical research. One interesting type of plywood is made from 4x8 foot panels bonded together by a special type of joint into a composite wallboard 8 feet wide and up to 20 feet long. These may be used as exterior panels in the finished home.

For interior purposes an unbleached muslin is bonded under heat with synthetic resin to the plywood, thus providing a permanently check-free surface for decoration which takes the place of one coat of paint. Only about 5 percent by weight of the finished product is synthetic resin, but without such plastic glass prefabrication of this type of home would be impossible.

Mahlon G. Milliken has said in a recent address, "Already the British are experimenting with plastic housing which they ex

the glass-and-plastic sandwich which is safety glass; plastic-coated decorative fabrics; plastic-impregnated glass wool pressed into a slab with heat-insulating and structural qualities; plastic surface coatings, clear and weather-resisting, for exposed metals; canvas impregnated with plastics and moulded into a light, strong and semi-rigid shape – like the seats now made for airplane pilots.'[31]

Thanks to progress in synthetic elastomers, which became essential as soon as the Japanese had cut off supply of Indonesian rubber trees, there were significant advances in pneumatic equipment in all fields. The British mass-produced inflatable tanks and landing craft for use as decoys in camouflage and diversionary operations, while the use of inflatable life rafts became increasingly common on ships and aircraft.[32] In construction, pneumatic structures appeared on building sites, with the American architect Wallace Neff using them as reusable moulds to make houses in sprayed-on concrete.

Raymond Dickey,
'The New World of Plastics', article in
The New Pencil Points,
January 1943.
CCA Collection

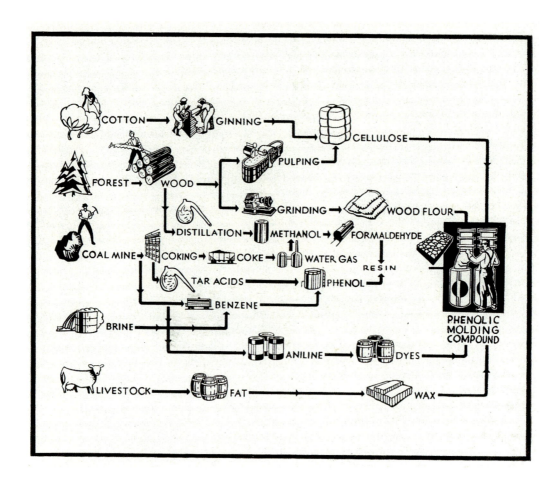

TRANSPARENT MODEL OF BLOWER SYSTEM

PLASTIC-PLYWOOD FUSELAGE, WEIGHT 75 LBS.

Recycling, Insulation and Substitution

The use of earth, plaster, particles and small pieces of wood was encouraged and became a major factor in industry. Recourse to these 'poor' materials cannot in any way be seen as a technical 'regression', for it relied on innovative production methods. In addition, every possible means was explored to organise the recovery and

Top: **The production of plastics**, diagram, in E. F. Lougee, *Plastics from Farm and Forests*, 1943. Getty Research Institute

Bottom: **'Plastics catalogue'**, illustration in *The Architectural Forum*, March 1943. CCA Collection

reuse of metals. In occupied Paris, monumental statues were dismantled and melted down, while in London a campaign to take down the fences around private squares was underway.[33] In Marseille, the engineer Robert Lavocat and the architect Jacques Coüelle invented 'ceramic spindles' in the form of truncated cones to enable the construction of inexpensive vaults.[34]

The energy consumption of dwellings was a particular focus of attention, and in America it led to what was no doubt the first campaign for thermal insulation, by means of insulating panels of wood scraps, compressed straw and cotton fibre, whose production grew rapidly.[35] The notion of conservation was applied to energy consumption, in building construction that used technologically simple materials in the place of thick masonry construction.

For the French, one German term more than any other came to express all the shortages of the occupation:

Ersatz (substitute), used in relation to coffee, chocolate, fabrics, etc. Issues of substitution were widespread during the war. In Paris, Henri-Marcel Magne, a professor at the Conservatoire National des Arts et Métiers and a member of the Collaboration group, organised in 1942 an exhibition on 'replacement materials' for the Société d'Encouragement pour l'Industrie Nationale.[36] This policy of substitution, carried forth on a global scale, occasionally led to strange results: in 1941, because the green colour on packs of Lucky Strike cigarettes contained metal, Raymond Loewy was asked to rethink the design of the packaging.

'Construction of a "balloon" house' [project by Wallace Neff], in *Techniques et architecture*, November 1945. CCA Collection

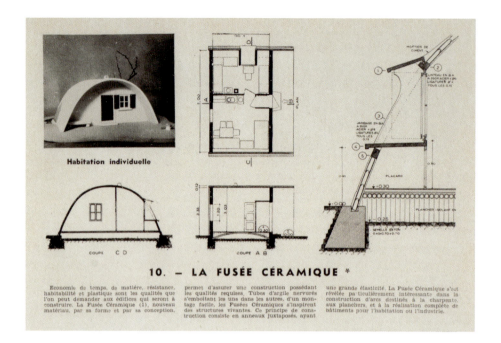

10. — LA FUSÉE CÉRAMIQUE *

Economie de temps, de matière, résistance, habitabilité et plastique sont les qualités que l'on peut demander aux édifices qui seront à construire. La Fusée Céramique (1), nouveau matériau, par sa forme et par sa conception, permet d'assurer une construction possédant les qualités requises. Tubes d'argile nervurés s'emboîtant les uns dans les autres, d'un montage facile, les Fusées Céramiques s'inspirent des structures vivantes. Ce principe de construction consiste en anneaux juxtaposés, ayant une grande élasticité. La Fusée Céramique s'est révélée particulièrement intéressante dans la construction d'arcs destinés à la charpente, aux planchers, et à la réalisation complète de bâtiments pour l'habitation ou l'industrie.

The Housewife, Combatant and Manager

While construction materials were being regulated through rationing and the administrative regulation of markets, households were also subject to significant programmes of restriction. The distribution of both organic and artificial substances, whether for food, for textiles, or for cleaning and repair of buildings was carefully and parsimoniously controlled. Cities were the bastions of the home front in the system put in place to wage total war and they in turn consisted of myriad small forts: each and every dwelling was mobilised from the very first days of war. War culture affected every practice within the house, and the domestic component was celebrated in the press and in film and radio just as much as the military component.[37] As had been the case twenty-five years earlier, a general policy of rationing was introduced in the warring nations, which regulated access to foodstuffs, textiles and tobacco. Highly visible campaigns were launched to convince families to consume materials sparingly and to recycle waste. Every form of persuasion was put to use and applied across the board, from food to underwear. The Scandale brand of girdles, for example, invited Frenchwomen under occupation to extend the life of their intimate apparel.[38] Transformed into a household manager – the French word *ménagère* (housewife) shares the same

Top: **The ceramic spindle barrel-vault hut**, in *Techniques et architecture*, July 1945. Collection of the author

'Save Fuel . . . Insulate your Home', poster, c. 1942. Harry Ransom Humanities Research Center, The University of Texas at Austin

SAVE FUEL..
INSULATE YOUR HOME

FUEL IS A WEAPON OF WAR...DON'T WASTE IT

86-S

**Ask your Building Materials Dealer about
Insulation Board for Homes..Attic rooms..Garages..Windows**

SPONSORED BY
INSULATION BOARD INSTITUTE
FOR U.S. GOVERNMENT

root as the English 'manager' – the mistress of the house was asked to 'plan', to 'conserve' and to 'recover', according to the terms of an American poster of 1942, entitled 'Homemaker War Guide'. The domestic battle station was transformed by these kinds of measures, and they affected the very concept of buildings and their interiors. In the United States, homes participating in these programmes displayed a sign on their window that stated 'This is a V Home'. Specific manuals were developed to help builders and residents follow the technical prescriptions, such as the *War-Time Guide Book for the Home*, whose subtitle was 'Make It Yourself, Fix It Yourself'.[39] The guiding principles were economy and self-sufficiency in maintaining and managing the home, which entailed significant revisions to home economics manuals, a very widespread literary genre.

In terms of food preparation, the war further extended the programmes for the rationalisation of domestic space that had started prior to 1914 with Christine Frederick and had developed after 1925 with the Frankfurt kitchen, the most radical form of a domestic space structured like a workspace. With the management of food supplies and the transformations in foodstuffs demanded by the war, it was no longer enough for women to simply be domestic producers. In the United States, in addition to the half a million women mobilised into the armed forces, another five million of them were employed in the defence industries.[40] In the absence of men, many women became both housewives and heads of family, and they were urged by official campaigns, by food corporations,

'Restrictions',
advertisement for Scandale
girdle, in *L'Illustration*,
24 May 1941.
Collection of the author

and by women's magazines, from the *Ladies' Home Journal* to *Good Housekeeping*, to become veritable managers at the heart of the home. They organised children into squads and assigned them tasks, they planned meals and food shopping in advance, they stocked the refrigerator judiciously, and used their rationing tickets carefully.[41] New types of prepared, ready-to-eat foods began to appear, in addition to the substitute foodstuffs that were currently on the menu for families of all countries, from saccharine and powdered eggs to coffee made from roasted cereals.

'Help Bring Them Back to You!', poster, 1943. The Wolfsonian-Florida International University, Miami Beach, Florida, gift of Leonard A. Lauder

From 'Useful Objects' to the Utility Scheme

Cultural institutions continued to play a distinct role in persuasion campaigns aimed at educating consumers and guiding them, when the market continued to function, towards reasonable purchases. In 1942, The Museum of Modern Art in New York put together an exhibition entitled 'Useful Objects in Wartime', imparting an aura to the most modest of domestic objects made from non-strategic materials. As the fifth in a series devoted to everyday objects costing less than ten dollars, this exhibition followed the criteria established by the Conservation and Substitution Branch of the War Production Board. The prescriptions of that administrative branch served as the programme for the exhibition, which consisted of three sections: 'Household objects made of non priority materials; articles asked for by men and women in the Army and Navy; and supplies necessary for adequate civilian defense'.[42] The exhibition fulfilled a double mission: to make consumers more vigilant in their decisions, avoiding 'critical' metals such as nickel, copper, aluminium, tin and steel, along with plastics such as lucite, Plexiglas,

'Useful Objects in Wartime', two-page spread in the *Bulletin of the Museum of Modern Art*, December 1942–January 1944. CCA

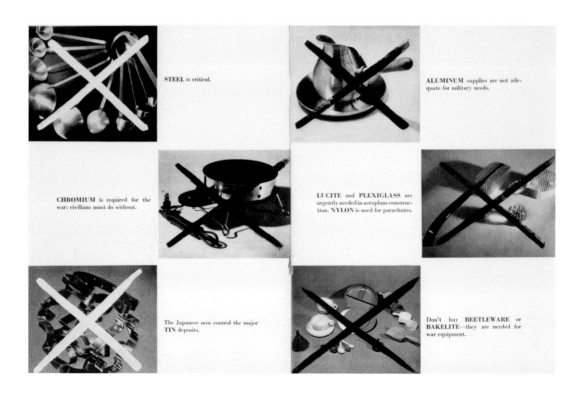

nylon, and other materials used for aircraft, and at the same time to help them acquire a taste for functional and innovative objects.

The rationing of consumer objects was already the rule around the world, but the most extensive policy was deployed in Great Britain, with the ambitious Utility Scheme, or public interest programme, elaborated by the Board of Trade in 1943. It put in place a veritable public administration for the production of everyday objects. Redefining the catalogue of producers, it promoted the most efficient use of materials and labour not only in the production of furniture, but also for glassware, clothing, lingerie and shoes.[43] This series of measures affected design as much as production, and aimed at drastically reducing the range of objects

Objects on display in the 'Useful Objects in Wartime' exhibition. Clockwise, from lower left: Russel Wright, *American Modern* salad bowl, glazed earthenware, manufactured by Steubenville Pottery Company, Steubenville, Ohio, 1937. Attributed to Paul V. Gardner, lower section of *Flameware* double boiler, Pyrex glass and wood, manufactured by Corning Glass Works, Corning, New York, c. 1940. Peter Schlumbohm, Chemex coffee pot, glass, wood and leather, manufactured by Chemex Corp., New York, c. 1939. Attributed to Paul V. Gardner, double boiler, Pyrex glass and stainless steel, manufactured by Corning Glass Works, Corning, New York,

c. 1937. Designer unknown, Silver Streak iron, Pyrex glass and chromium-plated steel, manufactured by Corning Glass Works, Corning, New York, and Saunders & Tool Corporation, Yonkers, New York, 1943. The Liliane and David M. Stewart Program for Modern Design Salad bowl, lower section of double boiler and coffee pot: gift of Dr Michael Sze Double boiler: gift of Eric Brill

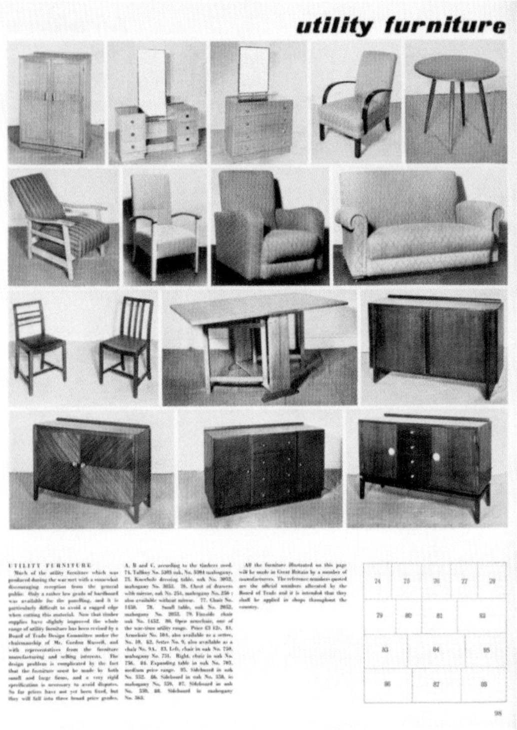
utility furniture
UTILITY FURNITURE

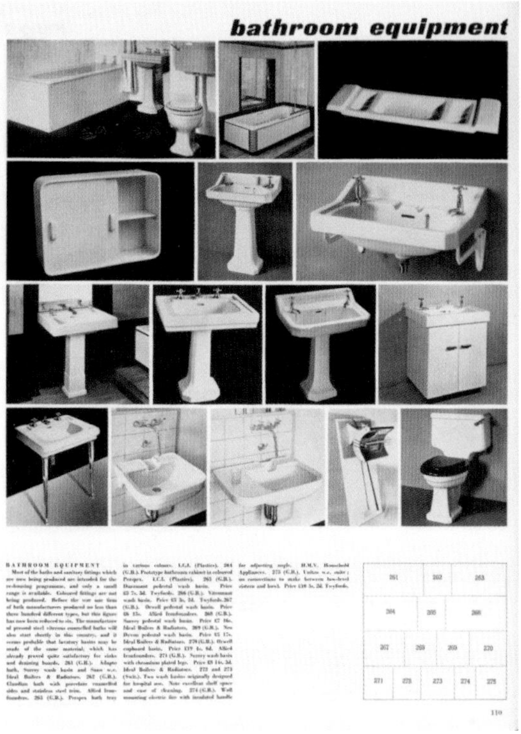
bathroom equipment
BATHROOM EQUIPMENT

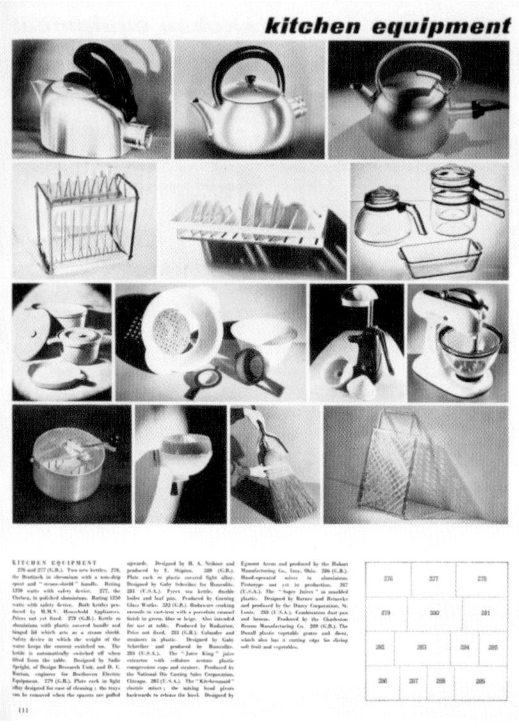
kitchen equipment
KITCHEN EQUIPMENT

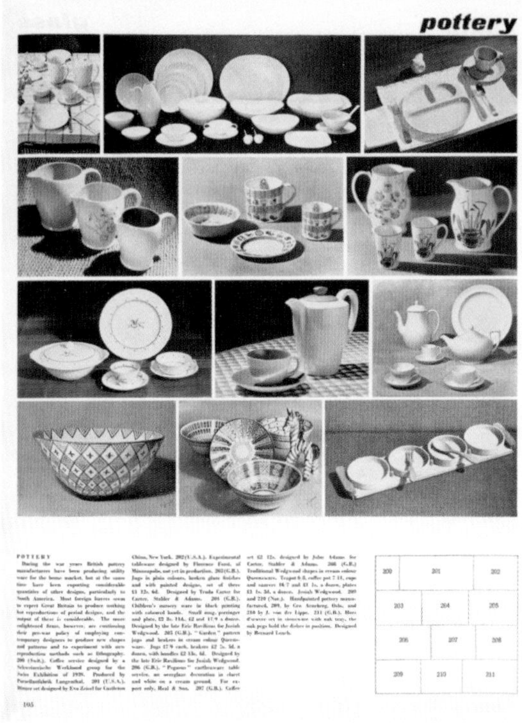
pottery
POTTERY

offered for consumption, shaping material culture in Britain for an entire decade. The programme was set up by a Utility Design Panel, under the direction of the designer Gordon Russell. It included manufacturers and designers, and was accompanied by a vigorous propaganda campaign, leading to exhibitions such as the one in the West End of London in 1942. Its programmes aimed at formal simplicity, at reducing redundancies between objects that simply differed in outward appearance, and especially at the elimination of decoration, which was considered too costly in terms of materials and labour. In keeping with these goals, the porcelain producer Wedgwood marketed a simplified Victory china.[44] As *The Architectural Review* would observe in 1946, 'Much of the utility furniture that was produced during the war met with a somewhat discouraging reception from the general public.'[45] The Czech architect Jacques Groag, a disciple of Adolf Loos, was one of Russell's principal collaborators. In 1946, Russell wrote up a very favourable account of the programme, and said of Groag: 'The modern movement was in his blood and he provided exactly the right counter-irritant to the most prosaic outlook which might so easily have grown up owing to the bludgeoning of difficulties and shortages of every kind. It was so

fatally simple to take the easiest solution, and let many details go on in the way the trade has always done them.'[46] The proponents of modern architecture expected this programme to bring to fruition those experiments in everyday objects that had taken place in the 1930s, particularly in the realm of public housing. The war would thus act as a kind of accelerator in the transformation of taste, as *The Architectural Review* indicated as early as 1943, formulating the expectation that the first attempts to link 'utility and austerity' would lead to 'utility furniture in thousands of houses, of the workmanship of this first batch and, on top of that, of cheerful design could indeed become a corner-stone of a successful housing policy. Once people could sincerely like their State-aided furniture purchases, besides appreciating their usefulness, they might very well, by such gaiety and pleasurable domesticity, be cured of their longing for bogus glamour.'[47] As Loosian a proposition as ever there was.

The Victory in the Garden
Even the garden went off to war, insofar as it was used for producing food that would offset some of the deficiencies and restrictions of rationing, or even sometimes

as a means of resistance, as was the case in the ghetto gardens and gardens in prison camps.[48] 'Victory gardens', which provided nourishment for families to supplement the foodstuffs commercially available, spread throughout Great Britain, Canada and the United States,[49] with daily labour in the flower beds serving as a simulacrum of normality, thereby boosting morale. The breakdown of economic networks and the evacuation of the cities led many families to rely on their personal agricultural activities to feed their families. This was the case of scores of architects who had been spared mobilisation but were deprived of professional employment. They transformed themselves into farmers, like Berthold Lubetkin, who withdrew to his farm in Wotton-under-Edge, in Gloucestershire. His colleague Wells Coates came upon him at work in his field and described him thus: 'The farm is a mixed one, that is to say it is partly dairy and partly arable. Nowadays, of course, everybody is growing as much food as possible and the farms of England haven't been so prosperous or so busy for a very long time. There are wheat, barley,

oats, dredge corn, root crops, potatoes and other growing crops, as well as about 40 heads of cattle.'[50]

In the United States, the wartime vegetable gardens continued the programme that the Homestead Movement had first formulated in the nineteenth century and that had been taken up again during the New Deal with the aim of giving each household one acre for a productive garden. This new development provided retrospective justification, while making it possible to produce conserved fruits and vegetables to feed families. By 1943, two-thirds of households would have a 'victory garden'. For his part, the Nazi landscape architect Alwin Seifert produced designs for wartime gardens that proliferated in Germany[51] as a continuation of the policy of the *Selbstversorgersiedlungen*, or self-sufficient housing estates, which had grown up around the periphery of large cities after the crisis of 1929. Thus the tendencies towards de-urbanism, or at least for some reconciliation of urban dwellers with the earth, took form, under the pressure of necessity, in concrete initiatives.

'Plant a Victory Garden', poster, 1943. The Wolfsonian-Florida International University, Miami Beach, Florida, gift of Leonard A. Lauder

PLANT A VICTORY GARDEN

OUR FOOD IS FIGHTING

A GARDEN WILL MAKE YOUR RATIONS GO FURTHER

OWI Poster No. 34.   Additional copies may be obtained upon request from the Division of Public Inquiries, Office of War Information, Washington, D. C.   U. S. GOVERNMENT PRINTING OFFICE : 1943—O—506617

1. 'Introduction', *The War-Time Guide Book for the Home* (New York: Popular Science Publishing Co., 1942).
2. Herbert L. Whittemore, 'Material Shortages: Redesign and Substitution', *Engineering News-Record*, 15 January 1942, 144–66. Quoted in Robert Friedel, 'Scarcity and Promise: Materials and American Domestic Culture During World War II', in *World War II and the American Dream. How Wartime Building Changed a Nation*, edited by Donald Albrecht (Washington: National Building Museum; Cambridge, Mass.: MIT Press, 1995), 55.
3. 'Design Review', *The Architectural Review*, vol. 96, no. 573 (September 1944), 87.
4. On the editing of the section, see Jill Seddon, 'The Architect and the "Arch-Pedant": Sadie Speight, Nikolaus Pevsner and "Design Review"', *Journal of Design History*, vol. 20, no. 1 (2007), 29–41.
5. 'Total War means All-Out Conservation', *The Architectural Record*, vol. 91, no. 1 (January 1942), 40–48.
6. Lessing J. Rosenwald, Bureau of Industrial Conservation, War Production Board, 'To the Architects and Engineers of the United States', *Pencil Points*, vol. 23, no. 5 (May 1942), 260.
7. Advertisement for the Portland Cement Association, *Pencil Points*, vol. 23, no. 6 (June 1943), 28.
8. Howard Robertson, 'Structural Economy', *The Architect and Building News*, no. 29 (March 1940), 298.
9. 'Wooden Springs', *Business Week*, 31 October 1942. '"Sleep Like a Log", on New Wood Springs', *Bruce Magazine*, May–June 1943, press clipping, IIT Archives, Chicago.
10. 'Materials for 194X', *The Architectural Forum*, vol. 80, no. 3 (March 1944), 12.
11. 'Le Bois', *Techniques et architecture*, vol. 2, nos. 7–8 (July/August 1942), 236–328.
12. 'Grande carpenteria in legno compensato', *Costruzioni Casabella*, vol. 26, nos. 184–85 (April/May 1943), 77.
13. Peter Sulzer, *Jean Prouvé: Complete Works, vol. II, 1934–1944* (Basel, Boston and Berlin: Birkhäuser, 2000), 284.
14. Nikolaus Pevsner, 'The First Plywood Furniture', *The Architectural Review*, vol. 84, no. 501 (August 1938), 75–76, and 'The History of Plywood',

The Architectural Review, vol. 86, no. 514 (September 1939), 129–130. In the same issue, the *Review* published a supplement on the uses of plywood, p. 133–42.
15. 'Plywood as a Material', *The Architectural Review*, vol. 86, no. 514 (September 1939), 134.
16. Al Bernsohn, 'The New Wood That Bends', *ID Designs*, April 1941, 22–23.
17. My thanks to Timo Keinänen at the Finnish Museum of Architecture for this information.
18. The rationing of wood started in Great Britain with a 'Control of Timber Order', issued as early as 5 September 1939.
19. Le Corbusier, *Les Constructions 'Murondins'* (Paris and Clermond-Ferrand: Étienne Chiron, 1942), 7.
20. See Erkki Helamaa, *40 Luku. Jorsujen ja jällenrakentamisen vuosikymmen* (Helsinki: Suomen rakennustaitee museo, 1983).
21. Carlo Mollino, 'Proposizioni sui mobili tipo che i costruttori di mobili sono invitati a leggere', *Stile*, no. 31 (July 1943), 33–37; quoted in Giovanni Brino, *Carlo Mollino. Architecture as Autobiography* (London: Thames and Hudson, 1987), 90.
22. Sergio Poretti, 'Modernismi e autarchia', in *Storia dell'architettura italiana*, edited by Giorgio Ciucci and Giorgio Muratore (Milan: Electa, 2004), 442–75.
23. Giuseppe Pagano, 'Variazioni sull'autarchia architettonica', *Casabella*, no. 129 (September 1938), 2–3, and no. 130, 2–3.
24. Carlo Emilio Gadda, 'I metalli leggeri', *L'Ambrosiano*, 2 September 1931, 1–2; referred to by Poretti, 'Modernismi e autarchia', op. cit. note 22, 459.
25. See Pep Aviles' unpublished paper 'Italy 1938: the Autarchic Debate', at the 'Front and Rear' conference held at New York's Institute of Fine Arts in March 2009.
26. Pier Luigi Nervi, 'Per l'autarchia. I problemi economici delle costruzioni e la politica dell'architettura', *Il Giornale d'Italia*, 23 July 1938, 3. Idem, 'Per la massima autarchia edilizia', *Costruzioni Casabella*, vol. 12, no. 147 (March 1940), 3. See Riccardo Dirindin, *Lo stile dell'ingegneria. Architettura e identità della tecnic a tra il primo modernismo e Pier Luigi Nervi* (Venice: Marsilio, 2010), 194–95.

27. 'The Voice of the Industry', *The Architect and Building News*, January 1940, 43–69, and 16 and 23 January 1942.
28. Roger Wade Sherman, 'What Priorities Mean to Building', *The Architectural Record*, vol. 90, no. 2 (August 1941), 37–40.
29. E. F. Lougee, *Plastics from Farm and Forests* (New York: Plastics Institute, 1943).
30. Stephen Phillips, 'Plastics', in *Cold War Hothouses. Inventing Postwar Culture from Cockpit to Playboy*, edited by Beatriz Colomina, Annmarie Brennan and Jeannie Kim (New York: Princeton Architectural Press, 2004), 90–123.
31. Robert F. Marshall, 'Plastics . . . Practically Speaking', *The Architectural Record*, vol. 93, no. 4 (April 1943), 54–55.
32. Roger N. Dent, *Principles of Pneumatic Architecture* (London: The Architectural Press, 1971), 32–33.
33. Celina Fox, 'The Battle of the Railings', *AA Files*, vol. 29 (1995), 50–59.
34. Pierre Vago, *Une vie intense* (Brussels: Archives d'Architecture Moderne, 2000), 200.
35. 'Insulation Board in Big War Boom', *The Milwaukee Journal*, 25 April 1943.
36. See his lecture, 'L'avenir de la qualité française dans la production européene', delivered on 10 May 1941, under the auspices of the Groupe Collaboration, at the Maison de la Chimie, Paris, 1941. Henri Poupée, biographical essay in *Les Professeurs du Conservatoire national des Arts et Métiers*, edited by Claudine Fontanon and André Grelon, vol. 2 (Paris: INRP/CNAM, 1994), 184.
37. Alistair Cooke, *The American Home Front, 1941–1942* (New York: Atlantic Monthly Press, 2006).
38. 'Restrictions: so that every woman can have a Scandale girdle, make the one you are fortunate to have last', *L'Illustration*, 24 May 1941, XXV. See Mike Brown and Carol Harris, 'Rationing', in *The Wartime House: Home Life in Wartime Britain 1939–1945* (Stroud, Gloucestershire: Sutton Publishing Ltd, 2001), 73–94.
39. See the *War-Time Guide Book for the Home*, op. cit. note 1.
40. D'Ann Campbell, *Women at War with America: Private Lives in a Patriotic Era* (Cambridge, Mass.: Harvard University Press, 1984).

41. Susan M. Hartmann, *The Home Front and Beyond: American Women in the 1940s* (Boston: Twayne Publishers, 1982).

42. 'Useful Objects in Wartime', *The Bulletin of the Museum of Modern Art*, vol. 2, no. 10 (December 1942–January 1943), 3.

43. *Utility Furniture and Fashion 1941–1951* (London: Geffrye Museum and Inner London Education Authority, 1974). Harriet Dover, *Home Front Furniture: British Utility Design 1941–1951* (London: Scholar Press, 1995). Judy Attfield, ed., *Utility Reassessed: the Role of Ethics in the Practice of Design* (Manchester: Manchester University Press, 1999).

44. Richard Stewart, *Design and British Industry* (London: John Murray, 1987), 64.

45. 'Utility Furniture', *The Architectural Review*, vol. 100, no. 598 (October 1946), 104.

46. Gordon Russell, 'National Furniture Production', *The Architectural Review*, vol. 100, no. 598, 184.

47. 'Utility and Austerity', *The Architectural Review*, vol. 93 (January 1943), 4.

48. Kenneth I. Helphand, *Defiant Gardens: Making Gardens in Wartime* (San Antonio: Trinity University Press, 2006).

49. A popular television programme on the BBC explored this subject: Jennifer Davies, *The Wartime Kitchen and Garden* (London: BBC Books, 1993). See also *Art of the Garden: the Garden in British Art, 1800 to the Present Day,* edited by Nicholas Alfrey, Stephen Daniels and Martin Postle (London: Tate Britain, 2004).

50. Wells Coates, letter to his daughter Laura Coates, 8 August 1943, CCA, Wells Coates fonds.

51. Charlotte Reitsam, *Das Konzept der 'bodenständigen Gartenkunst' Alwin Seifert: fachliche Hintergründe und Rezeption bis in die Nachkriegzeit* (Frankfurt-am-Main and New York: P. Lang, 2001), 190–91.

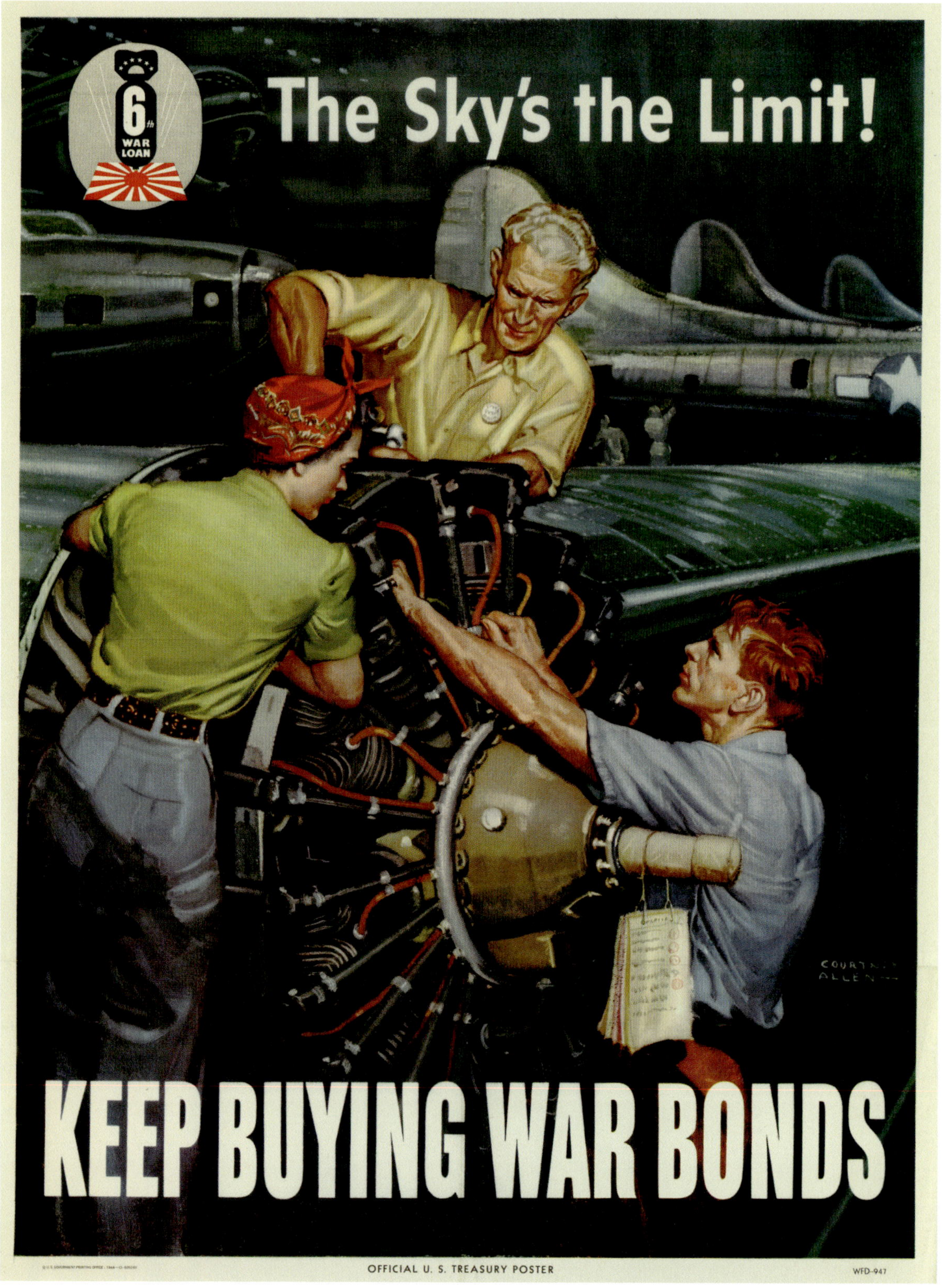
6th
WAR LOAN
The Sky's the Limit!
COURTNEY ALLEN
KEEP BUYING WAR BONDS
OFFICIAL U. S. TREASURY POSTER
WFD-947

4/ Producing Production and Workers' Housing

Guns, tanks, airplanes, ships and machine tools for defense require not only raw materials, transportation, factories and production schedules. They require men to make them, men working efficiently and, therefore, living as well as working in a satisfactory environment.
Albert Mayer, *The New York Times Magazine*, 1941[1]

Adequate housing for war workers becomes truly a part of our national assembly line. And it must be made progressively available as new war-production plants near completion. It must be timed to mesh with every cog in our gigantic wheel of preparation for victory. Housing needs must be anticipated. . . . We cannot allow production to be hampered by a dearth of adequate housing. Nor can we look with favor on an unplanned program of jerry building, which will only result in creation of vast suburban and rural slums in the immediate postwar future. Common sense and energy coupled with an understanding of the job to be done *must* provide the full housing equipment necessary to keep our war production geared to top speed.
Dorothy Rosenman, *The Architectural Record*, 1942[2]

In 1934, Lewis Mumford declared that he considered war to be the real mainspring of the Industrial Revolution, much more than the invention of the steam engine. 'The spread of conscription and volunteer militia throughout the Western World after the French Revolution made army and factory, so far as their social effects went, almost

Courtney Allen
**'The Sky's the Limit!
Keep Buying War Bonds'**,
poster, 1943.
Harry Ransom Humanities
Research Center, The University
of Texas at Austin

interchangeable terms. And the complacent characterizations of the First World War, namely that it was a large-scale industrial operation, has also a meaning in reverse: modern industrialism may equally well be termed a large-scale military operation.'[3] These considerations are all the more convincing in view of the fact that the Second World War, even more than the first, was an industrial war in its every dimension. Each army on the battlefield had its double: an army of productive workers whose ranks in every country outnumbered anything seen before. In 1943, the combined forces of industry and the military made up 37% of the active population in Germany, 45% in the United Kingdom, 54% in the USSR, and 35% in the United States.[4]

Despite all the bombardments, German production grew steadily until 1945,[5] while Soviet production, after being disrupted by the invasion of 1941, was redeployed to the Urals and beyond, and surpassed Germany's by 1943. The case of the United States is the most spectacular. There production increased by 15% every year between 1940 and 1944, despite the initial sluggishness of its 'industrial mobilisation'.[6] The construction of thousands of factories for the manufacture of airplanes, vehicles and munitions required an army of designers and draughtsmen, with civil engineers and architects playing a lead role. The production was so intense that it changed the relation of the United States to the world, as the country exhausted its resources of bauxite and became an importer of oil.[7]

A New Industrial Geography

The first step in the programme was to convert existing factories, especially as many of the large factories of the 1930s had actually been conceived with the production of military material and armaments in mind. This was obviously the case of airplane factories, but was also true of the car factories that embodied the spread of Fordism. In 1936, Fiat's new Mirafiori factory in Turin was built according to the results of a study trip to the United States by the engineer Victor Bonadè-Bottino, with a very different building plan from the legendary Lingotto factory, as it was all built on one level. As a result, even though the repeated bombings that started in 1940 destroyed the roofs over the assembly lines converted for war production and some of the machines, the production of vehicles for the army continued.[8] Fritz Kuntze conceived a first project for the KdF-Wagen, or Volkswagen, factory whose cornerstone was laid by Adolf Hitler in 1938, in Wolfsburg, in Lower Saxony. It was ultimately developed by three agencies that were required by the regime to combine their rival proposals: the project by Emil Mewes, who had been working for the Bochumer Verein AG, the project by Karl Kohlbecker, who was working for Daimler-Benz, and the project by Fritz Schupp and Martin Kremmer, who had designed numerous industrial installations, including the Zollverein mine in Essen.[9] This large covered volume, more than a kilometre and a half long, and punctuated by a series of large brick fore-buildings, was also conceived from the outset with a transformation to military purposes in mind. After 1939, the production of the 'people's car' would be abandoned and replaced first by the production of amphibious vehicles, and later the V-1 flying bomb.

The construction of new factories in France in the 1930s was accompanied by a new distribution of production sites throughout the country, placed as far as possible from the borders in order to protect them from aerial bombing. The author of a report to the Comité Supérieur d'Aménagement de la Région Parisienne feigned admiration at the concentration of enterprises in the French capital city. 'What a magnificent target is this Parisian region, with its concentrated groups of factories, three hundred kilometres from the border, at a juncture of waterways. On a clear night, the Oise and the Marne rivers, those soft ribbons of light, could so easily be used to guide flights of bombers.'[10] And Paul Vauthier noted as early as 1930 that 'industry must be removed from major cities'.[11]

Such a process had already been started in the Soviet Union, where the construction of hundreds of industrial cities was set in motion as part of the five-year plan of 1928–1932. Magnitogorsk, for example, would later be able to maintain production of a significant amount of the country's steel after the German occupation of the Ukraine in the summer of 1941. Most of the larger factories

Mario Puppo
'FIAT: Work and Weapons',
advertisement in *Costruzioni Casabella*, August 1942.
CCA Collection

FIAT   LAVORO E ARMI

were built to the designs of American firms such as Albert Kahn Associates and The Austin Company. In France, the vulnerabilities of the existing industrial framework were a subject of discussion right through the 1930s,[12] and in 1936 the government of the Popular Front linked nationalisations with industrial decentralisation. Some care was devoted to the architectural qualities of business headquarters, such as the SNCASO (Société Nationale des Constructions Aéronautiques du Sud-Ouest) – previously the Avions Marcel Bloch – which was built by Georges Hennequin at Châteauroux-Déols, and the Société Centrale des Alliages Légers, a producer of cold-rolled aluminium in Issoire, which was carefully designed by Auguste Perret in 1939–1940, at the request of the minister of armaments, Raoul Dautry. This group of buildings is one of the clearest expressions of Perret's approach. The main building of the seven, which he worked on before being replaced by some less expensive and more docile architects, is a great industrial palace with an imposing monumental order, rather than a simple shed. It is covered with

Top: Auguste Perret
Factory for the Société Centrale des Alliages Légers, Issoire, perspective view of rolling and finishing hall, 1940. CNAM/SIAF/CAPA, Archives d'Architecture du xxᵉ Siècle, Fonds Perret

Oliver Percy Bernard
Vickers Supermarine seaplane factory, Southampton, 1939, perspective view from the water. RIBA Library Drawings and Archives Collections

of factories in France, the Netherlands and Czechoslovakia. Great Britain followed a double course: decentralising large factories and developing a system of sub-contracting. In the Midlands, the principle of the 'ghost factory' was introduced at many sites. As the car factories had been equipped before the war to build airplane engines, each one separately made components that were then assembled (the possibility of adapting car factories to the production of airplane engines had already been considered as early as 1914–1918).[14] The ammunition plants of Woolwich Arsenal and Waltham Abbey, two of the three factories that existed in 1939, were considered to be easy targets, and a programme of decentralisation was undertaken, leading to the creation of forty-four new plants. Architects benefited from this programme, and the firm of Sir Alexander Gibb and Partners, whose designer-in-charge was William Holford, built three of them: in Swynnerton in Staffordshire, at Risley in Cheshire, and in Kirkby, near Liverpool.[15] The development of production throughout the Commonwealth, from Canada to South Africa, can also be thought of as an extreme form of global decentralisation.

The American programmes were distinguished by their scale and by the extensive migrations from the eastern part of the country to the Midwest and the West Coast. A second industrial revolution was taking place, made possible by federal funds that linked the extraction of raw materials, their transformation and fabrication – with particular emphasis on airplane production – and the energy these required. The completion of the Bonneville dam on the Columbia River in 1937 provided electricity to the shipyards of Portland, Oregon, to the

a concrete slab one metre thick that was supposed to protect it from bomb damage.[13]

The war would accelerate the trend towards decentralisation in Germany and Great Britain, and would initiate it in the United States as well, although at a slower pace until 1939. Under the threat of bombs, the Nazis moved their production sites towards the centre and the eastern part of the Reich and buried them as well. At the same time, the occupation of a large part of Europe allowed the Germans to take control

airplane factories of Seattle, and subsequently to the Hanford nuclear reactor. Gigantic factories were built by the Army Corps of Engineers in Kansas City, Tulsa, Omaha and Fort Worth.[16] California witnessed the creation of a powerful mining and metallurgical industry, which multiplied the number of aluminium and magnesium refineries. The industrialist Henry J. Kaiser was responsible for the creation of the Fontana steel mills, the first on the West Coast, which were designed by the firm of Birge M. and David B. Clark of Palo Alto. These metals were then used in shipyards and airplane factories.[17] The Greater Los Angeles urban region alone would count more than four thousand factories of various sizes and would become an important place of production for Liberty ships. The latter were also built at various places on the West Coast by the Kaiser Shipbuilding Company, which took a lead role in hiring women and making strides towards eliminating racial segregation in its factory.[18] The population of Los Angeles increased by 780,000 new inhabitants between April 1940 and 1944. It would employ as many as 228,000 workers in the aeronautic industry and become known as the 'boom town of aviation',[19] centred around the Douglas, Lockheed, North American and Northrop factories, which transformed the manufacture of standardised airplanes, rationalised through interchangeable equipment, into a truly massive system of production.

The Case of Kahn

In June 1942, *The Architectural Record* reported on the activity of the office of Albert Kahn Associates, based in Detroit, which the review described as a 'producer of

ALBERT KAHN.
ARCHITECT

PRODUCER OF PRODUCTION LINES

'Producer of Production Lines', article in *The Architectural Record*, June 1942. CCA Collection

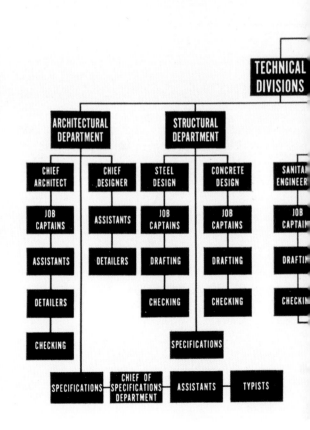

'The Kahn Organization',
illustration in *The Architectural Record*, June 1942.
CCA Collection

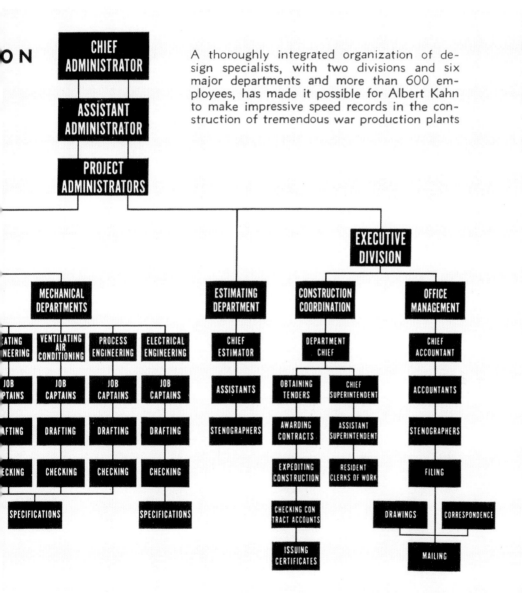

A thoroughly integrated organization of design specialists, with two divisions and six major departments and more than 600 employees, has made it possible for Albert Kahn to make impressive speed records in the construction of tremendous war production plants

production lines'. It described the 'magic formula' of their work, based on the 'coordination of experienced experts', and described the expansion of the team: 'Normally, the firm employs approximately 150 men and women – architectural designers and draftsmen, specification writers, estimators and expediters, field superintendents, mechanical, electrical and ventilation engineers and office workers. Now the organization has expanded; until this spring it was employing over 600, and was still increasing. Last year Kahn and his associates designed and supervised the construction of more than three-score buildings for the production of implements of war – armor plate foundries, synthetic rubber plants, airplane plants, naval bases. In telling how it was done, Mr. Kahn stresses three elements – organization, teamwork and business. It is the hard-hitting teamwork of real specialists.'[20] The immense projects that came out of the office joined that register of 'American technological sublime' that the historian David E. Nye described as starting with the construction of the first textile mills in Lovell, Massachusetts, and continuing with the Ford factory in Detroit, which had already been designed by the same firm.[21] The Kahn office itself took on a sublime dimension, with its rows of draughting tables extending into the distance, ready to take on every new

Albert Kahn Associates
Chrysler Tank Arsenal,
Warren Township, Michigan,
view of assembly building,
1940–1942. Photograph
by Bill Hedrich.
Chicago History Museum

commission, but all the while maintaining the architect's control over the projects.[22]

One of the most spectacular projects in this vein realised by the Kahn organisation was the Chrysler Tank Arsenal in Warren Township, Michigan, which was built between 1940 and 1942 in response to the complete lack of tanks in the American army's equipment. Inside its glazed envelope, 1,300 feet long and 500 feet wide, the different stages of production took place in a linear process, with the assembly line along the south side fed by pieces put together along the north side.

Albert Kahn Associates
**Ford Motor Company
Bomber Plant**
(1941–1943), Willow Run,
Michigan, model, 1941.
The Henry Ford Museum

Over the course of the war, the roughly five thousand workers in the arsenal would assemble more than 25,000 tanks.[23] Another comparable project was the Ford Motors Company Airplane Parts Manufacturing Building for the manufacture of bombers, which was constructed between 1941 and 1943 at Willow Run, in the same state. After initial planning to put together parts that would be assembled elsewhere, Ford ultimately undertook to assemble the B-24 Liberator bomber in a single building covering one million square feet, which contained workshops and assembly lines capable of 'turning out' one plane per hour, a rate that required employing 100,000 workers.[24] This 'gigantic symbol' of the armaments programme, which the local press did not hesitate to describe as the 'marvel of the industrial

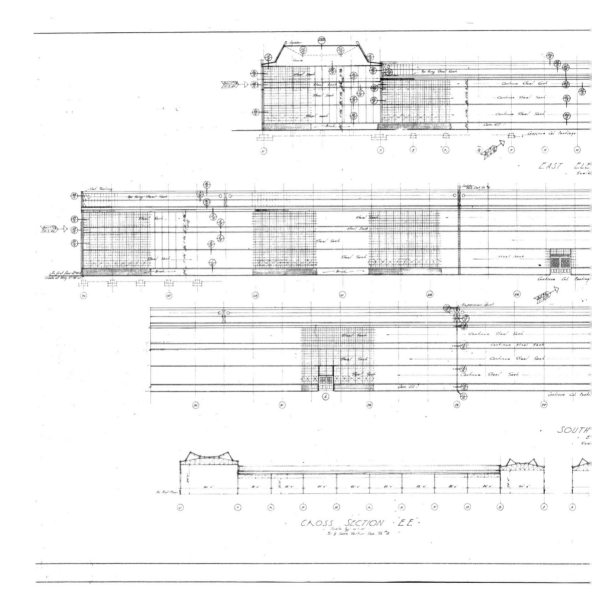

· EAST ELE

· SOUTH

CROSS SECTION ·E·E·

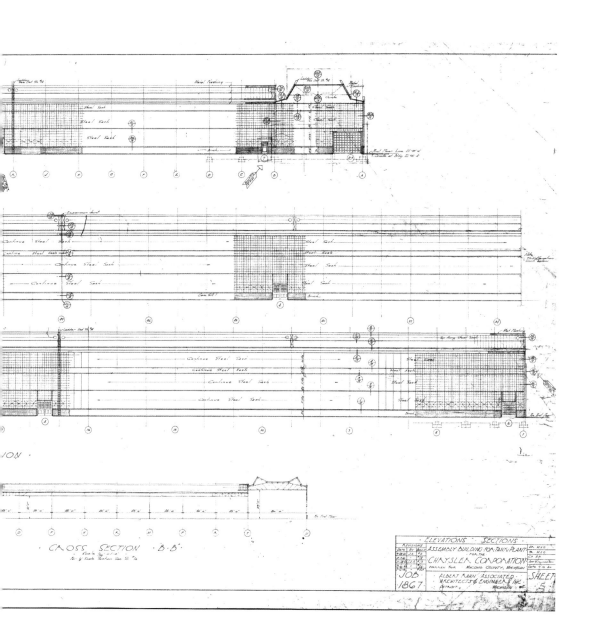

Albert Kahn Associates
Chrysler Tank Arsenal
(1940–1942), Warren
Township, Michigan,
elevation drawings, 1940.
Albert Kahn Collection,
Bentley Historical Library,
University of Michigan

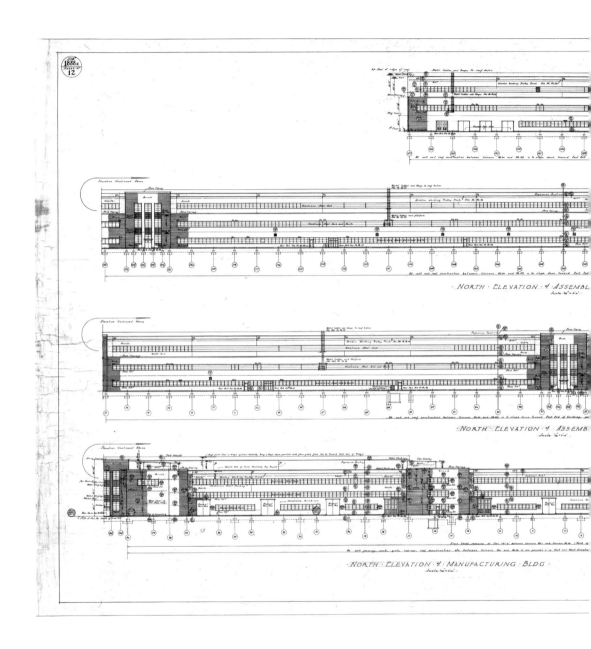

· NORTH · ELEVATION · ᵒᶠ · ASSEMBL

· NORTH · ELEVATION · ᵒᶠ · ASSEMB

· NORTH · ELEVATION · ᵒᶠ · MANUFACTURING · BLDG ·

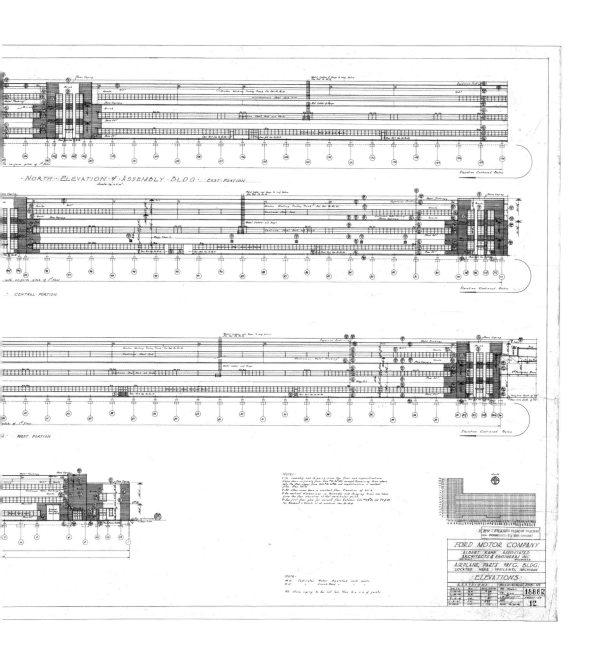

Albert Kahn Associates
Ford Motor Company
Bomber Factory (1941–1943),
Willow Run, Michigan,
elevation drawings.
Albert Kahn Collection,
Bentley Historical Library,
University of Michigan

world',[25] contained a remarkably complex heating and ventilation system, developed by Kahn and engineers from Ford, under the direction of the vice-president of the company, Charles Sorensen, who was directly involved in the conceptual design of the assembly line.[26] Nor did the site selection leave anything to chance. Ford was careful to place the factory on the other side of the county limit separating Wayne and Washtenaw counties, where the Republicans were in the majority and the unions had no legal standing. Kahn developed the final plan of the building as an L, a form that was less rational than a straight bar, but which avoided crossing this critical boundary. As we shall see, the related project for housing was not as ambitious as the factory.

Some of Kahn's other large projects included the ongoing enlargement of the Glenn Martin factory at Middle River, Maryland, which he had built in 1937.

'Building in One Package', article on The Austin Company in *The Architectural Forum*, January 1945. CCA Collection

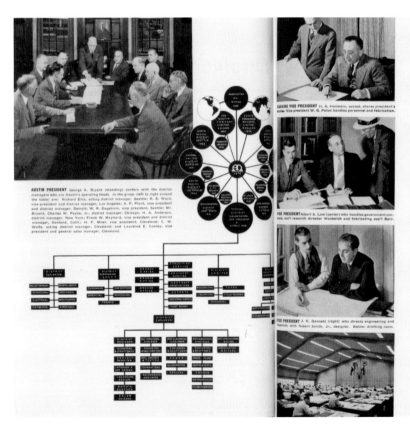

located underground so as not to stand in the way of later extensions, and to serve as shelters in an eventuality.[27] Kahn insisted on the importance of placing all the production under a single roof and following 'principles of sensible industrial building', namely 'an orderly straightforward arrangement, uniform as far as possible, designed for straight line quantity production, with the raw material entering at one point and the finished product leaving at the other without recrossing of steps'.[28] He was proud of having been able to circumvent building regulations in his constructions of 1941 and 1942 to make them lighter than normally required.

Despite the shortage of materials such as aluminium, zinc and tungsten, all necessary for electrical systems, Kahn Associates built hundreds of other projects, a level of productivity made possible by a hierarchical and standardised working method, a model of Taylorism applied to conceptual work, which embodied his famous aphorism, 'architecture is 90% business and 10% art'.[29] Such was Kahn's fame that he figured prominently in advertisements for building materials (and pencils), and his death in December 1942 was greatly mourned. His disappearance 'in the middle of the greatest industrial building program ever entrusted to a private architect' provided the press with an opportunity to underscore the originality of his working methods: 'While so many of his fellow architects wrestled with problems of exterior decoration for banks, state capitols and universities, he was quietly creating shelters for mass production on a scale that few men of his generation ever dreamed of. Oddly enough, it was not until the late years of his life that Kahn or his co-professionals

In 1941 alone, he completed the Curtiss-Wright factories in Buffalo and Columbus and the Wright Aeronautical factory in Lockland. The factories he had erected in the Soviet Union between 1928 and 1932 were put to similar use. His tractor factory in Chelyabinsk, built with the help of Russian architects such as Andrei Burov, was set up with equipment evacuated from the Kirov mechanical factory in Leningrad and the tank factory in Kharkov, to create the production centre known as 'Tankograd', under the supervision of General Izaak Moiseevich Zaltsman, who was named people's commissar for tank production – only to be thrown in prison by Stalin a few years later.

Kahn's basic concept for industrial buildings was fairly simple: single-storey volumes with steel-frame structures – subsequently replaced by concrete when steel became requisitioned for shipbuilding – lit from above and the sides, whose secondary spaces such as changing rooms, mess halls, cafeterias and toilets were

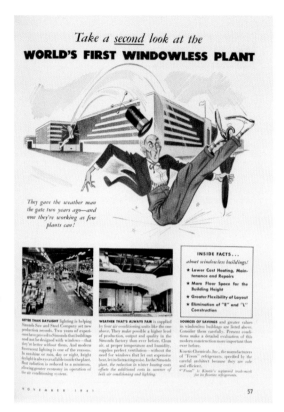

saw the real significance of his merging of
architecture and engineering to create and
entirely new types of building, but today the
record is clear for all to see.'[30] After Kahn's
death, the firm would continue under his
brother Louis.

The Kahn office was certainly not the
only organisation engaged in the serial
production of huge factories. The Austin
Company, founded in the nineteenth century,
consolidated in 1904, and based in Cleveland,
Ohio, completed significant 'turnkey'
industrial projects. The company applied
what it considered its specific 'method',
which integrated 'design, specifying and
contracting in a single organization', leading
some to consider them 'contractors trying
to masquerade as architects'.[31] Under its
president George A. Bryant, the company
established a network of offices in various
cities around the country and promoted
technological inventions: welded steel
structures, rather than bolted, prestressed
concrete, and glue-laminated wood. These
techniques were employed in three factories
for Boeing in Seattle, whose longest metallic
roof trusses measured 90 metres in length,
and in the Douglas factory in Chicago, with
wood framing pieces 45 metres long.
Workplaces such as these, along with
the Consolidated Vultee in Fort Worth
and the Douglas factory in Oklahoma City,
also looked to fibreglass panelling or found
solutions to make opaque walls 'breathe'.
The firm was less intent on architectural
qualities than Kahn's, but laid claim to define
'a fundamental flow diagram in which the
problem is presented in its simplest form'
and employed various solutions for the

secondary workshops and collective spaces.[32]
Although the firm was less active in Russia
than Kahn, it nonetheless built a number of
large factories, including the Avtostroi car
factory in Nizhny Novgorod (subsequently
renamed Gorky), which was converted to
military use like Kahn's factory in Chelyabinsk,
in this case for trucks. And when the Soviets
started building their own factories, in the
mid-1930s, their project manuals highlighted
the American examples.[33]

Factories without Windows

The Austin Company was closely involved
in the development of a new kind of industrial
building in response to the new production
requirements that came to the fore after
1940, that a factory be able to function
around the clock with all openings

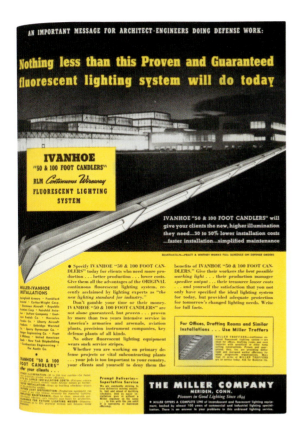

'Nothing less than this
Proven and Guaranteed
fluorescent lighting system
will do today', advertisement
in *The Architectural Forum*,
November 1941.
CCA Collection

blocked up effectively for blackout purposes.[34] Several techniques were employed to achieve this objective. The main structural elements – made out of steel, concrete or laminated wood – were designed for long spans and were clad in lightweight exterior materials, in sandwiches of waterproof and insulating materials. The resulting large interior spaces could be heated and air-conditioned, making them usable in every season. The largest air-conditioned building in the world remains the Consolidated Vultee factory at Fort Worth. Another important new feature of the time, fluorescent lighting, had the advantage of reducing the need for tungsten in a time of shortage. General Electric and Westinghouse marketed the lamps in 1938, and The Austin Company first used them in the Simonds Saw and Steel factory that same year, and for the General Motors aircraft engine factory in Austin in 1939. The use of white reflective flooring materials helped to ensure that the lighting was homogeneous, which further facilitated continuous production.[35]

While there was little resistance to the introduction of air-conditioning and fluorescent lighting, the idea of completely sealed factories was not universally accepted. The equipment manufacturers in question did not hesitate to plead their case to the architects: 'Two years

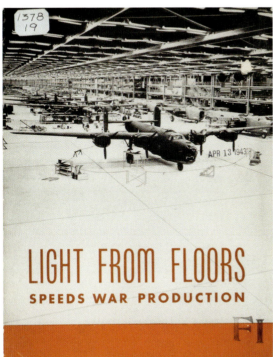

LIGHT FROM FLOORS
SPEEDS WAR PRODUCTION

'Light from floors
speeds war production',
cover of a promotional
brochure for the Universal
Atlas Cement Company, c. 1941.
CCA Collection

Ludwig Mies van der Rohe **Minerals and Metals Research Building, Illinois Institute of Technology, Chicago,** view of exterior, 1941–1943. Photograph by Ken A. Hedrich. Chicago History Museum

of experience have proved that buildings need not be designed with windows – that they're better *without* them. And modern fluorescent lighting is one of the reasons. In sunshine or rain, day or night, bright daylight is always available inside the plant. Heat radiation is reduced to a minimum, allowing greater economy in operation of the air conditioning system.'[36] In 1942, the Austin Company's choice of the 'windowless' option went against Albert Kahn's insistence on glazing in his 'windowed' approach.[37] The latter expressed his basic opposition to windowless factories, although he recognised their advantages in relation to blackout requirements, as well as the fact that they were 'faster and perhaps simpler to construct'. But 'they require artificial lighting all the time, as well as mechanical ventilation and air-conditioning', which he considered to be acceptable in wartime, under twenty-four-hour working conditions, but hardly appropriate to a return to the eight-hour workday during peacetime.[38] Of course, the manufacturers of metal windows and glazing shared the same point of view and made it known through their advertisements in architectural journals.

Producing for the Reich

The architects of factories built in Germany did not have access to American technological resources, even though General Electric's patent for fluorescent lighting had initially been granted to the Germans Meyer, Spanner and Germer in 1927. On the other hand, the design strategies they developed were just as modern as those employed on the other side of the Atlantic, especially after Hitler

launched his 'four-year plan' in 1936 to prepare the Reich for war. The prototype of the functional industrial building was without a doubt the factory for the airplane manufacturer Heinkel in Oranienburg, north of Berlin, which was designed by the young architect Herbert Rimpl, who had studied under Theodor Fischer in Munich. The metal structural framing, the large glazed areas and the large rectangular volume of the hangars provided a convincing demonstration of the application of the principles of modern architecture to the industrial programmes of the regime.[39] Rimpl's buildings, along with those constructed at almost the same time by Heinrich Bormann for the Salzgitter steelworks – a company owned by Hermann Göring – by Pius Pahl for a foundry in Linz, as well as Fritz Pfeil's work for the Junkers factory in Breslau, extended the research undertaken under the Weimar Republic to develop an architectural language for industrial programmes.

In terms of its organisation, Rimpl's office was the equal of Kahn's. He would employ as many as seven hundred architects and draughtsmen in open office spaces in the principal cities of occupied Europe. The staff included a number of former *Bauhäusler*, such as Bormann, Pahl, Gerd Balzer, Hubert Hoffmann, Walter Tralau and Gerhard Weber.[40] In addition to the Heinkel factory, Rimpl would develop projects for the Austrian steel company Montan, which had been integrated into Göring's *Konzern*, for the Krupp steel works in Breslau, the Wittkowitz/Vítkovice works in Moravia, and even as far as Madrid, where he worked for CASA Aeronáutica, which was licensed to manufacture the Messerschmitt Bf 109.

He would subsequently close his offices only *in extremis*, and abandoned his office in Paris only hours before the arrival of General Leclerc's tanks in August 1944.

For his part, Ernst Neufert had studied at the Weimar Bauhaus, and had then been the on-site supervisor for Gropius during the construction of the Dessau Bauhaus. He had subsequently gone on to join Albert Speer's team after the success of his bestselling *Bauentwurfslehre* (Architects' Data) in 1936. He would build projects for the Hagenuk telephone company in Berlin-Tempelhof; at Barth in Pomerania; and for Focke-Wulff as part of the 'Ostmark' industrial complex, which was spread over three sites, in Wiener-Neustadt, Maribor and Brno. He built an extraordinary factory for aeronautical electronics in Rhinau, in the Alsace plain, for the Heinrich List company, based in Berlin-Zehlendorf. With its modular concrete framing, it was an extreme application of the policy of standardisation

that he was a proponent of at the time, and was the equal in terms of rationality and abstraction to any of the American factories.

Other modernist architects, such as Bernhard Hermkes, were also involved in the construction of large factories for the war effort. Hermkes was employed by Rimpl and then recruited by Wilhelm Wichtendahl, for whom he built the Messerschmitt airplane factory in Regensburg, from 1936 to 1939, and especially the six enormous machine halls in the port of Hamburg for the manufacture of submarine engines for MAN Motorenwerk, before being conscripted in 1944. For his part, Rudolf Lodders was the architect for the Borgward company in Bremen, and designed extensions to the plant

Herbert Rimpl
Heinkel Aircraft Factory,
Oranienburg, 1939, view of
exterior, in Werner Rittich,
*Architektur und Bauplastik
der Gegenwart*,
3rd edition, c. 1940.
CCA Collection

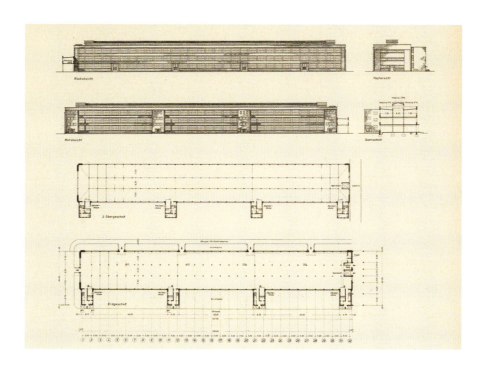

Top: Ernst Neufert
**Heinrich List Factory for
Aeronautical Electronics**,
Rhinau, plan and elevations,
in Ernst Neufert,
Bauordnungslehre, 1943.
CCA Collection

Bottom: Ernst Neufert
**Heinrich List Factory for
Aeronautic Electronics**,
Rhinau, view of exterior, c. 2008.
Service de l'Inventaire et du
Patrimoine, Région Alsace

throughout the war. After 1945, he developed the convenient myth that the construction of factories had been a 'refuge' for modern architects opposed to the Nazis.[41]

One of the most active modern architects in the war effort was Egon Eiermann, a former student of Hans Poelzig. After building the Degea AB factory in Moabit, in 1938–1939 and the Total KG factory in Apolda, in Thuringia (1938–1940), he worked on other industrial programmes, such as the elegant steel volumes of the Märkischer Metallbau factory for aeronautical parts in Oranienburg (1939–1941). His propeller factory for Gustav Schwarz in Eilenburg (1941–1945) and the other projects he proposed for this firm were particularly elegant. Concentrating on every project that might enable him to avoid being conscripted into the Wehrmacht, he designed and partially completed the factory-city of Udetfeld in Upper Silesia (Zendek-Mierzęcice today), which was part of the programme for the colonisation of Poland. It was centred around a repair firm for airplanes with an airfield – where one of the first squadrons of the Me 163 rocket-planes were based – and the adjacent town, an extension of the urban theories of Gottfried Feder.[42] Under the supervision of the Kriegsmarine, he built a shipbuilding hangar in Bremerhaven

(1939–1941) and worked on the construction of shipyards up and down Germany.[43]

The young Hermann Henselmann took over the Prague branch of the Godber Nissen firm and built an airplane engine factory in Letňany that was covered by thin concrete shells.[44] Schupp and Kremmer, who were also involved in the industrial policies of the expanded Reich after the conquests at the beginning of the war, created a branch in Gleiwitz. The most important of their buildings in Upper Silesia was the Oberschlesiche Hydrierwerke AG factory for synthetic fuel at Blechhammer/ Blachownia Slaska, which they worked on from 1939 to 1941 and whose workforce was drawn from the Auschwitz III-Monowitz concentration camp.

Towards the 'Green' Factory

In 1940, Le Corbusier took great delight in observing that 'five million workers, both men and women, are in the factories involved in the war. Throughout the country, industry has adapted to the needs of wartime. Intense production. Industry has become fabulously organised. It has made a gigantic

Bernhard Hermkes **MAN factory for submarine motors**, Hamburg, view from the Elbe, 1939–1942.

Photograph by Otto Reich. Akademie der Künste, Bernhard Hermkes Archiv, Berlin

leap forward. It is a new presence in the Land.'[45] He saw the call for decentralised manufacture as an opportunity for experimentation and criticised the existing 'black factories': 'The wartime factories, or at least some of them, which have been located by Fortune in pleasant sites, can now be "GREEN FACTORIES", places where work with tools or machines can be totally transformed, transplanted in a single step from the dreary and unhappy conditions that have been the norm until now in workshops, into happy places that make work friendly.'[46] This was a strange declaration to make when one takes into account the role of forced labour in French industry under the Vichy regime on behalf of the occupiers.

In a letter sent in May 1940 to the writer Jean Paulhan, Le Corbusier, who was writing *Sur les quatre routes* at the time, included a sketch that contrasted the war, with its 'revitalised industrial equipment', with the state of peace that would call for 'the equipping of the country in order to satisfy human needs'. He warned of a drastic vertical 'drop', a 'catastrophe, if preparations were not made for tomorrow'.[47] The idea was an expression of all his utopian expectations with regard to military production. Conceived

Le Corbusier
Project for a munitions factory, Lannemezan, general perspective view of the site, 1944. Fondation Le Corbusier

for a production line forming a continuous circuit on a single floor, the factory was meant to join together a 'strict organisation of work' with a *joie de vivre* that the existing chaos had 'banished'. The project was abandoned in 1940, although it was supposed to 'eventually serve as a pilot study'. In 1945, it would be presented as a solution for reconstruction.[48]

Extreme Solutions, from the Inflatable to the Tunnel

The spectrum of architectural solutions was particularly broad, ranging from imposing buildings like great boxes and fortified factories on the one hand, to a strategy of attenuation, even disappearance. The most radical proposal along the latter lines was developed by the American engineer Herbert H. Stevens for a large-scale pneumatic structure.[49] It followed in the footsteps of a series of experiments conducted since the First World War, when the British William Lanchester had first imagined an inflatable structure inspired by balloons that was to serve as a mobile military hospital, an idea he developed during the following years.[50] With a diameter of around 370 metres, Stevens' membrane was to be made of welded sheets of steel 1.7 millimetres thick, held up thanks to sixteen air pumps and anchored to concrete. The airlock that was required between interior and exterior was to be large enough to permit assembled sections of bombers to pass through. Hugh Ferriss's renderings of its air-conditioned interior illustrate how the inner surface of the metallic roof structure ensured even lighting conditions inside. As to the exterior of the low-slung dome, it could wonderfully lend itself to camouflage, especially as the building had no sharp ridges and would barely cast a shadow.

Herbert H. Stevens, Jr.
Project for an aircraft factory with a pneumatic structure, interior perspective, rendering by Hugh Ferriss.
Elaine Stevens Collection

The aim of concealing factories, sheltered underground and protected from the bombs, gave rise to an ambitious policy during the final years of the Third Reich. The idea of a 'retractable' factory had been proposed in England in 1939 in the form of a telescopic hangar that was designed to retract into the ground.[51] And after defeating France, the German forces were surprised to discover the underground airplane factory of Lioré & Olivier, set up in the tunnels of a former quarry in Creil, north of Paris. Pictures of that factory, along with press clippings for American projects, such as an 'aerial Gibraltar' for the US Navy in San Francisco, published in Germany before the war, were collected by engineers working for the Luftwaffe and by Junkers.[52]

With the intense allied bombing campaigns against airplane factories, the idea of a general programme to construct underground assembly lines was not long in coming. A network of underground factories was created in the centre and southern part of the Reich, sometimes using existing galleries. This was the case for the Mittlewerk group of underground factories, in the Hartz, which was created under the direction of Albert Speer, using galleries from abandoned mines to stockpile strategic materials. The production lines for the V-1 and A-4 (later V-2) were transferred there after Operation Hydra, which destroyed part of the facility at Peenemünde in 1943. Field research immediately after the war by an Anglo-American team documented two kinds of galleries, cut into sandstone or anhydrite, used at first to stock hydrocarbons, revealing a dense network of assembly halls.[53] Similar factories were also implanted in the annexed territories, like the ones created for the production of V-1's in a former mine in Thil, between Verdun and Luxembourg.[54] In 1944–1945, tunnels were dug throughout Germany for

Underground factory for V-1 flying bombs, Mittlewerk, Kohnstein, Hartz, view of an underground gallery. Photograph by O. Ang. Bundesarchiv, 183-1985-0123-027

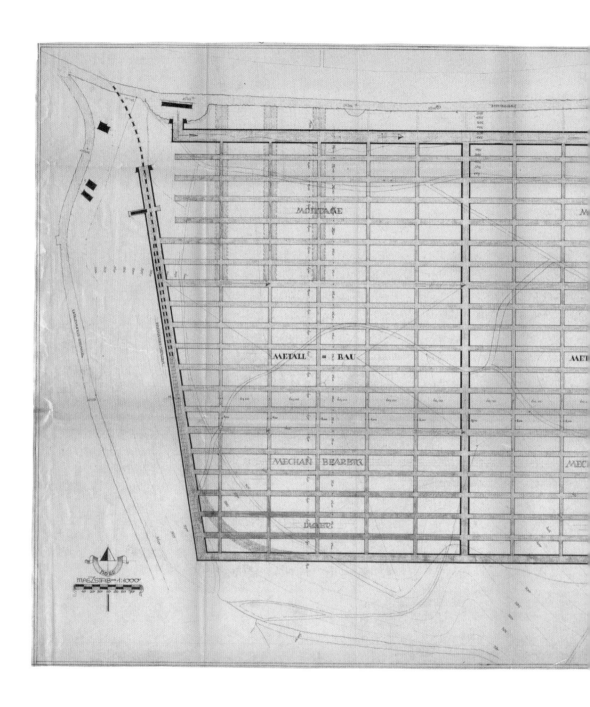

MONTAGE

METALL = BAU

MECHAN. BEARBTG.

LAGER.

MASZSTAB 1:1000

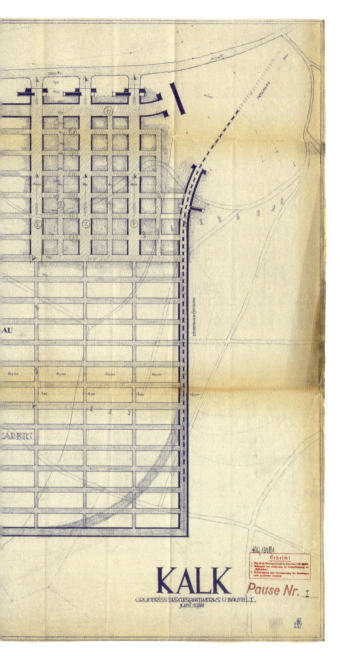

KALK
GRUNDRISS DESGESAMTWERKS U BAUTEIL I.
JUNI 1944

Pause Nr. I

the production of airplanes, after the creation of a specialised industrial department in October 1944, under the Reichsminister für Rüstung und Kriegsproduktion.[55]

As the Allied raids progressed, factories were buried in converted mine tunnels (*Stollen*) or in new underground complexes that were being developed at an ever-increasing rate in 1944 and continued to be built until the last weeks of the war. The Stuttgart architect Eberhard Kuen worked on several factories for Messerschmitt. His activities ranged from determining which sites would be best suited to excavation, as well as being sufficiently well connected to road and rail networks, to detailed projects. He studied both steel and wood support systems for underground galleries and the use of watertight doors. In January 1945, Kuen was still working for an aircraft manufacturer that was developing on its own construction programme, without recourse to the state, and he was designing tunnels for the 'Ring-Kalk' factory complex in Kelheim and the 'Weisse Tal' in Schelklingen-Allmendingen. The galleries had an elliptical profile with rails integrated into their concrete structure and rolling platforms that could move motors or components through these

Eberhard Kuen
Project for the 'Ring-Kalk'
underground aircraft factory
for Messerschmitt, Kelheim,
Bavaria, plan of underground
galleries, 1944.
Architekturmuseum
der TU München

invisible labyrinths, which were connected to railway lines. Kuen drew up elaborate systems of reinforced sealed doors designed to withstand impact from bombs.[56]

The Mobilisation of the Labour Force

The large increase in industrial production required millions of additional workers throughout the world. Many of these were female, notably in American cities, which became the world's major arsenals. In Los Angeles, 42% of the industrial workers were women, and the figures were comparable in Chicago.[57] A poster by J. Howard Miller in 1943 made Rosie the Riveter into a mythical figure to symbolise the six million women working in American industry.[58] The situation in England was similar, where women were employed in firms that were sometimes located far from the urban centres – and they too provided models for painters.[59] The phenomenon extended to architecture, with increasing numbers of women working for architectural firms. For example, Seattle-based Pietro Belluschi considered it worthy of note that during the war his office included five women.[60]

The industrial programmes orchestrated by belligerent states, often conceived as part of a strategy of decentralisation, required assembling a large labour force to be transplanted from existing cities or drawn from the countryside, necessitating corresponding projects for workers' housing. The scale of these programmes was far greater than those undertaken during the First World War, which had led to formal and technical innovations, especially in

Germany – for example, the complex designed by Paul Schmitthenner at Staaken, outside Berlin – and in the United States, where for the first time the federal government was playing a role in housing. These programmes were based on the premise that quality housing would be a productive factor in the great factory that the country had become. Such was the argument of proponents of social housing, whose vision extended past the war.

New Types of Habitation

Specific programmes emerged under the urgent conditions of the first years of the war; they led to significant innovations in the typology of housing units and their overall organisation, and these were sometimes directly linked to the sociological specificities of the labour force employed. The British architect William Holford, for example, while employed by the firm of Sir Alexander Gibb, worked on commissions to design several hostels for women workers in munitions factories – sixteen in Warrington, and eight in Swynnerton. He set a team of two hundred draughtsmen to work, under the direction of R. T. Kennedy, which included a number of modernist architects such as the young F. R. S. Yorke and émigrés such as Johannes Schreiner, who had been in charge of Erich Mendelsohn's office in Berlin.[61] Scattered across the countryside like villages, the complexes were each designed to house between one thousand and fifteen hundred women. Each was to be provided with advanced communal facilities and to be sited in carefully planted and camouflaged landscapes. The common room,

**Women workers
at the Boeing factory**,
Seattle, c. 1944.
Boeing Images

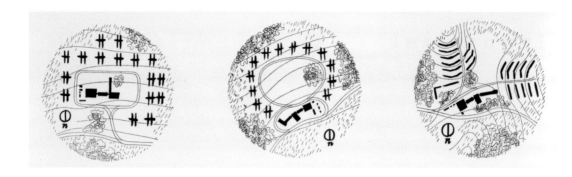

the kitchens, the dining halls and the numerous relaxation areas employed a wide range of materials – concrete, brick, lightweight framing – along with the architecturally successful incorporation of anti-aircraft shelters. The housing employed lightweight prefabricated elements, assembled into L-shaped, T-shaped or H-shaped plans built around a brick and concrete core. *The Architectural Review* stressed the importance of the 'social centre' in their conception: 'Their sites vary in size from fifteen to thirty acres, and from flat and featureless agricultural land of poor quality to fine parkland with good trees and interesting differences of level. Each hostel houses a thousand or more girls, and each

William Holford
Hostels for women workers in munitions factories (1941–1942), various site plans (top) and interior views of a community centre (bottom) in *The Architectural Review*, December 1942. CCA Collection

SOCIAL CENTRE

SOCIAL CENTRE

group of hostels is planned around its place of work rather like a ring of satellite villages. The girls are taken to them and from work by bus and have their mid-shift meal at the factory. A community in which there is no normal home-life and in which one sex is segregated, needs greater provision for social welfare and entertainment than a mixed community; and isolated as some of these wartime centres of industry are, most hostels have to aim at catering for the whole of the girl's leisure time.'[62]

The rapid and efficient construction of these clearly articulated and functional ensembles brought professional recognition to Holford, and he was quickly called upon by the Ministry of Town and Country Planning. These hostels were designed to be 'as attractive as possible' and to create a 'healthy and pleasantly designed environment',[63] but in fact they were not fully occupied, and some were used to house American forces.

The importance of these projects, which were widely disseminated in the profession, is that they were 'the largest, as well as among the first, war building schemes on which architects not on the staff of a Government department had just those responsibilities – no more and no less – which they would naturally have been given on a pre-war scheme of the same size'.[64] Projects for unmarried workers were also built at many American sites, both industrial – like the 'duration dormitories' designed by architects such as Paul Nelson and Eero Saarinen for the Federal Public Housing Authority – and administrative – such as those designed by George Howe for the Public Buildings Administration in Washington.[65] Frederick Ackerman, who had been actively involved in social housing since the 1920s, conducted a methodical examination of the issues involved in grouping together hundreds of workers in eight-hour shifts that required substantial communal services.[66]

The Lanham Act

The Housing Act of 1940 in the United States, named after the representative from Texas Fritz G. Lanham, gave rise to the most ambitious housing programme in the world. The act allowed massive federal funds to be used for the construction of public housing, under the control of the National Housing Agency, created in 1937 as part of the New Deal. Charles F. Palmer of Atlanta was appointed Defense Housing Coordinator in the summer of 1940. The programme was enthusiastically endorsed by architects in general and by modernist ones in particular, as it appeared open to innovative solutions in construction and distribution. Previous projects had generally deployed traditional architectural forms and site planning derived from the principles of the garden city adapted to the car, the prototype for which had been Radburn in New Jersey.

Some 625,000 units would be produced between 1940 and 1944 thanks to the Lanham Act (adding to the housing produced by private initiatives), 580,000 of which would be temporary, much to the indignation of Richard Neutra: 'Not all brains of the nation operate or are capable to operate in tank turrets or submarines. There is brain enough left for other needed employment. Housing of this day definitely casts a shadow into the post-war period. It is probably the ABC and backbone of post-war planning.

It must under all circumstances retain an element of pure vision. It must be differentiated and properly fitted into localities whether demountable, prefabricated or conventional in construction, whole villages for two, three, five thousand inhabitants built today, must have a post-war use value, which can be salvaged to a really high percentage. The idea of "temporary" dwellings is prolific in wastefulness and lasting danger. Temporary dwellings are the costliest thinkable.' He continued: 'So called temporary structures without fail become permanent slums, adding to the curse under which we have been laboring. But there is a difference. The old slums could be blamed on a few hardy exploiters; these new slums would stand, justly or unjustly, attributed to the incapacity of an administration or a government to engage in housing. Governmental action in this matter, so badly needed, where private enterprise cannot find reward, may be silenced and killed off for a decade.'[67]

In 1943, the new programme coordinator, the National Housing Administrator John B. Blanford, Jr., took account of an amendment to the Lanham Act which called for the temporary housing to be destroyed within two years after the war, and proposed a different course, through a programme to upgrade the housing, 'because of the serious shortages of critical materials, recent private war housing has been streamlined to meet war requirements in use of critical materials, with the result that some pre-war standards of equipment have necessarily gone by the board. However, many current private projects are been planned for use of temporary equipment which can be replaced with higher-quality items after the war.'[68]

Here we see a double time frame appearing: a long duration for the basic construction and a short one for the equipment.

The programme's concern for economy was praised by some architects, such as Antonin Raymond, who considered in 1941 that this arrangement would contribute to a virtuous modernisation of housing architecture: 'The limitations of the Lanham Act, coupled with intelligent administration, by eliminating waste, extravagance, and false pretention have brought about a radical change toward better understanding of the value of simplicity and direct solutions and is a safe approach toward better design and the true art of building.'[69] Along with Raymond, who had recently returned from twenty years in Japan, the leading figures of modern architecture in America participated in this programme, applying their various efforts to the composition of the complexes, the typology, the technical issues and the aesthetics of serial housing. As far as unit types were concerned, competition and emulation were the rule.[70]

The leaders of the movement for social housing – both architects and militants such as Catherine Bauer – were the most active at the beginning of the programme. Bauer saw hope for the coming years in the programme, writing: 'The war is giving us one thing that's been almost universally demanded for years. It's giving us vast laboratory experience with experimental building methods and prefabrication, with large-scale community planning, with rental management and upkeep, and with streamlined production processes. The present results may be reduced to barest bones, but this experience can revitalize

Robert Alexander
Clarence Stein
Workers' housing (1941–1942),
Baldwin Hills, Los Angeles,
view of a building, c. 1943.
Robert Alexander Papers,
Division of Rare and
Manuscript Collections,
Cornell University

the much-maligned building industry after the war.'[71] As for the architects, Clarence Stein, the subtle designer of garden cities, drew up numerous housing complexes in 1941 in Pennsylvania for the Federal Work Agency and the Allegheny County Housing Authority, notably at Clairton, Shaler Township, and Stowe Township. In Culver City, part of the Los Angeles agglomeration, he built the large complex of Baldwin Hills, combining some six hundred units in groups of two or four, with a large shared green space as its main element, which linked groups of houses as at Radburn. In a city where racial tensions were tending to become more of an issue during the war

years with riots by young Mexicans and the piling together of blacks in Little Tokyo, which had been emptied of its previous inhabitants, deported to camps such as Manzanar, and re-baptised 'Bronzeville' – Baldwin Hills was the first housing complex where a plurality of social groups was a government requirement, while the eight hundred units of housing at Aliso Village, built at the same time by Ralph C. Flewelling, George J. Adams, Eugene Weston, Jr., Lewis E. Wilson and Lloyd Wright in an area condemned as unsanitary, marked the first step in the urban renewal of Los Angeles.[72] The architect Joseph Allen Stein, who had previously worked in the Neutra office, was working in the research branch of the US Navy and had become interested in emergency shelters through work on installations for migrant workers. In 1942, he organised an exhibition at the San Francisco Museum of Art that presented 'Houses for War and Post-War'. Stein developed a structural system for single-family houses that consisted of a large roof, supported by angled wood supports.[73] The project was primarily a pedagogical expression of the basic tenets of the Allied struggle: 'War housing can be an example of our war aims. The new housing can raise the morale of workers and be a constant reminder of the meaning and promise of democracy, and the "Four Freedoms" we are fighting to preserve and enlarge. . . . It would be a national loss that any large part of the few hundreds of thousands units of war housing being constructed should not serve to advance the living standard of the people and the character of our communities.'[74] As early as 1940, Stein also collaborated with Gregory Ain, who had also worked with Neutra and was equally politically to the left, on the concept of a 'one-family defense house', with a 7.5 by 7.5 metres square plan. The project addressed several particular concerns of the time: the plumbing was 'compact', the four concrete angles were to be poured in plywood forms that would then serve as beams, and the flat roof prolonged by pergolas was supposed to facilitate the camouflage of the building.[75]

Modern Successes, from Channel Heights to Vallejo

The Museum of Modern Art was quick to grasp what was at stake. In May 1942, the museum opened the 'Wartime Housing' exhibition, with projects that were considered exemplary. When the exhibition travelled to London, its reception gave some idea of the importance of many of these projects in thinking about the post-war period: 'The programme is a triumph

for the architect and planner. It shows that America is developing a national architecture. Everywhere in the exhibition allowance has been made for differences in climate and material, yet the buildings themselves show that America is developing a vernacular as unmistakable and unique as her language.' The lesson here was twofold, ensuring that the errors of the interwar period could be avoided: the Americans 'show us that prefabricated houses, if they are properly sited and related to a communal pattern, can make worthy and beautiful homes. They show us how new housing estates and townships can be built in such a way that they are satisfactory in themselves and do not strangle the older centres to which they are attached.'[76]

Let us dwell for a moment on the completed projects by the principal American protagonists of what is generally called the 'Modern Movement'. Some of them were direct extensions of the European social-democratic experiments, for instance the Aluminum City Terrace in New Kensington, north-east of Pittsburgh, Pennsylvania, where the ALCOA factories were located. It was the last project that Walter Gropius and Marcel Breuer worked on together, after almost five years of collaboration.[77] This *Siedlung*, laid out on a verdant and very steep site, broke with the morphology advocated by Gropius in the first CIAM congresses. Essentially south-facing, the two-storey blocks containing eight units each were clad in wood and included long galleries and porches. Reflecting a desire for greater individuality, the blocks were not aligned with each other, the outer ones progressively freeing themselves from the centre of the complex as if subject to

REPLACE THIS

WITH THIS

Two children in the back yard of a three-room house with no bath, electricity or gas.

Nursery school of a Farm Workers' Community.

Slum interior.

Built by a community Housing Authority with USHA aid.

Laundry tubs.

Laundry and utility building in a Farm Security Administration camp for defense workers.

NOT THESE

BUT THESE

Architect:
Eero Saarinen

Architects:
George Howe
Oscar Stonorov
Louis I. Kahn

'Wartime Housing',
pages from *Wartime
Housing: an Exhibition
in 10 Scenes*,

The Museum of
Modern Art, May 1942.
CCA Collection, gift
from the Avery Library

a centrifugal force. *The Architectural Review* was quick to praise the 'delightfully planned informality' of its plan, which was in keeping with the magazine's editorial inclinations.[78] Although the complex was held up in the architectural press as 'almost a revolution in public housing, with their accustomed severity of exterior design and exceptionally open interior',[79] and was equally appreciated by its inhabitants as well, a hostile mayor saw only 'chicken coops' and refused to build an access road. The complex was not fully occupied until late 1943, eighteen months after its completion.

Projects proliferated in the industrial stateof Pennsylvania. After the lean years of the Depression, George Howe and Louis I. Kahn, based in Philadelphia, completed two projects between 1941 and 1943. Located in Pine Ford Acres and Pennypack Woods, in the suburbs of Philadelphia, they included five hundred and one thousand housing units

respectively, including single- and double-storey units, arranged in rows of blocks of four. The relatively modest project for Carver Court in Coatesville, financed by the FPHA and designed in collaboration with Oscar Storonov, was the most inventive. Designed to house a hundred families of black steelworkers, it was located in a former horse track. The houses were arranged in two rows around a looping pathway and had concrete structural walls. Open on the ground floor as a result, they seemed to echo Le Corbusier's 'réorganisation agraire' houses from the 1930s. In the catalogue for the exhibition at MoMA 'Built in USA 1932–1944', Elizabeth Mock noted that 'the scale is intimate. In every part of the community

Walter Gropius
Marcel Breuer
**Aluminum City
housing** (1941–1942),
New Kensington,

Pennsylvania,
model, c. 1942.
Harvard Art Museums,
Busch-Reisinger Museum,
gift from Ise Gropius

one is pleasantly aware of the shape and substance of the whole. Buildings have been skillfully arranged to preserve and enhance the natural character of the site.'[80] Storonov and Kahn also built the 475 units of the Lily Ponds Houses in Washington, with the emphasis this time on the prefabrication of the wood elements.[81]

Richard Neutra's office on the West Coast of the United States worked on much larger projects. The first, Avion Village, was built in Grand Prairie, between Fort Worth and Dallas, Texas, to house workers at the North American factory. This 'park living development' was planned in the spirit of Radburn, around a large open green space with communal amenities. Neutra described it as 'an extensive communal area, continuous, without interruption by through traffic, and a layout where all the dwellings face this green area. Houses have park addresses rather than street numbers.'[82]

This alternative to previous workers' housing was built in 1942 in collaboration with the architects Roscoe P. DeWitt and David R. Williams, and landscape architect Wynne B. Woodruff. Neutra concentrated on the prefabricated units. The project was praised by Albert Mayer, an architect who was active in social housing in New York and was subsequently the first planner of Chandigarh. Mayer, who was seeking to define criteria for the new federal programmes, considered Avion Village a worthy example of good planning'.[83]

The Channel Heights complex, built above San Pedro to the south of Los Angeles for workers in a US Navy shipyard, was more ambitious both in size and in the

Walter Gropius
Marcel Breuer
**Aluminum City
housing** (1941–1942),
New Kensington,

Pennsylvania,
partial view, c. 1942.
Harvard Art Museums,
Busch-Reisinger Museum,
gift from Ise Gropius

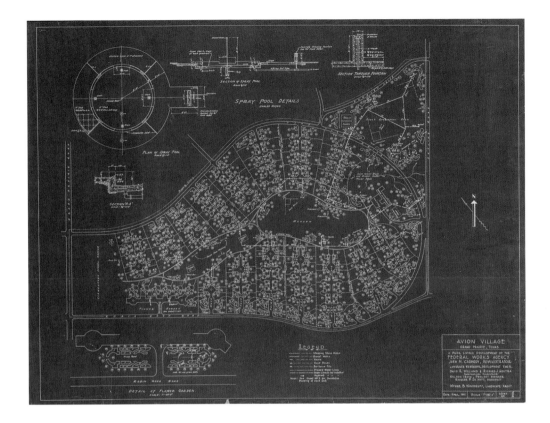

sophistication of the architectural solutions, to the point that Max Bill judged it in 1945 'the most successful of all the wartime projects'.[84] Six hundred permanent units were built on a 160-acre plot at the lowest density of any project built to date. The relative monotony of the plan is only an illusion, for the very dramatic site – with a 75-metres difference in elevation between top and bottom – created interesting contrasts in siting despite the regular arrangement of the houses. For Elizabeth Mock, 'The community is remarkably free of monotony. One reason is the superb site, but another is the variety and distinction of the houses and the skill with which they are grouped. Most of the houses are single story and all are planned for unobstructed view.'[85]

Neutra claimed to have made the best of the 'very rugged topography'. 'Illuminated underpasses under high road embankments serve pedestrian communication between recreational areas, as well as for surface drainage of several deep canyons and ravines. The idea that dwelling units face on finger-parks radiating from a central green area is maintained. Visitors enter through trellised pergolas onto park walks leading to the houses.' Defending himself pre-emptively against accusations of monotony, he declared that his complex 'is much more a *living entity* than is that checkerboard of 500 or 1,000 individual lots laid down in a rectangular street gridiron and carrying, side by side, miniature English cottages, Mexican ranchos, Cape Cod fishermen's

Richard J. Neutra
Avion Village Defense Housing, Grand Prairie, Texas, plan, 1941.
Richard and Dion Neutra

Papers, Charles E. Young Research Library, Department of Special Collections, University of California, Los Angeles

huts, and all that dubious variety of yesterday's speculative subdivision art'.[86]

The buildings at Channel Heights were indeed developed in a modern language without any concession to common practices, except for the use of wood for balconies and fittings. The sculptural qualities of the one- and two-storey houses is clearly evident, and their arrangement displays great ingenuity for compact workers' housing and is linked to a network of generous communal amenities, including a nursery and a supermarket – the latter a novelty in this kind of project. Neutra developed a line of wood furniture, from

Top: Richard J. Neutra
Channel Heights Defense Housing,
San Pedro, California, model, 1942. Photograph by Julius Shulman
Julius Shulman Photography Archive, Research Library, Getty Research Institute

Richard J. Neutra
Channel Heights Defense Housing,
San Pedro, California, exploded perspective view of a unit, 1942.
CCA Collection

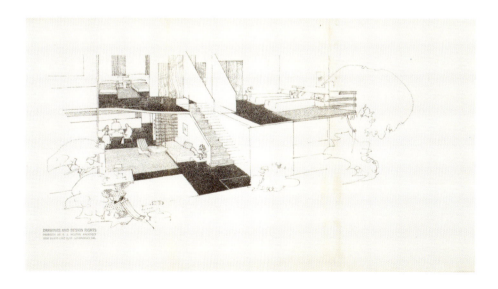

folding tables that maximised the use of the small living rooms to armchairs and storage units. After 1945, Neutra made no secret of the satisfaction he took in this project, which he expressed in modest, anonymous terms in a report he drew up for the first CIAM in Bridgwater: 'What can be called a contemporary trend of design is markedly gaining from Vancouver to San Diego, with possibly Los Angeles in the lead. The efforts of two decades to overcome historical imitations are evidently bearing fruit.'[87] French town planner Gaston Bardet, a fervent opponent of modern architecture, would be unsparing in his irony when criticising the monotony of the project, but his analysis was based only on the single published plan, not on the three-dimensional reality of the project.[88]

On an even larger scale, William Wurster's projects in Vallejo, north of San Francisco

(1941–1942), differed in two important ways. This was one of the largest programmes undertaken during the entire war, in a city whose population tripled between 1939 and 1945, with thousands of units laid out on a hilly landscape with the aid of landscape architect Garrett Eckbo. Most importantly, it was the most advanced and successful experiment in prefabrication of the time, based on the use of plywood panels for half of the house and panels of homosote nailed and glued to wood framing for the other. The goal was to 'increase the salvage value of the houses, which may not be needed after the war'.[89] In Carquinez Heights, Wurster

Top: Richard J. Neutra
Channel Heights Defense Housing, San Pedro, California, view of a living room, 1943. Photograph by Julius Shulman
CCA Collection

William Wurster
Defense Housing, Vallejo, California (1941–1942), views of manufacture and assembly of elements, page in *The Architectural Forum*, October 1941.
CCA Collection

DEFENSE HOUSES AT VALLEJO, CALIF.*   WILLIAM WILSON WURSTER, ARCHITECT

1. **2.** **3.**

Picture **1** shows Homasote sheets being wet down before use, in order to swell sheets so that subsequent shrinkage will stretch material on frames. **2** shows precutting of openings for electric outlet boxes, **3** precutting of studs and other framing lumber outside the plant.

4. **5.** **6.**

4, 5, and **6,** show assembly of a typical, room size wall panel on a "jig table" marked off in modular units. Door opening is cut after the sheet is applied, using plywood template and skill saw; sheets are glued and nailed to 2 x 3 studs, using mechanical glue spreaders.

7. **8.** **9.**

7, 8, and **9** show fabrication of a roof panel, complete with overhang and screened vent. Homasote ceilings are applied to furring strips on the bottom of the rafters, tops of rafters canted to receive sloping roof at job. Four such panels, plus seven smaller units, roof one house.

10. **11.** **12.**

10. Trailer-truck loaded with three complete houses ready for 29 mile trip to the site.

SITE PREPARATION. Picture **11** shows form for casting foundation piers in batches of 84 piers. **12** shows hole-boring apparatus for drilling foundation holes, and operation of setting piers.

*Constructing Agency: FWA Division of Defense Housing

121

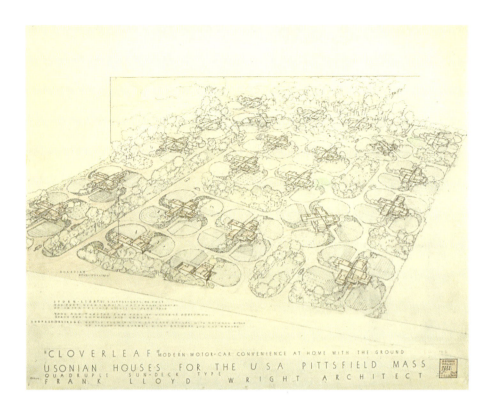

"CLOVERLEAF" MODERN-MOTOR-CAR CONVENIENCE AT HOME WITH THE GROUND
USONIAN HOUSES FOR THE USA PITTSFIELD MASS
QUADRUPLE SUN-DECK TYPE
FRANK LLOYD WRIGHT ARCHITECT

developed three prototypes using different techniques, in order to achieve maximum flexibility. At Chabot Terrace, he built three thousand units.[90]

A two-fold trend can be observed in these projects: a modernisation of the layout of the experimental garden cities from the 1920s; and a kind of organic disarticulation of the rigid functionalist schemas that structured the projects devised for European social democracies.

Modernist Failures, from Pittsfield to Willow Run

In addition to those projects whose influence continued on past 1945, some notable failures must be mentioned as well, although the reasons for failure varied. In 1941, Frank Lloyd Wright was given the commission for a workers' housing complex in Pittsfield, Massachusetts, for the Division of Defense Housing of the Federal Works Agency, under the direction of Clark Foreman. The latter advocated a high degree of experimentation in projects that he commissioned, which included the Aluminum City Terrace. Wright was very critical of the federal programmes, which he considered to be 'the most unfortunate of government activities', and he developed a configuration in which variants of his Usonian houses were grouped in fours, forming a cloverleaf pattern, hence the name 'Cloverleaf Housing'. These houses reflected his vision of a family controlled

Frank Lloyd Wright
Cloverleaf war industry housing project, Pittsfield, Massachusetts (unbuilt), overall perspective view, 1942. The Frank Lloyd Wright Foundation

by the mistress of the house from atop a mezzanine: 'I regard the units themselves as, primarily, little breeding stables to be made decent and convenient for the purpose of up to seven children . . . The house-wife is the captain of the ship and things should be on ball-bearings for her – in every way . . . A type of group building is needed that automatically keeps the neighborhood tidy and free of objectionable features . . . The garage should be a rendezvous for the father and the boys, as a kind of shop and loafing place.'[91] Wright's commission was cancelled, under pressure from John McCormack, majority leader in the House of Representatives, who insisted that it be given to a local architect, which was not a requirement of the Lanham Act, and a group of prefabricated houses called Victory Hill replaced the rejected project.

The inability of a group of modern architects to develop the projected new town near the Ford factory of Willow Run cannot be imputed to simple political patronage. Built in a rural part of Michigan, north of Ypsilanti, 'Bomber City' was predicated on the requirements of a workforce that could not be housed in Detroit, which was already experiencing an acute shortage of housing.[92] At first, the workers were conveyed by buses using an advanced highway system, built

with the help of Robert Moses, the developer of the parkways system in New York. The United Automobile Workers union was able to successfully petition Washington for the creation of a town for twenty thousand workers by the FPHA, while the press commented ironically on the miserable conditions of housing in 'Will It Run?', one of the many nicknames given to the site.[93] A smaller project for 6,000 families was designed, consisting of five 'neighborhood units' of 1,200 units each, which were soon reduced to three. The union, operating through the workers' groups, insisted on using the Radburn plan. But each of the three teams working on the project interpreted Radburn in its own way.

To the west, Albert Mayer and Julian Whittlesey arranged their neighbourhood around a circular lawn, dominated by the school. In the middle, Skidmore, Owings, and Merrill, in association with the engineer Andrews, laid out four complexes of double units along curving pathways. These were similar to their colleagues', but in a more modern style that employed industrial materials such as Cemesto. The third group, by Louis I. Kahn and Oscar Storonov utilised elevated houses 'ground-freed', like those initially developed at Carver Court. The configuration of the development displayed a more complex interrelationship between open spaces and residential streets.[94] The two architects described the lost project with no little nostalgia: 'The character of the town is neither urban nor suburban; its safety, spaciousness and convenience would have offered a powerful inducement to permanent settlement.'[95] Eliel Saarinen and Robert F. Swanson

Top: Louis I. Kahn, Oscar Storonov **Housing development project**, Willow Run, Michigan, aerial perspective, 1943. Louis I. Kahn Collection, The University of Pennsylvania and the Pennsylvania Historical and Museum Commission

Bottom: Eero Saarinen **Willow Run town centre project** (1943), Willow Run, Michigan, illustration in *The Architectural Forum*, March 1943. CCA Collection

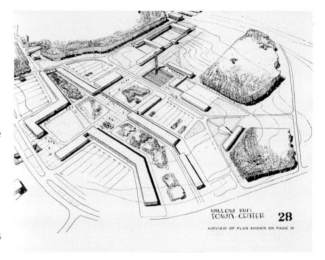

designed a new pedestrian centre defined by large slabs of shops and public buildings arranged around a water feature, not unlike the Technical Center of General Motors that Eero Saarinen would complete in Warren.

Despite the teams' imaginative approach and the support of Roosevelt's administration, the project was abandoned under pressure from Ford, who refused to allow it to be built on their land, and from the Republicans, who were afraid to lose their majority in the county. The federal agencies would ultimately build the complexes of Willow Village and Window Lodge, to house whites and blacks respectively. In the end, barely 15,000 of the 44,000 recruited workers would be housed onsite, many of them in shacks and trailers that formed a rural shantytown.[96] In 1943, the journal *Task*, published by the architecture school at Harvard, denounced Ford's manoeuvres and engaged in a heated discussion of the 'blue prints for the post-war never-never land' developed at Willow Run, arguing that the 'internecine squabbles, side-tracking details and concentration on minor issues' scuppered the project, and that 'housing cannot be achieved by a government agency in isolation, or by an architect or planner alone no matter how good his solution, or by a consumer group by itself. It is the collective responsibility of all these in recognizing the need, programming its solution and fighting, on the widest political, social and architectural front, for its consummation.'[97]

As the case of Willow Run vividly demonstrates, public programmes and planned projects were only a small part of the housing that was actually built during the war. The shortage of materials limited construction of individual houses, and complexes made up of huts, shacks and even tents proliferated. The more luxurious of these ephemeral lodgings were trailers, whose production and use increased during the war.[98] In 1940, the Trailer Coach Manufacturers Association approached the American government and proposed that it launch the production of trailers to house the workforce of the new industrial centres, and in 1942, the year when the lack of housing was most acute, fifty thousand of them would

In two of the four experimental types developed by TVA a slight shaping of undersides to accent the cantilever at ends, an eaves overhang front and rear and a slight projection of the roof along the side walls are reminiscent of traditional house design

THE TRAILER HOUSE

TVA's new approach to mobile shelter. By the staff of the Department of Regional Studies. Tennessee Valley Authority

come out of the factories. Designed in 1936, the Stout Folding Trailer, whose central segment could extend out on both sides, was highly popular for a while, but it was soon discredited because it leaked.[99] In the wake of the Federal Housing Administration's lack of enthusiasm for these products, a group of manufacturers designed a simple, economical model known as the 'committee trailer', which would be a lasting success. For its part, the Tennessee Valley Authority introduced mobile homes transported

'The Trailer House', article in *The Architectural Record*, February 1943. CCA Collection

Top: **Housing estate made from trailers**, Willow Run, Michigan, aerial view, 1943. The Henry Ford Museum

in sections, which prefigured techniques that would be widely used after the war.[100]

While the American case was unique, the problem existed worldwide. Giuseppe Pagano addressed the American policies in 1943 in one of the last issues of *Costruzioni Casabella*. Implicitly criticising fascism, he stressed two tendencies he observed in the United States: 'The first is the decentralisation of industry and the consequent relocation of workers' housing to the vicinity of the new centres of production, in conformity with the well-known principles of Ford. The second is to see the industry producing prefabricated houses as the prime resource and source of revenue for American capital after the war.'[101] But the article by the experts on popular housing, Irenio Diotallevi and Francesco Marescotti, 'La casa singola nella esperienza americana', only addressed houses built before 1939.[102]

In the Soviet Union, the relocating of the manufacture of equipment and armaments

to the east gave rise to a considerable need for housing. The growth of the new industrial centres created in the first five-year plans included the construction of new housing developments, some of them drawn up by architects who had been evacuated from the western parts of the USSR. Quarter no. 14 in Magnitogorsk, a new centre for metallurgy, was built in 1943 by a team from Leningrad consisting of Andrei Ol, Evgueni Levinson and Georgui Simonov. In another steelmaking centre, Nizhny Tagil, in the Urals, minimal two-family dwellings were constructed out of plaster panels, which were at that time the objects of extensive research in the USSR. In the field of energy, a plan for the expansion of the town of Guriev on the Caspian Sea, strategically important for the supply of petrol to the front, was drawn up by A. Arefyev, who, with V. Vasilkovsky, also made studies of the public infrastructure and dwellings using elements borrowed from the region's traditional architecture.[103] But much more than was the case in Michigan or in the American production zones, the majority of the dwellings produced were shacks, or *zemlianki*,

A. Arefyev
Workers' housing in Guryev,
elevation, c. 1942.
Shchusev State Museum
of Architecture

half-buried habitations covered with whatever scrap materials were available. The task of drawing up the plans for these dwellings was entrusted by the Academy of Architecture, which had relocated to Chimkent in Kazakhstan, to A. M. Saltzman.[104]

German Complexes and Camps

The development of the Nazi war industries from the mid-1930s onwards led to the creation of numerous housing complexes linked to factories. Their traditional style was in stark contrast to the modern construction of the production hangars. In Oranienburg, Herbert Rimpl built the Siedlung Leegebruch (1936–1938), which looked like a full-scale version of a village from a miniature train set.[105] The aviation, chemical and steelmaking industries provided the impetus for housing programmes whose construction continued during the first years of the war and whose scale was sometimes considerable. Rimpl

designed a whole town in Salzgitter, near Braunschweig, for the Hermann-Göring-Werke steel mills.[106]

Large-scale complexes were planned, like the Gemeinschaftssiedlung comprising 800 units that Heinrich Tessenow drew up for Junkers in Mosigkau, near Dessau, as a result of the direct intervention of his former pupil Speer, and the Gefolgschaftssiedlung that he designed for the same firm in Magdeburg. These two projects from 1940–1941 were a development of formal themes that Tessenow had explored as early as before 1914, but with large elongated blocks, lined with simplified houses.[107] The Stadt des KdF-Wagens, a new town for the Volkswagen factory workers based

Herbert Rimpl
Project for a city near Braunschweig for the Hermann-Göring-Werke, aerial perspective, in *Monatshefte für Baukunst und Städtebau*, 1939. CCA Collection

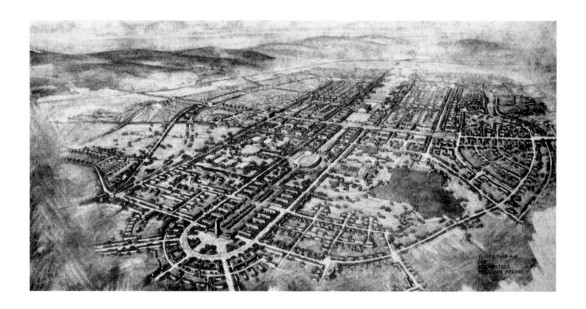

on the ideas of Nazi theoretician Gottfried Feder, was designed by Peter Koller, a former student of Tessenow's who had been recommended by Speer. It was built between 1939 and 1943, and combined dwelling areas with a central *Stadtkrone*. It was supposed to be able to expand to house 400,000 occupants, but only 3,500 dwellings were built before 1945 to accommodate German workers and employees, and after 1942 these were accompanied by an *Ostlager*, a camp of shacks for 20,000 prisoners and detention facilities for the camps of Neuengamme and Sachsenhausen.[108]

Indeed, the labour that the Axis countries extracted from the subjugated populations was decisive. The Polish and, above all, Russian campaigns, which provided Germany with millions of prisoners of war, and the creation of concentration camps gave rise to a new source of labour. Prisoners of war, political prisoners, deported Jews and forced labourers like the French workmen sent to Germany by the Service du Travail Obligatoire were all increasingly put to use in the production of equipment and armaments. An industrial economy founded on constraint, control and the cynical exploitation of labour was established, under the authority of Albert Speer and the SS architect Hans Kammler, linking factories and concentration camps: the factory became a camp, while the camp contributed to war production. The proximity of the camps to quarries used for large-scale projects, which had already frequently been the case before 1939, now became the rule and was characteristic of the war economy in general.[109] The new development was the establishment of smaller subsidiary camps

or small places of imprisonment to serve every military-industrial facility.

This was the case for the base at Peenemünde on the Baltic coast for the production and testing of rockets, where Walter Dornberger and Wernher von Braun's team used prisoners of war and political deportees, who were held in camps built nearby.[110] The base created by the Luftwaffe on the same site used prisoners sent from the Ravensbrück camp. Mittelwerk, in the Hartz, was able to function because of foreign workers requisitioned from the Buchenwald camp, seventy kilometres away, who were then transferred to a subsidiary camp named Dora. Under constant surveillance and ongoing threats from SS detachments, who watched over production and who punished any act considered sabotage with death, these deportees initially slept in the factory tunnels themselves, before a camp of shacks was set up in 1944. One third of the 60,000 prisoners so 'utilised' would not survive, while the number of victims of the V-1 and V-2 bombings in England and Belgium would not exceed 15,000.[111] The living conditions of these prisoners, who were engaged in the Reich's most advanced armaments programme, were such that Albert Speer subsequently made sure to deplore them in retrospect and to highlight his charitable interventions, all the while justifying the use of prisoners by the need for complete secrecy regarding this production.[112] Despite the bombings, prisoners and forced labourers provided the Luftwaffe with a growing volume of material, and by the end of 1944, they represented up to 60% of the workforce of certain airplane factories.[113]

1. Albert Mayer, 'Housing for Defense – and After', *The New York Times Magazine*, 21 September 1941.
2. Dorothy Rosenman, 'Housing to Speed Production', *The Architectural Record*, vol. 91, no. 4 (April 1942), 42.
3. Lewis Mumford, 'Agents of Mechanization', in *Technics and Civilization* (New York and London: Harcourt, Brace and Company, 1934), 84.
4. Alan Gropman, 'Industrial Mobilization', in Alan Gropman, *The Big 'L': American Logistics in World War II* (Washington: National Defense University Press, 1997), 82.
5. Alec Cairncross, *Planning in Wartime: Aircraft Production in Britain, Germany, and the USA* (New York: St. Martin's Press, 1991).
6. Donald Marr Nelson, *Arsenal of Democracy: the Story of American War Production* (New York: Harcourt, Brace and Company, 1946). Alan S. Milward, *War, Economy, and Society, 1939–1945* (Berkeley: University of California Press, 1977).
7. Gerald D. Nash, 'The Impact of World War II on the American Economy', in *World War II and the Transformation of Business Systems: the International Conference of Business History 20: Proceedings of the Fuji Conference*, edited by Jun Sakudo and Takao Shiba (Tokyo: University of Tokyo Press, 1994), 84–100.
8. On the war years in Mirafiori, see Duccio Bigazzi, 'Mirafiori e il modello americano, 1936–1960', in *Mirafiori 1936–1962*, edited by Carlo Olmo (Milan: Umberto Allemandi, 1997), 247–52.
9. Hans-Ernst Mittig, 'Industrie-Architektur des NS-Regimes: das Volkswagenwerk', in *Städtebau und Staatsbau im 20. Jahrhundert*, edited by Gabi Dolff-Bonekämper and Hiltrud Krier (Munich and Berlin: Deutscher Kunstverlag, 1996), 77–112.
10. Henri Puget, 'La région parisienne', *Vers un Paris nouveau, Cahiers de la république des lettres, des sciences et des arts*, 1929, 20; quoted by Lieutenant-Colonel Vauthier, *Le Danger aérien et l'avenir du pays* (Nancy, Paris and Strasbourg: Berger-Levrault, 1930), 338.
11. Ibid., 336.
12. Effi Markou, 'Militaires et urbanistes durant les années trente. L'aménagement urbain et la menace aérienne', *Les Annales de la recherche urbaine*, vol. 91 (December 2001), 18–26.

13. Jean-Pierre Côtre and Franz Graf, 'Les hangars, un type pleinement ouvert à l'expérimentation technique', in *Encyclopédie Perret*, edited by Jean-Louis Cohen, Joseph Abram and Guy Lambert (Paris: Éditions du patrimoine/Institut français d'architecture/Éditions le Moniteur, 2002), 100. Maurice Culot, David Peyceré and Gilles Ragot, eds., *Les Frères Perret. L'œuvre complète* (Paris: Institut français d'architecture/Norma, 2000), 273.
14. David Thoms, *War, Industry, and Society: the Midlands, 1939–45* (London and New York: Routledge, 1989).
15. Gordon E. Cherry and Leith Penny, *Holford: A Study in Architecture, Planning and Civic Design* (London and New York: Mansell, 1986), 80.
16. Joel Davidson, 'Building for War, Preparing for Peace: World War II and the Military-Industrial Complex', in *World War II and the American Dream. How Wartime Building Changed a Nation*, edited by Donald Albrecht (Washington: National Building Museum; Cambridge, Mass.: MIT Press, 1995), 195.
17. Gerald D. Nash, *The American West Transformed: The Impact of the Second World War* (Bloomington: Indiana University Press, 1985).
18. Gerald D. Nash, *World War II and the West: Reshaping the Economy* (Lincoln: University of Nebraska Press, 1989), 61–63.
19. 'City of Angels: Aviation's Boom Town', *Fortune*, March 1941, 90–95.
20. 'Producer of Production Lines', *The Architectural Record*, vol. 91, no. 6 (June 1942), 40.
21. David E. Nye, *American Technological Sublime* (Cambridge, Mass.: MIT Press, 1994), 109–42.
22. See the reminiscences of Henry J. Magaziner, 'Working for a Genius: My Time with Albert Kahn', *APT Bulletin*, vol. 32, no. 2–3 (2001), 59–64.
23. Anne M. Bos and Randy R. Talbot, 'Enough and On Time, The Story of the Detroit Arsenal', *Michigan History Magazine*, March–April 2001, 33.
24. 'Willow Run Bomber Plant', *The Architectural Record*, vol. 92, no. 3 (September 1942), 39–46.
25. The article is cited by Keith Sward, *The Legend of Henry Ford* (New York: Rinehart & Co., 1948), 430.
26. Charles Sorensen, with Samuel T. Williamson, *My Forty Years with Ford* (New York: Norton, 1956), 286.

27. Albert Kahn, speech to the Society of Automotive Engineers, Detroit, 28 April 1941, p. 7. Albert Kahn Collection, Bentley Historical Library, University of Michigan.
28. Albert Kahn, untitled note (with a handwritten mention 'Aircraft'), 28 November 1941, p. 8. Albert Kahn Collection, Bentley Historical Library, University of Michigan.
29. 'Art: Industrial Architect', *Time Magazine*, 8 August 1938.
30. 'Albert Kahn 1869–1942', *The Architectural Forum*, vol. 78, no. 1 (January 1943). See also 'Albert Kahn Architect', *The Architectural Record*, vol. 93, no. 1 (January 1943), 10 and 12.
31. 'Building in One Package', *The Architectural Forum*, vol. 82, no. 1 (January 1945), 93.
32. Ibid., 93–112; the article continues in *The Architectural Forum*, vol. 82, no. 2 (February 1945), 113–28. See also Martin Greif, 'Austin Goes to War', in *The New Industrial Landscape: The Story of The Austin Company* (Clinton NJ: Main Street Press, 1978), 129–33.
33. See for example Vladimir D. Tsvetaev, *Sovremennaia fabriko-zavodskaia arkhitektura* (Moscow and Leningrad: Gosstroiizdat, 1932). V. D. Gofman, *Osnovy proektirovania promyshlennykh zdanii* (Moscow: ONTI-Gosstroiizdat, 1934).
34. Nina Rappaport drew my attention to this programme.
35. Maurice Gauthier, 'The Lighting of Industrial Plants', *The Architectural Record*, vol. 92, no. 3 (September 1942), 77–80. Don Graf, 'For Better Sight: White Factory Floors', *Pencil Points*, vol. 23, no. 2 (July 1942), 77–80.
36. 'Take a Second Look at the World's First Windowless Plant', *The Architectural Forum*, vol. 75, no. 5 (November 1941), 57.
37. 'War Requirements Accelerate Progress in Design', *The Architectural Record*, vol. 91, no. 1 (January 1942), 66.
38. Albert Kahn, 'Aircraft' (28 November 1941), 5. Albert Kahn Collection, Bentley Historical Library, University of Michigan.
39. Hermann Mäckler, *Ein deutsches Flugzeugwerk: die Heinkel-Werke Oranienburg* (Berlin: Wiking-Verlag, n.d. [1939]). 'Ein Flugzeugwerk: Architect Herbert Rimpl', *Monatshefte für Baukunst*, vol. 24 (November 1940), 289–300.
40. Winfried Nerdinger, 'Bauhaus-Architekten im "Dritten Reich"', in *Bauhaus-Moderne im*

Nazionalsozialismus. Zwischen Anbiederung und Verfolgung, edited by Winfried Nerdinger (Munich: Prestel, 1993), 153–78.

41. Rudolf Lodders, 'Zuflucht im Industriebau', *Baukunst und Werkform*, vol. 1, no. 1 (1947), 39.

42. Gottfried Feder, *Die neue Stadt: Versuch der Begründung einer neuen Stadtplanungskunst aus der sozialen Struktur der Bevölkerung* (Berlin: Springer, 1939).

43. Sonja Hildebrand, *Egon Eiermann. Die Berliner Zeit. Das architektonische Gesamtwerk bis 1945* (Braunschweig: Vieweg, 1999), 181–233.

44. Hermann Henselmann, *Drei Reisen nach Berlin* ((East) Berlin: Henschelverlag, 1981), 182.

45. Le Corbusier, 'L'architecture et la guerre', *Gazette Dunlop*, vol. 19, no. 232 (May 1940), 10–13, typescript, FLC B3(5)204-206.

46. Le Corbusier, *Sur les quatres routes* (Paris: Gallimard, 1941), 12.

47. Le Corbusier, letter to Jean Paulhan, 23 May 1940, FLC E2(18)123.

48. The factory is presented as 'built for armaments in 1940': Le Corbusier, 'L'usine verte', in *Les Trois Établissements humains* (Paris: Denoël, 1945), 179–80.

49. Herbert H. Stevens, 'Air-Supported Roofs for Factories', *Architectural Record*, vol. 92, no. 6 (December 1942), 45–46.

50. F. W. Lanchester, 'An Unproved Construction of Tent for Field Hospitals, Depots and Like Purposes', patent drawing 1918, in Thomas Herzog, *Pneumatic Structures* (London: Crosby Lockwood Stapes, 1976), 34–35.

51. 'A Retractable Factory', *Flight*, vol. 35, no. 1585 (11 May 1939), 487.

52. See photos of the Creil underground galleries, with a stamp from the Ingenieurbüro Erich Neumann, in Cologne, as well as the press clipping 'Das Luft-Gibraltar am Goldenen Tor', pasted to letterheads of Junkers AG, and the issue of *Flight*, Deutsches Museum, LR 00275. The comparison seems to have been a popular one. See Bradley La Verne, 'San Francisco: Gibraltar of the West Coast', *National Geographic*, vol. 83, no. 3 (March 1943).

53. W. R. J. Cook, T. R. B Saunders, A. S. W. Thomson, S. W. J. Butler, J. H. Elstub, C. V. T. Campbell, D. N. Haird, K. D. Ellington, G. E. D. MacBride, R. N. Welch

and E. D. Eckel, 'Underground Factories in Central Germany', mission report, 1945, Deutsches Museum, 735 Peen, *CIOS XXXII-17*. See also André Sellier, *Histoire du camp de Dora* (Paris: La Découverte, 2010), 59–62 and 79–80.

54. C. N. Hickman, 'Visit to Underground V-1 Manufacturing Plant 23 September [1944], Combined Intelligence Objectives Sub Committee', 1944, Deutsches Museum, 735 Peen *CIOS II-12*.

55. See the plans published by Keith Mallory and Arvid Ottar, *The Architecture of War* (New York: Pantheon Books, 1973), 255–65.

56. Eberhard Kuen archive, Architekturmuseum Munich.

57. Perry R. Duis and Scott LaFrance, *We've Got a Job to Do. Chicagoans and World War II* (Chicago: Chicago Historical Society, 1993).

58. Sherna Berger Gluck, *Rosie the Riveter Revisited: Women, the War, and Social Change* (Boston: Twayne Publishers, 1987).

59. Brian Foss, '"These Most Exacting Jobs": Women's Work in Art and War', in *War Paint. Art, War, State and Identity in Britain, 1939–1945* (New Haven: Yale University Press, 2007), 81–115.

60. Pietro Belluschi, interviews with Meredith Clausen, 22 August–4 September 1944, Archives of American Art, Smithsonian Institution.

61. Cherry and Penny, op. cit. note 15.

62. 'Industrial Hostels, W. G. Holford, Architect', *The Architectural Review*, vol. 92, no. 552 (December 1942), 131.

63. Ibid.

64. 'Hostels', *The Architect's Journal*, vol. 95, no. 5 (March 1942), 167.

65. 'PBA Residence Halls for Women, Washington, DC', *The Architectural Record*, vol. 92, no. 1 (July 1942), 40–47.

66. Frederick L. Ackerman, 'Duration Dormitories. Notes on the Technical Problem', *The Architectural Record*, vol. 92, no. 2 (August 1942), 32–36.

67. Richard Neutra, 'Housing, Defense and Postwar Planning', typewritten, undated, UCLA, Richard and Dion Neutra papers, box 176, folder 4, pp. 2–3. See also Dorothy Rosenman, 'Housing for Defense: Are We Building Future Slums or Planned Communities?', *The Architectural Record*, vol. 90, no. 5 (November 1942), 56–58.

68. 'An Interview with John B. Blanford, Jr.', *The Architectural Forum*, vol. 79, no. 3 (September 1943), 61–64.

69. Antonin Raymond, 'Working with USHA under the Lanham Act', *Pencil Points*, vol. 22, no. 5 (November 1941), 693.

70. 'Housing for Defense. A Building Types Study', *The Architectural Record*, vol. 90, no. 5 (November 1942), 71–90.

71. Catherine Bauer, 'Wartime Housing in Defense Areas', *Architect and Engineer*, vol. 151, no. 1 (October 1942), 35.

72. Dana Cuff, *The Provisional City. Los Angeles Stories of Architecture and Urbanism* (Cambridge, Mass.: MIT Press, 2000), 152–69.

73. 'A Wartime Approach to Prefabrication. Joseph Allen Stein, Designer', *The Architectural Forum*, vol. 77, no. 2 (July 1942), 78–80.

74. Stephen White, *The Architecture of Joseph Allen Stein in India and California* (Delhi, Oxford and New York: Oxford University Press, 1993), 63.

75. 'One-family Defense House Project Design by Architect Gregory Ain', *The Architectural Forum*, vol. 73, no. 5 (November 1940), 450.

76. 'U.S. Wartime Housing', *The Architectural Review*, vol. 96, no. 572 (August 1944), 30.

77. 'New Kensington Housing Project', *The Architectural Forum*, vol. 80, no. 1 (July 1944), 75–76.

78. 'Wartime Housing Estate in Pennsylvania. Architects: Walter Gropius and Marcel Breuer', *The Architectural Review*, vol. 96, no. 573 (September 1944), 72.

79. 'New Kensington Politics', *The Architectural Forum*, vol. 80, no. 1 (July 1944), 76.

80. Elizabeth Mock, *Built in USA, 1932–1944* (New York: The Museum of Modern Art, 1944), 66. See also 'Carver Court', *The Architectural Forum*, vol. 81 (December 1944), 109–16.

81. For all of these ensembles, see David B. Brownlee and David G. De Long, *Louis I. Kahn: in the Realm of Architecture* (Los Angeles: Museum of Contemporary Art; New York: Rizzoli, 1991), 29–31. Their features are compared in '"Standards" Versus Essential Space, Comments on Unit Plans for War Housing by George Howe, Oscar Storonov and Louis I. Kahn', *The Architectural Forum*, vol. 76, no. 5 (May 1942), 308–11.

82. Richard Neutra, 'Peace Can Gain from War's Forced Changes', *Pencil Points*, vol. 23, no. 5 (November 1942), 29.

83. Albert Mayer, 'Housing for Defense – and After', *The New York Times Magazine*, 21 September 1942.

84. Max Bill, *Wiederaufbau. Dokumente der Zerstörung, Planungen, Konstuktionen* (Erlenbach and Zürich: Verlag für Architektur AG, 1945), 65.

85. Mock, op. cit. note 80, 68.

86. Richard Neutra, 'Peace Can Gain from War's Forced Changes', op. cit. note 83, 36, 38.

87. Richard Neutra, 'Report for the Bridgwater CIAM on the Situation of the West Coast', 1947, 5, UCLA, Richard and Dion Neutra Papers, box 168, folder 3.

88. Gaston Bardet, 'Le Dilemme de Neutra, ou l'urbanisme, antidote de la prefabrication', *L'Architecture française*, vol. 9, no. 83–84 (1948), 4–7.

89. 'Defense Houses at Vallejo, Calif.', *The Architectural Forum*, vol. 75, no. 4 (October 1941), 226. See also William Wurster, 'Carquinez Heights', *California Arts and Architecture*, vol. 58, no. 11 (November 1941), 34–40; 'Vallejo. War Housing Case History', *California Arts and Architecture*, vol. 59 (December 1942), 22–25.

90. Greg Hise, 'Building as Social Art: the Public Architecture of William Wurster, 1935–1950', in *An Everyday Modernism: the Houses of William Wurster*, edited by Marc Treib (San Francisco and Berkeley: University of California Press, 1995), 147–52.

91. Frank Lloyd Wright, letter to Clark Foreman, 1 December 1941. Frank Lloyd Wright Archives, Taliesin, quoted by Zenia Kotval, 'Opportunity Lost: A Clash between Politics, Planning, and Design in Defense Housing for Pittsfield, Massachusetts', *Journal of Planning History*, vol. 2, no. 1 (2003), 32.

92. See Alan Mather, 'Backhousing for Bomber Plants', *Pencil Points*, vol. 23, no. 6 (December 1942), 69–74.

93. 'No "Bomber City"', *Business Week*, 8 August 1942, 48. On this episode, see Lauren Jacobi, 'Willow Run's Bomber Plant and Housing Crisis: American Home-Front Conflicts during World War II' unpublished paper, New York, Institute of Fine Arts, 2005.

94. Brownlee and De Long, op. cit. note 81, 30–31.

95. 'The Town of Willow Run', *The Architectural Forum*, vol. 78, no. 3 (March 1943), 52.

96. Thomas W. Mackesey, 'The Conception of a Community to House Workers near Willow Run and How it Developed Technically until its Program was Changed', *The Architectural Record*, vol. 93, no. 1 (January 1943), 78–82; 'What Housing for Willow Run?', *The Architectural Record*, vol. 92, no. 3 (September 1942), 51–54.

97. Hermann H. Field, 'The Lesson of Willow Run', *Task*, no. 4, 17. See the historical analysis by Lowell J. Carr and James E. Stermer, *Willow Run: a Study of Industrialization and Cultural Inadequacy* (New York: Harper and Brothers, 1952).

98. See for example, Richard H. Foster Jr., 'Wartime Trailer Housing in the San Francisco Bay Area', *Geographical Review*, vol. 70, no. 3 (July 1980), 276–90.

99. Allan D. Wallis, *Wheel Estate: The Rise and Decline of Mobile Homes* (Baltimore: John Hopkins University Press, 1991), 91.

100. Department of Regional Studies, Tennessee Valley Authority, 'The Trailer House', *The Architectural Record*, vol. 93, no. 2 (February 1943), 49–52.

101. Giuseppe Pagano, 'La politica delle abitazioni in periodo di guerra e il programma di ricostruzione edile negli Stati Uniti', *Costruzioni Casabella*, vol. 16, no. 187 (July 1943), 2. Pagano also reprinted a text by the Danish economist Carl Major Wright, 'L'abitazione operaia e il rendimento industriale', ibid., 3–9, which had previously appeared in the *Revue Internationale du travail*, vol. 45, no. 3 (March 1943).

102. Irenio Diotallevi and Francesco Marescotti, 'La casa singola nella esperienza americana', *Costruzioni Casabella*, vol. 16, no. 188 (August 1943), 2–32.

103. Tatiana Malinina, ed., *Iz istorii sovetskoi arkhitektury 1941–1945 gg.: Dokumenty i materialy: Khronika voennykh let: Arkhitekturnaia pechat* (Moscow: Nauka, 1978), 83 and 85.

104. Report of the Architectural Academy of the USSR on the main topics of research work for 1942, ibid. note 103, 59.

105. Hermann Mackler, 'Wohnsiedlung eines deutschen Industriewerks', *Moderne Bauformen*, vol. 43 (January–March 1944), 1–11.

106. 'Die Stadt der Hermann-Göring-Werke, Architekt: Herbert Rimpl', *Der Städtebau*, vol. 34 (September 1939), 77–92. 'The Town of the Herman-Göring-Werke', *Journal of the Town Planning Institute*, vol. 26 (January–February 1940), 36–39.

107. Marco de Michelis, *Heinrich Tessenow, 1876–1950* (Milan: Electa, 1991), 322–24.

108. Christian Schneider, *Stadtgründungen im Dritten Reich: Wolfsburg und Salzgitter. Ideologie, Ressortpolitik, Repräsentation* (Munich: Heinz Moos Verlag, 1979). Marie-Luise Recker, *Die Großstadt als Wohn- und Lebensbereich im Nationalsozialismus. Zur Gründung der 'Stadt des KdF-Wagens'* (Frankfurt-am-Main: Campus, 1981).

109. Paul Jaskot, *The Architecture of Oppression: the SS, Forced Labor and the Nazi Monumental Building Economy* (London and New York: Routledge, 2000).

110. Christian Mühldorfer-Vogt, ed., 'Der Betrieb kann mit Häftlingen durchgeführt werden', *Zwangsarbeit für die Kriegsrakete* (*Peenemünder Hefte 3*) (Peenemünde: Historisch-Technisches Museum Peenemünde, 2009).

111. Sellier, op. cit. note 53, 409.

112. Albert Speer, *Inside the Third Reich*, translated by Richard and Clara Winston (New York and Toronto: Macmillan, 1970), 374–76.

113. Paul Erker, 'Emergence of Modern Business Structures? Industry and War Economy in Nazi Germany', in Sakudo and Shiba, op. cit. note 7, 168.

Albert Kahn Associates
**Ford Motors Bomber
Plant**, Willow Run,
Michigan, view of the
drafting room, 1942.
Photograph by
Bill Hedrich.
CCA Collection, gift
of Federico Bucci

Albert Kahn Associates
**Ford Willow Run Bomber
Plant**, Willow Run, Michigan,
exterior view of a hangar
(top), and view of the north
facade of hangar no. 1
(bottom), 1942.
Photograph by Bill Hedrich.
CCA Collection,
gift of Federico Bucci

Albert Kahn Associates
**Pratt & Whitney Aircraft
Engine Factory**, view of
the rear facade (top), 1940.
Wright Aeronautical

**Corporation Aircraft
Engine Factory**, view
of the main facade (bottom),
1944. West Hartford,
Connecticut.

Photograph by Bill Hedrich
CCA Collection, gift of
Federico Bucci

Top: Albert Kahn
Associates
**Wright Aeronautical
Corporation Aircraft
Engine Factory**, Lockland,
Ohio, view of the testing
cells, 1944. Photograph
by Forster Studio.
CCA Collection,
gift of Federico Bucci

Bottom: Albert Kahn
Associates
**Dodge Chicago Aircraft
Engine Plant**, Chicago,
view of the testing cells,
1943. Photograph
by Bill Hedrich.
CCA Collection,
gift of Federico Bucci

Top: Albert Kahn Associates **Curtiss-Wright Corporation, Airplane Division**, Robertson, Missouri, interior view of the assembly building, 1942. Photograph by Bill Hedrich. CCA Collection, gift of Federico Bucci

Bottom: Albert Kahn Associates **Glenn L. Martin Aeronautic Plant**, Middle River, Maryland, interior view of the assembly building under construction, 1941. Photograph by Bill Hedrich. CCA Collection, gift of Federico Bucci

Albert Kahn Associates
Detroit Arsenal Tank Plant,
Warren Township, Michigan,
view of the assembly building,
c. 1940–1942.
CCA Collection,
gift of Federico Bucci

Der Feind sieht Dein Licht!

Verdunkeln!

5/ The Menace from the Air

The next war . . . will be so horrible that all who experienced this one will look back on it with regret. The cities in the rear will be completely destroyed by aerial attacks.
André Maurois, *Les Discours du docteur O'Grady*, 1922[1]

The airplane has little concern for lines on the ground; it can cross borders to bring the battle into enemy territory; after that, it returns to its own field. All territory within range of the enemy's aircraft can suddenly find the enemy in the sky above, despite the presence of troops to guard the ground; the entire region subject to the attack of enemy aircraft is in fact an aerial border. But the crucial fact is that this border is no longer a line; it is a surface.
Lieutenant-Colonel Vauthier, *Le Danger aérien*, 1930[2]

The city will defend itself. Passive defence measures have taught it to dim all lights, to pass for the night itself, to create trained rescue teams. . . . An entire architecture is being created, which poses a number of specific problems. Modern architects need to provide us with 'complete' buildings in order for our cities to have the moral and material strength to endure the aerial ordeal, an architecture that allows life to go on under the threat from the skies, to go on working for the final success of our armed forces.
General René Keller, *L'Architecture d'aujourd'hui*, 1937[3]

In a special issue published in December 1937 on 'passive defence', the French magazine *L'Architecture d'aujourd'hui* included a series of remarks by General Niessel, a veteran of the First World War and the author of an alarmist book *Préparons la défense aérienne*, published in 1929, which deplored the 'errors' of all

Otto Sander-Herweg
'Make It Dark!', poster, 1940.
The Wolfsonian-Florida International University, Miami Beach, Florida, The Mitchell Wolfson, Jr. Collection

those who 'claim that one cannot defend oneself from the danger posed by aviation', and referred to examples of the 'results achieved in Germany and in the USSR through forceful action by the governing bodies'.[4] The allusion refers to the Nazi Reichsluftschutzverband, which had replaced the earlier Deutscher Luftschutz and the Deutsche Luftschutz-Liga, both of which were founded in 1927 and had organised major exhibitions on civil defence as early as the beginning of the 1930s.[5] Niessel also mentioned the Osoaviakhim, created in Moscow in 1927, an organisation that would subsequently grow to include more than fifteen million members.[6] In Italy, the UNPA, or Unione Nazionale Protezione Antiaerea, was created in 1936. During the summer of 1940, recruitment extended to include high school students, such as the future writer Italo Calvino, who left humorous accounts of his own nocturnal exploits.[7] Architect Pierre Vago evoked in *L'Architecture d'aujourd'hui* those 'tragic large-scale manoeuvres that were the wars in Spain and China' in order to focus the attention of architects: 'It thus seemed to us that architects should become completely up-to-date regarding the many technical problems posed by the need for Passive Defence. And if the large cities, as it would seem, are the most threatened, one should still not think that other locations in the rear are sheltered from the aerial danger. . . . Many coastal fishing villages in Catalonia were "sprayed" after some of the failed raids on Barcelona.'[8]

States responded to the ever-growing aerial threat on several levels, with architects playing an active role. In the early 1930s, architects took part in the technical and psychological preparation of populations that were potential targets. They contributed to preventive pedagogy and to propaganda, through publications and public lectures. Around the middle of the decade, they started to develop technical solutions for the protection of existing buildings, taking into account the various kinds of threat. Later, they established structural and spatial principles for building shelters. Finally, as war approached, they called for the evacuation of civilians and suggested various ways of dispersing urban and industrial agglomerations. These interventions saw architects and structural engineers forming alliances with the officers and political leaders militating for prevention, and sometimes coming into open conflict with others. Different requirements began to appear between the policies called for by the potential belligerents. The French, for instance, who still vividly remembered the bombardments of the previous war, tended to focus on the evacuation of civilians, whereas the Germans, whose experiences had been limited to the Russian bombardment of East Prussia, concentrated their protective measures in shelters.[9] But rapid circulation of information and studies across borders was now the rule, as the academic studies on this topic, such as the theses of Hans Schoszberger at the Technische Hochschule in Berlin (1934) and Henri Bahrmann's at the Institut d'Urbanisme de Paris (1935), clearly indicated.[10] Vauthier based his analysis on Italian, British, German and Russian works, most of which were read by the majority of

'Protection from Gas and from Aerial Attack', cover of *Gasschutz und Luftschutz*, September 1933, in Helga Schmal and Tobias Selke, *Bunker: Luftschutz und Luftschutzbau in Hamburg*, 2001. Avery Library, Architectural and Fine Arts Library, Columbia University

Bottom: Pierre Vago, 'The Aerial Danger', illustrated with the ruins of Guernica, article in *L'Architecture d'aujourd'hui*, December 1937. CCA Collection

GUERNICA, VILLE HISTORIQUE DU PAYS BASQUE, APRÈS UN BOMBARDEMENT AÉRIEN (1937)

LE DANGER AÉRIEN

his colleagues throughout Europe as well. The pages of *L'Architecture d'aujourd'hui* from that time contain illustrations borrowed from *Bauwelt* and *Casabella*, and this even before the American periodicals of the 1940s were to recycle material published in Great Britain. In general, between 1936 and 1940 most professional journals devoted special issues or dossiers to the question of anti-aircraft protection. This was the case in Great Britain for *The Architects' Journal*, *The Architect and Building News* and *The Builder*; in Italy, *Casabella* and *L'Ingegnere*; in Germany *Bauwelt* and the *Deutsche Bauzeitung*; in France, *Le Génie civil* and *L'Architecture d'aujourd'hui*, as well as *L'Ossature métallique*; in the United States, *The Architectural Forum* and *Pencil Points*.

Warnings and Precautions: Paul Vauthier

Another propaganda campaign was undertaken in the 1930s to mobilise public opinion and to prepare urban populations for attacks on their cities. Apocalyptic visions

of cities either incinerated or rendered uninhabitable by gas were proliferating in Europe and the United States, while the governments, concerned about potential panic or revolt that air raids could set off, saw them mainly as potential sparks for urban uprising. In 1938, the hoax radio broadcast by Orson Welles, which gave a realistic account of a supposed Martian invasion, was the occasion for a full-scale test run of panic on a massive scale.[11] The warnings from military officers had considerable impact on public opinion, amplifying Douhet's prophecies and giving them a more rational basis. In Great Britain, Air Commodore Lionel Evelyn Oswald Charlton, who had resigned his commission in the RAF after refusing to bomb Iraqi villages, published *War over England* in 1936, written along the lines of Douhet. He subsequently participated in putting together a work of popularisation, *The Air Defence of Britain*, published in 1938 by the very widely read Penguin Books.[12]

A regular presence on the public scene, Vauthier insisted as early as 1930 that the 'weak points of the country are extremely numerous', claiming that 'there is a danger from the sky that should be studied as a whole'.[13] He reviewed the various means of defence: searchlights and obstacles such as barrage balloons, and paid particular attention to 'means of leading enemy attacks astray' by emitting smoke and by blackouts, a difficult policy to implement that would be checked by 'police airplanes' flying over large urban areas. He also proposed the exact opposite: a blinding 'halo of light' that included creating 'false lighted targets' like those imagined during the First World War. But Vauthier insisted on the importance of 'educating the population' and on preventive measures: 'One cannot resist the aerial danger by high morale alone, for the simple reason that a living being cannot breathe phosgene gas or survive exploding bombs, even light ones. Proper defensive organisations, including a well-organised alert system, shelters from explosives and gas, and rapid rescue operations would do much more for morale than any eloquent speeches and beautifully organised lectures.'[14]

Vauthier made a fundamental contribution on another point, 'equipping the country' against the danger from the skies. Here he explicitly addressed architecture, starting with a quote from the Russian Kozhevnikov: 'It is incomprehensible that civil architecture would continue to think that it has nothing to do with the defence of the country, when it is clear to anyone with an open mind that every large city can and will be a target of aerial attacks in any future war.'[15] Vauthier observed that 'modern architecture has a first-class fireproof material at its disposal, namely reinforced concrete' and that it would make sense to reduce the size of built-up areas, in short, to 'rebuild the cities on a new basis'.[16] Taking up ideas proposed by his Russian colleagues and the Japanese general Nagaska,[17] he drew up an 'essay on the organisation of the future city', in which he mentioned studies for underground garages in Paris, reviewed the height regulations for buildings in Paris and New York, and most importantly, referred

to the new ideas put forward by Albert Guérard in his book *L'Avenir de Paris*[18] on the layout of urban areas. Vauthier referred to the stepped-back apartment buildings of Henri Sauvage, as well as to projects for towers by Auguste Perret and Le Corbusier. He also took into account the issues of public order and its policing in the face of insurrections. Nor did he forget to express his support for conserving some older buildings. From his extensive analysis, he concluded: 'Both solutions that emerge from theories of urbanism – the horizontal, spread-out city or the city of vertical extension – can be usefully employed to resist aerial attacks. The first model would apply to villages and smaller cities; the second would be better suited to larger cities.' Vauthier's preferred options for big cities 'always leaned towards Le Corbusier's system', albeit with some small modifications, especially as he had established contact with the latter in 1929.[19] In essence, his 'very simple programme' 'for laying out a large city, and Paris in particular, from the fourfold points of view of town planners, guardians of public order, archaeologists, and the consideration of the aerial threat', tended to 'open up' Paris, to reduce congestion by the removal of government and heavy industry, to create a Paris whose 'business district, in the heart of the city, would be organised into residential towers, isolated buildings, separated one from another by large planted areas.' If one takes into further consideration that the plan of these concrete towers 'will take on cruciform or related shapes', one will have little difficulty recognising Le Corbusier's Plan Voisin.[20]

The architect was quick to seize on this unexpected support for his own ideas,

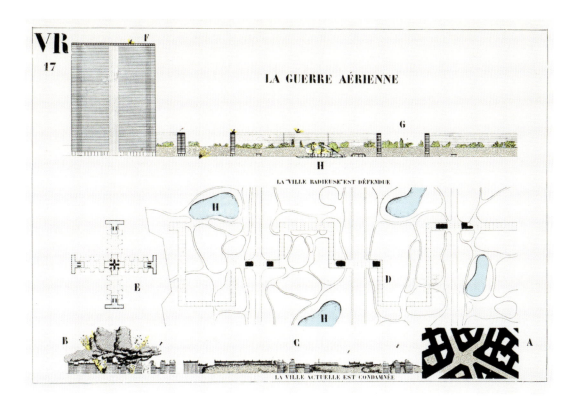

Le Corbusier
'Aerial Warfare', plate
from *La Ville radieuse*, 1935.
CCA Collection

especially since Vauthier would affirm in 1934 that his own studies derived from the architect's,[21] who thereupon responded in turn: 'Rest assured that I have a very strong sympathy for you, if I may say so, for you represent a clairvoyant and courageous quality of spirit which is not commonly to be found. As for our questions of urbanism, cowardice in all its forms along with greed and thirst for money are so prevalent that I am coming to the conclusion that only a serious case of the jitters will shake people up sufficiently, that perhaps the fear of aerial torpedoes will be what ultimately leads to the complete transformation of cities, through their demolition and reconstruction.'[22]

The spectre of a future war in the air provided a justification for the urban concept of his 'Ville Radieuse'. Upon its publication in 1935, plate 17 of this project, drawn in 1930, was accompanied by Vauthier's analysis: while on the one hand 'the current city is condemned', on the other, 'the radiant city is defended'.[23] In his sketches he shows, from top to bottom, that on the higher levels 'the inhabitants [take] refuge above the gas and behind the shielding', since 'the entire ground plane of the city is free (*pilotis*) [and] the winds easily disperse the gases', and that underground 'the production of pure air continues to work behind its shielding and to supply the inhabitants'.[24] This idyllic vision of a system that is practically impervious to explosives, gas and fire was the complement to

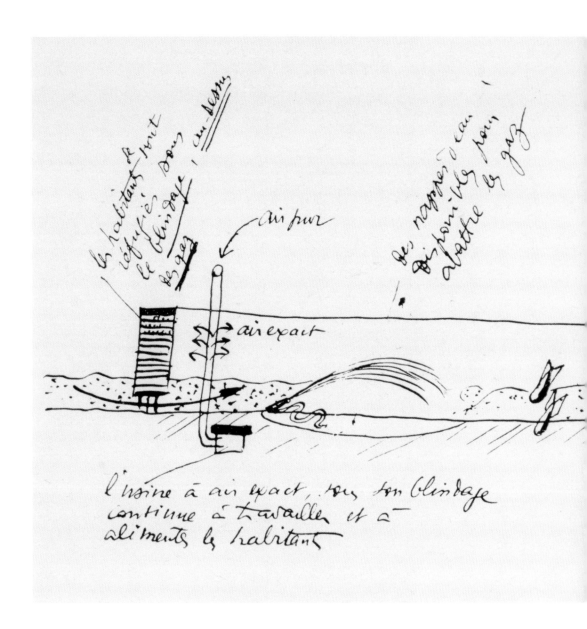

air pur

air expat

le habitant sont
réfugiés sous
le blindage
des gaz

au-dessus

des nappes d'eau
disponibles pour
abattre les gaz

l'usine à air expat, sous son blindage
continue à travailler et à
aliments les habitant

a diatribe entitled 'Et la guerre aérienne?', in which he puts Vauthier to good use without actually naming him, and claims that 'the general staff have made their unexpected verdict known: given the current state of urbanism, only cities conceived along the lines of the "Ville Radieuse" are capable of successfully withstanding aerial warfare.' Le Corbusier uses more threats to advance his gambit: 'Through the horror thus evoked, attention must be drawn, opinion must be mobilised and a decision perhaps made. Let the filth of odious war furnish the pretext for coming together, for overturning normal usage, and announcing the prospect of the "Ville Radieuse".'[25]

In 1937, Vauthier made a presentation to the fifth Congrès International

Le Corbusier
**'Protection against
aerial warfare'**,
illustration in
La Ville radieuse, 1935.
CCA Collection

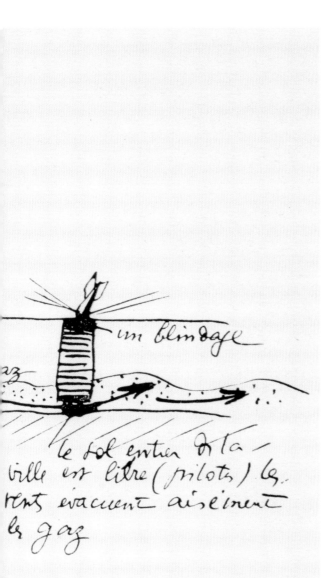

another. Against explosives, the argument for reducing the built area becomes even stronger. Furthermore, there is reason to isolate functions from each other (dwellings, factories, circulation), so that the same projectile cannot have several different effects (whence two requirements: zoning that separates out the functions of dwelling, commerce and industry, and the prohibition of building at the street edge). Against gas, it is necessary to isolate constructions, to eliminate "continuous street fronts", and to have ponds available.' And as far as architecture is concerned, 'air raid shelters' will be built with their 'enclosing walls independent of the structural framework'.[26]

The Analyses of
Hans Schoszberger

Three years earlier, in 1934, Vauthier had directed Le Corbusier's attention to the publication of Hans Schoszberger's doctoral thesis, *Bautechnischer Luftschutz* (Aerial protection through construction).[27] The analyses of this architect, trained in Vienna, Brno and Berlin, provided new support for the solutions proposed by the Parisian architect, and Schoszberger sent a copy of his book to Le Corbusier with an admiring inscription, writing that Gropius had assured him of his 'keen interest in the questions addressed in [his] work'.[28] The book starts out with a presentation of plans for ideal fortified cities from the Renaissance, before going on to attempt a definition of the ideal city for anti-aircraft defence, based on the corpus of modern architecture after 1920.[29]

d'Architecture Moderne, which was held in Paris, on the subject of 'urbanism and architecture in the face of aerial danger', in which he acted as a spokesman for the ideas of his host and plagiarised Le Corbusier's slogans in his list of the town planning measures to be taken: 'Against fires, it makes sense to reduce the built area . . . and to separate buildings one from

In his eyes, 'A new urban form must be found, which avoids the inconveniences of older cities but retains their advantages.' He addressed the issue of decentralisation within this perspective, but rejected any idea of the 'dissolution' of cities, because aerial defence also requires a concentration of labour and material. So the issue is more some form of *Auflockerung* (a loosening in density), which still maintains a 'temporal proximity'.[30] As a result, the Plan Voisin, which he admired, remained only a 'transitional solution'. Despite what Vauthier thought at the time, Schoszberger preferred the Obus plan for Algiers of 1932, which he considered a better application of the French officer's ideas and principles.

After considering several German theoretical projects – in particular the parallel blocks proposed by Gropius in 1931 and a centralised scheme developed in 1933 by Paul Wolf – the analysis focused on the hypotheses put forward by the Russian Nikolai Milyutin, which were widely known in Germany. Schoszberger claimed these to be *the* pertinent response: 'The linear city is an urban form that compares favourably

Top: Le Corbusier
Walter Gropius
**Urban projects for
Karlsruhe, Paris and Berlin**
(1929, 1925 and 1930),
double-page spreads
in Hans Schoszberger,
Bautechnischer Luftschutz, 1934.
CCA Collection

Cover of Hans
Schoszberger,
*Bautechnischer
Luftschutz*, 1934.
CCA Collection

to any other city that has been proposed for the future. The balance between city and country, an economic requirement, is still assured by the linear city. The gradual transformation of our cities into linear cities is not only a possibility, it has in fact already begun. Anti-aircraft protection demands the form of the linear city. This requirement for defence will overshadow every criticism of the linear city. The linear city is the city of the future.'[31] So as not to completely cede the field to the Soviet projects, which had become slightly heretical after the Nazis had come to power, a theoretical project developed in 1933 by the architect Karl Friedrich was presented as responding to the same criteria.[32]

Moving on to issues of architecture, Schoszberger considered that a new 'element distinguishes the built forms of anti-aircraft protection from the forms built before the war. The considerations that protection from the attacker's bombs require of construction are none other than the requirements of modern architecture, designed for the well-being and health of the people.'[33] In short, the Neues Bauen project could be advanced as a preparation for war. As for Schoszberger himself, subsequent events would see him working after 1940 on projects for bunkers as a member of Ernst Neufert's team. When José Luis Sert

Nikolai Milyutin
Projects for linear cities in the USSR (1930), double-page spread in Hans Schoszberger, *Bautechnischer Luftschutz*, 1934.
CCA Collection

BLACKOUT

published *Can Our Cities Survive?* in 1942, which developed and illustrated the conclusions of the fourth CIAM (Congrès International d'Architecture Moderne), held in Athens in 1933, he affirmed that 'we cannot ignore the air-raid menace' and found the best response in radical projects. Like Schoszberger, he reproduced images of 'high dwelling blocks widely spaced and surrounded by park land', and noted that 'a hit is comparatively difficult, and the high buildings may offer greater possibilities for an efficient shelter system'.[34]

The Play of Light and Shade
The fear of bombs led to the publication of a multitude of manuals, and also to the production of life-size models of cities to train rescue teams, as in Los Angeles, where a sort of 'ghost town' called 'Central City', or 'Bombville', was built in the summer of 1943, deemed necessary following the recent bombing of Hamburg. At the corner of Third Street and Vermont Avenue, teams of volunteers and personnel from the Warner Brothers studios erected buildings whose

Margaret Bourke-White
'Blackout' [of Los Angeles],
illustration in *The Architectural Forum*, January 1942.
CCA Collection, copyright of the Estate of Margaret Bourke-White / Licensed by VAGA, New York, NY

sole purpose was to be burned. As the review *Civilian Defense* put it,[35] the techniques of the mushroom cities of the West were combined with those of Hollywood set construction to give a sense of realism to the operation. Each large American city undertook full-scale exercises, and so no less than eight hundred airplanes coming in from seven directions were employed in 1943 to simulate an air raid on Chicago.[36]

One of the most widespread techniques of passive defence would be the blackout, a darkening of cities that required the active participation of the inhabitants, who were persistently reminded in every city at war

Air raid guidelines,
Tokyo, 1943.
The Wolfsonian-Florida International University,
Miami Beach, Florida
The Mitchell Wolfson, Jr.
Collection

not to let light filter out that might be visible to pilots. The blackout became a project in itself, to the extent that, in 1942, *The Architectural Forum* suggested that it was the 'No. 1 weapon of US civilians in their passive defense against hostile bombers', and to define it thus: 'The three-fold purpose of blackout is 1) to obliterate the tell-tale light patterns of communities which would facilitate the spotting of specific air raid objectives, 2) to conceal the identity of localities which enemy airmen might use as sign posts on their way to more important military and industrial objectives, and 3) to discourage haphazard civilian bombardment resorted to by hostile aircraft which, unable to find their assigned targets, dump their bombs on any recognizable scenes of activity before returning to their bases.'[37] This was clearly an architectural issue, whether it consisted in eliminating or masking sources of light; in blocking up windows with wood panels, paint, adhesives or shutters; in creating spaces that functioned as light locks at the entrance to buildings that needed to be used during the blackout; and lastly in rendering public lighting more adjustable and discreet. A new market in light-blocking devices emerged. Knowledge of construction elements and their coordination became an important area of expertise, and teams in the United States made sure to learn from European experiences, as in San Francisco, for example, where Serge Chermayeff spoke as a recent émigré.[38]

There were plenty of ideas as to how to enable city dwellers to find their way about in the dark. In Berlin, for example, phosphorescent flowers to attach to one's jacket were sold in the streets. In 1942, Norman Bel Geddes tried to obtain a

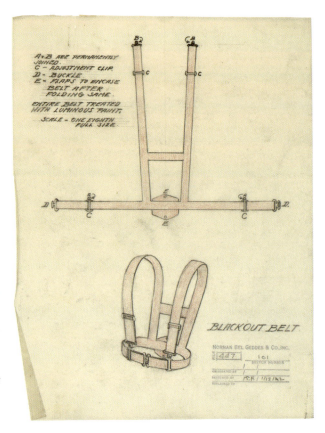

Norman Bel Geddes
Project for a **'blackout belt'**,
elevation and perspective
sketch, 1942.
Courtesy of the Estate of
Edith Lutyens Bel Geddes,
Harry Ransom Humanities
Research Center, University
of Texas at Austin

patent for a 'blackout belt', which would soon become commercially available from better-organised manufacturers. Italo Calvino tells of the games played by adolescents, who enjoyed tricking passers-by in the dark.[39] At the same time, the nocturnal spectacle became a source of fascination to photographers. Bill Brandt describes how 'the darkened city, illuminated only by moonlight, was more beautiful than it had been before or ever would be subsequently. It was fascinating to walk the deserted streets and to take pictures of houses that I knew so well,

but which had lost their three-dimensionality and become flat like painted stage sets.[40] His friend Brassaï, whose volume *Paris de nuit* had been a considerable success in 1932, published his photographs of the darkened city in 1940, as a pictorial essay in the English pocket magazine *Lilliput*.[41] The first raids instigated a new and changing dialectic between the static and darkened city, plunged into obscurity, and the beams of anti-aircraft searchlights sweeping the sky, a dialogue between light and dark that was interrupted by the impact of projectiles and the explosions of crashing airplanes. In Paul Virilio's recollection, it was an extraordinary 'lightshow [in English in the French text]'.[42]

Protecting Existing Buildings

The adaptation of existing construction to the triple threat of explosive bombs, incendiary devices and poison gas posed difficult problems that civil engineers and architects attempted to resolve in advance, by developing typical solutions that could be rapidly put into effect by a workforce formed at short notice. No part of buildings went unexamined, from the basement to the attic and roof, from the exterior walls and their openings to interior partitions, ventilation and electrical systems. Attention focused on the different types of bombs and their effects, and continued with the evaluation of different types of building, questions that were never completely lacking in ideology. One of the most symptomatic studies was the *Défense passive et organisée*, published in 1936 by commander Charles Gibrin, a specialist in

'**Protection afforded by a house in reinforced concrete**', plate from Commandant Gibrin, Louis C. Heckly, *Défense passive organisée*, 1936. Collection of the author

Top: Cover of Commandant Gibrin, Louis C. Heckly, **Défense passive organisée**, 1936. Collection of the author

anti-aircraft protection, and the civil engineer Louis-Clovis Heckly, no doubt the most prolific builder in modern Paris, where he erected almost fifteen thousand dwellings in the 1930s.[43] Both authors were concerned about the collapse of masonry buildings built before 1910, whereas they considered more recent constructions of reinforced concrete to be 'monolithic by their very nature' and to be 'resistant to deformation under conditions quite different from the original criteria for stability', such as the impact of a bomb; on the other hand, their basements tended to be too small to serve as shelters.

The consolidation of cellars was a particularly important issue, for they offered possibilities for shelter throughout the city. As for the roof terraces of concrete buildings, they could be reinforced with 'bursting' paving slabs, which could absorb some of the energy of exploding bombs. In this context, the various construction methods available at the time were studied for their predictable behaviours, both in the case of traditional materials such as brick and newer ones such as reinforced concrete.[44] Each building component, from walls and floors to roofs – was studied for its intrinsic resistance and for its potential for reinforcement. Inside the dwellings, various protective measures were suggested – some slightly fanciful, such as using adhesive tape as protection from gas or splintering glass and making piles of books on window sills.

ILLUSTRATION 4.—A STOUT BOOK-CASE, STUFFED TIGHTLY WITH OLD BOOKS, PROTECTS ONE WINDOW. OR A TABLE CAN BE USED WITH BOOKS 2 FT. 6 IN. THICK PILED ON IT. IF THE BOOKS ARE LOOSE, ROPE THEM DOWN FIRMLY.

But aesthetic concerns did not disappear altogether. In 1940, the German periodical *Der Baumeister*, using a two-part layout inspired by Paul Schultze-Naumburg's *Kulturarbeiten*, contrasted, with the aid of photographs, 'ugly' solutions for protecting the openings in houses with those that were deemed 'good', or at least 'acceptable'. The editors maintained that 'today's architect must become familiar with the detailed requirements for protecting buildings from the air and must be able to respond to these with as much ease and assurance as other questions of construction'.[45]

Policies for Shelters

The 1937 issue of *L'Architecture d'aujourd'hui* devoted to 'passive defence' was illustrated with photographs of the bombardment of Madrid, and a number of the protective measures contained in the magazine were borrowed from Gibrin and

Top: **Protection of the interior with piles of books**, illustration in *Your Home as an Air Raid Shelter*, 1940. CCA Collection

Using cellars as public shelters, plate from *L'Architecture d'aujourd'hui*, December 1937. CCA Collection

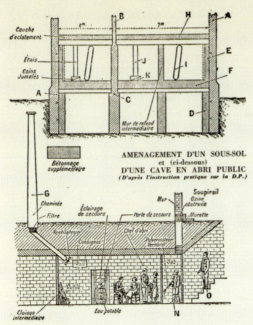

AMENAGEMENT D'UN SOUS-SOL
et (ci-dessous)
D'UNE CAVE EN ABRI PUBLIC
(D'après l'instruction pratique sur la D.P.)

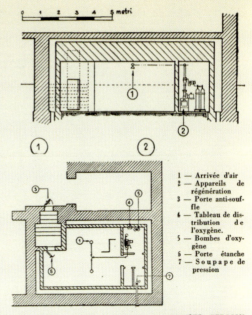

1 — Arrivée d'air
2 — Appareils de régénération
3 — Porte anti-souffle
4 — Tableau de distribution de l'oxygène
5 — Bombes d'oxygène
6 — Porte étanche
7 — Soupape de pression

ABRI POUR 30 PERSONNES DE LA SOCIÉTE BERGOMI
D'après Casabella

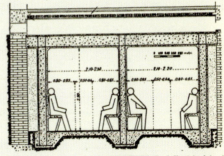

DEUX ABRIS POUR 30 PERSONNES, REALISES DANS LES CAVES D'IMMEUBLES EXISTANTS (CORTELLETTI, Ingénieur)
D'après Casabella

COUPE D'ABRI A DEUX COMPARTIMENTS (R. Colletti ingénieur)
D'après Casabella

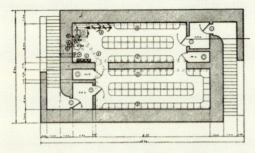

ABRI BETONNÉ POUR CENT PERSONNES

1: Portes étanches — 2: Filtre. — 3: Appareil régénérateur. — 4: Ventilateur électrique et à double pédalier. — 6: Bouteilles d'oxygène. — 7: Aspiration étanche d'air extérieur — 8: Canalisation de reprise d'air vicié. — 9: Répartition d'air frais ou régénéré
D'après C. M.

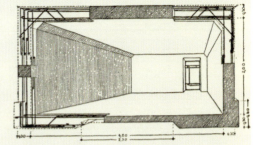

PROTECTION PAR CADRE MONOLITHIQUE EN BÉTON ARMÉ

Charge utile 50/1200 - 2.500 kg./m².
Charge de rupture (verticale): 7.500 kg./m² env.
Charge de rupture (horizontale): 9.200 kg./m² env.

D'après Bauwelt

155

Heckly's *Défense passive organisée*. Other projects for consolidation were borrowed from the reviews *Bauwelt* and *Casabella*. Finding support in previous analyses by the Italian colonels Francesco Laviano and Alessandro Romani, along with their Rumanian and German counterparts, Popescu and von Keller,[46] Vauthier was one of the first to emphasise the limitations of the transformation of cellars into shelters and to ask 'if it wouldn't be better to create special shelters from scratch' and to 'look at using metropolitan railway tunnels', providing they were compartmentalised to prevent gases from spreading.[47] Gibrin and Heckly followed suit, but were concerned about their narrow access points and suggested this as a systematic recourse only in 'overpopulated' – i.e., working class – quarters of Paris.[48] Their preference would be for the creation of collective shelters forming a defence group comprising several apartment buildings. But the suggestion of using subways in times of war was not completely ignored. It provided the impetus for a significant modification of the Moscow subway project, which had initially been conceived as a shallow, surface excavation, but was ultimately dug much deeper in order to be able to serve as a shelter. This would in fact turn out to be the case in 1941–1942.[49]

The policy of creating shelters was not limited to the sphere of dwellings. In Italy, where Douhet's theories were taken very seriously, reflections on anti-aircraft protection were all the more accurate and precise in that the fascist regime did not hesitate to use aviation against civilian targets, first in Ethiopia, and later in Spain. From the outset, the new industrial complexes were planned with air warfare in mind. The

FIAT factory in Mirafiori, for example, included fourteen kilometres of tunnels dug beneath the buildings, so that production could be withdrawn into them in case of threat.

During the 1930s, the issues surrounding shelters mobilised the attention of architects in a variety of contexts. These concerns were so explicit that when the functionalist architect Ernst Neufert published his *Bauentwurfslehre* in 1936 – a systematic presentation of the dimensional requirements of building – he devoted a full page to typical

Top: Margaret Bourke-White **'The Subway Shelter'**, view of the Moscow subway (1942), illustration in *Shooting the Russian War*, 1942. CCA

'Dispersion and evacuation [of the 15th arrondissement of Paris]', plate from *L'Architecture d'aujourd'hui*, December 1937. CCA Collection

solutions for the protection of civilians, after specifying the standard dimensions for all spaces in a dwelling.[50] At the end of the decade, Henri Bahrmann had called for the deployment of shelters in the city as a form of public facility. Their 'distribution and locations' would be 'a problem analogous to the distribution of schools'.[51] In northern Europe, another important figure in modern architecture, Alvar Aalto, was the winner of a competition in Helsinki to design a gigantic anti-aircraft shelter under the Erottaja intersection, in the very centre of town, where the Bulevardi, the Esplanadi and the Heikinkatu (today the Mannerheimintie) meet, but the project was built only in a very scaled-down version by the city authorities.[52]

Evacuation and Urban Dispersal

Two policies, developed in relation to distinctly different time frames, were formulated to empty cities of their inhabitants. The first one, the temporary evacuation of populations under threat, required the creation of accommodation outside the cities and the provision of routes to get there. The second, the dispersal of the inhabitants as a preventive measure, would need new principles of urban development.[53] Vauthier stressed that 'the evacuation of the population of large cities would tend to reduce their vulnerability as sensitive points. That way at least, if the cities burn, or if they are destroyed by explosives, the evacuated inhabitants

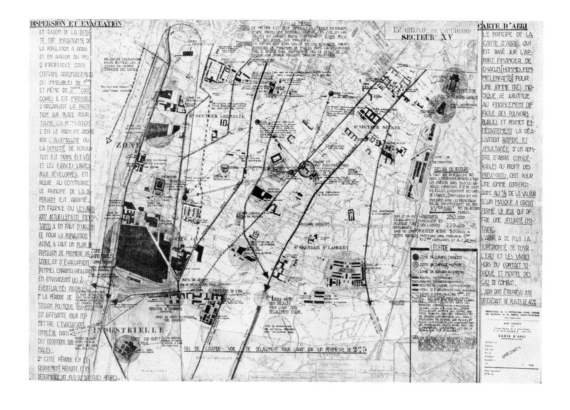

will be at some remove from these miseries: they will not suffer from them directly. In this way, one of the worst dangers of aerial warfare can be avoided: the panic of the population. One will thus have safeguarded one of the most precious forms of resilience: the morale of the country.'[54]

In an examination of Paris in 1937 from the point of view of its vulnerability to bombs, P. H. Rey proposed an analytic zoning in the pages of L'Architecture d'aujourd'hui that was both functional and morphological. He suggested a programme of collective shelters 'located in principle in open spaces so as to avoid protest or any infringement on private property'. But above all, he considered urban form from the perspective of the evacuation of a significant part of the population to 'refuge-camps, in which each quarter would already have its itinerary set out for it, its location indicated, and its edges marked out'. Located about seven kilometres from Paris, 'in open spaces, elevated, and sparsely wooded (because of gas), close to roads and regional bus terminals, the camps would be set up to take in as much of the population as possible . . . which would be rapidly evacuated by every means possible on the roads, and would also mean that the boarding and unboarding areas would have to be equipped beforehand. This dispersal would be planned only for the duration of the aerial attacks themselves and the cleaning up period that would follow.'[55] These proposals led Rey to a critique of the deficiencies of the existing road system, and to propose overpasses at exchanges, as well as bypasses around the centres of old villages in the vicinity. Gibrin and Heckly pursued similar ideas in calling for the creation of 'special evacuation roads',

CURRENT ARCHITECTURE

E V A C U A T I O N   C A M P S

ALISTER G. MACDONALD
AND SIR JOHN BURNET,
TAIT AND LORNE*

SITE PLAN

new national roads linking Paris to the dispersal sites.[56] As for Henri Bahrmann, he called for the construction of 'underground motorways', but remained sceptical as to the possibility of evacuating a large city to 'zones of dispersion' that would be difficult to keep supplied.[57]

The creation of camps like these called for architectural work, such as Ernö Goldfinger's in London in 1939 and 1940. There were few 'natural' sites such as the caves in Chislehurst, in Kent, which would

Alister G. Macdonald,
Sir John Burnet, Tait and Lorne,
'Evacuation Camps', article
in The Architectural Review,
February 1940.
CCA Collection

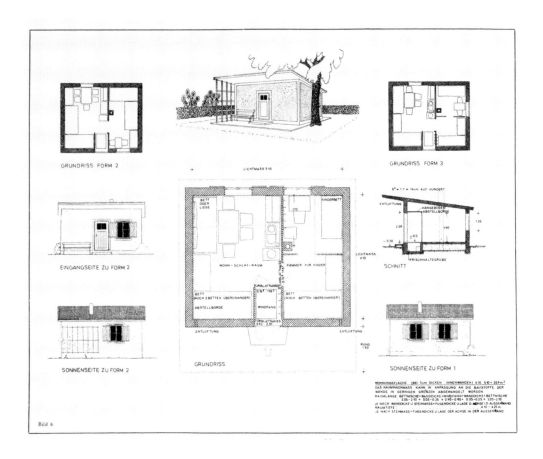

GRUNDRISS FORM 2

LICHTMASS 3.10

GRUNDRISS FORM 3

EINGANGSEITE ZU FORM 2

SCHNITT

SONNENSEITE ZU FORM 2

GRUNDRISS

SONNENSEITE ZU FORM 1

Bild 6

be used during the Blitz, and a programme of urgent construction was proposed in a report by the Association of Architects, Surveyors and Technical Assistants (AASTA) as an alternative to the policy of the National Camps Corporation, which was in the process of building forty camps to designs by architect Thomas Tait, who could also claim authorship of a charming poured concrete shelter in an acacia grove on the grounds of his private garden.[58] Projects for young children and their mothers were displayed in March 1940 at the London gallery of Paul and Marjorie Abbatt. Different groupings of low, camouflaged buildings were proposed by Justin Blanco White and Birkin Howard, and by Goldfinger and Mary Crowley, who also devised a prefabricated wooden system for building them.[59] A number of articles appeared in the press about these projects, no doubt because there were so few other ones that could be published without being subject to military censorship.[60]

In Germany, no specific architecture seems to have been proposed for the Erweiterte Kinderlandverschickung programme, which was introduced in 1940 and consisted of sending children away to the countryside for an extended period of time.[61] The Deutsche Wohnungshilfswerk

Hans Spiegel
Shelters for evacuees
(1943), plan, elevations
and section, plate from
*Der soziale Wohnungsbau
in Deutschland*,

January 1944,
reproduced in Tilman
Harlander, *Gerhard Fehl,
Hitlers sozialer
Wohnungsbau*, 1986.
CCA Collection

(German Assistance for Dwelling) programme started up in September 1943 under the direction of the Nazi Robert Ley. Its goal was to construct a million minimal dwelling units of approximately 20 square metres, and a design was developed by Hans Spiegel, but it only very partially came to fruition.[62] The aid promised to the evacuees, who were supposed to build their dwellings themselves and to survive off their gardens, did not make up for the lack of building materials. And Ernst Neufert's project for the construction of BfB (*Behelfsunterkünften für Bombengeschädigte*) – emergency housing for victims of the bombardments consisting of single-storey shacks for sixteen families each – would meet with little more success.

In *L'Architecture d'aujourd'hui*, the young town planner Gaston Bardet, who argued for both an underground urbanism and garden cities, criticised in 1937 the notion of 'passive' defence and claimed that 'everything that is not aggressive, is still active'. Bardet stressed above all that cities must be expected to 'be able to live a double life: a normal, peaceful life, with its long rhythms and continuous evolution, and a life of crisis, with its jerks and jolts, with brusque and sudden changes, with periods whose duration would remain unpredictable.' In times of approaching crisis, he foresaw 'the dispersal of three-quarters of the population of large urban centres' and the 'protection of sensitive points: the protection of foodstuffs, which would perhaps entail the dispersal of major markets, the concealment of industrial facilities, the organisation of shelters up to the task, the reorganisation and interconnection of electrical lines'. But like his colleague Henri Bahrmann,

who was an advocate of garden cities and linear cities, Bardet presented proposals for a longer time frame as well: 'Aside from these extremely urgent measures, others must be undertaken that are more long-term, and that are in perfect harmony with the wishes of town planners: reducing the density of outlying industrial areas, grouping certain industries together in clearly identified parts of the country; promoting the decentralisation of the population by creating garden cities in the English manner adjacent to those industries, or even completely breaking down some industry into home-work, which would still enable the fabrication of certain standardised parts.'[63]

A policy along these lines was established in Italy by the Unione Nazionale Protezione Antiaerea, which developed a plan in 1938 for a necklace of a dozen or so *borgate satelliti* around Rome, located near the great radial roads that derived from Antiquity. The plan received support the following year from Gustavo Giovannoni, an architect-town planner who favoured the respectful modernisation of cities, but who was also a proponent of a certain *deurbanizzazione* – which gained in legitimacy from the aerial threat.[64] The same set of issues were addressed by the engineer Vincenzo Civico, who called for a decentralisation of employment in preparation for the urban planning law of 1942.[65]

Although his ideas on the city and architecture were poles apart from Giovannoni's, when Frank Lloyd Wright introduced his Broadacre City to the press, on the occasion of his exhibition at The Museum of Modern Art, he called it 'a bomb proof city'. Wright declared that 'I would not say that the bombing of Europe is not

AERIAL BOMBARDMENT EFFECTS AND DEFENCE IN BARCELONA

[By F. SKINNER]

a blessing, because at least it will give the architects there a chance to start all over again. Concentration of population is murder – whether in peace time or in war.' And he added that 'the only bomb-proof city I know of is this one, which I call Broadacre City. It is so spread out that scarcely any real damage could be done. This is what the community of the future will be like. The trend of population now is to the country and all the cities are dying.'[66] Perspectives on the war in Europe also influenced the thinking of American critics such as Douglas Haskell, who took the question of evacuation as a starting point for an undogmatic call for change in urban policy: 'The needs of

Francis Skinner,
'Aerial Bombardment:
Effects and Defence
in Barcelona', article
in *The Architects' Journal*,
23 June 1938.
CCA Collection

air defense and peacetime planning both favor decentralization. But, having different aims, they call for decentralization of different kinds. Therefore glib optimism on the subject must yield to careful study. Evacuation after hostilities have begun is a horrible prospect at best. Long-range air defense planning must seek to keep its industrial and population centres permanently hard to reach, hard to find, and hard to strike effectively by an enemy air force.'[67] This set of issues, which would only become sharper with the development of the atomic bomb, was formulated as succinctly as possible by Ludwig Hilberseimer in *The New City* of 1944: 'Modern aerial warfare has made all city concentrations dangerous. Protection in the future must be accomplished by disurbanization and dispersal.'[68]

The Controversy over Shelters in Great Britain

The issue of protecting civilian populations was discussed along similar lines throughout Europe, but these took on particular acuity in London in the late 1930s, where radical architects became engaged in a direct political conflict with conservative forces regarding the Air Raid Precautions, or ARP.[69] The war in Spain was closely studied for its lessons on the subject, and British architects – more than any others – took a leading role in the debate over the protection of civilian populations that developed in response to the images of destruction in Madrid and Barcelona. Discussions of the issue had already started in 1924, after the German raids on London during the First World War, with the creation of the subcommittee for Air Raid Precaution, headed by John Anderson, who was at the time Permanent Under-Secretary of State at the Home Office. This body, part of the Committee of Imperial Defence, continued to update and study the files up until the next conflict.[70] But preparations for civil defence were closely correlated to anti-rioting measures that were meant to be put into effect in the event of a general strike, giving rise to a plan overseen by Anderson whereby a grid surveillance system was applied to England. These reflections and those of the ARP department established within the Home Office in 1934 remained essentially theoretical, insofar as they did not include any actual budgets, especially for the construction of shelters.[71] When a first booklet was sent out to local authorities in 1935, the stress was deliberately placed on gas, and not on explosive or incendiary bombs. Protection was described as a primarily individual affair, not a collective one, and a manual entitled *The Protection of Your Home Against Air Raids* was distributed in 1938 to that effect.[72]

In June 1938, the RIBA organised a three-day conference on civilian protection. In the spring of that same year, Francis Skinner, a partner in the Tecton group, as well as a member of the British Communist Party and a militant of AASTA and ATO – the Architects' and Technicians' Organisation – had travelled to Catalonia. Upon his return, he published an account of the effects of the bombardments of Barcelona in *The Architects' Journal*. Skinner provided specific and detailed examples of destruction, which he documented in drawings and photographs, and claimed

that the precautions taken 'are synonymous with the provision of shelter against high explosive bombs'. He insisted on the fact that the shelters he illustrated, initially located near military installations, had subsequently been built 'in the most thickly populated parts nearer the centre of the city'.[73] Notes based on the Spanish experiences were circulating in London and were drawn from the best sources.[74] Ramon Perera, an engineer who was at the head of the Junta de Defense Passiva de Catalunya, created in Barcelona in July 1937, related his experiences in 1939 at a meeting of the Air Raid Protection Institute in London; the engineer Cyril Helsby, who had travelled to Barcelona in order to observe the war and had subsequently shared his experiences with the general public, had helped Perera to find refuge in Britain, with the support of the British secret services. Perera considered that it was the use of four different kinds of shelters – 'the large cellular type, the tunnel type, the adaptation of basements and the covered trench' – that had made it possible to keep the number of deaths to 246 despite some 200 raids on the city.[75] These accounts called into question the official British doctrines for the protection of civilians from air raids that had been developed since the early days after the First World War.

A first set of directives and handbooks, including one by the engineer Charles Glover, was circulated in order to mobilise public opinion, particularly after the Munich Agreement of September 1938. But this did little to quell the opposition of a group of left-wing scientists that included the physicists C. P. Snow and J. D. Bernal, the biologist Julian Huxley and the geneticist

J. B. S. Haldane.[76] The Cambridge Scientists Anti-War Group, founded in 1932, published its first work in 1937, followed by *Air Raid Precautions*, both of which appeared in the same collection of the Left Book Club, a publishing house with communist sympathies. The handbook was put together by Haldane, who had first-hand experience of bombs during the First World War.[77] Unlike the official doctrine, these analyses dwelled on the damages that could result from explosive devices and incendiary bombs, based on observations conducted in Spain, and called for the creation of collective shelters for the population. Haldane had a field day with his ironic comments on some of the solutions

'Residential shelter',
perspective section,
illustration in Charles W.
Glover, *Civil Defence*, 1941.
McGill University Library,
Montréal

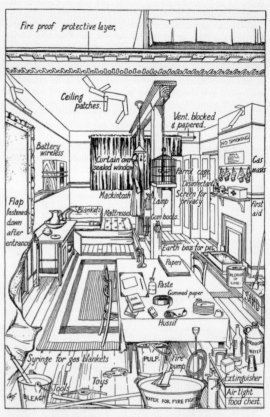

Transforming the house into a gas-proof refuge (1938), illustration in Charles W. Glover, *Civil Defence*, 1938. CCA Collection

FIG. 6.—The gas-proof refuge ready for occupation.

included in the handbook, *The Protection of Your Home Against Air Raids*, fourteen million of which had already been published and distributed, when he wrote: 'The official handbook does not distinguish sharply between an air raid and a picnic. In Spain the distinction is quite obvious.'[78]

In 1939, the engineer Felix Samuely, an associate of Helsby who had presented a very detailed report on Barcelona to his colleagues at the Institution of Civil Engineers, published a technical work on the issue, and several young architects studied the resistance of buildings to bombs with J. D. Bernal, on behalf of the Building Research Station.[79] For his part, Serge Chermayeff argued for civil defence to be the object of a general policy, and that its findings be 'correlated in one central piece of executive machinery', while the architectural press called for a 'Ministry of Civil Defence'.[80] The architects of the Tecton group commissioned at their own expense two rigorous reports written by the engineer Ove Arup, which analysed the risks and proposed their most rational solutions.[81] In effect, the government transferred the task of foreseeing protective measures for civilians to the local authorities, and a series of municipalities embarked on this policy, as Chermayeff observed.[82] John Anderson, who had become the Lord Privy Seal in Neville Chamberlain's Cabinet, set in place a system of state control along the lines of Napoleon's prefectures, but he rejected the idea of building deep shelters, using for support the report prepared by an ad hoc conference under the presidency of Lord Hailey.[83] The stance was rather

hypocritical, however, because at that very time an underground 'citadel' under Whitehall to shelter the agencies of government was being built.[84]

Arup's project, promoted by the members of Tecton, was based on the opposite premise, and was popularised in *Planned A.R.P.*, a book illustrated with amusing vignettes by Gordon Cullen. In this book, soon thereafter published in the United States as well, they presented research undertaken for the London borough of Finsbury, the fiefdom of the Labour Party, at the request of Harold Riley, an elected official charged with the ARP, and who had already been the source of Tecton's commission for the Finsbury Health Centre. Tecton was asked to look

Tecton Architects
Cover of *Planned A.R.P.*
[Air Raid Protection], 1939.
CCA Collection

and hence that the circle was the best shape 'Firstly, a circle is the geometrical figure which has the shortest perimeter in proportion to its area. . . . Secondly, a circular wall has greater resistance to the pressure exerted by the explosion of bombs outside it.' The Tecton group proposed 'a cylinder sunk into the ground, several storeys in height, and having strong side-walls and a protected roof'.[87] Employing Arup's precise calculations that followed from Haldane's previous work, on the 'danger volume' as a function of the type of protection, the distance from the bombs and their weight, Tecton called for the creation of a system of large shelters, capable of taking in 50, 270, 830 or even 7,600 people, so as to shelter the entire daytime population of the borough.[88] These shelters were to be large helicoidal constructions, 37 metres in diameter, whose continuous ramps would be accessible to both pedestrians and cars, and which spiralled down to 20.5 metres underground. These subterranean ramps are reminiscent of the Penguin Pool built by Tecton and Arup at London Zoo in 1934, which makes the latter appear in retrospect a sort of reduced scale model for the project.[89]

into the 'highest standard of protection that can be reasonably expected for money spent'.[85] They criticised the official policy of creating trenches in the neighbourhoods. 'There appears to be no reason why the long, narrow corridor form, originally evolved to meet purely military needs, should be adhered to in the case of civilian shelters. Indeed since trenches in the usually accepted sense of the word have so many disadvantages, there is no reason why other forms, more suited to the traffic problems with which they will have to cope, more easily supervised and controlled, and having other advantages from the psychological point of view, should not be investigated.'[86]

Tecton rejected that solution, as well as the idea of reinforcing existing cellars, based on the analysis of the Madrid experiences and a comparison between the conditions in Paris and London. The group proposed some simple alternatives: circular shelters linked one to another, or large shelters at the surface. Above all, they stressed that the surface area of the roof of any shelter should be as small as possible,

The proposal, accompanied by sharp criticisms of the official policy, was based on sophisticated calculations of probabilities, which further clarified the efficiencies of large shelters in relation to individual ones. The construction methods of these shelters was extraordinarily well thought out, with the structure being poured progressively from the ground surface to the bottom level. While each structure was developed as an independent piece of construction,

Tecton Architects
Ove Arup, engineer
**Project for an air raid
shelter for 7,600 people
in the borough of Finsbury**,
section view, 1939.
RIBA Library Drawings
and Archives Collections

Fig. 36.—INTERIOR VIEW OF A SHELTER FOR 7,600 PEOPLE.
(1) Air extract. (2) Lavatories. (3) Air extract. (4) Telephone switchboards and chief warden's room. (5) First-aid post. (6) Loud-speakers. (7) Air inlet. (8) Emergency exit with trapdoor. (9) Movable benches. (10) Bombproof outer wall. (11) Baffle walls, which also support floor above and act as buttresses against external shockwaves.

Tecton Architects
Ove Arup, engineer
**Project for an air raid
shelter for 7,600 people
in the borough of Finsbury**
(1939), interior view,
illustration in *Planned A.R.P.*
[Air Raid Protection], 1939.
CCA Collection

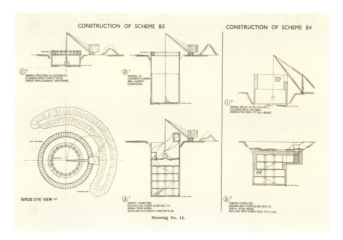

Ove Arup
**Contruction sequence
for an air raid shelter for
7,600 people**, illustrations
in *Design, Cost, Construction,
and Relative Safety of Trench,
Surface, Bomb-proof and
Other Air-raid Shelters*, 1939.
CCA Collection

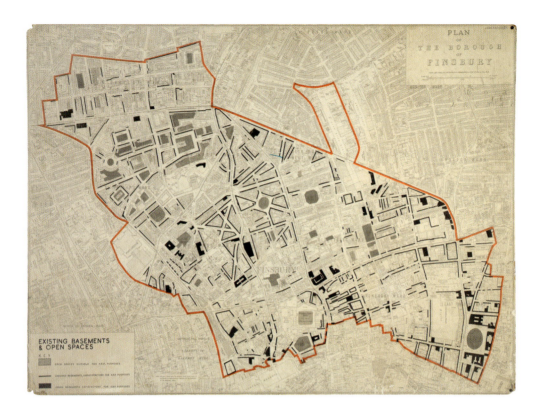

the distribution of the fifteen shelters throughout the borough was equally an object of rigorous study, such that the distances to be covered in the event of an alert would be minimised as much as possible. In June 1939, Haldane commented very favourably on *Planned A.R.P.* in the pages of *The Architectural Review* and declared that he had 'some faith in' and 'no doubt at all as to the efficiency' of the 'famous Finsbury shelter', although he retained his doubts as to its cost. He wondered above all about the overly theoretical aspect of the exercise.

Top: Tecton Architects
Plan of the existing basements and open spaces in the borough of Finsbury, 1939.
RIBA Library Drawings and Archives Collections

Cover of ***What Is Wrong With Official Shelter Policy?***, brochure, 1940.
CCA Collection

ERECTING AN ANDERSON SHELTER.

A COMPLETED ANDERSON SHELTER.

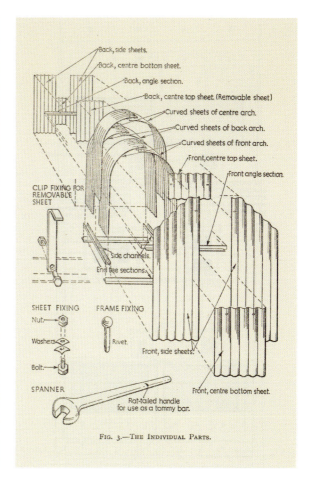

Back, side sheets.

Back, centre bottom sheet.

Back, angle section.

Back, centre top sheet. (Removable sheet)

Curved sheets of centre arch.

Curved sheets of back arch.

Curved sheets of front arch.

Front, centre top sheet.

Front angle section.

CLIP FIXING FOR REMOVABLE SHEET

Side channels.

End tree sections.

SHEET FIXING

Nut.

Washers.

Bolt.

FRAME FIXING

Rivet.

Front, side sheets.

SPANNER

Rat-tailed handle for use as a tommy bar.

Front, centre bottom sheet.

FIG. 3.—THE INDIVIDUAL PARTS.

'Throughout the authors have been handicapped by lack of vitally important information. If our government does not possess it, that is a scandal. If they do, but keep it secret, that is a scandal too. It appears only too probable that the data needed for designing shelters will first be furnished by actual raids on Britain in the near future.'[90] On the other hand, Winston Churchill employed classic forms of understatement when he stated that he was 'not favourably impressed' by *Planned A.R.P.*, and he did not hesitate to let Lubetkin know that 'the wide circulation of such a book would not be helpful at the present juncture'.[91]

Nonetheless, Lubetkin pressed forward with a propaganda campaign for his ideas, using every possible medium, both the classic ones – a conference under the aegis of the AASTA, for example – or more experimental ones – such as his appearance on a television broadcast on 15 February 1939.[92] The Finsbury borough council, for its part, decided to move forward with a variant of the Tecton shelter at Busaco Street in June 1939, despite

Left: **The Anderson shelter:** its construction and the completed shelter, illustrations in *Your Home as an Air Raid Shelter*, 1940. CCA Collection

Right: **The Anderson shelter:** the individual parts, illustration in *Air Raid Precautions Training Manual no. 1*, 1939. CCA Collection

the hostility of the government, that is, until its funding was cut off and Riley removed.[93] In retrospect, Lubetkin's judgment was that 'the truth is that the government saw our shelters as being morale-sapping. People would run to the shelters when the sirens sounded – but the government preferred that they should take a fatalistic approach and carry on with the manufacture of munition.'[94] Arup continued his campaign against dispersal and individual shelters until 1941, but without fully committing to defending the Finsbury project, which Lubetkin would reproach him for. Instead, he had to make do with building a few shelters for municipalities, firms and private individuals.[95]

SHELTER at home

3d. ISSUED BY THE MINISTRY OF HOME SECURITY AND PUBLISHED BY H.M. STATIONERY OFFICE

Cover of the brochure
Shelter at home,
featuring a Morrison
shelter, 1941.
CCA Collection

After the successful distribution of thirty-eight million gas masks, government policy remained deliberately oriented towards the reinforcement of cellars and especially towards individual shelters, while the poor organisation of defence groups demoralised the volunteers, as the anthropological studies of the Mass Observation group indicated.[96] A sheet-metal shelter designed by the engineers William Patterson and Oscar Carl Kerrison in 1938, and named the Anderson type, after the Home Secretary, was meant to be built out of fourteen pieces of corrugated metal and installed in gardens, over a shallow excavated pit, and then covered with earth. Some 2,250,000 of these 'doghouses', which caricaturists could not help but ridicule, would be built in the threatened regions of the kingdom, at no cost to the poorest families. The Morrison shelter – named after Herbert Morrison, Anderson's successor at the Ministry of Home Security, and designed by John Baker, the head of the Department of Civil Engineering at Cambridge, was meant to be used inside dwellings. In the form of a bed-cage that could be transformed into a table during the day, it was intended to protect those inside from falling walls. Half a million of these erector sets were distributed at the end of 1941, to be assembled by the inhabitants: the kits came in 219 pieces, not counting the bolts. But neither the Anderson nor the Morrison shelter took into account the living conditions of the worker population inside blocks of flats. Brick shelters called Sandwiches were

Shelter in the London Underground, view of a dormitory, 1942. Photograph by Sidney W. Newberg. Architectural Press Archive, RIBA Library Photographs Collection

Bottom: Frederick Herrmann **Project for underground shelters for Home Office officials**, Belsize Park, London, plan and sections, 1940. RIBA Library Drawings and Archives Collections

whose 'base' would be the population of the large shelters. Haldane made reference to the example of the ring of forts around Paris, used by Adolphe Thiers against the Commune in 1871: a population incapable of protecting itself from repressive bombardment would be more docile.[97] Churchill's declarations from as early as 1934 gave substance to this interpretation: 'We must expect that under the pressure of continuous air attack upon London, at least three million or four million people would be driven into the open country around the metropolis. This vast mass of human beings, numerically far larger than any armies

built for them, and these sometimes trapped their occupants under a layer of debris.

Haldane clearly perceived the class connotations of these measures, and he was only too happy to point out that the policy of the Conservative government was an expression of its fear of a popular revolt

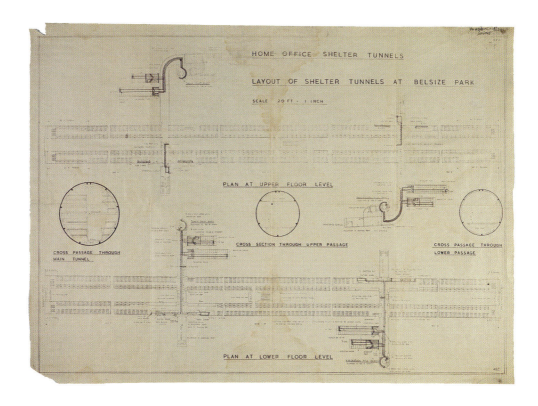

which have been fed and moved in war, without shelter and without food, without sanitation and without special provision for the maintenance of order, would confront the Government of the day with an administrative problem of the first magnitude, and would certainly absorb the energies of our small Army and of our Territorial Force.'[98]

Inhabited Tunnels under London

With the beginning of the Luftwaffe raids on London, the protection of officials and civilians took on a new dimension. The creation of collective shelters deep below the surface could no longer be excluded on principle, and the underground parts of the city were occupied in a variety of ways. Despite the prime minister's pronouncements, Winston Churchill's war Cabinet buried itself for months at a time,[99] but the most memorable experiences took place in the London Underground, which was transformed into a network of shelters that the population could use as soon as the sirens sounded. This approach had been rejected at the time of the attacks in 1918, as the government had given priority to uninterrupted use of the transport system at the time. It had not even been considered in 1939. On 27 September 1940, almost eighty Underground stations would shelter as many as 177,000 people, yet this amounted to only 5% of the population that had remained in London.[100] In the practice and mythology of the Blitz,

scenes of life on the platforms of the Underground remain among the most memorable. In a celebrated series of photographs, Bill Brandt captured *tableaux* of life during the nights when they alert had been given.[101] In his sketches, Henry Moore captured the poses of the shelters' occupants, and the Hungarian artist Joseph Bató published a book of drawings on the same theme.[102]

Winkel anti-aircraft shelter (c. 1936), illustration in Charles Glover, *Civil Defence*, 1938. CCA Collection

COMMUNAL SHELTERS 207

FIG. 91.—German ant-hill type of public bomb-proof shelter in reinforced concrete 80 ft. high, to accommodate 300. It is circular on plan and its steeply sloping sides minimise danger of undeflected impact.

Encouraged by this successful adaptation of part of the civilian infrastructure, the government would finally launch a programme of some scope. The ministries undertook studies for shelters to house their own personnel. Frederick Herrmann, a student of Paul Bonatz, who had built social housing in Berlin before emigrating and had subsequently spent some time in an internment camp,[103] studied the possibilities of shelter-tunnels to house employees of the Home Office at Belsize Park, under Haverstock Hill. This complex was to consist of a series of parallel and interconnected tunnels. And the creation of a set of deep shelters linked to the Underground and for the use of the population was also undertaken in October 1940.[104] Comparable in capacity to the shelters proposed by Tecton, they were meant to shelter 9,600 people and consisted of two parallel tubes 3,800 metres long and 2.11 metres in diameter, with cylindrical entrances at the surface. These were implanted at the level of existing stations at Stockwell, Camden Town, Belsize Park, Chancery Lane, and at Clapham South, Clapham Common and Clapham North. Designed and constructed by a group of contractors and engineers, the first of these shelters was completed in March 1942, but these were put to other uses until the V-1 and V-2 attacks of 1944, during which they were still not filled to capacity.[105]

Although they were marginalised from the implementation of official projects, architects still participated in the anti-aircraft protection effort in their own ways. Ernö Goldfinger served in the Home Guard and also as a guard for civil defence, for lack of finding another job.[106] Skinner served in the Royal Engineers. Finding the daily work too boring, he volunteered for the teams in charge of detonating unexploded bombs.[107] At the same time, the publicity surrounding the British projects had its effect: L'Architecture d'aujourd'hui reproduced Gordon Cullen's illustrations for Planned A.R.P., as well as Helsby's analyses of the experience of Barcelona.[108] The Russians studied the English experiences with shelters, and their ambassador in London requested a copy of Arup's studies.[109] The British experience was disseminated in the United States, for example when the president of the London County Council, Emil Davies, spoke before his colleagues, the American councilmen.[110] But Augustin M. Prentiss's book Civil Air Defense (1941), which was based on British handbooks without covering the Blitz, was judged obsolete by Chermayeff.[111]

The Blitz provided many lessons for the various belligerent countries. Designing civilian shelters suitable for schools became a concern in America, and the students at the Pratt Institute studied the question in 1942.[112] For his part, the young French architect André Wogenscky drew up a 'sketch for a shelter-refuge during the war'.[113] In Germany, anti-aircraft protection had not led to any important programmes before the war, but the situation changed as soon as the Nazi rulers realised that bombs could also fall on the cities of the Reich. On 10 October 1940, Adolf Hitler launched a Sofortprogramm (a programme of immediate urgency) for the construction of shelters in the cities, using in particular the spaces between buildings. The architectural responses varied. Without a doubt the strangest were the shelter-towers proposed by the firm of Leo Winkel

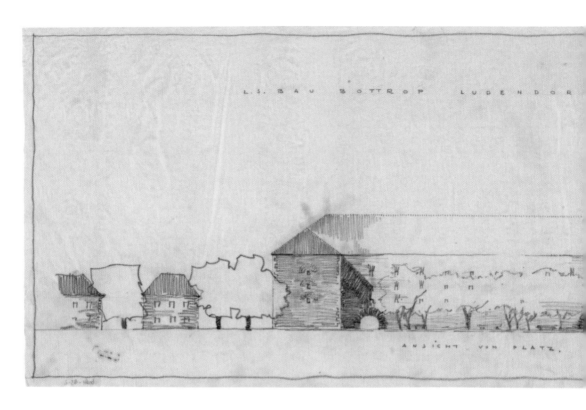

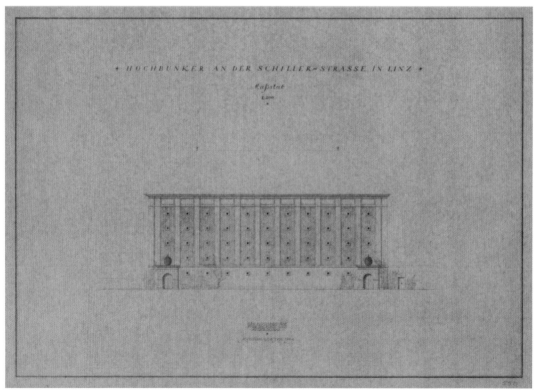

Fritz Becker
**Project for an
anti-aircraft shelter,**
Lüdendorfplatz and
Hindenburgstraße,
Bottrop, elevation, 1941.
Architekturmuseum
der TU München

Bottom left:
Roderich Fick
**Project for an
anti-aircraft shelter,**
Schillerstraße, Linz,
elevation, 1944.
Architekturmuseum
der TU München

Roderich Fick
**Competition project for
an anti-aircraft shelter,**
perspective view, 1942.
Architekturmuseum
der TU München

in Duisburg, whose conical structures could hold up to five hundred people, but left no room for decoration and looked more like industrial buildings or termite mounds.[114] On the other hand, the towers built in Hamburg by Konstanty Gutschow, cylinders with conical roofs, resembled nothing so much as windmills or medieval fortifications. But they turned out to be ineffectual in the face of attacks different from those they had been so systematically designed for. During the firestorm of July 1943 that resulted from Operation Gomorrah, their occupants were asphyxiated due to lack of oxygen, a possibility that even the most visionary of the prophets of war had never considered.

Although they were not affected by the Axis raids, the Americans nonetheless followed British experiences and projects closely. After being transferred from London to San Francisco, Serge Chermayeff criticised a report issued by the Washington branch of the AIA, laying claim to his own clear and uncontested expertise, insofar as he brought his own first-hand experience of the bombardment of London to bear on the subject.[115] In 1941, *The Architectural Forum* considered that *Planned A.R.P.* afforded 'striking evidence of the value of architectural services for civilian defense', while also praising the principles of camouflage, 'of especial interest and value to architects . . . because they are perhaps the best equipped for such work of all professional groups'.[116] The episodes described below will tend to confirm this assertion. Aerial warfare that is conducted for political imperatives that are not justified by actual events on the ground can be seen as a distant echo of the controversy surrounding the destruction of Lisbon in the earthquake of 1755. In his *Poème sur le désastre de Lisbonne*, Voltaire had found confirmation for his own pessimism, and deploring God's injustice, he asked himself: 'Was then more vice in fallen Lisbon found, than Paris, where voluptuous joys abound? Was less debauchery to London known, where opulence luxurious holds her throne?'[117] Rousseau was to write back in his 'Letter on Providence', in relating destruction to the vices of men, that 'Of the many people crushed under the rubble of Lisbon, some, no doubt, escaped greater misfortunes.'[118] It is undoubtedly possible to liken the critics of the raids over Germany that started in 1942 under Air Marshall Arthur 'Bomber' Harris to Voltaire, and to see their partisans as latter day fellows of Rousseau. But the bombardments of the Second World War were of a completely different order. They found their justification in what they helped avoid (although to an extent that will always remain impossible to measure): the victory of the Axis.

1. André Maurois, *Les Discours du docteur O'Grady* (Paris: Grasset, 1922), quoted by Lieutenant-Colonel Vauthier, *Le Danger aérien et l'avenir du pays* (Nancy, Paris and Strasbourg: Éditions Berger-Levrault, 1930), 77.
2. Vauthier, op. cit. note 1, IX–X.
3. General René Keller, *L'Architecture d'aujourd'hui*, vol. 8, no. 12 (December 1937). Keller was the inspector general of air defence.
4. General A. Niessel, ibid., 3. In collaboration with Rémy Alphonse Chabord and G. de Guilhermy, Niessel wrote, *D. A. T: Défense aérienne du territoire* (Paris: Éditions cosmopolites, 1934).
5. Peter Fritzsche, 'Machine Dreams. Airmindedness and the Reinvention of Germany', *American Historical Review*, vol. 98, no. 3 (June 1993), 685–709.
6. The acronym of the *Obshchestvo sodeistviia oborone i aviatsionno-khimicheskomu stroitelstvu SSSR*. Vauthier refers to it as early as 1930.
7. Italo Calvino, 'Le notti dell'UNPA', in *Romanzi e racconti* (Milan: Mondadori, 1991).
8. Pierre Vago, 'La Guerre aérienne', *L'Architecture d'aujourd'hui*, vol. 8, no. 12 (December 1937), 5.
9. Julia S. Torrie, 'Preservation by Dispersion: Civilian Evacuations and the City in Germany and France, 1939–1945', in *Endangered Cities: Military Power and Urban Societies in the Era of the World Wars*, edited by Marcus Funck and Robert Chickering (Boston: Brill Academic Publishers, 2004), 47–62.
10. For Schoszberger, see below. Henri Bahrmann, *L'Urbanisme et la défense du pays* (Paris: Institut d'Urbanisme de l'Université de Paris, 1935) and 'L'urbanisme et la défense du pays', La Vie urbaine, vol. 17, no. 34 (July–August 1936), 207–48.
11. Joseph W. Konvitz, 'Représentations urbaines et bombardements stratégiques 1914–1945', *Annales ESC*, vol. 64, no. 4 (July–August 1989), 823–47.
12. L. E. O. Charlton, *War Over England* (London: Longmans, 1936). L. E. O Charlton, Geoffrey T. Garratt and Reginald T. H. Fletcher, *The Air Defence of Britain* (Harmondsworth: Penguin, 1938).
13. Vauthier, op. cit. note 1, 54–55.
14. Ibid., 54–55.
15. M. A. Kozhevnikov, 'Puti stroitelstva i planirovki gorodov i vazhneishchikh

tylovykh punktov v usloviakh sovremennoi vozdushnoï i khimicheskoi voiny', *Voina i Tekhnika*, nos. 258, 268, and 278–79, cited in Vauthier, op. cit. note 1, 213.
16. Vauthier, op. cit. note 1, 213.
17. He cites General Nagaska, *Les Ailes*, 11 April 1929; ibid., 352–53.
18. Albert Guérard, *L'Avenir de Paris* (Paris: Payot, 1929).
19. Vauthier, letter to Monsieur Jeanneret [*sic*], 22 December 1929, FLC R3(6)90.
20. Vauthier, op. cit. note 1, 289.
21. Vauthier, letter to Le Corbusier, 21 November 1934, FLC R3(6)91.
22. Le Corbusier, letter to Lieutenant-Colonel Vauthier, 6 December 1934, FLC R3(6)92.
23. Le Corbusier, 'La guerre aérienne', in *La Ville radieuse* (Boulogne-sur-Seine: Éditions de L'Architecture d'aujourd'hui, 1935), 171. Vauthier's text is an extract from the report he presented to the Comité Supérieur de l'Aménagement de la Région Parisienne on 14 March 1933.
24. Le Corbusier, sketch in ibid., 61.
25. Le Corbusier, 'Et la guerre aérienne?', FLC A3(2) 248 to 253, also in ibid., 60–61.
26. Lieutenant-Colonel Vauthier, 'L'urbanisme et l'architecture devant le danger aérien', 21 June 1937. Typewritten text, FLC D2(11)545.
27. Vauthier, letter to Le Corbusier, 21 November 1934, FLC R3(6)91.
28. Hans Schoszberger, letter to Le Corbusier, 15 September 1934, FLC R3(3)171. Schoszberger's dedication, 'Le Corbusier in Verehrung zuigenet vom Verfasser', in Schoszberger, FLC, Le Corbusier's personal library, Z 108. The book is cited in a note in *La Ville radieuse*, p. 60, as well as Vauthier's book. Gropius provided Schoszberger with the Frenchman's address.
29. Hans Schoszberger, 'Luftschutz und Städtebau. Vorschläge für eine "luftsichere Idealstadt"', *Monatshefte für Baukunst und Städtebau*, no. 10 (October 1933), 476–79.
30. Hans Schoszberger, *Bautechnischer Luftschutz. Grundsätze des bautechnischen Schutzes gegen Fliegerbomben bei der Landesplanung, beim Aufbau der Gebäude und beim Schutzraumbau* (Berlin: Bauwelt-Verlag, 1934), 179.
31. Ibid., 206.
32. Schoszberger cites Karl Friedrich,

'Verschiedene, bisher unveröffentliche Arbeiten über Luftschutz und Landesplanung', *Wissen und Fortschritt*, no. 3, 1934.
33. Schoszberger, op. cit. note 30, 221.
34. José Luis Sert, *Can Our Cities Survive?* (Cambridge, Mass.: Harvard University Press, 1942), 69.
35. Samuel L. Friedman, 'Los Angeles Goes in for Realism', *Civilian Defense*, vol. 2 (August 1943), 5–7.
36. Ralphe H. Burke, 'The 'Bombing' of Chicago', *Civilian Defense*, vol. 2 (June 1943), 5.
37. 'Blackout', 'Civilian Defense Reference Number', *The Architectural Forum*, vol. 76, no. 1 (January 1942), 6.
38. Serge Chermayeff, 'San Francisco Blackout', *Pencil Points*, vol. 23, no. 1 (January 1942), 27–28.
39. Italo Calvino, op. cit. note 7.
40. Nigel Warburton, ed., *Bill Brandt: Selected Texts and Bibliography* (Oxford: Clio Press, 1993), 30.
41. Brassaï, 'Blackout in Paris', *Lilliput*, vol. 6, no. 6 (June 1940), 509–16.
42. Paul Virilio and Marianne Brausch, *Voyage d'hiver, entretiens* (Marseille: Parenthèses, 1997), 23.
43. Commandant Gibrin and Louis C. Heckly, *Défense passive organisée. Personnel et matériel* (Paris: Dunod, 1936).
44. R. C. Butler and L. W. Burridge, 'Bricks in Wartime', *The Architects' Journal*, 18 July 1940, 47. Giuseppe Stellingwerff, *La protezione dei fabbricati agli attachi aerei. L'applicazione del cemento armato nella protezione antiaerea* (Milan: Reggia Scuola d'Ingegneria, 1933).
45. Blei, 'Luftschutz und Baugestaltung', *Der Baumeister*, vol. 38, no. 1 (January 1940), 1–3.
46. Vauthier mentioned the following articles, translating their titles into French: Colonel Francesco Laviano, 'La défense contre les attaques aériennes', *Rivista di Artiglieria e Genio*, May 1928; Lieutenant-Colonel Alessandro Romani, 'Abris de défense antiaérienne', *Rivista di Artiglieria e Genio*, May 1927 and July 1929; Colonel Popescu 'La protection de la population contre les gaz toxiques', *Rivista Antigaz*, November 1927; Colonel von Keller, 'La protection passive des villes, de l'industrie et du commerce dans la guerre aérienne', *Das Wissen vom Kriege*, 18 May and 1 June 1927.
47. Vauthier, op. cit. note 1, 162.

48. Gibrin and Heckly, op. cit. note 43, 180.

49. Josette Bouvard, *Le Métro de Moscou: la construction d'un mythe soviétique* (Paris: Sextant, 2006).

50. Ernst Neufert, *Bauentwurfslehre* (Berlin: Bauwelt-Verlag, 1936), 255.

51. Bahrmann, loc. cit. note 10, 236.

52. *See Arkitekten-Arkkitekti*, no. 1 (1942), 9–11.

53. A. E. Kabel, 'Forderungen des baulichen Luftschutzes bei der Planung, Bebauung und Entwicklung des Großstadtraumes', *Baulicher Luftschutz*, vol. 10, no. 5 (May 1940), 19–22. Erich Bauer, 'Baulicher Luftschutz und Städtebau', *Zentralblatt der Bauverwaltung*, vol. 68, no. 5–6 (1943), 49–57.

54. Vauthier, op. cit. note 1, 152.

55. P. H. Rey, 'Paris objectif important', *L'Architecture d'aujourd'hui*, vol. 8, no. 12 (December 1937), 31–33.

56. Gibrin and Heckly, op. cit. note 43, 170.

57. Bahrmann, op. cit. note 10, 233.

58. 'Mr. Tait's Air Raid Shelter', *The Architects' Journal*, 23 November 1939.

59. Robert Elwall, *Ernö Goldfinger* (London: Academy Editions, 1996), 58.

60. Ernö Goldfinger and Mary Crowley, 'Evacuation Buildings for Mothers and Children', *Keystone, The Official Journal of The Association of Architects, Surveyors, and Technical Assistants* (March 1940), 2–6. 'Permanent Evacuation and Holiday Camps', *The Local Government Chronicle*, 23 March 1940, 291. Roy Nash, 'Homes From Home; Is This the Solution To The Evacuation Problem', *The Star*, 28 March 1940. 'Evacuation camps for Mothers and Children', *The Architect and Building News*, 27 October 1940, 138–40, and 27 October 1940, 615–16. 'Evacuation: the "Under Fives"', *The Builder*, 27 September 1940, 312–13. 'Evacuation: the "Under Fives"', *The Architects' Journal*, 3 October 1940, 267–68.

61. Marie-Luise Recker, 'Wohnen und Bombardierung im Zweiten Weltkrieg,' in *Wohnen im Wandel: Beiträge zur Geschichte des Alltags in der bürgerlichen Gesellschaft*, edited by Lutz Niethammer (Wuppertal: Peter Hammer Verlag, 1979), 418–19.

62. Hans Spiegel, 'Gestaltung und Ausführung des Behelfsheims', *Der Wohnungsbau in Deutschland*, vol. 4, no. 1–2 (January 1944), 1–12.

On the Deutsche Wohnungshilfswerk, see among others Marie-Luise Recker, 'Staatliche Wohnungsbaupolitik im Zweiten Weltkrieg', *Die alte Stadt*, vol. 5 (1978), 134–37.

63. Gaston Bardet, 'L'urbanisme et la défense passive', *L'Architecture d'aujourd'hui*, vol. 8, no. 12 (December 1937), 30.

64. Gustavo Giovannoni, 'Urbanistica antiaerea' (Rome: n.p., 1939). Diagram reproduced in Alessandro Del Bufalo, *Gustavo Giovannoni. Note e osservazioni integrata dalla consultazione dell'archivio presso il centro di studi di storia dell'architettura* (Rome: Kapp, 1982), 115. In Luigi Manzione, *Déclinaisons de l'urbanisme comme science. Discours et projets: Italie et France (1920–1940)*, doctoral thesis, Université de Paris 8, 2006, ill. facing p. 356. See also Giuseppe Stellingwerff, *La protezione antiaerea nel quadro del piano regolatore di Roma imperiale* (Rome: Istituto Nazionale di Studi Romani, 1939).

65. Vincenzo Civico, 'Distribuire il lavoro per distribuire la popolazione', *Critica fascista*, May 1942.

66. Frank Lloyd Wright. '"Bomb-Proof City" Shown as Model. Wright, the Architect, Holds Community of the Future Will Be Spread Out', *The New York Times*, 11 November 1940.

67. Douglas Haskell, 'What Does Military Design Offer to the Planning of Peace?', *The Architectural Record*, March 1939, 75.

68. Ludwig Hilberseimer, *The New City. Principles of Planning* (Chicago: Paul Theobald, 1944), 40.

69. An illuminating comparison between British and German policies can be found in Bernd Lemke, *Luftschutz in Großbritannien und Deutschland. 1923–1939. Zivile Kriegsvorbereitungen als Ausdruck der staats- und gesellschaftspolitischen Grundlagen von Demokratie und Diktatur* (Munich: Oldenbourg Verlag, 2005).

70. Arthur Marwick, *Britain in the Century of Total War: War, Peace, and Social Change, 1900–1967* (Boston: Little, Brown and Co., 1968).

71. Joseph S. Meisel, 'Air Raid Shelter Policy and its Critics in Britain before the Second World War', *Twentieth Century British History*, vol. 5, no. 3 (1994), 302–04. Uri Bialer, *The Shadow of the Bomber: The Fear of Air Attack and British Politics,*

1932–1939 (London: Royal Historical Society, 1980).

72. See the material collected by Terence H. O'Brien, *Civil Defence. History of the Second World War*, United Kingdom Civil Series (London: Her Majesty's Stationery Office, 1955), 153.

73. Francis Skinner, 'Aerial Bombardment. Effects and Defence in Barcelona', *The Architects' Journal*, 16 June 1938, 1017–21 and 23 June 1938, 1057–61. Cited on pp. 1017 and 1058. On the Barcelona shelters, see Judit Pujadó i Puigdomènech, *Oblits de rereguarda: els refugis antiaeris a Barcelona (1936–1939)* (Barcelona: Federació de l'edificació de Catalunya, 1998).

74. Goldfinger preserved a note of warning by the colonel of the Republican army, Frederico de la Iglesia, who found refuge in Great Britain: 'Comment l'attaque aérienne se produirait', typewritten, in French, no date [1938], Ernö Goldfinger Papers, series 47, box 410.

75. Ramon Perera, 'ARP in Calalonia', *The Architect and Building News*, vol. 160, no. 15 (December 1939), 258. John Pinckheard, 'Lessons of Barcelona in Air-Raid Shelter Design', *Architectural Design and Construction*, vol. 9, supplement to no. 5 (May 1939), 12–15. 'Air Raid Precautions in Catalonia', *Journal of the Air Raid Protection Institute*, February 1940, 88.

76. John Desmond Bernal had discussed the links between research and war in *The Social Function of Science* (London: Routledge, 1939). He participated in the collective publication, *Science in War* (Harmondsworth: Penguin, 1940).

77. Cambridge Scientists Anti-War Group, *The Protection of the Public from Aerial Attack*, (London: Victor Gollancz, 1937). John Burdon Sanderson Haldane, *Air Raid Precautions*, (London: Victor Gollancz, 1938).

78. Haldane, op. cit. note 77, 119.

79. Cyril Helsby, 'Air Raids, Structures, and A.R.P. in Barcelona Today', *Structural Engineer*, vol. 17, no. 1 (January 1939), 2–39. The discussion continued in the next issue, pp. 117–23. Felix J. Samuely, *Civil Protection: the Application of the Civil Defence Act and Other Government Requirements for Air Raid Shelters* (London: The Architectural Press, 1939). Samuely also commented very

favourably on the Tecton projects: Felix J. Samuely, 'Aspects of A.R.P.', *Focus*, vol. 2, no. 3 (spring 1939), 48–52.
80. Serge Chermayeff, *Plan for the A.R.P. A Practical Policy for Air-Raid Precautions* (London: Frederick Muller, 1939). F. E. T. [Towndrow]. 'A.R.P.: The New Arm, The Case for a Ministry of Civil Defence', *Architectural Design and Construction*, vol. 9, no. 3 (March 1939), 82.
81. Ove Arup, *Air Raid Precautions: Report to the Finsbury Borough Council*, London, 1939. *Design, Cost, Construction, and Relative Safety of Trench, Surface, Bomb-Proof and Other Air-Raid Shelters* (London: Concrete Publications Limited, 1939).
82. Chermayeff, op. cit. note 80.
83. *The Times*, 21 April 1939. 'Home Office Engineers' Report on Air Raid Shelter Policy', supplement to *The Builder*, vol. 116, no. 5012 (24 February 1939).
84. On this double language, see Duncan Campbell, *War Plan UK: the Truth about Civil Defence in Britain* (London: Burnett Books, 1982), 62–68.
85. Tecton Architects, *Planned A. R. P. Based on the Investigation of Structural Protection Against Air Attack in the Metropolitan Borough of Finsbury* (London: The Architectural Press, 1939), 11.
86. Ibid., 43.
87. Ibid., 75 and 77.
88. See the calculations of John Burdon Sanderson Haldane, 'The Mathematics of A.R.P.', *Nature*, vol. 142, no. 3600 (29 October 1938), 791–92.
89. John Allan, *Berthold Lubetkin, Architecture and the Tradition of Progress* (London: RIBA Publications, 1992), 352–63.
90. John Burdon Sanderson Haldane, 'Shelter', *The Architectural Review*, vol. 85, no. 511 (June 1939), 305.
91. O. Harrington, private secretary to Winston Churchill, to Lubetkin, 20 March 1939. RIBA, Berthold Lubetkin Papers, series 10, box 11, LUB/11/1/15.
92. Berthold Lubetkin, 'Principles of Design for Air-Raid Shelters', *The Architect and Building News*, no. 17 (November 1939), 160.
93. *The Times*, 18 July 1939.
94. Berthold Lubetkin in 'Samizdat', typewritten memoires, 1978, 1987, 1993, p. 33. RIBA, Berthold Lubetkin Papers, series 13, box 25, LUB/25/4/3.
95. Ove Arup, *London's Shelter Problem* (London: D. Gestetner Ltd,

1939). Jones mentions some thirty shelters built by him: Peter Jones, *Ove Arup. Masterbuilder of the Twentieth Century* (London and New Haven: Yale University Press, 2006), 83.
96. Tom Harrison and Charles Madge, eds., *War Begins at Home* (London: Chatto & Windus, 1940).
97. John Burdon Sanderson Haldane, *Air Raid Precautions*, p. 234, quoted by Joseph S. Meisel, op. cit. note 71, 310–11.
98. Winston Churchill, *House of Commons Debates*, 28 November 1934, vol. 295, p. 859.
99. Claudio Magris on the Cabinet War Rooms in London: 'A Londra sono tornato scolaro', *Il Corriere della Sera*, 1 April 1988.
100. Alan A. Jackson and Desmond F. Croome, *Rails Through the Clay, A History of London's Tube Railways* (London: Routledge, 2006).
101. Joanne Buggins, 'An Appreciation of the Shelter Photographs taken by Bill Brandt in November 1940', *Imperial War Museum Review*, 1989, 32–42.
102. David Mitchinson and Roger Tolson, *Henry Moore, War and Utility* (London: Imperial War Museum, 2006). Angus Calder, *The Myth of the Blitz* (London: Jonathan Cape, 1991).
103. Charlotte Benton, *A Different World: Émigré Architecture in Britain, 1928–1938* (London: RIBA Publications, 1995), 169–70. See the memoirs of this architect: F. H. Herrmann, *F. H. Herrmann: an Architect at Work* (London: Goethe Institut/RIBA, 1977).
104. See 'Deep Tunnel Air Raid Shelters', *The Engineer*, 27 November 1942, 445–46; 4 December 1942, 456–58; 11 December 1943, 472–74.
105. John Gregg, *The Shelter of the Tubes. Tube Sheltering in Wartime London* (Harrow Weald: Capital Transport Publishing, 2001). Andrew Emmerson and Tony Beard, *London's Secret Tubes: London's Wartime Citadels, Subways, and Shelters Uncovered* (Harrow Weald: Capital Transport Publishing, 2007).
106. File with correspondence, target papers and various souvenirs: RIBA, Ernö Goldfinger papers, series 47, box 410, GolEr\410\1-2.
107. John Allan, 'Obituary: Francis Skinner', *The Independent*, 17 January 1988.
108. 'L'Experience de Barcelone', *L'Architecture d'aujourd'hui*, vol. 10, no. 8 (August 1939), 11–12.

109. Jones, loc. cit. note 95, 83.
110. Alderman Emil Davies, 'What American Cities Can Learn from Wartime England', *The American City*, vol. 57, no. 1 (January 1942), 43–45.
111. Serge Chermayeff, 'Textbooks and Actuality', *Pencil Points*, vol. 23, no. 6 (December 1941), 777–78. See Augustin M. Prentiss, *Civil Air Defense* (New York: McGraw Hill), 1941.
112. 'Bombproof and Splinterproof construction. Pratt Institute Makes Series of Models for the Study of Shelter Types', *Pencil Points*, vol. 23 (March 1942), 136–37.
113. Paola Misino and Nicoletta Trasi, *André Wogenscky, raisons profondes de la forme* (Paris: Le Moniteur, 2000), 187.
114. Michael Foedrowitz, *Luftschutztürme und ihre Bauarten 1934–1945* (Eggolsheim: Nebel, 2003).
115. Serge Chermayeff, 'Is High Explosive the Greatest Danger?', *Pencil Points*, vol. 23, no. 1 (July 1941), 489–90, and 'ARP and Our Office of Civilian Defense', *Pencil Points*, vol. 22, no. 3 (September 1941), 591–93.
116. 'Books', *The Architectural Forum*, vol. 75, no. 4 (October 1941), 44.
117. Voltaire, 'Poem on the Lisbon Disaster,' in *Portable Voltaire*, edited by Ben Ray Redmann (New York: Penguin Books, 1977), 560.
118. Jean-Jacques Rousseau, letter to Voltaire. In Jean-Jacques Rousseau, *The Discourses and Other Early Political Writings*, edited by Victor Gourevitch, vol. 1 (Cambridge and New York: Cambridge University Press, 1997), 235.

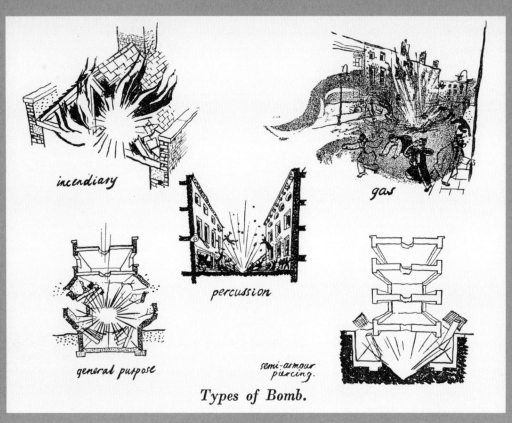

incendiary

gas

percussion

general purpose

semi-armour piercing.

Types of Bomb.

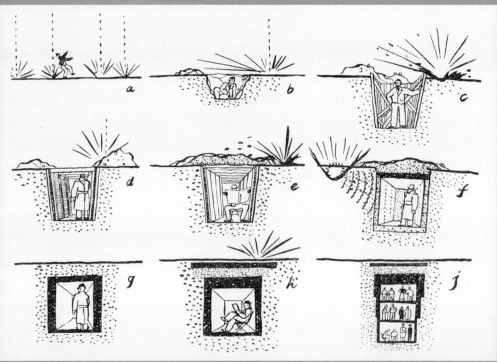

Gordon Cullen
**Design, construction and
everyday life in anti-aircraft
shelters**, illustrations in
Planned A.R.P, 1939.
CCA Collection

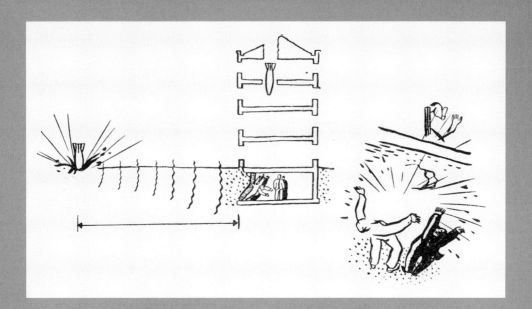

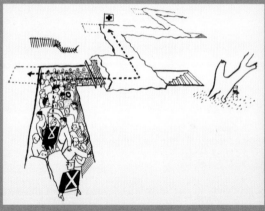

6/ Camouflage, or the Temptation of the Invisible

'War of Production' sounds the note of reality for today, and tomorrow. But in our world, there is still a role to be played by magic.
Salvador Dalí, 'Total Camouflage for Total War', 1942[1]

Camouflage is functional design *par excellence*. **Its only** *raison d'être* **is to conceal effectively. Whether this is done with aesthetically valuable or indifferent results cannot matter in the least to those who commission and pay for it. Yet – as it is mostly done by artists or at least experts of aesthetic sensibility – the results of camouflage often have a distinct visual charm and a curious similarity to the creations of modern art.**
'Art by Accident', *The Architectural Review*, **1944[2]**

Whether advantageous, dangerous or indifferent, the call of invisibility illustrates a fundamental need that seems in some cases to develop independently of the advantages or disadvantages it might entail, as if it had become an end in itself.
Roger Caillois, *Le Mimétisme animal*, **1963[3]**

The attempt to partially or completely conceal targets from their attackers, instead of trying in vain to withstand bombardment, led to elaborate strategies involving architects. The strategy adopted against daylight raids was camouflage, and for night raids, the blackout – in certain respects the most extreme attempt at invisibility.[4] One of the broadest definitions of the practice of camouflage can be found in the opening pages of the manual published in 1942 by Major Robert P. Breckenridge of the American Corps of Engineers: 'Camouflage, or protective concealment, may be defined as the science of disguising or hiding a target from an enemy, including any and every method of confusing him as to its location, strength and purpose.'[5] One can retrace the history and precedents, with examples from previous times dating back to Antiquity, of all the ruses employed to deceive the enemy as to the strength of the troops deployed. One can find many an echo of Malcolm's strategy, when he managed to move Birnam Woods in Shakespeare's *Macbeth* by hiding his soldiers under its branches.

The origins of the term camouflage are still obscure, even if Paolo Fabbri provocatively ties it to *carmen* and hence to charm, seeing it as a form of charming, or 'casting a spell'.[6] Camouflage is related to strategies found in the animal kingdom, as has been highlighted by the many books written on the subject, which has become all the more popular since it became a source of inspiration for fashion designers.[7] The book published in 1909 by Abbott H. and Gerald H. Thayer, *Concealing Coloration in the Animal Kingdom*, remains a key reference work in terms of observation.[8] Roger Caillois' reflections on the subject of animal mimicry gave it a theoretical framework that remains current today. For Caillois, 'merging into the background, into the environment' revealed

A team of camouflage designers at work at Fort Belvoir, Virginia, illustration in Robert P. Breckenridge, *Modern* Camouflage: The New Science of Protective Concealment, 1942. McGill University Library, Montréal

man's 'permanent wish' for invisibility:
'Man has not invented any better means
of camouflaging himself, his devices, and
his constructions than those employed by
snakes and leaf insects: disruptive colours,
and recourse to leaves. Canvases painted
with large and dazzling spots of colour
break up the form and make it disappear.
At one time, sticks and branches were
there for cover. But, as always, it is human
imagination that one should look to first
for the true response to the fantasy fixed
in the anatomy or instinct of insects.'[9] But
there is no better way to understand the
characteristics of camouflage as practiced
in the Second World War than to compare
it with the initial experiments undertaken
in the previous conflict.

Lucien Haye
Paul d'Espagnat
**'The Camouflage
Artist'**, cover
illustration of *La Guerre
documentée*, 1918.
Collection of the author

Bottom: **'Le faux Paris'**,
urban camouflage project,
regional layout of the
project, illustration
in Paul Vauthier,
Le Danger aérien, 1930.
Collection of the author

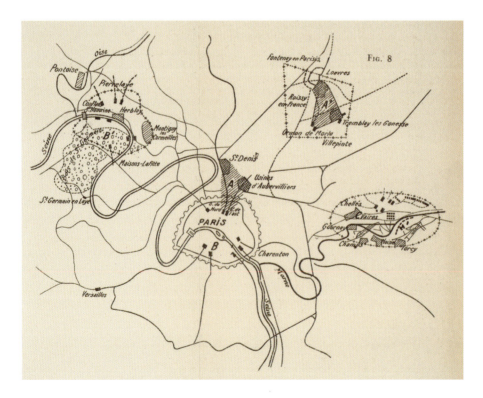

The Legacy of the 'Camouflage Section'

During the First World War, camouflage was essentially the work of artists. They were responsible for the vivid colours of the 'dazzle painting' that was applied to the ships of the Royal Navy, an approach first thought up by the painter Norman Wilkinson.[10] But artists were primarily employed in the concealment of land forces. The link between camouflage and modern art could not have been stated more clearly than in Picasso's memorable reaction to seeing a camouflaged vehicle on the Boulevard Raspail with Gertrude Stein: 'Yes, it is we who made it, that is Cubism.'[11] Cocteau reported that Picasso had also claimed that the best way to render an army invisible would be to dress the soldiers as harlequins.[12]

In France's case, the Section de Camouflage, created in February 1915 on the Picardy front at the instigation of Lucien-Victor Guirand de Scévola, would comprise three thousand men by 1918. It remained a secret until the Armistice, when its achievements were revealed by the press, which listed the names of the artists involved, including the painters Forain, Dunoyer de Segonzac, Devambez and Laurens, and the sculptors Landowski and Bouchard, together with a few architects.[13] Documentation of the work of the brigade was to be found in the notebooks of some of its members, like interior decorator André Mare, the designer of the *Maison cubiste* of the Salon d'Automne of 1912.[14] His drawings showed how they attempted to visually break up the recognisable forms of artillery and vehicles. A similar unit was created in 1916 by the British Royal

Engineers, through the initiative of the painter Solomon J. Solomon, and Franz Marc painted canvas tarpaulins for the German army in the manner of Kandinsky. After the founding of the New York Camouflage Society by the painters Barry Faulkner and Sherry H. Fry, the Americans entrusted the camouflage of Pershing's expeditionary corps in 1917–1918 to the 40th Engineers, under the direction of officers Dwight Bridge and Homer Saint-Gaudens, the son of the sculptor Augustus.

The camouflage artists of the First World War were primarily concerned with concealing troops and their equipment, either at the front or immediately behind it. The only major exception, one that was particularly spectacular, was the creation of a 'faux Paris' to deceive the zeppelins that bombarded the French capital at night. In an area to the north-west of Paris, where the Seine follows a course between Conflans Sainte-Honorine and Maisons-Laffitte that echoes its path through the city, the electrical engineer Fernando Jacopozzi laid out a network of fake streets and squares, as well as fake railway stations meant to recreate Paris. The movement of trains at night was simulated by lines of electrical lights that turned on in sequence over two kilometres. A first attempt at simulating the Gare de l'Est was laid out in the Orme de Morlu area, between Sevran and Villepinte – at the current location of the Roissy-Charles de Gaulle airport – with imitations of glazing obtained by stretching out shiny canvas on the ground. The Armistice would put an end to work on this scale. It was revealed to the public in 1920 in *L'Illustration*, and Vauthier devoted a number of pages to it ten years later in *Le Danger aérien*.[15] Jacopozzi

'**Le faux Paris**',
urban camouflage project,
detailed plan, illustration
in Paul Vauthier,
Le Danger aérien, 1930.
Collection of the author

would put the same imagination he had deployed in these kinetic lighting solutions to enchanting nocturnal use in 1925, by using 250,000 light bulbs attached to the Eiffel Tower as an advertisement for Citroën.

Painters' Comments

During the Second World War, architects almost completely supplanted painters in the field of camouflage. Studies had continued uninterrupted since 1918 and camouflage departments now occupied an important place in all the armed forces. Vauthier refers to the work of the Italian colonels Laviano and Merzari,[16] and there was much activity in Germany and the Soviet Union. Some artists tried their luck again in 1939. During the Phoney War of 1939–1940, the painter Charles Lapicque, who had been trained as an engineer and specialised in optics, flew over France with aviator and writer Antoine de Saint-Exupéry on behalf of the newly formed Centre National de la Recherche Scientifique, which had asked him to research night vision.[17] Fernand Léger, who had previously served in the camouflage section, offered his services to the director of the École des Beaux-Arts, Georges Huisman, and stressed the affinities of camouflage with the artistic avant-garde: 'I am sure you have a say in this camouflage commission. Don't forget that imagination is much more on the side of the "moderns" than on the rue Bonaparte.'[18] Léger subsequently emigrated to America, and shortly thereafter, the director of exhibitions at MoMA, Monroe Wheeler, referred to Léger's expressed hope of becoming

involved. But Homer Saint-Gaudens, who had returned to head the American Camouflage Engineers, based at Fort Belvoir, considered him too old for the job.[19]

In Great Britain, the Air Ministry set up a Directorate of Camouflage, under the direction of Captain L. M. Glasson, in 1938. Its principal task was to prepare camouflage for the most exposed industrial targets. Quartered in 1939 at Leamington Spa under the auspices of the Ministry of Home Security, the team consisted primarily of artists and sculptors. Physicists were added in increasing numbers, in order to strengthen the scientific component of the projects;[20] advanced experiments were conducted in an ingenious 'vision chamber', making it possible to study the various proposals under different lighting conditions, as well as in a 'moonlight vision chamber' for nocturnal views. There were individual initiatives, as well. In London, the architect

Ernö Goldfinger added a private 'industrial camouflage unit' to his office at 7 Bedford Square. He became the technical advisor to a team of four Surrealist painters, Bill Hayter, Roland Penrose, Julian Trevelyan and John Buckland Wright, and used a heliometer to study the effect of natural lighting on buildings. Given the lack of commissions – the main one being the Imperial Tobacco cigarette factory in Bristol – the principal results of this cooperation were, on a practical level, the charming *Home Guard Manual of Camouflage*, illustrated

by Penrose, who had become an instructor at the War Office School for Instructors to the Home Guard,[21] and at a more theoretical level, the analyses of Trevelyan on 'The Technique of Camouflage', which would be published by *The Architectural Review* in a special issue in 1944.

For Trevelyan, who in the meantime served in the Camouflage and Training Centre of the Royal Engineers at Farnham Castle, camouflage was 'visual warfare' practiced 'at once as an art, a craft and a science'. He pointed out that the perception of camouflage depends on one's point of view: 'To the soldier, it is the ubiquitous set with a few pieces of scrim tied to the corner which he is supposed to throw over his truck when parking; to the architect it is the lozenges of green and brown paint that obliterate the features and symmetry of his buildings. To the ordinary citizen it is something between a sort of magic cloak of invisibility and a bad joke in *Punch*.' Although it has to be perfect to fool photographers, camouflage can be more approximate if the sole aim is to confuse pilots. 'In the last instance, the whole subject is bound up with that faculty for visual awareness that it is now recognized our society has lost to such a dangerous degree.' In every case, Trevelyan insists on 'the most neglected principle of camouflage: siting to conform to the pattern of the country', and hence

CAMOUFLAGE

aesthetics and technique

'Camouflage: aesthetics and technique', article in *The Architectural Review*, September 1944. CCA Collection

Total Camouflage for Total War

As the War for Survival demands some new, more general type of camouflage, why not employ psychological control of vision?

by SALVADOR DALI
•ARTICLE•

R

TO BE or not to be (Shakespeare). To see or not to see (Dali). That is the question, or more precisely, the problem. At the beginning of the last war it was Picasso, inventor of Cubism, who found the solution. This is the authentic story.

Seated in the spring sunshine on the terrace of the famous Rotonde in Montparnasse, Picasso and a group of his ardent admirers were sipping their absinthe, with the familiar ritual of the sugar spoon. The talk was naturally of war. But with this group of youthful innovators in the arts, the conversation was given to imaginative flights, rather than weighty considerations. Somebody threw out the strategic suggestion of making an army invisible.

"That's perfectly possible!" cried Picasso. Everybody kept still, waiting for the great painter to launch one of those ideas with which he always managed to eclipse other contributions to the conversation, no matter how original. And Picasso went on:

"If you want to make an army invisible, all you have to do is dress the soldiers like harlequins. At a distance the diamond patterns will merge into the landscape, and nobody will be able to see them."

Thus out of the casual and offhand talk bandied about among a handful of still little-known artists, was born the principle of camouflage so effectively used in the last war. It was not long indeed till one saw heavy guns, cuirassiers, cruisers, tanks, all covered with the same fancifully colored arabesques that figured simultaneously in the perturbing canvases of the new painters. At first people did not realize that this very same Cubism which created such a scandal in the art galleries as being too trivial for days occupied with matters of such grave moment, was already operating with high efficiency on the fields of battle.

The profound lessons of history repeat themselves, but never in quite the same way. Outwardly they change, often beyond recognition. And just as the camouflage of 1914 was Cubist and Picassan, so the camouflage of 1942 should be Surrealist and Dalistic. For this time, the discovery is mine—namely the secret of total invisibility and the psychological camouflage. More of this later.

The discovery of "invisible images" was certainly part of my destiny. When I was six years old, I had astounded my parents and their friends by my almost mediumistic faculty of "seeing things differently." Always I saw what others did not see; and what they saw, I did not.

Among countless examples, there is a striking one which dates from that period of my life. Every Saturday I received a juvenile publication to which my father had sub-

scribed for me. Its final page was always devoted to a puzzle picture. This would present, for instance, a forest and a hunter. In the tangled underbrush of the forest the artist had cleverly concealed a rabbit; the problem was to find it. Or, again, a doll must be discovered, lost by a child in an apparently empty room. My father would bring me the puzzle, and what was his astonishment to see me find, not one but two, three or four rabbits; not a single doll but several—and never the one which the artist had meant to conceal. Still more astonishing was the fact that my rabbits and my dolls were much clearer and better drawn than the ones which had been intentionally hidden. As soon as I outlined them with my pencil, everybody could see them as clearly as I could, and exclaimed over them in surprise.

But my seeing several rabbits where others could find only one after long study and turning the page this way and that—was not all. The really phenomenal part of it was that in the same image I could see a mosquito, an elephant, a bathtub, or anything else, just as well as a rabbit.

It was in psycho-pathology that I later found the explanation of this mysterious ability to see whatever I chose, wherever I chose. I had the paranoiac mind. Paranoia is defined as systematic delusion of interpretation. It is this systematic delusion which, in a more or less morbid state, constitutes the basis of the artistic phenomenon in general, and of my magic gift for transforming reality, in particular.

Watching fanciful images taking on more and more definite form, while gazing at the damp spots on an old wall, was one of the favorite and fascinating games of my childhood. I could see almost anything too, in the ever-changing shape of the clouds—so prolific a source of paranoiac visions. What was my amazement, in the course of later studies, to find that back in the days before Christ, Aristophanes in *The Clouds* had declared them "the masters of delusion"—melting from the form of a leopard into the graceful contours of a nude woman, and evolving thence into the shape of a nose. In the same way, I was to read the advice of Leonardo da Vinci, who counseled his pupils to seek inspiration for painting an equestrian battle, by gazing in a certain mental state at the spots of dampness on an old wall, in order to see the desired images arise out of chaos. The very same clouds and damp old walls which had evoked the hallucinations of my childhood.

Long before Aristophanes, indeed, the cave man, whose animal engravings of magic import simply followed certain lines of relief on the walls of the cave, in which he saw the forms which obsessed him, was obeying the

same paranoiac principle—the systematic delusion of interpretation.

And well before the cave man, even before man appeared at all on the surface of the earth, the same principle reigned in nature, taking the form of that most mysterious and least known of all phenomena—mimetism. In the beginning . . . was camouflage, the invisible!

The leaf-type insects represent one of the most subtle forms of mimetic camouflage in nature. Some of them not only take on the exact form and color of leaves, but even imitate their slightest surface conformations —tiny holes corresponding to drops of water pierced by a ray of sunlight, gossamer traces of mildew, the notched edges made by the gnawing of certain insects. Others imitate rotting twigs or thorny stems so closely as to be indistinguishable from the originals. Thus we might say that reality playing at illusion, becomes illusion; and being illusion—and therefore invisible—can serve equally well as a mechanism of defense or offense.

The leopard's spots and the tiger's stripes, imitating the effects of light and shade in the jungle, the markings of all animals in fact, obey this same obscure principle, whose least developed and most elementary manifestation is among the mammals. On the other hand, there is a variety of African sole which

Continued on next page

REPRINTED FROM VOGUE © CONDE NAST PUBLICATIONS, INC.

This bit of visual drollery is really the reverse of those on the opposite page. Dali here asks you to visualize the incongruous image suggested somewhere in this picture (try holding the page at a distance and squinting your eyes)—and then compare your version with his on the next page.

on the importance of reading landscapes, which would lead to the employment of architects who have an understanding of territorial patterns.[22]

Writing in New York in 1942, on 'Total Camouflage for Total War', Salvador Dalí remained in the realm of pure painting when he proclaimed: 'Just as the camouflage of 1914 was Cubist and Picasso, so the camouflage of 1942 should be Surrealist and Dalistic.' He announced that he was a specialist in 'invisible images'; he invoked the hidden figures in the enigmatic drawings published in children's books, and gave examples of forms rendered unreadable by their context. Dalí claimed that his 'most pressing project' was to 'to perfect for the United Nations a system of camouflage based on my radical theory of invisibility'.[23] No less!

The Agency of Architects

Architects were called upon because they had the ability to read the built landscape, as well as geometric skills – perspective and shading – and the graphic and pictorial techniques required. Furthermore, as early as 1919, Saint-Gaudens had claimed that 'our best officers were architects. They not only understood the principles of form and colour, but they had been faced with clients who would have the linen closet, the stairs, and the chimney all in the same place.'[24] For his part, Le Corbusier, drawing on his experiences during the First World War, saw in the camouflage of 1923 the negative influence of De Stijl: 'Polychromy on the outside produces the effects of camouflage; it destroys, disarticulates, divides and thus

works against unity.'[25] Iakov Chernikhov, an architect chiefly known for his prodigious output of graphic work, designed a set of motifs for camouflage during the first months of the Russian campaign in 1941.

At the beginning of the war at least, camouflage also became a potential market for architects who had not been mobilised, but who were no longer in a position to design real buildings. They resorted to various initiatives to sell skills that often remained without any outlet during the war. Hoping to run the large model shop set up to make models for General Motors' Futurama pavilion, the centrepiece of the New York World's Fair in 1939, Norman Bel Geddes besieged the offices of the US Army to obtain a commission to study the camouflage of factories in three dimensions. He also visited Albert Kahn, noting to his team that 'Mr Kahn was very much impressed with our idea on this and made the statement that compared with applying camouflage to a completed building, if anyone would plan to do it this way in the start, he felt confidence that the difference in cost would be as much as a 50% saving. . . . Another thing is the Government is forcing them to make these buildings as cardboardish and flimsy as possible.'[26] The project was so unrealistic – it used layers of concrete and earth that were much too heavy – that Saint-Gaudens was still mocking it in 1946.[27] Never at a loss for ideas, Geddes proposed a camouflaged tent to the National Inventors' Council of the Department of Commerce in Washington. His prospective clients noted that 'the camouflaged tent will be of extreme importance in operations in Alaska, where it could be camouflaged to look like a hill

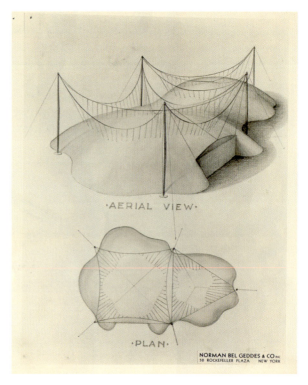

of snow or a green mound, and there
is also a tropical design for islands
in the Pacific or for the deserts',[28] but
they did not pursue the matter further.

Percival Goodman, an architect based
in New York, created the Camouflage
Engineering Company with some friends
from different professional backgrounds,
in order to carry out military and industrial
projects. He succeeded in obtaining a
commission from the engineering base
at Fort Belvoir, in Virginia.[29] His Parisian
colleague, Charles Siclis, known primarily

Top: **'Join an Air Force
Camouflage Batallion'**,
poster, 1941–1945.
The Wolfsonian-Florida
International University,
Miami Beach, Florida,
gift from The Ringling
School of Art and Design,
Sarasota, Florida

Norman Bel Geddes
**Portable camouflaged
tent hangar**, perspective
and plan, 1941.
Courtesy of the Estate of
Edith Lutyens Bel Geddes,
Harry Ransom Humanities
Research Center,
University of Texas
at Austin

for his modern theatres, arrived in New York in 1940 with the stated intention of offering a 'secret method' of camouflage to the American army, which had been developed during the French campaign, or so he declared to the press.[30] But he died in 1942 before revealing the still mysterious secrets.

Didactics of Camouflage, from Chicago to Brooklyn

The demand for camouflage even reached teaching institutions, from the most conservative to the most innovative. As opportunistic as ever, the École des Beaux-Arts in Paris devoted the Prix Labarre of 1939 to the theme 'A camouflaged city' and gave its seal of approval to the fogged watercolours of its students Roland Sonrier, Alexandre Colladant, Michel Oberdoerffer, Félix Le Saint and Pierre-Georges Lozouet.[31] The British Percy Johnson-Marshall taught camouflage in India and Burma as part of an engineering programme.[32] Louis I. Kahn, at the time a young professional in Philadelphia, followed courses in camouflage at the University of Pennsylvania and became particularly interested in decision theory, which seems to have influenced his post-war vision of urbanism.[33] Jean Labatut, a French architect who had been teaching at Princeton since 1928, conducted a course in camouflage in 1942–1943 that included experiments in painting the students' faces, as well as retrospective reflections on the transformations that had occurred since 1914.[34] The epidemic raged on, and in 1942 *The Architectural Forum* announced in the same issue that both Yale University and New York University (under the directorship of William A. Rose) were starting courses in camouflage for architects, engineers, industrial designers and factory managers.[35]

Artists started their own programmes. While Arshile Gorky was creating a course in camouflage at the Grand Central School of Art in New York, a unique experiment was taking place at the School of Design in Chicago. László Moholy-Nagy, a former *Meister* at the Bauhaus, and the painter György Kepes, who had worked with Le Corbusier, were involved in the effort to provide the municipality of Chicago, one of the most important centres of the American war effort, with anti-aircraft protection. Their programme for camouflaging the main buildings was so ambitious that it prompted the press to exclaim 'How Chicago May Hide from Bombers', referring to Kepes' course, while Moholy-Nagy imagined the possibilities of changing the edge of Lake Michigan, which he studied during observation flights.[36] It is certainly true that proposals like covering the superstructures of the Chicago Board of Trade with synthetic plants were not lacking in audacity.

In June and July 1942, Kepes took part in a workshop at the Fort Belvoir engineering school that covered the general principles of camouflage and aerial photography. Thanks to the support that Moholy-Nagy had managed to extract from Roosevelt, Kepes set up a course that ran for the rest of the summer in the countryside, and then resumed in Chicago from September 1942 to January 1943. The Office of Civilian Defense in Washington stated that it 'encourages architects and engineers to take the course [as] they are the ones to whom protective concealment problems will best be referred when such decisions are made by the War Production Board'. Chemists, psychologists

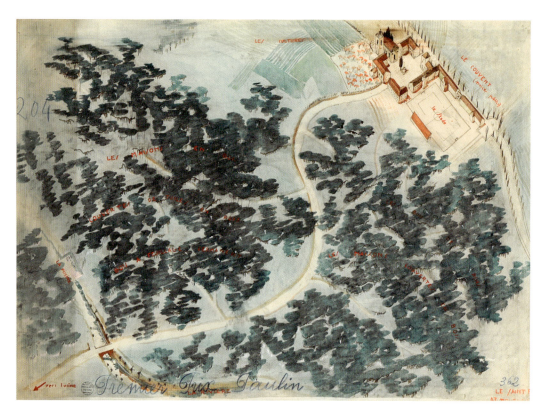

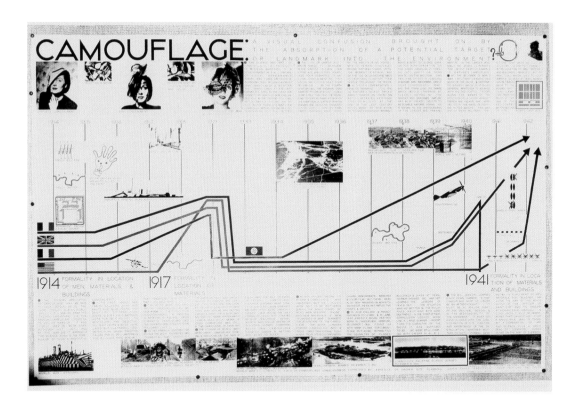

CAMOUFLAGE: A VISUAL CONFUSION BROUGHT ON BY THE ABSORPTION OF A POTENTIAL TARGET OR LANDMARK INTO THE ENVIRONMENT

1914 FORMALITY IN LOCATION OF MEN MATERIALS & BUILDINGS

1917 FORMALITY IN LOCATION OF MATERIALS

1941 FORMALITY IN LOCATION OF MATERIALS AND BUILDINGS

and specialists in optics were called upon to consult with architects such as George F. Keck, who taught at the school, and with landscape architects such as Ralph R. Root, together with military men, to define the goals and method of teaching.[37] The call was for integration, as opposed to the First World War, in which 'in camouflage the painter saw only painting problems, the architect only architecture, the engineer only engineering. They were unable to coordinate their expert knowledge with the necessary flexibility which emerges from a mutual grasp of each others problems.'

Moholy-Nagy and Kepes applied the Bauhaus theories of visual language to these problems: 'To grasp an object one needs first to isolate it from its surroundings by its outline. To understand its form one has to evaluate its constituent shapes by their tone, colour and texture values. These are among the basic elements of a visual language conscious possession of which gives the main direction toward the solution of every camouflage problem.' The pedagogy that was developed in Weimar and Dessau was applied to 'basic investigation of point, line, tone, colour, shape, etc., put in all their

Top: Félix Le Saint
'A Camouflaged Town', project for the Labarre prize at the École des Beaux Arts de Paris, 1939. École Nationale Supérieure des Beaux-Arts, Paris

Bottom: Pierre Georges Henri Lozouet
'A Camouflaged Town', project for the Labarre prize at the École des Beaux Arts de Paris, 1939. École Nationale Supérieure des Beaux-Arts, Paris

Jean Labatut
The development of camouflage from 1914 to 1941, didactic presentation board for students at Princeton, 1941. Department of Rare Books and Special Collections, Princeton University Library

School of Design in Chicago

247 East Ontario Street • Telephone Delaware 5775 and 5779

The course in the

Principles of Camouflage

approved by the OCD, Washington, D.C. has opened with 90 students.

Mr. George Kepes, head of the Light and Color Workshop who attended a camouflage instruction course given by the Army Engineer School at Fort Belvoir, Virginia, is in charge of the class.

The Office of Civilian Defense in Washington, D.C., especially encourages "selected professionals"

architects and engineers

to take this course. They are the ones to whom protective concealment problems will best be referred when such decisions are made by the War Production Board. In our Camouflage Course information will be given which will qualify those taking the course to prepare plans, in accordance with principles established by the O.C.D. in Washington, D.C.

We are entitled to give to such participants, after their successful graduation, certificates issued by the O.C.D., Washington, D.C., as shown on opposite page.

Enrolment for the course is still open. New students will receive a transcript of the lecture already given. The second class will meet next Wednesday evening at 6:30 P.M. The panel of lecturers for the course include the following military and civilian experts:

Dr. Theodore Ashford	Instructor in Dept. of Chemistry, University of Chicago
Mr. J. Copeland	Riggs Optical Co.
Prof. Milton Fox	Chairman of Camouflage Committee, Cleveland, Ohio.
Mr. Johns Hopkins	Senior Engineer of Blackout, Camouflage, and Protective Construction, Sixth Regional Office of Civilian Defense.
Mr. Otto Jelinek	Chief of Techniques, Chicago Metropolitan Area
Mr. George Fred Keck	Architect, Head of Architectural Dept. School of Design
Mr. John Moyer	Field Museum, Chicago.
Captain G. G. Preston	Royal Air Force
Mr. R. R. Root	Landscape Architect, author of "Camouflage with Planting"
Dr. Christian Ruckmick	Psychologist
Mr. M. B. Sweet	Northern Pigment Co. Pres. Color Research Assn.
Col. A. D. Tuttle	Medical Director, United Air Lines
An officer from Col. Goddard's Staff	Wright Field, Dayton, Ohio.

The class meets every Wednesday evening from 6:30 to 9:00 P.M. The fee for the Sixteen week course is $30.00.

possible interrelationships.' The psychology of form was the focus, through the study of 'psychological and physiological phenomena such as figure/ground relationship, effects of similarity, closure, inclusiveness, submergence, optical mixture of tone and color values, border, successive and simultaneous contrast, various forms of visual illusion'.[38] The final exercise was the camouflage of an air base.

The notes taken by the students, of whom there would be 110 in all, confirm the importance accorded to questions of vision and illusion, which were presented with great precision, along with very technical teaching on painting techniques, as well as the use of smoke emissions, netting and plants.[39] Already anticipating *Vision in Motion*, which was published in 1947

after Moholy-Nagy's death, Kepes insisted on the 'mobile elements' of camouflage: 'The air observer is mobile, the sunlight is mobile, the shadows are mobile.' He also stressed that 'the target has three-dimensional volume', and summed up the problem thus: 'The bombardier must perceive this three-dimensional volume. The camoufleur must detect this three-dimensional volume and eliminate it from aerial observation.'[40] No Daliesque magic here, but rather a rational approach that

'The Course in the Principles of Camouflage', leaflet, Chicago School of Design, Chicago, c. 1942. The Wolfsonian-Florida International University, Miami Beach, Florida, The Mitchell Wolfson, Jr. Collection

derives from the close intellectual relations between modern architecture and the psychology of form. In his classic work entitled *Gestalt Psychology*, the principal theoretician of this approach, Wolfgang Köhler, focused his attention on 'this real art for making objects disappear'. He describes it thus: 'The objects themselves are destroyed as optical realities and in their place appear meaningless patches which do not arouse military suspicion, since similar patches are produced constantly by the accidental properties of country and sea.'[41]

In 1942, Moholy-Nagy and Kepes, along with John L. Scott, published three articles in *Civilian Defense* that encapsulated their teaching and brought together material from the courses at the School of Design.[42] They based their work on an extensive analysis of the perception of light and shadow, but also took into account developments in photography, such as panchromatic films sensitive to infrared, which thus transformed the methodology of camouflage: 'To the naked eye, the real cannot be distinguished from the artificial, so colour in camouflage must be treated not from the standpoint of the bombardier but from the standpoint of the aerial photographer who precedes him.'[43] They devoted particular attention to light and shade. As they admitted, the goal was not to conceal objects such as grain silos, large bridges, gas storage tanks, water reservoirs, tall smokestacks or skyscrapers, but rather to deform them sufficiently so that pilots and bombardiers would be momentarily perplexed, just long enough to make them miss their targets.

Whereas this programme was solidly grounded in scientific observation, the teaching of Konrad F. Wittmann at the Pratt Institute in Brooklyn was in a completely different spirit. Wittmann published some critical and slightly moralistic articles in the American professional press on the urban landscape and the need for national planning.[44] He was more convincing when

Materials for the Camoufleur

Part III of "Civilian Camouflage Goes Into Action" takes up the various devices a camoufleur has at his disposal for getting the effects he wants. They range all the way from transplanted trees and shrubbery to the use of blowtorches for discoloring large grassed areas

BY JOHN L. SCOTT
in collaboration with
L. MOHOLY-NAGY
and
GYORGY KEPES
of The School of Design, Chicago

IN CIVILIAN camouflage, as in so many other wartime production operations, results are dependent on the economy and availability of materials. Shortages, priorities, and outright bans on the supplies and equipment he needs both tax the camoufleur's ingenuity and limit his methods. Many of his projects are large-scale undertakings, covering a wide area and consequently requiring an abundance of material, and the importance of the job must always be balanced against its cost.

Camouflaging an airport is a good case in point. It's one thing to conceal an oil tank or a small factory building, but something entirely different to disguise an airfield runway measuring some 250 feet in width by a mile or so in length. Such a project was recently handled, though, by covering an

September 1942   13

entire runway with a bituminous emulsion applied with a big sprinkler. Then a covering of wood chips was spread over the area and sprayed with paint of a color to match the surrounding grass. The air gun used for spraying the paint was mounted on a truck and the entire operation was performed in a relatively small time.

But airports don't just disappear overnight. And it seemed rea-

FIG. 22. The telltale regularity of a cylindrical object may be camouflaged with paint, with partial obliteration, with false shadow formation, or with all three, as was done here. The paint distorts the object through optical illusion, while the scaffolding at the top and side, covered with osnaburg or some other garnish, partially conceals the object and likewise throws confusing shadows

sonable to assume that this particular airport was already established in the enemy's records and calculations, so the whole operation had to be performed over again— in reverse. The airport, or something that looked exactly like it, had to be moved somewhere else so that when enemy planes came looking for it they wouldn't have any trouble in finding it.

As a result, a similar plot of

László Moholy-Nagy
György Kepes
'Materials for the Camoufleur',
illustration in *Civilian Defense*,
September 1942.
General Research Division,
The New York Public Library, Astor,
Lenox and Tilden Foundations

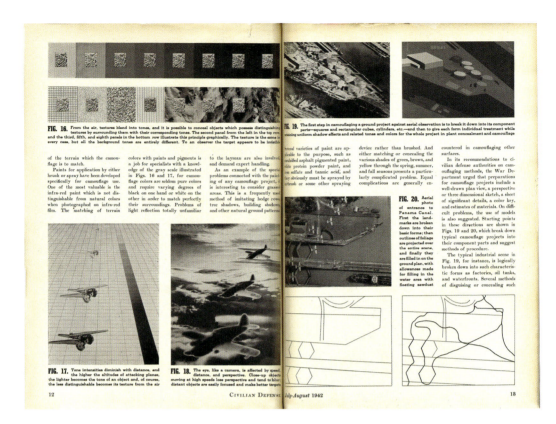

he criticised the prevailing state of affairs, one month after Pearl Harbor, and pointed out that: 'Here we have no standardized designs, no trained and experienced contractors, no material which we can pick out confidently from a catalogue and no assurance that untested ideas are really effective.' He dismissed the British precedents, with their stories about 'the frog, the moth, and the copperhead', and noted that 'camouflage is still considered in too many quarters a job for brush and paint pot as it was in World War I'. But the books 'dealing with protective coloration in the animal kingdom' can only lead to 'fallacious hopes and disastrous failures'. Camouflage 'cannot be accomplished through the study of zoology. It is a complex requiring the combined efforts of architects and technicians, industrial manufacturers, chemical experts, and town planners.'

For Wittmann, the camouflage of industrial installations was conceptually different from the camouflage of forces deployed at the front, which were essentially mobile. The problem was at the level of industry and engineering rather than of painting, and this was the basis for using architects, for 'the final goal of camouflage and industrial protection is a revision in principles of design. This involves making, perhaps for the first time, a search for principles in industrial design to be used in place of those hitherto dictated by arbitrary adherence to usage, plus the desire for easy production profits.'[45]

László Moholy-Nagy
György Kepes
A bird's eye view of
camouflage, double-page
spread from *Civilian Defense*,
July–August 1942.
Chicago Public Library

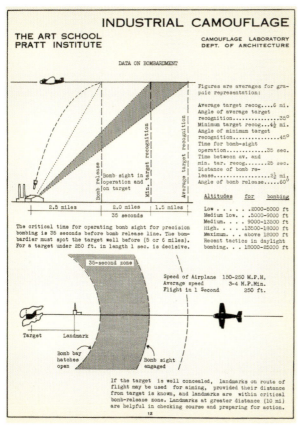

INDUSTRIAL CAMOUFLAGE

THE ART SCHOOL
PRATT INSTITUTE

CAMOUFLAGE LABORATORY
DEPT. OF ARCHITECTURE

DATA ON BOMBARDMENT

Figures are averages for graphic representation:

Average target recog....6 mi.
Angle of average target recognition..............35°
Minimum target recog..4½ mi.
Angle of minimum target recognition............45°
Time for bomb-sight operation.............35 sec.
Time between av. and min. tar. recog.......25 sec.
Distance of bomb release.................2½ mi.
Angle of bomb release.....60°

Altitudes	for	bombing
Low	. .2000-5000 ft
Medium low. .	.5000-9000 ft
Medium. . . .	9000-13500 ft
High.	13500-18000 ft
Maximum. . . .	above 18000 ft
Recent tactics in daylight bombing. . .	18000-25000 ft

The critical time for operating bomb sight for precision bombing is 35 seconds before bomb release line. The bombardier must spot the target well before (5 or 6 miles). For a target under 250 ft. in length 1 sec. is decisive.

35-second zone

Speed of Airplane 150-250 M.P.H.
Average speed 3-4 M.P.Min.
Flight in 1 Second 250 ft.

Target   Landmark

Bomb bay hatches open
Bomb sight engaged

If the target is well concealed, landmarks on route of flight may be used for aiming, provided their distance from target is known, and landmarks are within critical bomb-release zone. Landmarks at greater distance (10 mi) are helpful in checking course and preparing for action.

12

Data on bombardment, page from Konrad F. Wittmann, *Industrial Camouflage Manual*, 1942. CCA Collection

Wittmann's *Industrial Camouflage Manual*, published under the auspices of the Pratt Institute and dedicated to Homer Saint-Gaudens, remains one of the most popular books on the subject in North America. It came out of work carried out in a 'camouflage laboratory' established within the department of architecture and contains a set of precepts illustrated by lively graphic images, in the style of a comic strip. On the subject of industrial complexes, it deals with the decentralisation of the units of production, organic plans rather than orthogonal ones, and taking advantage of existing natural landscapes. On the subject of buildings, it covers the distortion of form and the distortion of shadows, studied by means of a 'sun machine', the transformation of the roof outline and roofing materials, and the use of irregular textures (natural or artificial plants, nets). The book studies some of the most tricky examples, notably cylindrical or spherical reservoirs, water tanks, chimneys and vertical silos.[46] The distribution of this simple, practical book was accompanied by articles presenting its contents in more accessible form illustrated with some of its most striking images,[47] while Wittmann disseminated his teachings in conferences, for example in Philadelphia, where Louis I. Kahn was in the audience.

Louis I. Kahn
Civilian camouflage drawing, the University of Pennsylvania, 1943.
Louis I. Kahn Collection,

The University of Pennsylvania and the Pennsylvania Historical and Museum Commission

Designing Camouflage

In addition to these training programmes, the armies also recruited architects directly. Some were given honorific positions; others were entrusted with delicate missions. In 1940, the French air ministry turned to Émile Maigrot, president of the SADG (Société des Architectes Diplômés par le Gouvernement) to direct work on camouflage.[48] On the other side of the Channel, a complex system was set up, starting with the creation of a sub-committee for camouflage for passive defence, within the Committee of Imperial Defence, established in 1936. After the Munich Agreement, a section for civilian camouflage was set up, until the Civil Defence Act of 1939 created the Civil Defence Camouflage Establishment, with Dr Stradling as the chief scientific advisor, with the director of the Royal College of Art having an advisory role. Ultimately, a Directorate of Camouflage was created, with Wing Commander

Hugh Casson
Camouflaged airfield, perspective, 1943. Victoria and Albert Museum, London, Archives of Sir Hugh Casson and Margaret MacDonald Casson, gift of the Casson daughters

Bottom: Hugh Casson **Revised camouflage scheme for Gloucester**, perspective, 1942. Victoria and Albert Museum, London, Archives of Sir Hugh Casson and Margaret MacDonald Casson, gift of the Casson daughters

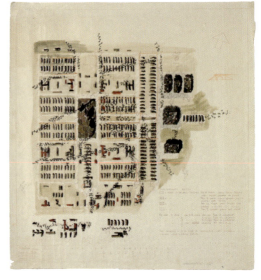

Hugh Casson
Camouflage gasometre,
perspective, 1944.
Victoria and Albert Museum,
London, Archives of Sir
Hugh Casson and Margaret
MacDonald Casson, gift
of the Casson daughters,

T. R. Cave-Browne-Cave as director. He sent missions abroad that included a trip by Captain Glasson to Russia in July 1941 and a series of lectures by the deputy chief of design Ironside to Canada and Washington. After the creation of the Civil Camouflage Assessment Committee at the beginning of 1942, only some two hundred sites were deemed to require protection against daylight raids; these were selected both for their monumental character and for the extent to which camouflage projects were already underway. But by June 1943, the various actions by the Admiralty, the War Office and the Air Ministry involved no fewer than 8,031 locations.[49]

In terms of concrete work, the Camouflage Development and Training Centre at Farnham Castle included architects such as Stirrat Johnson-Marshall and David Medd, under the direction of the set designer James Gardner. The bulk of their work consisted in the creation of decoys – false vehicles, tanks and other objects – which were used extensively and seemingly with relish by the British on battlefields from Tobruk to Normandy.[50] The contributions of an architect such as Hugh Casson were quite different. As the district Superintending Engineer of the Works & Buildings Department of the Air Ministry, he was based in Cheltenham, Gloucestershire,

from 1940 to 1943.[51] His letter of recommendation from the librarian of the RIBA to the RAF in 1940 provides insight into what was expected of a modern camouflager. 'In all his work, Mr Casson has shown himself a person of quite outstanding competence, both as regards the structural and planning and general architectural sides of his work. He is also an artist of great ability.'[52] Casson has left behind charming watercolours of camouflaged hangars and gas tanks, along with documentation of his work that enables us to reconstruct his process, based on aerial photographs and analytic sketches of the landscapes, in which airfields are located, the general plans of camouflage of the buildings are set forth, and drawings of the motifs selected for the standard Bellman or Robin hangars. He also developed schemes for the 'planned cultivation' of the land to obscure the orthogonal shapes of the hangars with vegetation.

In 1944, when *The Architectural Review* became interested in the meeting between the 'consciously functional' and the 'accidentally aesthetic' in camouflage, Casson affirmed, contrary to Dalí, that 'camouflage is not magic. Despite popular belief to the contrary, particoloured patterns, violently contrasted, confer no mantle of invisibility upon the object to which they are haphazardly applied. They may, indeed, do the reverse.' But he pointed out the discovery of a new kind of beauty: 'To see a camouflaged building looming through a grey November morning or aflame in the angry light of a June sunset, is to receive a tremendous visual thrill from the flow and flicker of its fantastic patterns and strange colours. The fact that this aesthetic experience is, so to speak, accidental, does not blunt the sharpness of its impact, but its nature perhaps cannot be accurately assessed without some knowledge of the true aims and principles of camouflage of which this beauty is so exciting a byproduct.'[53] Casson listed the progression of techniques from the 'infantile' stage to the 'adolescent' ones to the 'mature', and while acknowledging visual relationships with the paintings of Joan Miró and Juan Gris, whose work helped to foster an appreciation of abstract forms, as well as with Rococo architecture, he criticised any approach that was too overtly aesthetic. 'It would be only a slight exaggeration to say that the more intense the aesthetic effect, the less successful is likely to be the camouflage. If the shapes are exquisitely formed, then almost certainly the designer has been obsessed with pattern making.' Individualistic approaches are also subject to criticism: 'Certain designers even developed so personal a pattern style that those who were familiar with it could recognise at moderate range a camouflaged object as being the work of A or B. This may have been aesthetically amusing but it was probably poor camouflage.'

Casson was especially aware of the paradox of seeing architects who had actively promoted modern forms being employed to create illusions, and he expressed this in one of the most subtle remarks of the time on this theme: 'Architects are men trained in precision and in the sensitive expression of structure. Between the wars these qualities had crystallised into a sort of Puritanism. Ornament disappeared,

form was meticulously, almost anatomically expressed, materials were left unassisted to explain themselves. Buildings, crisp, gleaming, shapely, were designed and placed to contrast rather than merge with their surroundings. War, with its shortages, utility products and general austerity aggravated this rigorous approach. Yet here, in the midst of war, is two-dimensional ornament of the most sensational and boisterous kind, applied not to emphasise structure, but to destroy it. Solid is suggested where there is void, recession hinted at where there is projection. Beneath the rhythm of pattern, form seems to melt away. Here is strangeness indeed.' In the field, architects were recruited at every level of the chain of camouflage. At the conceptual level, one finds the French Prix de Rome winner Bernard Zehrfuss, who had joined the army of Marshal Weygand in the Near East at the beginning of the war, before pursuing his work in Tunisia after the arrival of the Allies.[54] At the level of implementation, the young Paolo Soleri, still a student at the Politecnico of Turin, worked unenthusiastically for twenty-two months in a camouflage unit of the Italian corps of Engineers.[55]

National Variations

The most extravagant projects were sometimes undertaken furthest from the theatres of operation. For example, the airplane factories on the West Coast of the United States were the object of particularly elaborate treatments in the months following Pearl Harbor, when the threat of Japanese air raids was taken very seriously. A special unit

of the Corps of Engineers was assembled for this purpose on the base at March Field, near Riverside, by Colonel John F. Ohmer, who recruited set designers from the main Hollywood studios – Metro-Goldwyn-Mayer, Disney, Fox, Paramount and Universal – to develop projects for the camouflage of some thirty military bases.[56] As for the factories, their enormous rectangular volumes for assembly lines were covered over with simulacra of residential blocks of detached family houses. This was the case of the Boeing Plant 2 in Seattle, where the architect William J. Bain, at the time the camouflage director for the state of Washington, constructed an entire landscape with Ohmer's help, which included some fifty houses, with trees and cars covering the more than five acres of assembly halls for B-17's and B-29's.

Further to the south, in the Los Angeles urban area, the Corps of Engineers worked on the Lockheed Vega factory in Burbank with a team of a dozen or so illustrators and decorators from the Disney studios, located in the same city, who were directed by Hal Adelquist.[57] And in Santa Monica, the most elaborate of these measures were

taken for the concealment of the Douglas factory by the architect H. Roy Kelley, a trusty specialist in houses in Colonial and Spanish revival styles, and the landscape architect Edward Huntsman-Trout, with the help of a team from the Warner studios.[58] An expanse of netting supported by four hundred poles canopied all the buildings on the site, upon which reduced-size wooden houses, as well as trees and pastures in feathered flocking were recreated, along with streets and fake cars at night. The illusion of a suburban neighbourhood was so successful that, according to legend, some pilots were unable to find the airfield, while the Warner studio, worried that they might be taken for a factory, adopted similar measures. The Douglas factory in Long Beach took a simpler approach, laying out a motif of streets on the roofs. However, once the United States had gained the strategic advantage in the Pacific, after the Battle of Midway in June 1942, the need for these measures would be called into question.

Camouflage of Boeing Plant 2, Seattle, aerial view, 1942.
Boeing Images

Given that wartime camouflage also required people with an understanding of topography and a knowledge of plants and their methods of cultivation, landscape architects inevitably also had a key role to play. The *Reichslandschaftsanwalt* (landscape advocate) Alwin Seifert, who had been appointed by Fritz Todt to work on the integration of motorways into the landscape for the Reich, was also part of camouflage operations.[59] In 1942, the Florentine

Top: **Camouflage of the Douglas aircraft factory**, Santa Monica, structure and canvas panels, seen from ground level, 1942. Santa Monica Public Library Image Archives, gift of the Museum of Flying

Bottom: **Camouflage of the Douglas aircraft factory**, Santa Monica, structural elements and fake vegetation and housing, seen from above, 1942. Santa Monica Public Library Image Archives, gift of the Museum of Flying

landscape architect Pietro Porcinai taught at the Italian engineering school in Civitavecchia. There he worked on projects for the camouflage of munitions

depots at Magliana, on the outskirts of Rome, and at Frosinone, and developed a principle of *mimetizzazione ideale* (ideal camouflage) for munitions depots, which he disguised as large farms, whose buildings were arranged in U or L shapes.[60] With the architect Nello Baroni, who had won the competition for the Florence railway station as a member of the Gruppo Toscano, Porcinai proposed creating a department of military engineers specialised in camouflage.

Differences in technical and military cultures shaped the field of camouflage, of course, as suggested by the differences in meaning between the French and English terms of 'camouflage', the Italian term *mimetizzazione*, the German term *Tarnung*, and the Russian term *maskirovka*. These differences were apparent in the different national styles. Some, like the Japanese, limited their practice to 'dazzle painting'. Others tended to the over-refined. In the Russian case, the policy of 'masking' included a number of measures that went beyond tactical camouflage to include

the large-scale concealment of civilian and military installations. Soviet camouflage manuals were more precocious than those of the other warring nations and included such interesting notions as *maskangar* for airplanes, an abbreviation for *maskirovanny angar* (camouflaged hangar), which became an important part of the landscape.[61]

Camouflage was clearly a less depressing sight than that of ruins and corpses, and it became an object of information campaigns, even propaganda, for the general public. Before the United States entered the war, The Museum of Modern Art in New York held an exhibition from May to September 1941 entitled 'Britain at War', a whole section of which was devoted to camouflage, which it presented as a shared activity of specialists complementing each other. As the painter Carlos Dyer wrote in the

German project for a camouflaged underground hangar, illustration in E. F. Burche, *Maskirovka v rabote vozdushnykh sil*, 1936. Collection of the author

catalogue, 'The practice of camouflage requires the collaboration of the military strategist, the architect and the artist. The military strategist decides what should be camouflaged, the architect and the artist possess, each in his field, the knowledge and technical ability required to meet the problems of camouflage design – they understand the fundamental relationships of plastic and graphic representation through the use of color, form and texture.'[62] One year later, in August and September 1942, the museum mounted a travelling exhibition entitled 'Camouflage for Civilian Defense', put together by Dyer with the help of the Pratt Institute and the informed advice of Homer Saint-Gaudens.

From the Battlefield to the Displacement of Cities

Accounts of the war tell of the major camouflage operations of the armed forces, by which the general staffs attempted to deceive their enemy as to their strategic or tactical intentions. The Russians and the British excelled at this. The former simulated preparation for attacks that would never take place, which kept German forces in place, while the British created phantom armies, at the Battle of El Alamein in North Africa for example,[63] and in the Operation Fortitude South, for which an entire fictional invasion force was assembled in Kent to divert attention from the preparations for the landing in Normandy. These operations were not only visual, they also included simulated radio traffic and sound, employing techniques from film with the help of experts such as Harold Burris-Meyer, who had worked on Disney's *Fantasia*.[64]

The use of camouflage in large cities remains to this day one of the most extraordinary chapters in the implementation of this strategy, for it dealt with the perception of a landscape of infrastructure, blocks, monuments and streets that was more complex than any countryside or desert. Camouflage started at the most basic level, at the very sources of information, with the organisation of ignorance. It started with pure and simple censorship of city plans and aerial photographs. For example, two overhead views of the port of Marseille were censored in the last issue of *L'Architecture d'aujourd'hui* in 1940 and replaced with white spaces.[65] Another technique, the systematic alteration of city plans, was widely practiced in the USSR, where every plan was a trick.

On the ground, urban camouflage aimed at producing large-scale illusion. It was not simply a matter of ambiguity in the perception of a factory, some hangars or a landing field. Its goal was rather to erase or displace an extremely recognisable sight, as the French had thought to do twenty years previously with their 'faux Paris'. During the Libyan campaign, which included extensive deception of every sort and played a decisive role in the British victory at El Alamein, the port of Alexandria, an essential element to the British logistics, was visually displaced in June 1941 and recreated further south at Maryut Bay, where the Luftwaffe planes dropped their bombs on a canvas decor. The project was overseen by the Royal Engineers' director of camouflage in the Middle East, filmmaker Geoffrey Barkas, with the help of the 'magic gang' of the illusionist Jasper Maskelyne, who pushed concern for verisimilitude to the point of simulating the after-effects of raids through fake ruins.[66]

The Russians were aware of the 'faux Paris' precedent[67] and worked at faking Moscow. Only four days after the beginning of Operation Barbarossa, General N. K. Spiridonov presented two solutions for camouflaging the Kremlin to Lavrenti Beria, the deputy chairman of the Council of People's Commissars. The first proposal consisted in concealing the gold roofs of the churches, removing the crosses and reproducing the colours of the Kremlin on nearby roofs and neighbouring spaces. The second consisted instead of simulating housing blocks on the Kremlin itself and constructing a false port on the Moskva River. All of this had the purpose of rendering it difficult to make out the Kremlin against the backdrop of the city and to limit the effects of potential dive-bombing. It was suggested to recruit from the staff of architects working on the construction of the Palace of the Soviets – which was meant to be built nearby – and to use 'important theatrical set designers'.[68] Lenin's mausoleum was wrapped in a wooden structure to look like a church.

Margaret Bourke-White went to Moscow to photograph the Russian war effort. It was particularly easy for her to witness the painting of Manezh Square, as she was staying in the American embassy, which at the same time overlooked the square, in a neo-Palladian apartment building by Ivan Zholtovsky. She described the spectacle in *Shooting the Russian War*: 'Moscow went paint mad. Rooftops began appearing in flat wash tones in all squares and plazas.

Margaret Bourke-White
'Camouflaging Moscow',
Moscow (1941), view of Manezh
Square from the American
Embassy, photograph
reproduced in *Shooting
the Russian War*, 1942.
CCA, copyright of the Estate of
Margaret Bourke-White / Licensed
by VAGA, New York, NY

Imitation windows were painted realistically on the pavement, with shadows indicated around the edges to give the illusion of depth. Little artificial villages were erected in unexpected spots here and there and moved about from time to time, to distract the enemy from their real objectives. Artificial rooftops were thrown across the banks of the rivers to mislead enemy planes that might try to follow the rivers from the air.'[69] Other comparable programmes were developed for Leningrad: during the summer of 1941, the architect Nikolai Baranov deployed nets and false foliage to camouflage the old monastery of Smolny, which had housed the Congress of Soviets in 1917, before Lenin had established the power of the Bolsheviks. The objective in this case was to protect an emblematic site of the new regime, but more readily identifiable elements of the old city were concealed as well, such as the Admiralty, a key landmark forming the base for the 'trident' of the city's main avenues, which the architects Yulia P. Gremiachinskaia, N. Navrotskaia and Fiodor F. Oleinik concealed under vegetation.[70] Guided by specific directives from the professional organisations, architects played an important part in disseminating the principles and techniques of *maskirovka*.

In July 1942, the board of the Union of Architects of the USSR adopted a 'resolution on the issues of camouflage' assessing the work of the 'hundreds of qualified architects' working on the ground and pursuing research with the Academy of Sciences. The resolution emphasised the lack of proper materials, especially paint colours, which required the development of alternatives, and it insisted on a series of measures, like working on entire cities, while at the same time placing 'strict limits' on the number of objects to be camouflaged, scaling down projects, in some cases to simple colouring, as well as calling for the effective use of decoys and the use of found materials.[71] In particular, it called for better training of architects through the development of a course of instruction and a specific manual. The latter would

Nikolai Baranov
Project for the camouflage of the Smolny monastery,
Leningrad, perspective, 1941.
Shchusev State Museum of Architecture

The centre of Hamburg
and the Innenalster,
initial and camouflaged
states (1942), illustrations
in F. Werner, *Das Gesicht der
Hansestadt Hamburg im Wandel
der Jahre 1939–1945*, 1945.
CCA Collection

be published in 1944, at a time when the camouflage of cities was being slowly abandoned.[72]

In a number of German cities, from Berlin to Munich, similar measures were taken to disguise the most characteristic urban elements: the streets, squares and monuments. The most discussed visual manipulation of the urban landscape during the war took place in Hamburg, where a large-scale operation was undertaken during the winter of 1941 to visually 'displace' a very distinctive part of the city. The primary aim of the operation was to protect the main railway line from bombing. To this end, a part of the Aussenalster, a lake extending to the north-east, was covered with almost ten acres of false islands built on floats in order to simulate the Binnenalster nearby. The Lombardsbrücke and the railway bridge thus became less visible and were also replicated 600 metres further away. The main railway station itself was disguised by painting large motifs simulating streets on its glass roof. These measures were very soon fairly widely known, to the extent that Wittmann – who was very familiar with Hamburg – criticised it in his manual. 'The pattern of the faked city blocks is generally too bold and lacks detail, showing flat roofs instead of the detailed pattern of pitched roofs in this, the very oldest part of Hamburg. The false bridge . . . is dull and flat in appearance, too definitely contoured, and with not enough texture. The depth effect of shadow is lacking.'[73] For his part, Casson would see it as a 'mature' and 'bold' example of camouflage. He judged the treatment of the railway station to be a success, even though the tracks running in from the south, which

had not been camouflaged, betrayed the actual arrangement of the site.[74] At any rate, none of these ingenious measures bothered the British airmen, who successfully destroyed the city centre during Operation Gomorrah in July and August 1943.[75]

Camouflage strategies had their limits, at least in the photo-interpretation units.[76] The use of stereo-photography enabled the identification of two-dimensional forms that appeared as volumes to the naked eye, rendering the large-scale constructions

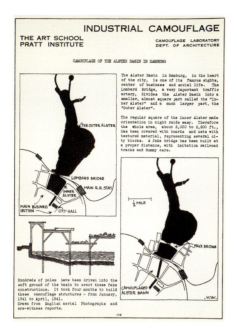

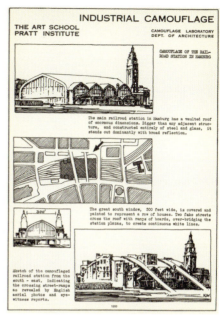

of the kind made in Moscow and Hamburg essentially futile. Furthermore, infrared photography, which Kodak had developed by 1937, made it possible to recognise simulated plants, which are less reflective than natural flora. It also led to the rapid development in Germany of reflective chemical agents, a new form of camouflage in response to this new technique of detection. But the objectivity of vision was not necessarily the main issue, and Casson was correct in emphasising that the goal of camouflage 'was to deceive the eye of the pilot (*not* of the camera) in such a way that recognition of the target is delayed or prevented for as long a time as possible. As he approaches his target, the pilot . . . is a busy and probably uncomfortable man, clumsily clothed, beset by complicated instruments, harried perhaps by fighters or flak.'[77]

Despite its limitations due to improvements in photographic technology and, on the Allied side, to the development of bomb sights, the use of camouflage went far beyond the saga of successful exercises in deception and found resonance with art historians sensitive to

psychological issues. For example, in *Art and Visual Perception*, Rudolf Arnheim, writing on the subject of lighting, explained that 'the effect of illumination can be compensated by appropriate shading so that the roundness of the volumes becomes invisible: the principle is used in camouflage'.[78] Few overall accounts would be drawn up regarding the considerable effort on each side to conceal its cities, forces and intentions. Homer Saint-Gaudens produced one of the most lucid analyses, in which he expressed his admiration for the achievements of the Germans, who used fewer means and in more 'scrupulous' ways. He felt that the Allies' success in concealing and protecting targets was due more to their air superiority than the effectiveness of their camouflage, which with hindsight often proved futile.[79]

Analysis of the camouflage of the centre and railway station of Hamburg, plates from Konrad F. Wittmann, *Industrial Camouflage Manual*, 1942. CCA Collection

1. Salvador Dalí, 'Total Camouflage for Total War', *Esquire*, vol. 18, no. 2 (August 1942), 130.
2. 'Art by Accident', *The Architectural Review*, vol. 96, no. 573 (September 1944), 63.
3. Roger Caillois, *Le Mimétisme animal* (Paris: Hachette, 1963), 51.
4. In the 1930s, the two approaches were combined in the quest for anti-aircraft protection: Alfred Giesler 'Tarnung, Verdunkelung, Scheinanlagen und die Räumung großer Städte bei Luftangriffsgefahr', *Gasschutz und Luftschutz*, vol. 2, no. 1 (January 1932), 4–6.
5. Major Robert P. Breckenridge, *Modern Camouflage, The New Science of Protective Concealment* (New York: Farrar & Rinehart, Inc., 1942), 3.
6. Paolo Fabbri, 'Estrategias del camuflaje', interview with Tiziana Migliore, *Revisa de Occidente*, no. 330 (November 2008), 89–110. See also Massimo Scolari, 'La costruzione dell'invisibile: occultamento e camouflage nella guerra moderna', *Eidos*, no. 6 (1990), 56–78.
7. Among recent works, see Timothy Newark, *Camouflage: Now You See Me, Now You Don't* (London: Thames and Hudson, 2007). Peter Forbes, *Dazzled and Deceived: Mimicry and Camouflage* (New Haven and London: Yale University Press, 2009).
8. Gerald H. Thayer, *Concealing Coloration in the Animal Kingdom, an Exposition of the Laws of Disguise, through Color and Pattern, Being a Summary of Abbott H. Thayer's Discoveries* (New York: Macmillan, 1909).
9. Roger Caillois, 'Camouflage', in *Méduse et Cie* (Paris: Gallimard, 1960), 115–16.
10. Albert Roskam, 'Dazzle Painting: arte come camuffamento, camuffamento come arte', *Casabella*, no. 557 (May 1989), 24–26.
11. Gertrude Stein, *Picasso* (London: B. T. Batsford, 1938), 11.
12. Roland Penrose, *Picasso, His Life and Work* (London: Granada, 1981), 199.
13. Jean de Pierrefeu, 'La section de camouflage (1915–1918)', *L'Illustration*, 3 January 1920, 14–18.
14. André Mare, *Cubisme et camouflage: 1914–1918* (Bernay: Musée Municipal des Beaux-Arts, 1998).
15. 'Un faux Paris imaginé par la DCA', *L'Illustration*, 2 October 1920, 245–46. 'Planned to Build Three False Parises; Elaborate Project to Fool Air-Bombers

Was Afoot When the Armistice Came', *The New York Times*, 2 October 1920. Lieutenant-Colonel Vauthier, *Le Danger aérien et l'avenir du pays* (Nancy, Paris and Strasbourg: Éditions Berger-Levrault, 1930), 140–43. See also Lieutenant-Colonel Delanney, 'L'attaque aérienne massive du territoire', *Revue des forces aériennes*, May 1930, 503–07.
16. Colonel Laviano, 'La défense contre les attaques aériennes', *Rivista di Artiglieria italiana*, July 1928; Colonel Manlio Merzari, 'La défense aérienne du territoire', *Rivista militare italiana*, July 1928; in Vauthier, op. cit. note 15, 149.
17. See the biography published in Bernard Dorival, *Lapicque* (Zurich: Galerie Nathan, 1978), 92.
18. Fernand Léger, letter to Georges Huisman, AN F 213972, cited by Pierre Assouline, *L'Homme de l'art. D. H. Kahnweiler 1884–1979* (Paris: Folio, 1989), 489.
19. MoMA Archives, dossier to Exhibition #190, 'Camouflage for Civilian Defense'.
20. Guy Hartcup, *Camouflage. A History of Concealment and Deception in War* (Newton Abbott, London and Vancouver: David and Charles, 1979), 51ff. Henrietta Gooden, *Camouflage and Art: Design for Deception in World War 2* (London: Unicorn Press, 2007), 22–23.
21. Roland Penrose, *Home Guard Manual of Camouflage* (London: George Routledge & Sons Ltd., 1941).
22. Julian Trevelyan, 'The Technique of Camouflage', *The Architectural Review*, vol. 96, no. 573 (September 1944), 68–70.
23. Dalí, op. cit. note 1, 65 and 130.
24. Homer Saint-Gaudens, 'Camouflage and Art', *Art Bulletin*, vol. 2, no. 1 (September 1919), 26, cited by Roy R. Behrens, *Camoupedia: A Compendium on Art, Architecture, and Camouflage* (Dysart, Iowa: Bobolink Books, 2009), 30.
25. Le Corbusier, 'Deductions consécutives troublantes', *L'Esprit nouveau*, no. 19, December 1923, n.p., quoted by Bruno Reichlin, 'Le Corbusier vs. de Stijl', in Yve-Alain Bois, Jean-Paul Rayon and Bruno Reichlin, *De Stijl et l'architecture en France* (Liège: Mardaga, 1985), 103.
26. Norman Bel Geddes, meeting notes from a meeting with Albert Kahn in Detroit, 15 May 1942, Bel Geddes

archives, Harry Ransom Center, University of Texas, Austin, dossier 462/2.
27. Homer Saint-Gaudens, 'Camouflage – World War II', *Military Engineer*, vol. 38, no. 7 (July 1946), 289.
28. Lawrence Langner, Secretary NIC, to Thomas R. Taylor, Director of Staff, NIC, 2 February 1942, Harry Ransom Center, University of Texas, Austin, dossier 342.
29. Taylor Stoehr, 'The Goodman Brothers and *Communitas*', in Kimberly J. Elman and Angela Giral, *Percival Goodman. Architect, Planner, Teacher, Painter* (New York: Columbia University, Miriam and Ira D. Wallach Art Gallery, 2001), 33.
30. 'New Camouflage to be Offered U.S. French Designer Has Secret Method for Use on Planes and Munition Works', *The New York Times*, 14 November 1940.
31. École Nationale Supérieure des Beaux-Arts, Paris, architecture student drawings, LAB 96–99.
32. Percy Johnson-Marshall Archives, University of Edinburgh.
33. Louis I. Kahn Collection, University of Pennsylvania, Folder 030.II.A.68.16. See Andrew Shanken, 'The Uncharted Kahn: The Visuality of Planning and Promotion in the 1930's and 1940's', *The Art Bulletin*, vol. 88, no. 2 (2006), 310–27.
34. See the documents held at the Princeton University Library, Jean Labatut Papers, 1915–1983, sub-series 3D. See Jorge Otero-Pailos, *Architecture's Historical Turn: Phenomenology and the Rise of the Postmodern* (Minneapolis: University of Minnesota Press, 2010), 27–32.
35. *The Architectural Forum*, vol. 77, no. 3 (September 1942), 194.
36. 'How Chicago May Hide From Bombers!', *Chicago Herald-American*, 12 January 1942. See also 'Kelly and Army Plan Hiding of City from Foe', *Chicago Daily News*, 8 May 1942. Sybil Moholy-Nagy, *Moholy-Nagy, Experiment in Totality* (Cambridge, Mass.: MIT Press, 1969), 184. On the programmes at the school during this period, see Alain Findeli, *Le Bauhaus de Chicago: l'œuvre pédagogique de László Moholy-Nagy* (Sillery: Septentrion, 1995), 87–108.
37. Prospectus for the School of Design, 1942. The Wolfsonian, Miami Beach. See also the certificate given to Kepes by Captain Chas. J. Craig, Corps of Engineers Secretary, The Engineer

School, Belvoir, Virginia, Archives of American Art, 5303.

38. 'Outline of the Camouflage Course at the School of Design in Chicago 1941–1942', IIT Archives, Chicago, Institute of Design Records. Acc. #1998.31, box 3, folder 4.

39. Findeli, op. cit. note 36, 95.

40. M. Seklemian, 'A Study in the Principles of Camouflage, Conducted at the School of Design, Chicago', 1942, IIT Archives, Chicago, Institute of Design Records. Acc. #1998.31, box 3, folder 4. See also the version by Patrick O'Reilly Bird, 'A Study in the Principles of Camouflage', ibid.

41. Wolfgang Köhler, *Gestalt Psychology* (New York: Liveright, 1929), 131.

42. John L. Scott, László Moholy-Nagy and György Kepes, 'Civilian Camouflage Goes into Action', *Civilian Defense*, vol. 2 (June 1942), 7–11 and 33–34; 'A Bird's-Eye View of Camouflage', July–August 1942, 10–14 and 37; 'Materials for the Camoufleur', September 1942, 13–16.

43. Scott, Moholy-Nagy and Kepes, 'A Bird's-Eye View of Camouflage', op. cit. note 42, 37.

44. Konrad F. Wittmann, 'American Architecture Viewed Objectively', *Pencil Points*, vol. 21, no. 3 (March 1941), 109–202. 'Planning for Victory is Planning the Future', *Pencil Points*, vol. 23, no. 5 (May 1942), 301–02.

45. Konrad F. Wittmann, 'The Camouflage Dilemma', *Pencil Points*, vol. 23 (January 1942), 13–14.

46. Konrad F. Wittmann, *Industrial Camouflage Manual, Prepared for the Industrial Camouflage Program at Pratt Institute, Brooklyn, New York* (New York: Reynold Publishing Co., 1942).

47. 'Putting Blinders on the Axis. Industrial Camouflage Hampers Accurate Bombing Raids', *Popular Science*, October 1942, 90–94.

48. See the administrative documents conserved in the Fonds Maigrot, Cité de l'Architecture et du Patrimoine, Fonds 82 IFA 001.

49. Ministry of Home Security, *Camouflage of Vital Factories and Key Points* (London: Ministry of Home Security, 1946).

50. Andrew Saint, *Towards a Social Architecture: the Role of School Buildings in Post-War England* (New Haven: Yale University Press, 1987), 17–31.

51. A drawing from his studio is published in Hugh Casson, 'Christmas Eve at the Site', *The Architects' Journal*, 23 December 1943; reproduced in Gooden, op. cit. note 20, 77.

52. Edward Carter, RIBA librarian, to the State Undersecretary for the Air, 4 July 1940, Victoria and Albert Museum, Archives of Hugh Casson and Margaret MacDonald Casson.

53. Hugh Casson, 'The Aesthetics of Camouflage', *The Architectural Review*, vol. 96, no. 573 (September 1944), 63.

54. Bernard Zehrfuss, autobiographical account assembled by Philippe Simon, *Mini PA* no. 20 (Paris: Pavillon de l'Arsenal, 1991).

55. Sherwood Davidson Kohn, 'Paolo Soleri Thinks Very Big', *The New York Times*, 26 July 1970, 30.

56. United Scenic Artists Archives, microfilm, 1897–1978, New York University, Bobst Library.

57. Behrens, op. cit. note 24, 19.

58. 'U.S. at War: The Camoufleurs', *Time Magazine*, 6 August 1945.

59. Thomas Zeller, '"Ganz Deutschland sein Garten". Alwin Seifert und die Landschaft des Nationalsozialismus', in *Naturschutz und Nationalsozialismus*, edited by Joachim Radkau and Frank Uekötter (Frankfurt-am-Main: Camus Verlag, 2003), 273–308.

60. Pietro Porcinai, 'Mimetizzazione ideale dei depositi di munizioni', 11 December 1942, Porcinai archives, Florence. My thanks to Valentina Mulas for pointing me in this direction.

61. E. F. Burche, *Maskirovka v rabote vozdushnykh sil* (Moscow: Voenizdat, 1936).

62. Carlos Dyer, 'The Role of the Artist in Camouflage', in *Britain at War*, edited by Monroe Wheeler (New York: The Museum of Modern Art, 1941), 90–91.

63. Henrietta Gooden, 'Desert Camouflage' and 'Operation Overlord', in op. cit. note 20, 105–31.

64. Philip Gérard, *Secret Soldiers: How a Troupe of American Artists, Designers, and Sonic Wizards won World War II's Battles of Deception Against the Germans* (New York: Dutton, 2002), 100–21.

65. 'L'aménagement du port de Marseille', *L'Architecture d'aujourd'hui*, vol. 11, no. 3–4 (1940), 16–17.

66. David Fisher, *The War Magician* (New York: Coward-McCann, 1983), 85–97. On decoys, see Charles Cruickshank, *Deception in World War II* (Oxford and New York: Oxford University Press, 1979).

67. E. F. Burche reproduces it, op. cit. note 61, 50.

68. N. K. Spiridonov, note to L. I. Beria, 26 June 1941, in V. S. Khristoforov and V. S. Vinogradov, *Lubianka v dni bitvy za Moskvu* (Moscow: Zvonnitsa, 2002), 32.

69. Margaret Bourke-White, 'Camouflaging Moscow', in *Shooting the Russian War* (New York: Simon & Schuster, 1943), 77.

70. See the plan in Yu. Yu. Bakhareva, T. V. Kovaleva and T. G. Shishkina, *Arkhitektory blokadnogo Leningrada* (Saint Petersburg: Gosudarstvenny Muzei Istorii Sankt-Peterburga, 2005), 45.

71. *Rezolyutsia soveshchania pri Pravlenii SSS SSSR po voprosam maskirovki*, 1 and 2 July 1942, TsGALI Moscow, collection 674, op. 2, dossier 100, pp. 34–35, in *Iz istorii sovetskoi arkhitektury 1941–1945 gg.: Dokumenty i materialy: Khronika voennykh let: Arkhitekturnaia pechat*, edited by Tatiana Malinina (Moscow: Nauka, 1978), 45.

72. K. S. Alabian, F. F. Kizelov and Iu. Savitskii, *Spravochnik maskirovshchika* (Moscow: Gosudarstvennoe arkhitekturnoe izdatelstvo Akademii arkhitektury SSSR, 1944).

73. Wittmann, op. cit. note 46, 121.

74. Casson,op. cit. note 53, p. 65.

75. Davide Deriu, 'Between Veiling and Unveiling: Modern Camouflage and the City as a Theater of War', in *Endangered Cities: Military Power and Urban Societies in the Era of the World Wars*, edited by Marcus Funck and Roger Chickering (Boston: Brill Academic Publishers, 2004), 15–34.

76. See the recollections of a photo-interpreter: Ursula Powys-Lybbe, *The Eye of Intelligence* (London: W. Kimber, 1983).

77. Casson, op. cit. note 53, 64.

78. Rudolf Arnheim, *Art and Visual Perception: a Psychology of the Creative Eye* (London: Faber & Faber, 1956), 255.

79. Saint-Gaudens, loc. cit. note 27, 287–90.

INDUSTRIAL CAMOUFLAGE

**THE ART SCHOOL
PRATT INSTITUTE**

CAMOUFLAGE LABORATORY
DEPT. OF ARCHITECTURE

PRINCIPLES OF INDUSTRIAL CAMOUFLAGE
Texture of Roofs

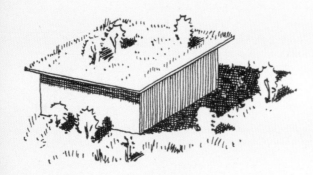

Roofs which are planted with grass, or even with small shrubs can match their surroundings almost entirely, under all weather and light conditions.

Surrounding with trees gives better concealment and natural irregularity of light and shadow. Trees play an important part in the design of natural camouflage.

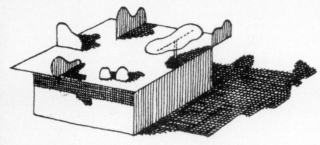

Vertical, irregular slabs, or horizontal slabs, elevated several feet, cast irregular shadows to distort the monotony of large roofs. Gravel, cinders, and stones of lightweight, porous concrete give rough texture.

COLORATION AND COLOR TRANSFORMATION

Camouflage net is
sprayed with paint.

Vividly-dyed fabrics
are spread on roof.

Whatever the original color of the texture material, it will
fade in time, get dirty and dusty, and will finally appear
gray. Restoring the colors will be necessary. In addition
it is imperative to synchronize camouflage colors with those
of the adjacent landscape for each season of the year.

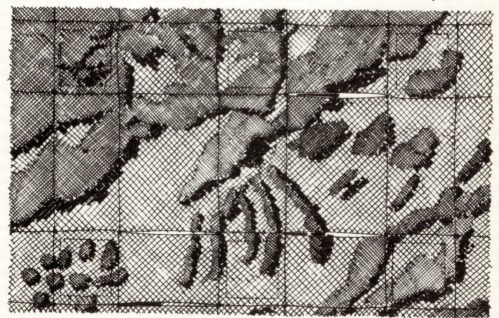

Color transformation can be made in two ways: 1-Spraying the
nets (or texture) from above, and 2-Displaying vividly painted boards or fabrics on the roof, below the camouflage construction. This color shines through the openings of the
net and gives additional coloration. The pattern should be
varied and spotty - not too uniform - with some boldness of
detail.

64

**'Coloration and color
transformation'**, plate in
Konrad F. Wittmann, *Industrial
Camouflage Manual*, 1942.
CCA Collection

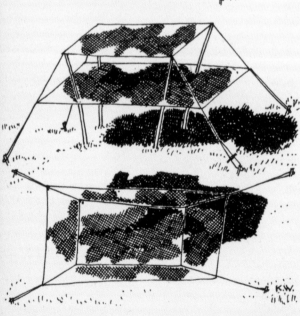

ARTIFICIAL TREES I

Artificial trees are built not only to hide installations underneath, but to change the pattern of the landscape all around the factory. Instead of eliminating shadows, they are built to create them.

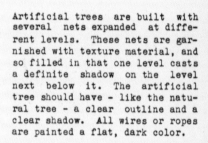

Artificial trees are built with several nets expanded at different levels. These nets are garnished with texture material, and so filled in that one level casts a definite shadow on the level next below it. The artificial tree should have - like the natural tree - a clear outline and a clear shadow. All wires or ropes are painted a flat, dark color.

Poles of any kind may be used, provided they are painted dark. Three or four poles are used to produce tall and spreading trees, forming a supporting frame for the highest net, which is garnished like a flat-top. This garnishing should not be too flat or too dense, but should show a loose pattern of spreading branches, casting shadows to the second net and to the ground.

'**Artificial trees**', plate in Konrad F. Wittmann, *Industrial Camouflage Manual*, 1942. CCA Collection

INDUSTRIAL CAMOUFLAGE

**THE ART SCHOOL
PRATT INSTITUTE**

CAMOUFLAGE LABORATORY
DEPT. OF ARCHITECTURE

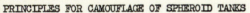

PRINCIPLES FOR CAMOUFLAGE OF SPHEROID TANKS

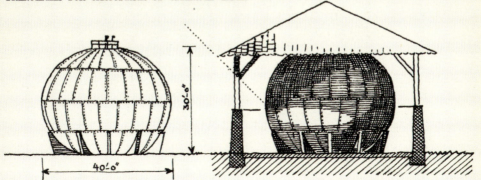

These tanks are mostly of bright metal and, by their spherical form, reflect the light strongly.

A practical and permanent method of concealing such tanks would be to build a square roof over them, imitating a house, with a protecting wall to avoid inundation and spreading fire. This is advisable however, only in a surrounding of similar structures.

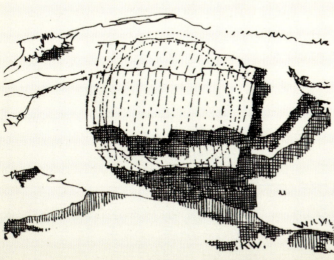

If embankments and varied terrain can be created, a light "roof" of irregular shape is advisable. This roof can be constructed of light trusses, and lightweight boards, in order to produce irregular shadowlines, which will blend with the shadows of the terrain.

90

'Principles for camouflage of spheroid tanks', plate in Konrad F. Wittmann, *Industrial Camouflage Manual*, 1942. CCA Collection

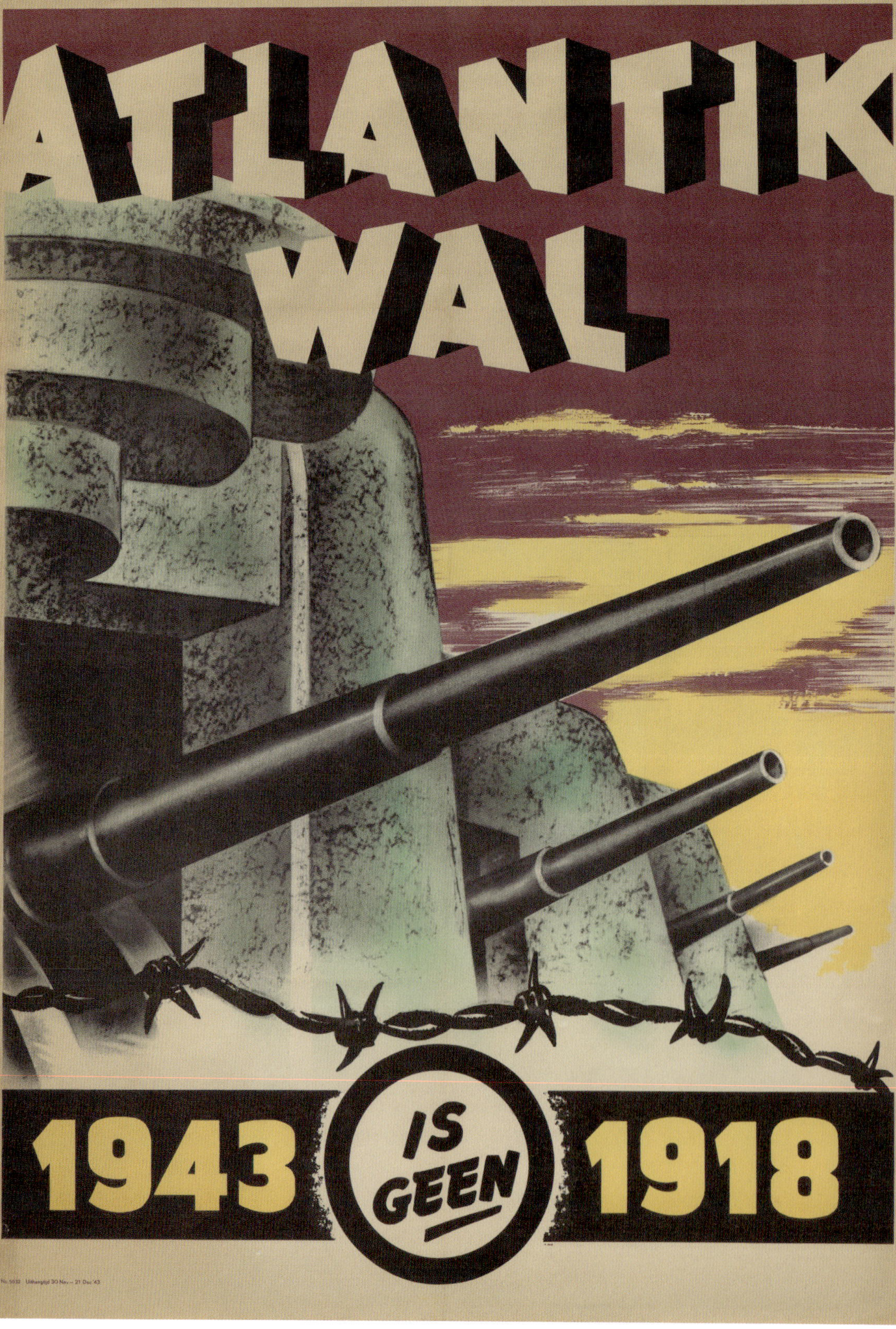

Uithangtijd 30 Nov — 21 Dec '43

7/ Architects and Bombs, from Bunkers to Napalm

Fortress Europe was three dimensional, the casemates on the beaches complemented the anti-aircraft shelters of the cities, the submarine bases were but the counterparts of industry's subterranean bases. Space was at last homogenised, absolute war had become a reality, and the monolith was its monument.
Paul Virilio, *Bunker Archeology*, 1975[1]

The portrait of the architect that Vitruvius presents in his *Ten Books of Architecture* is both that of a technician in the erection of defensive works and an inventor of machines to ruin them. This double game would also be played out in the Second World War, although the dialectic between the defensive and the offensive would be vastly different in scale, given all the technical revolutions that had taken place since the invention of gunpowder, and particularly since the invention of aerial warfare. The professionalization of the art of war, which was conducted by military men trained in modernised schools, left little place for architects as independent experts when it came time to designing things that would be of direct use in conflict. The laws of chemistry relating to explosives and ballistics took precedence over spatial and aesthetic considerations, although

'Atlantic Wall, 1943 is not 1918', German poster printed in the Netherlands, 1943. The Wolfsonian-Florida International University, Miami Beach, Florida, The Mitchell Wolfson, Jr. Collection

the latter were not neglected altogether. Architects were still involved at various levels in the conduct of the war, on the defensive side in the construction of fortifications – on first a national and then a continental level – and in various ways on the offensive side, applying their expertise both to planning effective bombing and simultaneously to the 'enlightened' protection of heritage.

Fortified Fronts

The most extensive and massive works created before and during the war were fortifications, whose only precedents in territorial extent were the Great Wall of China and the ring of citadels by Vauban. Although architects were only marginally involved in their design and construction, the construction, logistical and design issues involved intersected at many points with their practice within the opposing camps. In actual fact, the Second World War combined the most rapid military operations, made possible by mobility on land, at sea and in the air, with traditional warfare of position. Significant works were created for the latter. In the realm of fortifications, the era of 'lines' preceded the era of ramparts (the term *Wall* is used in both German and English). The French preparations for war were marked by the saga of the Maginot Line. To use perhaps abusively Bernard Rudofsky's terms, the Maginot Line was, like many defensive works, an eminent example of 'architecture without architects'.[2] And its construction provides evidence to support the hypothesis of the continuity between the two wars, for it was based on the model of the fort of Verdun, which had remained almost completely intact after all the battles of 1916.

After the creation of the Commission de Défense des Frontières in 1922 and extensive debate during the 1920s, the idea of a continuous fortification from Alsace to Belgium was officially proposed in 1927, with the support of Marshal Pétain and General Weygand. It was approved in 1929 by the minister of war, André Maginot, its strongest political supporter, who likened it to 'an underground fleet'.[3] The work was undertaken on a discontinuous front stretching from the Mediterranean to the Lorraine region, and although it was the subject of intense public debate and differences of opinion, it would be justified after 1932 as a project that offset the economic crisis, and it was completed in 1936. The work was hierarchically organised, with two 'fortified regions' separated by the Sarre gap, each of which consisted of four 'fortified sectors' of five to fifteen fortifications. Each of these, in turn, combined *grands ouvrages*, which could contain as many as a thousand persons, with *petits ouvrages* and casemates. Beneath the ground was a complex maze of spaces that were protected from gas and used to garrison troops. Many of these were linked by galleries and electric rail lines. Its protrusions above ground gave little sense of its size and it had little visible impact on the landscape. The different parts were also meant to be able to defend each other

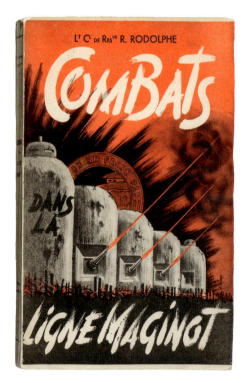

in the case of attack. But they would hardly have the chance to do so, as Guderian sent the Wehrmacht armoured forces through the poorly defended sector of the Ardennes, which Pétain had mistakenly thought to be impassable.[4] Other parts of the line did resist the German attacks, which the Germans had trained for in the Heuberg camp, using sheet metal replicas of the line's casemates. Finally, in the latter stages of the war, some of the largest bunkers that had remained completely intact were used for the manufacture of German military equipment.

After 1936, the organisation set up by the Nazi engineer Fritz Todt for the construction of the motorway system was redeployed in the construction of the Westwall, which the allies would call the 'Siegfried

Cover of Lieutenant-Colonel René Rodolphe, **'Battles in the Maginot Line'**, 1949. Collection of the author

Line', referring to the German defensive installations of the First World War. It would extend some 560 kilometres from Switzerland to the Netherlands, and to far greater depths than the Maginot Line. But the Siegfried Line was conceived very differently, as a double set of 'belts' of unequal strength, and tied to a more mobile doctrine of defence. Eisenhower's procrastination in September 1944 would allow the Germans to reinforce it and to hold out until March 1945.

Other important systems of defence were erected in Europe during the 1930s. The Czechs constructed a solid ring of works inspired by the French model. It would be conquered without a single shot being fired by the Germans in 1939, as soon as the Munich Agreement had cleared their way. The 'réduit national' (national redoubt) constructed in Switzerland between 1940 and the end of the war, on the other hand, was not a continuous system. It consisted of three fortresses – at Saint-Maurice, in the massif of Saint-Gothard, and at Sargans – along with other fortifications spread out in the north of the country. On the Soviet side, construction of the Stalin Line, with its three thousand positions extending across a front stretching 1,835 kilometres, was undertaken

in 1936. The policy of Mikhail Frunze, a proponent of fortification, had prevailed over the concept of defence in depth propounded by Mikhail Tukhachevsky. And faced with Stalin's forces, the Finns set up the Mannerheim Line, which was a theatre of intense combat during the winter of 1940.

According to one cliché, the Royal Navy was there to provide a rampart for Great Britain, but in the face of the German invasion threat, a decision was made in 1940 to build coastal batteries. These were completed in 1942–1943 as autonomous units, built on land and towed into position out at sea, where they were sunk to shallow depths. The naval forts were supported by two cement pillars, while the army forts were on three legs of steel. Both were designed by the engineer G. A. Maunsell, who had proposed them to the government. This is one of the rare cases where the designer of such a project is clearly known.[5]

G. A. Maunsell
Shivering Sands Fort (1943) for the British Army, off Whitstable, Kent, illustration in Reyner Banham, *Megastructure: Urban Futures of the Recent Past*, 1976. CCA Collection

The latter type was one of the strangest constructions of the entire war and paved the way for oil drilling platforms. Reyner Banham considered them precursors of the theoretical projects of Archigram in the 1960s.[6]

'Europe's Construction Site'

The most important fortification project undertaken during the war itself was the Atlantic Wall, which the Wehrmacht's propaganda publication *Signal* proclaimed was 'Europe's construction site'.[7] The first German measures were offensive. They consisted of the construction of gun batteries at Cap Gris Nez, at the narrowest point of the Channel, to provide support for the planned invasion of Britain, which was to be called *Unternehmen Seelöwe* (Operation Sea Lion). When the Germans turned to a defensive posture and the United States entered the war, a first directive prescribed a Westwall Standard, whose purpose was to rationalise construction all the way from Spain to the North Cape. On 23 March 1942, a specific directive was issued by Hitler defining the precise objectives of the work, and the largest construction site of the century, stretching over 2,685 kilometres, could begin. Its 15,000 concrete elements would consume more than 45 million tons of material.

In the meantime, Todt, the central figure for both the engineers and the architects, was killed in a plane accident.[8] But despite the loss of its leader, the construction project set up by Todt for all of occupied Europe was pursued on a number of fronts, enlisting the service of hundreds of architects and structural engineers, among them Fritz Leonhardt. The latter had been in close contact with Todt, whom he had met when

at a presentation of his project for a giant suspension bridge over the Elbe at Hamburg, and had always held him in great affection. Leonhardt, who was a member of the Nazi Party – and was in retrospect very critical of Speer, whom he had witnessed close up at work – worked under the direction of the architect Hermann Giesler, who was in charge of construction in the Baltic region.[9] In 1943, he was entrusted by the Organisation Todt with the construction of the Baltöl factory, a bituminous schist refinery in

Top: **Todt battery**, Cap Griz Nez, view from the land side, 1942–1944. Photograph by Maier. Bundesarchiv, Bild 146-1973-036-01

Bottom: **Impassable rampart of the Atlantic Wall**, 1941–1943. Photograph by O. Ang. Bundesarchiv, Bild 146-1998-036-21A

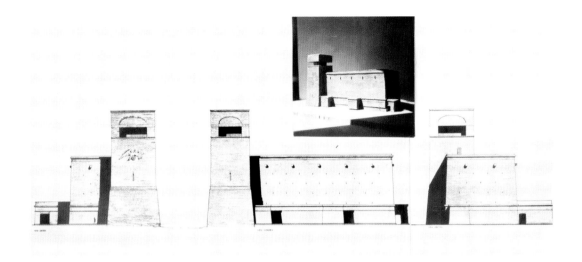

Estonia, which he completed with the help of architects from Paul Bonatz's office. He also designed bridges with the assistance of French engineer Eugène Freyssinet, the inventor of prestressed concrete, with whom he established cordial relations. The transfer of the techniques of prestressing to Germany during the war remains an obscure episode in the 'collaboration' between Vichy France and the occupier.

Leonhardt was also asked for his expert opinion on the strength of the submarine shelters that the Germans had built in Brest. His calculations showed that the 7-metre-thick roof still remained vulnerable to English bombs.[10] Subsequently, Leonhardt was assigned Project Riese ('Giant') for an underground general headquarters

Top: Sergius Ruegenberg **Project for a bunker for the Luftwaffe**, elevations and model, 1940. Berlinische Galerie, Ruegenberg Estate

Bottom: **Lorient submarine base,** with U-67 entering the dry dock, 1942. Photograph by Dietrich. Bundesarchiv, Bild 101II-MW-5335-30

Apeldoorn, Bunker Seyss-Inquart

for Hitler at Waldenburg (Wałbrzych), in
the Eulengebirge mountains of Silesia, built
by prisoners from the Groß-Rosen camp.
Leonhardt also used his analyses of the
Atlantic Wall to design bomb-proof factories
in Bavaria.[11] Meanwhile in Berlin, Sergius
Ruegenberg, Mies van der Rohe's former
office manager, designed bunkers on behalf
of the Luftwaffe. The role of architects and
companies from the occupied countries
in the construction of Fortress Europe,
which employed 1.4 million workers, is
all the more of a mystery as many of the
archives that would have made it possible
to document it were destroyed.[12] The French
firm of Perret Frères worked on a number
of construction sites, along with the major
firms working on public projects.

On the other hand, the chapter that
concerns what one could call the encounter
between the Atlantic Wall and the cities is
better known, especially in its effects on
the ground, which are still visible today
due to the fact that many of the surviving
structures are essentially indestructible.[13]
In some cases the urban fortresses were
built for purely defensive purposes. In others
their purpose was primarily offensive. The
twin towns of The Hague and Scheveningen
in the Netherlands can be counted among
the former. Although the port did provide
shelter for fast torpedo launches, the towns
were primarily the seat of the administration
of occupied Holland. They had been emptied
of their population and transformed into
fortified camps, in the middle of which
the Nazi high commissioner, Arthur

Seyss-Inquardt established his general
headquarters. For his staff headquarters,
he had a large bunker camouflaged to
look like a farm built by the architect Karl
Gonser. His own residence, an apparently
unremarkable house in Apeldoorn, was
in fact a bunker in disguise, which, like
many of the other projects in the town,
was designed by his brother-in-law,
Walter Münster, an architect who had
practiced in Vienna before the war.[14]

The Germans pursued a similar policy
of evacuating port cities in France. In
Cherbourg, almost thirty-eight thousand
of the fifty-one thousand inhabitants were
evacuated in 1943–1944, not for the purpose
of protecting civilians from Allied bombs,
but so the Nazis could use its buildings free
from any bothersome witnesses. In that
city, as in Saint-Nazaire and Bordeaux,
the creation of coastal fortifications went
hand in hand with the construction of bases
for Admiral Dönitz's submarines, similar
to those built in German ports to protect
the Hamburg shipyards of Blohm und
Voss, Howaldtswerke and Deutsche Werft,
the Bremen shipyards of Vulkan, and many
others.[15] The advanced techniques employed
included prestressing and the massive
use of concrete, with plates as much as
five metres thick.

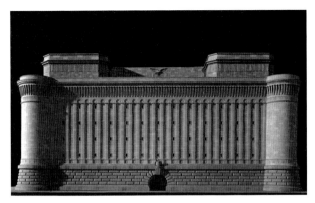

construction stemmed from an order of Hitler's aimed at preventing Allied planes from flying over government quarters. The Führer himself is supposed to have made a sketch of one of these structures, which included a large shelter for as many as ten thousand people and platforms for anti-aircraft guns, and was topped with gun control towers. Tamms completed eight of them in total: they were located in Berlin (at the Zoo, in Friedrichshain and at the Humboldthain), Hamburg (at the Heiligengeistfeld and in Wilhelmsburg) and Vienna (at Arenberg Park, at the Augarten, and at the Stiftskaserne). Additional towers planned for these cities, as well as for Bremen and Munich, were not built.[16] It was clear that once they were constructed, these gigantic structures were meant to remain in place after the war, and Tamms imagined them both in their simplest form during the conflict – in raw concrete, perhaps painted in camouflage – and in a later version, in which they would be given an architectonic treatment. The designs that Tamms proposed included a base with rustication, an order of pilasters and an entablature carried on a sequence of consoles. The towers were clearly related to theoretical projects such as those of Claude-Nicolas Ledoux and the 'city gates' imagined in the 1780s by Étienne Louis Boullée, an illustration of which had been published in 1933 by Emil Kaufmann in *Von Ledoux bis Le Corbusier*.[17]

The theme of bunkers appealed to the imaginations of a wide range of architects with varying poetic and visionary sensibilities. In 1943, while his father was building shelters in Turin, Carlo Mollino imagined an underground shelter for a fighter plane,

Designing Bunkers

While the construction of bunkers was generally carried out by the Organisation Todt or public works companies, it nonetheless involved architects as well. One of the most visible components was the construction of *Flaktürme*, or anti-aircraft towers, designed by the architect Friedrich Tamms, a student of Heinrich Tessenow and Hans Poelzig. Their

Top: Friedrich Tamms
Project for a *Flakturm*, on the Heiligengeistfeld, Hamburg, model, c. 1943.
Berliner Unterwelten e.V.

Bottom: Friedrich Tamms
Project for a *Flakturm* with proposed post-war decoration, model, c. 1943.
Niels Gutschow Archives

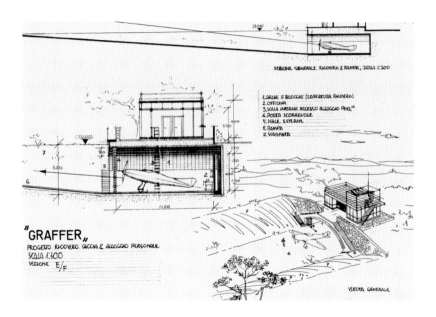

"GRAFFER"
PROGETTO RICOVERO CACCIA & ALLOGGIO PERSONALE
SCALA 1:100
SEZIONE E/F

above which he placed the pilot's lodgings. He envisaged them in groups of three at the end of a landing strip. This multi-use proposal, apparently a personal initiative of Mollino's – who was an aeronautical enthusiast – was dedicated to Giorgio Graffer, a fighter pilot of the Reggia Aeronautica, shot down in 1940. It resembles a half-buried version of the House of Tomorrow designed by George Fred Keck in 1933 for the Century of Progress Exposition, which consisted of a polygonal house superposed over a hangar.[18] Mollino's project combined engineering (the hangar) and architecture (the dwelling).

In the domain of pure invention, the drawings Hugh Ferriss made of a project for the creation of rock caverns near New York are of particular note. The project was initiated by the contractor George J. Atwell, whose intentions seem to have been primarily to obtain publicity, but it had a certain historic dimension: 'One of the oddest contradictions in our supermechanised, global war is that the cave has been raised to a position of usefulness and general esteem it

has not enjoyed since man's worst enemy was the mastodon. Powerful planes and four-ton block busters have done terrific damage since the war began, but the places equipped with good old fashioned caves – Malta, Chunking, Gibraltar – have carried on very well in the face of both raids and threats.'[19] Whence the idea of creating shelters a mile and a half deep in the Palisades, with the use of explosives. These shelters were to be 30 metres high and 60 metres wide and cut into the cliffs of the Hudson Palisades along the New Jersey side, and were to house planes, factories and hundreds of thousands of people. The weaknesses of the project were underscored by John Evans, the chief engineer of the Port of New York Authority, who described the potentially 'disastrous process' of an evacuation of the population of Manhattan by boat.

Carlo Mollino
Project for the 'Graffer' pilot's house and hangar, section and perspective, 1943.

Sistema Bibliotecario del Politecnico di Torino, Biblioteca Centrale di Architettura-Archivi di Architettura, Fondo Carlo Mollino

Within the very real parameters of commissions from the British army, Ove Arup built a number of underground works, including the general headquarters of the Coastal Command at Northwood, an underground bunker 60 metres long and 15 metres wide, under very difficult geological conditions, in the midst of menacing masses of fluid clay.[20] In a speech given to the Association of Supervisory Staffs and Engineering Technicians in 1943, he dwelt on the legacy of wartime construction methods. He asked himself 'whether this merging of essentially two different types of organisation, bureaucratic control and competitive contracting is likely to prove successful in the long run' and declared himself to be in favour of 'a high degree of control in the building industry', as long as 'such a control can be organised without destroying the individual's incentive to give of his best'. This required designing simple projects and promoting mechanisation while taking into account the expectations of workers. Above all, it entailed responding to 'the necessity for combining the knowledge and experience of the contractor with that of the designer'.[21]

Housing Airplanes and Soldiers

In addition to work on fortifications, the war also gave rise to a series of programmes that were specifically military in nature, but were not fundamentally different from civilian programmes. Housing the military required the construction of barracks, sometimes on a truly urban scale, and these were designed in the style favoured by the individual architect recruited for the purpose. Almost all the Nazi projects

Hugh Ferriss
'Caves for New York',
illustration in
The Architectural Forum,
February 1943.
Saint Louis Art Museum,
gift of Hugh Ferriss

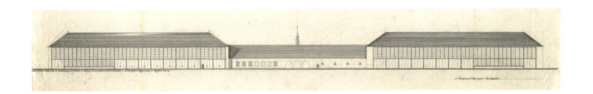

for housing troops, such as those of Roderich Fick in Bavaria and Austria, were designed in the modern traditionalist vein advocated by Paul Schmitthenner, with the occasional modern element in the form of warehouses. The general headquarters of the Luftwaffe planned for Stuttgart was clearly anti-modernist in intent, since it was supposed to be located on the site of the Weissenhofsiedlung, the main manifesto for the *Neues Bauen* ("new way of building") at the time of the 1927 Stuttgart exhibition.

Elsewhere, the militarisation of a country could give rise to modern projects. For example, the Neapolitan architect Luigi Cosenza, assigned to the Ufficio

Addestramento of the general staff of the royal army, worked with O. Blatto on a project for 'military housing estates' intended to be located on the coast at Naples.[22] These large complexes were designed on the scale of a city and were sited in the landscape as autonomous entities. For Giulio Carlo Argan, they formed 'the new concept of an organism both social and architectural at the same time'. He saw

Top: Roderich Fick **Project for an artillery barracks,** Klagenfurt, elevation, 1940. Architekturmuseum der TU München

Pier Luigi Nervi **Concrete hangars for seaplanes** (1940), Orbetello, illustration in Alberto Sartoris, *Encyclopédie de l'architecture nouvelle*, 1957. CCA Collection

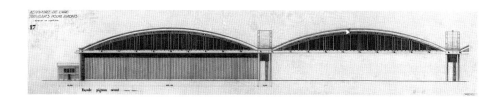

Auguste Perret
**Aircraft hangars
for L'Arc airport**,
Marignane, elevation
of the front gable, 1943.

CNAM/SIAF/CAPA,
Archives d'Architecture
du xxᵉ Siècle,
Fonds Perret

them as a critique of monumental urbanism: 'As opposed to the frequent reduction of urbanism to a dilettante's *mise en scène*, or worse yet, to the materialisation of a generic monumentality, whose neutrality makes it incomprehensible, this project is an indication of the methodical rigour of a completely functional urban principle, which adheres to the concrete requirements of the organisation, to the point of constituting an absolutely autonomous social unit, all the while respecting the limits of the conditions required of such particular users.'[23]

Providing shelter for airplanes and dirigibles obviously called for a completely different set of solutions. Also in Italy, the engineer Pier Luigi Nervi built two extraordinary hangers between 1939 and 1941 in Orbetello, north of Rome, that combined a structural grid of prefabricated reinforced concrete beams with a thin shell of the same material on top. Destroyed by the Nazis during their retreat, these seaplane shelters were a convincing demonstration of the stimulating effects of the policy of autarchy on the invention of alternatives to steel structures, but they were mostly appreciated for their visual power.[24] For his part, in 1942 Perret started working on studies for the L'Arc airport, in Marignane, in response to a commission from the secretariat for aerial defence and the local chamber of commerce. He collaborated with the engineer Nicolas Esquillan to build hangars out of concrete. They were initially designed for seaplanes, building on Esquillan's prior experience in building hangars for the construction of seaplanes

by the SNCASE (Société Nationale de Constructions Aéronautiques du Sud-Est) on the same site before the war. Perret's contribution was to give an elegant form to these large volumes covered by double curvature vaults 100 metres across. Only a set of two hangars would be built after the war.[25]

'Destroy, They Said': the Dugway Experiment

During the war, architectural skills were also called upon in certain engineering units for the purposes of destruction, particularly in urban combat or for the effective mining of bridges, viaducts and tunnels. In fact, the military only called upon the skills of architects on very rare occasions, not to resolve their building problems or adjust their tactics, but to develop new weapons of strategic importance. This made the experiment on an American base in Utah involving a group of European émigrés in 1943 all the more remarkable. These architects were asked to help develop a new type of incendiary bomb on the Dugway Proving Grounds, established by the American army and navy some eighty-five miles from Salt Lake City, for the purposes of experimenting with chemical and biological weapons.[26]

The starting point for the project was Roosevelt's creation of the National Defense Research Committee in July 1940, under the direction of Vannevar Bush. One of the most promising projects undertaken under the auspices of the committee was conducted by the Harvard University chemistry professor Louis F. Fieser. In collaboration with the army's Chemical Warfare Service and his colleagues at the Massachusetts Institute of Technology, he devised an incendiary bomb using a gel composed of naphthene of aluminium, palmitate and gasoline to produce naphthene palmitate, soon known as napalm.[27] The production of the M-69 bombs using this new compound was entrusted to the Standard Oil Development Co., but experimental testing was required to see how it would perform on credible replicas of buildings from the target cities, and Dugway was to serve as a full-scale laboratory.

In March 1943, the Chemical Warfare Service organised a meeting in Elizabeth, New Jersey, and invited several architects as consultants: Erich Mendelsohn, Konrad Wachsmann and Antonin Raymond were in attendance. Each of them brought his own specific expertise to bear. Ironically, Mendelsohn, who had been an ardent supporter of the modernist flat roof versus the sloped roof in the conflict that raged during the Weimar Republic, submitted a report analysing the materials used for roofing in German cities, in order to classify them according to their combustibility. For his part, Wachsmann, with his experience of building in wood for the construction company Christoph & Unmack, was asked to specify the types of wood that would have been used and the hygrometric conditions prevalent in Germany.[28] Based on these analyses, the Ford J. Twaits Co. of Los Angeles erected Building 8100,

the 'German village'. It consisted of two longitudinal buildings reproducing housing from Rhineland and central Germany. The different housing types 'precisely reproduced authentic German construction, with wood panels, masonry interior dividing walls and facades, mortise and tenon construction and typical roofing materials'.[29] But the quest for realism did not stop with the structural characteristics of the dwellings: interior furnishings were also made with the help of the German émigrés Paul Zucker, an architect and art historian, together with Hans Knoll and George Hartmueller, furniture designers, who specified furniture for the different rooms – the living and dining rooms, the kitchen and bedrooms. The furniture was then produced using the workforce of the Authenticity Division of the RKO Pictures studio in Hollywood.[30]

In addition to the two buildings of the 'German village', a three-block fragment of a Japanese city, consisting of twenty-four wooden houses, was built by the Czech-born architect Antonin Raymond, who had worked for eighteen years in Tokyo and had published an important book on Japanese construction.[31] In his memoirs, he states that he had 'passionately studied Japanese construction methods' and had been particularly interested in details 'as being the very basis for projects'. As Wachsmann had done for German woods, Raymond researched the best ways of substituting American construction woods for Japanese varieties. The houses were built using structural elements made in New Jersey and rattan infill, with the facades subsequently coated with clay. According to Raymond's account, 'We constructed a prefabrication

CONFIDENTIAL

FIGURE 1

GENERAL VIEWS OF DUGWAY STRUCTURES

CONFIDENTIAL

Antonin Raymond
Erich Mendelsohn
Konrad Wachsmann
**Japanese village
and German village**,

Dugway Proving Grounds, Utah,
view of the buildings, 1943.
National Archives and
Records Administration,
Washington

233

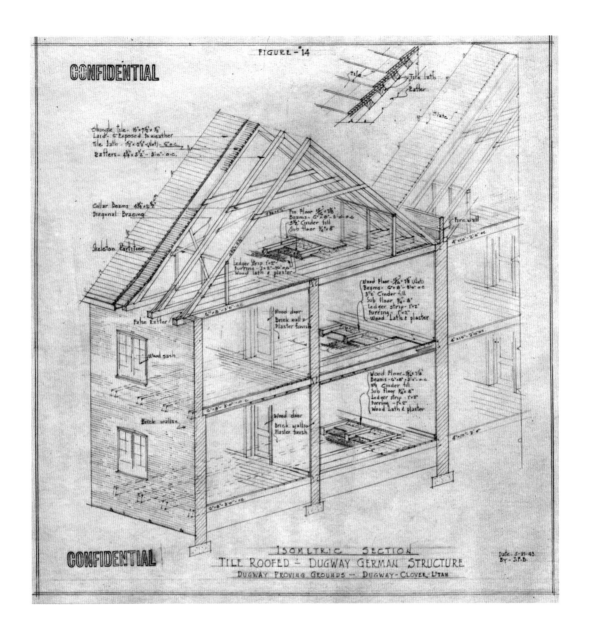

Erich Mendelsohn
Konrad Wachsmann
German village, Dugway
Proving Grounds, Utah,
isometric view of the structure
of a tile-roofed building, 1943.
National Archives and
Records Administration,
Washington

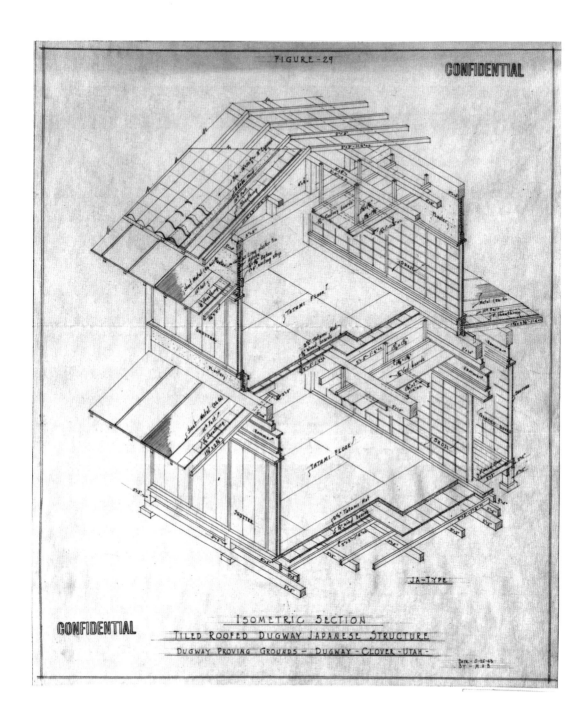

Antonin Raymond
Japanese village, Dugway
Proving Grounds, Utah,
isometric view of the structure
of a tiled roof building, 1943.
National Archives and
Records Administration,
Washington

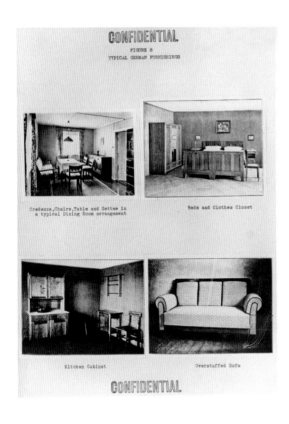

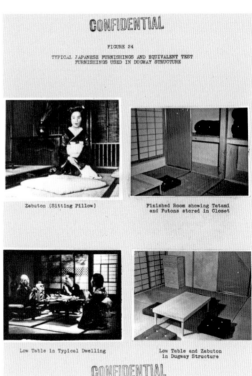

factory near Fort Dix, and established a line of trucks from Dix in Jersey to the Utah Proving Grounds, thousands of kilometres away, to transport the prefabricated parts. The parts were then assembled at the Proving Grounds and were subject to bombarding. As soon as they were destroyed, new ones were erected, until the result was satisfactory. The buildings were fully furnished with *futon*, *zabuton* and everything one finds usually in a Japanese house. They even had *amado* (sliding shutters), and bombarding was tried at night and in the daytime, with the *amado* closed and open.'[32] The wood elements came from the Pemberton Lumber & Millwork Co., and the furniture, which was selected with the further aid of the decorators at RKO, came from the Union National Co., in Youngstown, New York. The tatamis were 'borrowed' from the Japanese neighbourhoods in

Hawaii and transported by airplane. On site, the assembly was overseen by the Ford J. Twaits Co., which produced the mud coatings using Native American workers.[33]

The bombs that were tested at Dugway would be used to set ablaze Japanese cities, for example in the devastating raid of 9 March 1945, when eighty thousand residents of Tokyo perished in a firestorm. But the contributions of the architects recruited to work on full-scale tests of these devastating bombs did not end there. 'One of Germany's former leading industrial architects', in actual fact Erich Mendelsohn, was also consulted in May 1943 by the Standard Oil

German village (left),
Japanese village (right),
Dugway Proving Grounds,
Utah, research on interior
furnishings, 1943.
National Archives and
Records Administration,
Washington

JOBS

PREFAB TARGET
Antonin Raymond duplicates Japanese workers houses for U. S. Army.

New York architect Antonin Raymond, who lived 18 years in Japan, knows almost as much about Japanese building as the Japanese themselves. Early in 1943 Raymond got a strange order from the Standard Oil Development Co. of Elizabeth, N. J. Standard Oil wanted Raymond to design replicas of Japanese workers' housing, life-size and exact—right down to the 3 x 6 floor mats and the rice paper sliding screens. Moreover, the 24 houses were to be designed for factory prefabrication and rapid site assembly, and were to be accompanied by a big stockpile of extra structural parts. But the strangest part of the strange order was its single purpose: the

Joints were mortised and doweled

houses were to be burned to the ground immediately after construction.

Just released by Army censors, pictures (see cuts, right) are the only remaining record of one of the war's most meticulous design jobs. As fast as the houses could be erected, U. S. Army bombers, thundering over their desert Utah site, demolished them with incendiary bombs. On the basis of this experiment, directed by the Army's Chemical Warfare Service and by the National Defense Research Committee, the Army choose the incendiary bomb which destroyed 18 square miles of Tokyo last March and which was used by the 20th Air Force to destroy some 160 square miles of property in Japan's industrial cities.

About 60 per cent of the industrial area of Japan's cities is covered with workers' houses, most of them with tile or sheet metal roofs. How fast they could be fired was a prime factor in how fast adjacent war industry could be knocked out.

In New Jersey the Pemberton Lumber & Millwork Co. drew upon plenty of prefab experience to cut the thousands of wooden structural parts.

The Union National Co., Youngstown, N. Y. turned over its entire plant for two weeks to produce furniture. The Ford J. Twaits Co. of Los Angeles handled site assembly, brought Indians to the job to apply the adobe plaster. Within 67 days after the job was assigned, the prefab Japanese houses were ready for destruction.

TOKYO WORKERS HOUSING (above view shows typical tile roofs) was duplicated by U. S. prefaber. Because Japanese houses are based on modular system (which in turn is based on the 3 x 6 floor mats) they were easy to adapt to prefab construction. Architect Raymond designed houses from memory.

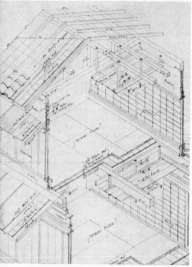

STRUCTURAL FRAME (above) was reinforced by rattan weave. Adobe was applied (bottom picture) and wall finished with lime plaster coat.

HOUSES were set on square concrete piers. Fire walls (lower right), not used in Japan, were built between every two units to limit bombing effect.

SPARSE FURNITURE of Japanese houses was exactly reproduced. A bomber flew to Hawaii to collect enough floor mats from Japanese community.

11

'**Prefab Target**, Antonin Raymond duplicates Japanese workers housing for the U.S. Army', article in *The Architectural Forum*, January 1946. CCA Collection

FIGURE 7
FORD FACTORY, COLOGNE

FIGURE 19
WAREHOUSE, KOENIGSBERG (EAST PRUSSIA)

Development Co. in Elizabeth to produce a report on 'the construction of typical German factories and penetration results on typical German factory roofs given by various incendiary bombs'. The report was submitted to N. F. Meyers, in charge of project 30601, and was entitled 'German Industrial Structures, Construction and Incendiary Bomb Penetration'. According to the report's author, 'his preliminary data were checked by other ex-German architects', and the report 'represents what is believed to be an authoritative and reliable description of this construction'.[34] The report was a methodical analysis of construction techniques used throughout Germany, along with an assessment of their resistance to bomb impact, as confirmed by experiments conducted on similar buildings in the United States. Despite the complete lack of any references to these activities in Mendelsohn's correspondence and archives, we thus have a good idea of his actual contribution to the development of strategic bombing, which was both analytic – as in his expert reports on the roofing of dwellings and factories – and practical, in regards to the realisation of the German 'village' of Dugway.

Protecting Artworks, in Defence and Attack

In the dialectic of attack and defence, historical edifices and artworks were in a sense sandwiched in between. Their protection took two forms, both of which would be accompanied by concrete action on the part of architects and historians. In targeted cities, action on the ground was required, either by evacuating works or protecting them in situ. For the attackers, those who did not wish to destroy an architectural heritage enlisted the aid of architects and historians, who worked as consultants to the military, almost as if sitting alongside them in their cockpits.

After the traumatic episodes of destruction during the First World War in Belgium and France, there had been considerable thought given during the 1930s to the policies that would be required in a subsequent conflict. The League of Nations addressed the problem in 1937–1938 through its International Commission for Intellectual Cooperation.[35] In Italy, Great Britain, France and Germany, specific measures were discussed that were basically similar to those that applied to persons. The measures entailed evacuating what could be evacuated and protecting in situ that which could not – such as immovable artworks and buildings.[36]

After losing the Battle of Britain, the Luftwaffe began a longer-term campaign aimed at cities other than London. Seeking to create the kind of shock to the populace that had accompanied the German bombardment of Rheims Cathedral in 1914, German bombing raids targeted historic cities. After the destruction of Coventry on 14 November 1940, subsequent raids on selected cities in the winter and spring of 1942 were 'justified' by the British bombing of Lübeck and Cologne, and were described

Erich Mendelsohn
Report on the construction of German factories and penetration of their roof structures by incendiary bombs, views of the Ford Cologne factory (top) and of a warehouse in Königsberg (bottom), 1943.
National Archives and Records Administration, Washington

City Companies' Halls

by the German propagandist Gustav Braun von Stumm as reprisals aimed at bombing 'every building in Britain marked with three stars in the Baedeker Guide'.[37] This policy of high symbolic intent led to the attacking of a number of English cities, including Exeter, York and Bath.[38] While the public press and *The Architectural Review* conducted a sort of running chronicle of the ruins, German architects documented the destruction immediately after each raid. For example, Konstanty Guschow's assistant, Richard Zorn, assembled a systematic documentation of the ruins of Hamburg after the incendiary bombardment of 1943.[39]

If the Baedeker guides were presented by the Germans as a menu for the selective destruction of British cities, they played precisely the opposite role in the work of the Commission for the Protection and Salvage of Artistic and Historic Monuments in War Areas, set up in 1943 under the presidency of judge Owen J. Roberts, whose assistant was David E. Finley, the first director of the National Gallery of Art in Washington.[40] The commission enlisted dozens of historians of art and architecture from Harvard University and from New York to establish systematic lists of objects *not* to target, which were to be communicated to American pilots who practiced 'precision' bombing, at least until the latter stages of the war and the carpet bombings of Air Marshal Arthur H. Harris. After a long process of research, discussion and cartographic analysis, these lists were distilled down to a drastically reduced number of monuments to be protected, sometimes as few as five per Italian city.[41] In the end, the destruction caused by Allied bombing in Europe would be far greater in Germany, where it reached 20% of all

Top: **'City Companies' Halls'**, page from *The Architectural Review*, July 1941. CCA Collection

ACLS staff preparing maps, illustration in the *Report of the American Commission for the Protection and Salvage of Artistic and Historic Monuments in War Areas*, 1946. CCA Collection

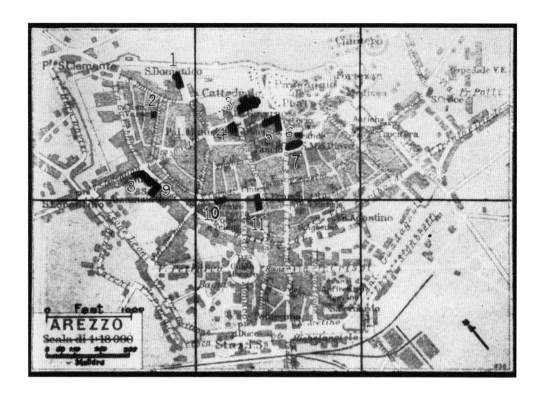

monuments, as opposed to 5% in Italy and
2% in France. It is still difficult to gauge
the responsibility of the experts on the
commission, who included the American
Craig Hugh Smyth, the permanent or
temporary émigrés Erwin Panofsky, Paul
Frankl, Lionello Venturi and Sigfried Giedion,
along with members of the recently formed
Society of Architectural Historians, for the
'precision' that was hoped for revealed itself
in the course of aerial actions to be an illusion.
The Columbia University archaeologist
William Bell Dinsmoor expressed his fears
upon his return from Europe: 'I very much
fear that, unwittingly, we have been engaged
in a city planning program and that some of
the towns, in which the most severe fighting
has occurred, now very closely resemble
our maps, with only the marked protected
monuments now standing.' He cited a French
report according to which 'the specially
marked maps handed over to the liberating

bombardiers have been of remarkable
efficacy'.[42] Dinsmoor no doubt exaggerated
the effects of the maps given to the airmen,
and the chains of causality that resulted
in images of flattened cities in the middle
of which the walls or spires of a cathedral
could be seen standing were undoubtedly
much more complex. For it was doubtless
their masonry construction, much stronger
than that of the buildings around them,
rather than their selection as objects to
be preserved, that resulted in their relative
survival. It nonetheless remains the case that
the choice of churches and palaces as being
worthy of greater protection was part of a vision
of preservation that was limited to unique
objects, to the detriment of the urban fabric.[43]

Map of Arezzo indicating which buildings not to bomb, illustration in the *Report of the American Commission for the* *Protection and Salvage of Artistic and Historic Monuments in War Areas*, 1946. CCA Collection

1. Paul Virilio, *Bunker Archeology*, translated by George Collins (New York: Princeton Architectural Press, 1994), 40.
2. Bernard Rudofsky, *Architecture without Architects: a Short Introduction to Non-Pedigreed Architecture* (New York: The Museum of Modern Art, 1965).
3. Keith Mallory and Arvid Ottar, *The Architecture of War* (New York: Pantheon Books, 1973), 95.
4. Among the principal studies: Kurt Grasser, *Westwall, Maginot-Linie, Atlantikwall. Bunker-und Festungsbau 1930–1945* (Leoni am Starnberger See: Druffel-Verlag, 1983); Anthony Kemp, *The Maginot Line. Myth and Reality* (London: Frederick Warne, 1981); J. E. Kaufmann and H. W. Kaufmann, *Fortress France: the Maginot Line and French Defenses in World War II* (Westport, Conn.: Praeger Security International, 2006).
5. John Albert Posford, 'The Construction of Britain's Sea Port', in *The Civil Engineer in War. A Symposium of Papers on War-Time Engineering Problems* (London: The Institution of Civil Engineers, 1948), 3, 132–63.
6. Reyner Banham, *Megastructure: Urban Futures of the Recent Past* (London: Thames and Hudson, 1976), 28–29.
7. 'Baustelle Europas', *Signal*, no. 2 (January 1943).
8. He was celebrated as a true hero of technology. See for example G. H. [Guido Harbers], 'Dr. Fritz Todt', *Der Baumeister*, vol. 40, no. 3 (March 1942), 26.
9. Hermann Giesler, *Ein anderer Hitler: Bericht seines Architekten Hermann Giesler, Erlebnisse, Gespräche, Reflexionen* (Leoni am Starnberger See: Druffel, 1977).
10. Fritz Leonhardt, *Baumeister in einer umwälzenden Zeit. Erinnerungen* (Stuttgart: Deutsche Verlags-Anstalt, 1984), 99–100.
11. Joachim Kleinmanns and Christiane Weber, eds., *Fritz Leonhardt 1909–1999. Die Kunst des Konstruierens* (Stuttgart and London: Edition Axel Menges, 2009), 170–73.
12. Jak P. Mallmann Showell, *Hitler's U-Boat Bases* (Annapolis: Naval Institute Press, 2002), 5.
13. On the results of Allied bombing, see some two hundred studies of the United States Strategic Bombing Survey.

14. For the Dutch shelters and much more, see the remarkable book by Koos Bosma, *Schuilstad, Bescherming van de bevolking tegen luchtaanvallen* (Amsterdam: SUN, 2006).
15. Jak P. Mallmann Showell, *U-Boats in Camera, 1939–1945* (Phoenix Mill: Sutton Publishing, 1999).
16. Michael Foedrowitz, *Die Flaktürme in Berlin, Hamburg und Wien 1940–1950* (Wölfersheim-Berstadt: Podzun-Pallas, 1996).
17. Jörn Düwel and Niels Gutschow, 'Luftschutzsichere Städte – eine Illusion', in *Fortgewischt sind alle überflüssigen Zutaten. Hamburg 1943: Zerstörung und Städtebau* (Berlin: Lukas Verlag, 2008), 39–48. Emil Kaufmann, *Von Ledoux bis Le Corbusier, Ursprung und Entwicklung der autonomen Architektur* (Vienna and Leipzig: Verlag Dr. Rolf Passer, 1933), 39–48.
18. Mollino archives, Politecnico di Torino, P.8C, 39. *Carlo Mollino 1905–1973*, edited by Fulvio Irace (Milan: Electa, 1989), 175.
19. 'Caves for New York', *The Architectural Forum*, vol. 78, no. 2 (February 1942), 2.
20. Peter Jones, *Ove Arup. Masterbuilder of the Twentieth Century* (London and New Haven: Yale University Press, 2006), 102.
21. Ove Arup, 'Address to the Association of Supervisory Staffs and Engineering Technicians', 7 April 1943, Cambridge University, Churchill Centre, Arup Papers, 5/1; in Jones, op. cit. note 20, 103.
22. O. Blatto and Luigi Cosenza, *Città militari* (Rome: Tipografia Regionale, 1940).
23. Giulio Carlo Argan, 'Città militari', *Le Arti*, vol. 3, no. 4 (April–May 1941), 289–90. Giuseppe Pagano, 'Nuovi orizzonti di urbanistica militare', *Costruzioni Casabella*, no. 161, 1941; also in *Comando*, no. 6, 1940. In *Luigi Cosenza. L'opera completa*, edited by Giani Cosenza and Domenico Moccia (Naples: Electa Napoli, 1987), 121–22.
24. Agnoldmenico Pica, 'Nuove tipe di aviorimesse', *Architettura*, vol. 17, no. 3 (March 1938), 143–48. See the analysis of Mario Sassone and Eduardo Piccoli, 'Otto aviorimesse in cemento armato', in *Pier Luigi Nervi. Architettura come sfida*, edited by Carlo Olmo and Cristiana Chiorino (Cinisello Balsamo: Silvana Editoriale, 2010), 146–51.

25. Bernard Marrey, *Nicolas Esquillan, un ingénieur d'entreprise* (Paris: Picard, 1992), 68–79. Maurice Culot, David Peyceré and Gilles Ragot, eds., *Les Frères Perret. L'œuvre complète* (Paris: Institut Français d'Architecture / Norma, 2000), 296.
26. See the excellent essay by Enrique Ramirez, 'Erich Mendelsohn at War', *Perspecta*, no. 41 (2008), 83–91. 'Fata Morgana', *Thresholds*, no. 33 (2008), 51–60. The first study of this episode was by Mike Davis, 'Berlin's Skeletons in Utah's Closet', in *Dead Cities and Other Tales* (New York: W. W. Norton, 2002), 64–83.
27. Louis F. Fieser, *The Scientific Method: A Personal Account of Unusual Projects in War and in Peace* (New York: Reinhold, 1964), 25–33.
28. Standard Oil Development Company, *Design and Construction of Typical German and Japanese Structures at Dugway Proving Grounds, Utah*, SOD Project 3061, SPCWT 161, 27 May 1943, National Archives, Washington, DC, 4–5.
29. Historic American Engineering Record, National Park Service, Department of the Interior, *Dugway Proving Ground, Dugway, Tooele County, Utah: Written Historical and Descriptive Data*, HAER UT-92A, UT 0568, 2 April 2001, p. 7. According to this document, Mendelsohn's drawings are conserved at Dugway.
30. Standard Oil Development Company, op. cit. note 28, 7–8, figs. 8–12.
31. See his illustrated volume Antonin Raymond, *Architectural Details* (Tokyo: A. Raymond, 1938).
32. Antonin Raymond, *An Autobiography* (Rutland, Vt.: C. E. Tuttle, 1973), 189.
33. The only published trace of the Dugway programme is: 'Prefab Target: Antonin Raymond Duplicates Japanese Worker Houses for U.S. Army', *The Architectural Forum*, vol. 84, no. 1 (January 1946), 11.
34. Standard Oil Development Company, note to N. F. Meyers, 5 May 1943, National Archives. My thanks to Enrique Ramirez, who put me in contact with David Tucker, who generously provided me with this document.
35. 'Résolution de la Commission Internationale de Coopération Intellectuelle du Conseil et de l'Assemblée de la Société

des Nations, Protection des monuments et œuvres d'art en temps de guerre (1937)', *Mouseion*, vol. 39–40, nos. 2–4 (1938), 262ff. My thanks to Johanna Blokker for this information.
36. Karl F. Kühn, *Fliegerschutz für Kunst- und Kulturdenkmale. Ein technischer Wegweiser* (Brno, Vienna and Leipzig: Rudolf M. Rohrer Verlag, 1938). See Sandra Schlicht, *Krieg und Denkmalpflege: Deutschland und Frankreich im Zweiten Weltkrieg* (Schwerin: Helms, 2007).
37. A. C. Grayling, *Among the Dead Cities* (New York: Walker Publishing Company Inc., 2006), 50–52.
38. 'Bath: What the Nazis Mean by a "Baedeker Raid"', *Picture Post*, 4 July 1942.

39. Düwel and Gutschow, op. cit. note 17, 101–03.
40. On Finley's role, see David A. Donehy, *David Finley. Quiet Force for America's Arts* (Washington, DC: National Trust for Historic Preservation, 2006), 205–35.
41. The final report is: *Report of the American Commission for the Protection and Salvage of Artistic and Historic Monuments in War Areas*, Washington, DC, United States Government Printing Office, 1946. The documents pertaining to the commission's activities are at the National Archives, Washington, DC.
42. William B. Dinsmoor, 'Lecture on the Preservation of Monuments', presented at the meeting on 'Europe's

Monuments as Affected by the War', Archaeological Institute of America and The Metropolitan Museum of Art, New York, 29 December 1944. Cited by Lucia Allais, 'Will to War, Will to Art: Cultural Internationalism and the Modernist Aesthetics of Monuments, 1932–1964', Ph.D. dissertation, Massachusetts Institute of Technology, 2008, 217.
43. An evaluation of this policy is to be found in Lieutenant-Colonel Sir Leonard Woolley, 'The Preservation of Historical Architecture in the War Zones', *RIBA Journal*, vol. 53, no. 2 (December 1946), 35–41.

Guido Guidi
**Atlantic Wall bunker at
Vlissingen**, the Netherlands,
view in 2005.
Collection of the artist

Guido Guidi
**Atlantic Wall bunker
at Christianstad**, Norway,
view in 2005.
Collection of the artist

Guido Guidi
**Atlantic Wall bunker
at Løken**, Denmark,
view in 2005.
Collection of the artist

Guido Guidi
**Atlantic Wall bunker
at Hirstals**, Denmark,
view in 2005.
Collection of the artist

pages 250–51:
Anne Garde
**Submarine base
in Bordeaux**, interior
of a submarine pen, 1987.
Collection of the artist

ENGINEERING
NEWS-RECORD

NEWS ISSUE—OCTOBER 26, 1944

Demountable war houses are floated 577 mi. down Ohio for reuse at Camp Breckenridge.

8/ Mobility and Prefabrication

Architecture and urbanism have no need for the pomp
and power of strong materials and delicate assemblies
chosen to endure the passage of time; before the war,
these heavy and expensive things had crushed with
all their weight any propositions for developing our
machine civilization. But a great step forward can be
taken with precarious or provisional buildings, that
will only last for an uncertain time . . . Temporary
elements can be like 'models' of future enterprises
and serve as a first test . . . The shacks of wartime
can be thought of as an *inclined plane* leading
with ease and simplicity to social developments in
the near future. These numberless sheds, in which
users will conduct their first experiments, will be,
in a word, the birth of function, the birth of life.
Le Corbusier, 'L'Architecture et la guerre', 1940[1]

Any unit or combination of units manufactured or
cut to size before being brought to the building site
can, in a literal sense, be called **PREFABRICATION**.
California Arts and Architecture, July 1944[2]

The forces engaged in the Second World War
were much more mobile than in any previous
conflict. After wars conducted by the
infantry and cavalry on land, the American
Civil War and the Franco-Prussian war
inaugurated the use of railways, and
the First World War had been the first to
use cars. The extension of the theatre of
operations to four continents required an
intensive movement of men, equipment
and raw materials, with forces that were
capable of operating thousands of miles

**'Demountable war houses
are floated 577 miles
down the Ohio for reuse
at Camp Breckenridge'**,
cover of *Engineering News-
Record*, 26 October 1944.
CCA Collection

from their base. With the mechanisation of
the conflict, some architects and designers
set out to give form to the new combat
vehicles. For a time, Norman Bel Geddes
apparently thought seriously about applying
the principles of streamlining to tanks and
combat vehicles, as if the appearance of
armaments needed to be brought in line
with the modernist design principles he
had already applied to boats and cars.[3]
For his part, the Milanese architect
Giuseppe de Finetti, who had been an
early anti-fascist, concerned himself
with what could be called the degree zero
of mobility, the infantryman carrying his
equipment on his shoulders. To this end,
he proposed in 1939 the *reggicarichi
universale*, a harness that would enable
the rifleman to carry his equipment.[4]

Somewhere between the immovability
of fortifications and the extreme mobility
of aerial forces, land operations were
characterised by the large-scale movement
of mechanised and armoured forces,
accompanied by support and supply units
whose roles would turn out to be decisive.
The Wehrmacht's inability to ensure support
for its operations across large expanses
of territory was one reason for its defeat in
Russia, while on the other hand the excellent
planning and proper functioning of the Allied
supply system would be a decisive factor
in the success of the landing in Normandy.
Even though the underlying issues were
hardly new, the new notion of logistics would
become a crucial part of military planning,
which required the creation of transport

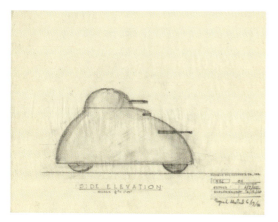

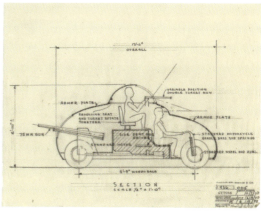

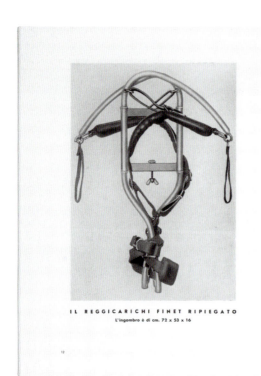

IL REGGICARICHI FINET RIPIEGATO
L'ingombro è di cm. 72 x 53 x 16

12

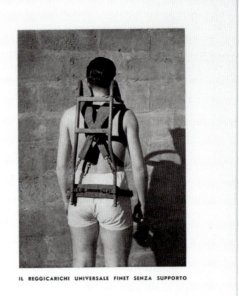

IL REGGICARICHI UNIVERSALE FINET SENZA SUPPORTO

13

Top: Norman Bel Geddes **Project for a streamlined tank**, elevation and longitudinal section, 1942. Courtesy of the Estate of Edith Lutyens Bel Geddes, Harry Ransom Humanities Research Center, University of Texas at Austin

Bottom: Giuseppe de Finetti **'Finet' universal load carrier** for the Italian infantry, views of harness folded up and mounted on a man's back, 1940. CCA Collection

links by land and sea, and the deployment of the requisite equipment behind the fronts.[5]

Construction methods that had been developed since the Crimean War for the creation of transportable buildings had transformed the panoply of military expeditions, which from Antiquity up until that time had essentially consisted of tents. The First World War saw the production of hundreds of thousands of British Nissen huts, made from sheet metal, the German wooden shanties of Christoph & Unmack and the French Adrian shacks, made out of wood and metal.[6] With the approach of the new conflict, military and civilian initiatives proliferated. The armed forces equipped themselves with buildings that could be disassembled and transported in order to provide shelter for their men and equipment in faraway theatres of combat, while the governments called for housing that was quick to erect and to relocate in order to house the workers in armament factories.

Demountable Airplane Hangars

The air forces were among the most active in researching the possibilities for structures that could move with air squadrons from one airfield to another, or that could be set up on rough and ready fields. In Great Britain, the Air Ministry put out a call for tenders for transportable airport hangars in 1936. As part of this programme, several types of steel-framed constructions clad in corrugated metal would be produced in 1939–1940, including four hundred Bellman hangars.[7] The most advanced work in France was carried out by Jean Prouvé. In 1936, with Eugène Beaudouin and Marcel Lods, he designed the clubhouse at Buc airfield,

and in 1937–1938, together with the Forges de Strasbourg, the three men worked on the BLPS project for metal houses. Prouvé then designed demountable sheds for the French Air Ministry, developing a variant with an external structure and a variant with a portico, which was soon patented and would form the basis for many of his subsequent houses. With his workshop, he was able to design and construct a prototype of a demountable hut with an external skeleton for the engineering corps within a single week in 1939, several hundred of which would be built.[8] His experiments for the military led him to work with Le Corbusier in 1940 on a project for 'flying' schools. Their structure drew on the portico structure of Prouvé's sheds for the Air Ministry, and the envelope was composed of lightweight metal panels, which Prouvé had previously experimented with on the Maison du Peuple in Clichy. These modular structures could be rapidly assembled or taken apart in order to move with travelling populations. They were also designed to be used after the war as 'temporary housing for the inhabitants of certain quarters undergoing transformation' or to serve as day nurseries, village clubs and even holiday camps.[9] Shortly thereafter, Prouvé started working with Pierre Jeanneret, who had just parted company with Le Corbusier because of their differences over the war – Jeanneret would join the French Resistance, whereas his cousin for quite some time sought support from the Vichy regime. With Georges Blanchon, the three of them worked on a group of demountable metal lodgings for a factory that produced lightweight alloys, the Société Centrale des Alliages Légers, built by Auguste Perret at Issoire.

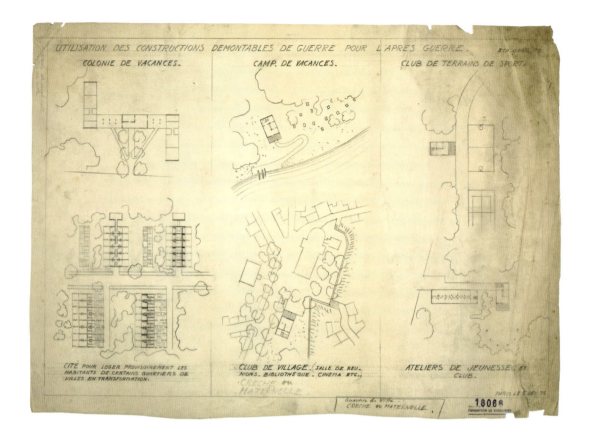

This was the first time he would employ the steel portico frames that would form the structure for his demountable houses in the following decades.[10]

Fuller's Dymaxion Deployment Unit

Like Jean Prouvé, whose research on lightweight metallic structures was accelerated by the preparations for war, the prolific and equally marginal American inventor R. Buckminster Fuller was able to reach the production stage of a transportable dwelling under similar conditions. More than ten years after his proposal for the Dymaxion House in 1927, which was meant to be suspended by cables from a central mast, with floor panels and a ceiling of casein, Fuller adapted the proven construction techniques used for corrugated steel grain silos. Working on a commission from the British War Relief Organisation for temporary housing for families displaced by bombing, he recalled the silos he had seen when crossing the Midwest by car.[11] These silos were mass-produced by the Butler Manufacturing Company of Kansas City for a programme that was part of the New Deal. They were six metres in diameter, with a cylindrical bearing surface on the outside and a cone-shaped roof. Fuller adopted the

Le Corbusier
Project for 'flying schools',
with proposals for their reuse
after the war, site plans, 1940.
Fondation Le Corbusier

corrugated metal, with its structural stiffness, for his Dymaxion Deployment Unit, which he developed with the financial support of the writer Christopher Morley, redesigning the doors and porthole openings. Fuller applied for a patent from the United States Patent Office in March 1941,[12] even before a first unit could be assembled and examined by officials at Haynes Point Park in Washington the following month. He pierced the roof, made from sheet metal, with small oculi and topped it with a mechanical ventilator to ensure that the interior remained comfortable in all seasons. The units were originally intended as housing and were to be grouped in pairs, with a separate cylindrical bathroom in the second one.

The construction sequence called for a central mast for temporary support of the roof. After the construction of the wall, the mast could then be disassembled.[13] Storage and furnishings, which were fixed to the walls and movable partitions of canvas, rendered the unit fully habitable.

Because the use of steel for military purposes was given top priority, the British abandoned the project, but not before the US Signal Corps had ordered a number of them to house the crews for its radars. Butler would manufacture as many as a

R. Buckminster Fuller
Dymaxion Deployment Unit, elevation, plan and construction details, 1941. Courtesy of the Estate of R. Buckminster Fuller

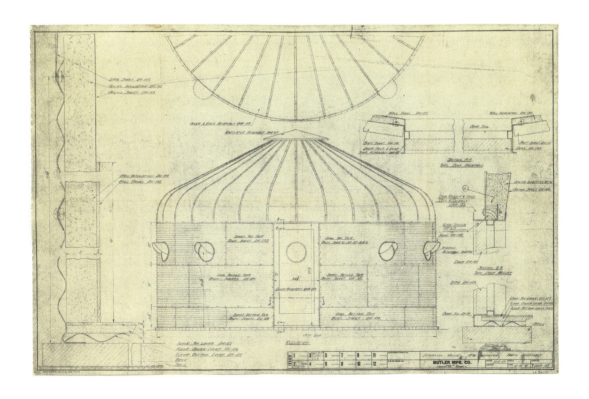

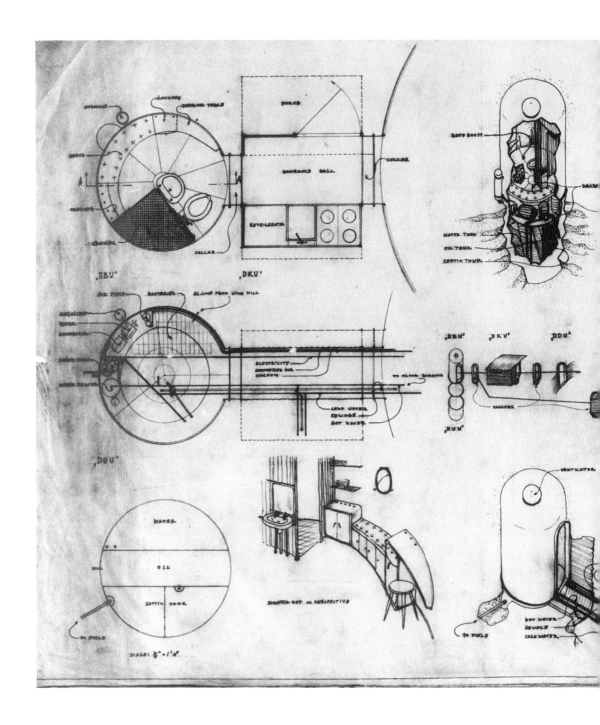

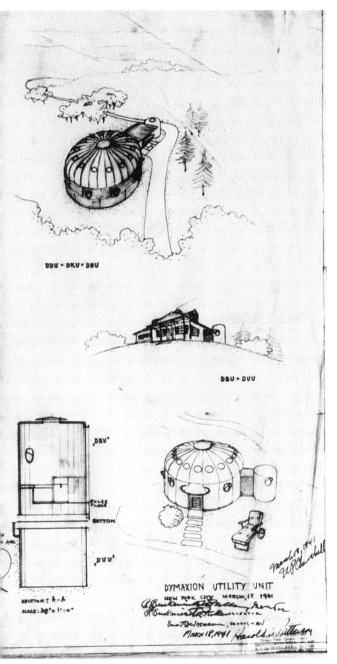

DYMAXION UTILITY UNIT
NEW YORK CITY   MARCH 18 1941

thousand of them per month, primarily
for use in the Persian Gulf by the American
military and by the Russian ferry crews of
the Lend-Lease programme.[14] From October
1941 to May 1942, a pair of the units, dubbed
the Defense House, were set up in the garden
of The Museum of Modern Art in New York,
where *Vogue* used them as a backdrop for
fashion photographs.[15] Fuller described
the house as an anti-aircraft shelter that
could be used in peacetime as 'a beach
or guest house'. He used whatever
arguments he could to justify its round
shape. 'The round house is the easiest to
camouflage from the air as it coincides with
nature-forms such as trees and hillocks.
The ventilator may support camouflage
netting or shading screen. Translucent
plastic water-tight ventilator panels let
in light from above, but all panels may be
closed for blackout without interrupting
air circulation. . . . The Dymaxion House is
simply an attitude, an interpretive principle
– a principle of doing the most with the least
in consideration of a mobilizing, integrating
society.'[16] A model of the unit was also
on display at the Cincinnati Art Museum
in November and December 1942, as part
of the exhibition 'Shelter in Transit and
Transition: An Exhibition revealing a
New Phase in Architectural Activity'.

R. Buckminster Fuller
Dymaxion Utility Unit,
plans and detail views,
plate, 1941.
Courtesy of the Estate
of R. Buckminster Fuller

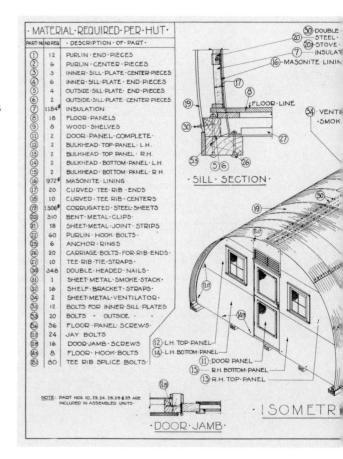

The Triumph of the Quonset Hut

By the modest standards of Fuller's previous experiments, the Dymaxion Deployment Unit was an unqualified success. But the greatest American achievement in the field of demountable structures was the Quonset hut. Like Fuller's Dymaxion Deployment Unit, it made use of corrugated metal, a material invented in the 19th century and used after the 1920s in the aviation industry – notably in the German Junkers planes – and subsequently used in the car industry, by Citroën to clad its vans. The Quonset hut also derived from an earlier structure, the Nissen hut of 1916, designed during the First World War by Peter Norman Nissen, a lieutenant-colonel of the Royal Engineers. Two models were produced at that time, with steel ribs for the structure and curved corrugated panels for the enclosure. Some 100,000 Nissen Bow Huts, measuring 16 feet by 27 feet (4.8 x 8.1 metres), and 10,000 Nissen Hospital Huts, measuring 20 feet by 60 feet (6 x 8 metres) were deployed in war zones.[17]

The project was developed at the base that the United States Navy had created at Quonset Point, Rhode Island, which was chosen the following year as the bridgehead for the first consignments of American aid to Great Britain. The George A. Fuller construction company, which had been contracted to build the base, received an additional request for the serial production of huts that would improve upon the Nissen.[18] The design was completed in less than a month by a team led by the architect Otto Brandenberger, who had studied at the Zürich Polytechnic and worked in the offices of Ernest Flagg and of Shreve, Lamb & Harmon, where he participated

in the design of the Empire State Building. Fuller and Brandenberger retained the structural principle and overall shape of the Nissen hut, but their principal contribution was to provide insulation by lining the inside with pressed wood panels, which enabled them to be used under the most extreme climate conditions. The first order was placed by the navy in April 1941 for bases in Scotland and Northern Ireland, and the Fuller factory immediately began mass production.

More than 153,000 of the different versions of the hut, which was initially called a 'temporary installation for aviation' and then, in July 1941, officially renamed as the 'Quonset', would end up being produced.

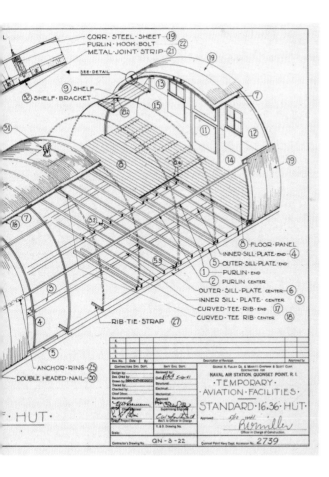

CORR·STEEL·SHEET ⑲
PURLIN·HOOK·BOLT ㉒
METAL·JOINT·STRIP ㉑

SEE·DETAIL

⑨ SHELF
㉜ SHELF·BRACKET
⑬
⑮
⑱
⑪
⑫
㉛
⑦
⑲
⑲
⑧
⑭
⑯
㉜
㉕
⑤·³
⑤
③
④
⑤
RIB·TIE·STRAP ㉗
ANCHOR·RING ㉕
DOUBLE·HEADED·NAIL ㉚

⑧ FLOOR·PANEL
INNER·SILL·PLATE·END ④
⑤ OUTER·SILL·PLATE·END
① PURLIN·END
② PURLIN·CENTER
OUTER·SILL·PLATE·CENTER ⑥
INNER·SILL·PLATE·CENTER ③
CURVED·TEE·RIB·END ⑰
CURVED·TEE·RIB·CENTER ⑱

·HUT·

4.				
3.				
Rev. No.	Date	By	Description of Revision	Approved by
Contractor's Eng. Dept.		Navy Eng. Dept.	GEORGE A. FULLER CO. & MERRITT·CHAPMAN & SCOTT CORP. CONTRACTORS FOR	

NAVAL AIR STATION, QUONSET POINT, R.I.
·TEMPORARY·
·AVIATION·FACILITIES·
STANDARD·16.36·HUT·

Contractor's Drawing No. QN-3-22 — Quonset Point Navy Dept. Accession No. 2739

Their dimensions and certain details of construction varied. The first 'T-Rib' units measured 16 x 36 feet (4.8 x 10.8 metres) and could accommodate about ten soldiers in its dormitory version. It was replaced in October 1941 by the 'Quonset Redesign', designed by Brandenberger in accordance with suggestions from the Stran-Steel Corporation, which was initially a sub-contractor to Fuller but soon became the primary producer. Brandenberger's redesign no longer used simple curved T sections, but I sections instead, onto which the metal sheets could simply be nailed.[19] The basic hut, whose parts took up less space than a tent of comparable capacity, could be erected in a single day by ten men equipped only with hand tools.[20] It would see a wide variety of uses, from billeting troops and officers to lodging visiting families, from administrative offices to infirmaries,

Top: Otto Brandenberger, for the George Fuller Co. **Quonset hut**, isometric drawing of temporary aviation facilities, standard-1636 hut, 1941. Rhode Island Historical Society

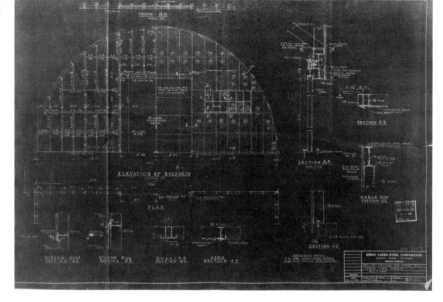

Great Lake Steel Corporation, Detroit, Michigan **Quonset hut**, principal section and construction details, 1942. CCA Collection, Myron Goldsmith fonds

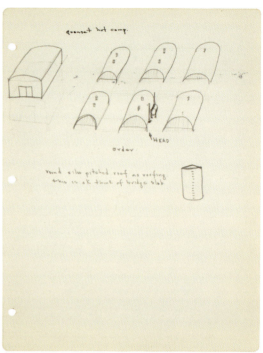

Myron Goldsmith
Quonset huts, exterior
and interior sketches,
between 1942 and 1945.
CCA Collection,
Myron Goldsmith fonds

to use as temporary morgues in the first days of the American occupation of Germany. Quonset huts were used extensively, especially in remote territories such as Alaska, where 30,000 of them would serve as lodgings for many of the 300,000 members of the armed forces posted there during the war, and for thousands of civilian workers recruited for infrastructure projects.[21]

The Mero System,
or the Triumph of the Node

Although Quonset huts were a brilliant technological and logistical success, as their widespread and continued presence on sites that carry the traces of the war can attest, they did not employ any heroic architectural principles, nor even any particularly advanced ones.

A far more inventive and rigorous system of metal construction was developed by the German engineer Max Mengeringhausen. A specialist in the relatively unglamorous domain of central heating, he published a text on metal tubes in the 1930s and became interested in the properties of polyhedra and structural skeletons, which he studied under August Föppl, a professor of statics and mechanics in Munich. He also began to explore crystallography and the work of the Frenchman Auguste Bravais.[22] As a specialist in domestic heating and plumbing systems, he worked on several modern projects such as the Siemenstadt housing estate, where he collaborated with Walter Gropius, and published a study on silent piping systems.[23] Mengeringhausen was an aviation enthusiast, and in the 1930s he met Ernst Udet, a First World War fighter ace and aerobatic pilot, who became head of the technical unit for the Luftwaffe in 1939. For Udet, he developed a prototype

of a prefabricated garage with a tubular metal skeleton, whose parts were produced at the engineering school of Berlin-Neukölln. The ultra-rapid assembly of this small shelter convinced Udet to entrust him with the design of a building that would be fully transportable by airplane.

Mengeringhausen imagined a modular system of construction consisting of nodes and metal rods of standardised lengths. At a time when Le Corbusier was developing his Modulor system of proportions, Mengeringhausen shared Ernst Neufert's passion for modularity and further developed the research of the engineer Walter Porstmann, the inventor of the DIN (Deutsche Industrie-Normen). Like Porstmann, he relished the ratio of $1/\sqrt{2}$. In 1940, he formulated the 'law of regular spatial structures' and worked on the division of the cube into sectors. He developed a polyhedral node with three principal axes, which could be used to join up to eighteen elements either orthogonal or inclined at 45 degrees, using standard threading. In 1942–1943, he completed two types of light demountable buildings that could be transported by airplane, the *flugzeugverladefähige Kleinsthaus* (airborne minimal house) and the *flugzeugverladefähige Planetarium* (airborne planetarium), but they were still not produced in any quantity.[24] After being interrupted in 1945, mass production of

Max Mengeringhausen
The MERO system,
potential uses proposed
in 1943: on the right,
the 'minimum house';
on the left, a planetarium;
in the background,
antenna towers; illustration
in *Raumfachwerke aus
Stäben und Knoten*, 1975.
Collection of the author

the elements started up again in 1948 under the name MERO – an acronym of Max Mengeringhausen Rohrbauweisen – and would succeed at every scale of construction in the post-war period.

Wachsmann's Ingenious Connectors

Mengeringhausen's fellow countryman Konrad Wachsmann pursued a similar line of research into the three-dimensional assembly of industrialised elements. But despite the apparent similarity, there were significant differences between the former, a specialist in steel tubing, and the latter, who worked entirely with elements in wood. Wachsmann had initially been trained as a cabinetmaker, before studying architecture with Hans Poelzig at the Technische Hochschule in Berlin. His mentor recommended him to the firm of Christof & Unmack in 1926 – Europe's biggest timber building manufacturer – to work in their factory in Niesky, in Silesia. Wachsmann rationalised the company's design operations, and he also designed and made a very special kit house: Albert Einstein's weekend house in Caputh, near Potsdam (1929).[25]

Wachsmann drew on his research into structures for the military and those intended for civilian use. After a time in Rome, he stayed in Grenoble and in the South of France, where he worked on a demountable airplane hangar in 1939.[26] This project would provide the starting point for a system for making prefabricated hangars out of steel tubing, which he designed in 1944 for the Atlas Aircraft Product Corporation. Called the Mobilar, it was included in an exhibition at The Museum of Modern Art in 1946.[27] The system consisted of an enclosing surface assembled from tubes connected by 'open' connectors that could accommodate up to six pieces and ingenious moveable vertical partitions.[28] The issue here was not so much that the whole building could be transported, but rather that it could be assembled rapidly or transformed from being fully enclosed into an open shelter in a few minutes.

During his imprisonment by the Vichy government in 1940, Wachsmann studied a first system of assembly using prefabricated panels. In 1941, he was able to flee to the United States, where he joined up with Walter Gropius again. The former director of the Bauhaus had long held a passionate interest in prefabrication and was fascinated by the example of car manufacture. In Dessau, he had conducted two types of experimentation, one with reinforced concrete elements, and one with metal panels. In Berlin, he had worked on refining the Hirsch system of houses in copper.[29] At Harvard, Gropius worked with Martin Wagner, who had formerly been chief planner in Berlin, and who was also interested in prefabrication. Wagner was working on his own system of 'igloo houses', in faceted cone shapes. Discussing the merits of spherical and box-like structures, Wagner combined economic reflections and aesthetic considerations in a text entitled 'Rundbauten oder Kubusbauten',[30] and with Gropius petitioned the American authorities for a strong policy of prefabrication. Associating prefabrication with mobility, they both claimed to 'create a new kind of inexpensive, high quality housing, with the latest equipment, consisting of standardized

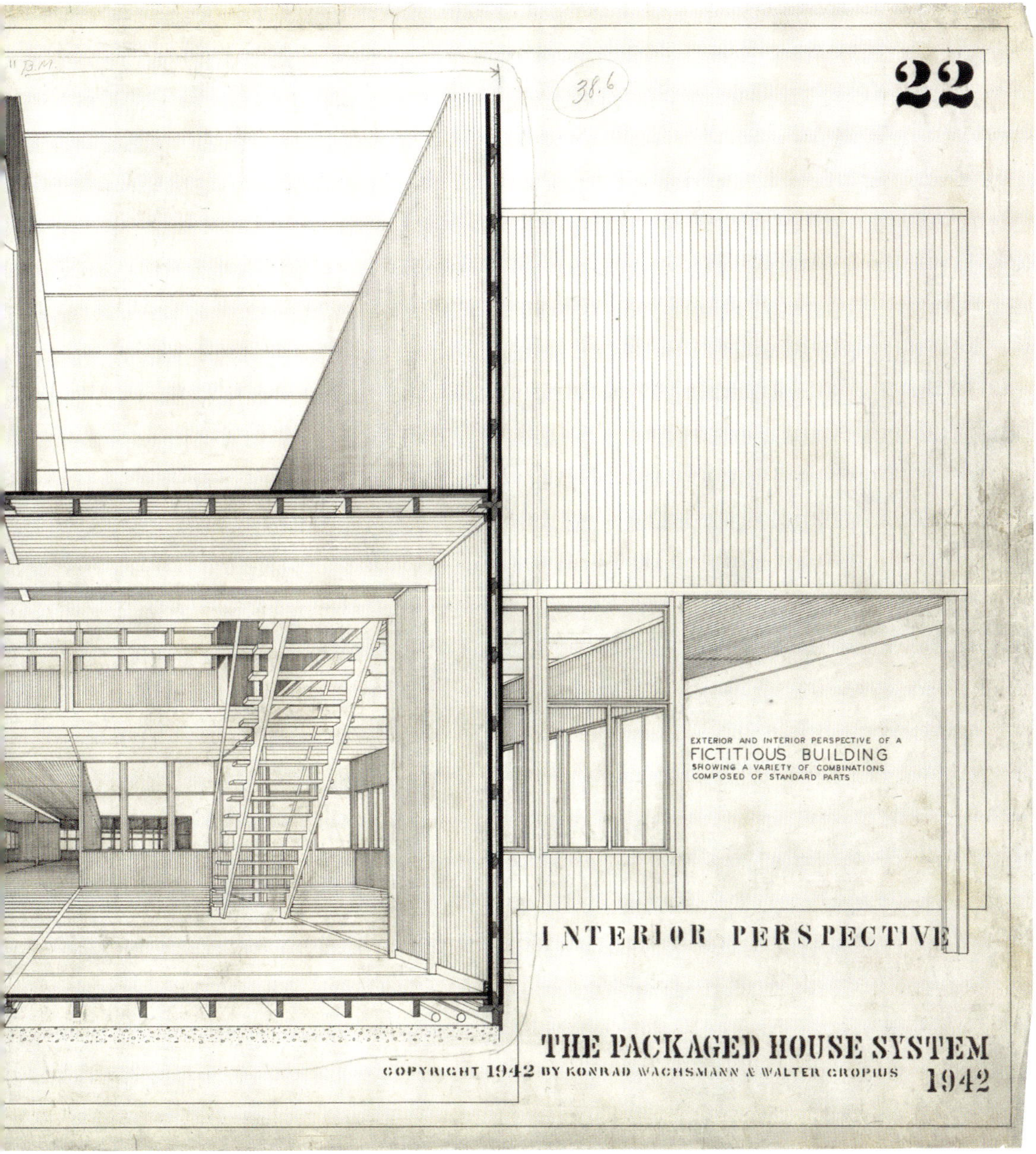

Walter Gropius
Konrad Wachsmann
The Packaged House system, section / perspective of 'fictitious building showing a variety of combinations composed of standard parts', 1942. Akademie der Künste, Konrad Wachsmann Archiv, Berlin

and interchangeable parts, to be used in different types of houses of different size. These lodgings would need to be demountable and transportable, but would also need to serve as permanent homes, depending on the circumstances.'[31]

In late 1941 and early 1942, Wachsmann worked in Gropius's office on transforming his French sketches, based on the metric system, into a more advanced system using imperial measurements, for which he developed a new type of metal connector.[32] At the suggestion of the dean of the school at Harvard, Joseph Hudnut, it was called the 'Packaged House' and an application to patent a 'prefabricated building' was submitted in May 1942.[33] As Gilbert Herbert has pointed out, the system was both closed and open at the same time in that it used prefabricated panels yet permitted a variety of configurations. The panels measured 40 x 120 inches (101 x 304 centimetres) and were either solid or glazed, incorporating specially built windows and doors. A wide range of combinations was possible thanks to the system's most innovative feature, the wedge connector, which enabled four panels to be joined together.[34]

Gropius called on his network of friends to promote the project, while a first experimental house was built in Somerville, near Boston, in February 1943, on the grounds of the US Plywood Corporation, following the setting up of the General Panel Corporation as a result of a meeting between Wachsmann and the New York financier Jack Marqusee. The architectural press hailed the birth, thanks to the war, of 'one of the first prefabricated, fully demountable systems that consistently uses the same module for all dimensions,

Konrad Wachsmann
General panel system,
prototypes of metal connecting pieces conserved in a Lufthansa cigar box, 1944. Akademie der Künste, Konrad Wachsmann Archiv, Berlin

horizontal, vertical and lateral, a truly *three-dimensional module*'.[35] But the orders did not come in – at least not before Wachsmann had made other financial arrangements in California, as we shall see later.

A Proliferation of Systems

Although refined projects such as Wachsmann's did not manage to reach the stage of mass production, almost seventy American companies produced more than 200,000 prefabricated lodgings during the war.[36] Hundreds of architects shared the ideal of a house that could be manufactured in a factory and easily transported, but few managed to attain that goal. Among the unfortunate inventors was Marcel Breuer, who had worked with Gropius until the completion of Aluminum City. In 1942, he developed the Nomadic Nests, later known as Yankee Portables, compact single-storey houses made out of wood panels that could accommodate families of different sizes. His project for workers' housing in Wethersfield, Connecticut, used the same constructional principle, in conjunction with a V-shaped roof. The following year, Breuer developed the Plas-2-Point house, whose roof rested on a single main beam sitting on two vertical supports that also held up the floor. The plywood cladding of this house, which seemed to float, was impregnated with a plastic resin produced by Monsanto to render it waterproof.[37]

Another inventor was Bertrand Goldberg, a young Chicago architect more interested in mobile systems. Goldberg had briefly studied at the Bauhaus, and was employed by the Board of Economic Warfare, Reoccupation and Reconstruction Division of the Office of Strategic Services. In that capacity, he worked on a programme for mobile sanitary equipment, recasting a project for 'ice cream carts' he had developed in 1939.[38] In 1943, he made studies for mobile delousing units for use during military operations in North Africa. Consisting of folding canvas panels stiffened with cable, it could be erected directly from a truck.[39] He subsequently proposed a Mobile Penicillin Lab, made out of two streamlined plywood volumes assembled at right angles to each other in a T-shape, one part being used to cultivate the mould, the other to incubate the penicillin.[40] In response to a more prosaic programme, Goldberg did

manage to build a number of prefabricated houses at Suitland, Maryland, and at the Indian Head naval base, also in Maryland.[41]

For his part, Richard Neutra emphasised the aesthetic dimension in 1943, when he claimed in the pages of the review *California Arts and Architecture*, which published projects for prefabricated houses, that 'it is untrue that a fabricated house can offer no esthetical satisfaction; it may of course be true that the beauties derived from rare handiwork cannot be duplicated. . . . Quality in housing the multitudes certainly will have to be founded on something else than rarity.' Neutra saw great promise in the experiences of the war: 'If we fabricate the dwelling commodity in lightweight units at centers where industrial tools and skills have been piled high by the armament effort, we may spread and distribute this vital product, as we do with other essentials of contemporary living to people who live in decentralized areas where no comparable materials, tools and skills are brought together in economical effectiveness.'[42]

The appeal of prefabrication was far from being exclusive to America, and seems instead to have played an important part in the thinking of architects far and wide, whether in response to a specific programme such as evacuation, housing workers, billeting troops or the rapid creation of distant bases, or whether the idea of prefabrication was simply an extension of primarily technical concerns. In Vichy France there was much research, but it had little practical application, because construction materials were mostly requisitioned for the projects of the occupiers.[43] In Great Britain, Ernö Goldfinger developed designs for prefabricated units

TRUCK EQUIPMENT

1 HOT WATER FURNACE.
2 CHEMICAL STORAGE (36 CU. FT.)
3 FUEL STORAGE (500 GAL.)
4 SHOWER WATER TANKS (300 GAL.)
5 DRINKING WATER STORAGE (100 GAL.)
6 CHEMICALS STORAGE.
7 SUPPLIES STORAGE.
8 BUNKS (TWO).
9 SUPPLIES STORAGE.
10 AERATION CHAMBERS (TWO).
11 FUMIGATION CHAMBERS (TWO).
12 PUMP AND CHLORINATION UNIT.

PLAN OF OPERATION

TRAFFIC.
① REGISTER AND ENTER.
② DISROPE.
③ DISINFECTANT SPRAY.
④ SHOWER.
⑤ DRESS.
⑥ EXIT.

EQUIPMENT.
Ⓐ REGISTRATION DESK.
Ⓑ INFECTED CLOTHING RACKS.
Ⓒ BENCHES.
Ⓓ LATRINES, INFECTED.
Ⓔ LATRINES, DISINFECTED.
Ⓕ FUMIGATION CHAMBER.
Ⓖ AERATION CHAMBER.
Ⓗ STORAGE LOCKER.
Ⓙ TRUCK CAB.
Ⓚ CHECK RACK.
Ⓛ CREW'S MESS
(SUNDECK AND BUNKS ABOVE)

OPERATION PER 10 HOUR DAY.
⚡ 1. 4 MIN. SHOWER - 900 PERSONS.
⚡ 2. 5 MIN. SHOWER - 720 PERSONS.
⚡ 3. 6 MIN. SHOWER - 600 PERSONS.

MATERIALS REQUIRED PER DAY.

OPERATION	WATER (GAL.)	GAS (CU. FT.)	DISINFECTA (GAL.)
⚡ 1.	5400	1800	25
⚡ 2.	5400	1440	18
⚡ 3.	5400	1200	16.5

PERSONNEL (TRAVELING).
I 1 RECEPTIONIST.
II 1 MALE NURSE.
III 1 FEMALE NURSE

PERSONNEL (SITE).
IV 1 STOKER
V 1 DRESSING HELPER - FEMALE.
VI 2 DRESSING HELPERS - MALE.
VII 1 TRANSLATOR.

ERECTION

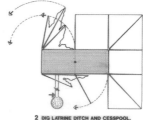

1 JACK WEIGHT OFF SPRINGS.
ERECT METAL CHIMNEY.
STAND HINGED MAST UPRIGHT.

2 DIG LATRINE DITCH AND CESSPOOL.
UNFURL CANVAS FROM SPARS AND
UNFOLD SPARS TO PROPER POSITION.

3 DRIVE STAKES IN GROUND AND FASTEN SPARS
WITH GUYS FROM MAST AND FROM STAKES.
TIGHTEN GUYS. TAKE LOOSENESS OUT OF
CANVAS ROOF BY TIGHTENING ROPE BETWEEN SPARS.

O.S.S. MOBILE DELOUSING STATION AFRICAN

BERTRAND GOLDBERG ASSOCIATES INC.
ARCHITECTS   ENGINEERS

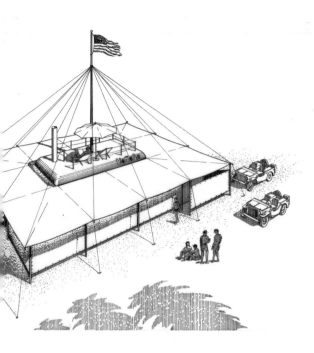

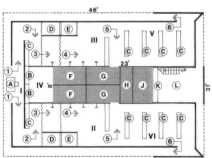

L INTERMEDIATE STANCHIONS FOR
S PARTITIONS. INSTALL LADDER TO
ECK AND TOP DECK STANCHIONS.

5 INSTALL CANVAS PARTITIONS.
INSTALL BENCHES, CLOTHES RACKS,
AND MISCELLANEOUS EQUIPMENT.

EATER 1943

to be used in the camps for mothers and children evacuated from London. These were exhibited at the Paul and Marjorie Abbatt Gallery. Over the course of the war, British proposals continued to proliferate under the aegis of the Burt Committee, organised at the inter-ministerial level to stimulate research and organise competition between manufacturers, with these parallel research projects exploring different uses of materials and methods of assembly.[44] For his part, Ove Arup designed a prefabricated house and hangar out of aluminium in 1945. Arup was opposed to temporary solutions. He sought to link prefabrication with the use of new materials and was critical of projects presented in the press. In a letter to the *RIBA Journal*, he wrote: 'Prefabrication is only incidental to certain modern production methods which exploit the economical possibilities of quantity production. . . . If the task is to provide a large quantity of goods which have to fulfil the same purpose then standardisation and, wherever possible, machine production is the way to do it economically.'[45] In Russia, Andrei Burov sharply admonished his fellow directors of the Architects' Union in 1943 and urged them to learn from the American example in both industry – which he was well acquainted with since working with Albert Kahn – and agriculture, particularly in regards to light demountable structures, which he contrasted with the heavy systems of construction used in the USSR.[46]

DUPLEX DORMITORY FOR 6 CHILDREN

ENTRANCE TO COMMUNAL BLOCK

HOLIDAY & EVACUATION CAMP FOR FAMILIES II

Ernö Goldfinger
Prefabricated construction,
project for holiday and
evacuation camps for
families, perspective
views, 1940.
RIBA Library Drawings
and Archives Collections

Wartime Meccano:
the Bailey Bridge

Along with the Quonset hut, the greatest
success in the field of transportable
construction was the bridge designed by
the British engineer Donald C. Bailey to
replace the tubular trusses of the Inglis
bridges, which had been invented during
the First World War and used widely up
until that time. The advantages of the
Bailey bridge were particularly remarkable:
the basic elements could be assembled
in an almost unlimited number of
configurations. This was one of the first
practical illustrations of the principles
of so-called 'open' prefabrication, which
would be so widely promoted during the
1960s and 1970s. Bailey had worked for
the Experimental Bridging Establishment,
where he had started developing his ideas,
and had become its chief designer in 1941.
Not unlike Joseph Paxton, who sketched
his initial design for the Crystal Palace
on a piece of blotting paper, according
to myth Bailey drew his basic idea on
the back of an envelope, in a car, one
night around the end of 1940.[47]

Bailey's ingenious Meccano was based
on a combination of modular steel panels
all measuring 10 x 5 feet (approximately
3 x 1.5 metres), which could be placed on top
of each other or assembled end-to-end using
a very simple system of pins. Strong enough
to support loads up to 70 tons, it could bear
the heaviest of convoys. The panels could
be carried on 3-ton trucks. They did not
require any special transport vehicles and
could be assembled by as few as six men.
Bailey explained that 'the panel is built up
by welding from standard rolled sections
in high-tensile structural steel. . . . These
panels are connected together, end to end,
to form girders or trusses of various length.
The strength of the girders can be adjusted
by arranging that there are one, two, three,
or even four trusses, side by side.'[48] After
a year of design work, production began in
early July 1941. Six hundred and fifty British
companies were involved in manufacture,
using unskilled labour, whereas the earlier
bridges could only be produced in a limited
number of specialised factories. In discussions
held after the war at the London Institution
of Civil Engineers, one participant stressed
'the outstanding ingenuity of the authors in
producing not only a unique and versatile
design, but also a system of inspection
and inspection gauges which permitted
fabrication by unskilled and semi-skilled
labour to a degree of accuracy hitherto

Donald Bailey
Bailey bridge standard panel
(1941), isometric view, plate
in *The Civil Engineer in War*, 1948.
Rare Books and Special
Collections Library, McGill
University, Montréal

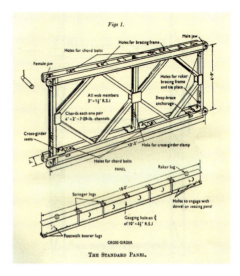

considered to be outside the range of constructional steelwork, especially since a large amount of the manufacture was distributed among firms not accustomed to structural steelwork'.[49]

The universal possibilities of the system were in marked contrast to the American pontoon treadways and to the Inglis bridge, which was difficult to assemble. By combining the panels in different ways, it was easy to make large bridges, pontoons, floating bridges, docks and jetties, and even suspension bridges with spans up to 150 metres long. The first bridge was built in November 1942, in Tunisia. Between 1942 and 1945, 500,000 tons of material were used to produce 700,000 standard panels; in the European theatre alone, 1,500 bridges would be built.[50] After

widespread use during the Italian campaign and in the Netherlands, Bailey bridges would be used to cross the Rhine in the final offensive of the war. The Sussex Bridge, built in 1945 in the German city of Xanten, would be the longest of them, at 650 metres in length. Production was also undertaken in the United States, where the panels were manufactured by general construction companies.

Arthur Ensor
**Installing an access
ramp to a Bailey bridge**,
watercolour, n.d.
Beaverbrook Collection
of Military Art,
Canadian War Museum

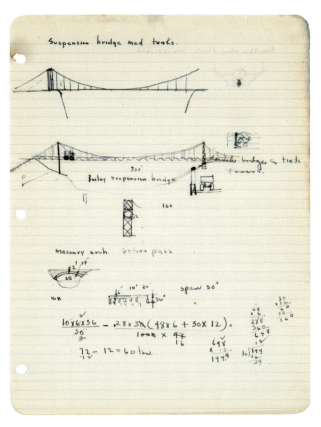

Work on the project for two harbours – Mulberry A at Omaha Beach and Mulberry B at Arromanches – started in September 1943, following an Allied conference in Quebec, and it drew on knowledge gained from the construction of two floating portsin Faslane, on the Gare Loch, and on Loch Ryan, import points for troops and equipment arriving from America. Each had three major components. Offshore, the port was to be protected by a breakwater made up of concrete caissons (known as Phoenixes) and scuttled 'block ships' (known as Gooseberries). The caissons measured 18 x 60 x 15 metres and were constructed in the docks of the port of London. They were stockpiled underwater, then refloated and towed across the Channel, to be filled with stones and sunk into position, together with the block ships. Floating breakwaters, nicknamed Lilos, and later Bombardons, were positioned outside these breakwaters to protect them during construction. The docks themselves were to be connected by floating bridges, called Whales, which would connect to the shoreline, supported on concrete Beetles. The most remarkable features of this system were its flexibility and its capacity to adjust to the motion of the sea.[52] Prefabrication on this scale was unprecedented. The construction of the elements of the ports mobilised hundreds of contractors, 200 of them for the Whales alone, and 45,000 workers, who produced 16 kilometres of floating

Floating Prefabs: the Mulberries

British engineers were also responsible for the largest prefabricated works of all time, the two Mulberry harbours that ensured the success of the Allied landing in Normandy in 1944. Planning and design of the project within the Royal Engineers was supervised by Bruce White and Allan Beckett, who were implementing an idea developed by J. D. Bernal, but usually attributed to Churchill. A note from the prime minister to Lord Mountbatten, dated 30 May 1942, is often cited in this regard: 'Piers for use on the beaches. They must float up and down with the tide. The anchor problem must be mastered. Let me have the best solution worked out. The difficulties will argue for themselves.'[51]

Myron Goldsmith
Bailey suspension bridge
(between 1942 and 1945),
sketches and calculations, n.d.
CCA Collection,
Myron Goldsmith fonds

bridges, 10 kilometres of caissons and 23 bridgeheads, all of which were sunk in estuaries in the south of England before being towed in June 1944, at a speed of three knots, towards the coast of Normandy.[53] Although Mulberry A was almost completely destroyed in a storm and remained out of commission for some time, no less that 326,000 men, 54,000 vehicles and 100,000 tons of material would pass through Mulberry B, before the Allies were able to take control of Caen and Cherbourg and start using the permanent ports. The installations would function until the end of 1944.

These 'portable ports'[54] were a remarkable and ingenious feat of design, which addressed conflicting concerns as to the advance preparation of the

No 5 Army Film &
Photographic Unit
**Mulberry artificial harbour
at Arromanches**, a convoy
of ambulances on the floating
roadway, September 1944.
Imperial War Museum

elements, their installation in situ and their subsequent use. Did the young Bruno Zevi really work on this enormous project, as he claimed? His diary simply indicates that he worked from 22 February to 30 June for the Design and Engineering Section of the Office of the Chief Engineer of the American army. Its chief, Colonel W. J. Lyles, praised his work, which 'consisted principally of general design of military buildings, layout of military installations and drafting'.[55] At any rate, Ove Arup's participation in the study of certain subsystems of the Mulberries has been confirmed. The War Office accepted his application, for he had gained solid experience in constructing jetties and docks during the 1930s. His principal contribution, with Ronald Jenkins, was the development of an ingenious type of shock absorber, which was essential for securing the LST's (landing ships, tanks) to the floating bridges and making it possible to transport armoured vehicles, equipment

Mulberry artificial harbour at Arromanches, remains of a caisson, 1987. Photograph by Anne Garde. Collection of the artist

and troops.[56] These were secondary but effective components that contributed to the strategic success of a large-scale prefabrication operation, enabling the landing to take place where the Germans least expected it, on relatively flat beaches that were the least defended. Albert Speer was to state in his memoirs that the Atlantic Wall consumed 13 million cubic metres of concrete and 1.2 million tons of steel, only to be bypassed and be rendered irrelevant 'by a single brilliant technical idea'.[57]

Neufert's Machine for Laying Houses

While the complex machinery of British engineering was setting up the network of construction sites and docks to produce the components for the Mulberries, Ernst Neufert was thinking about severing the factory from its site, using the model of railway convoys used to repair damaged tracks and the experience he had gained building fortifications. The Hausbaumaschine, the plans of which he published in 1943 in his *Bauordnungslehre*, was a hybrid project

in which the techniques of the Atlantic Wall were adapted to apartment buildings. To be transported on tracks, in an unknown direction (perhaps to the east), the Gußhaus (shed for the pouring of concrete) resembled a large shelter on wheels. At the front end, trucks would bring concrete, to be poured inside the shelter. The machine would move forward, and like a snail leaving a trail of slime, would leave a continuous building of potentially infinite extension: 'In its winter coat, the construction shell (Bauschale) produces week in and week out, without concern for ice or snow, by day as by night, house after house.'[58]

Neufert's machine would have produced identical ground plans and identical facades, a result he defended on the grounds that the building types of German cities are very similar one to another, and that the most pleasing towns have uniformly lined streets. Whereas the experiments in lightweight prefabrication were linked to ideas of mobility and the permanent reconfiguration of the deployment of force, Neufert's ponderous machine, anchored to its rails, attempted laboriously – and not without unwitting irony – to provide some meaning to the equipment accumulated for the fortification of Europe. Along with other Nazi projects, such as the *Breitspurbahn*, the broad-gauge railway that Fritz Todt had dreamed up and studied down to the streamlined design of its trains and that was to provide a high-speed link between the cities of a Nazi Europe,[59] it provides the image of a perverted modernism, whose networks would have been in the service of oppression.

Ernst Neufert
House-building machine,
general view on its rails,
erection process and
cross-section, illustrations
in *Bauordnungslehre*, 1943.
CCA Collection

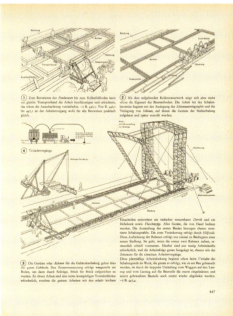

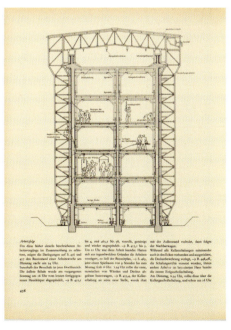

1. Le Corbusier, 'L'architecture et la guerre', *Gazette Dunlop*, vol. 19, no. 232 (May 1940), 10–13. Typewritten text, FLC B3(5)204-206, pp. 10–13.
2. *California Arts and Architecture*, vol. 61, no. 7 (July 1944), n.p.
3. See the drawings of Norman Bel Geddes, HRC, folder 342.
4. Giuseppe de Finetti, *Reggicarichi universale 'Finet'* (Milan: Giuseppe de Finetti, 1940).
5. Roland G. Ruppenthal, *United States Army in World War II, European Theater of Operations, Logistical Support of the Armies* (Washington, DC: Office of the Chief of Military History, 1953). Jerome G. Peppers, Jr., *History of United States Military Logistics 1935–1985, A Brief Review* (Huntsville: Logistics Education Foundation Publishing, 1988).
6. Keith Mallory and Arvid Ottar, *The Architecture of War* (New York: Pantheon Books, 1973), 75–83.
7. Paul Francis, *British Military Airfield Architecture from Airships to the Jet Age* (London: Patrick Stephens Ltd.), 100–10.
8. Peter Sulzer, *Jean Prouvé: Complete Works, vol. 2, 1934–1944* (Basel, Boston and Berlin: Birkhäuser, 2000), 230–36 and 258.
9. Le Corbusier, 'Utilisation des constructions démontables de guerre pour l'après-guerre', 1940, FLC, drawing 24139.
10. Sulzer, op. cit. note 8, 265–71.
11. R. Buckminster Fuller and Robert Snyder, *Autobiographical Monologue / Scenario* (New York: St. Martin's Press, 1980), 78–79.
12. Building Construction – Dymaxion Deployment Unit, US Patent Office, no. 2.343.764, deposed 21 March 1941, no. Serial 384.509, granted 7 March 1944.
13. Martin Pawley, *Buckminster Fuller* (London: Trefoil, 1990), 91–93.
14. George C. Herring, *Aid to Russia. 1941–1946: Strategy, Diplomacy, the Origins of the Cold War* (New York: Columbia University Press, 1973).
15. Beatriz Colomina, 'DDU at MoMA', *Architecture New York*, no. 17 (January 1997), 49–53.
16. R. Buckminster Fuller, in 'Museum of Modern Art Exhibits Portable Defense Housing Unit and Bomb Shelter Made from Steel Grain Bin', The Museum of Modern Art, Press Release 411009-77, 1941.
17. Fred McCosh, *Nissen of the Huts* (Bourne End: B. D. Publishing, 1997).

18. George A. Fuller Company, *The George A. Fuller Company: War and Peace, 1940–1947* (New York: George A. Fuller Company, 1947), 60–62.
19. See the remarkable work by Julie Decker and Chris Chiei, *Quonset Hut: Metal Living for a Modern Age* (New York: Princeton Architectural Press, 2005), 1–29.
20. United States Navy, *Building the Navy Bases in World War II*, Washington, Government Printing Office, vol. 1, 162, in Decker and Chiei, op. cit. note 19, 24.
21. Steven Haycox, 'Quonsets, Alaska and World War II', in Decker and Chiei, op. cit. note 19, 31–45.
22. For these precursors, see August Föppl, *Drang und Zwang* (Munich: Oldenburg, 1920); Auguste Bravais, *Mémoire sur les systèmes formés par des points distribués régulièrement sur un plan ou dans l'espace* (Paris: Bachelier, 1850).
23. Max Mengeringhausen, *Geräuschlose Wasserleitungen. Noiseless water-systems. Conduites d'eau silencieuses* (Frankfurt-am-Main: Internationaler Verband für Wohnungswesen, 1934).
24. Max Mengeringhausen, 'Zur Geschichte der 'Berliner Raumstrukturen', *Bauwelt*, vol. 61, no. 6 (1970), 226–30.
25. Konrad Wachsmann, *Holzhausbau, Technik und Gestaltung* (Berlin: Wasmuth, 1930).
26. Konrad Wachsmann, 'Projekt für zerlegbare Flugzeughallen', Vence, April 1939, heliographic print, Akademie der Künste, Berlin, KWA 5.3-001.
27. *Architecture in Steel: An Experiment in Standardization by Konrad Wachsmann*, The Museum of Modern Art, Exh. #308, 5 February–6 March 1946. See Robertson Ward Jr., 'Konrad Wachsmann: Toward Industrialization of Building', *AIA Journal*, March 1972, 33–43.
28. Konrad Wachsmann, *Wendepunkt im Bauen* (Wiesbaden: Krausskopf-Verlag, 1959), 56–57.
29. Gilbert Herbert, *The Dream of the Factory-Made House: Walter Gropius and Konrad Wachsmann* (Cambridge, Mass.: MIT Press, 1984), 119–59.
30. Martin Wagner, *The Prefabricated MW House*, 1940–1942, GSD, Frances Loeb Library. 'Rundbauten oder Kubusbauten', Frances Loeb Library.

31. Walter Gropius and Martin Wagner, 'How to Bring Forth an Ideal Solution to the Defense Housing Problem', in US 77th Congress, 1st Session, House Select Committee Investigation National Defense Migration, 1941, H. Doc. 17, p. 6949–956. Quote p. 6956. In Herbert, op. cit. note 29, 238.
32. See his recollections in Michael Grüning, *Der Wachsmann–Report; Auskünfte eines Architekten* (Basel, Berlin and Boston: Birkhäuser, 2001), 454–57.
33. Patent Serial 445216, patent application deposed by Konrad Wachsmann and Walter Gropius, 30 May 1942.
34. Herbert, op. cit. note 29, 254–56.
35. Willo von Molke, 'Prefabricated Panels for Packaged Buildings', *The Architectural Record*, vol. 93, no. 4 (April 1943), 50.
36. Herbert, op. cit. note 29, 276. Herbert cites Burnham Kelly, *The Prefabrication of Houses* (Cambridge, Mass.: Technology Press/Wiley, 1951), 60.
37. Advertisement 'From Wartime Plastics-Bonded Plywood . . . This "Plas-2-Point House" for Postwar Living', *Monsanto Magazine*, October–November 1943. On these two projects, see Peter Blake, *Marcel Breuer Architect and Designer* (New York: The Museum of Modern Art, 1949), 80–81 and 84. Joachim Diller, *Marcel Breuer. Die Wohnhäuser 1923–1973* (Stuttgart: Deutsche Verlags-Anstalt, 1998), 217. Barry Bergdoll and Peter Christensen, eds., *Home Delivery. Fabricating the Modern Dwelling* (New York: The Museum of Modern Art; Basel, Boston and Berlin: Birkhäuser, 2008), 86–89.
38. 'Ice Cream Store on Wheels, Chicago; Bertrand Goldberg and G. V. Black, Architects', *The Architectural Forum*, vol. 71, no. 2 (August 1939), 29–30.
39. Drawing at The Art Institute of Chicago, Bertrand Goldberg Archive, RX 23664/158.2.
40. Michel Ragon, *Goldberg: dans la ville / On the City* (Paris: Paris Art Center, 1985), 138.
41. Bertrand Goldberg and Betty J. Blum, 'Oral History of Bertrand Goldberg' (Chicago: The Art Institute of Chicago, 1992), 143. Cited by Lori Hanna Boyer, 'Bertrand Goldberg and the Legacy of 1945', in *1945. Creativity and Crisis: Chicago Architecture and Design of the World War II Era*, edited by Robert V.

Sharp and Elizabeth Stepina (Chicago: The Art Institute of Chicago, 2005), 10.

42. Richard Neutra, 'Planning Postwar Fabrication', *California Arts and Architecture*, no. 60 (1943), 23–24.

43. Between 1941 and 1942, the magazine *Techniques et architecture* explored the entire spectrum of usable materials.

44. R. B. White, 'War-Time Committees and Temporary Houses', in *Prefabrication. A History of its Development in Great Britain* (London: Her Majesty's Stationery Office, 1965), 122–65.

45. Ove Arup, letter [apparently unpublished] to the *RIBA Journal*, 14 November 1943, in Peter Jones, *Ove Arup. Masterbuilder of the Twentieth Century* (London and New Haven: Yale University Press, 2006), 104–06.

46. Andrei Burov, statement to the 11th plenum of the directorate of the Architects' Union of the USSR, 16 August 1943, in *Iz istorii sovetskoi arkhitektury 1941–1945 gg.: Dokumenty i materialy: Khronika voennykh let: Arkhitekturnaïa pechat*, edited by Tatyana Malinina (Moscow: Nauka, 1978), 84 and 86.

47. Brian Harpur, *A Bridge to Victory: the Untold Story of the Bailey Bridge* (London: Her Majesty's Stationery Office, 1991), 3.

48. Sir Donald Coleman Bailey, Robert Arthur Foulkes and Rodman Digby-Smith, 'The Bailey Bridge and its Development', in *The Civil Engineer in War. A Symposium of Papers on War-Time Engineering Problems* (London: The Institution of Civil Engineers, 1948), 374–75.

49. *The Civil Engineer in War*, op. cit. note 48, 453.

50. R. E. Stewart, 'Military Bridging', *Structural Engineer*, vol. 24, no. 11 (November 1946), 565–89.

51. Cited in Neil Parkyn, *Superstructures. The World's Greatest Modern Structures* (London: Merrell, 2004), 134.

52. Allan Harry Beckett, 'Some Aspects of the Design of Flexible Bridging, Including "Whale" Floating Roadway', in *The Civil Engineer in War*, op. cit. note 48, vol. 2, 385–400.

53. John Holmes Jellett, 'The Lay-Out, Assembly and Behaviour of the Breakwaters at Arromanches Harbour (Mulberry "B")', in *The Civil Engineer in War*, op. cit. note 48, 291–312. The best account by a protagonist of the operation is W. J. Hodge, 'The Mulberry Invasion Harbours.

Their Design, Preparation and Installation', *The Structural Engineer*, vol. 24, no. 3 (March 1946), 125–92. See also Guy Hartcup, *Code Name Mulberry. The Planning, Building and Operation of the Normandy Harbours* (Newton Abbott, London and Vancouver: David & Charles, 1977).

54. 'Portable, Prefabricated Harbors are the Allies' Newest Weapon in the Vital Battle of Supply', *The Architectural Forum*, vol. 81, no. 6 (December 1944), 166–72.

55. Colonel W. J. Lyles, certificate delivered to Bruno Zevi, 29 June 1944, Fundazione Bruno Zevi, Rome.

56. Jones, op. cit. note 45, 107. On this aspect of the works, see W. J. Hodge, 'The Mulberry Invasion Harbours. Their Design, Preparation and Installation', *The Structural Engineer*, vol. 24, no. 3 (March 1946), 140 and 142.

57. Albert Speer, *Inside the Third Reich* (New York: Simon & Schuster, 1970), 353.

58. Ernst Neufert, *Bauordnungslehre* (Berlin: Volk und Reich Verlag, 1943), 471.

59. Anton Joachimsthaler, *Die Breitspurbahn Hitlers* (Freiburg: Eisenbahn-Kurier Verlag, 1981).

9/ Macro and Micro, or the Issue of Scale

The main trend of our time is toward bigness. The general belief seems to be that things become better as they become bigger. Everyone is greatly impressed by bigness. Only a few are aware of the dangers of substituting quantity for quality, a value only human beings can create. Ludwig Hilberseimer, 'Bigness and its Effect on Life', 1944[1]

The great exists in the midst of the small; it precedes its environment. The great is not born of the small, but the small, the common, the everyday, draws its existence from the great. At the beginning was the great! Friedrich Tamms, 'Das Grosse in der Baukunst', 1944[2]

In March 1941, *The Architectural Record* showed a chart of forthcoming construction projects under the rubric of 'large-scale operations'.[3] An extension of the public programmes of the New Deal, these would be, above all, complex operations involving many protagonists and dealing with difficult functional requirements, but on a scale that would of itself entail a whole new dimension to the work. Among the principal belligerents, the scope of the organisational, economic and scientific tasks at hand led well before 1939 to the undertaking of colossal planning and construction projects. These included projects directly linked to combat operations, the expansion of the

George Edwin Bergstrom
David Witmer
War Department, Pentagon (1941–1943), Arlington, Virginia,
aerial view of the Pentagon courtyard, 1949. National Archives and Records Administration, Washington

administrative sphere in the economy and the armed forces, the creation of centres for scientific research and experimental production, and ultimately to the massive exploitation and extermination of prisoners.

The first major construction project of this type was without a doubt the Maginot Line, a project whose complex spatial organisation has been described above, and which would be followed by other operations that stretched for greater distances – but were discontinuous and less complex – such as the Atlantic Wall. But these large constructions were more remarkable for the logistics involved than for their role in battle.

Infrastructure and Superfactories

These planning programmes and constructions were a specific expression of 'bigness', the actual benefits of which were contested by Ludwig Hilberseimer, who favoured a planned decentralisation.[4] But the roads, camps and structures built in the United States for the war can also be seen as the militarisation of the American technological sublime mentioned above.[5] Although mega-projects were built in various countries, more were built in the United States than in all the other warring countries put together. This was also true of the First World War, with Cass Gilbert's Army Supply Base (1917) in Brooklyn being the largest building in the world at that time. This double block 800 metres long, where troops and equipment transferred from trains to ships, was finally put to full use between 1941 and 1945. The description provided by Gilbert of the building, underscoring the restraint of his design, could equally apply to the designers who followed him during the Second World War. 'The whole system of building is characterized by extreme simplicity – there is not one moulding or ornament of any kind. The structures are impressive and majestic because of their vast scale, severe design, and fine proportions.'[6]

Strategic threats led to extensive road projects, the most memorable of which were the construction of the Burma Road and the Alaska Highway. The latter was intended to enable the transport of reinforcements and equipment to Alaska in the event of a Japanese invasion – which their attack on the Aleutian Islands rendered plausible. Started in February 1942 and completed eight months later, the Alaska Highway was over 1,645 miles (2,600 kilometres) long.[7] Difficulties encountered during construction included swamps and permafrost. The CANOL (Canada Oil) pipeline was built alongside it, and the route was transformed from the emergency road it had been when work started to a permanent roadway that could be used year-round. After that, it lost its strategic importance as the Japanese threat receded. It would still serve a crucial role in the transfer of almost eight thousand airplanes to the Soviets starting in 1942, and would function both as a guide and service road for landing strips located along its length. The urban planner Benton MacKaye was even more ambitious than the developers of the road and urged in vain that it be extended all the way to

Siberia, across the Bering Staits.[8] In the Far Eastern theatre, the Burma Road, which had initially been built by the British and Chinese, then in turn by the American army in 1940, was intended to convey Allied equipment to China as part of the Lend-Lease programme, and connected Lahio, in Burma, with Kunmung, in the Yunnan. This project would be no less difficult to complete than the North American road.[9]

For its part, industry called for construction on the scale of small cities or whole neighbourhoods, as illustrated by a montage from 1943, in which *The Architectural Forum* superimposed an image of all of downtown Manhattan and the new Dodge factory in Chicago, built with a new technique of ribbed concrete arches.[10] Few superlatives were spared in descriptions of the enormous volume of the Ford factory in Willow Run, Michigan – 'the most enormous room in the history of man'. Charles Lindbergh, the aviation hero, was recruited by Ford to speak for the factory. In 1942, comparing it to an archetype of the sublime, he described it as a 'stupendous thing – acres upon acres of machinery and jigs and tarred wooden floors and busy workmen . . . a sort of Grand Canyon of a mechanized world'.[11] The title of champion could also be claimed by the Grand Coulee dam, which after 1942 provided electricity to the factories of the West Coast of the United States, and was the basic source of energy for the production of steel and aluminium. At the same time, the construction of a powerful fleet – which would include ten thousand ships in 1945, ten times the number from five years previously – required the creation of 'superdocks' after 1930, in Norfolk, Philadelphia and New York.[12]

DODGE CHICAGO PLANT DIVISION OF CHRYSLER CORP.

Manufacturing and administration required a massive workforce, whose movements needed to be controlled. The rational assembly and dispersal of large numbers of people, be they workers, employees, soldiers or prisoners, became one of the basic elements of wartime logistics. Services that accompanied mobilisation, such as mail, led to the construction of giant buildings, like the gigantic military post office built in 1944 in Long Island City by the Corps of Engineers, under the direction of Colonel Edgar W. Garbisch. Built in three and a half months on the site of the former Madison Square Garden boxing stadium, it covered 680,000 square feet (63,000 square metres) near the tracks of the Pennsylvania Central, and ensured the circulation of mail between the railway, roads, ships and planes in all directions worldwide.[13]

Albert Kahn Associates
Dodge Chicago Plant
(1943), Chicago, plan of
the factory superimposed
over an aerial photograph
of Lower Manhattan,
illustration in
The Architectural Forum,
December 1943.
CCA Collection

The Pentagon,
a Modern Labyrinth

The New York post office, which was built late in the war, was only one of the many significant projects undertaken in the fields of communications and bureaucracy as part of the war effort, which was marked by a spectacular expansion of administration. Architects were involved in this process and sought to find their place in the increasingly extended branches of the federal government. A photomontage from *The Architectural Record* of March 1942 shows a cohort of men with their matching hats and briefcases marching towards the Capitol building, together with a map of Washington showing ten or so government departments where their skills might be put to good use.[14] These would soon be lost among the proliferation of different administrative branches, the principal one being, of course, the one directly responsible for the conduct of the war, which was so badly housed that its offices overflowed onto the Mall, where a dozen or so office buildings were aligned in a row, as if on parade.[15] The largest war project, built with the aim of rationalising military bureaucracy, was the complex of offices to house the Department of War in Arlington, Virginia, named after its form– an equal-sided pentagon. The idea of providing a single building to house the three armed services, which were dispersed over seventeen sites throughout the Washington area, led Roosevelt to instigate the project to build a single administrative seat of 500,000 square feet (46,000 square metres) at Foggy Bottom. But by mid-1941 this building was already proving to be too small, as the secretary of war Henry L. Stimson would point out. The president, who had been assistant secretary of the navy during the First World War, did not want a proliferation of temporary buildings in the capital and supported the idea of a large building in the suburbs. Management of the project was assigned to Brigadier General Brehon B. Somervell, head of the Construction Division of the Quartermaster Corps, who had previously been in charge of the Works Project Administration in New York City, where he had seen the building of La Guardia Airport to completion. The job subsequently fell to Colonel Leslie R. Groves, of the Army Corps of Engineers, who had been responsible for all the projects linked to the mobilisation of 1941–1942, about fifteen times the size of the proposed project for Washington in total. Groves is known for having bought at some point half of the annual production of timber in all the United States.[16]

The site that was initially chosen, west of the Potomac, had once been part of Robert F. Lee's plantation and had been conserved since the beginning of the century for the creation of a park or the extension of the Arlington Cemetery. A first design was proposed by George Edwin Bergstrom, an experienced professional from Los Angeles, where he had been the associate of John Parkinson, working on the headquarters of the *Los Angeles Times*, the Hollywood Bowl and the Pasadena Civic Center, among other projects. Bergstrom had been recruited through the engineer and landscape architect Gilmore Clarke, chairman of the National Commission of Fine Arts. He was assisted and then replaced by his colleague David Witmer, who had previously been architectural supervisor of the Southern California District of the Federal Housing

Leet Brothers photo

"ON TO WASHINGTON?"

Authority. Witmer was at one point in charge of a hundred architects and as many engineers, providing jobs for fifteen thousand workers employed by the general contractor John McShain.

The initial proposal was for a complex of five-storey office blocks covering 4 million square feet (371,500 square metres) and served by a complex highway interchange. It formed a rectangular space surrounded by roads. One of the access roads sliced off a corner, turning it into an irregular pentagon. The complex consisted of two

series of buildings: two continuous buildings in five segments with secondary buildings attached to them at right angles. This overall form was retained when the project was transferred to a new site. The original site had aroused strong opposition, since the new building risked blocking the view from the Lincoln Memorial towards the cemetery. In Gilmore Clark's view, this would profane the view from L'Enfant's tomb[17] and destroy that gesture of reconciliation represented by the direct visual link between Lee's mansion and the Lincoln Memorial. So the entire project was relocated a mile down the Potomac, to Hell's Bottom. It would occupy the site of an abandoned airfield and railway switchyard, home to a sparse array of obsolete buildings and inhabited by fifty black families, who were displaced forthwith.

George Edwin Bergstrom
David Witmer
War Department, Pentagon, Arlington, Virginia, version with a central tower, 1941. Library of Congress, Prints & Photographs Division, Theodor Horydczak Collection

Top:
'On to Washington?', illustration in *The Architectural Record*, March 1942. Photograph by Leet Brothers. CCA Collection

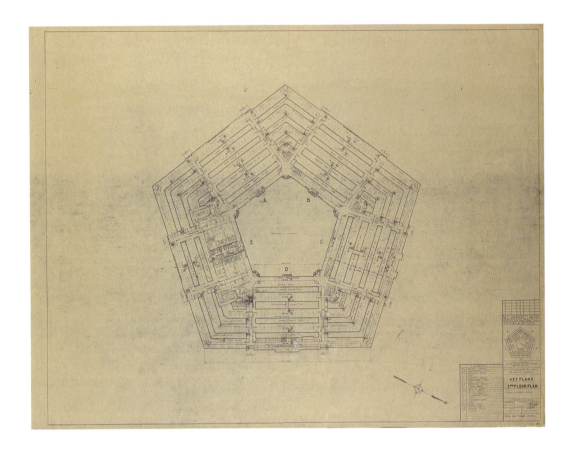

The first meeting with the architects took place on 17 July 1941, and the overall plan was drawn up over a weekend. The pentagonal shape, now regular, with the secondary buildings eliminated, allowed for an effective use of the site. The parallel rows of buildings were set on a single two-storey base. The extraction of 700,000 tons of sand and gravel for use as aggregates in the concrete created a pond that still exists, to the east of the building. The reinforced concrete structure, left raw with the imprints from its formwork exposed – except where the exterior facades were clad in stone – rested on 41,492 concrete columns, which were chosen over a steel frame so that the metal could be used for naval and mechanical projects. The choice is supposed to have saved enough steel to have built a battleship. The tower initially planned at its centre was abandoned and replaced with a courtyard, which resulted in both savings in costs and a height limit of 77 feet 3½ inches (24 metres), which was required to maintain the view of Arlington Cemetery. Cost considerations resulted in the elimination of elevators as well, which were replaced by ramps. Access to the offices was through five concentric polygonal rings and ten radial corridors, making it possible to cross the building diagonally, so that no trip from one office to another, along the 26 kilometres of

George Edwin Bergstrom
David Witmer
War Department,
Pentagon (1941–1943),
Arlington, Virginia,
ground floor plan,

May 1942.
Department of Special
Collections, University
of California, Los Angeles,
Richard and Dion Neutra
Papers

corridors, took more than seven minutes. The polygonal shape itself was less important in this respect than the fact that the building was basically circular, so that routes between remote points were like diameters. *The Architectural Forum* took evident delight in claiming that 'here is the picture of a future architecture in which buildings will be linked to their users by smooth-flowing traffic networks'.[18] A signage system was clearly essential, and each floor is colour-coded, while the offices are numbered in sequence: a letter or number indicates the floor (B=basement, M=mezzanine, 1 through 5 the floors), another letter indicates which ring the room is located on, a number indicates the corridor and two final numbers the specific row of offices. Although the building had 'gained

a reputation as the latest word in modern elaboration of the labyrinth', observers noted that 'getting lost in the building actually requires a special gift of bewilderment'.[19]

A new network of roads was constructed around the building itself, including 48 kilometres of new roadway, 21 bridges and 3 interchanges on a site of 576 acres, of which 67 acres were devoted to parking in order to accommodate almost 10,000 vehicles. The pace of construction was brisk. Work onsite started on 11 September 1941, and the first occupants started moving in less than eight months later, on 30 April 1942.

George Edwin Bergstrom
David Witmer
**War Department,
Pentagon** (1941–1943),
Arlington, Virginia,

overall view from
the air, 1953.
National Archives and
Records Administration,
Washington

The work would be completed on
15 January 1943, when Roosevelt was
attending the Casablanca conference,
at which the Allies decided that the final
objective of the war was nothing less
than Germany's unconditional surrender.

The rushed construction process inspired
many an anecdote, like the one told by
Alan Dickey, a member of the project team.
When a colleague asked him 'How big should
I make that beam across the third floor?'
he answered: 'I don't know, they installed
it yesterday.'[20] The total floor area of the
completed Pentagon is six million square
feet. Its 125 telephone switchboards were
supplemented by a system of pneumatic
tubes for sending paper. These modern
touches were offset by the layout of the
cafeterias, restrooms and other sanitary
equipment, each built in duplicate, one

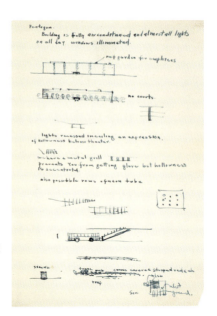

Top: Myron Goldsmith
**War Department,
Pentagon** (1941–1943),
Arlington, Virginia,
sketch, n.d., between
1942 and 1945.
CCA Collection,
Myron Goldsmith fonds

George Edwin Bergstrom
David Witmer
**War Department,
Pentagon** (1941–1943),
Arlington, Virginia, overall
aerial view with roadways
and parking areas, 1952.
National Archives and
Records Administration,
Washington

WATROUS FLUSH VALVES
installed in the
new War Department
Pentagon Building—WORLD'S
LARGEST OFFICE BUILDING

3,004 Watrous Flush Valves will bring to the new War Department Pentagon Building the "all-out" water and maintenance saving performance for which Watrous Valves are famous. Here in the world's largest office building these valves will demonstrate the tremendous extra savings that are possible when each valve can be *adjusted* to the actual water requirements of the fixture on which it is installed.

For detailed information on Watrous Flush Valves, including the new "V" model which is now available for essential applications, write for Bulletin No. 858-W or see the new 1943 Sweet's Catalog File, Catalog No. 39, Section 27.

THE IMPERIAL BRASS MFG. CO., 1238 W. Harrison St., Chicago, Ill.

Top: George Edwin Bergstrom
David Witmer
War Department, Pentagon
(1941–1943), Arlington,
Virginia, view of access
doors to the interior ramps,
illustration in *The Architectural
Forum*, January 1943.
CCA Collection

Bottom: **'Watrous flush
valves installed in the new
War Department Pentagon
Building'**, advertisement
in *The Architectural Forum*,
January 1943.
CCA Collection

for blacks and one for whites, until Roosevelt asked that the signs saying 'Whites only' be removed.

As *The Architectural Forum* wrote shortly before the completion of construction, 'The Pentagon is not big – it is super.'[21] The building's horizontality and the complete lack of the structural heroics so typical of vertical construction appeared to be in stark contrast, for example, to the designs of the engineer and architect Myron Goldsmith, who served during the war as a bridge designer for the US Army Corps of Engineers, and would publish some reflections on 'the effects of scale' in 1953.[22] Yet the Pentagon still shared some of the same underlying attitudes. *The Architectural Forum* saw in the Pentagon the beginnings of the end to the relationship between the building and the city: 'Perhaps the greatest lesson of the Pentagon is here: as building approaches the scale technically feasible, the distinction between architecture and city planning vanishes. Despite its shortcomings, The Pentagon gives a real foretaste of the future.'[23] The future would prove this correct. In one of the most effective metonymies of modern history, the Pentagon to this day denotes the entire American military apparatus, and the 'foretaste' provided by the building was that of wars to come. This was not necessarily going to be the case, because the first idea for the building's post-war use, advanced by Roosevelt, was to transform it into a central archive, a project whose load requirements had already been taken into account in the design of the floor slabs. Some elected officials would inevitably see this gigantic complex as a dangerous symptom of the hypertrophy of the state. Robert Rich, for example, a senator from Pennsylvania called out to the executive branch in these words: 'Where are you going? Where are you taking this nation? No place except to national bankruptcy and ruin.'[24] As for the urban plan of Washington, the Pentagon marked a break with the principles of L'Enfant, as the landscape architect Elbert Peets observed: a centripetal logic of concentration was taking the place of a centrifugal logic for the distribution of public buildings in the grid. 'The government capital is running away from the city; the government buildings are being concentrated together and separated from the buildings of the city.'[25]

Auschwitz, a Place for All Industries

A very different future was coming into sharper focus in the successive plans for an industrial town whose central core was the Silesian village of Oświęcim (Auschwitz), where the Austrian army had built a garrison during the First World War. This place of the most extreme and methodical barbarity did not go untouched by architects, as Deborah Dwork, Robert Jan van Pelt and Niels Gutschow have shown.[26] The Nazis did not invent the camps in general, nor concentration camps in particular – this type of place of confinement was invented by the British during the Boer War[27] – but they were the first to combine confinement, industrial production and industrialised murder, and Auschwitz was the largest camp created in Europe by the Reich, both in its size and in the flow of humanity that passed through it.[28] Its location was determined primarily by the conjunction

of several factors: the central location of the region and its rail connections to western, eastern and southern Europe, its proximity to mineral resources, its water supply and the availability of good land for cultivation.

The rather complex episodes of planning have been meticulously analysed by Niels Gutschow, who has given an account of the projects developed, on the one hand, for the town of Auschwitz and the residential areas planned for its extension, and on the other hand, for the different elements of the concentration camps and their distribution in the region. Auschwitz was an industrial programme even before becoming a camp, and the first projects were developed with that intent. They were carried out jointly by the German civil authorities, the central administration of the SS and the giant conglomerate of I. G. Farben, which was drawn by the region's potential, as Otto Ambros, who was in charge of industrial chemicals for the Ministry of Armaments and director of the firm, would recall after the war.[29] It was an ambitious undertaking, a veritable new city linked to a regional and ecological vision that left little to chance. It was a response to the labour requirements of Buna, a subsidiary of I. G. Farben that produced synthetic rubber from coal and oil, and to the requirements of SS companies such as the Deutsche Ausrüstungswerke, the Deutsche Erd- und Steinwerke and Golleschauer Portlandzement AG, as well as a number of mining concerns. It was also the result of methodical collaboration between numerous local, regional and Berlin-based administrative entities, all under the control of the Reich's political and economic leaders.

The first phase of the project for the town and the studies for the development of the

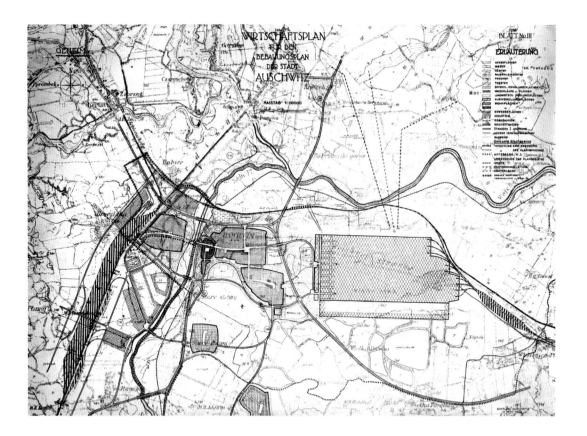

region were coordinated by the Breslau architect Hans Stosberg, who had received his professional training in Munich and Hanover, and had written a thesis on urban history. In early 1941, Stosberg was put in charge of the *Landesplanung* of a zone that was to accommodate forty thousand inhabitants. To this effect, he produced a *Raumordnungskizze* (a sketch development plan). At the same time, starting in 1940, shortly after Rudolf Höß was named commandant of the first camp installed in the Austrian barracks, the architects Fritz Ertl, who had been a student at the Dessau Bauhaus from 1928 to 1931, and August Schlachter, originally from Biberach, set up a first design office to oversee the planning and construction of the camp itself.

Auschwitz was more than a single camp, in fact. It was a network of three main camps: Auschwitz I, the *Stammlager*,

or base camp, laid out in a trapezoidal plan to the southwest of Oświęcim, which included the administrative centre, the central services and offices; to the west, laid out in a rectangular plan, was Auschwitz II, or Birkenau, the extermination camp with its gas chambers and crematory ovens, with an archipelago of smaller agricultural camps attached to it; and to the east, the still larger rectangle of Auschwitz III, or Monowitz, adjacent to the Buna chemical factory of I. G. Farben, with extensions for a series of mines and industrial camps. At its peak, the Auschwitz complex would hold 135,000 prisoners in a region previously

Hans Stosberg
Auschwitz, economic
development plan for
the town, October 1942.
Panstwowe Muzeum
Auschwitz-Birkenau

only sparsely inhabited; 1.1 million people would be murdered there.[30]

In 1941, Stosberg restored the town hall and worked on setting up public facilities, declaring that he was engaged in 'the construction of a new German city and the reconstitution of the old Silesian annular town square'.[31] As Stosberg imagined it, the new town of Auschwitz would combine urban areas and country zones in a unique form, that would hold to the theoretical principles of *Stadtlandschaft* – the city conceived as landscape. Equally careful architectural refinements and ecological considerations were incorporated into the project, especially in regards to the use of water resources for drinking purposes as well as for industrial uses, and water purification, especially the polluted waters from factories.[32] His plan of August 1942

was a particularly detailed application of the principles of low-density housing drawn from the German experiments of the 1920s, with its hierarchies of blocks and social centres. Stosberg laid out two *Neustädte* (new towns) around the old town and its castle, one to the east and one to the west, along with a *Bereitschaftsiedlung*.[33] Architect Clemens Anders, who trained in Munich and was employed by I. G. Farben, would design houses as part of the plan. The landscape architect Werner Bauch, the Reichslandschaftsanwalt (landscape advocate) for the Beskiden region, designed a 'green belt' between the camp and the

Auschwitz, *The Bauleitung* (construction office), interior view of the offices, c. 1942. Panstwowe Muzeum Auschwitz-Birkenau

town, as well as rural developments at Rajsko.[34] A series of wooded zones were to be created to cut off any view of the camps from the neighbourhoods of the new town. Camill Santo, an engineer trained in Karlsruhe and Braunschweig, and head of construction for I. G. Farben, sought to give the technical facilities at Monowitz a 'coherent architectural face'.[35]

Ertl was subsequently employed by the Zentrale Bauleitung der Waffen SS und Polizei Auschwitz, under the direction of the engineer Karl Bischoff. The latter had been recruited by the SS Hans Kammler, an architect trained in Danzig and Munich, who had been a draughtsman for Paul Mebes in Berlin before working in several research agencies for housing and planning during the Weimar Republic. Krammler, who had previously worked for the Luftwaffe, was in charge of construction for all the Reich's camps, directing operations with an iron fist. It was there that he had known Bischoff, who was building military landing fields in France. In 1941, Ertl drew up several versions of the plans for the new camp in Birkenau in the region administered by the SS. It was designed for 97,000 prisoners, using the standardised barracks designed by Kammler's department. Kammler also included sheds initially intended as stables, and the complex was built by Russian prisoners at a terrible cost in lives.[36] The Birkenau camp was laid out in an implacable serial arrangement, with only a gigantic assembly ground to interrupt the endless rows of sheds.

After the Wannsee conference of 20 January 1942, which was to ratify the 'final solution', that is to say, the fully planned extermination of the eleven million European Jews, construction started on the gas chambers of Birkenau and the capacity of the camp set at 200,000, before being limited to 140,000. The Austrian builder Walter Dejaco and the architect Georg Werkmann had drawn up the first crematoria in 1941, for the disposal of the corpses of Soviet prisoners, with the help of the firm of Topf und Söhne. Dejaco and Ertl would subsequently design and equip the gas chambers located under the crematoria. These were first used in March 1943.

While Ertl was working on the camp buildings, Lothar Hartjenstein, who had studied in Hanover, Karlsruhe and Stuttgart with Paul Schmitthenner, drew up studies for the open spaces. In November 1942, he completed a 'Generalbebauungsplan' for the western part of the town, whose picturesque layout contrasted sharply with the repetitive rows of the camp. In Rajsko, Joachim Caesar, who was in charge of the camp's agricultural department, oversaw facilities for the cultivation of *Taraxacum*, or kok-saghyz, a Russian dandelion with a rubbery sap that was supposed to be a substitute for the rubber tree, *Hevea braziliensis*.[37]

The professionals who worked on the creation of the new town of Auschwitz were thus products of the best German schools. They represented practically all the architectural trends of the 1920s and 1930s, with experienced traditionalists working alongside radical modernists such as Ertl, under the remote but effective champion of state modernisation, the demonic Kammler, who reviewed the basic designs of the buildings. At the bottom of the chain of command, within the Bauleitung, were to be found the prisoners recruited for their skills as engineers and architects, such as Szymon Syrkus, a pioneer of modernism in Poland since the 1920s, who designed the greenhouse for the Rajsko camp, used for the cultivation of kok-saghyz. Another insight into this policy can be gained by the fact that in 1941, Bischoff had asked, apparently in vain, to use three 'German architect detainees' from Buchenwald.[38]

At the end of the war, the Auschwitz area had become one of the largest industrial enclaves of Europe. A new form of urban development had appeared, extending far beyond the perimeter of the camp. It combined technological experimentation with the forced labour of 'inferior' populations, in a sort of industrial despotism that was carefully designed architecturally. While there can be little doubt as to the cynical functionality of the systems put in place for production and for methodical extermination, one can still recognise in the large roofs, the chimneys and even the openings in the crematoria, whose machinery has been studied by Jean-Claude Pressac,[39] those formal themes found in the works of Paul Mebes, Werner Lindner, Georg Steinmetz and Friedrich Ostendorf, in which a learned

Werner Lindner
'Buildings for the state saltworks', illustration in *Bauten der Technik*, 1927. Collection of the author

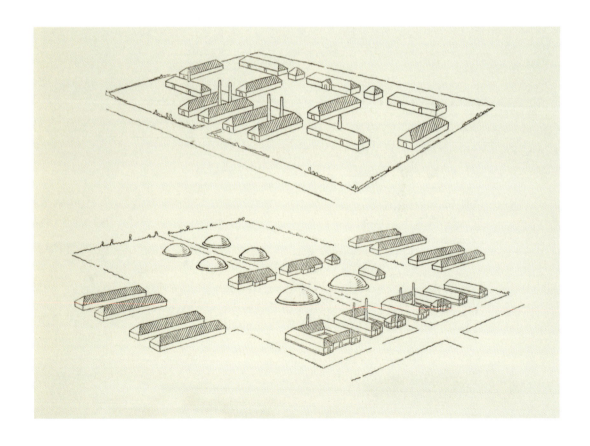

nostalgia for the buildings of the agrarian economy is presented as a relevant response to the programmes of large-scale industry. These evocations of what might be called the industrial vernacular had been used in the reconstruction of East Prussia after 1918 by the *Heimatschutz* (homeland protection) movement as a way of both preserving and modernising German traditions.[40] Reference to such a tradition was evidently perfectly at home within the context of the particular activities that were part of the colonisation of the east, namely the industrial enslavement and extermination of 'inferior' peoples. But above and beyond issues of architectural language, Auschwitz raised the problem of the ethics of its designers. Albert Speer attempted to justify his actions by claiming that his 'obsessive fixation on production

and output statistics' had 'blurred all considerations and feelings of humanity'.[41] But in the case of the architects of the Bauleitung of Auschwitz, who could not be unaware of the horror at work some metres away from their drawing board, this pale excuse cannot even be contemplated.

Peenemünde: Rockets in the Pinewood

Five years before the Americans started to work on developing a nuclear weapon with their Manhattan Project, the Germans,

Szymon Syrkus
Greenhouses for horticulture in the camp annex of Rajsko, Auschwitz, interior view, 1943. Panstwowe Muzeum Auschwitz-Birkenau

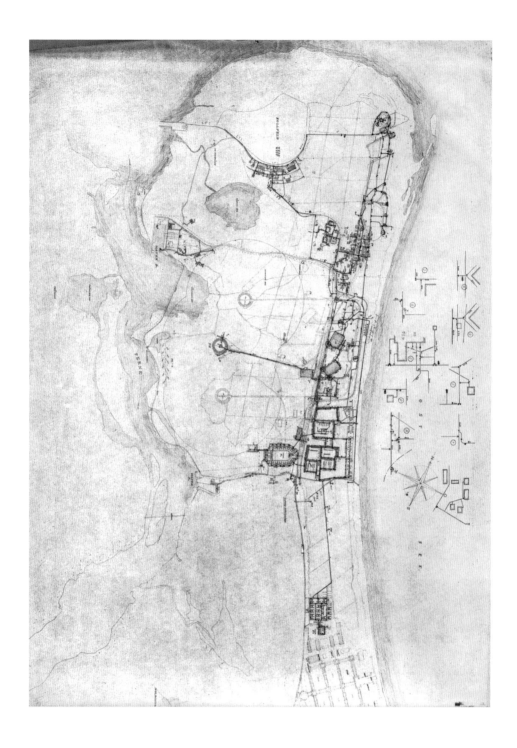

**Army testing facilities,
Peenemünde**, general site
plan including mechanical
conduit networks, 1944.
Deutsches Museum

where the rockets could be tested in flight, and an industrial complex where they were manufactured. The overall project was run by the Wehrmacht, and construction started before the war with the Siedlung Karlshagen for housing scientific and technical staff. It was designed in 1939 by Hans Simon and Dipl.-Ing. Fritz Pötschke. Laid out on an axial plan, according to the principles of traditional town planning, the housing complex was linked to the railway station by a monumental entrance generally known as the 'Brandenburg Gate',[43] because of its main portico. In 1939, construction of a coal-fired electrical plant, indispensable to the production of liquid rocket fuel, was contracted out to the construction department of Siemens. Completed in 1942, it was similar in design to the buildings designed by Hans Hertlein for the Berlin branches of the company at Siemensstadt. On 15 September 1940, responsibility for the project as a whole fell to Albert Speer, the Generalbauinspektor für die Reichshauptstadt. Speer assigned it to the *Baugruppe* (architectural team) of the architect Walter Schlempp, who had previously constructed the neoclassical building of the Deutsche Gemeindetag on the east-west axis of the new Berlin under Speer's direction. The local coordinator for construction was the engineer Heinrich Lübke. The staff of Albert Speer and Heinrich Eggerstedt also worked on a project for another *Siedlung* between Zinnowitz and Trassenheide, but only the housing for prisoner workers would be built.

As regards the base itself, which covered about twenty square kilometres, a single

whose atomic research fortunately remained at an embryonic stage, began developing ballistic missiles. In the unequal symmetry of these installations, the counterpart to the atomic sites of Los Alamos and Oak Ridge was the research and testing facility at Peenemünde. This ultra-secret complex was created in 1936 on the Baltic coast, at the very north-western tip of the island of Usedom. Its construction was assigned to a Bauleitung that was headed by Dipl.-Ing. Johannes Müller, later replaced by the Dipl.-Ing. Abendroth and Hans Simon, and consisted of as many as fourteen departments.[42] The first major element of the base was the HVA (Heeresversuchsanstalt Peenemünde), or army research centre, which came under the Wehrmacht's jurisdiction, and whose purpose was the production and testing of the A-4 (Aggregat-4) rocket, later called the V-2. In 1938, Peenemünde-West was built and given over to the Luftwaffe. Its role was primarily as a testing facility for rocket-propelled aircraft such as the Heinkel He 176 and the Messerschmitt Me 163, and for the Fieseler Fi 103 flying bomb, later known as the V-1. The HVA was by far the more complex of the two. It included a research laboratory, a place

Walter Schlempp
**Army testing facilities,
Peenemünde**, launch
pad VII, general view,
aerial perspective, 1942.
Deutsches Museum

Walter Schlempp
**Army testing facilities,
Peenemünde**,
F1 assembly building,
general view, exterior
perspective, 1942.
Deutsches Museum

Walter Schlempp
**Army testing facilities,
Peenemünde**, staff
dwellings, aerial
perspective, 1942.
Deutsches Museum

architectural language was used for the production and testing facilities – the halls where the propellant fuels (liquid hydrogen and oxygen) and rockets were made, the weapons assembly halls and the firing ranges. Test stand VII, for example, combined an architecture of strong tectonic expression, notably in the rocket assembly building. The general appearance was that of a modern factory, with a concrete skeleton and brick infill, set in a pine forest. The launch pad was protected by an elliptical embankment. The only buildings designed in a nostalgic style were the first structures built to house the Bauleitung in 1936. With these two adjacent universes, Peenemünde, like most aeronautical sites, was a compact symbol of the contradictory pluralism of the Third Reich. Returning to the ultimate goal of this work, 282 A-4 (later known as V-2) rockets would be launched from Peenemünde between June 1942 and February 1945, under the direction of the general of artillery Walter Dornberger and the scientific team of Wernher von Braun. The massive and successful British

bombing raids of Operation Hydra on 17 and 18 August 1943 would permanently cripple the large-scale production of missiles and would mark the 'beginning of the end' for the site, whose purpose had been discovered fairly early on by the Allies.

The inverted double of Peenemünde was an underground megaproject, which was built in response to this bombardment and led to the relocation of experimental activity to Blizna, in Poland. On Hitler's orders, the manufacture of 'secret' weapons was relocated in October 1943 to the centre of Germany. A former mine near Nordhausen, in the Harz Mountains, which had previously been used to stockpile strategic materials, was transformed into a place of production directly under Speer, who created the Mittelwerk GmbH for this purpose. It operated with equipment evacuated from Peenemünde and other sites. Under the direction of Hans Kammler, who had impressed the Nazi leadership so much that at one point he was in line to replace Speer, the SS took over operations, transforming the subsidiary of the Buchenwald camp, known as Dora, into a camp called KZ Mittelbau.[44] Almost 6,000 V-2's and thousands of V-1's would be produced in the tunnels of Mittelwerk, where up to 4,000 prisoners and 500 free labourers worked alongside each other.[45]

Oak Ridge, Atomic and Secret

Shortly after the capitulation of Japan, the world would discover the 'birthplace of the atomic bomb' in the heart of the United States. *The Architectural Record* revealed 'a secret city of 75,000 people busily working on they knew not what', which it turns out was 'one of the largest construction projects of the war', and wondered which epithet would best describe it: 'Mighty, staggering, solid, permanent, vast, utilitarian?'[46] Oak Ridge, which had previously remained entirely in the shadows, was only one of the ten or so operations set up by the Manhattan Engineer District, a programme set up in July 1942 with the aim of developing an atomic bomb before the Germans, who were suspected at the time of having their own military nuclear programme. The starting point of the programme was a now famous letter that Albert Einstein sent to Franklin D. Roosevelt on 2 August 1939. The programme was set up by Vannevar Bush, the head of the Office of Scientific Research and Development, and by James B. Conant, the president of Harvard University, who both pushed for the creation of a programme 'Napoleonic' in scope.[47]

The editors of *The Architectural Forum* did not hesitate to claim in 1945 that 'Atom City' was not only 'unquestionably the biggest job of quick town building ever attempted in the USA', but that it was also 'the best job of emergency housing to come out of the war'.[48] Not all reviews were as positive. For others, the 'functionalist spirit' of the town only occasionally resulted in 'interesting design'.[49] The location for Oak Ridge was chosen because of its good electricity supply. It housed several production units for nuclear fuel, but was only one of the three principal sites of the Manhattan Project, which would employ up to 125,000 people, from manual labourers to Nobel laureates in physics, including legions of women working in the factories and thousands of young physicists in the Special Engineering Department, recruited from every university in the country.

Site X – its first code name – was not as extensive as site W, at Hanford, Washington, on the banks of the Columbia River, where the plutonium used at Nagasaki was produced in factory B, designed by the University of Chicago, led by Enrico Fermi,[50] but it was much larger than site Y, at Los Alamos, New Mexico – also known by its address: P.O. Box 1663 in Santa Fe – where the bombs were assembled with the fissile material already

'Concrete and steel frame buildings that house atomic diffusion processes at Oak Ridge, Tennessee', cover of *Engineering News-Record*, August 1945. CCA Collection

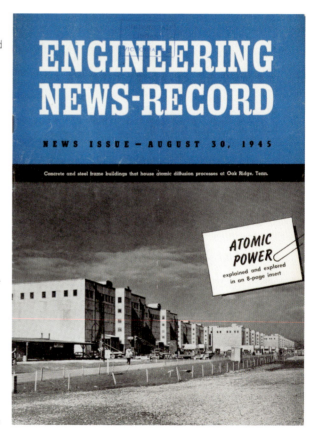

produced, and where the physicist J. Robert Oppenheimer conducted the scientific part of the programme with a staff of five thousand.

In September 1942, Leslie R. Groves was put in charge of the Manhattan Project. Groves had demonstrated his organisational skills during the construction of the Pentagon, leading to his promotion to the rank of general. The project entailed the creation of a large number of scientific and industrial sites of varying sizes. In an issue of 1945, which raised 'the giant curtain of secrecy' hanging over the programme, the *Engineering News-Record* considered that the planning and 'construction for production of the atomic bomb was probably the largest and most rapid coordinated building job ever undertaken'.[51] Several years later, the *Journal of the AIA* described Oak Ridge as the very example of a successful new town, 'the basic program stated the danger factor, the secrecy factor, the need for cheap electricity. The decision was made to build a new permanent town for about three thousand families somewhere fairly well away from civilization, where there was adequate electric power and the topography would permit the segregation of the town from the plant.'[52] The proximity of the Norris and Watts bar dams, built by the Tennessee Valley Authority during the New Deal, was a factor in the decision, as was the pressure that Kenneth D. McKellar, head of the Senate Appropriations Committee, put on Roosevelt. The site, which was initially called Clinton Engineer Works, included three main facilities.

The X-1 nuclear reactor was the first to be built, followed by the Y-12 isotope separation factory, run by the Tennessee Eastman Corporation. Twenty-two thousand people worked at Y-12, where uranium-235 was produced by an electro-magnetic process, using calutrons – a method suggested by the University of California at Berkeley. The third and final piece was the gigantic K-25 plant for separating out uranium hexafluoride by gaseous diffusion, which went into operation in February 1945. The name K-25 was a combination of the K from the Kellex Corporation, the company selected to design it, before Union Carbide took over contracting, and the last two digits of the isotope it was to produce. Built from high-strength cement by the J. A. Jones Construction Company of Charlotte, North Carolina, the factory used a process developed at Columbia University. It was housed in a three-storey U-shaped building, 800 metres long by 300 metres wide, covering a total of 44.5 acres. It contained three thousand 'cascades' to enable the progressive separating out of fissile uranium, with the isotope 238 remaining as a residue, as well as hundreds of kilometres of nickel piping that needed to be perfectly sealed.[53]

The nearby town built to accommodate the workforce formed a rectangle one mile by six miles, located in the heart of almost 60,000 acres of land, some of it ruthlessly expropriated by the army. The initial project to house three thousand inhabitants – which turned out to be off by a factor of ten – was given to the engineering firm of Stone and Webster. The military considered the design inadequate and had concerns not just about its technical quality, but also about aspects of the architectural and landscaping. In February 1943, they recruited the John B. Pierce Foundation and the architectural firm of SOM (Skidmore, Owings & Merrill), which

had been founded in Chicago in 1936. John Merrill drew up a preliminary design using unlabelled topographic plans and aerial photographs, well before being informed of the actual location of the project and being allowed to visit the site. The final programme called for a total population of 42,000, and in 1944 it was decided that the housing would be transformed into a permanent town. The existing landscape was largely conserved in the laying out of the main east-west axis, Tennessee Avenue, from which secondary roads extended to the north and south.

Most of the dwellings were prefabricated: 3,000 were built by the Pierce Foundation out of Cemesto panels. Others were brought in from Dallas by road in 'room sections' and assembled together in place. Still others came from Indiana and West Virginia. SOM developed assembly-line techniques inspired by the car industry. By 1945, 10,000 single-family houses had been constructed, along with accommodation for 13,000 in well-equipped apartment buildings and in sometimes primitive dormitories, together with 5,000 trailers and 16,000 'hutments' or shacks, the only dwellings provided for the African American workers. The latter were limited to low-level jobs and were squeezed together six to a space measuring 25 square metres. In the winter of 1945, the population of the town reached 100,000, and the factories worked nonstop. The need for housing would never be fully satisfied, even though the army had delegated construction and management of the housing to a private company, the Roane-Anderson Company, a subsidiary of the Turner Construction Company of New York.

K-25 Gaseous Diffusion Building for isotope separation (1944–1945), Oak Ridge, Tennessee, aerial view of the complex, 1945.

Photograph by H. B. Smith. National Archives and Records Administration, Washington

Community facilities were created at the same time as the housing for the workers and scientists (known as the 'long hairs' by the military, who watched over them closely)[54] and included a network of shopping malls with galleries. The main one, Jackson Square, served as the town centre, with its cinemas, schools and basic services such as the post office. *The Architectural Forum* would praise its reductive aesthetics: 'Unfinished walls look better than gingerbread.'[55] For their part, the military were aware of having an unusual opportunity and admitted that 'most of us have never been, or will never again be in a position to build our own community – to our own specification'.[56] The reality would not be quite so rosy, and tensions abounded between the different groups gathered together for a single purpose – to produce the bomb before the Nazis.[57] When some German visitors were invited a few years later to take a look at a city 'built on a powder keg', they would be impressed by the 'coherent style of this ultra-modern city designed by a single Chicago firm', but somewhat less enthusiastic about a way of life where 'everything was planned'.[58]

Skidmore, Owings & Merrill
Oak Ridge, town and administrative centre
(1944–1945), Oak Ridge, Tennessee, aerial view, 1945. Photograph by J. E. Westcott. National Archives and Records Administration, Washington

Enormous but Invisible

These four projects were very different in
their territorial extent – from the Pentagon,
which was concentrated in a point, to the
Manhattan Project, spread out over an entire
continent, and the Nazi installations that
mobilised entire regions. They were also
very different in their prominence, ranging
from being apparently completely visible
to total concealment. They were both vast
and hidden, and were in each case subject to
a rigid security policy that masked their true
purpose. If the main features of the Pentagon
were visible to the public, even though its
operation was not, Oak Ridge remained a
town hidden from everyone, whose purpose
was even concealed from thousands of its
workers. Auschwitz and Peenemünde were
shielded by Nazi censorship and by the use
of semantic artifice to conceal, even in the
archives, the machinery of the 'final solution'.
As the Red Army was approaching, the
Nazis tried in vain to eradicate all traces

of the Holocaust by blowing up
the gas chambers and crematoria and
exterminating any remaining witnesses.

David E. Nye has quite appropriately
included the atomic tests and the Manhattan
Project in the category of the 'technological
sublime'.[59] There is no doubt that these four
projects, looked at from this perspective,
were linked to that other form of the
sublime which is state action. They were
condensations of the administrative,
productive and scientific intentions of the
Allies, on the one hand, in their struggle
to defeat fascism, and of the Nazis, on
the other hand, bent on creating a racist
and repressive order across a continent.
In more specifically architectural terms,

Skidmore, Owings
& Merrill
**Oak Ridge, collective
dwellings** (1944–1945),
Oak Ridge, Tennessee,
exterior view, 1945.

Photograph by
Bill Hedrich.
National Archives
and Records
Administration,
Washington

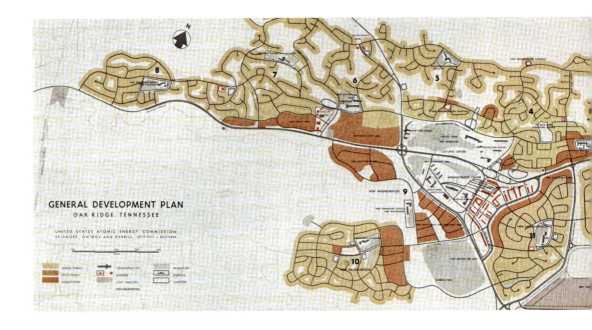

GENERAL DEVELOPMENT PLAN
OAK RIDGE, TENNESSEE

UNITED STATES ATOMIC ENERGY COMMISSION
SKIDMORE, OWINGS AND MERRILL, ARCHITECT – ENGINEER

Friedrich Tamms, an experienced specialist in large-scale construction, who had worked for the Organisation Todt in road bridge construction before building the fortified towers of Berlin, Hamburg and Vienna, compared the 'rigorous law of architecture' to the law of the monument, which he defined in terms of its grandeur. He linked it to other scales when he claimed that 'the small, the common, the everyday draw their existence from the great'.[60] The megaprojects presented here are in fact closely linked to work on a small scale that was equally characteristic of the programmes carried out during the war.

Norms and Modules

The object of Tamms' critique in his text on the 'great' in architecture was the 'gentle law in art' outlined in 1943 by the traditional architect from Stuttgart, Paul Schmitthenner.[61] This plea was an attempt to aestheticise one of the most widespread phenomena of wartime

construction, namely the reduction in size of structures used to shelter both civilians and combatants. Discussions about the need to limit dimensions and appeals for greater standardisation were widespread, as they were a response to the preoccupation with economising on space and materials. The question of standards, which was the central subject of this discussion in all countries, was posed in terms of the experimental investigations of the 1920s and 1930s, which themselves should be understood as part of a much longer process. For Lewis Mumford, the turning point had been the need to clothe the army of 100,000 created by Louis XIV, and he claimed that this 'was in fact the first large-scale demand for absolutely standardised goods'.[62]

The standard is not an absolute category, but rather a field of interaction between states, architects, businesses and industrialists rife with contradictory tendencies. The aim, depending on the specific case, was either to adapt peacetime standards, reducing them so as to simplify

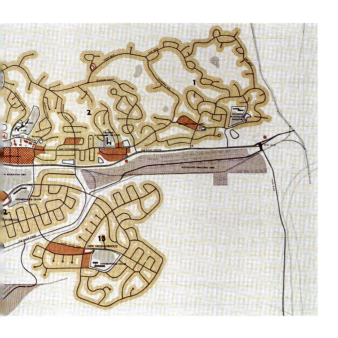

and increase production, or else to create
new standards in order to establish new
rates of production. In early 1942, Talbot F.
Hamlin issued a warning to his profession:
'One the most important tasks facing the
architectural profession is the preservation
of standards – standards of all kinds –
standards of construction, standards of
design, standards of practice, and especially
standards of thinking. The *temptation* to
lower standards is terrific.'[63] Hamlin's
call to avoid impoverishment was written
under American conditions. The direction
followed by the other warring nations was
different, especially in relation to standards
in dimensions, whose promulgation was
unavoidable in all cases. The First World
War had led to the first steps towards
the establishment of standards in
the United States and Germany, with the
creation in 1917 of the Normalienausschuß
für den allgemeinen Maschinenbau, at
the instigation of Heinrich Schaechterle,
the engineer at the head of the Spandau
Königliche Fabrikationsbüro. In 1917,

this became the Normenausschuß der
deutschen Industrie, which was the source
for the DIN (Deutsches Institut für Normung)
standards. In France, the Commission
Permanente de Standardisation, set up
in 1918 at the behest of minister Étienne
Clémentel, paved the way for the creation of
the Association Française de Normalisation,
or AFNOR, in 1926. During the Vichy regime,
a Commissariat à la Normalisation was
established to coordinate the work of the
committee for standards of the association
of architects, the organisation committee
for the building trade and civil engineering,
and the committee for producers of
materials. Shortly after its creation, the
committee for standards of the association
of architects issued the norm NFP01-001
regarding 'modulation', which was adopted
in September 1942, establishing a module
of 10 centimetres. This research on an
'elementary unit of measure' to govern
the dimensions of structures and elements
of construction, a path that the French
developers of standards undertook jointly, was
presented more as a measure of social order
than a response to an emergency situation.[64]

At the same time, the Organisation Todt
was committed to a definition of dimensional
norms and standards that was to be valid
for all the work it was commissioned to
carry out throughout occupied Europe.
As the *Handbook of the Organisation Todt*,
published in 1945 by the Allies, would point
out, 'Standardisation – always dear to the
Germans and carried almost to the level of
a religion by the Nazis – is the keynote of all
OT construction work.'[65] The organisation
put some of its best minds to work in order
to produce a set of standards that would

apply not only to fortified structures, but also to all the annexes. Thus Rimpl, who was put in charge of the Prüfstelle für Großbauvorhaben (test station for large structures) by Speer in 1942, also worked on standardisation, and Fritz Leonhardt became head of the division for 'Bauforschung, Entwicklung und Normen' (building research, development and standards) of the Todt Organisation in the summer of 1944.

The goal of mastering dimensions was obviously shared by all the belligerents, with the aim both of economising on materials and resources and speeding up design and execution. Thus alongside the macroscopic projects, now extending across large regions, microscopic projects, or rather projects reduced to minimal dimensions, were undertaken in the realm of housing and of course in places of detention. The most extreme compression of human bodies within buildings was instituted in the Nazi concentration camps. A monumental language requiring a certain architectural expertise was occasionally employed on the perimeter walls and entry pavilions, but professional designers would also make their own contributions to the design of the interiors of the barracks. As early as 1934, Richard Riemerschmid, who had been an active member of the reform movements

in southern Germany at the turn of the century, had drawn up plans for *Arbeitslager* buildings that combined minimal cells with 'living rooms' without natural light.[66] Subsequently, along with the reuse of barns and stables, the specification of simplified construction and crowded conditions would be pushed to unimaginable extremes in the prescriptions of the Organisation Todt and in the work of the Nazi Bauleitung offices. It was a kind of sadistic radicalisation of the research on the minimal habitation that had been conducted under the Weimar Republic by architects in Berlin and Frankfurt, whose purpose was the large-scale production of affordable modern housing for large urban populations. The concentration camp version of the *Existenzminimum* was compressed beyond any imaginable limits. In the case of the first constructions for Soviet prisoners at Auschwitz, they would not exceed 0.3 square metres (3 square feet) per person, which was less than one tenth of the area allotted in most projects for barracks housing.[67] These sheds were designed by the Bauleitung of Karl Bischoff, and the plans were approved

Fritz Ertl
Auschwitz-Birkenau
concentration camp
(1942–1943), detention sheds, overall view, November 1944. Panstwowe Muzeum Auschwitz-Birkenau

in Berlin by Hans Kammler, which gave them the status of actual political policy.

But the policies of the Reich should not be reduced to the two extremes of planned cities like Wolfsburg and Salzgitter on the one hand, and inhumanly crowded shelters for deportees on the other. A social housing policy was introduced on 15 November 1940, by order of the Führer, and was initially implemented under the Reichskommissar für soziale Wohnungsbau, Robert Ley, and developed further under Speer, which consisted largely of building *Volkswohnungen* (popular housing). Although this was rationalised, industrial housing, it was built to a fairly high standard.[68] The policy was geared to look ahead to the post-war years, especially in the programmes of 1941–1942, but from 1943 it needed to address the needs for emergency wartime housing, conceived

along rational lines, but in conjunction with an articulation of traditional building types and stylistic details that conformed to the precepts of *Heimatschutz*. At first, a *Landschaftsnorm* (landscape norm) was decreed, but this was abandoned after Speer was named Generalbevollmächtigter für die Regelung der Bauwirtschaft (director general for building regulation) in 1942.[69] At that point, research led to the development of a *Kriegseinheitstyp für den Wohnungsbau* (uniform type for wartime housing), which was studied in all its construction details by Ernst Neufert, with very small footprints

Ernst Neufert
Uniform wartime dwelling type (1943), rows of dwellings, plans, section and elevations, illustration in *Der soziale Wohnungsbau in Deutschland*, July 1943.
CCA Collection

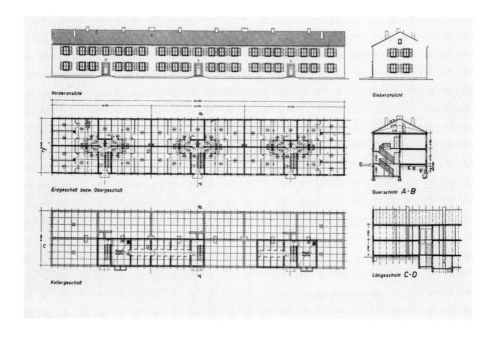

and techniques of wood construction enabling them to be built by an 'unskilled labour force' – a euphemism for slave labour.[70] For his part, as we have seen, Hans Spiegel, who was in charge of implementing standardisation for the Deutsche Akademie für Wohnungswesen, helped develop the *Behelfsheim* (emergency housing).[71] The norms he proposed for the Deutsches Wohnungshilfswerk were reduced: the standard plans assigned 4.1 x 5.1 metres for a unit, with one adult's bed and one child's bed above it. Adhering to this basic measure, combinations of several houses and local variants were allowed, as long as the basic unit did not exceed 20 to 22.5 square metres (215 to 240 square feet) and the height remained between 2.2 and 2.8 metres.

Neufert's Universal Measures

In 1945, in response to a commission from Swiss industrialists seeking to export their prefabricated houses, Swiss modernist architect and artist Max Bill drew up a first account of the reconstruction of Europe, still in its very beginnings. He drew attention to a book published in 1943 by Ernst Neufert, as an example of a useful work. This large, heavy tome, resembling a slab of cut stone, was the *Bauordnungslehre* (architect's data). Bill described it as 'a fundamental work by that well-known German theoretician, permeated with the ideas of the "thousand-year Reich", but whose core would survive it.'[72] In 1939, Neufert began working for the Reich's Ministry of Aeronautics on the definition of standard plans for the production of airplanes and their equipment, which led him in 1942 to the formulation of an *Industriebaumaß*, or IBA, based on

a 2.5-metre grid, which could be applied to all construction projects and would be codified by the norm DIN 4171.[73] The *Bauordnungslehre* outlines a complete world based on norms derived from the subdivision of the metre into eight basic modules of 12.5 centimetres, whence the notion of the 'octametric' norm.

The chain extends uninterrupted from the smallest unit of the brick – whose customary dimensions and local variations were replaced by the dimensions of 24 x 11.5 x 11.5 centimetres, with an added joint thickness of 1 centimetre to complete the module, up to the other extreme of large hangars and factories using large multiples of the basic module, which Neufert illustrated ironically by redrawing the entablature of a Doric Greek temple to conform to his norms. The development of the principles formulated in the *Bauordnungslehre* would lead to the DIN 4172 standard for *Maßordnung* (dimensional ordering) based on the module of 12.5 centimetres, a development that Fritz Leonhardt worked on.[74] The development of this single modular system applicable to production at every level illustrated, more than any other project, the possibilities for standardisation afforded by the war to German industry. This system was not the only one, but it unquestionably remains the most ambitious, if not the most extraordinary.

Ernst Neufert
'Human beings: their dimensions and spatial requirements', plate from the *Bauentwurfslehre*, 1936. CCA Collection

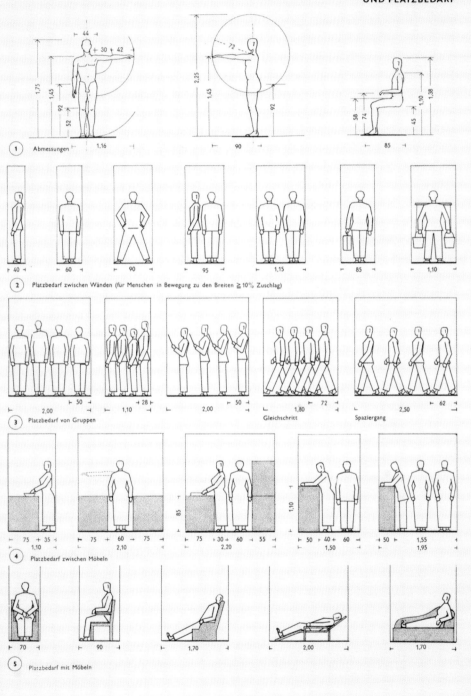

① Abmessungen

② Platzbedarf zwischen Wänden (für Menschen in Bewegung zu den Breiten ≧ 10% Zuschlag)

③ Platzbedarf von Gruppen   Gleichschritt   Spaziergang

④ Platzbedarf zwischen Möbeln

⑤ Platzbedarf mit Möbeln

311

1. Ludwig Hilberseimer, 'Bigness and its Effect on Life', in *The New Regional Pattern. Industries and Gardens, Workshops and Farms* (Chicago: Paul Theobald, 1949), 130.
2. Friedrich Tamms, 'Das Grosse in der Baukunst', *Die Baukunst*, supplement to *Die Kunst im Deutschen Reich*, vol. 8, no. 3 (March 1944), 50.
3. 'The Architect in Large-Scale Operations', *The Architectural Record*, vol. 89, no. 3 (March 1941), 89.
4. Hilberseimer, loc. cit. note 1, 130. Hilberseimer refers to Morris L. Ernst, *Too Big* (Boston: Little, Brown and Co., 1940), a book critical of large-scale business.
5. David E. Nye, *American Technological Sublime* (Cambridge, Mass.: MIT Press, 1994).
6. Cass Gilbert, 'The Brooklyn Army Supply Base', 30 December 1919, quoted by Mary Betts, 'Cass Gilbert, Twelve Projects', in *Inventing the Skyline: the Architecture of Cass Gilbert*, edited by Margaret Heilbrun (New York: Columbia University Press, 2000), 135.
7. Heath Twichell, *Northwest Epic: The Building of the Alaska Highway* (New York: St. Martin's Press, 1992).
8. Benton MacKaye, 'Alaska-Siberia Burma Road', *The New Republic*, 2 March 1942, 292–94.
9. Tan Pei-ying, *The Building of the Burma Road* (New York and London: Whittlesey House and McGraw-Hill, 1945).
10. 'Dodge Chicago Plant', *The Architectural Forum*, vol. 70, no. 12 (December 1943), 49.
11. Charles Lindbergh, quoted by Andrew Scott Berg, *Lindbergh* (New York: G. P. Putnam's, 1998), 439–40.
12. Hugh Conway and James E. Toth, 'Building Victory's Foundation: Infrastructure', in Alan Gropman, *The Big 'L': American Logistics in World War II* (Washington: National Defense University Press, 1997), 199–200 and 217–18.
13. 'Army Post Office', *The Architectural Forum*, vol. 81, no. 5 (November 1944), 85–94, 166.
14. 'On to Washington?', *The Architectural Record*, vol. 91, no. 3 (March 1942), 38–40.
15. 'Boomtown', in David Brinkley, *Washington Goes to War* (New York: Alfred A. Knopf, 1998), 104–37.

16. William Lawren, *The General and the Bomb: a Biography of General Leslie R. Groves, Director of the Manhattan Project* (New York: Dodd, Mead, 1988), 59.
17. Gilmore Clarke, *Report of the Commission of Fine Arts, NARA DC RG66*, cited by Steve Vogel. *The Pentagon: a History: the Untold Story of the Wartime Race to Build the Pentagon and to Restore it Sixty Years Later* (New York: Random House, 2007), 65. Pierre Charles L'Enfant designed the basic plan for Washington.
18. 'Pentagon Building Arlington, VA', *The Architectural Forum*, vol. 93, no. 1 (January 1943), 40.
19. Alfred Goldberg, *The Pentagon: The First Fifty Years* (Washington: Historical Office, Office of the Secretary of Defense, 1992), 85.
20. Brinkley, op. cit. note 15, 75.
21. 'Pentagon Building Arlington, VA', op. cit. note 18, 39.
22. Myron Goldsmith, 'The Tall Building: the Effects of Scale', master's thesis, Chicago, Illinois Institute of Technology, 1953. A revised version appears in 'The Effects of Scale', *Buildings and Concepts* (New York: Rizzoli, 1987), 8–23.
23. 'Pentagon Building Arlington, VA', op. cit. note 18, 39.
24. Brinkley, op. cit. note 15, 73.
25. Elbert Peets, cited by Jane Jacobs, *The Death and Life of Great American Cities* (New York: Random House, 1971), 173.
26. Robert Jan van Pelt and Deborah Dwork, *Auschwitz: 1270 to the Present* (New Haven and London: Yale University Press, 1996). See also Niels Gutschow, *Ordnungswahn: Architekten planen im 'eingedeutschten Osten' 1939–1945* (Gütersloh: Bertelsmann; Basel, Boston and Berlin: Birkhäuser, 2001). I have dealt briefly with this question in Jean-Louis Cohen, '"La mort est mon projet": architectures de la déportation', in *La Déportation et le Système concentrationnaire nazi*, edited by François Bédarida and Laurent Gervereau (Paris: Musée d'Histoire contemporaine BDIC, 1995), 32–41.
27. Giorgio Agamben, *Homo Sacer: Sovereign Power and Bare Life*, translated by Daniel Heller-Roazen (Stanford: Stanford University Press, 1998).

28. Ulrich Herbert, Karin Orth and Christoph Dieckmann, eds., *Die nationalsozialistischen Konzentrationslager 1933 bis 1945. Entwicklung und Struktur* (Göttingen: Wallstein, 1998).
29. Gutschow, op. cit. note 26, 82.
30. Frantiszek Piper, 'Die Rolle des Lagers Auschwitz bei der Verwirklichung der nationalsozialistischen Ausrottungspolitik', in Herbert, Orth and Dieckmann, eds., op. cit. note 28, 390–414.
31. Gutschow, op. cit. note 26, 111.
32. Robert Jan van Pelt, 'Auschwitz: From Architect's Promise to Inmate's Perdition', *Modernism/Modernity*, no. 1 (1993), 80–120.
33. Hans Stosberg, *Generalbebauungsplan* for the city of Auschwitz, August 1942, coll. Gutschow. In Gutschow, op. cit. note 26, 104–05. For an analysis of the successive stages of the plan, see ibid., 115.
34. On the environmental policies of the Third Reich, see *How Green were the Nazis?: Nature, Environment, and Nation in the Third Reich*, edited by Franz-Josef Brüggemeier, Mark Cioc and Thomas Zeller (Athens: Ohio University Press, 2005).
35. Minutes of the meeting held on 24 March 1941. Gutschow, op. cit. note 26, 201.
36. Van Pelt and Dwork, op. cit. note 26, 263–75.
37. My mother, who was a chemist by profession, and a political prisoner, worked in this section of the camp.
38. Note from Karl Bischoff, State Museum, Auschwitz, 1941, in Gutschow, op. cit. note 26, 130.
39. Jean-Claude Pressac, *Les Crématoires d'Auschwitz, la machinerie du meurtre de masse* (Paris: CNRS Editions, 1993).
40. Werner Lindner, *Bauten der Technik, Ihre Form und Wirkung* (Berlin: Wasmuth, 1927). Idem, *Georg Steinmetz, Die Ingenieurbauten in ihrer guten Gestaltung* (Berlin: Wasmuth, 1923). Paul Mebes, *Um 1900, Architektur und Handwerk im letzten Jahrhundert ihrer traditionellen Entwicklung* (Munich: F. Bruckmann, 1908). Friedrich Ostendorf, *Sechs Bücher vom Bauen* (Berlin: Wilhelm Ernst & Sohn, 1913). Georg Steinmetz, *Grundlagen für das Bauen in Stadt und Land*

(Berlin and Munich, Callwey, 1917–1928).

41. Albert Speer, *Inside the Third Reich* (New York: Simon & Schuster, 1970), 375.

42. Botho Stüwe, *Peenemünde-West. Die Erprobungsstelle der Luftwaffe für geheime Fernlenkwaffen und deren Entwicklungsgeschichte* (Esslingen and Munich: Bechtle, 1995), 63.

43. Günter Wiechmann, *Peenemünde-Karlshagen 1937–1943. Die geheime Siedlung der Wissenschaftler, Techniker und Arbeiter* (Frankfurt-am-Main: Peter Lang, 2006).

44. Jens-Christian Wagner, *Produktion des Todes. Das KZ Mittelbau-Dora* (Göttingen: Wallstein, 2004).

45. Johannes Erichsen and Bernhard M. Hoppe, eds., *Peenemünde. Mythos und Geschichte der Rakete 1923–1989* (Berlin: Nicolai, 2004), 231. Rainer Fröbe, 'KZ-Häftlinge als Reserve qualifizierter Arbeitskraft', in Herbert, Orth and Dieckmann, eds., op. cit. note 28, 647–50.

46. 'Birthplace of the Atomic Bomb', *The Architectural Record*, vol. 98, no. 3 (September 1945), 10 and 13.

47. James G. Hershberg, *James B. Conant: Harvard to Hiroshima and the Making of the Nuclear Age* (New York: Alfred A. Knopf, 1993), 159–62.

48. 'Atom City', *The Architectural Forum*, vol. 83, no. 4 (October 1945), 103.

49. 'Birthplace of the Atomic Bomb', op. cit. note 46, 14.

50. Harry Thayer, *Management of the Hanford Engineer Works in World War II* (New York: American Society of Civil Engineers Press, 1996). Michele Stenehjem Gerber, *On the Home Front: The Cold War Legacy of the Hanford Nuclear Site* (Nebraska: University of Nebraska Press, 1992).

51. 'Construction for Atomic Bomb Production Facilities', *Engineering News-Record*, vol. 135, no. 24 (13 December 1945), 112.

52. David S. Geer, 'Oak Ridge: A World War II New Town', *Journal of the AIA*, vol. 15 (January 1951), 17.

53. William Wilcox, *A Brief History of K-25: The Biggest Secret City Secret* (Oak Ridge: Secret City Store, 2006).

54. Louis Falstein, 'The Men Who Made the A-Bomb', *The New Republic* (26 November 1945), 707–09.

55. 'Atom City', op. cit. note 48, 107.

56. Captain P. E. O'Meara, 'Message from the Town Manager', *Oak Ridge Journal*, 2 October 1943, cited by Charles W. Johnson and Charles O. Johnson, *City Behind a Fence: Oak Ridge, Tennessee, 1942–1946* (Knoxville: University of Tennessee Press, 1981), 33.

57. Russell B. Olwell, *At Work in the Atomic City: a Labor and Social History of Oak Ridge* (Knoxville: University of Tennessee Press, 2004).

58. W. Peiner, 'Besuch in der Atomstadt Oak Ridge', *Baukunst und Werkform*, vol. 7–8 (1954), 388–92.

59. David E. Nye, 'Atomic Bomb and Apollo XI: New Forms of the Dynamic Sublime', op. cit. note 5, 224–56.

60. Tamms, loc. cit. note 2, 50; republished in an edited version in Friedrich Tamms, *Von Menschen, Städten und Brücken* (Vienna and Düsseldorf: Econ Verlag, 1974), 127.

61. Paul Schmitthenner, *Das sanfte Gesetz in der Kunst* (Strasbourg: Hünenburg Verlag, 1943). See the analysis by Hartmut Frank, 'La loi dure et la loi douce: monument et architecture du quotidien dans l'Allemagne nazie', in *Les Années 30; l'architecture et les arts de l'espace entre industrie et nostalgie*, edited by Jean-Louis Cohen (Paris: Éditions du patrimoine, 1997), 200–06.

62. Lewis Mumford, *Technics and Civilization* (New York: Harcourt Brace & Company, 1934), 92.

63. Talbot F. Hamlin, 'Design Standards in War Time', *Pencil Points*, vol. 23, no. 2 (February 1942), 67.

64. See the article by the president of the commission for standardisation in construction, L.-P. Brice,

'Du rôle social de la normalisation', *L'Architecture française*, vol. 4, no. 30 (April 1943), 23–24. And the 'Normalisation' issue of *Techniques et Architecture*, vol. 3, no. 1–2 (January 1943).

65. *Handbook of the Organization Todt*, Supreme Headquarters Allied Expeditionary Force. Counter-Intelligence Sub-Division, 1945, p. 51.

66. These drawings are held at the Munich Städtische Galerie, and were shown in the 'Kunst und Diktatur' exhibition in 1994 at the Vienna Künstlerhaus.

67. Van Pelt and Dwork, op. cit. note 26, 103–04.

68. Tilman Harlander, 'NS-Wohnungsbau und Planungskonkurrenz', in *Ernst Neufert: normierte Baukultur im 20. Jahrhundert*, edited by Walter Prigge (Frankfurt-am-Main: Campus Verlag, 1999), 358–75.

69. Tilman Harlander and Gerhardt Fehl, eds., *Hitlers Sozialer Wohnungsbau 1940–1945* (Hamburg: Christians, 1986), 32–44.

70. Ernst Neufert, 'Die Pläne zum Kriegseinheitstyp', *Der Wohnungsbau in Deutschland*, vol. 3, no. 13–14 (July 1943), 233–40. Reproduced in Harlander and Fehl, eds., op. cit. note 69, 312–19.

71. Hans Spiegel, 'Gestaltung und Ausführung des Behelfsheims', *Der Wohnungsbau in Deutschland*, vol. 4, no. 1–2 (January 1944), 1–12; vol. 4, no. 9–10 (May 1944), 97–108; and no. 13–14 (July 1944), 145–64.

72. Max Bill, *Wiederaufbau. Dokumente über Zerstörungen, Planungen, Konstruktionen* (Erlenbach-Zurich: Verlag fur Architektur AG, 1945), 174.

73. Wolfgang Voigt, 'Vitruv der Moderne', in Prigge, ed., op. cit. note 68, 20–34.

74. Fritz Leonhardt, *Baumeister in einer umwälzenden Zeit. Erinnerungen* (Stuttgart: Deutsche Verlags-Anstalt, 1984), 101.

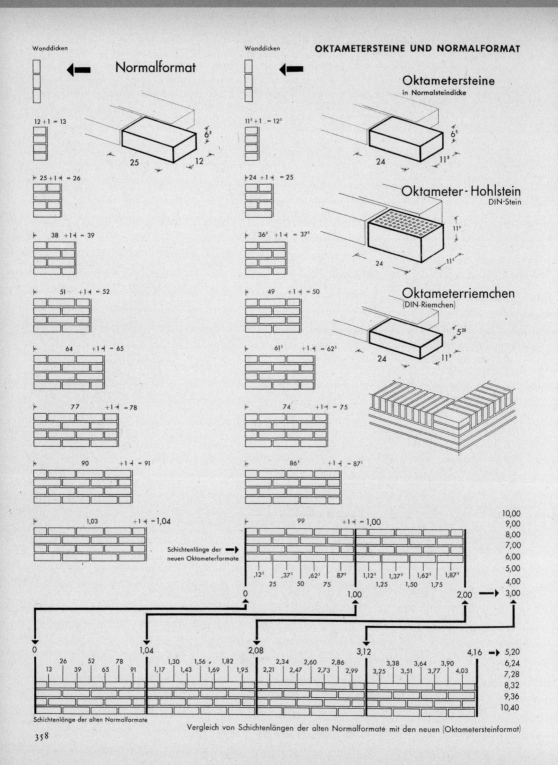

Wanddicken

Normalformat

$12 + 1 = 13$

6^5

25 12

$25 + 1 = 26$

$38 + 1 = 39$

$51 + 1 = 52$

$64 + 1 = 65$

$77 + 1 = 78$

$90 + 1 = 91$

$1,03 + 1 = 1,04$

Schichtenlänge der neuen Oktameterformate

Wanddicken

$11^5 + 1 = 12^5$

Oktametersteine
in Normalsteindicke

6^5

24 11^5

$24 + 1 = 25$

$36^5 + 1 = 37^5$

Oktameter - Hohlstein
DIN-Stein

11^5

24 11^5

$49 + 1 = 50$

Oktameterriemchen
(DIN-Riemchen)

5^{25}

24 11^5

$61^5 + 1 = 62^5$

$74 + 1 = 75$

$86^5 + 1 = 87^5$

$99 + 1 = 1,00$

,12⁵	,37⁵	,62⁵	87⁵
25	50	75	

10,00
9,00
8,00
7,00
6,00
5,00
4,00
3,00

$1,12^5$ $1,37^5$ $1,62^5$ $1,87^5$
$1,25$ $1,50$ $1,75$

0   1,00   2,00

0   1,04   2,08   3,12   4,16   5,20

| 26 | 52 | 78 | | 1,30 | 1,56 | 1,82 | | 2,34 | 2,60 | 2,86 | | 3,38 | 3,64 | 3,90 | |
| 13 | 39 | 65 | 91 | 1,17 | 1,43 | 1,69 | 1,95 | 2,21 | 2,47 | 2,73 | 2,99 | 3,25 | 3,51 | 3,77 | 4,03 |

6,24
7,28
8,32
9,36
10,40

Schichtenlänge der alten Normalformate

Vergleich von Schichtenlängen der alten Normalformate mit den neuen (Oktametersteinformat)

358

|◄— 1,12⁵ —►| |◄——— 1,25 ———►| |◄——— 1,37⁵ ———►| |◄——— 1,50 ———►|

Menschenreihen usw. immer davon ausgegangen werden kann, daß der angezogene Mann mit Mantel mindestens eine Breite von 62,5 cm und das Menschenpaar eine Breite von 1,25 m beansprucht.

Wenn 1, 2 und 3 Menschen nebeneinander gerechnet werden müssen, dann sollten diese Grundmaße als Mindestmaße gelten. Größere Reihen lassen Beschränkungen dieses Einheitsmaßes zu, so daß das Maß aus der Vielfalt von 1,25 m auch als Wandmittenmaß der raumumschließenden Wände, besonders bei Tafelbauweisen gelten kann.

Der Platzbedarf der Frau in der Breite ist etwa 12,5 cm schmaler als beim Mann. 50 cm ist hier das Regelmaß und entsprechend kleiner ist der Platzbedarf von Mann und Frau oder von Frauen miteinander.

Einige entsprechende Maßstaffelungen von 25 cm bis 2,50 m zeigen die Bildfolgen auf S. 36 und 37. Darüber hinaus ist eine vielfältige Art anderer Benutzungskombinationen möglich, die man sich an Hand der Aufbaufolge leicht selbst zusammenstellen kann.

Alle diese Platzmaßangaben lassen natürlich in der Praxis Abweichungen nach oben und auch in geringerem Maße nach unten zu.

Erfahrungsmaße der Praxis

Vergleicht man die vorstehend beschriebenen Maße mit den in der BEL, → L. 2, S. 24, 64, 212, und anderen für die gleichen Zwecke angegebenen Maßen, die dazumal ohne Hinblick auf eine übergeordnete Maßsystematik aus der Praxis entnommen wurden, so muß selbst ein Skeptiker die erstaunliche Paßfähigkeit des Moduls 12,5 zugeben.

Solche Vergleiche sind naturgemäß richtiger als theoretische Maßnahmen an Menschen und Dingen ohne Berücksichtigung der Bewährung dieser Maße in der Praxis. Es ist deshalb unbedingt notwendig, die Erfahrungsmaße unserer Vorfahren zu untersuchen, um daran die Gebrauchsfähigkeit der vorgeschlagenen Baumaße zu ergründen. → S. 38 ff.

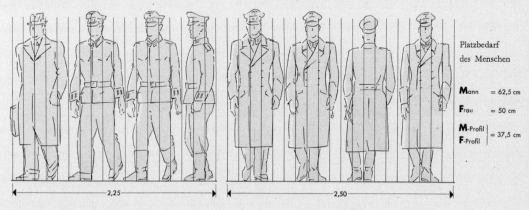

Platzbedarf des Menschen

Mann = 62,5 cm

Frau = 50 cm

M-Profil ⎤
F-Profil ⎦ = 37,5 cm

|◄——— 2,25 ———►| |◄——— 2,50 ———►|

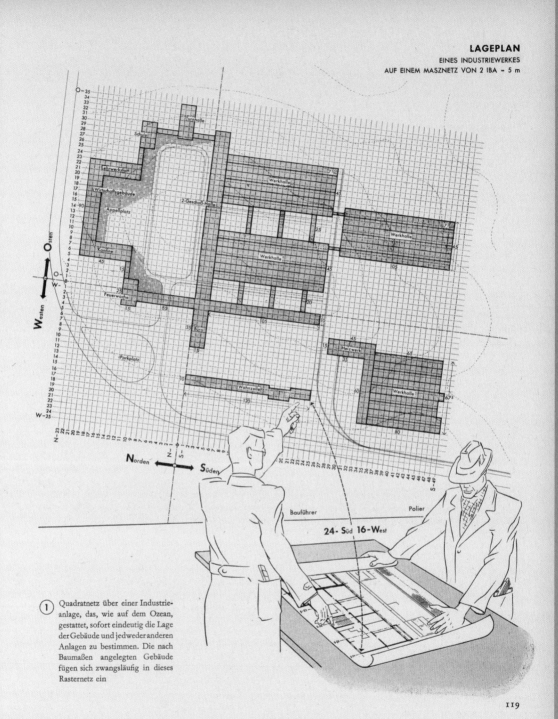

① Einfache Lagerhallen mit Bogenbindern

② Flugzeughallen mit Herabführung der Bogenbinder bis zum Erdboden mit eingesetzten Seitenwänden, entsprechend 4 und 5

③ Flugzeughallen mit Anbauten, in denen die Bogenfüße verschwinden

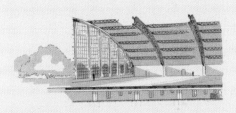

Bogenfläche, die als Reflektor die allgemeine Verteilung des Lichtes in Richtung auf die Arbeitsebene unterstützt.

Äußere Gestaltung

Auch das Äußere der Bogenhallen kann der heutige der Technik aufgeschlossenere Industriearchitekt schön und überzeugend gestalten.

Er wird nicht wie der frühere historisch gebundene Architekt die Bogenform hinter einem Scheingiebel irgendwelcher elektizistischer Form verstecken, sondern als ein wesentliches Element der Gesamterscheinung formal nutzen. → B. 211,1.

④ Weitgespannte Bogenhallen mit Unterkellerung. Träger der Kellerdecke sind zugleich Zugbänder für die Bogenbinder

Bogenführung

Als Bogenform wurde der Kreis gewählt, weil er der statisch günstigsten Parabelform am nächsten ist und dieser gegenüber einfacher in Zeichnung und Werkstatt darzustellen ist. Zur Festlegung der Bogenhöhe wurde von dem erfahrungsgemäß günstigsten Stichverhältnis - $1/8$ der Spannweite ausgegangen. Bei den Walzträgerbogen, bei denen in einem Fall 3, im anderen Fall 5 Träger über einen Lehrbogen gebogen werden sollen, mußte dieses ideale Stichverhältnis so vermittelt werden, daß der Bogen der jeweils geringsten

⑤ Bogenhallen, deren Licht durch verglasten Giebel einfällt

213

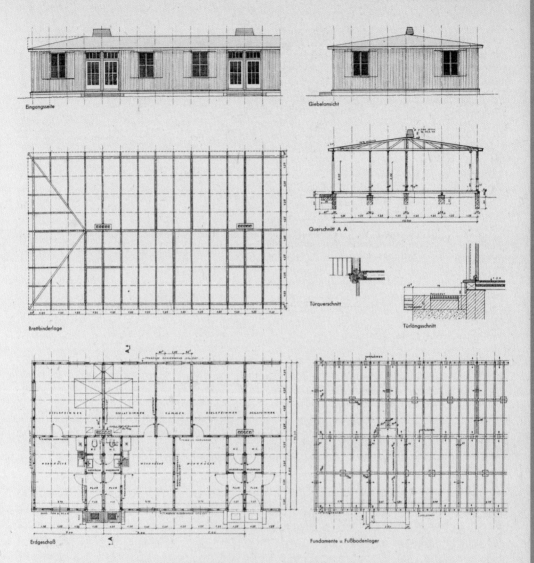

Für die Bedürfnisse der Rüstungsindustrie oder für Not-
wohnungen bevorzugt man *ortsfeste* Holzbauweisen. Auf
S. 320 wird eine solche Bauweise beschrieben, die eine gute
Wärme- und Schalldämmung bietet.

Obenstehende Darstellung zeigt dazu ein Ausführungsbei-
spiel mit 2- und 3-Zimmerwohnung mit einem Innenabort
je Wohnung, der über Dach entlüftet wird und seine Zuluft
vom Flur, durch einen Schlitz unter der Aborttür, erhält.

21 *

Ernst Neufert
**'Accommodation
in emergency shelters'**,
plate from the
Bauordnungslehre, 1943.
CCA Collection

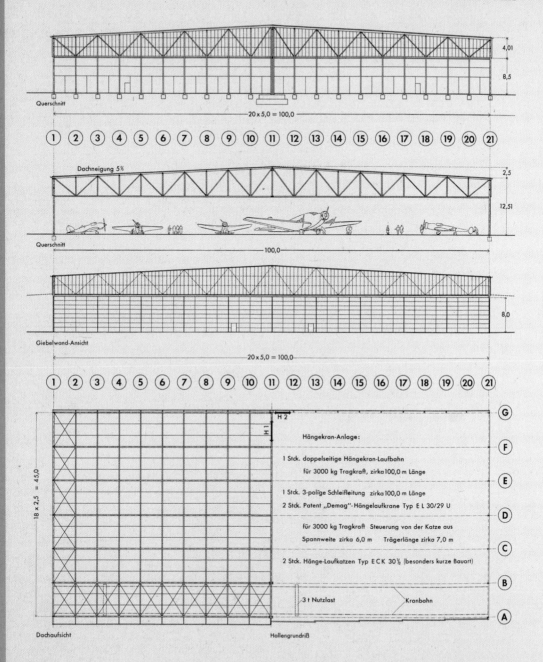

Ernst Neufert
'Aircraft hangar', plate from
the *Bauordnungslehre*, 1943.
CCA Collection

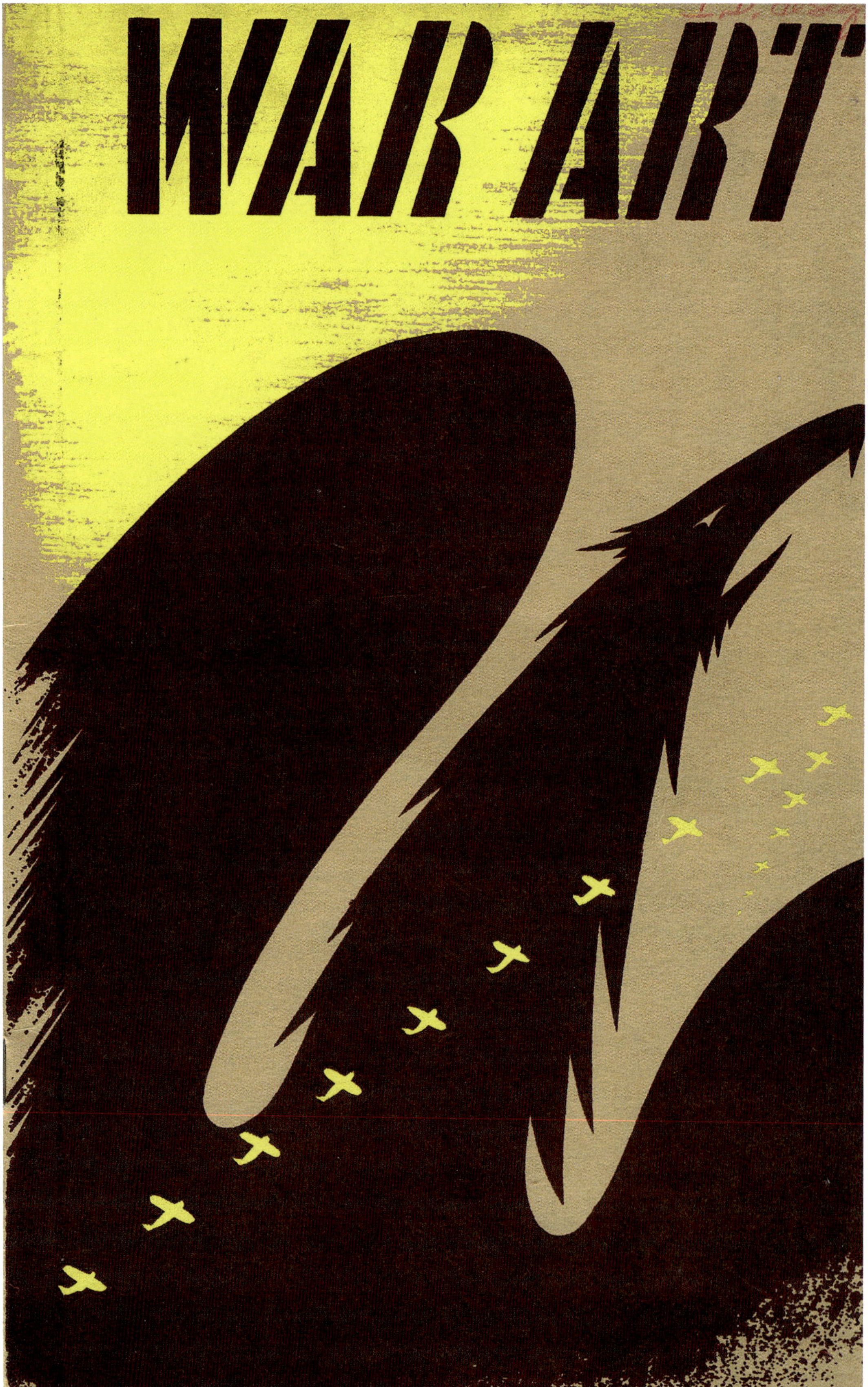
WAR ART

10/ On the Information Front

In no other field of art and architecture have the war years brought us so generous and so healthy a harvest as in exhibition design.
'The Wartime Exhibition', *The Architectural Review*, 1944[1]

In the defense of a civilization, there need to be as little a break with or indifference to the civilizing arts as possible, and as much continuity and persistence as we can manage. The artist is a consummate specialist, and yet even with the best intentions, he cannot become a first-rate soldier. His talent is required for posters and camouflage, as everyone knows. And the art of painting as such can serve the common cause.
Monroe Wheeler, 'The Artist and National Defense', 1941[2]

The Second World War was not only solidly rooted in production and administration, but it also took the form of a war of information. Information was ever-present – at the level of strategy and tactics, as part of decision-making and operations, in the persuasion of the mass of fighting forces and civilians – and it took a wide number of forms. It was particularly prevalent in the field of visual representation: maps, diagrams, photographs and caricatures that were tailored to their recipients, from political decision-makers and military staff to troops in the field and civilians manipulated by propaganda in the cities. The material apparatus was no less diverse, from secret documents to posters, the press, exhibitions, and newsreels that brought glimpses of the reality of war to cinemas where people went for entertainment.[3]

György Kepes 'War Art', cover to the exhibition catalogue for the Renaissance Society of the University of Chicago, 1942. Illinois Institute of Technology Archives

Visual information was essential for conducting military operations, which relied more than ever before on the systematic collection of data about production, construction of fortifications, territorial organisation and, of course, on the deployment of forces. In these efforts, aerial reconnaissance, which required some level of command of the skies, played an essential role. Aerial views were analysed in a constant attempt to uncover the ruses of camouflage. It could be said that one of the reasons the Allies won the war is that they could 'see' further than the Axis forces, due to a combination of superior aerial reconnaissance and better coordination of the material by intelligence services and resistance networks on the ground. The contributions of the scientists mobilised by the general staffs were crucial in the development of different types of radar – an important factor in the British victories during the battles of Britain and the Atlantic – and of sonar. Thanks to Operation Ultra, whose existence would only be revealed to the public in 1974, researchers were able to break the German codes after the capture of Enigma machines and intensive mathematical analysis. Through Operation Purple, the Americans were able to break the Japanese code they referred to as JN-25.[4] And the Colossus calculator, developed for the requirements of British code-breakers, along with the American ENIAC machine, were the immediate precursors of electronic computers.

Situations and Simulations

Collecting data was one thing, but assembling and interpreting it were different matters, and it was here that visual experts, artists and architects made significant contributions in creating environments dedicated to information. Wartime 'situation rooms' were set up for conducting operations using maps, photographs, statistics and diagrams to create panoptic systems that made it possible to view the 'theatres' of operation from the best seats available. With statistical and numerical information, the territories that were represented changed status. One could say they became quantified. The production of thematic maps and diagrams accelerated and intensified, whether their purpose was to survey German airplane manufacture in order to decide which factories to bomb, to convince the British public that the cities of the Reich were subject to destruction as well as their own, or to explain the major issues of the war to the heads of American companies.

The most advanced undertaking of the war in this connection was the Visual Presentation Branch, later renamed the Presentation Division, created in November 1941 as part of the Office of Strategic Services (OSS), and directed by economist Hubert C. Barton.[5] It sought both to investigate the different industrial and military dimensions of the conflict and to develop techniques of visually conveying these analyses. Artists, architects and filmmakers such as Walt Disney and John Ford[6] were employed to that end. The most ambitious of the projects undertaken by this team, which had been recruited by William J. Donovan, the founder of the OSS, was the presidential situation room, which was to be built beneath the White House and was inspired by British precedents. The project was launched in 1941 and given the code name 'Q-2'. It involved an unprecedented collaboration between the three main American industrial designers, Henry Dreyfuss, Raymond Loewy and Walter Dorwin Teague. Norman Bel Geddes was kept out of it, no doubt for being too whimsical. The documents that have been preserved also show traces of input from Buckminster Fuller, Bertrand Goldberg and Louis I. Kahn, as well as Lewis Mumford.[7]

As drawn up by Dreyfuss, the installation that was meant to 'dramatise' events for Roosevelt consisted of a group of curved screens for viewing diagrams, maps and photographs, onto which several layers of images could be simultaneously superimposed, using techniques like the epidiascope. The shape of the screens derived from those on the walls of the Socony-Vacuum Touring Service Bureau, installed in 1936 in Rockefeller Center. The project would be abandoned after an administrative reorganisation, but the team would continue its work into the post-war period. For his part, Henry Dreyfuss completed a 'situation room' for the US Navy, whose main element was a concave curved wall with a map of the world applied to it. Additional information could be tacked to it or projected from behind. The suspended loudspeakers were an indication of the increased role of long-distance conversations by telephone and radio.[8]

Many diverse talented individuals contributed to designs for graphic representation and their communication, and a number of them were architects.

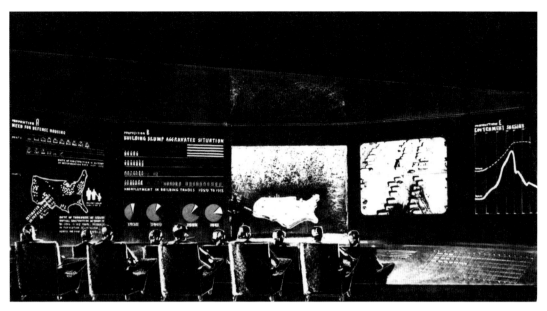

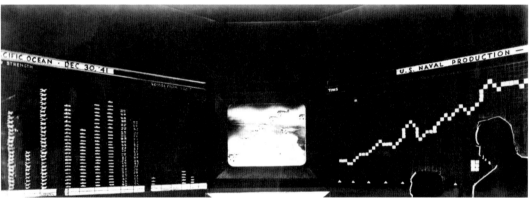

They included Benjamin Thompson, who would be one of the founders of The Architect Collaborative with Walter Gropius, Oliver Lundquist, a New York architect who had previously worked for Raymond Loewy, as well as his colleague Donal McLaughlin, a graduate of Yale, who in turn recruited Eero Saarinen, who would be responsible for the Special Exhibits Division, while also producing technical handbooks for the OSS. The most spectacular of the projects that incorporated the different techniques of Saarinen's team was set up in an auditorium of the Pentagon in 1943, in order to present the general issues of the war to an audience of economic and political decision makers. It included a full-scale recreation of a situation room.[9]

The modelling of situations, coupled with the analysis of the circulation of information,

Henry Dreyfuss
Project for a Presidential 'Situation Room' beneath the White House, Washington, perspective views, 1941. National Archives and Records Administration, Washington

was a basic part of operations research, a fundamental contribution of the war to the management of organisations and networks. The techniques of operations research originated in the work of Patrick Blackett on the distribution of British radar stations during the Battle of Britain. It was applied to artillery fire, to determining the optimal sizes of Atlantic convoys and even to issues such as the camouflage of airplanes to hunt submarines. It was developed in the United States before being applied to a wide range of military and economic problems.[10]

More primitive forms of simulation made use of simplified reproductions of reality, which fell within the field of competence of architects. This was the case for pilot trainers that simulated flying an aircraft, which were quite popular during the

Henry Dreyfuss
Weather map in the
Presentation Room of the
Combined Chiefs of Staff
Building, overall view,
Washington, 31 October 1942.
Official US Navy photograph.
Henry Dreyfuss Archive,
Cooper Hewitt National
Design Museum, Smithsonian
Institution, New York

THE ARCHITECT IN THE COCKPIT

Mr. R. Myerscough Walker, seated in the cockpit of one of the R.A.F. Link Trainers, for which he has designed the landscaped cycloramas illustrated on pages 230-231.

Second World War, because they allowed expensive aircraft to be replaced by simplified machines. The visual skills of architects enabled them to provide the trainee pilots with a semblance of realism. In 1939, such a fine perspective renderer as Raymond Myerscough-Walker designed 'cycloramas' to be used as backdrops for the Royal Air Force's Link Trainers, flight simulators named after the American organ manufacturer Edwin Link, who had invented them in 1928.[11]

Raymond Myerscough-Walker
'The architect in the cockpit',
for which he designed
landscaped cycloramas,
illustration in *The Architect
and Building News*, March 1940.
RIBA Library Photographs
Collection

The Narrative Models of Norman Bel Geddes

Pictorial reconstructions called on the figurative skills of architects, but their experience of miniaturisation was also put to good use, for example in Norman Bel Geddes's activity throughout the duration of the conflict. As an architect, set designer and industrial designer, Bel Geddes had tried in vain, as we have seen, to obtain commissions for camouflage to keep his model workshop, established for the Futurama exhibition in 1939, working to capacity. Like Dreyfuss, he could point to his extensive experience with the World's Fair, and he was not short of bold ideas, such as creating 'layered air maps' of the European landscape to help American pilots in their raids. Three-dimensional

Norman Bel Geddes
War manoeuvre models,
created for *Life Magazine*, page
from the *Norman Bel Geddes:
War Maneuver Models Created
for Life Magazine* catalogue,

The Museum of Modern Art, 1944.
Courtesy of the Estate of
Edith Lutyens Bel Geddes,
Harry Ransom Humanities
Research Center, University
of Texas at Austin

maps constructed out of wood would be photographed and used on the ground, but they would also be projected in the planes during flight. He explained that 'although qualified to be aviators so far as mechanical and flight knowledge is concerned', the pilots 'are not seasoned and are without experience in flying over terrain and countries strange to them'.[12]

Bel Geddes's only true success occurred at the intersection of propaganda and journalism, when *Life Magazine* commissioned him to construct a series of gigantic models to reconstruct battle sequences on land and sea, which were photographed to recreate their hour-by-hour progress, and published with a wealth of details. Elaborate techniques were employed: the scale models of the warships were made out of silver, using jewellers' and dentists' tools, with their wakes made initially out of sugar, and subsequently from bicarbonate of soda as an economy measure. The mountains were made of asbestos, and

oat grains were used for rocks, while the plumes from the explosions and columns of smoke from the fires were simulated by absorbent cotton held by thin steel wire. The models included the battles of the Coral Sea, Guadalcanal and the Aleutians in the Pacific, the invasion of Sicily and the battle of Orel on the Russian front.[13] Bel Geddes even anticipated some events and started work on a model of the 'battle of Gibraltar', which ultimately never took place. He had also started reproducing all the warships of the US Navy even before Pearl Harbor and thus had a 'library' of models at his disposal to deploy like the ships and armoured vehicles that served as his models.[14]

Norman Bel Geddes
Box containing sixteen model warships for use in model photography of naval battles, 1945. Courtesy of the Estate of Edith Lutyens Bel Geddes, Harry Ransom Humanities Research Center, University of Texas at Austin

The programme was publicised
in two ways. During the winter of 1944,
the techniques used to design and make
the models were revealed to the general
public in an exhibition at The Museum
of Modern Art. The public's fascination
for miniatures facilitated the presentation
of a sanitised representation, almost playful
in form, while the military censors were
careful to expunge any intensely bloody
images from photographic reports.[15] In
the museum galleries, 'The day-by-day
construction of a large model showing
various aspects of the war as it progresses,
[gives] the onlooker not only a graphic
presentation of phases of actual battle

but also enables him to see how ingeniously
the Geddes war maneuver models are
constructed.'[16] Elevated ramps were also
used to give a sense of the pilot's point of view
as he flew over the sites at high altitude.

The models were advertised by the
museum and by Bel Geddes himself as a
'new form of picture journalism', one that
could keep up with rapid changes and be
used under any circumstance.[17] After the
war, Bel Geddes would attempt to recycle
his techniques for historical purposes,
by making models of the construction
of the Pyramids, or developing models
for post-war planning purposes by
building a model of Toledo, Ohio in 1945,

with the aim of prompting public debate on the developments proposed by the municipality.[18] After 1945, he would also construct an elaborate model of the Battle of Midway for the navy's public relations purposes. The mini construction site for the model, which mobilised thirty model makers in a hangar on Pier 5 at South Ferry, was itself a kind of military feat.[19]

Diagrams and Images

The documentation and communication of the destruction caused by the war was an important aspect of communications policies. A remarkable example of this work was provided by the architect Constantinos Doxiadis during the German occupation of Greece and after its liberation.[20] After fighting in Albania in 1940, Doxiadis became the head of the urban and regional planning department for the Ministry of Public Works by day, and head of the resistance group Midas 614 by night. He kept an extremely detailed account of the damage the war caused to the Greek economy, which included keeping track of the loss of farm animals, the reduction in industrial manufacturing and the destruction of artworks both by the regular armies and the resistance groups. To communicate the information obtained through hundreds of architects and engineers throughout the country, Doxiadis employed graphic techniques that had been developed

in the 1920s by the Viennese philosopher Otto Neurath. With the help of the German graphic designer Gerd Arntz, Neurath had created the Isotype system (International System of Typographic Picture Education) for transposing statistics into pictograms. Doxiadis had first been exposed to the system while he was still a student at the Athens Polytechnic, when it was discussed at the CIAM (Congrès Internationaux d'Architecture Moderne) in Athens in 1933,[21] and remembered it when shaping his visual statistics.

In 1946, Doxiadis published a book in a giant format, with text in Greek, English, French and Russian, entitled *Sacrifices of Greece in the Second World War*. It was intended to accompany a travelling exhibition, whose purpose it was to make world opinion aware of the extent of Greece's distress. The book contained several dozen plates that he worked on during the war, which synthesised the information and painted a powerful picture of the ravaged countryside and ruined cities. Far more effectively than the photographs of demolished houses, scorched fields and bombed out factories that were common currency in the publications of the time, the graphic presentation of what Doxiadis modestly called 'a summary picture' transposed quantified information that measured the extent of devastation into a sort of 'datascape' before its time.[22]

Norman Bel Geddes
'Coral Sea: Norman Bel Geddes' models re-enact naval battle', photograph of a model published in *Life*, May 1942.
CCA

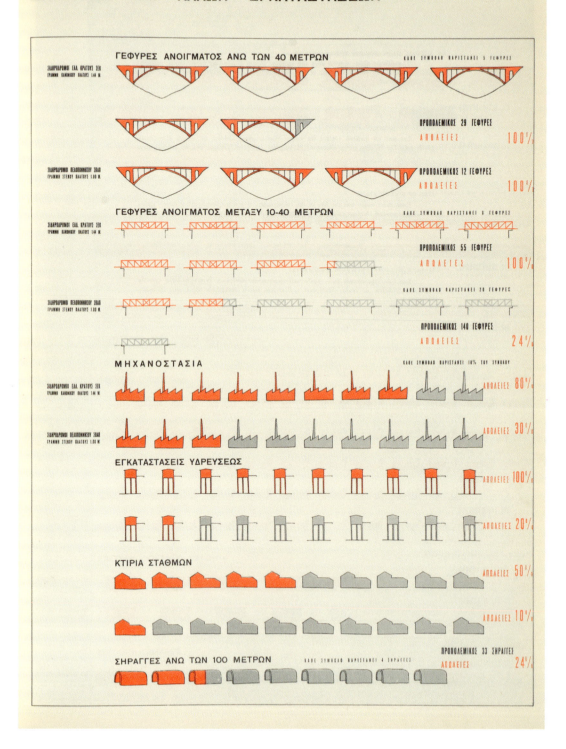

ΚΑΤΑΣΤΡΟΦΕΣ ΣΙΔΗΡΟΔΡΟΜΙΚΩΝ ΓΕΦΥΡΩΝ ΣΗΡΑΓΓΩΝ ΚΑΙ ΑΛΛΩΝ ΕΓΚΑΤΑΣΤΑΣΕΩΝ

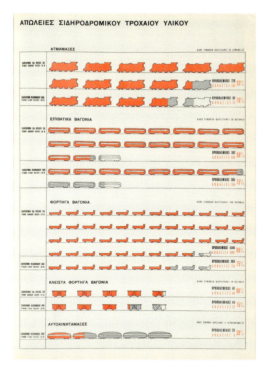

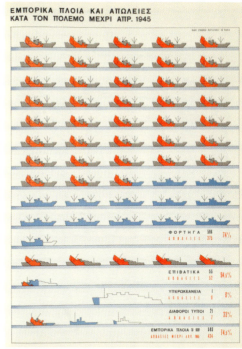

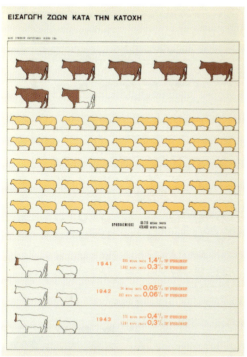

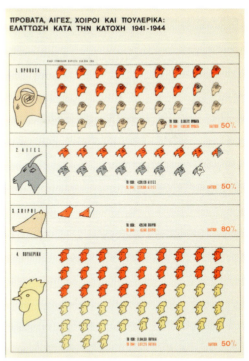

Left: Constantinos Doxiadis
Greece's Sacrifices during the Second World War,
plates illustrating the 'destruction of bridges, railway overpasses, etc.', 1946. University of Guelph Library

Constantinos Doxiadis
Greece's Sacrifices during the Second World War,
plates illustrating the 'importation of livestock during the occupation', the 'losses of rolling stock', the 'reduction in number of sheep, goats, pigs, and poultry' during the occupation, and the 'losses in the merchant marine during the war, up to the month of April 1945', 1946. University of Guelph Library

Wartime Exhibitions

The requirements for communication brought on by the war were addressed in academic institutions, such as the School of Design in Chicago, where Moholy-Nagy and Kepes put together accelerated courses in wartime communications, which included the construction of model airplanes and concepts for travelling exhibitions.[23] Artists of every stripe were recruited to design posters, which ranged in style from the most obsessive naturalism to Expressionism and Surrealism. Posters were a particularly important means for mobilising public opinion, and striking images were created in all the countries at war, often making use of the same rhetorical registers.[24] They were frequently supplemented by propaganda exhibitions, another manifestation of the presence of the war in the heart of capital cities. Some of the exhibitions reinforced the policies of the occupiers, such as the one entitled 'Le Juif et la France' (The Jew and France) held in 1941 at the Palais Berlitz, in the middle of German-controlled Paris. They were instrumental in the mobilisation of public opinion, and attempted to convey a reassuring vision that was both epic and spectacular, and that sometimes included material from the front. In 1941, for example, Alexei Shchusev designed a 'Pavilion of Trophies' for the Gorky Central Park of Culture and Leisure in Moscow. As a large watercolour of the project that featured a captured Junkers Ju-88 airplane reveals, this large exhibition hall, with a large timber frame, was meant to house airplanes and vehicles abandoned by the Germans in the course of the battle for Moscow, the first defeat of the Nazi forces on land, and a strategic turning point of the war in the east.[25]

This full-sized presentation was more the exception than the rule. Most of the exhibitions were set up in museums and galleries and made heavy use of photography. The design of these programmes provided work for many unemployed architects, who were often unable to join the army even when they wanted to. This was the case with Ernö Goldfinger, who had remained in London after the Blitz, and who remarked bitterly in 1942 that 'architecture has ceased to exist in my sense, everything is done by official bodies, and it is not easy for me to fit in there'.[26] Exhibitions gave him a new outlet for his talents: he designed an exhibition on the airplane manufacture for the Ministry of Information, which presented in detail the system for producing the components of the Lancaster bomber in decentralised factories.[27] The exhibitions he designed for the Army Bureau of Current Affairs contributed to propaganda regarding the domestic economy during the war, such as 'Food' and 'Planning your Kitchen', in 1943 and 1944 respectively. After organising an exhibition of paintings in 1941, entitled 'Aid to Russia', in his own modern house in Hampstead, he subsequently designed the 'Eastern Front Exhibition' in order to present the Soviet war effort to the British public.[28]

In 1943, Gerhard Kallmann, a German émigré and the future designer of Boston's City Hall, attempted to define the specific qualities of 'the wartime exhibition' in the pages of *The Architectural Review*. The effect of 'surprise' resulting from

Gerhard Kallmann
'The Wartime Exhibition',
article in *The Architectural
Review*, October 1943.
CCA Collection

the wartime exhibition

by G. S. Kallmann

In no other field of art and architecture have the war years brought us so generous and so healthy a harvest as in exhibition design. Not only are there more exhibitions and larger crowds in the exhibitions than ever before, not only do they spread to the smallest country towns and villages, to stores and shops, canteens and British Restaurants, but their average quality is infinitely higher, their contemporary impact infinitely stronger than anybody could have ventured to hope in 1937 or 1938. And, to make the surprise doubly bewildering and gratifying, this achievement is due to a Government department, the Exhibition Division of the Ministry of Information. How can this apparent miracle be explained ? How is it that the same Government which must accept responsibility for the insipid and hackneyed new Whitehall waterfront and which always hesitated in international exhibitions to commit itself to advanced æsthetic standards, should now make it its official policy to canvass for ideas by means of the idioms of Stockholm 1930, and Le Corbusier ? In London, such a dynamic synthesis of drama and lightheartedness had, before the war, only been seen in the MARS Exhibition of 1938 and in exhibition stands of such enlightened firms as Venesta, Ascot Heaters, and a few others ? The answer to this question is given in the following pages, written by a young architect of special exhibition experience. He discusses in detail the hopes and pitfalls of the new exhibition technique, the collection of an exhibition from general idea via scenario to the finished show, the social implications of the propaganda and the educational exhibition, the various æsthetic approaches used, and the high standard achieved. The style of to-day's exhibitions will, it must be hoped, become an integral part of post-war visual planning. For here, evolved in the happy atmosphere of the ephemeral and none-too-serious, appears that very interpenetration of the Baroque spirit (with its frank delight in the spectacular) and a strictly contemporary idiom which will be needed to convert a style of a few intellectuals and artists into a welcome vernacular of the many. And, strangely enough, wherever in these wartime exhibitions the results have been most convincing, they fit curiously into the best and truest English tradition of Romanticism and the Picturesque.

Preamble

LARGE scale exhibitions as a hallmark and stocktaking of our civilization are less than a hundred years old. The 1851 paragon was the first-born of the new species. More followed, and as time went on, they recurred with increasing frequency. Paris came after London, then London again, Vienna, Chicago, St. Louis. In the years between the two wars we had an international exhibition every five years, and somehow there happened to be somewhere a fairly big exhibition every summer. These great peaceful contests of nations were lavish spectacles. The great powers bolstered their prestige with colossal structures, while some of the small nations put up smaller, more delicate and sensitive pavilions, and received the first prizes, the well-earned fruits of a higher civilization. We had the great trade shows, and those which advertised a profession, and then the art exhibitions in the museums, way off the track of ordinary people's lives and just a little aimless in a world that had not much use for what they offered.

When war broke out, it seemed only natural that the end of exhibitions had come, that they would go overboard together with all our other cultural activities. The Finnish and Swedish pavilions at the World Fair in a still peaceful America gave us a last nostalgic vista of an exhibition art developed to utter perfection, yet a flower of luxury with not a hope of survival in the frosty season of war.

But things did not work out that way. On the contrary, there are now more exhibitions than ever. Going through the streets, wherever we may walk in the familiar places, we find exhibitions of one sort or another, nearly all of them well attended, attracting the ever curious, who will go and see anything if it costs nothing, and those who will only go if it costs something. What is it

EXHIBITIONS EVERYWHERE

at the Wallace Collection

on the bombed site of John Lewis's

under a marquee in a country town

on a gun post in the Middle East

the quality and impact of these exhibitions was all the greater as far as the journal was concerned since they were created at the instigation of the Ministry of Information, and Kallmann marvelled at this 'apparent miracle': 'How is it that the same Government which must accept responsibility for the insipid and hackneyed new Whitehall waterfront and which always hesitated in international exhibition to commit itself to advanced aesthetic standards, should now make it its official policy to canvass for ideas by means of the idioms of Stockholm 1930, and Le Corbusier?'[29]

Under the influence of Franck Pick – the principal visionary of the London Underground during the 1930s – the MOI (Ministry of Information) called on a design team that included the atypical architect Misha Black, who had designed the 1938 'New Architecture' exhibition of the MARS group (Modern Architecture Research Society),[30] the graphic designers Milner Gray and Peter Ray, and various outside contributors to produce a number of different types of exhibition, ranging from the small 'presentations' that could be exhibited in vitrines or small spaces, to large exhibitions planned for the United Kingdom or the rest of the world. These exhibitions were but one of the political resources put to use by the ministry to reassure the population – especially against the largest of the air raids – to stigmatise the Germans, to promote the economic use of resources, to endorse the contributions of the Americans, and to contain British communists.[31]

'Exhibitions Everywhere', illustration in *The Architectural Review*, October 1943. CCA Collection

'MOI [Ministry of Information]', illustration in *The Architectural Review*, October 1943. CCA Collection

MOI

The first show

London Pride, at Charing Cross Underground Station, on a small scale, but already with the full orchestra of Corbusier–MARS effects.

The smallest shows

Two scenes from an exhibition to attract women into part-time war work. The third picture is of a window display in a country town. It also canvasses for women's war work by showing public nursery school facilities.

Charing Cross

Used by the MOI for showing exhibitions in London before they go on into stores in the country. The site was already before the war familiar for exhibitions. Frank Pick had frequently permitted its use for campaigns with which he was in sympathy. For London Pride see above, for Fire Guard page 102 ; the Story of Lin was propaganda for China.

The show trailers

An experiment in minimum exhibitions and a most promising revival of the Renaissance Trionfo. The exhibition illustrated in the three pictures is advertising salvage. The outside panels are of the comic strip type, with cut-out figures.

The team's first success was the 'London Pride' exhibition in response to the Blitz. The public subsequently learned about the material necessary for combat in 'The Equipment of a Division', designed by the designers B. Katz and Frederic Henri Kay Henrion, together with the architect Frederick Gibberd. It was a great success and was seen by 1.5 million visitors. The general public saw its own circumstances portrayed in 'Off the Ration', an exhibition organised at the London Zoo. Both the ABCA (Army Bureau of Current Affairs) and the CEMA (Council for the Encouragement of Music and the Arts) – the predecessor of the Arts Council – recruited architects: Ralph Tubbs would design 'The Englishman Builds' and Ernö Goldfinger would design 'Cinema'.

Kallmann saw the prolific production of exhibitions as part of an attempt to popularise culture, which itself was part of a broader policy. 'The exhibitions are never isolated; they provide the climax or the opening bars of a campaign which is staged by radio, press, film and posters. Whether it is a many-pronged attack with a number of small local exhibitions, or a massive monster show as focal point, they always fit into the pattern of a wider strategy.'[32] But Kallmann did not ignore the risks of manipulating public opinion that this entailed.

In terms of presentation, he called for a combination of scholarly and popular presentations within the same exhibition, the use of photomontage, which could avoid the 'pictorial' excesses of photography, and the 'semi-typographical, semi-representational symbols' of the Isotype. To maintain 'the dynamic qualities of the message', he favoured the techniques of the Surrealists: 'Their shock tactics of baroque perspective, nightmare panic, and sudden illumination of subconscious contexts, their literary mannerisms and ability to tell a strong story strongly – all these are admirably suited to exhibition technique. . . . Moreover, aloof as the surrealists seem, where their paintings, collages and objects are supposed to be appreciated as pure art, in a propaganda exhibition, their technique has proved to be able to bridge the gap between aesthetic conception and mere receptivity.' Kallmann's analysis of the dozen or so exhibitions produced in London during three years of the war led him to see them not as high art, but rather as a 'new vernacular'. In his eyes,

there was no doubt as to their experimental qualities: 'The folkloristic aspects of exhibitions should be made the starting point for the creation of a new medium . . . similar to jazz and swing, a Cinderella art more genuine than any diluted form of fine art.'[33]

Compared to the British output, France's was far more meagre and was, of course, completely different in nature, as its purposes were part of the occupier's propaganda and that of the Pétain regime. The exhibition 'L'âme des camps (vie intellectuelle, spirituelle et sociale)' – The Spirit of the Camps (Intellectual, Spiritual, and Social Life) – deserves mention, as it was prepared in 1943 for the French Red Cross by Henry Bernard, an architect who

'Britain Shall Not Burn', view of the exhibition, illustration in *The Architectural Review*, October 1943. CCA Collection

MoMA's Road Maps

From May to September 1941, The Museum of Modern Art in New York began its wartime programming with 'Britain at War', the aim of which was to prepare public opinion for the imminent conflict.[36] The visual material assembled by Monroe Wheeler was powerful: soldiers at the front, airplanes, convoys at sea, dramatic night-time photographs of London during the Blitz in the autumn of 1940, drawings by Henry Moore of scenes in Underground stations, as well as watercolours by Raymond McGrath of the ruins of bombed airplane factories and of the vegetable gardens planted in the moat around the Tower of London. As we have seen, the museum presented the British contributions to camouflage. The most extraordinary part of the exhibition was devoted to 'War-time forms'. In his introduction to a group of photographs of fortifications that illustrated the inventive forms prompted by war, E. J. Carter, RIBA librarian, claimed that 'every bomb that falls is a stimulus to creation'.[37]

The influence of the British exhibition techniques and those of the continental avant-garde were clearly evident in the variously sized exhibitions that MoMA organised after Pearl Harbor. Some of them, such as 'The Road to Victory', under the artistic direction of the photographer Edward Steichen, at the time a lieutenant commander in the US Navy, brilliantly exploited the capacity of photography to structure a dramatic itinerary through the exhibition. The exhibition provided a 'procession of photographs of the nation at war', punctuated by large prints, with an installation by Herbert Bayer. Over the course of the exhibition, whose main spatial element was a winding ramp that

had returned from captivity and was named general commissioner. He had the support of a 'steering committee' chaired by the novelist Georges Duhamel.[34] Works of art, drawings and architectural models were gathered from the camps and brought to Trier, before finding their way to Paris. The exhibition was set up in the Grand Palais, with a rotunda at its centre and a ring of large stele around it, with engravings by the painter Charles Pinson. This exhibition was a fine example of the continuity between Vichy France and liberated France: it opened originally only a few days before the Parisian insurrection of August 1944 and was closed shortly afterwards, only to reopen in the autumn with a few changes, like the removal of images of Pétain, and the new title 'Le Front des barbelés' (The Barbed Wire Front), implying that prisoners had been part of the Resistance.[35]

Henry Bernard
Charles Pinson, artist
'Spirit of the Camps'
exhibition, Paris,
sketch of the entrance,
August 1944.

Académie d'Architecture,
Cité de l'Architecture
et du Patrimoine,
Archives d'Architecture
du xxᵉ Siècle, Fonds
Henry Bernard

provided views of dozens of images at once, one could find traces not only of Bayer's exhibition of the *Neues Bauen* in Paris of 1930, but also many of the experimental rhetorical strategies developed by Alexander Rodchenko and El Lissitzky in the pages of the large-format magazine *SSSR na stroike* (USSR in Construction). Rather than providing apparently objective documentation of the war fronts – both near and far – the exhibition was structured into four sections: national resources, production, the war in action and people. It dramatised the spectacles of combat and production, and featured giant photographic prints portraying the faces of anonymous heroes both at the front and at home. The poet Carl Sandburg, Steichen's brother-in-law, celebrated the 'man behind the gun' using rhetoric that was close to socialist realism: 'They dig out ore from deep down in the dark, they shoot the oil wells, they

chase the slag out of copper, steel-driving men they drill and twist deep rock, they hammer steel bars for rifle and cannon, they rivet the steel sheets and sew them tight with steel buttons to meet storms or torpedoes – listen, they clank and boom the mighty song of steel – the breath of their assembly lines is in miles of tanks – their thumbprints are on bombers over five oceans.'[38] The museum, in a propaganda operation that also served its own interests, took pains to celebrate a 'combination of creative writing and pictorial art of the same inspiration', which 'moves with magnificent simplicity and a kind of visual eloquence from the landscape of the primeval continent through the folkways of simple Americans,

Herbert Bayer
'Road to Victory' exhibition,
The Museum of Modern Art,
exhibition entrance, 1942.
The Museum of Modern Art,
New York, Photographic Archive

the extraordinary mechanism of peace and war, to the cavalcade of men flying and sailing and motoring and marching to the defense of that continent'.[39] This exhibition would be presented in London, in 1943 under the title 'America Marches'.

Other exhibitions at MoMA were closer to those themes addressed during the 1930s. In 1942, 'Wartime Housing' extended the exploration of social housing presented in the all-too-famous 'Modern Architecture: International Exhibition' of 1932, whose catalogue had established the 'International Style' as a catchword, and in 'America Can't Have Housing', held in 1934. Designed by Eliot F. Noyes, the director of the then Department of Industrial Design, it displayed illustrations of the most innovative operations up until then, and developed an argument through ten 'scenes' in a logical and apparently implacable line of development, with victory depending on productivity, and productivity

depending on proper housing for workers. The visual dialectic followed a well-trodden path of opposing pre-war slums with idyllic proposals. The campsites and shacks made of materials scavenged from around airplane factories were not edited out of the picture. The text addressed producers and potential inhabitants, few of whom were likely to be present among the museum visitors to read it, but nonetheless urged them to contact their elected representatives to demand well-equipped and comfortable housing. The long-term effects of the emergency housing policies were considered within the perspective of the country's ongoing modernisation. 'The smartest thing

Eliot F. Noyes
'Wartime Housing'
exhibition, The Museum
of Modern Art, view of a
gallery, 1942. Photograph
by Samuel H. Gottscho.
The Museum of Modern Art,
New York, Photographic Archive

a town can do is to start thinking right now what it wants to be when the war is over. The community can benefit or suffer as a result of this housing. War work can be the best thing that ever happened to a town – or the worst.'[40] An installation of three aerial photographs encapsulated the exhibition's thesis: in the middle, a view of a small existing city with two arrows pointing to either side, and a caption asking 'Which way?'. On one side was an image of a dense and monotonous suburb, and on the other an open 'neighbourhood unit' in an organic composition. As the extension of a transatlantic dialogue beginning in 1941, the exhibition would be shown in London in 1944, at the RIBA, and would be considered at the time as 'a triumph for the architect and planner'.[41]

From July to October 1943, the 'Airways to Peace' exhibition at MoMA continued to raise post-war issues for its visitors. The principles previously explored in 'The Road to Victory' were further developed, ranging from a consideration of the implications for roads to the aeronautical issues in the title. But this time the medium was different, consisting mainly of geographical maps instead of photographs. A map in relief of Europe, by Norman Bel Geddes, and didactic maps of airplane routes and globes, including one belonging to Franklin D. Roosevelt, were arranged in a new space laid out by Bayer to present an essay written by Wendell L. Willkie, the former progressive Republican candidate in the presidential elections of 1940, and Monroe Wheeler. It was initially to be entitled 'Global War for Global Peace'. The vision of the world it conveyed was innovative in several respects: in response to the contributions of the prophet of air

power, Alexander de Seversky, the strategic importance of the polar regions was pointed out, while a concave globe created by Bayer enabled the potential new links between continents to become more visible, be they for bombs or passengers. In Willkie's words, 'the modern airplane creates a new geographical dimension', and 'the American people must grasp these new realities if they are to play their essential part in winning the war and building a world of peace and freedom'.[42] What was at stake was not just winning the war, but establishing a position for the new geopolitical situation that would result from it.

Few themes would go unaddressed in the museum's programme, and every department was involved, from painting and sculpture to architecture and design.[43] Architectural issues would also appear in unexpected places, on the fringes of the exhibitions. At the time of the Salvador Dalí retrospective in 1941, James Thrall Soby described his work as anticipating architectures of war: 'One may ask which type of architecture more accurately diagnosed the hidden psychosis of the years just before the war: *machines à habiter*, with their flat white roofing and broad areas of glass; or the small, dark, womblike houses which Dalí proposed to build as retreats from a mechanical civilization and which, as air raid shelters, recently covered the landscape of England.'[44] In 1944, the museum set out to participate in post-war arrangements by giving an account of the years since 1932, highlighting the projects for housing by Clarence Stein, William Wurster, Kahn & Stonorov and Richard Neutra. Modern factories remained undocumented because of censorship,

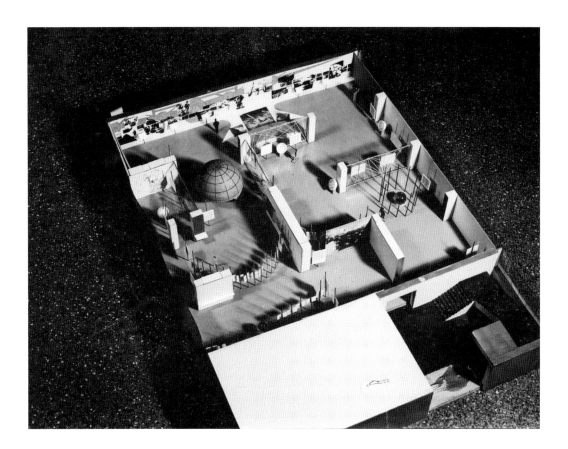

aside from one building of Albert Kahn's that was already well known in 1940. With the publication of Mies van der Rohe's Minerals and Metals Building for IIT, his first building in America, the museum continued it efforts to bring him to the fore.

Photography, from Document to Emotion

The production of visual images relating to the war fulfilled various needs, ranging from the preparation and documentation of battles – for example through aerial reconnaissance – to persuasion and to the intimate accounts of the protagonists and witnesses to the war. During this same period, the supports for these representations were transformed. The graphic and painterly techniques used

by painters and architects for the armies continued relatively unchanged, especially in Britain and in Germany, where the painter Ernst Vollbehr, who had previously made drawings of the First World War and devoted paintings to the construction of the motorway system by the Organisation Todt,[45] would distinguish himself by painting realistic accounts of the invasion of Poland and the French campaign. But in addition to the small sketchbook, so easy to slip into the pocket of a combat jacket, small-format still or movie cameras would become the new instruments of vision. In this new context,

Herbert Bayer
'Airways to Peace'
exhibition, The Museum
of Modern Art, model, 1943.
The Museum of Modern Art,
New York

Bridge abutment on Dunajek
Morning on 19.8.44

what did architects draw when they were
involved on multiple fronts? Some furnished
accounts of troop movements through
unharmed or devastated territories,
both in their advances and their retreats.
For example, Norman Braun, a former
student of Heinrich Tessenow who was
employed by Egon Eiermann, drew the
countryside of Ukraine and East Prussia
during his service in the engineering corps.[46]

Nor did the architects remain untouched
by the melancholy of ruins. Arkady Mordvinov
drew the ruins of Stalingrad after the battle
of 1943, and many of his colleagues who had
remained in Leningrad documented with
extreme care and precision the destruction
of the city's palaces, notably the Peterhof.
But the sublimity of great works touched
them as well, as much as the almost
poignant fragility of temporary constructions
built on military bases and landing fields,
as rendered by Hugh Casson. More rarely,
they made portraits of combatants they
encountered at the front, such as those

drawn by Giuseppe Terragni on the Russian
front, which were included in an exhibition
of Italian artists under the colours, presented
in Berlin, Munich and Vienna in late 1942
and early 1943 to reassure the local public
of the loyalty of the southern tip of the Axis.[47]

These drawings and paintings remain,
it must be admitted, rather weak in
comparison to photographic images.
Alongside the objective mechanical precision
of the cameras of the reconnaissance
planes, which the camouflage programmes
set out unsuccessfully to outwit, intensive
photographic reporting took place on
the ground, controlled and utilised by
the military, for example in the Nazi
reviews *Signal* and *Adler*. Thousands
of photographers joined the American

Norman Braun
**'Bridge abutment near
Dunajek** [near Goldap,
in East Prussia], the morning
of 19 August 1944', page from
a watercolour notebook.
Akademie der Künste,
Norman Braun Archiv, Berlin

forces, consuming almost all the Kodak film
produced during the war and stimulating
further innovations in fine-grain photographic
emulsions. Other forms of reporting
sometimes escaped direct control. The most
expressive photographs described the field
of combat or conveyed the atmosphere
at the rear, as did Margaret Bourke-White
in her publication of photographs entitled
Shooting the Russian War. Daily life
in the shelters and on the platforms of
the Underground did not escape the eye
of photographers such as Bill Brandt.

Landscape photography did not
disappear, however, and it took its place
in the propaganda system, especially in
attempts to reinforce the aura of the national
landscapes. The series of photographs
entitled 'The Land We Are Fighting For',
published by the *Picture Post* in 1940,
fed the patriotism of British readers, while
the photo albums celebrating the Germanic
nature of the countryside of Alsace and
the Moselle, which had been re-annexed
by the Germans, served to integrate these
new territories into an idyllic vision of the
extended *Heimat*. But these observations
became immediately obsolete when pictures
of the Blitz and the Allied bombardments
transformed images of rich landscapes
and artworks into inventories of damage,

with both undertakings making use of
existing historical narratives or aligning
themselves with the nationalist discourses of
the time.[48] Thus photography would help set
the emotional conditions for reconstruction,
first by simply documenting the current state
of the sites, as did August Sander in the
still-smoking rubble of Cologne (see pages
48–53).[49] Most architectural periodicals
refrained from demoralising visual accounts
of the destruction of monuments and cities.
The only one that did not pass over the
destruction nor the aesthetic potential of
ruins was *The Architectural Review*, but
when one of its editors sought 'to give dignity
and permanence to a picturesque ruin as
the eighteenth-century landowner used
to do it, if he was fortunate enough to count
a mediaeval ruin among his possessions',[50]
this was perhaps more a form of nostalgia
for romantic *mise en scène*, or simply
an expression of pessimism in the face
of the huge task of reconstruction.

Hugh Casson
**Construction of a Nissen
hut on an airfield**,
watercolour, 1941.
Victoria & Albert Museum,
London, Archives of
Sir Hugh Casson and
Margaret MacDonald
Casson, gift from the
Casson daughters

Giuseppe Terragni
**'German combattant
on the eastern front'**,
portrait in *Feldgraue
italienische Künstler
stellen aus*, 1942.
The Wolfsonian-Florida
International University,
Miami Beach, Florida,
The Mitchell Wolfson, Jr.
Collection

1. Introduction to G. S. Kallmann, 'The Wartime Exhibition', *The Architectural Review*, vol. 94, no. 562 (October 1943), 95.
2. Monroe Wheeler, 'The Artist and National Defense', in *Britain at War*, edited by Monroe Wheeler (New York: The Museum of Modern Art, 1941), 10.
3. Paul Virilio, *La Machine de vision* (Paris: Galilée, 1988), 115–16. In English: *The Vision Machine*, translated by Julie Rose (Bloomington: Indiana University Press, 2009).
4. Gustave Bertrand, *Enigma ou la plus grande énigme de la guerre 1939–1945* (Paris: Plon, 1973). Francis Harry Hinsley and Alan Stripp, *Codebreakers: The Inside Story of Bletchley Park* (Oxford: Oxford University Press, 1993).
5. For the work of this organisation, see *The Secrets War: the Office of Strategic Services in World War*, edited by George C. Chalou (Washington, DC: National Archives and Records Administration, 1992).
6. See the remarkable article by Barry Katz, 'The Arts of War: "Visual Presentation" and National Intelligence', *Design Issues*, vol. 12, no. 2 (summer 1996), 3–21.
7. 'Presentation History', National Archives and Records Administration, Washington, OSS Record Group 226, entry 99, box 76, file 44a, 5.
8. Russell Flinchum, *Henry Dreyfuss, Industrial Designer: the Man in the Brown Suit* (New York: Cooper-Hewitt National Design Museum and Rizzoli, 1997), 84–87.
9. Katz, op. cit. note 6, 14.
10. Erik P. Rau, 'The Adoption of Operations Research in the United States During World War II', in *The Systems Approach in Management and Engineering. World War II and After*, edited by Agatha C. Hughes and Thomas P. Hughes (Cambridge, Mass.: MIT Press, 2000), 57–92. Idem, 'Combat Science: the Emergence of Operational Research in World War II', *Endeavour*, vol. 29, no. 4 (December 2005), 156–61. Guy Hartcup, *The Effect of Science on the Second World War* (London: Macmillan, 2000), 100–21.
11. 'Cycloramas for the RAF "Visual Link" trainers designed by Raymond Myerscough Walker', *The Architect and Building News*, 1 March 1940, 230–31. The architect is photographed in a trainer, ibid., 219.
12. HRC, Job 465. Layered air maps, 'Three Dimensional Course Guide for Pilots', p. 1.

13. 'Coral Sea. Norman Bel Geddes' Models Re-enact Naval Battle', *Life*, 25 May 1942, 21–25. 'The Desert Battlefield is the Doorway to Rich Nile Delta, Suez and the East', *Life*, 20 July 1942, 26–27. 'The Aleutians. Bel Geddes' Models Show Jap Bases on the Craggy Doorstep of North America', *Life*, 28 September 1942, 36–37. 'Guadalcanal. On an Island 100 Miles Long, Two Nations Dispute a Small but Priceless Airfield', *Life*, 9 November 1942, 32–34. 'Amphibious War. Geddes Models Explain Land-&-Sea Attack', *Life*, 16 November 1942, 115–23. 'Red Army Fights Battle in Depth. Topographical Model Reveals Russians' Strategy and Tactics', *Life*, 26 March 1943, 100–01. 'Sicily Invasion Goes Well', *Life*, 26 July 1943, 25–28. 'How the Russians Took Orel. Models by Norman Bel Geddes Show Red Tactics in Winning their First Big Summer Victories', *Life*, 6 August 1943, 21–27.
14. 'Prefabricated History: Designer Geddes Makes Battles to Order for Life Magazine Before they Happen', *The Architectural Forum*, vol. 80, no. 3 (March 1944), 4–6 and 150.
15. The exhibition was on view from 26 January to 5 March 1944. See the catalogue: *Norman Bel Geddes War Maneuver Models Created for Life Magazine* (New York: The Museum of Modern Art, 1944).
16. 'Museum of Modern Art Schedules New Exhibitions Including War Maneuver Models and Modern Drawings', press release, 1944, MoMA archives.
17. HRC, file 356, flat box 14: publicity material describing the models as 'a new kind of journalistic technique' which can also be 'ready in 48 hours'.
18. 'The Building of the Great Pyramid. Bel Geddes Models Reconstructs for "Encyclopaedia Britannica" How Biggest Pyramid Was Built', *Life*, 3 December 1945, 75–79. 'Toledo. A Model of Proposed Changes in the Transformation Pattern Arouses Citizen Interest in Planning the City's Future', *The Architectural Forum*, vol. 83, no. 2 (August 1945), 119–23.
19. 'Midway Models Reconstruct War's Decisive Naval Battle', *Life*, vol. 20, no. 7 (18 February 1946), 93–101.
20. Mark Mazower, *Inside Hitler's Greece: the Experience of Occupation, 1941–44* (New Haven: Yale University Press, 1993).

21. Nader Vossoughian, *Otto Neurath: the Language of the Global Polis* (Rotterdam: NAI Publishers, 2008).
22. Constantinos Doxiadis, *The Sacrifices of Greece in the Second World War* (Athens: Ministry of Reconstruction, 1946).
23. Alain Findeli, *Le Bauhaus de Chicago: l'œuvre pédagogique de László Moholy-Nagy* (Sillery: Septentrion, 1995), 96.
24. Marianne Lamonaca and Sarah Schleuning, *Weapons of Mass Dissemination: the Propaganda of War* (Miami Beach: The Wolfsonian, Florida International University, 2004).
25. Andrew Nagorski, *The Greatest Battle. The Fight for Moscow 1941–42* (London: Aurum Press, 2007).
26. Ernö Goldfinger, letter to his brother George, 24 January 1942, in Nigel Warburton, *Ernö Goldfinger. The Life of an Architect* (London: Routledge, 2004), 92.
27. MOI Exhibition, MAP Oxford Street, 'Building a Lancaster' section, RIBA, Goldfinger archive, PA 640.
28. Nigel Warburton, op. cit. note 26, 100–08.
29. Introduction to G. S. Kallmann, loc. cit. note 1, 95.
30. Misha Black, *Exhibition Design* (London: The Architectural Press, 1950).
31. Ian McLaine, *Ministry of Morale: Home Front Morale and the Ministry of Information in World War II* (London and Boston: Allen & Unwin, 1979).
32. Introduction to G. S. Kallmann, 'The Wartime Exhibition', op. cit. note 1, 103.
33. Ibid., 106.
34. See the material assembled by Henry Bernard, IFA, 266 AA 14/6, 77/2 and 56/8.
35. 'De "l'Âme des camps" au "Front des barbelés"', *Le Parisien libéré*, 1 November 1944.
36. For MoMA's position, see 'The Museum and the War', *The Bulletin of the Museum of Modern Art*, vol. 10, no. 1 (October–November 1942).
37. E. J. Carter, 'Architectural Reconstruction and War-Time Forms', in *Britain at War*, edited by Monroe Wheeler (New York: The Museum of Modern Art, 1941), 74.
38. Carl Sandburg, 'Road to Victory', *Bulletin of The Museum of Modern Art*, vol. 9, no. 5–6 (June 1942), 7–8.
39. Monroe Wheeler, ibid., 19–20.

40. 'Wartime Housing', *Bulletin of The Museum of Modern Art*, vol. 9, no. 4 (May 1942), n.p.

41. Richard Sheppard, 'US Wartime Housing', *The Architectural Review*, vol. 96, no. 572 (August 1944), 30–60.

42. Wendell L. Willkie, 'Airways to Peace', *Bulletin of The Museum of Modern Art*, vol. 11, no. 1 (August 1942), 226. My thanks to Enrique Ramirez for pointing out the significance of this exhibition.

43. Edgar Kaufmann Jr., 'The Department of Industrial Design', *Bulletin of The Museum of Modern Art*, vol. 14, no. 1 (1946), 2–14.

44. James Thrall Soby, *Salvador Dalí. Paintings, Drawings, Prints* (New York: The Museum of Modern Art, 1941), 27.

45. Ernst Vollbehr, *Mit der OT beim Westwall und Vormarsch* (Berlin: Elsner, 1941).

46. Norman Braun, *Brückenanschlag bei Dunajek, Morgens am 19. 8. 44* and *In Ostpreussen 1944*, watercolours, Akademie der Künste, Berlin.

47. Generalstab der Kgl. Italienischen Heeres, *Feldgraue italienische Künstler stellen aus* (Rome: Druckerei Novissima, 1942), nos. 390 to 394.

48. 'Recuperating Ruins', in Kitty Hauser, *Shadow Sites: Photography, Archaeology, and the British Landscape, 1927–1955* (Oxford: Oxford University Press, 2007), 201–54. Walter Hotz, *Kunstwerk und Landschaft im Elsass*, photographs by Theodor Seeger (Berlin: Rembrandt-Verlag, 1941).

49. Winfried Ranke, *August Sander: Die Zerstörung Kölns. Photographien 1945–1946*, with a text by Heinrich Böll (Munich: Schirmer/Mosel, 1985).

50. 'Save our Ruins', *The Architectural Review*, vol. 95, no. 765 (January 1944), 14.

U.S. ATTACK ON JAPS CAME AT 10:20 A.M. JUNE 4 WHEN PLANES FROM "ENTERPRISE" AND "YORKTOWN" SET FIRE TO THREE JAP CARRIERS

U. S. PLANES ATTACK THE ENEMY FLEET

At 9 a.m. on June 4 some 80 Japanese ships were still converging rapidly on Midway. In the nine climactic hours from 9:20 a.m. to 6:30 p.m. this fleet was stopped in its tracks.

It was an action of carrier against carrier. By 7 a.m. on the 4th the three U. S. carriers were judged close enough to the enemy task force to launch planes for attack. Before planes from the *Hornet* and *Enterprise* had reached their target (*Yorktown* planes were held briefly in reserve), the Jap fleet suddenly turned north and headed away from Midway. Torpedo Squadron 8 from the *Hornet*, failing to find the enemy, turned north. At 9:20 it found the target. In the next 2½ minutes the 15 planes of Torpedo 8 attacked the whole Jap striking force. Only one man, Ensign George Gay, survived. By 10:15, however, confusion over the whereabouts of the enemy was corrected and wave upon wave of dive bombers and torpedo planes began to hit the Jap fleet. In a few minutes three carriers, the *Akagi*, *Kaga* and *Soryu*, were crippled, two battleships were damaged and the rest of the striking force was in retreat. Meanwhile a fourth Jap carrier was launching its planes for counterattack on the *Yorktown*.

BURNING JAP CARRIER, the *Akagi*, tried to launch planes after being dive-bombed. Jap bombers had just returned from attack on Midway, were caught on their carriers.

TORPEDOES from U.S. submarine *Nautilus* finish off Jap carrier *Soryu*. The *Nautilus* had been tracking the enemy, closed in on the crippled *Soryu* after dive bombers hit her.

JAPS COUNTERATTACK SIMULTANEOUSLY

"YORKTOWN" WAS DEFENDED by her fighters in fierce fight. Attacking bombers came from *Hiryu*, still unscathed and heading northward. This was 12:06 p.m. June 4.

"YORKTOWN" WAS HIT at 12:13 p.m. by three bombs. Splashes left and right are Jap bombers which scored hits and crashed. Escorting ships circled, throwing up ack-ack.

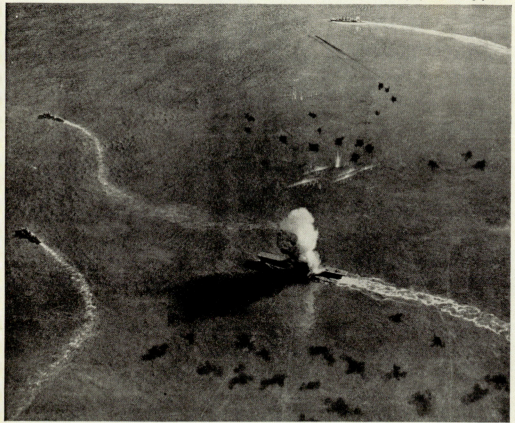

"YORKTOWN" WAS HIT AGAIN at 2:15 on port side amidships by two torpedoes from *Hiryu* planes. Previous bombing had blown out *Yorktown* boiler fires, but she had made repairs, was doing 20 knots. After torpedoes hit, she listed heavily and order was given to abandon ship. Men had to fight their way upward through wreckage in darkness.

CONTINUED ON NEXT PAGE

The main battle took place Thursday and Friday, May 7 and 8, in the Coral Sea off the northeastern coast of Australia. This is the bright and cloudless scene of the first important naval defeat suffered by Japan since it acquired a Navy in 1870.

The first Jap carrier hit and sunk burns at lower center, an oil slick spreading out from its fuel tanks. A Jap cruiser and destroyer start to lay a smoke screen around it but it is too late. Other destroyers race up to help survivors, if possible, mean-

while filling the air with the puffs of anti-aircraft fire. They have visibly brought down three U. S. planes. Three more at upper left head for the second Jap carrier at upper right, whose convoy destroyers are also starting a smoke screen. This carrier has

24

presumably sent up most of its fighter planes. Soon after, the Americans got several dive-bomber hits on this carrier's deck and several torpedo hits below the water line. The carrier was believed to have sunk later. At the height of the battle, when MacArthur's land-based planes arrived on the scene, 500 planes had been involved. The American Army fliers took aerial photographs of the damage their Navy colleagues were doing. It was, in fact, the U.S. Navy's day. The Jap loss of two carriers will never be made up by Japan in this war. That fact far outweighs the Japs' incidental occupation of the Louisiades. Furthermore, the U.S. Navy, despite painful losses in planes and fliers, had proved that it could outsmart and outhit the Japs.

Norman Bel Geddes
'Coral Sea: Norman Bel Geddes' models re-enact naval battle', photograph of model in *Life*, May 1942.
CCA

FIRST TROOPS TO LAND BATTLE TO WIN BEACH HEAD

The most delicate and savage period of a beach-head landing is shown in pictures on these pages. A touch of rough weather could play havoc with the whole operation. A piece of luck one way or another may be all-important. But now the light tanks plunge down steel runways into the shallow water and wallow ashore like hippopotamuses. The men get wet to the waist but the next half-hour's action will dry the clothes on them or kill them. Here they match cour-age, weapons and wits with the enemy. The position of these troops, tactically, is that they are all front, exposed flanks, and no rear. They have no place to re-treat to. They must go forward. They must go as far as possible as fast as possible and they must entrench well enough to hold off the inevitable counterattack. They are lost if their heavy supplies and artillery are not presently landed safely behind them. It is up to them to hold the beach until the big stuff comes in.

ACTUAL LANDING on the hostile beach is the ticklish moment of transferring from water to land. Only a flat shore-line without sand bars will do to land tanks and heavy sup-plies, hence the enemy has put trenches and holding forces be-hind all the sloping beaches. Anything spilled here can be sal-vaged. Now the enemy machine-gun and rifle bullets spatter the sides of the tank barges and drop the first men in their tracks. Machine guns from the barges try to keep the enemy's heads down. Assault troops charge through the barbed wire

THE GAME OF WAR is now played out on the beach. The enemy still holds in thin force the first line of trenches above the beach. Follow the tank tracks up from the beach. Each heads for a machine-gun nest or to enfilade a trench. The tanks are under fire from enemy howitzers on the hilltop which is itself under fire from our naval guns. Some fool on a ship has even plopped two shells dangerously close to the advancing American line. At the bottom of the picture come the swarming rubber boats. One landing boat has been sunk.

CONTINUED ON NEXT PAGE

Norman Bel Geddes
'Amphibious War: Geddes' models explain land- & sea-attack', photograph of model in *Life*, November 1942.
CCA

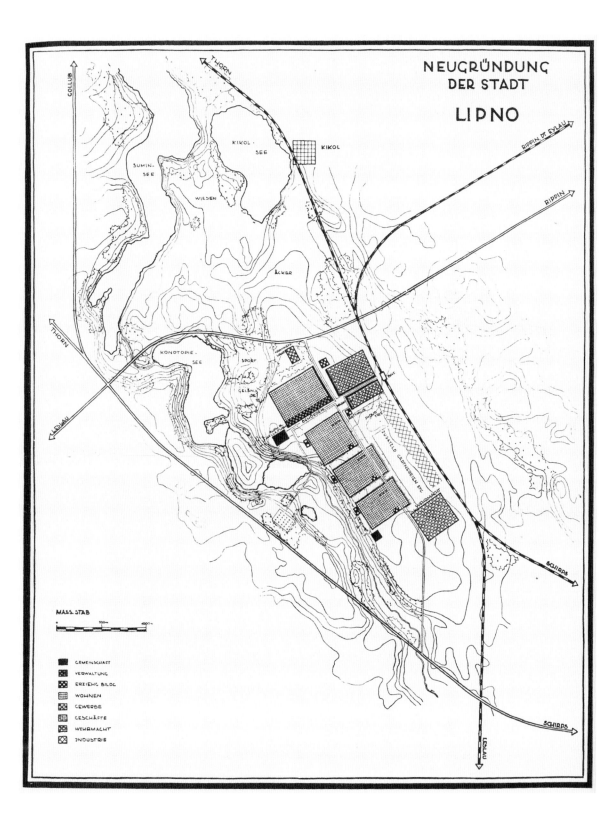

NEUGRÜNDUNG
DER STADT

LIPNO

11/ Alternative Futures: Occupation and Reconstruction

Through a thorough redevelopment and to a large extent through plentiful new construction, the towns and villages of the new German territories to the East will take on a distinctly German face.
Heinz Haacke, president of the Deutscher Heimatbund, 1940[1]

We should see in this time of stagnation a welcome pause in our, in many ways, obsolete prewar activities – a time of mental preparation for a new activity far beyond the dreams of our young years, as well as those of generations that preceded ours. Believe me, the world is going to be rebuilt, and America is too, on a greater scale – the scale of America's highways, parkways, reclaimed areas and power dams – but not necessarily in a way that leads to bigger cities. This will be done through imaginative planning that takes mechanization and accepts technology as ABC, through rejecting retrospective sentimentalism, and through the directive power of the most creative and courageous men in our profession all over the world. This is the unchangeable message of war and evolution.
Erich Mendelsohn, 'Architecture Today', lecture, 22 April 1942[2]

The war unfolded according to different temporal rhythms – at the pace of a battle, at the pace of a campaign or at the pace of an industrial policy that transformed whole regions. These events defined the present or the short-term, but at the same time state policies were being developed that aimed at the long-term, and the contrasting war objectives of the opposing camps were defined in spatial terms. Even during the conflict, the warring nations looked ahead to creating a future order – but from diametrically opposed perspectives, of course. These included envisaging a Europe or Asia under Axis rule, planning for a democratic welfare state in the post-war West, and preparing the stage for the triumph of a Soviet Russia reconciled with national values. For territories occupied by Russia and Japan, whether they were annexed outright or transformed into fictitious protectorates, projects aimed at colonisation and territorial demarcation were devised. At the same time, the first plans for the reconstruction of destroyed cities were set out, first of all in Franco's Spain, at the instigation of the Dirección General de Regiones Devastadas and the Dirección General de Arquitectura under the architect Pedro Muguruza, and then in the Finnish cities bombarded by the Soviets starting in late 1939, during the Winter War, images of which were disseminated by Alvar Aalto in the United States. Reconstruction would subsequently become policy in France, Britain and the Netherlands, then in the USSR. From 1943, Albert Speer began devoting some of his energy to working with a team of architects on the reconstruction of devastated Germany.[3]

Ewald Liedecke
Development plan for the new town of Lipno in occupied Polish West Prussia (1941), illustration in *Raumordnung und Bauforschung*, April 1941. Collection of the author

New Roles for Existing Buildings

The mobilisation of state resources for war extended not only to the construction industry, but also to all existing buildings, irrespective of whether they were built for military or civilian purposes. By being requisitioned, an existing construction could be assigned new functions, from housing troops to holding the wounded or keeping prisoners, demonstrating the latent adaptability of buildings. Likewise, facilities built for military use, insofar as they are not directly shaped by the requirements of battle, as is the case with fortifications, can be adapted for civilian life at the end of hostilities, which is usually marked by extreme need as a result of destruction and the movement of populations. Some facilities would in fact be explicitly conceived in this way: between the late 1930s and the mid-1940s, the construction and use of certain buildings exhibited a double flexibility, with some passing from a civilian to a military state, and vice versa.

The practice of functional transmutation in both directions occurred before the appearance of the term *flexibility*, whose first occurrence was detected by Adrian Forty in a text published by Walter Gropius in 1954.[4] Forty has identified three strategies leading to flexibility: 'redundancy', 'flexibility by technical means' and flexibility 'as a political strategy' in the manner advanced by the Situationists.[5] The war highlighted two other approaches. One was flexibility by default, that is to say the military use of civilian buildings – housing transformed into barracks, schools transformed into hospitals, neighbourhoods transformed into urban prisons, as in the case of the ghettos created by the Nazis – not to mention the urban areas used for battlefields. The other was based on anticipation, with military infrastructure that would one day be demobilised being converted to civilian life for various uses: barracks became housing, while medical facilities were turned into office buildings.

The Architecture of Occupation

Before changing function, buildings sometimes had their exteriors reworked. These transformations could be almost cosmetic, as part of an architectural 'cleansing' of a newly annexed territory, as was the case for example soon after the conquest of Poland. In 1942, for example, the *Deutsche Bauzeitung* reported on the Germanisation of the Rynek Główny of Kraków, which was renamed the Adolf Hitler Platz: the monument to the poet Adam Mickiewicz was removed, and the Dom Feniksa (Phoenix Building), built by Adolf Szyszko-Bohusz in 1932, was cleansed of its excessively 'exotic' facade by the engineer Stahl, the head of the new department for construction, who erased all traces of the efforts of 'Polish, and especially Jewish architects' with the aim of administering a 'fatal blow' to the medieval square by building 'American-style concrete boxes'.[6] Similar policies were followed in western Europe. In Alsace, from 1940, a methodical process of *Entwelschung* (extirpation of Latin culture and language) or 'purification' was undertaken at the instigation of the municipal architect, Richard Beblo. Apartment buildings that were deemed too tall were cut down and Art Deco architectonic elements were replaced by traditional arrangements.

As in every *Gau* of the Reich, a manual, or *Baufibel* (building primer), for the construction of authentic German houses was prepared as a guide to architects.[7]

When buildings in annexed countries were assigned new uses, local architects were mobilised against their will, or it occurred in their absence. One of the most revealing cases is that of the La Muette housing estate, built in 1934 in Drancy by Eugène Beaudouin and Marcel Lods, in collaboration with Jean Prouvé.[8] Built at the behest of Henri Sellier, the major advocate of social housing in the Paris region, the project

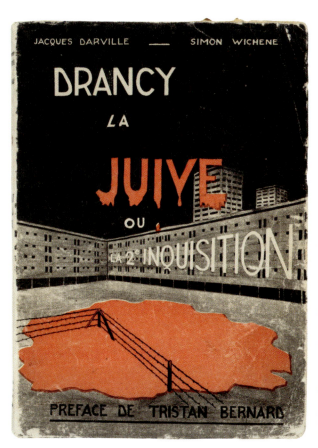

Jacques Darvillé
Simon Wichené,
***Jewish Drancy or the 2nd
Inquisition***, book cover, 1945.
Collection of the author

was experimental in form – five fourteen-storey towers and low buildings – and in technique: it was built with precast concrete panels attached to a steel frame. It was also included in 1942 by José Luis Sert in *Can Our Cities Survive?*, as a model example of the new kinds of housing that could be expected after the war.[9] And yet at that very time, it had become a principal intermediate station for the deportation of Jews from France. Its isolated location in the middle of fields and houses, as well as the conflicts with the municipality before the war, had already resulted in the estate being assigned to the gendarmerie. So the guards were already in place. The transformation of the site into a camp was made possible both by the presence of militarised staff and by the fact that in 1940 a large U-shaped building was still unfinished and would be simple to transform into a place of detention and surveillance by virtue of its panoptic aspect. Almost seventy thousand Jews would be held there, guarded first by the French gendarmes and later by the SS, before being transferred to the extermination camps.[10] Aside from practical considerations – availability of the site, ease of surveillance – this archetype of the post-war 'grands ensembles' (large-scale housing projects) seems to have been predestined to serve as a place of confinement not so much as a consequence of its system of construction, based on the techniques of the engineer Mopin, or of its architectonic qualities, but because it formed a perfect geometrical enclave set among the suburbs. This heterotopia was meant to improve the quality of life of its inhabitants, drawn from the working classes. Instead, it was transformed into a repressive and murderous space.

Occupation and Total Planning: the Generalplan Ost

Aesthetic 'purification' and the requisition of existing buildings were the most benign aspects of the actions undertaken by the Nazis in the cities they controlled, some of them for five years. In the long-term vision of a Germanised Europe, industrial and agricultural policies were linked to a spatial policy that was methodically developed by a large number of organisations, staffed by experts of every stripe, recruited from the municipal offices of Germany, in the service of a project of systematic exploitation and subjugation, whose visual dimension was by no means neglected. A great deal of attention was given to the concept of *Raum*, or space, which formed the basis for reflection and action on the part of a group of experts assembled after 1935 in the Reichsarbeitsgemeinschaft für

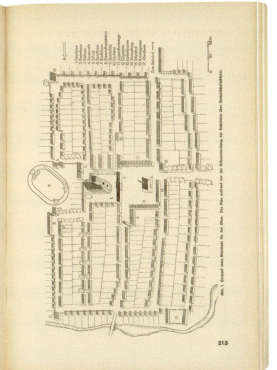

Raumforschung, whose political positions were explicitly racist, and whose house organ was the review *Raumforschung und Raumordnung*, published from 1936 to 1944. With the war, the work group gained new strength by calling on pro-Nazi intellectuals of renown, such as the Catholic law theorist Carl Schmitt, to define a 'new concept of space'.[11]

Architects, town planners and landscape architects were active participants, alongside the engineers, rural planners and researchers from all disciplines, in the elaboration of the different versions of the Generalplan Ost, devised between January 1940 and May 1942 for the Germanisation of more than 200,000 square kilometres of territory that were previously Polish, Baltic, Ukrainian, Belorussian and Russian.[12] The planning applied specifically to Poland, which had been annexed and divided into three entities: the *Gauen* of Danzig / East Prussia, the Wartheland and the overall government centred in Kraków. The leading figure in the initial conception of the plan was Konrad Meyer, a specialist in rural development, an early and devoted Nazi who worked on behalf of the head of the Sicherheitspolizei (security police), Heinrich Himmler, who had been named Reichskommissar für die Festigung deutschen Volkstums (Reich Commissar for the Strengthening of Ethnic Germandom) in October 1939.[13] Approximately thirty million inhabitants were to be pushed further east to make room for the settlement of German

The movement of populations linked to the 'return to the homeland' of 'ethnic Germans' in the Greater Reich, propaganda map, 1941. Deutsches Historisches Museum, Berlin

Top: Erich Böckler **'The form of the German city in the East'**, double-page spread in *Raumforschung und Raumordnung*, April 1941. CCA Collection

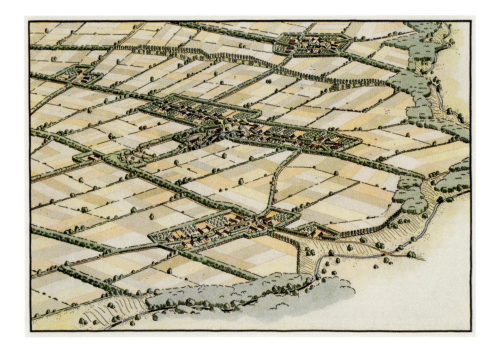

colonists.[14] Other institutions set to work with Himmler's service, including the Akademie für Städtebau, Reichs- und Landesplanung (Academy for Town, State and Rural Planning), whose president Herbert Boehm insisted in 1939 that the visual landscape of the cities in the new German East have a clear design. The Deutsche Arbeitsfront (German Labour Front) participated in the methodical preparations for colonisation, as is evident from the articles written by its expert Erich Böckler, who analysed small medieval towns in order to derive principles for laying out the new towns.[15]

The geographer Walter Christaller, a former social democrat turned Nazi, was employed by the Reichskommissar für die Festigung deutschen Volkstums, and brought his theory of the *zentralen Orte* (central places), which he had formulated in 1933 in relation to southern Germany, to bear on the East, by drawing up a map of the *zentralen Orte in den Ostgebieten*.[16]

The plan drew on the research that had been conducted since 1935 within the Reichsstelle für Raumordnung (Reich Office for Spatial Planning) as part of a general plan for the Reich.[17] The landscape was a fundamental issue for the project, as is clear from a very specific set of instructions from Heinrich Himmler specifying the form to give to villages and groups of dwellings in zones that had been modernised and mastered down to the smallest detail.[18] Within his Reichskommissariat, the landscape designer Heinrich Wiepking-Jürgensmann, who had been appointed to supervise the *Landespflege* (care of the landscape), developed the concept

Development project for the village of Minden (1942), near Ciechanów/Zichenau, in occupied Poland, aerial view of the proposed landscape, illustration in *Gestaltung der neuen Siedlungsgebieten*, edited by Heinrich Himmler, 1942. CCA Collection

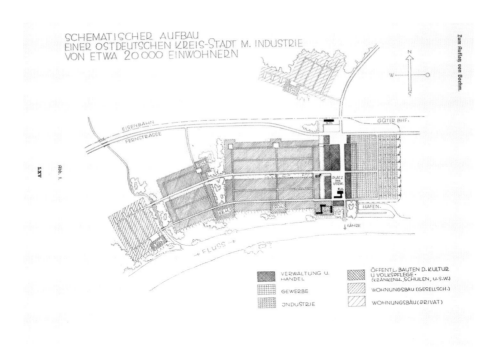

of the *Wehrlandschaft*, or military
landscape, conceived for the needs of both
attack and defence.[19] He was competing
with a group of Landschaftsanwalte to
control the vast market for housing in
the East. The most important of them,
Reichslandschaftsanwalt Alwin Seifert, was
also a member of the Wirtschaftsstab Ost,
where he laid out the route of the highway
that was meant to link Kraków to the
Crimea.[20] Seifert was a staunch supporter
of the racial measures of the regime and
was a declared enemy of the *Versteppung*
(desertification) of Germany, which he
intended to combat through colonisation
of the east. He did not hesitate to write:
'If the East is to become a homeland for
Germans from every region, and if it is to
grow and become as beautiful as the rest
of the Reich, then it is not enough to free the
cities from the effects of the Polish presence
and to build clean and pleasant villages.
The landscape must be re-Germanised
as well.'[21] This issue of the landscape

was judged to be of capital importance by
the legal expert Erhard Maeding, who was
also involved in the Generalplan, when he
published his *Landespflege: die Gestaltung
der Landschaft als Hoheitsrecht und
Hoheitspflicht* in 1942: 'The Germans will
be the first Western people to establish their
mental environment through the landscape
and, for the first time in human history, to
create a form of life in which a people itself
completely defines the local conditions of
its material and spiritual well-being.'[22]

Josef Umlauf, advisor for town planning
to the Reichskommissar für die Festigung
deutschen Volkstums, played a crucial role,
aided by architect Udo von Schauroth, who
proposed the theory behind the project

Herbert Boehm
**Schematic plan for
an industrial town** of
approximately twenty
thousand inhabitants in
the German East, plate
in *Raumforschung und
Raumordnung*, April 1941.
CCA Collection

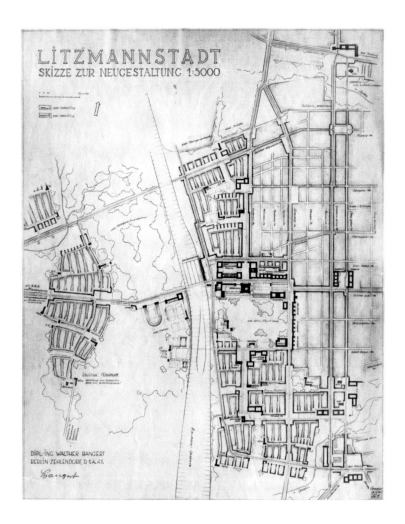

LITZMANNSTADT
SKIZZE ZUR NEUGESTALTUNG 1:5000

DIPL-ING. WALTHER BANGERT
BERLIN-ZEHLENDORF, D. 1.4.41.
Bangert

in 1941 and went on to formulate general recommendations for structuring towns in 1942, which were endorsed by Himmler.[23] Among other modern architects, Hans Bernard Reichow, the head of construction in Stettin, developed a plan for the industrial development of Posen, the capital of the new *Gau* of Wartheland, whose plan, drawn up by Walter Bangert, was to be centred on a monumental classical *Gauforum* that was to accentuate the German aspect of the city. Most importantly, he proposed a generic city plan for the eastern territories.[24] With the collaboration of the Amt für Schönheit der Arbeit (Office for the Beauty of Labour)

and the working group Schönheit des Wohnens (Beauty of the Dwelling), he prepared an integrated aesthetic programme for the Wartheland. Bangert subsequently worked on the plan for the *Neuordnung* of Łódź/Litzmannstadt, part of whose population was to be expelled so that the city could become a German industrial centre. Construction was started on a *Siedlung* for the German workers,

Walter Bangert
**Plan for the redevelopment
of Łódź/Litzmannstadt,**
July 1941.
Niels Gutschow Archives

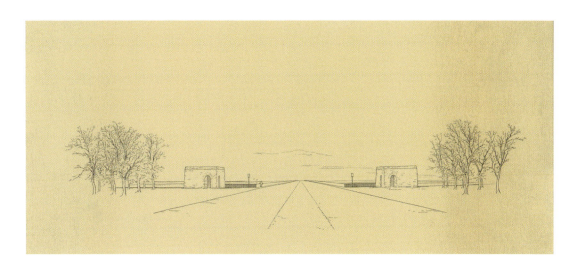

designed by Hans Bartning, while Herbert Rimpl was invited to work on a project for a factory hall.[25] Among the other architects working to develop the general plan, Carl Culemann, based in Danzig, proposed a functionalist strategy for the plan of the new urban areas.[26]

The Reichskommissar organised competitions for the architectural design of the new areas, covering not only the layout of the villages, but also the composition of their centre.[27] A tight network of projects was developed interlinking the Germanisation of existing centres, their extension, the creation of German villages and the construction of concentration camps, all based on forced labour and massive executions. Hans Stosberg's plan for the new town of Auschwitz, far from being an exception, was instead a particularly elaborate version of this integrated form of planning, in which every level of development was carefully considered. In addition to declared Nazis such as Friedrich Tamms, other architects who were not directly involved with the administration of colonisation also ended up working on civil engineering structures, such as Heinrich Tessenow, whose only known perspective of a bridge to span the Vistula was flanked by two towers that could be used to house artillery.[28]

In Warsaw, now demoted from its rank as the capital city of a state – which was itself dissolved by then – the head of the construction administration of Würzburg, Hubert Groß, who had been appointed by

Hubert Ritter
Overall development plan for Kraków, March 1941.
Architekturmuseum der TU München

Top:
Heinrich Tessenow
Project for a bridge over the Vistula, perspective view from one end, 1940.
Kunstbibliothek, Berlin

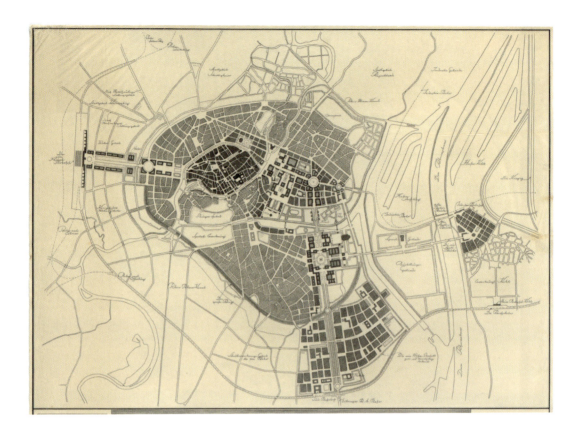

the governor general Hans Frank, initiated between the end of 1939 and the spring of 1940 a project for the complete demolition of the existing conurbation, which had already been partially destroyed by the Luftwaffe, and which was slated to be replaced by a mid-sized German city of 120,000 inhabitants. To this end, Friedrich Papst, Hans Hubert Leufgen and the jurist Friedrich Gollert would continue to work on a redevelopment project that entailed the complete destruction of the Jewish neighbourhoods, as well as the royal palace.[29] The plan for Kraków prepared

Paul Schmitthenner
**Competition project
for the 'New Straßburg'**,
overall plan, 1942.
Architekturmuseum
der TU München

by Hubert Ritter, an architect based in Leipzig and a specialist in hospitals, took a very different approach. The old city was to be conserved and 'cleaned up' through the 'complete disappearance of Jews', among other things, and to be 'completed' for the purposes of its Germanisation by the construction of an area for the German government and a ring of new *Siedlungen*.[30]

There were projects concerning other regions, although they were not as radical and far-reaching as the one devised for Poland. The protectorate set up in 1939 in Bohemia-Moravia was also considered as a *Planungsraum*,[31] and teams of architects and town planners were put to work after 1940 in French territories that were now attached to the Reich, in both Alsace and Moselle. The more important projects under consideration included

the extension of Strasbourg through the
creation of a new area between the city and
the Rhine, a territorial mark of its return
to the bosom of the Reich. A competition
was held in 1942 for its plan, in which the
project of Paul Schmitthenner stood out for
its elegance. In the Lorraine steelworking
valley, Rudolf Schwarz, an architect from
Cologne, developed a plan for the conurbation
of Thionville, which combined strings of
industrial villages, clustered around the
historic city, in an extended and hierarchical
Stadtlandschaft.[32] At the same time, smaller
projects were undertaken in the villages that
had been destroyed in 1940, such as Boust,
which the modern traditionalist architect Emil
Steffann worked on. Designs were also drawn
up for the *Erbhöfe*, or hereditary farms, that
were created in Moselle and Alsace for the
settlement of German colonists transferred
from eastern Europe.[33] Not far from there,

Emil Steffann
Emergency barn, Boust,
Moselle, photography
of the rebuilt section, 1941,
in *Baumeister* no. 8, 1950.
CCA Collection

in Luxembourg, Hubert Ritter would also work
on a plan for the city, after leaving Kraków in
1941. On this hilly site, he proposed placing
a cultural forum on the Kirchberg plateau
and a system of ring roads connected to
the German Autobahn system.[34]

At that point, all of Europe was considered
to be *Planungsraum*. In late 1942, Konrad
Meyer established a *Generalsiedlungsplan*
under the supervision of Himmler.
It covered the Polish territories, the
Baltic countries, Bohemia, Moravia, Alsace,
Lorraine and Luxembourg. The plan took
stock of the potential Germanisation
of the different territories, estimated the
investments necessary for their development
and specified the steps required for the
transformation of the cities and the creation
of new towns and villages.[35] Although
Himmler at one point asked for the plan
to be extended to include several regions
of the USSR, the strategic reversal that
resulted from the defeat at Stalingrad
and Hitler's subsequent announcement
of 'total' war caused these continental
planning projects to be abandoned.

HOFPLEIN - ROTTERDAM

ONTWERP J.J.P.OUD

Nazi Internationalism

Elsewhere, the Nazis exerted varying
degrees of supervision, sometimes relying
on certain members of the local elites,
or at least tolerating them, in a sort of
internationalist development that did not
lead to any single architectural language.
After 1942, in completely occupied France,
German interventions remained fairly
minimal once the Vichy government was
put in place and provided with its own
supervisory instruments, the Délégation
Générale à l'Équipement National,
responsible for economic and spatial
planning for the entire territory, and
the Commissariat à la Reconstruction
Immobilière, which was responsible for
interventions in the cities. This state system
relied primarily on engineers, especially
those of the Ponts et Chaussées, but
architects and town planners were
mobilised under their control as well
to work on plans for reconstruction
and development. A range of visions were
proposed for a France whose industry
was largely decentralised, ranging from
the most conservative operations, which

J. J. P. Oud
**Project for the reconstruction
of the Hofplein**, Rotterdam,
overall axonometric view, 1943.
Nederlands Architectuurinstitut

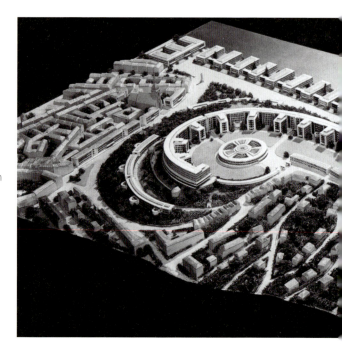

tended to highlight historical urban forms and regional construction within these looser, more open fabrics,[36] to more general schemes, like the ones proposed by Le Corbusier and François de Pierrefeu in *La Maison des hommes* in 1942, whose architectural elements such as the 'unité d'habitation de grandeur conforme' (standard-sized dwelling unit) were to be in a modern style. During the last two years of the occupation, Le Corbusier gathered a group of young architects and various specialists around him, into the ASCORAL (Assemblée de Constructeurs pour une Rénovation Architecturale), under the banner of which he published a book in 1945 that proposed the 'trois établissements humains' (three human establishments) as the elements of a general transformation of the country.

In the Netherlands, J. A. Ringers, the commissioner for reconstruction and building (Regeringscommissariaat), who had been appointed to the post just before the country capitulated, was kept in place under the Nazis up to the moment of his arrest in April 1943.[37] Ringers created a Stichting Ratiobouw, which worked on rationalising the building industry. In matters of town planning, while a city like The Hague was completely militarised, the reconstruction of Rotterdam, a city of fundamental importance for the Ruhr and western Germany, was undertaken under the supervision of the occupier. The planner Willem Gerrit Witteveen, who had occupied his post since 1924, was head of the ASRO (Adviesbureau Stadsplan Rotterdam), while the business community supported the OPRO (Opbouw Rotterdam) under the leadership of Piet Verhagen.[38]

In Belgium, the Commissariaat-Generaal voor's Lands Wederopbouw (general commission for the reconstruction of the country) worked closely with the Germans under the supervision of the politician Charles Verwilghen. His younger brother Raphaël, a town planner, directed the department of reconstruction and recruited architects known for their modern views, notably Henry Van de Velde, who was in charge of architecture until he resigned in 1943. As to its ideology, the Commissariaat-General pursued the course followed by Henri de Man's Planists, while in terms of architectural style, it fostered a modern

Hans Luckhardt
Wassili Luckhardt
**Competition project for
a university campus in
Bratislava**, model, 1942.

Photograph by
Arthur Köster.
Akademie der Künste,
Luckhardt und
Anker Archiv, Berlin

Top: Kunio Maekawa
**Competition project for
the Japanese cultural centre
in Bangkok** (1943), aerial
perspective, illustration
in *Shinkenchiku*, January 1944.
Collection of Benoît Jacquet

Bottom: Kenzo Tange
**Competition project for
the Japanese cultural centre
in Bangkok** (1943), aerial
perspective, illustration in
Shinkenchiku, January 1944.
Collection of Benoît Jacquet

approach through a system of public competitions whose juries included German officers.

One of the most remarkable episodes in the policy carried out under Nazi hegemony took place in Bratislava, capital of the Prvá Slovenská Republika (First Slovak Republic) which was set up in 1939 under Nazi supervision. A competition was organised there in 1942 for the design of a *Hochschulstadt* (university campus) on the hill where the castle is and on the banks of the Danube. It was unique in that it brought together experts who all came from the Axis countries. The participants in the competition included the excellent Slovakian architect Emil Belluš, as well as many Germans. These included the Berlin architects Hans and Wassili Luckhardt, who had been among the most conspicuous of the modern professionals under the Weimar Republic. They proposed a large complex that combined a row of low buildings at the level of the river, with higher buildings forming a spiral on the hill above that would have towered over and dominated the city below. No first prize was awarded, but the second prize went to the less grandiloquent, rather restrained composition of the Roman architects Attilio and Ernesto La Padula, the latter being the designer of the Palazzo della Civiltà Italiana at the EUR.[39]

The oriental component of the Axis, Japan, also organised competitions for public buildings intended to glorify the expansion of the empire. The competition for the design of Japan's cultural centre in Bangkok was notable for the entries by modernists such as Kunio Maekawa and Kenzo Tange, the winner, who proposed variations on historical Japanese themes.[40]

Planning and Designing on the Fringes

While some their colleagues worked on reconstruction for the Vichy government, or in the case of some of the younger ones, attempted to avoid compulsory service in the Reich by taking part in the Chantier 1425, a survey of rural construction undertaken by the Musée des Arts et Traditions Populaires directed by Georges-Henri Rivière, 448 French architects were held prisoner in Germany. The professional institutions maintained contact with them and kept the rituals of the École des Beaux-Arts alive by organising architectural competitions that were judged in Paris, once the drawings made in Pomerania or East Prussia had been transported there. In October 1942, watercolours extending 400 metres, produced in Germany for the prisoners' 'concours d'études provinciales', were exhibited in the galleries of the Palais de Chaillot, in Paris, before travelling to Vichy. Responding to the campaign by the Pétain regime for a 'return to the land',[41] they featured designs for the 'house of an agricultural worker' and the house of an 'artisan', as well as city houses and farmhouses clearly rooted in the traditional architectural style of a specific region. The reconstruction authorities then attempted to enable the prisoners to work on projects awarded to their free colleagues, so as to have a share in the small amount of work available. A year later, the prefecture of the Seine sponsored another competition for several urban sites in Paris: the porte Saint-Denis, the square in front of the Val-de-Grâce and the place Clichy.[42]

Henry Bernard, a winner of the Prix de Rome who was critical of the competitions

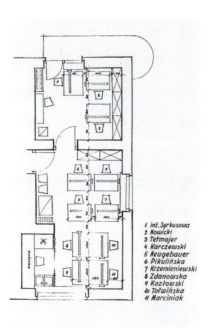

1 inž. Syrkusowa
2 Nowicki
3 Tetmajer
4 Karczewski
5 Neugebauer
6 Pikulińska
7 Krzemieniewski
8 Zdanowska
9 Kozłowski
10 Tołwińska
11 Marciniak

for provincial studies, described the living conditions of the prisoners, who recreated workshops in their Oflagers (officer camps) that were similar to those of the Beaux-Arts. He underscored that 'rare freedom of thought that came from almost complete destitution and a meagre pittance'. Amongst themselves, they discussed reforms to the teaching methods of architecture and made plans for the post-war period with the engineers and builders among their fellow prisoners: 'The barbed wire disappeared. The studio was born. On all these different faces, in all these expressions, a faith, a certainty; same sentiments, same reflex; from this diverse crowd, from all these different individuals, it was clear right away that we were effortlessly forming

Clandestine bureau of architecture and urbanism, 18 Krasińskiego Street, Warsaw, plan dated 9 January 1942, illustration in Niels Gutschow, Barbara Klain, *Vernichtung und Utopie: Stadtplanung Warschau 1939–1945*, 1994. CCA Collection

Top left: Henry Bernard **Competition project for the Church of the Prisoner**, elevation, plan and study sketch, 1940–1942. Académie d'Architecture, Cité de l'Architecture et du Patrimoine, Archives d'Architecture du xxᵉ Siècle, Fonds Henry Bernard

Top right: Allard, Boudoin, Bourget, Eschmann, Kindermans, Léotey, Porcher, Robert, Teppe, Vigier, Warnesson, prisoner architects **'A farm in the Val-de-Loire'**, axonometric drawing, illustration in *L'Architecture française*, September–October 1942. CCA Collection

a monolith.'[43] In the Stablack camp in East Prussia, the very Catholic Bernard designed a monument to Jeanne d'Arc, reflected on religious architecture, and took part in a competition for the 'Church of the Prisoner'.[44]

The British architects had similar experiences. The RIBA organised a 'Prisoners of War Book Scheme'[45] to provide intellectual sustenance to those detained, while some of them prepared for professional examinations from afar. James Kennedy-Hawkes, for example, detained at the Oflag 7B in Eichstätt in Bavaria, would carefully preserve the notebooks containing his notes for the RIBA examination and some record of his readings, including the Italian review *Casabella*.[46] Conversely, the British detained a number of architects among their Axis prisoners, for example the Roman Lodovico Quaroni, who, like his colleague Frederico Gorio, was held in a YOL (Young Officers Leave) Camp, where twenty thousand Italians were detained in the Himalayas. In this setting, he worked on a pilgrimage church for the town of Dehradun.

Some architectural projects carried out in occupied Europe escaped the control of the occupiers altogether. The most remarkable case was the clandestine bureau of town planning, which operated for four years in occupied Warsaw. The PAU (Pracownia Architektnoniczo-Urbanistyczna, studio for architecture and town planning) was created by Szymon Syrkus and started work in 1941 on the reconstruction of two housing estates, one of which was commissioned by organisations in the Jewish community, and on future plans for Warsaw. The studio was run by Syrkus and his wife Helena, Barbara Brukalska, Jan Chmielewski, Roman Piotrowski

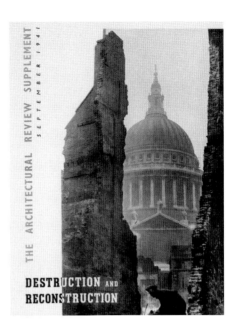

and Zigmunt Skibniewski, who had founded the avant-garde group Praesens in the 1920s and were members of CIAM, along with colleagues such as Marian Spychalski and Stanisław Tołwiński. They did not escape Nazi repression, and Szymon Syrkus in particular would, as we have seen, be imprisoned in Auschwitz from 1942 to 1945.[47]

British Post-War Visions

Like the Poles who clung to visions of the post-war period under the most extreme conditions of occupation, the Allies also imagined a completely different future from that envisaged by the Nazis: in their conception, planning was seen as a means of social modernisation, not an instrument of colonisation. Although some plans were shared and experiences constantly exchanged, their policies were still characterised by a high degree

'**Destruction and Reconstruction**', article in *The Architectural Review*, September 1941. CCA Collection

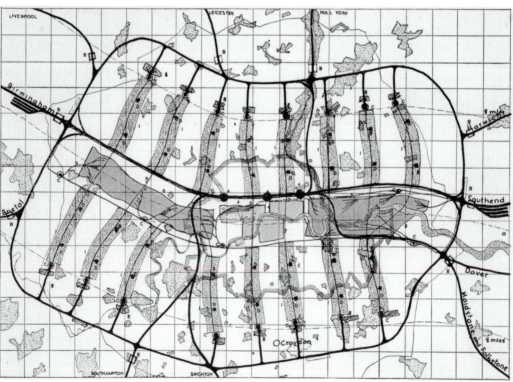

Top: Patrick Abercrombie
John Henry Forshaw
**London reconstruction
plan**, development

and zoning plan,
plate from the *City
of London Plan*, 1943.
CCA Collection

Bottom: Modern
Architecture
Research Society
MARS plan for London,

1942, illustration in
*The Architectural
Review*, January 1942.
CCA Collection

of state involvement. In each case, the professionals involved in development took on the roles of administrators and project managers. As early as 1940, prominent figures in London, such as the art critic Herbert Read, who spoke on BBC radio,[48] addressed the issue of Britain's post-war future. The architectural press, for its part, became interested in much earlier precedents, such as nineteenth century Paris, which was examined by art historian Francis Klingender.[49] *The Architectural Review* abandoned its ostrich-like policy of 'deliberately' ignoring the war, and published a supplement in 1941 and 1942 entitled 'Destruction and Reconstruction'. While also publishing notes by the historian John Summerson on the buildings destroyed in London, the magazine reviewed recent experiences by asking 'What happened last time?' in order to avoid the mistakes of the policies adopted after the First World War.[50] In 1943, the magazine put together a large dossier entitled 'Rebuilding Britain', followed by 'a tribute to the greatest of modern town-planners', who included Frenchman Tony Garnier.[51]

These developments took the form of projects, but were also reflected at the institutional level. There was a consensus between the Conservative and Labour parties to plan for the country after the end of the war. This was illustrated by William Beveridge's report of 1942 in which he outlined how the social measures of the welfare state could make up for the shortcomings of the pre-war period. For its part, the Town and Country Planning Association dedicated itself to the promotion of the idea of comprehensive planning, already outlined in the Barlow Report of 1940 on the 'Distribution of the Industrial Population'.[52] A specialised arm

of the state was created to deal with these issues, initially through the Ministry of Works and Planning, from 1942 to 1943, then through the Ministry of Town and Country Planning, created in 1943. William Holford was hired for the purpose, in light of his administrative talents, which he had demonstrated in the construction of workers' housing. The discourse around planning contained many semantic ambiguities, as Ove Arup would point out in 1943.[53]

On the ground, the preparation of plans started forthwith, at the instigation of public organisations and sometimes of independent groups. In 1942, Donald Gibson, city architect for Coventry, the emblematic target of the Nazi air raids, Patrick Abercrombie and J. Paton Watson in Portsmouth in 1943, and finally Abercrombie and John Henry Forshaw, with their *County of London Plan*, provided the three most important public initiatives. London was defined, following a number of surveys, as an assemblage of 'social communities', so the composition of the city as a whole was not rethought. Rather, the existing fabric would be modified and modernised. Published in book form, this plan would be widely disseminated throughout Europe before 1945. Speer's Arbeitsstab Wiederaufbau (working group for reconstruction), which was already working on the reconstruction of German cities in 1943, quickly became aware of it.[54] The MARS group was the most active of the unofficial groups and developed its own plan for London that drew on pre-war studies, even before the official document appeared. Maxwell Fry had shown himself to be overly pessimistic when he wrote to Neutra in 1940: 'We had gone far with proposals for the replanning of London and if peace had

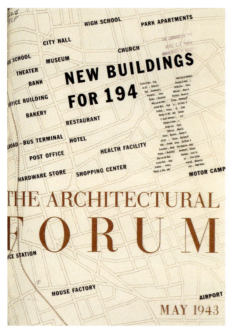

metaphorical as real. The engineering
and architecture professions developed
an obsession with planning and plans.
Another émigré, the Swiss architect
William Lescaze, who was working on
social housing, wrote that 'the free world
is not only our opportunity, it is also the
most challenging responsibility we have ever
faced. If we are not "Master Builders", let us
be sure that we are the master planners.'[58]

But preparing to become 'master planners'
presupposed a number of changes. The
discourse of modern architecture would
have to become more accessible. Some
organisations undertook the task, as well
as isolated individuals such as the brothers
Percival and Paul Goodman, who, in a 1941
grant project for the Guggenheim, proposed
'a synthesis of the major architectural
theories', especially those of Le Corbusier
and Frank Lloyd Wright, inasmuch as 'one
way or another, there will be an enormous
world-wide post-war expansion in building',
which would entail an 'analysis of the
writings and works of the modern masters'

continued would have published some of our
findings. . . . But nothing further will happen
until the war ends.'[55] Like the official plan, the
MARS plan was widely disseminated, so that
by 1944 Ludwig Hilberseimer was stressing
its 'great freshness of conception'.[56]

The United States
and Visions of 194X

Reconstruction was a galvanising term for
mobilisation, even in cities that were beyond
the reach of Axis bombers, such as those
in the United States. The German-born
critic Walter Curt Behrendt wondered, in a
rhetorical and somewhat paradoxical way,
what was holding back the 'reconstruction'
of cities.[57] After Roosevelt's New Deal and
the initial phases of industrial mobilisation,
the term took on a sense that was as much

to be put forward in a manner intelligible to the public.[59] In fact, another profession, or rather another field of competence was being outlined, in which new capacities would be mobilised. The Goodman brothers also lucidly pointed out, and deplored, the inadequacies of the architectural system put in place during the first years of the war, claiming: '(1) that with some exception the military architecture is stand-put and has analyzed nothing, though the navy and the new air forces have done some fine work; (2) that the defense housing sponsored by government and agitated for by labor, has slipped into a garden-city orthodoxy that was excellent fifty years ago but has already become pernicious; (3) that the industrial architecture has most often adjusted to expanding production by enlarging old plans, without analyzing the new technical and community problems that arise when the big becomes gigantic; (4) that plenty of "temporary" work is being done "in haste" that will yet outlive its authors; (5) and that the profession of architecture has taken

Louis I. Kahn
Oscar Storonov
Project for a hotel for 194X,
overall perspective, 1943.
Louis I. Kahn Collection,
The University of Pennsylvania
and the Pennsylvania Historical
and Museum Commission

a beating and should be reorganized on a new basis for large-scale projects.'[60]

A magic number seemed to condense all the aspirations for the reconstruction of America through its buildings thanks to the opportunity afforded by the war: 194X. Although only a distant horizon in 1943, despite the strategic turn that was occurring on the ground, this fictional time provided a challenge to the professions, to industry and policy-makers, as indicated by a series of articles in, and special issues of, *The Architectural Forum*, which managed to form a sort of choir of the most passionately engaged planners and architects. For the next two years, three main themes were considered, which marked a real turning point in American modernisation. 'The New House 194X', in 1942, 'New Buildings for 194X', in 1943, and 'Planned Neighborhoods for 194X' on two occasions, in 1943 and 1944.[61] In this way, the elements of a different urban society were outlined in a periodical whose structure distinguished between different building types and different urban forms in a manner that harkened back to the town planning manuals of the beginning of the century, thanks to the influence of the architects and town planners most committed to a renewal of the professional culture.

From the outset, these reflections were part of the magazine's aim to 'dramatise the contribution of modern design to the building of a better America'. *The Architectural Forum* pleaded for designers to free

themselves from the constraints of the present, by presenting the hypothesis of a post-war era open to every possibility. As for the house, 'Assuming prefabrication – and taking into account the tremendous increase in productive capacity which the war has brought about, wartime elimination of restrictive practices, the availability of new materials and fabrication methods, new and higher standards of illumination, thermal comfort, atmospheric composition, and so on – how can the House of 194X be made the most-wanted commodity in the competitive postwar market place?'[62] Thirty-three architects provided their own answers to the question, with exploratory technical solutions and spatial and tectonic responses.

A few months after this first publication, some twenty 'New Buildings for 194X' were presented in a portfolio assembled by the designer George Nelson, which avoided the approach of a catalogue. The projects proposed a vision for the future of a city of seventy thousand inhabitants, whose central core was rethought as if it had been bombed, a rather provocative concept, especially as this enterprise was linked to a joint initiative of *Forum* and *Fortune* – two publications belonging to Henry Luce – for the redesign of the town of Syracuse in upstate New York. In a discussion very favourably disposed towards big business, *Forum* published the arguments of Alvin Harvey Hansen and Guy Greer for an urban planning policy based on public control of the land.[63]

his name to Gruen – designed the shopping centre with Elsi Krummeck. Charles Eames provided a design for the city hall, and Mies van der Rohe worked on the best-known of all the projects, the museum, which he presented through a series of remarkable collages.[64] On this model site, the urban landscape of post-war America appeared in project after project.

If the 'new buildings' were paradigms for the subsequent modern reconstruction America, the 'Planned Neighborhoods for 194X' can be seen as syntagms affecting the quantification and structuring of the constituent elements of cities.[65] These entailed not only territorial or spatial reconfigurations, but also new modes of collaborative work in the fields of town planning and urban design. These countered the unlimited growth of the metropolises with a model of small and mid-sized towns composed of units 'regaining a human scale'.[66] The issues addressed ranged from transport to the infrastructure of shops and schools, as well as the mix of social groups within neighbourhoods. The notion of 'satellite towns' was proposed, with the support of the Stran-Steel Corporation, the manufacturer of Quonset huts.

The credits for this virtual Syracuse read like a 'Who's Who' of modern professionals, and included several recent immigrants. Each of them formulated his own vision, ranging from the most traditional to the most innovative. Serge Chermayeff studied collective housing, while Caleb Hornbostel proposed a 'house factory' that was quite appropriate to the occasion, as was Ernst Payer's motor camp. The team of Storonov and Kahn designed a hotel that combined a high-rise section in the form of a parallelepiped with a low building, which presaged the hotel chains of the 1950s. Among the newer functions, William Lescaze designed a service station, Antonin Raymond the airport, and Victor Gruenbaum – who would soon change

New solutions for the urban renewal of Syracuse, the southern part of Manhattan and Harlem were proposed, as well as for the other extremes of territorial occupation, for the small towns of Massachusetts, of the Tennessee Valley, and in southern Arizona. An overall picture of synchronous but unfocused planning energy emerges, with negotiations between public interventions and the market that were sometimes very ingenious.

The Elasticity of Planning

While the Americans set about
modernisation without paying much
attention to regional specificities or local
history, other reconstruction policies, be
they regional or architectural, or even
policies concerning specific details of
proposed buildings, would take local,
regional and national conditions into
account. The important difference between
the United States and those countries
bearing the traumatic scars of war was
the sense of mourning that resulted from
the destruction. As a result, the relation
to history and the land was deeply
imbued with emotion. Three cases can be
mentioned to clarify this type of attitude.

The first relates to the work of Alvar Aalto
following the Winter War of 1939–1940, as
a result of which the Soviet Union annexed
11% of Finland's territory and claimed 30%
of the economic resources for itself, and
also during the subsequent conflict known
as the Continuation War, starting in the
summer of 1941. While reconstruction plans
were being prepared for towns destroyed

Alvar Aalto
Kokemäenjok River Plan,
overall layout, 1940–1941
Alvar Aalto Museo

in battle, such as Viipuri, Aalto oversaw
the master plan for the Kokemäenjok River
valley, a prosperous agricultural region
near the town of Pori, in the western part
of the country, which included the town
of Noormarkku, where he had built the
Villa Mairea. Aalto rejected the idea of
planning based on an urban model, and
sought inspiration in the intrinsic qualities
of this rural territory, which enabled him to
formulate a vision of a flowing landscape,
founded on self-regulation rather than
new infrastructures. Even if this was not
an area directly affected by combat, its
development was still rendered necessary
by the circumstances of the war. Aalto's
plans for the Oulu and Imatra rivers were
part of an energetic development strategy.[67]

In Greece under Nazi occupation, a very
different enquiry was undertaken at the
instigation of Constantinos Doxiadis and his
'circle of technical experts' in Athens. Based
on collective research in different regions of
the country, in which his friends undertook
an analysis of popular culture, language
and habitations, Doxiadis attempted to

develop a new doctrine – *Chorotaxia* –
for the organisation of space, in a manner
reminiscent of the German *Raumordnung*,
whose theories and programmes he knew
well.[68] This undertaking sought to remedy
the disorder of Greek towns by looking
to popular residential architecture as a
source of principles of development that
would respect regional cultures, based
on the study of their built, artistic and
poetic artifacts. Doxiadis' utopian attempt
to deal with the contradictions between
modernism and regionalism addressed
the same issues that the Vichy policies,
for example, were incapable of resolving,
torn between a folkish and reactionary
vision of the land and the technocratic
prospect of a national infrastructure built
by the Ponts et Chaussées engineers.

Georgui Goltz
**Project for the reconstruction
of Smolensk**, 1943,
elevation on the Dnieper.
Shchusev State Museum
of Architecture

Plans for reconstruction developed in the Soviet Union were deeply paradoxical. Economic planning in its most rationalised forms had been at the heart of the country's economic policy since the 1920s. The successful defence of the country was in large part made possible by the industrial development of the Urals and regions further east. Yet the plans for reconstruction were marked for the most part by archaism. Even before the end of the battle of Moscow, Alexei Shchusev worked on a plan for the reconstruction of the town of Istra, using for the first time architectural elements derived from Russian history.[69] This marked a significant break with the historical references advocated by the adherents of socialist realism during the 1930s, which were to be derived almost exclusively from the Italian Renaissance. References to the monuments of Saint Petersburg and the Russian architecture of the sixteenth and seventeenth centuries would blossom in many of the plans. After the strategic turning point of the battles of Stalingrad and Kursk, the outlines of victory over the Nazis began to appear and these coloured the architectural projects, bringing a profusion of triumphal accents. The main avenues of reconstructed cities such as Stalingrad, which was the object of several concurrent projects by Karo Alabian, Lev Rudnev and Alexei Shchusev, seemed designed not so much for existing motor traffic, and destined to remain so for decades, but more for endless victory parades.[70]

International Networks and Exchanges

Swiss architect Max Bill was one of the first to provide an outline of the post-war period in 1945. Thanks to his privileged position of neutrality 'above the fray', he was able to gather material from various countries and to provide an assessment of the 'new forms of habitation', and particularly the experiments in prefabrication conducted during the war.[71] Switzerland had also been a place of refuge for architects fleeing persecution, including the Milanese architect Ernesto Nathan Rogers, who had been a militant against fascism within the Partito d'Azione. After taking refuge there in 1943, he created the Centro Studi per la Ricostruzione Italiana and devoted himself not only to thinking about architectural problems, but also about the moral problems of his country.[72]

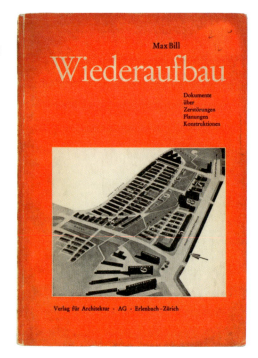

Max Bill
'Reconstruction',
cover of *Wiederaufbau*, 1945.
CCA Collection

Although the CIAM (Congrès International d'Architecture Moderne) was based in Zurich and its secretary-general Sigfried Giedion lived there, it remained dormant during the war, despite the latter's activism. On the other hand, its American branch was active after 1944 thanks to the creation of the CIAM Chapter for Relief and Postwar Planning, hosted by Greek architect Stamo Papadaki at the New School in New York. Its president was Richard Neutra, assisted by Knud Lonberg-Holm, José Luis Sert and Paul Nelson, with Harwell Hamilton Harris as secretary. Aside from organising conferences in schools, its primary activity consisted in gathering material on prefabrication.[73] Other organisations created before the war, such as the International Federation for Housing and Planning, continued to operate at reduced levels, but nonetheless their publications circulated between the Allied and the Axis countries, and made the circulation of certain projects for reconstruction possible, even through the tightest barriers.

But when it came to imagining the post-war world, the most fecund relations were established in bilateral configurations, even more than within these organisations. We have already referred to the presence of the United States on the British scene and in its publications. In a similar fashion, and without waiting for the war to end, Free France proceeded to collect information in Washington through the intermediary of Paul Nelson, a former American student of Auguste Perret's. This information-gathering laid the foundations for the study trips that the Ministry of Reconstruction and Urbanism would organise after the war.[74] In 1944–1945, the National Council of American Soviet Friendship set up an architects' committee chaired by Harvey Wiley Corbett, in a sort of extension of the Lend-Lease agreements between the United States and Russia. Responding to the numerous publications in which Soviet architects looked to suburban American housing for the best solution to the housing issues of the USSR, and with the help of The Museum of Modern Art, the committee organised an exhibition shown briefly at the centre for architects in Moscow in March 1945,[75] followed by an American-Soviet Building Conference in New York, with the participation of Corbett, Serge Chermayeff and Simon Breines.[76] And AMTORG, the commercial representatives of the Soviet Union in the United States, sought to promote American building techniques in the USSR, before the Cold War would dampen its enthusiasm.[77]

1. 'Richtlinien zur Pflege und Verbesserung des Ortsbildes im deutschen Osten', *Zentralblatt der Bauverwaltung*, 1940, 867; quoted by Johanna Blokker, '"Kirche in Trümmern". World War Two and the Reconstruction of Church Architecture in Cologne, 1945–1963', Ph.D. thesis, New York University, 2011, 83.
2. Erich Mendelsohn, 'Architecture Today', in *Three Lectures on Architecture Today* (Berkeley and Los Angeles: University of California Press, 1944), 31.

3. For the Arbeitsstab Wiederaufbau that Speer assembled for this purpose, see Werner Durth, *Deutsche Architekten: biographische Verflechtungen, 1900–1970* (Brunswick: F. Vieweg & Sohn, 1988), 203–09.
4. Walter Gropius, 'Eight Steps towards a Solid Architecture', *The Architectural Forum*, vol. 100, no. 2 (February 1954), 156–57; republished in Joan Ockman, *Architecture Culture, 1943–1968: a Documentary Anthology* (New York: Rizzoli, 1993), 177–80.

5. Adrian Forty, *Words and Buildings: a Vocabulary of Modern Architecture* (London: Thames & Hudson, 2000), 143–48.
6. Herbert Urban, 'Krakaus Adolf-Hitler-Platz zeigt wieder ein deutsches Stadtbild', *Deutsche Bauzeitung*, vol. 11, no. 5 (March 1942), 108.
7. Wolfgang Voigt, 'Épuration et manuel d'architecture: les idées d'intervention pour le Strasbourg allemand', in *Planifier et construire dans les territoires annexés,*

architectes allemands en Alsace
de 1940 à 1944 (Strasbourg:
Publications de la société
savante d'Alsace, 2008), 127–46.
8. Robert Weddle, 'Housing and
Technological Reform in Interwar
France: the Case of the Cité de la
Muette', *Journal of Architectural
Education*, vol. 54, no. 3 (2001), 167–75.
9. José Luis Sert, *Can Our Cities
Survive?* (Cambridge, Mass.:
Harvard University Press, 1942), 59.
10. Jacques Darvillé and Simon
Wichené, *Drancy la Juive ou
la 2e inquisition* (Paris: A. Bréger, 1945).
11. Carl Schmitt, 'Der neuer Raum-
begriff in der Rechtswissenschaft',
Raumforschung und Raumordnung,
vol. 4, no. 1–2 (1940), 440–42.
12. Mechthild Rössler and
Sabine Schleiermacher, eds.,
*Der 'Generalplan Ost'. Hauptlinien
der nationalsozialistischen Planungs-
und Vernichtungspolitik* (Berlin:
Akademie Verlag, 1993). See also
Götz Aly and Susanne Heim, *Vordenker
der Vernichtung. Auschwitz und die
deutsche Pläne für eine europäische
Ordnung* (Hamburg: Hoffmann und
Campe, 1991).
13. Mechthild Rössler, 'Konrad Meyer
und der "Generalplan Ost" in der
Beurteilung der Nürnberger Prozesse',
in Rössler and Schleiermacher, eds.,
op. cit. note 12, 356–68.
14. See Konrad Meyer's outline of
the doctrine, 'Planung und Ostaufbau',
Raumforschung und Raumordnung,
vol. 5, no. 3–4 (1941), 392–401. The most
precise documentation of the plan
is: Konrad Meyer, *Generalplan Ost.
Rechtliche, wirtschaftliche und räumliche
Grundlagen des Ostaufbaues*, June 1942.
Reproduced in *Vom Generalplan Ost
zum Generalsiedlungsplan*, edited
by Czesław Madajczyk (Munich,
New Providence, London and Paris:
K. H. Saur, 1993), 91–130.
15. Erich Böckler, 'Die Gestalt
der deutschen Stadt im Osten',
Raumforschung und Raumordnung,
vol. 5, no. 3–4 (1941), 212–20.
16. Walter Christaller, *Die zentralen
Orte in den Ostgebieten und ihre
Kultur- und Marktbereiche* (Leipzig:
Koehler, 1941). This publication
was part of a series devoted to
the 'Struktur und Gestaltung der
zentralen Orte des deutschen Ostens'.
17. Elke Pahl-Weber, 'Die Reichsstelle
für Raumordnung und die Ostplanung',
in Rössler and Schleiermacher,
eds., op. cit. note 12, 149–53.

18. Heinrich Himmler, 'Allgemeine
Anordnung Nr. 20/VI/42 über die
Gestaltung der Landschaft in den
eingegliederten Ostgebieten
vom 21. Dezember 1942', in Rössler
and Schleiermacher, eds., op. cit.
note 12, 136–47.
19. Gert Gröning and Joachim
Wolschke-Bulmahn, *Die Liebe
zur Landschaft. Teil 3. Der Drang
nach Osten. Zur Entwicklung der
Landespflege im Nazionalsozialismus
und in den 'eingegliederten Ostgebieten'
während des Zweiten Weltkriegs*
(Munich: Minerva, 1987), 85.
20. Madajczyk, op. cit. note 14, 41–42.
Thomas Zeller, '"Ganz Deutschland
sein Garten": Alwin Seifert und die
Landschaft des Nationalsozialismus',
in *Naturschutz und Nationalsozialismus*,
edited by Joachim Radkau and Frank
Uekötter (Frankfurt-am-Main: Campus
Verlag, 2003), 273–308.
21. Alwin Seifert, 'Die Zukunft der
ostdeutschen Landschaft', *Flüssiges
Obst*, vol. 12, 1941, no. 1–2, 108–10, cited
by Joachim Wolschke-Bulmahn, 'Gewalt
as Grundlage Nazionalsozialistischer
Stadt- und Landschaftsplanung in
den "eingegliederten Ostgebieten"',
in Rössler and Schleiermacher,
eds., op. cit. note 12, 329.
22. Erhard Maeding, *Landespflege:
die Gestaltung der Landschaft als
Hoheitsrecht und Hoheitspflicht*
(Berlin: Deutsche Landbuchhandlung,
1942), 215.
23. Josef Umlauf, 'Zur Stadtplanung
in den neuen deutschen Ostgebieten',
Raumforschung und Raumordnung,
vol. 5, no. 3–4 (1941), 100–22. Umlauf's
set of instructions was published under
the title 'Allgemeine Anordnung Nr. 13/II
des Reichsführers SS, 30. Januar 1942',
in Rössler and Schleiermacher, eds.,
op. cit. note 12, 259–70.
24. Hans Bernard Reichow,
'Grundsätzliches zum Städebau im
Altreich und im neuen deutschen Osten',
Raumforschung und Raumordnung,
vol. 5, no. 3–4 (1941), 225–30.
25. Niels Gutschow, 'Stadtplanung
im Warthegau 1939–1944', in Rössler
and Schleiermacher, eds., op. cit.
note 12, 232–58.
26. Carl Culemann, 'Die Gestaltung
der städtischen Siedlungsmasse',
Raumforschung und Raumordnung,
vol. 5, no. 3–4 (1941), 122–34.
27. [Guido] Harbers, 'Wettbewerb
für den neuen Dorfmittelpunkt
in den eingegliederten Ostgebieten',
Der Baumeister, vol. 40, no. 9

(September 1942), 119–20.
28. Marco De Michelis, *Heinrich
Tessenow, 1876–1950* (Milan: Electa,
1991), 324.
29. Barbara Klain, 'Warschau 1939–1945:
Vernichtung durch Planung', in Rössler
and Schleiermacher, eds., op. cit.
note 12, 294–307. Niels Gutschow and
Barbara Klain, *Vernichtung und Utopie:
Stadtplanung Warschau 1939–1945*
(Hamburg: Junius, 1994), 21–41.
30. Hubert Ritter, 'Der
Generalbebauungsplan von Krakau',
c. 1941, presentation binder,
Architekturmuseum, Munich,
Ritter archives.
31. Wilhelm Fischer, 'Das Protektorat
Böhmen und Mähren als Planungsraum',
Raumforschung und Raumordnung,
vol. 5, no. 10 (1941), 502–15.
32. Jean-Louis Cohen and Hartmut
Frank, eds., *Les Relations franco-
allemandes 1940–1950 et leurs effets
sur l'architecture et la forme urbaine*,
research report (Hamburg: Hochschule
für bildende Künste; Paris: École
d'architecture Paris-Villemin, 1989).
33. Curt Schiebold, 'Die Neuordnung der
bäuerlichen Verhältnisse in Lothringen',
Raumforschung und Raumordnung,
vol. 8, no. 2 (1944), 51–56.
34. Guy Thewes, 'City Planning as
an Instrument of National Socialist
"Germanization" Policy: Hubert Ritter's
Development Plan for Luxembourg',
in *Endangered Cities: Military Power
and Urban Societies in the Era of the
World Wars*, edited by Marcus Funck
and Roger Chickering (Boston: Brill
Academic Publishers, 2004), 161–76.
35. 'Dispositionen und
Berechnungsgrundlagen für einen
Generalsiedlungsplan', 29 October
and 23 December 1942, BAK,
R 49/984; reproduced in Rössler
and Schleiermacher, eds., op. cit.
note 12, 96–117.
36. Danièle Voldman, *La Reconstruction
des villes françaises de 1940
à 1954: histoire d'une politique*
(Paris: L'Harmattan, 1997), 17–42.
37. Cor Wagenaar, W*elvaartsstad
in wording. De wederopbouw
van Rotterdam 1940–1952*
(Rotterdam: NAi Uitgevers, 1992).
38. Noor Mens, *W. G. Witteveen
en Rotterdam* (Rotterdam:
Uitgeverij 010, 2010), 212–15.
39. Dr. Krebs, 'Internationaler
Wettbewerb für eine Hochschulstadt in
Preßburg', *Deutsche Bauzeitung*, vol. 76,
no. 16 (12 August 1942), 367–85. Giulio
Roisecco, 'Concorso per la sistemazione

urbanistica ed architettonica della città universitaria di Bratislava', *Architettura*, vol. 22, no. 1 (1943), 1–9.

40. See Benoît Jacquet, *Les principes de monumentalité dans l'architecture moderne. Analyse du discours architectural dans les premières œuvres de Tange Kenzô (1936–1962)*, doctorate thesis, Université de Paris 8, 2007, 439–53.

41. 'Les concours d'études provinciales des architectes prisonniers de guerre', *L'Architecture française*, vol. 3, no. 23–24 (September–October 1942), 15–20.

42. 'Le concours d'architecture d'ensembles urbains de la préfecture de la Seine pour les architectes prisonniers de guerre', *L'Architecture française*, vol. 4, no. 38 (December 1943), 3–10.

43. Henry Bernard, 'Les architectes prisonniers de guerre', *L'Architecture française*, vol. 4, no. 38 (December 1943), 11–17.

44. See the drawings for this project held at the IFA, fonds Henry Bernard, 266 AA 14/4, 7/8, 233 and 56/4.

45. See the calls for donations and letters of gratitude from the prisoners in *RIBA Journal*, vol. 51 (November 1943), 13.

46. James Kennedy-Hawkes, notebooks, RIBA, K-HaJ/1 box 2, folders 2 and 3.

47. Gutschow and Klain, op. cit. note 29, 57–73. See also Stanislaw Jankowski, 'Warsaw: Destruction, Secret Town Planning 1939–44, and Postwar Reconstruction', in *Rebuilding Europe's Bombed Cities*, edited by Jeffry Diefendorf (New York: St. Martin's Press, 1990), 77–93.

48. Nicholas Bullock, *Building the Post-War World; Modern Architecture and Reconstruction in Britain* (London and New York: Routledge, 2002), 8–9.

49. Francis D. Klingender, 'Daumier and the Reconstruction of Paris', *The Architectural Review*, vol. 90 (September 1941), 55–60.

50. J. M. Richards, 'Planning and Reconstruction', *The Architectural Review*, vol. 89, no. 534 (June 1941), 117–88. 'What Happened Last Time', *The Architectural Review*, vol. 90, no. 535 (July 1941), 3–5.

51. 'Rebuilding Britain', *The Architectural Review*, vol. 93, no. 556 (April 1943), 85–112. The 'homage' is on p. 113ff.

52. Royal Commission on the Distribution of the Industrial Population, *Report*, London, H.M.S.O., 1940.

53. Ove Arup, 'Planning Vocabulary Needed', letter published in *The Architects' Journal*, 3 June 1943, 362–63. On the political repercussions in the United States, see W. S. Morrison, 'The Work and Establishment of the Ministry of Town and Country Planning', *Journal of the American Planning Association*, vol. 11, no. 1 (March 1945), 5–9.

54. *County of London Plan, Prepared for the London County Council by J. H. Forshaw and Patrick Abercrombie* (London: Macmillan, 1943).

55. Maxwell Fry, letter to Richard Neutra, 9 April 1940, Thomas Hines collection, Los Angeles.

56. Ludwig Hilberseimer, *The New City. Principles of Planning* (Chicago: Paul Theobald, 1944), 152.

57. Walter Curt Behrendt, 'What Retards Urban Reconstruction', *New Pencil Points*, vol. 23, no. 6 (June 1942), 48–51.

58. William Lescaze, 'Architecture in War and in Peace', manuscript, 29 October 1942, William Edmond Lescaze Archive, Special Collections Research Center, Syracuse University, Syracuse, NY.

59. Percival Goodman, project for the Guggenheim Foundation, 1942, cited by Taylor Stoehr, 'The Goodman Brothers and *Communitas*', in Kimberly J. Elman and Angela Giral, *Percival Goodman. Architect, Planner, Teacher, Painter* (New York: Columbia University and Miriam and Ira D. Wallach Art Gallery, 2001), 49.

60. Percival Goodman and Paul Goodman, 'Architecture in Wartime', *The New Republic*, 20 December 1943, 878–79.

61. Andrew M. Shanken, *From Total War to Total Living: American Architecture and the Culture of Planning, 1939–194X*, Ph.D. thesis, Princeton University, 1999. Idem. *194X. Architecture, Planning, and Consumer Culture on the American Home Front* (Minneapolis: University of Minnesota Press, 2009).

62. 'The New House 194X', *The Architectural Forum*, vol. 77, no. 3 (September 1942), 65.

63. Alvin Harvey Hansen and Guy Greer, *Urban Redevelopment and Housing*, Washington, DC, National Planning Association, 1941. See Shanken, op. cit. note 60, 29–39.

64. 'New Buildings for 194X', *The Architectural Forum*, vol. 78, no. 5 (May 1943), 69–152.

65. 'Planned Neighborhoods for 194X', *The Architectural Forum*, vol. 79, no. 4 (October 1943), 65–140 and vol. 80, no. 4 (April 1944), 71–151.

66. 'Planned Neighborhoods for 194X', *The Architectural Forum*, vol. 80, no. 4 (April 1944), 72.

67. Eeva-Liisa Pelkonen, *Alvar Aalto: Architecture, Modernity, and Geopolitics* (New Haven: Yale University Press, 2009).

68. John Papaioannou, 'C. A. Doxiadis' Early Career and the Birth of Ekistics', *Ekistics*, vol. 41, no. 247 (June 1976), 314. My thanks to Ioanna Theocharopoulou for bringing this undertaking to my attention.

69. Alexei Shchusev, *Proekt vosstanovlenia goroda Istry* (Moscow: Akademia Arkhitektury SSSR, 1946).

70. See the (poorly) reproduced plans in *40 Let Velikoi Pobedy*, edited by Yuri Volchok (Moscow: Stroiizdat, 1985). See also *URSS anni '30-50. Paesaggi dell'utopia staliniana*, edited by Alessandro De Magistris (Milan: Mazzotta, 1997).

71. Max Bill, *Wiederaufbau. Dokumente über Zerstörungen, Planungen, Konstruktionen* (Erlenbach-Zurich: Verlag für Architektur AG, 1945), 37–52 and 67–80.

72. Renata Broggini, *Terra d'asilo. I rifugiati italiani in Svizzera 1943–1945*, (Bologna: il Mulino, 1993), 516–17, 524–25, 561–63 and 684. See Luca Molinari, *Continuity and Crises: The Experience of Ernesto Nathan Rogers within Modernist Architectural Culture (1909–1969)*, doctoral thesis, Technische Universiteit Delft, 2008.

73. The principal sources on the exchanges within this chapter are to be found in their correspondence: Sert papers, CIAM archives, gta, ETH Zurich, 42 JLS. Stamo Papadaki Papers, Princeton University Library, Manuscripts Division, box 12, folder 2.

74. Danièle Voldman, 'À la recherche de modèles, les missions du MRU à l'étranger', in *Images, discours et enjeux de la reconstruction des villes françaises après 1945, Les Cahiers de l'IHTP*, no. 5 (June 1987), 103–18.

75. 'Exhibition of Prefabricated Houses in the United States', *VOKS Bulletin*, no. 3–4 (1945), 76.

76. Louise Cooper, ed., *Proceedings, American-Soviet Building Conference [. . .] New York City, May 5, 1945, under the Auspices of the Architects' Committee of the National Council of American-Soviet Friendship, in Cooperation with the New York Chapter of the A. I. A.*, New York, 1945.

77. Richard Anderson, 'USA/USSR: Architecture and War', *Grey Room*, no. 34 (2009), 80–103.

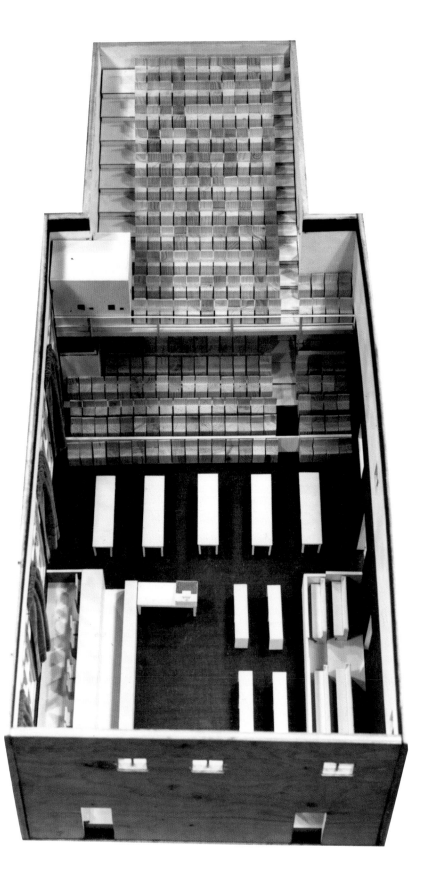

12/ Recycling, Recalling, Forgetting

We are starting to suspect what this war will have brought us in terms of innovations in the technical domain. . . . The application of these discoveries to peacetime ends will appear slowly and inevitably. This is a very small compensation for the enormous suffering that humanity has just endured.
Robert L'Hermitte, 'Progrès scientifique et matériaux de construction', 1945[1]

New industrial plants and implementation, new useful methods of production and products, improvised substitutes as ancestors of valuable new materials, above all new skills and attitudes have been the best residuum of wars.
Richard Neutra, 'Housing, Defense and Postwar Planning', undated[2]

Contrary to the myth of the *Stunde Null*, the zero hour corresponding to the moment of the Nazis' unconditional surrender, on 9 May 1945, at zero hours, summer time in the centre of Europe, which became a metaphor for the defeat,[3] the break between the war years and those that followed was in no way a radical one, except of course for the military and political order, since liberation and the Allied victory brought new forces to power throughout Europe, and later China. As we have seen, in terms of general reflection on the prospects for a desirable yet still hazy world, the post-war period began as early as 1942. There was a sort of overlap between historical periods: projections about the future started early,

Dan Kiley
Courtroom for the trial of the Nazi leaders, Nuremberg, view of the model, 1945. National Archives and Records Administration, Washington

and traces of fortifications and destruction would long remain in the landscape – indeed, many of them can still be seen. Despite the launch of the first reconstruction sites, which in Europe got underway as early as 1940, the cities cleared of rubble and partially rebuilt would long remain like the canvas villages erected by Count Potemkin for Catherine II to see on her travels: new streets could barely hide the piles of ruins and the emergency shacks, some of which would become permanent. German cities such as Dresden would have to wait until the reunification of 1990 for the most emblematic ruined structures, such as the Frauenkirche, to be rebuilt.

The Opportunity of Ruins
Captured on film by Roberto Rossellini in *Germania anno zero* (Germany, Year Zero), the landscape of Berlin would for a long time be marked by the wastelands left by the destruction of the railway tracks.[4] When he emerged from his internal exile, Hans Scharoun, who devised the first reconstruction plan, saw in the 'mechanical destruction' of the city an opportunity to 'compose that which is overwhelming and scale-less into manageable parts, and to order these parts into a beautiful landscape – like forest, fields, hills and lakes',[5] in other words, as the source of a purified *Stadtlandschaft*. Even during the war itself, the aesthetic potential of ruins and devastated landscapes had been pointed out by architects on both sides, who sought

a certain poetic promise in them. In *Inside the Third Reich*, Albert Speer wrote: 'By using special materials and by applying certain principles of statics, we should be able to build structures which even in a state of decay, after hundreds or (such were our reckonings) thousands of years would more or less resemble Roman models.'[6]

Between the first Blitz of 1940 and the second – that of the V-1's and V-2's of 1944 – J. M. Richards, the editor of *The Architectural Review*, described their aesthetic potential: 'Most people look at the charred ruins of this war with the disgust for things that were useful and are now no use. Only very few can detach themselves from

**The ruins of Dresden
as seen from the
town hall**, 1945.
Photograph by Richard Peter.
Deutsche Fototek

A FOREWORD BY THE DEAN OF ST. PAUL'S

As a member of the Bishop of London's Commission on the City Churches I am precluded from expressing an individual opinion on the best way to treat any particular bombed church in the City of London, but I gladly commend the suggestion in this number of THE ARCHITECTURAL REVIEW to the consideration of those who are concerned with the rebuilding of cities and towns in which ancient churches have been completely ruined. Nothing but good can come from the expression of opinions by experts on this subject. The danger that we must guard against is that of being too exclusively "practical" and utilitarian. Beauty and dignity cannot be given a cash value, but they are necessary elements in the good life and they bring in dividends which are not the less important because they are intangible and spiritual. The cities which men make reflect their souls. Those who have mean thoughts of themselves and their fellows will build mean and ugly cities, and those who respect themselves and their fellows and desire a worthy life for all citizens will build cities which express their spirit and are an abiding witness of their quality to those who come after. No one doubts that the London of the future must be a centre of commerce and finance, but if it is nothing more, it will be no city at all, but simply a place where people work and from which they flee as soon as they can. The devastation of war has given us an opportunity which will never come again. If we do not make a City of London worthy of the spirit of those who fought the Battle of Britain and the Battle of London, posterity will rise and curse us for unimaginative fools.

W. R. Matthews

SAVE US OUR RUINS

Ruins need not be a disfigurement. They can be of great picturesque beauty, as the eighteenth century knew. The above engraving of St. Botolph's, Colchester, is from Grose's Antiquities.

ARGUMENT The following article and the drawings accompanying it propose a new solution to the problem of the future of some of the bombed churches in Britain. This solution is in no way meant to prejudice any of the other solutions now under discussion by various commissions and committees. The City of London has been chosen to illustrate the suggested treatment of damaged churches, because the problem here is especially extensive, complicated and urgent, and because the acceptance of the solution advocated would have the most beneficial results on visual planning in that general sense which the introductory article to this number of THE ARCHITECTURAL REVIEW is putting forward. It is proposed that a few of the bombed churches of Britain be selected to remain with us as ruins, essential in the state in which bombing has left them, that they be laid out and planted appropriately, and that they be regarded as permanent places of open-air worship, meditation and recreation, as national war memorials of this war and focal points of picturesque delight in the planned surroundings of the post-war world.

WORSHIP In the debates on the future of the City churches nobody seems to deny that there were more of them than the needs of congregations justified. Should they be rebuilt, or should their sites be sold to use the sums raised for erecting churches in suburban areas with inadequate numbers of churches? Both proposals will no doubt be followed. THE ARCHITECTURAL REVIEW's is a third, applicable to only a few, say two or three in the city and one each in some other towns and cities. The need for short services for city workers, chiefly in the mornings and at lunch-time, is undeniable. The war has shown that such services can be held in the open. Our climate does by no means rule out open-air worship and open-air recreation. The middle ages in Britain had their church processions. Later centuries, right down to the nineteenth, had a well-developed open-air life though not a spiritual one. Vauxhall, Ranelagh, Spring Gardens and many other worldly assembly places attest that. Where chapels and altars are still roofed and usable open-air services should be an established and would be a welcome element in the week-to-week life of the City. The ruined churches which it has been decided to keep as ruins would provide the best setting for them. Seats would be distributed in such a way that quiet prayer would also be possible.

MEDITATION There is only a short step from quiet prayer to meditation. One is as imperative a need in the life of the city as the other. Both take the office worker out of his daily routine into short moments of a fuller and more genuine life, the life of religion and philosophy—usually, in the untrained mind, religion and philosophy applied to some

Ruins as a setting for open-air services. Some of the ruins would be major and commemorative of the dead on the home-front and over-seas. Some would be smaller and ministering to the needs of the city worker.

13

---

utilitarian, humanitarian or educational viewpoints to see ruins as objects picturesque and pleasingly horrifying. Not all individual ruins have these qualities; a great many (of original good or bad buildings) are devoid of them. But all ruined districts possess some of the beauty of Rome before it was tidied up or of Timgad and Baalbek.'[7] This analysis follows the same lines as Nikolaus Pevsner's contemporaneous reflections on the picturesque, which he thought of as an antidote to the excesses of functionalist urban design.[8] In 1944, the *Review* would go so far as to propose the partially ironic slogan 'Save our Ruins': 'It is proposed that a few of the bombed churches of Britain be selected to remain with us as ruins, essential in the state in which bombing has left them, that they

'**Save Us Our Ruins**', article in *The Architectural Review*, January 1944. CCA Collection

be laid out and planted appropriately, and that they be regarded as permanent places of open-air worship, meditation and recreation, as national war memorials of this war and focal points of picturesque delight in the planned surroundings of the post-war world.'[9] In 1945, these analyses would be assembled together in a book and published under the title *Bombed Churches as War Memorials*.

The tragic vision was also shared by the defeated, such as Friedrich Tamms, who had already written in 1942 that 'only the very large can become monumental, and the constructions of industrial architecture, even though they are often thought of as "great", cannot achieve this state as long as they continue to serve profane ends. It is only when they are in a state of ruin, once they no longer retain their utilitarian side, that they can come to produce a monumental effect'.[10] The least one can say about the Allied raids is that they led to a monumental result. So two opposing strains of thought were brought to bear: the English picturesque and the German sublime – at least until after the war, when the picturesque became predominant in relation to preserved ruins, whether they be the remnants of the Kaiser-Wilhelm Gedächtniskirche in Berlin, linked to two glass and concrete volumes by Egon Eiermann, or Coventry Cathedral, whose shell was reinforced but remains essentially as the raids left it, alongside a new cathedral by Sir Basil Spence built on adjacent land. This was the picturesque of regret and repentance, leading Le Corbusier, who had rejected Camillo Sitte's theories after first acclaiming them, to confide in a letter to Raoul Dautry, the minister for reconstruction, that Saint-Dié-des-Vosges was 'an urban area destroyed in a particularly beneficial way', this to justify a sublime project for a new town consisting of a group of *unités d'habitation* set on the cleared site and bearing no relation to the previous urban form.[11]

Mise en Scène in Nuremberg

The unprecedented event of judging the criminals of the Third Reich at Nuremberg, staged by the American intelligence agencies, also called upon architects. Dan Kiley, a young landscape architect recruited, with the help of Eero Saarinen, to the Presentation Division of the Office of Strategic Services, coordinated the efforts of the service to set up the event. The project put to good use the team's experience in mounting the other major spectacle of the immediate post-war period, the founding United Nations Conference on International Organization, held in San Francisco from 25 April to 26 June 1945. For the occasion, Oliver Lundquist and Donal McLaughlin, who had been assigned, along with Saarinen and some thirty other designers, to create the setting for the event, also designed the logo that the organisation still uses six decades later.

In the spring of 1945, Kiley was given the mission of completely rebuilding the courthouse at Nuremberg for the trial of the Nazi war criminals, after he had tried in vain, as he would recount in his memoirs, to use the setting of the town's opera house.[12] He scoured a devastated Germany for

bricks and plywood panels: 'We reopened factories, extracted the remains of ruined public buildings and purchased materials on the black market to construct a venue for the most profound human judgments and newest media technologies.'[13] The construction project employed as many as 875 workmen. The trial, which lasted from 20 November 1945 to 1 October 1946, took place in a completely transformed environment. Kiley's design placed the members of the tribunal and the accused across from each other behind long tables, with simple lines to the tables and chairs. This conformed to the internal notes of the Presentation Division, which specified that 'the courtroom proper should have the architectural and functional *simplicity* of the traditional court. Materials and furnishings should be improvised on the site selected. There should be no allowance in design and layout for purely decorative, propagandistic, or journalistic purposes.'[14]

In addition to Kiley's work on the spatial principles of the courtroom and the design of the furniture, the Presentation Branch prepared graphics and charts, such as the one detailing the extensive structure of the Nazi Party throughout Germany, and those that specified the mechanisms of the occupation of Europe. The same division put together the montages of photographs from the concentration camps that were projected during the hearings. The courtroom became a kind of retrospective situation room, in which the victors took apart for the vanquished the mechanisms of their lost empire. The experiments of the Presentation Division would continue for some fifteen more years in other projects, such as the

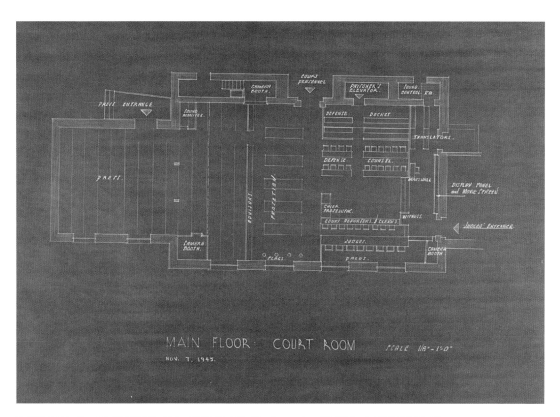

Top: Dan Kiley
**Courtroom for the trial
of the Nazi leaders**,
Nuremberg, plan, 1945.
Frances Loeb Library, Harvard
Graduate School of Design

Dan Kiley
**Courtroom for the trial of the
Nazi leaders**, Nuremberg, views of
the chamber during the trial, 1945.
National Archives and Records
Administration, Washington

multi-screen display by Charles and Ray Eames for the 'American National Exhibition' in Moscow of 1959, which was openly inspired by the dark rooms that allowed the general staff to wage war in real time.[15]

The Research Legacy

While the ruins were gradually being taken over by armies of workmen and the Nazi war criminals faced their judges and world opinion, the legacy of the war also made itself felt in the more immaterial field of skills and experience. The victors conducted a general examination of the resources left by the war, be they industrial or scientific.

When the United States considered relocating its airplane factories to the interior of the country in 1945, in the face of a potential future conflict with the Soviet Union, the aircraft manufacturer Donald Douglas focused on the immaterial aspects of the war's legacy. He insisted that 'we cannot trust the destiny of our future generations to the safety of a Maginot Line, in fortifications, or in plants'. He also stressed the importance of the strong research sector that had emerged since 1940, claiming that 'constant, intelligent technological research and development will provide a more dependable and elastic defense from sudden attack than mere removal of aircraft plants from their present locations'.[16] The most direct consequence of this exchange was the creation of RAND (Research ANd Development) in 1948,

a non-profit association that came out of the programmes of the aircraft manufacturer and would remain a permanent consultant of the Pentagon for decades.

On the ground, the built infrastructure that had been the scientific and technical underpinning of the Allied victory would be extended, in a new bout of gigantism. At Oak Ridge, the Cold War led to a further round of production of fissile uranium, and in 1948 SOM was invited by the Atomic Energy Commission to develop a new master plan, extending the town and expanding it from five to thirteen neighbourhood units (see pages 306–307). The Pentagon, which

Marcel Lods' atelier
at work on the reconstruction of Mainz, 1947.
Académie d'Architecture, Cité de l'Architecture et du Patrimoine, Archives d'Architecture du xxᵉ Siècle, Fonds Lods

Roosevelt had imagined being transformed into a repository for archives after the victorious end to the war, increased its physical and political presence and power in Washington and beyond. While the institutions endured and expanded, human factors remained equally important, and researchers who had been part of the teams working for the war effort would go on to make many of the important scientific breakthroughs of the post-war period. William Shockley, the co-inventor of the transistor in 1947, had been at the head of a working group for anti-submarine defence for the Tenth Fleet of the US Navy, and Francis Crick, the co-discoverer of DNA in 1953, had worked on acoustic and magnetic mines for the Royal Navy.

One of the major results of the policies pursued by the Allies was the development of operations research, which had originated, as we have seen, in a military context. In a lecture to the RIBA in 1946, crystallographer J. D. Bernal, who had participated in the preparations for the Normandy landings by analysing the compressive strength of the sand from its beaches, gave an account of the transformations taking place in research in the previous few years: 'In the early days of the war, the whole emphasis of science in war was science in relation to scientific gadgets. . . . But, as the war progressed, it became noticed that it was not so much the scientific gadgeteering side which was important; it was the scientific approach to the problems raised by the military situation generally; problems raised in the factory, production problems, planning problems in the preparation of war weapons, and finally, towards the middle and the end of the war, the problems of actual operations.'

In addressing 'science in architecture', he raised the issue, among others, that architects were completely unaware of the work of women in the house, and he argued for research that would be as sociological as it was technological: 'The real problem is to analyse bit by bit what the operations that occur in any building are and to see how these operations can most advantageously be carried out so as to give the minimum cost, the maximum speed and the minimum labour hours on the job itself.' The conclusions were clear: 'When the rate of change in society goes beyond a certain amount, it cannot be left to the individual genius of the architect, though he may be himself a scientist; you have to bring in the scientist, because he is the person who weighs up and assesses the result of any change.'[17]

This sudden emergence of science at multiple levels, which also occurred in the public system of architecture in Britain, was indicative of the new importance accorded to experts by society. Architects and town planners were not immune from this movement. Some of them, such as the Roman Luigi Moretti, who was very keen on mathematics, would become explicitly interested in operations research after the war, which would provide them with a scientific model for the optimisation of complex construction projects.[18] Training programmes were set up to provide the necessary spatial expertise for post-war town planners. The most structured of these was organised by Jacqueline Tyrwhitt at the Architectural Association in London. The courses could be followed by correspondence, thus enabling architects who had been mobilised to take up their studies once more from a distance.[19]

The allied armies, for their part, recruited urban planners to analyse the condition of cities and to propose solutions to their problems. In the occupied part of southwest Germany, the French asked Marcel Lods to oversee preparation of a plan for Mainz, and Georges-Henri Pingusson found himself at the head of a team of town planners in the Sarre that remained active until 1949.[20] Although the Americans were less interventionist in their sector, they did call on Walter Gropius, who was taken on a tour of Germany in 1947 by airplane, but this did not lead to any concrete result except for a report he submitted to General Lucius Clay, the commander of the occupation forces.[21]

Flexible Construction

Clearing of rubble generated millions of tons of material, some of which was reusable, making it possible to recycle parts of the edifices of the vanquished. Legend has it that the Soviets built the apartment buildings on Gorky Street in Moscow with the red granite that the Nazis had prepared for raising their memorial to victory over Russia, and that the Soviet memorial to victory over the Reich, designed by architect Yakov Belopolsky and sculptor Yevgeny Vuchetich, erected in Berlin-Treptow in 1946, used stone blocks from Hitler's Chancellery. Other kinds of recycling occurred, on the scale not of granite blocks but of whole buildings, especially when they were virtually indestructible, like the *Flaktürme* that Friedrich Tamms had intended to decorate with classical details after the war. In this case, 'Bunker-Hotels' made their appearance, along with emergency housing for refugees. In Braunschweig, the 'Central Hotel' opened in 1948 in one of the towers, after a few windows had been pierced through the concrete with great difficulty.[22]

But even before these forms of reuse occurred, propelled by urgent circumstance and lack of resources, the issue of flexibility had already been explicitly addressed in projects previously proposed for the post-war period in the United States. The question of flexibility could be found throughout the issue that *The Architectural Forum* devoted in 1942 to 'The New House 194X'. Most projects combined an exterior envelope and fixed primary structure with moveable interior partitions, which could be adapted to changes in the family unit – a particular experience that had been common in the course of migrations and mobilisation. The founding partners of SOM had been committed to developing a language of construction that would lead to 'flexible space, zoned and conditioned for satisfaction', and asked themselves: 'How may space be enclosed? Expansive rectangular form, completely spanned, has inherent flexibility and structural simplicity. . . . The basic units can be thought of as Vocabulary, their considered relation to each other as Grammar, and the final expression in space as Composition. . . . The plans have been developed with progressive change in mind. Utilities should be replaced when obsolete, not necessarily as a complete room. Families may increase or shrink. Flexible space provides one answer.'[23] For his part, William Wurster, who had become dean of the architecture school at MIT, was thinking along the same lines, as if he was already imagining the post-war baby boom: 'There should be no boxlike

Yakov Belopolsky
**Monument to the victory
over Nazism**, Treptow, Berlin,
general perspective, 1946.
Shchusev State Museum
of Architecture

permanent rooms on this living floor – just
space. Initially, this space would be divided
only by a completely prefabricated kitchen
bay, bathroom and closets. Later on, with
children, it would be further divided into
smaller separated areas or rooms through
the addition of closet units.'[24]

The preoccupation with reconversion
operated at every scale. Workers' housing
estates were analysed for their long-term
potential, and strategies for converting them
into 'planned neighborhoods' had appeared
as early as 1943.[25] On occasion, architectural
inventiveness was applied to recycling the
waste from the American logistical system
during the war, which had littered the planet
with crates and containers, whose movement
had been facilitated by widespread use of

forklifts. On the Allied side, the consumption
of packaging of every sort had quintupled
during the war, and Bertrand Goldberg
designed a shipping crate for the 90 mm
Bofors anti-aircraft gun that could be
converted into housing for troops. He
proposed to cut round holes in the sides,
and to transform one side into a facade panel
that could swing up and serve as an awning.
A limited series of these would be built.[26]

Recycling Quonset Huts

After four years of production, tens of
thousands of metal huts had been produced
and were available for civilian life. The sheer
quantity of them required both that they be
recycled and that the production lines be
redirected to new ends. By the beginning
of 1944, Stran-Steel, a division of the Great
Lakes Steel Corporation, and the main
producer of Quonset huts that were by now
much improved over the original version,

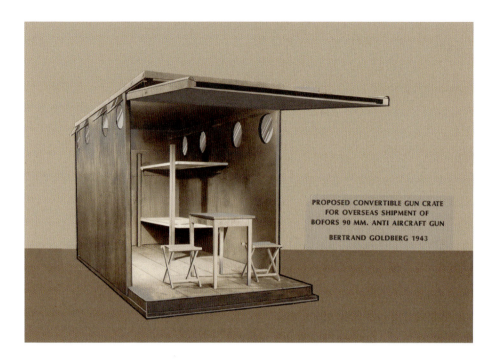

PROPOSED CONVERTIBLE GUN CRATE
FOR OVERSEAS SHIPMENT OF
BOFORS 90 MM. ANTI AIRCRAFT GUN

BERTRAND GOLDBERG 1943

raised the question of how to pass from 'hutments to houses'. They advanced the hypothesis that this kind of building 'can be applied in substantially its present form to a number of peacetime purposes, such as garage buildings, and can be adapted to other uses like greenhouse construction', which drawings produced by the Detroit firm of Smith, Hinchman & Grylls purported to demonstrate. The fact that many candidates for these new uses would probably have someone among their neighbours with 'military experience setting up huts'[27] was clearly an advantage. Elsewhere, the firm's advertisements presented them quite unapologetically as 'the sportsman's dream with real steel',[28] and myriads of variants were put on the market, either as individual elements or as three of four units assembled together to make larger covered envelopes.

Specific projects were published in the reviews alongside the advertisements. In 1946, Ben Rosen, Harold Jensen and Vincent Solomita, three American military

men stationed near Oxford, imagined using the structures of their base to create communal facilities to house the British wounded. They assigned the Nissen huts to be individual homes and sought to make apartments, a shopping centre and a social centre with clusters of Romlin huts. The first coverage in continental European magazines of 'l'habitation américaine' (American housing), such as Louis-Georges Noviant's publication of the J. D. Pierce Foundation's 'Victory House', built from a Quonset hut,[29] were widely reproduced. The half-barrel shape of that project resembled the semi-circular houses that Jacques Couëlle built out of 'Ceramic spindle'.[30]

But the most creative approach of all was taken by the American architect Bruce Goff. After being enlisted in the Seabees, he built

Bertrand Goldberg **Proposal for the conversion of a shipping crate for Bofors anti-aircraft guns** into a dwelling, 1943.

Department of Architecture and Design, the Archive of Bertrand Goldberg, gift of his children through his estate, The Art Institute of Chicago

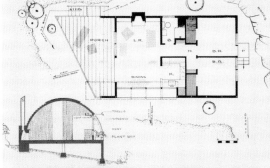

John Campbell
Worley K. Wong
**Transformation of
a Quonset hut into a
dwelling**, Fallen Leaf
Lake (1946), illustrations
in *Arts & Architecture*,
December 1946.
CCA Collection

Bottom: Bruce Goff
**Ruth and Sam Ford
House no. 1**, Aurora,
Illinois, elevation,
1947–1949.
Department of
Architecture and
Design, The Art
Institute of Chicago,
gift of Shin'enkan, Inc.

the mess and dormitory for single officers at the naval base of Dutch Harbor, in the Aleutian Islands. In 1944, he was stationed at Camp Parks, in Dublin, California, where he designed the interior of the Star Bar (1944) in a wood-framed hut. And using mostly Quonset elements, he built the McGall Memorial Chapel at the same camp in 1945, by assembling two 'elephant' format huts end-to-end, placing stone walls at the ends, and opening up the top line of panels to bring in light from above.[31] The church was subsequently purchased by the parish of San Lorenzo, not far from Oakland, where it was reconstructed in 1947. It was here that it earned the approbation of Erich Mendelsohn, who was looking at the time for a modern form for a synagogue.[32] After the war, Goff put together various assemblages of Quonset huts of different heights for the purpose of producing standardised housing, as well as designing a workshop for himself, all of which he then deconstructed.

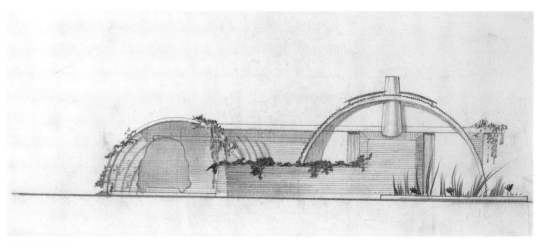

Top: Bruce Goff
McGall Memorial Chapel built from Quonset hut elements, Camp Parks, California, 1945.
Department of Architecture and Design, The Art Institute of Chicago

Bottom: Bruce Goff
House no. 1 based on the Stran-Steel Quonset, elevation, 1945–1946.
Department of Architecture and Design, The Art Institute of Chicago, gift of Shin'enkan, Inc.

He recycled various structural elements and reused them to make a central mast, comparable to the one in Fuller's Wichita House, enabling him to design larger houses, such as the painter Ruth Ford's house in Aurora, Illinois (1947–1949), with its circular plan, which drew strong reactions from the press.[33]

The very widespread distribution of the Quonset hut had turned it into one of those products that could symbolise the capacity of wartime industry to respond to civilian needs, at a time when whole complexes were put together out of hundreds of huts in a row, such as the Rodger Young Village in Los Angeles, which was used to house war veterans until 1954.[34] The review *California Art and Architecture* presented it in 1944 in support of post-war policies. In 1946, it published a project for a 'converted Quonset' built by John Campbell and Worley K. Wong at Fallen Leaf Lake, California. Comparing its pure cylindrical form to the pure cube, it proposed to 'look at the Quonset again with a more analytical attitude and an open mind. Let's stop thinking of the Quonset as a stop-gap emergency shelter or as a poor relation to a real house.' Charles and Ray Eames would answer the call with their Qwikset Lock House,[35] whose name and curved roof were an explicit reference to the Quonset hut, even though the material was now plywood. Another memorable use of the Quonset hut was by Pierre Chareau, shortly before his death, when he built Robert Motherwell's studio at Easthampton, Long Island. He lifted up the structure by setting it on five rows of cinderblock and replaced some of the sheet metal with panes of glass.

Fuller's Wichita House

In the case of the Quonset hut, recycling was being applied to a specific object, whose overall design remained unchanged in the conversion. Such was not the case with attempts to redirect the work of airplane factories to the production of metal houses. The contrasts and contradictions between the publicity surrounding a project and the reality of its production – or lack of production – were nowhere so apparent as in the case of Buckminster Fuller's Wichita House, in which he applied the ideas for the post-war period that he had submitted to the Board of Economic Warfare in 1944.[36] With advice from the unionist Harvey Brown, he convinced the Beech Aircraft Corporation, founded in 1932 in Wichita, Kansas, to launch production of a hybrid of the first Dymaxion House and the Dymaxion Deployment Unit, or DDU. The Wichita House used the former's central supporting mast and the latter's circular plan and ventilator. But its diameter was twice that of the DDU, which made its floor area far more habitable. Its amenities were also more elaborate, as they included two Dymaxion bathrooms and motorised storage units in a continuous loop that he called 'O-volving shelves', modelled on Paternoster lifts. More than any of Fuller's previous projects, it incorporated mechanical elements that had become more widespread during the war and addressed the expectations of American housing reformers.[37]

The Wichita House made use of both the experience of wartime airplane construction – the advances in lightweight steel construction and the widespread use of Plexiglas – and critical assessments of the tensile structures used by the army.

Fuller wrote, 'I wanted to have a relatively rigid affair, a composition of tension and compression that would not give like a bed spring. The rigidity advantage was gained by positioning a compression ring, i.e. a horizontal arch, at a considerable distance outward from the mast and at as flat an angle as was reasonable within the limitation of tension metallurgy. . . . By this method we can enclose a large space very rapidly, that is why circuses and armies employ tents.'[38] Weighing a total of 3.5 tons, this metal tent was packaged in a metal cylinder that was easy to transport by truck. The first house was presented to the public in October 1945, and only one

Top: R. Buckminster Fuller
Dymaxion Dwelling Machine,
Wichita, Kansas, attaching
the ventilator, 1945.
Courtesy the Estate of
R. Buckminster Fuller

R. Buckminster Fuller
Dymaxion Dwelling Machine,
Wichita, Kansas,
original model, 1945.
The Museum of Modern Art,
New York, gift from the architect

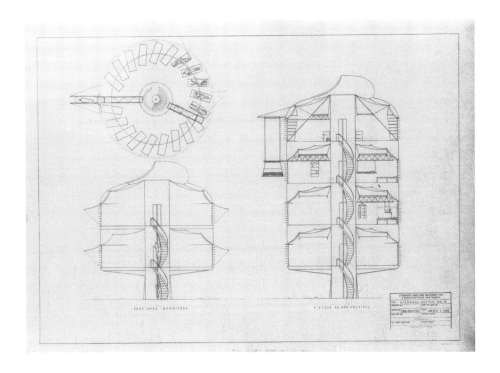

prototype survives. Some sixty thousand units were slated to be produced per year, but production never started up, even though Fuller received no fewer than 3,500 orders. He was forced to liquidate the enterprise, a victim of his own perfectionism and his conflicts with his financial backers. In the meantime, Fuller had imagined an assemblage of houses piled on top of each other that he called the 'Airbarac', but this was equally unsuccessful. His attempt to 'convert all Earthian industrial productivity from killingry to livingry products and service systems'[39] would ultimately lead nowhere.

Prefabricating Post-War Times

The manufacturers of prefabricated houses, who had up to that time focused on workers' housing, prepared themselves to conquer the post-war markets. One representative of their organisation described the trend: 'Automobiles, vacuum cleaners, mechanical refrigerators, radios, and other labor saving, job creating mass produced conveniences of the post-war interlude will be followed by domestic adaptation of airplanes, electronic devices, television, and equally phenomenal developments in other lines now beyond the horizon of our imagination. . . . It is inconceivable that the lessons learned and the products devised will not also be adapted to the field of housing.'[40] The heralded turnover from an administered economy to a market economy did not necessarily entail the end of action on the part of the state, quite to the contrary. The Veterans' Emergency Housing Program was launched in February 1946 and would come close to its goal of financing 1.2 million dwellings in that year alone, before a new Republican congress managed to close down the

R. Buckminster Fuller
'**Airbarac' project
for the stacking of
Dymaxion Dwelling**
Machines, plan
and sections, 1946.
Courtesy the Estate of
R. Buckminster Fuller

programme in January 1947. In anticipation of such a programme, Bill and Alfred Levitt, who had served in the Seabees, bought property in Hempstead, Long Island in 1944, where they would start building inexpensive housing on an immense scale.

The architects and critics most open to innovation prepared themselves for this turn of events. Also in 1944, *California Arts and Architecture*, at the instigation of its editor John Entenza, and with the help of Charles and Ray Eames, Eero Saarinen and Buckminster Fuller, devoted a special issue to prefabricated houses, illustrated with photomontages by the Swiss graphic designer Herbert Matter. It was more a sort of hymn than an actual report. The review was at pains to clarify that 'prefabrication is not just a trick to save labor in the building of a house; is not a super industrialized method to be used for the reproduction of the architecture of the past; is not merely an ingenious meccano-set of parts which, when put together, forms walls, roofs, shells of buildings; is not the use of the factory as a catch for all obsolete building crafts; is not a new sales promotion package for the purpose of marketing streamlined versions of old products.'[41] Entenza would immediately follow up on his stated programme by starting the Case Study Houses project, but these would make only slight use of prefabrication.

Meanwhile, Konrad Wachsmann finally managed to relaunch his Packaged House in 1946, and two test houses were built in Queens, New York, before the company relocated to the West Coast. Wachsmann and Gropius established an agreement with the Celotex Corporation, which had worked with SOM on the Cemesto houses for Oak Ridge, and which had adapted a Lockheed

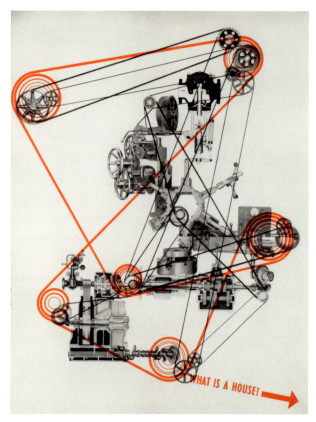

aircraft factory in Burbank, California, for the purpose of mass-producing the house. In July 1947, the factory started production of panels whose basic size was 8 feet 3 inches high by 3 feet 4 inches wide (243 x 101 cm). Gropius set to work on new projects using the system, as did Paul Bromberg, Elsa Guidoni and Richard Neutra.[42] But the optimistic forecasts for production – of ten thousand units per year – were soon adjusted downwards. Production would cease a few years later, with Wachsmann continuing his research in a purely theoretical context at the Illinois Institute of Technology.[43]

Herbert Matter
'Prefabrication', photomontage,
page in *Arts & Architecture*,
July 1944.
CCA Collection

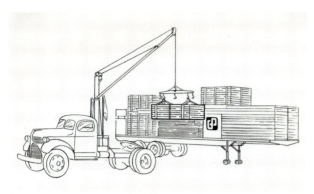

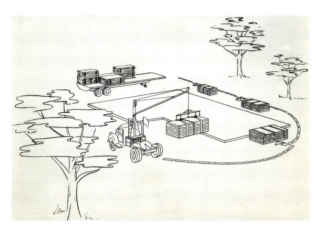

At that point, the only significant success in the field of prefabrication was to be the Lustron Homes, whose lacquer-coated steel parts were produced in the Curtiss-Wright aircraft factory in Columbus, Ohio, starting in 1948. Under the direction of Chicago industrialist Carl Strandlund, 2,500 units would be produced, each of which could be delivered on a single truck carrying all the parts of the house. Production would cease in 1950, however, and with the Korean War, the factory returned to its original purpose. Another relatively successful industrial project were the three thousand Kaiser Community Homes, built in Panorama City in the San Fernando Valley by the steel and aluminium producer Henry J. Kaiser. Their exterior forms were completely traditional. Edward Larrabee Barnes, a young architect

recently demobilised from the navy, worked with Henry Dreyfuss in Los Angeles on the manufacture of houses made of aluminium and paper panels, for the aircraft manufacturer Consolidated Vultee. Only two prototypes would be built in South Pasadena.[44]

The number of homes produced in the United States was ridiculously small, and Gropius had some reason to report on the 'failure of prefabrication', to which he had devoted so much energy,[45] especially in the light of what Great Britain had managed to achieve, despite the difference in scale between the two countries and the extent of damage. The American press referred to 'Mr. Churchill's Prefab' with a tinge of jealousy, and asked itself 'Is the Ministry of Works a forerunner of the industrialized house that may come from giant US war plants now turning out steel ships and tanks?'[46] The British government recruited J. D. Bernal to help identify the systems with the most potential for industrialisation. At the head of a committee at the Ministry of Works, he evaluated the hundreds of methods that had emerged after 1942 at the instigation of various ministerial committees.[47] But very discreetly, the ministry developed the Temporary Housing Programme, which would produce 130,000 houses of four types.[48] The Arcon was designed by a group of architects using ready-made elements available on the market, with 40,000 units being built. The Uni-Seco, of which 29,000 were built, used a timber frame and asbestos panels. And the Tarran, of which 8,000 would be built, was designed

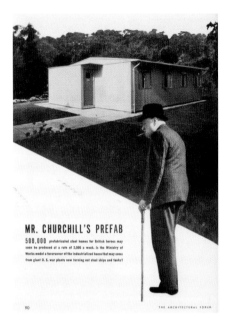

by the architect Alfred C. Bossom and used plywood panels covered in asbestos.[49]

The most successful design was the AIROH house, whose name was an eloquent acronym of the Aircraft Industry Research Organisation of Housing. Some 55,000 units would be produced at the Weston-Super-Mare factory of the British Aeroplane Company. Made from stamped and riveted aluminium sheets, they were produced on an assembly line in sections 7 foot 6 inches (228 cm) wide and were transported fully equipped by truck to the construction site.[50] The experiment was extended most successfully to school construction, especially in Hertfordshire, where a realistic system of construction would be developed in the 1940s.[51] But heavier construction was not altogether ignored. The Wates houses were built of concrete panels, and a number of them were purchased by the French authorities in Morocco and erected in Casablanca.

In Germany, aircraft builder Willi Messerschmitt, who had been banned

by the Allies from making airplanes, turned in 1947 to the manufacture of metal kit houses, with the encouragement of the French occupation authorities, who intended to import them into their zone. Research into prefabrication had been undertaken in France itself after 1940. After his split from Le Corbusier, Pierre Jeanneret had been asked in 1940 to study emergency housing solutions for the central department of new construction at the Ministère de l'Armament, and had continued his research with Jean Prouvé and Georges Blanchon in the Bureau Central de Construction set up in Grenoble.[52] During the occupation, Prouvé continued to develop several prototypes of metal-framed houses with Marcel Lods, although production would be quite limited after 1945. But it was symptomatic that the 'compass' and characteristic beams typical of Prouvé's houses appeared on

'Mr. Churchill's Prefab', article in *The Architectural Forum*, June 1944. CCA Collection

'A section of house' [AIROH house], illustration in *The Architects' Journal*, 21 June 1945. CCA Collection

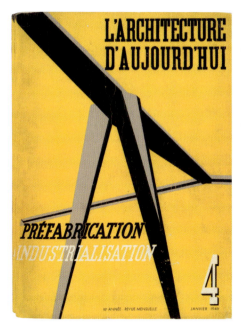

'Prefabrication, Industrialisation', cover of *L'Architecture d'aujourd'hui*, January 1946. CCA Collection

the cover of a special issue on prefabrication of *L'Architecture d'aujourd'hui*, which had resumed publication after the liberation.[53]

For a brief moment, it seemed that American experiments could be transplanted to France, as indicated by Paul Colin's poster for the 'Exposition des techniques américaines de la construction et de l'urbanisme 1939–194X', held in Paris in the summer of 1946, featuring an image of a complete house being unloaded from a Liberty ship. The exhibition was designed by Paul Nelson, with the help of Frederick Gutheim, Louis I. Kahn and young architect Anatole Kopp, who had returned from the United States, where he had emigrated during the war. In the great nave of the Grand Palais, the exhibition displayed the projects published during the war as part of the 194X series, from neighbourhood units to kitchen interiors, together with prototypes of prefabricated homes. They were accompanied by full-size models of the British units used on a housing estate built in Noisy-le-Sec, to the north-east of Paris.

And starting with its first post-war issue, the review *L'Architecture française*, which had a lot to answer for (it had been the official organ of the profession under the Vichy regime), offered a column to Louis-Georges Noviant, who presented the abandoned projects for Willow Run, before the magazine opened its pages to the ambiguous diatribes of Gaston Bardet on the subject of Neutra. Despite the appeal of the American model and the arguments of Marcel Lods, French reconstruction would concentrate on reinforced concrete.[54] The American programmes for workers' housing, which conservatives in American itself would not hesitate to condemn as 'socialist' in inspiration, would provide food for thought in Europe and beyond through American propaganda programmes. MoMA's travelling exhibition 'Built in USA', which gave these extensive coverage, was widely circulated after 1945, and its catalogue was translated into German in 1947.

The Victory of the 'Big Box'

If the conversion of factories producing military equipment into assembly lines for prefabricated building elements remained extremely limited, the use of large, windowless sheds, designed for American industry at the beginning of the war in a response to the blackout and the 24-hour production cycle, became widespread. Like the skyscraper, the first example of which had been erected in Chicago during the 1880s, and like the apartment block for collective housing, this building genre was unprecedented. And like them, it became one of the principle building types invented by the artisans of modernity.

Already widely published during the war years in the United States, the 'windowless factories' came to the attention of the rest of the world and would be used in many different projects: warehouses and factories, of course, but also sports halls, schools and community centres. To begin with, the two principal protagonists of the construction campaign of the early 1930s, Albert Kahn Associates and The Austin Company, were in a position, each in its own way, to draw on their experience in evaluating this revolutionary way of building. The spokesmen for Kahn, who had never been particularly enthusiastic about the 'windowless factory', claimed that its extensive use was not inevitable. They expressed their position with the observation that: 'We believe the blackout plant feasible for precision manufacturing operations which require temperature and humidity control. But there is not yet available conclusive data to show that it is practical for other operations, or that the lower maintenance costs will offset the extra investment required in conditioning equipment.'[55] According to the Kahn office, the principal lessons to be drawn from the wartime programmes, aside from the necessity of creating parking structures for the generally anticipated boom in car use, was the creation of 'facilities for improving morale and preventing costly disruption of production'.

But the message of The Austin Company's technicians was a different one. It was less concerned with mere technical solutions and more focused on finding a method for putting together a 'building in one package' – a term that would be much used – and on the emergence of new forms of practice,

because 'especially since the war, former distinctions between purely architectural and purely engineering services have broken down almost entirely'.[56] But the exploits of the war years, such as the 300-foot (90-metre) trusses in the Boeing factories and structures made from laminated wood were linked to the progress in exterior cladding and lighting. The lessons to be gained from these operations were quickly drawn in Europe. In the first edition of *The Architect's Year Book* in Britain, Howard C. Crane, who happened to be a specialist in cinemas, attempted to impart the results of this experiment, by announcing, without undue stress on

'Building in One Package: Consolidated Vultee's Plant', article on The Austin Company

in *The Architectural Forum*, January 1945. CCA Collection

the 'windowless factory', that what had been previously known as 'factory buildings' had acquired the status of 'industrial architecture' during the war.[57] Nor would the lessons of the American programmes be lost on the vanquished. In German industrial architecture, Functionalism, which Eiermann and Neufert continued to pursue, would soon be combined with its more recent echoes arriving from the other side of the Atlantic.

Ernö Goldfinger
Project for a Plexiglas radio
for the Design Research Unit, elevations, sections and axonometric views, June 1945. RIBA Library Drawings and Archives Collections

The Lure of New Materials

One of the most violent contradictions of the immediate post-war period was the extreme contrast between the impoverished conditions of the European countries and Japan and the affluence in the United States, along with the profusion of American products worldwide. The sudden availability of assembly lines freed from the demands of producing bombers and tanks opened up new possibilities, captured in a collage by Herbert Matter in a double spread of *California Arts and Architecture* in 1944, in which he combined wood panels, airplane motors and sections, trucks and containers.[58] The quantities produced by

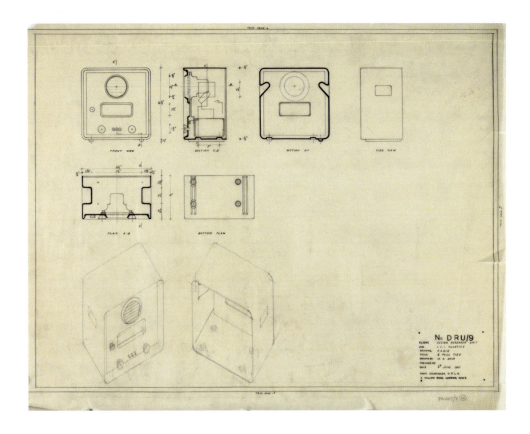

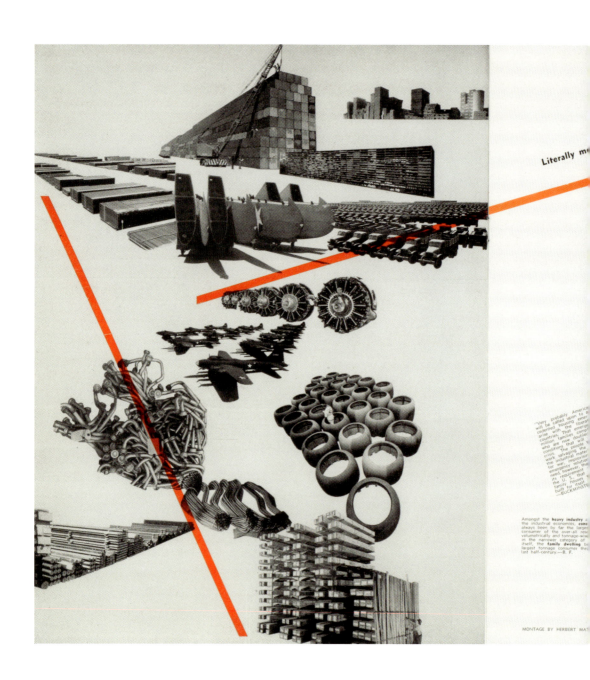

Literally me

MONTAGE BY HERBERT MA...

material have been created by

industry under the pressures of war conditions. Not only American industry but also world industry has fully demonstrated its ability to create an abundance of goods for man's needs. But more important than this important fact is man's growing awareness of his real power through the machine. His absolute knowledge of not only an industrial potential but also the accomplished fact of an industrial reality so vast, so overpowering that it becomes the one great common denominator of the life of all mankind.

True mass production has won the respect of all people because it has been able to put into their hands the weapons by which their lives have been saved in war. Man now knows that mass production properly directed and properly disciplined will not only save lives but also set them free. The one outstanding fact of our time is that this c a n be done. We no longer lack the means. It is now only a matter of directing our wills and our intelligence to the proper use of the mountains of materials and technologies at our disposal in order to solve the most pressing problems which concern the material welfare of mankind.

Science in industry cannot be expected to function if it must make compromises in terms of political minorities, commitments-to-the-past or prejudices concerning the future.

Herbert Matter **'Literally mountains of material have been created** by industry under the pressure of war conditions', photomontage in *Arts & Architecture*, July 1945. CCA Collection

the gigantic machine that the home front had become, had changed the status of certain materials, which were now readily available. Metals such as aluminium that had previously been restricted to the airplane industry were now available for domestic use. This had been to some extent the case after the First World War: the food drawers of the Frankfurt kitchen, for example, were made from the same metals used for munitions boxes.[59] But this time, a whole new range of materials made their appearance, starting with plastics.

The potential of the new materials had already been considered before the end of the war, for example in the pages of *The Architectural Forum* which, unsurprisingly, unveiled the 'Materials for 194X',[60] or in the 'Design Review' edited by Sadie Speight for *The Architectural Review*, where bakelite, which was already available before the war, was now joined by a range of new plastics produced in quantity by DuPont and American Cyanamid.[61] In 1943, *Newsweek* was already offering a glimpse ahead to a 'plastic postwar world',[62] whose field would extend from nylon textiles to clear plastic shells of Plexiglas (Perspex in Great Britain). The latter had been used for airplane cockpits and became available for civilian use after 1945. On behalf of the Design Research Unit created in 1943 by Herbert Read, and at the request of Frederick Gibberd, Ernö Goldfinger designed radio receivers (see page 403), chairs, bathroom equipment and even a tea set for architects out of this miracle material.[63]

In the kitchen, electric appliances were becoming widespread and plastic dishware suddenly appeared, ranging from plates and bowls in melamine to the containers that

THE
AIRPLANE
HELPS BUILD
THIS HOUSE

Earl Tupper named after himself in 1946, after manufacturing parts for gas masks and lights for the navy. New technology also made its appearance in home furnishings. At The Museum of Modern Art in 1946, Charles and Ray Eames presented furniture that was radically different from the first projects by Charles that they had shown in 1940, because, as Edgar Kaufmann, Jr., the director of the museum's design department observed, 'to the original concepts [he] had added a wealth of personal experimentation and knowledge acquired during his war production career'. The basic principle was to use 'rubber shock-mounts electronically glued to metal and plywood, a process perfected in wartime aircraft factories'.[64] In Italy, Marco Zanuso developed seating using Pirelli's 'gommapiuma', which was derived from the foams used to protect the fuel tanks of the Reggia Aeronautica airplanes from shocks.

Transfers between the industrial sphere and the domestic sphere occurred in the field of lighting, as well. New mercury discharge fluorescent lamps allowed architects 'to choose from numberless variations of the lighting system which most effectively solves their problem'.[65] And in a major innovation, frozen foods started to appear in homes, a consequence both of the shortage of tin, which was reserved for the tinned goods of the military, and the growing production of conserved food in the home, which was encouraged by official policy. As a temporary measure, collective freezers were set up in cities, but these would not long satisfy the individualistic aspirations of homemakers.[66]

Eyes That Do Not See: Jeeps

Very significant amounts of stockpiled material were dispersed all over the planet by the war, whether it was equipment intended for troops in faraway theatres, the deliveries of equipment as part of Lend-Lease, or in preparation for reconstruction and as contributions to post-war markets. The dominance of the United States in this matter was overwhelming, and led to the accumulation of what would soon be called 'surplus', which could be further broken down into 'surplus capacity, surplus stock, and surplus scrap'.[67] These were not just items of equipment or material, but also included whole technological procedures, such as those transferred to civilians by the Corps of Engineers, whether in Europe or North Africa, which would set the direction of post-war public works, above and beyond the proliferation of bulldozers.[68]

So as not to endanger whole branches of industry and trade by having to compete

Photographs by Charles Eames

**'Beauty had to be thrust
upon us'**, page in
*California Arts &
Architecture*, January 1943.
Photographs by Charles Eames.
CCA Collection

• The "jeeps" have been with us for some time. Their "naked truth" no longer shocks us. We have found that the lack of chromium and streamlining hasn't slowed them down or cramped their style. They have plenty of power even though the hood is just big enough to house the engine. They have not just been "accepted." Actually, they have been coveted by almost every man, woman, and child. We all would like to have one—because we like their "looks." It is true they are "romantic" and "timely," but it may also be true that a nation of super slick autos has been hungry for forms growing out of some reason and goodness. A feeling for the beauty of such forms has been growing in a thousand different ways, but before that feeling could actually become a part of our lives, it seems that

BEAUTY HAD TO BE THRUST UPON US

It's too bad it took a war to do away with the "frosting," but with that frosting gone we see the real side of many things for the first time. The honest and orderly forms we have been forced to use in order that we may survive make past attempts at styling look insipid and self-conscious and somehow rather stupid by comparison. When the "duration" is over we can expect to swing back to self-conscious "hopped-up" design, but we wonder if it will be the same. The change back to the easy life and meaningless form will surely not be as fast as we think and the rich feeling of "appropriateness" in war forms will certainly have some lasting effect. One thing becomes increasingly evident—that most of the "design" which is lacking in the "jeep" is something that was never really design anyway.

with new material released from military stockpiles, the US Army undertook the massive destruction of certain types of equipment, such as photographic cameras. In other domains, surplus material flooded leisure activities, especially camping, and provided materials for schools and summer camps. Surplus played a fundamental role in the post-war period, both in its materiality and as a metaphor of the remainders, of the excess of military production, as a sort of accursed share, to use George Bataille's expression.

In fact, a veritable aesthetic of surplus would make its appearance. Participants at the International Congress of Modern

Architecture in Aix-en-Provence in 1952 would remember seeing Alison and Peter Smithson arriving from London at the wheel of the same Jeep that they had made sure to have Nigel Henderson photograph them in, while parked in front of their Hunstanton School.[69] From the time of its appearance in Great Britain in 1943, the Jeep was seen by *The Architectural Review* as a lesson for car manufacturers, because it demonstrated its 'efficiency for the American army and nothing of the glamour of the luxury car'. As a result, 'the American motor industry is shaken from its rut of slickness in design. The Jeep is no family car, but it has points that private-car designers might very well study. Will the American car to come still be showy, or will the contrast of the Jeep shame their designers into something like honesty of design?'[70]

The aesthetic and almost ethical power of the Jeep was conveyed in an extraordinary page of *California Arts and Architecture*, with photographs by Charles Eames, that celebrated the 'naked truth' of a vehicle 'coveted by almost every man, woman and child', whose lack of chrome or streamlining had in no way diminished its style. The editor of this unsigned page – John Entenza or Eames himself? – wrote that 'A feeling for the beauty of such forms has been growing in a thousand different ways, but before that feeling could actually become a part of our lives, it seems that beauty had to be thrust upon us. . . . One thing becomes increasingly evident – that most of the "design" which is lacking in the "jeep" is something that was never really design anyway.'[71] Here the Jeep provided a lesson in method, perhaps even a definition of a new way of designing.

'Britain Can Make It'

In early 1939, the critic Douglas Haskell asked himself in a rather rhetorical fashion 'What does military design offer to the planning of Peace?' He looked at the potential impact of anti-aircraft measures on both individual buildings and whole cities, and wondered how it would be possible to transform the 'plowshare into [a] sword'.[72] It would take more than five years for a possible answer to emerge and to reverse the formula, on the occasion of an exhibition that was intended to mark the resurrection of Great Britain in the eyes of the world and its citizens.

The exhibition 'Britain Can Make It', which opened in September 1946 on two floors of the Victoria and Albert Museum, was organised by the Council of Industrial Design. The COID, which grew directly out of the Utility Design programme, was founded in 1944 under the chairmanship of Sir Thomas Barlow. For the event, originally meant to be called 'Swords into Ploughshares; British Goods for the New Age',[73] the COID mobilised manufacturers from all over the country, who presented more than five thousand objects to the public, ranging from furniture to textiles, sports equipment to perfumes, toys to books. The section entitled 'War to Peace', located in the ground-floor pavilion at the corner of Exhibition Road and Cromwell Gardens, formed the prologue, a required passage in a long circuit, was also the linchpin in the event's overall message. The exhibition design, overseen by designer and graphic artist James Gardner, a camouflage officer, played on the metaphor of a blackout being dissipated.[74]

Some twenty objects, all developed using technology from the aviation and armament industries, were presented at the very beginning of the exhibition, spotlit in a manner that evoked anti-aircraft searchlights. Two objects were presented at a time, one intended for wartime, the other for peace: the inflatable fake gun to be used as a decoy led to pneumatic seating, airplane canopies and plastic grenades led to dishes, lamps and radio sets made of the same material.[75] According to the press at the time, 'Munitions inspired new designs for the home.'[76] A contemporary article entitled 'Spitfires to Saucepans', published by the Board of Trade to accompany the exhibition, reprised the theme of transmutation. It addressed the housewife who had had to 'give up her pots and pans to provide the material for much-needed Spitfires', explaining that the same refractory process developed to give a life-span of two thousand hours to the airplane exhaust had been applied to the manufacture of pans.[77]

'Britain Can Make It'
exhibition, Victoria and Albert Museum, view of the section 'From War to Peace', 1946. Design Council, University of Brighton Design Archives

Spitfires to saucepans

THE factory floor was a forcing bed during the war for day-to-day research into the possibilities of new materials, new techniques, and new designs, with the result that British industry gave to our armed Forces, and to those of our allies, the best weapons that scientific forethought could produce.

The march of events is swift ; memory is short. It is, perhaps, not out of place to remind ourselves and our friends overseas that British scientists were the pioneers of radar and jet propulsion, a British scientist discovered penicillin, and British engineers designed the Bailey Bridge, the oil pipe-line across the Channel and the Mulberry Harbour which helped to make possible the invasion of France.

ROCKET RADIO DEVELOPED FROM HIGH-SPEED TELEGRAPHY INSTRUMENT USED IN EUROPEAN UNDERGROUND MOVEMENT DURING THE WAR.

DOMESTIC WATER TAP DEVELOPED FROM AIRCRAFT HYDRAULIC JACK.

The threat of national extinction provided the impetus for our war achievements. In the face of yet another threat – the threat to our overseas trade – industry is maintaining this impetus, freed from aerial attack, reinforced in spirit and body by the men and women returning from the Forces. By no means the least contribution towards an export-conscious industrial reconversion is the unrivalled knowledge of overseas conditions and requirements brought back from every part of the globe by men and women of the Forces.

Can there be any doubt that the quality, mechanical reliability and excellent design of our munitions are being eclipsed by the goods of peace which are now pouring from our factories in daily increasing quantities ? It might well be that among our overseas friends there are some who wonder if it is possible for a beautiful hat to produce yet more rabbits. We ourselves, after twelve months of peacetime austerity, might reasonably be a little impatient to see what next is coming out of the hat. The "Britain Can Make It" Exhibition will serve in some measure to end both the doubts and the impatience.

Of the title "Britain Can Make It", the President

of the Board of Trade has said, "I think it is a good title, signifying as it does that we have passed from the years of endurance to the years of achievement, from destruction to creation". This keynote to the Exhibition is struck in the first display that the visitor will see. It is called "War to Peace". Here, side by side with their war-like origins, will be shown some twenty domestic articles which have been evolved from the new processes, new materials and new techniques developed during the war. Beams of light will pierce the blackout to reveal, against a vivid background of bomb-shattered London, Industry's newest contribution to domestic comfort and convenience.

In 1940 the housewife gave up her pots and pans to provide the material for much-needed Spitfires. In the "War to Peace" display she will see beside the exhaust stub of a wrecked Spitfire the saucepan that will be returned to her. It is reliably claimed for this saucepan that the attractive enamelling will not crack over the flame ; that the food is less likely to burn in it ; that it will wear considerably longer than saucepans did before. Why ? Because in the early days of the war it was found that exhaust stubs under conditions of high speed burned out in as little as ten flying hours. A refractory process was invented which extended the life of the stub to over 2,000 hours, with internal temperatures of 1,400 degrees centigrade and an outside temperature of minus 40 degrees centigrade. This process has been applied to the manufacture of saucepans.

Next to a Lancaster bomber fuel valve component will be gaily-coloured precision-engineered toys made of aluminium alloy by the same skilled hands and the same machines that twelve months ago were working to half-thousandth of an inch turning out fuel system components for twenty-seven aircraft types.

A steel one-man shelter standing amidst bomb rubble has been transformed into a brightly lit

FLAPJACK, WITH FINE DESIGN IN GOLD, ADAPTED FROM THE AIRMAN'S GOGGLES WITH GOLD FILTER LENSES SHOWN ON THE LEFT.

show-case for decorated glassware. A pair of Mark VIII airman's goggles coated with a fired deposit of gold to reflect heat and soften glare, will be shown next to a black glass cover for women's flapjacks, decorated in gold by the same process. Further war-time developments of this process resulted in the glass radar dial with its fine, fired-gold graticules and in the glass deflection plate used on the sighting apparatus of anti-aircraft rocket batteries. It was also applied to fired enamel graduations on hypodermic syringes. These war-time developments will be seen in company with such domestic articles as a glass tankard decorated with a fired enamel design, a radio dial, and a decorative glass panel in transparent and black enamels–an inexpensive substitute for genuine stained glass.

During the war, the textile industries applied their highly developed technical and chemical research organisations to the problems of protecting exposed Service personnel against the extremes of heat and cold, rain and sea-water. The products of their research will be seen in warm, damp-proof, "ack-ack" gun-crew suits, in the waterproof suits that protected naval ratings and troops against rain and cold and in the impregnated fabric waterproof suits used by commandos and paratroops. These fabrics have been readily adapted to such civilian uses as a raincoat which "breathes", with the waterproofing qualities in the weave, a thick, warm but extremely light blanket, and a waterproof beach-bag.

The urgent demands of war brought about an immense acceleration in the fabrication and applica-

tion of plastics which are now being used in a wide range of domestic goods. This simple adaptation of a complex industrial process is demonstrated by the juxtaposition of such exhibits as a Hurricane pilot's post-formed plastic seat and a domestic tray, a plastic grenade with a cigarette box, and a Perspex gun turret with a pair of lady's evening shoes.

When the furniture makers of this country turned their wide experience to the fabrication of aircraft frames, fuselages and fittings, they discovered new uses for wood which they are now incorporating in new furniture. They discovered new ways of laminating and shaping resin-bonded, multi-plywoods to stand up to the great stresses to which the wooden fuselage of the Mosquito aircraft was subjected when flying at speeds of over 400 miles per hour in Arctic conditions or through tropical monsoons. This, too, will be demonstrated in the "War to Peace" display.

Gaping holes in shored-up walls will reveal such surprising "debris" as a newly-designed household tap evolved from aircraft hydraulic equipment, and a portable radio receiver no bigger than a folding camera, made possible by development work on a high-speed radio-telegraphy instrument dropped by parachute to European underground movements during the war.

These, and many more exhibits, will be a fitting introduction to the gay and colourful settings which reveal the contribution our industries are making to a hard-won peace.

TOY MANGLE DEVELOPMENT FROM LANCASTER FUEL VALVE.

There was nothing fortuitous about the comparison. Steel airplane exhaust pipes had already been singled out as examples of technologies that could be transferred to the home, and above all, the Spitfire had been described during the war in the pages of *The Architectural Review* as a prime example of successful standardisation, a demonstration of how 'a scientific approach to design, pride in the appearance and performance of a product, and manufacturing on the largest scale can enhance aesthetic qualities while spectacularly reducing costs. . . . If the same method of research and production were applied to peace time needs.'[78] And keeping with this same example, it is amusing to note that an American advertisement for Armco would ask in 1943 the rhetorical question 'What's an airplane exhaust got to do with roof drainage?'[79]

Further on in the exhibition, the shadow cast by the war industries could be discerned in the cast aluminium BA3 chairs by Ernest Race, who would produce 250,000 of them between 1945 and 1964 from of a stock of recycled metal. New packaging techniques were on display, as well as the objects derived from them, for the initial aim included presenting 'some form of packaging which has been used during the war, such as the compressed paper container which carried a small number of mortar bombs, and compare this with one of the new lightweight suitcases or handbags which are already in production for use in connection with

'Spitfires to Saucepans', double-page spread in *Britain Can Make It*, supplement to the *Board of Trade Journal*, 28 September 1946. Victoria and Albert Museum, London

air travel'.[80] The public came in droves –
more than 1.5 million visitors – but remained
unconvinced by these promises of abundance
regained. Resigned to the products of the
Utility programme, which would not be
completely discontinued until 1953, the public
considered that the products on display,
in an exhibition aimed primarily at exports,
to be unaffordable, to such an extent that the
press had a field day referring to the exhibition
as 'Britons Can't Buy It'.[81] Yet despite the
limitations of its message, the exhibition
would serve as a precedent, along with those
mounted during the war by the Ministry of
Information, for the great spectacle of the
Festival of Britain in 1951, with the distinctive
contributions of Ralph Tubbs, Misha Black
and Milner Gray, under the direction of the
ubiquitous Hugh Casson.[82]

Architecture of
Memory and Oblivion

While public events shortly after the war,
such as 'Britain Can Make It' and the
'Exposition des techniques américaines'
in Paris, attempted to look beyond the

previous six years of hardship, which did not
end with the German surrender, issues of
commemoration – of the losses of the victims
and the triumph of the victors – became of
central concern in architectural theories.
The first important monument of the period
was erected in 1942, in the Valle de los Caídos,
not far from the Escorial, to commemorate
Franco's victory. It would not be completed
until 1959 and would remain the only major
project of the sort. In fact, almost none of
the projects that had been planned for the
conquered territories in the east of the Reich
would be built. Their design was overseen
by Wilhelm Kreis, one of the most prolific
builders of monuments to Bismarck during
the Second Reich before 1914, and the
creator of many commemorative monuments
during the First World War.[83] His projects
echoed those of the early twentieth century,
such as the Monument to the Battle of
the Nations in Leipzig by Bruno Schmitz,

Pedro Muguruza
Diego Méndez
Monument to the
Francoist victory (1950–
1959), Valle de los Caídos,
longitudinal section,

illustration in *Informes
de la Construcción*,
December 1959.
Universitat Politècnica
de Catalunya,
Barcelona

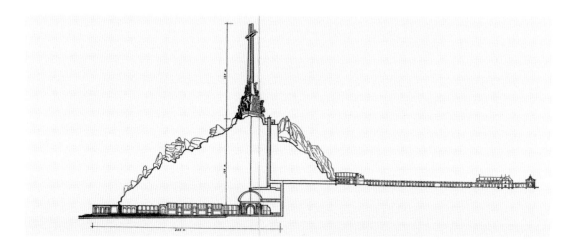

which the young Le Corbusier had harshly criticised. Despite his explicit but measured pro-modern positions under the Weimar Republic and his links to certain Jewish artists, Kreis had been appointed in 1941 by Albert Speer, who regarded him as 'brilliant', to the post of Generalbaurat für die Gestaltung der deutschen Kriegerfriedhöfe (Architect General for the Design of German Military Cemeteries). His memorial projects dotted the Wehrmacht's various theatres of combat. His designs to commemorate the French campaign in the Ardennes, at Meaux, Faux and Noyer-Pont-Maugis, were relatively modest. However, in his elegant ink drawings his imagination ran free, producing designs inspired by the buttresses of Egyptian temples (for a proposed monument to Rommel's Panzers in Africa) and hybrid forms ranging from his projects dating from the period of the Kaiser to Greek acropolises for a monument in Macedonia called 'At the Foot of Olympus'. His most

ambitious project, designed in 1941 and to be located on the banks of the Dnieper, was a *Totenburg* (fortress of the dead) in the shape of a gigantic cone, with a large interior chamber.[84] It was more than a simple monument to the dead: its upper part, 130 metres above the ground, was to serve as a belvedere from which to contemplate the conquered territories. The historian George Mosse has underscored the harkening back to medieval themes (such as the Teutonic knights) evident in these projects.[85] Tamms saw Kreis's projects as 'symbols of the faith and unity of the Germans' and associated them with 'truly divine edifices, evocations of eternity and the power of creation'.[86] They also seemed to be the very kind of monument to which Speer attributed

Wilhelm Kreis
Project for a military cemetery, Meaux, perspective, 1941. Architekturmuseum der TU München

Wilhelm Kreis
Project for a *Totenburg*
(fortress of the dead)
on the banks of the
Dnieper, elevation, 1941.
Architekturmuseum
der TU München

a 'Ruinenwert' (ruin value), allowing them to become as powerfully evocative as Roman monuments.[87]

The Soviet architects in central Asia, who were far from any actual building site, engaged in a sort of parallel race to the gigantic. They too began to imagine immense tumuli to commemorate the first victories over the Nazis. The project by Grigory Zakharov and Zinaida Chernyshova for a pantheon to the war heroes, designed in 1942–1943, shared a similar source of inspiration, although it resembled a hollow tumulus rather than a fortress.[88] The common source for that project, for Kreis's *Totenburg* and for the triumphal arch in homage to the 'defenders of the Russian homeland' designed by Leonid Pavlov, a former student of Ivan Leonidov's, was none other than Boullée. And the same was true of Tamms' *Flaktürme*. The images of the Parisian architect's ideal architecture carried echoes of the wars of revolution and empire that resonated in both camps. There were many parallels between the projects, because of the appeal of archetypes for many architects otherwise separated by opposing ideologies. The idea of a gigantic hollow edifice was also basic to two projects by the former Constructivist Andrei Burov for monuments and museums commemorating the defenders of Stalingrad. The first was a stepped pyramid containing an enormous cavity for the display of trophies conquered from the Germans, and the general ground plan is reminiscent of the Mundaneum

Zinaida Chernyshova
Grigory Zakharov
Iosif Rabinovich, sculptor
Competition project
for a **Pantheon of**
the heroes of the
Great Patriotic War,
perspective, 1943.
Shchusev State Museum
of Architecture

project designed by Le Corbusier – whom Burov had been close to – during his first stay in Moscow, in 1928. In a second, stranger project, the longitudinal cavity was enclosed by a building with cupolas whose undulating facades punctuated with openings evoked African constructions.[89]

Certain Japanese projects bear comparison in several respects to the Soviet and German creations, although it is inconceivable that there had been a direct influence. A competition for a Memorial Tower for the Fallen Soldiers to be built somewhere in Asia had been organised in 1939. It was very popular, attracting more than 1,700 entries. The projects of Kunio Maekawa and Junzo Sakakura both used the theme of the pyramid. Another architectural competition was held in 1942, as part of the Daitôa, or 'Greater East Asia Co-Prosperity Sphere', a euphemism by which the Japanese referred to their newly extended empire, for a memorial to be built at the foot of Mount Fuji. The winner was Kenzô Tange, with second

prize going to the team of Makoto Tanaka, Eiji Dômyo and Harumasa Sase, young architects from the office that Kunio Maekawa had set up in occupied Shanghai. The winning project consisted of a fairly steep pyramid and a compartmented plan that were reminiscent of the Mundaneum.[90] Tange combined the

Top: Andrei Burov
Project for a museum and memorial to the defence of Stalingrad, overall perspective, 1943–1944. Shchusev State Museum of Architecture

Ilya Golosov
Project for a museum and memorial to the defence of Moscow, 1943. Shchusev State Museum of Architecture

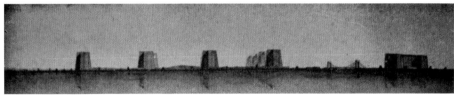

traditional temple forms with a portico whose plan seems to hearken back to Michelangelo's designs for the Capitoline Hill, which Tange had studied. Maekawa's own design – not entered for the competition – for a complex of vertical apartment buildings that also seemed saturated with Corbusian accents, even in its military ambitions – or raison d'être. In Maekawa's words, 'These skyscrapers are not to be left to the vagaries of capitalism. They cannot be vulgar high-rise buildings. They must express the will of the state, be nourished by the sensibility of the people. They must be an architecture worthy of our land. And in an emergency, these tall buildings could be used for anti-aircraft defence, just as they are.'[91]

Aside from the monuments designed for the battlefields and the extensive territories temporarily held by Japan – which Maekawa regarded as the 'East Asia road' – additional projects brought the memory of the war into the very heart of the cities. This was the case of the memorial museums for the battle of Moscow, proposed in 1943 for the Red Square, replacing the GUM department store. Ilya Golosov's project reproduced the murals of the Kremlin, which it faced, like a

Top: Kenzo Tange **Project for a memorial for the Daitôa** ('Greater East Asia Co-Prosperity Sphere') (1942), perspective, illustration in *Kenchiku zasshi*, December 1942. Courtesy Benoît Jacquet

Bottom: Kunio Maekawa **Project for a memorial for the Daitôa** ('Greater East Asia Co-Prosperity Sphere') (1942), perspective illustration in *Kenchiku zasshi*, December 1942. Courtesy Benoît Jacquet

Nello Aprile,
Mario Fiorentino,
Giuseppe Perugini
Mirko Basaldella,
Francesco Coccia,
sculptors
**Monument to the
victims of the Fosse**

Ardeatine massacre,
Rome, overall view,
1944–1949.
Photograph by
George E. Kidder Smith.
Architectural Press
Archive, RIBA Library
Photographs Collection

reflection in a mirror, along with a
statue of a proletarian Saint George
slaying a dragon, while Lev Rudnev's
project centred on an ornate rotunda,
adorned with happy Italianate touches.

There was nothing surprising about
the way the Soviet projects drew openly
on historical architectural languages,
because the doctrine of socialist realism
had rendered legitimate, if not compulsory,
the monumentality previously rejected by
avant-garde figures – exemplified by the
violent critiques of the Mundaneum by
El Lissitzky and Karel Teige. The about-face
of the modern critics and architects was
equally significant, such as it was articulated
in the 'Nine Points on Monumentality' drafted
by Sigfried Giedion, Fernand Léger and José
Luis Sert in 1943[92] and subsequently in a
series of exchanges in which the symbolic
dimension was to make a certain return in
modern discourse. In contrast to the academic
approach to collaboration between architects,
sculptors and painters that was based on the
traditional alliance of the three arts, some
architects were able to respond in a creative
manner to the proposals of modern artists.

Such was the case of Marcel Breuer,
for example, when in 1945 he designed a
memorial to the armed forces in Cambridge,
in which Mies van der Rohe, van Doesburg
and Piet Mondrian seemed to come
together.[93] Mondrian's two-dimensional
reticulation, as interpreted during the
1930s by Edoardo Persico, was evident
in another project dating from the same
period: a monument to the victims of the
concentration camps in the monumental

cemetery of Milan, designed by the three
survivors of the BBPR team, Belgiojoso,
Peressutti and Rogers (the fourth founding
member, Gian Luigi Banfi, had died in
Gusen).[94] That same year, a competition
was held for a monument to the victims
of the Fosse Ardeatine massacre in Rome,
on 24 March 1944. The project by the team
of Mario Fiorentino, which was inaugurated
in 1949, presents an almost point-by-
point contrast to that abstract solution.
This 'nuovo altare della patria' (Altar of
the Fatherland, or Monument to Vittorio
Emanuele), as it was called by the Italian
government of the liberation,[95] was on
the contrary designed entirely around
the concrete experience of the 335 victims.
The progression through the cavern
leads the visitors to the collective concrete
tombstone, under which the sarcophagi
are arranged in rows. This contrast between
an ascetic, intellectualised approach and
one filled with vibrant human reminiscences
also reflected the differences between
the Milanese architectural culture and
the Roman one, as Manfredo Tafuri was
able to demonstrate so clearly.[96] Belgiojoso
was not the only survivor of Mauthausen
to render homage to his companions in
captivity. His comrade, André Bloch, known
as Bruyère when he was in the Resistance,

would sketch out the French monument
at Mauthausen (1950), which was built by
the Viennese architect Wilhelm Schütte.
The latter had taken refuge in Turkey during
the war, and had managed from there to
keep his wife Grete, the architect of the
Frankfurt kitchen, from being executed.
Before that, Bruyère set the stage for the
memorial rally at Compiègne by creating
a 20-kilometre-long composition of anti-
aircraft searchlights along the banks of the
Oise (1946). He subsequently proposed a
split hollow tower for a projected national
monument to the victims of the war (1946)
on a nearby site, which remained unbuilt.[97]

Architects' Memoirs and Careers

Aside from a handful of resistance fighters
who were determined to be the only ones
to set in stone the memories of repression
and extermination, the work of recollection
took on extreme forms during the years after
the war. An insistence on memorialising
– a hypermnesia, one could call it, for the
victims and combatants against Nazism and
fascism – was matched by a hypomnesia,
even an amnesia, on the part of those who
had pursued or advanced their careers,
with varying degrees of enthusiasm. While
the urge to forget all the suffering and

humiliation was understandable for those
whose lives and those of their loved ones
were torn apart by oppression, in their
case there was no justification for lies and
omissions. During the brief phase of active
pursuit of Nazis, the Allied investigations
were made all the more difficult by the
concealment of careers and the cleansing
of the archives. Nor would this facilitate
the work of historians seven decades later.

The most monumental act of rewriting
was on the part of Albert Speer, during the
two decades he spent in Spandau prison,
after his conviction at Nuremberg. In his
memoirs, he denied having played any part
in the use of forced labour from the camps.
His rival Hans Kammler died in Prague,
in May 1945, under circumstances that
were never clarified, so he was never held
to account for his 'exploits' at the head of
the architectural services of the SS. Hans
Stosberg, one of the architects of Auschwitz,
would become the head of town planning
in Hanover in 1949, where he would practice
for twenty more years.[98] His colleagues
Walter Dejaco and Fritz Ertl were found
not guilty after a trial in Vienna in 1972.
For his part, former prisoner Szymon
Syrkus resumed his architectural career
in communist Poland and was one of the
authors of the reconstruction of Warsaw.

In general, the post-war purges spared
the architects. Wilhelm Kreis, who tried to
assume the apolitical mantle of 'architect
of Germany',[99] was able to avoid prosecution,
and Marcello Piacentini, the veritable
godfather of Italian architecture under
fascism, managed to minimise his role.

Le Corbusier followed a similar strategy. He had remained violently anti-German, but in his biographical notes written in 1945, he took care to erase the eighteen-month period he spent in Vichy. For his part, Perret said nothing about the work carried out by his firm on the construction sites of the Atlantic Wall, while some less cautious bit-players were being excluded from the profession for the same reasons.[100] The major French public works contractors, who had emerged more modernised from these projects, would emphasise the importance of continuing their work to justify themselves.[101] And voluntary lapses in memory would also help to camouflage compromising projects. When the Luckhardt brothers published a selection of their more important projects in 1958, they prudently predated their 1942 project for Bratislava to 1933.[102]

The post-war period would afford brilliant careers to some of the architects studied in action in the preceding sections. Friedrich Tamms would become Düsseldorf's chief town planner. Walter Schlempp, the architect behind Peenemünde, would form a partnership with Werner Hebebrand and Kurt Freiwald in Frankfurt-am-Main and build a number of hospitals. Herbert Rimpl and Ernst Neufert distinguished themselves in industrial architecture and tried to make everyone forget their active roles in serving Nazi industry. When Rimpl published a small book in 1953 on the 'spiritual foundations' of modern architecture, he limited himself to the platitude that 'in times of war, techniques contribute to the destruction of human goods'.[103] And as for the engineer Heinrich Lübke, who had coordinated construction at Peenemünde, he would be the second president of the German Federal Republic from 1959 to 1969.

A Modernised Profession

On the Allied side, the professionals who had proved themselves in the large-scale war programmes would become the central figures in post-war reconstruction and modernisation, whether these were run by the state, in the case of William Holford's work in Britain, or driven by the market, as in the United States, where SOM would expand and thrive. 'The Expanding Scope of Architectural Service' forecast by *The Architectural Record* at the beginning of 1941[104] was to become a reality, but at the price of becoming an architecture of 'bureaucracy' rather than an architecture of 'genius', something that Henry-Russell Hitchcock observed two years after the Japanese surrender.[105] In several countries, architects abandoned the exclusive relations they had with private clients before the war in order to serve the state. The clearest example of this displacement was in Britain, under the impulsion of the policies introduced by the Labour Party in response to the effects of the war. In 1953, *The Economist* would observe that 'the social changes which have taken place since 1945 have overset the traditional order of things for the architectural as well as for the medical profession'.[106] Other experiences came into play in the reconfiguration of the values and goals of architectural practice. Domestic interiors were influenced by the compact spaces created in vehicles, airplanes and ships, just as they had been influenced by the example of the sleeper train compartment in the 1930s. Marco Zanuso worked on modular compact kitchens, picking up on the research undertaken in Frankfurt.[107]

The work on camouflage died down after the war, but for Hugh Casson it provided a 'post-war contribution' that could be both 'entertaining' and 'valuable'. It made it possible to reintroduce chromatic qualities into architecture at a time when the question of the picturesque was again being raised in English debate: 'Camouflage can help – not in its narrow war-time idiom – but in the broader sense, as the scientific use of texture, tone and colour, to complement instead of to disguise form. The handling of colour in this way to create accents or to emphasise different materials, planes or changes of direction, has been greatly developed recently in interior decoration. Its possibilities in the street have never – at last in this country – been explored. Used with imagination, control and the knowledge gained from war-time experience, it could surely be of the greatest and most stimulating assistance to those who will be faced with the task of bringing coherence and vitality into the post-war street scene.'[108]

Some of Casson's British colleagues held very different views concerning the role of architects in the production process. David Medd, an architect employed by Stirrat Johnson-Marshall, who worked in the Camouflage Centre during the war, and subsequently on prefabricated schools for Hertfordshire, recalled the constant to-and-fro between the drawing board, production facilities and operation in the field that was part of the wartime projects: 'We, as designers, were part of a chain in a complete cycle which didn't repeat, but evolved as it went round: policy, thinking, designing, making, using, new policy, rethinking and so on. The designer was a link in a complete chain, not a detached component.'[109] Here was the formulation of an intense and reciprocal bond between project, production and use.

Resilient Networks

Aside from accelerating the careers of some, the war also led to more diffuse effects, creating in every country long-lasting networks between architects, as well as between architects and potential clients. On the German side, after a few difficult months, the members of Speer's Arbeitsstab Wiederaufbau got back together and remained in touch with each other in the Western part of the country.[110] In France, the ties established in exile and within France Libre in Algiers continued to hold inside the cabinet of Eugène Claudius-Petit, when he became minister of reconstruction and town planning and recruited Marcel Roux and André Sive, whom he had met in North Africa.

In London, the painter Robin Darwin, dean of the Royal College of Art and the former secretary of the Camouflage Committee, looked to his wartime colleagues for his teaching staff, starting with Hugh Casson.[111] In the United States, the career of Eliot Noyes took an important turn when he met Thomas J. Watson, the son of the founder of IBM, in the cockpit of a bomber based in England, which led to his being the consulting architect and design director for the firm.[112] For his part, Max Abramowitz saw his contacts with pilots bear fruit when he became the advisor to the US Air Force, which had become a separate arm of the American military and was planning a worldwide network of bases.[113] These generational ties, stemming from camaraderie in uniform or in the underground resistance, ran through the transnational systems that helped structure the world after 1945. Architects held prisoner had been exposed to other cultures, such as the British who were 'forced' to read

Casabella or the French who read the German works found in their camp library.[114]

The American cultural hegemony was unquestionably facilitated by the prestige of the technical objects that the GI's took with them around the world, from the walkie-talkie to the Jeep, but it also took on specific forms, such as the funding by the USIS (United States Information Service) of the *Manuale dell'architetto*, published by Mario Ridolfi, and the Paul Nelson exhibition held in Paris. Exhibitions were also organised for the Soviets in 1946, drawing lessons from the American industrial programmes, while the publications of Amtorg analysed the large factories built during the war, together with the housing complexes and house types that had been built since the New Deal.[115] Other migrations of forms and techniques were occurring at the same time, for example from Great Britain to France and Germany, where the architects were interested in organic plans for reconstruction and the processes of prefabrication. And symmetrically, when the Yalta agreements ratified the division of the world, the USSR established its cultural hegemony over its future satellites and sympathisers.

Barely a year after the end of the First World War, John Maynard Keynes published his celebrated work *The Economic Consequences of the Peace*.[116] It would take more time after the Second World War for its effects to be gauged with any detachment, and the accounts of the direct protagonists as well as the analysts would soon diverge considerably.[117] With the end of the Cold War and new access to the archives hidden in the vaults of the socialist bloc, along with the simple passage of time, historians today are better able to understand the upheavals that affected every sphere of society by what still remains the most murderous chapter in the history of human conflict.[118]

Architecture could not escape the convulsions that took place after 1945. Wartime unity, forged in common work or in the resistance, could not withstand the return to political conflict, although a certain shift to the left within the professions was apparent in Western Europe, or at least in Great Britain, France and Italy. Returning to civil life, in every sense of the word, architects lived in a wide range of times: a present marked by destruction and shortage, a sense of loss ceaselessly reinforced by the presence of ruins and the absence of those who had died, the promises of reconstruction and the exciting programmes that it sometimes entailed. And except for the short-lived Soviet 'camp', where the doctrine of socialist realism was abandoned in 1954, the alliance between modernist aesthetics and technical as well as social modernisation would become an enduring one everywhere. Instead of being a parenthesis, the Second World War, whose shadow reaches into the third millennium, crystallised and accelerated both history and architecture.

1. Robert L'Hermitte, 'Progrès scientifique et matériaux de construction', *Techniques et architecture*, vol. 5, no. 5–6 (November 1945), 115. L'Hermitte was at the time the director of the state laboratories for building and public works.
2. Richard Neutra, 'Housing, Defense and Postwar Planning', typewritten, undated, Dion and Richard Neutra Papers, UCLA [Box 176] [Folder 4], 1.
3. Wolfgang Malanowski, ed., *1945: Deutschland in der Stunde Null* (Reinbek bei Hamburg: Rowohlt, 1985).
4. Clara Magdalena Oberle, 'City in Transit: Ruins, Railways, and the Search for Order in Postwar Berlin (1945–1948)', Ph.D. thesis, Princeton University, 2006.
5. Hans Scharoun, lecture given on 5 September 1946, in Peter Pfankuch, *Hans Scharoun: Bauten, Entwürfe, Texte* (Berlin: Akademie der Künste, 1974), 158. See also Florian Urban, 'Recovering Essence through Demolition. The 'Organic' City in Postwar West Berlin', *Journal of the Society of Architectural Historians*, vol. 63, no. 3 (September 2004), 354–69.
6. Albert Speer, *Inside the Third Reich* (New York: Simon & Schuster, 1970), 56.
7. J. M. Richards, 'The Architecture of Destruction', *The Architectural Review*, vol. 94, no. 559 (1943), 23–36.
8. Nikolaus Pevsner, *Visual Planning and the Picturesque*, edited by Mathew Aitchison (Los Angeles: Getty Research Institute, 2010).
9. 'Save our Ruins', *The Architectural Review*, vol. 95, no. 565 (January 1944), 13. On the same topic, see Geoffrey A. Jellicoe, 'The Landcape Architect Speaks', ibid., 15–17.
10. Friedrich Tamms, 'Das Grosse in der Baukunst', *Die Baukunst*, supplement to *Die Kunst im Deutschen Reich*, vol. 8, no. 3 (March 1944), 50.
11. Le Corbusier, letter to Raoul Dautry, 21 December 1945, FLC H3(18)146. On Corbusier's misadventures in this town, see *Le Corbusier et Saint-Dié* (Saint-Dié: Musée municipal, 1987).
12. Dan Kiley, *North by Northeast*, vol. 3, no. 3 (July 1988), 6–9, 24, cited by Barry Katz, 'The Arts of War: "Visual Presentation" and National Intelligence', *Design Issues*, vol. 12, no. 2 (summer 1996), 19.
13. Dan Kiley and Jane Amidon, 'Philosophy, Inspiration, Process', in *Dan Kiley. The Complete Works of America's Master Landscape Architect* (Boston, New York and London: Bulfinch Press, 1999), 12 and 204.
14. 'Problems Related to the Selection or Construction of the War Crimes Courtroom', National Archives and Records Administration, Washington, OSS Record Group 226, entry 85, box 42, file 687, 1.
15. See the enlightening article by Beatriz Colomina, 'Enclosed by Images: The Eameses' Multimedia Architecture', *Grey Room*, vol. 2 (winter 2001), 39.
16. Donald Douglas, in United States Congress, Senate, *Truman Committee Hearings*, 1945, part 31, 15, 590, cited in Gerald D. Nash, *World War 2 and the West: Reshaping the Economy* (Lincoln: University of Nebraska Press, 1989), 88.
17. J. D. Bernal, 'Science in Architecture,' *RIBA Journal*, vol. 53, no. 5 (March 1946), 155 and 158.
18. Annalisa Viati Navone, '"Un nuovo linguaggio per il pensiero architettonico'. Ricerca operativa e architettura parametrica', in *Luigi Moretti. Razionalismo e trasgressività tra barocco e informale*, edited by Bruno Reichlin and Letizia Tedeschi (Milan: Electa, 2010), 409–19.
19. Inès Zalduendo, 'Jacqueline Tyrwhitt's Correspondence Courses: Town Planning in the Trenches', lecture at the annual convention of the Society of Architectural Historians, Vancouver, April 2005.
20. Jean-Louis Cohen and Hartmut Frank, 'Architettura dell'occupazione: Francia e Germania 1940–1950', *Casabella*, vol. 54, no. 567 (April 1990), 40–58.
21. Walter Gropius, 'Reconstruction: Germany', *Task*, no. 7–8 (1948), 35–36.
22. Michael Foedrowitz, *Bunkerwelten. Luftschutzanlagen in Norddeutschland* (Berlin: Ch. Links Verlag, 1998), 143–51.
23. Louis Skidmore, Nathaniel A. Owings and John O. Merrill, 'Flexible Space', *The Architectural Forum*, vol. 77, no. 3 (September 1942), 100–01.
24. William Wurster, 'The New House 194X: Flexible Space', *The Architectural Forum*, vol. 77, no. 3 (September 1942), 140.
25. 'Converted War Housing, San Francisco', *The Architectural Forum*, vol. 79, no. 4 (October 1943), 69–75.
26. See the montage in the collections of The Art Institute of Chicago, RX 23664/161.1.
27. 'Hutments to Houses', *The Architectural Forum*, vol. 80, no. 2 (February 1944), 91–94.
28. 'Sportsman's Dream Made with Real Steel', advertisement for Stran-Steel, *The Architectural Record*, vol. 96, no. 4 (October 1944), 39.
29. 'Emergency Housing: Existing Military Installations Could Provide Stop-Gap Shelter for Britain's Bombed-out Citizenry,' *The Architectural Forum*, vol. 84, no. 2 (February 1946), 110–12.
30. Louis-Georges Noviant, 'L'Habitation américaine', *L'Architecture française*, vol. 6, no. 48 (July 1945), 19.
31. 'Navy's Architecture', *The Architectural Forum*, vol. 83, no. 6 (December 1945), 73–79. Jeffrey Cook, *The Architecture of Bruce Goff* (London: Granada, 1978), 24–29.
32. Erich Mendelsohn, 'My Approach to Building a Modern Synagogue', *The Architectural Forum*, vol. 98 (April 1953), 108. David G. De Long, *Bruce Goff. Toward Absolute Architecture* (Cambridge, Mass.: MIT Press; New York: The Architectural History Foundation, 1988), 73.
33. 'The Round House', *Life*, vol. 30 (19 March 1951), 70–75; 'Umbrella House', *The Architectural Forum*, vol. 94, no. 4 (April 1951), 118–21; De Long, op. cit. note 32, 95–96.
34. Dana Cuff, *The Provisional City. Los Angeles Stories of Architecture and Urbanism* (Cambridge, Mass.: MIT Press, 2000), 172–207.
35. 'Converted Quonset', *California Arts & Architecture*, vol. 63, no. 11 (December 1946), 35.
36. Martin Pawley, *Buckminster Fuller* (London: Trefoil, 1990), 95–114.
37. Claude Lichtenstein, '"Spirit House" and "Steppenwolf" Avant-Garde. American Origins in the Dymaxion House Concept', in *New Views on R. Buckminster Fuller*, edited by Hsiao-Yun Chu and Roberto G. Trujillo (Stanford: Stanford University Press, 2009), 76–85.
38. R. Buckminster Fuller, *Designing a New Industry. A Composite of a Series of Talks by R. Buckminster Fuller, 1945–1946* (Wichita: Fuller Research Institute, 1948), quoted in Joachim Krausse and Claude Liechtenstein, *Your Private Sky: R. Buckminster Fuller, the Art of Design Science* (Baden: Lars Müller, 1999), 238.
39. R. Buckminster Fuller, 'Can't Fool Cosmic Computers', in *Grunch of Giants* (New York: St. Martin's Press, 1983), 86.

40. Harry H. Steidle, 'A Statement from the Prefabricated Home Manufacturers Association', *California Arts and Architecture*, vol. 61, no. 7 (July 1944), 41.

41. *California Arts and Architecture*, vol. 61, no. 7 (July 1944), unpaginated.

42. 'House in "Industry"', *Arts and Architecture*, vol. 64 (November 1947), 28ff. 'The Industrialized House', *The Architectural Forum*, vol. 86, no. 2 (February 1947), 115–20.

43. Wachsmann would publish illustrations of the General Panel system and the production line in Burbank in his large-format post-war book *Wendepunkt im Bauen* (Wiesbaden: Krausskopf-Verlag, 1959), 135–59. In a letter of 22 January 1950, he asked Le Corbusier for support. FLC R3(7)6, partially reproduced in Le Corbusier, *Le Modulor 2. La parole est aux usagers* (Boulogne-Billancourt: Éditions de l'Architecture d'aujourd'hui, 1955), 170.

44. For these projects, see *Home Delivery. Fabricating the Modern Dwelling*, edited by Barry Bergdoll and Peter Christensen (New York, Basel, Boston and Berlin: The Museum of Modern Art, Birkhäuser, 2008).

45. Walter Gropius, *Apollon in the Democracy: the Cultural Obligation of the Architect*, p. 97, as quoted by Gilbert Herbert, *The Dream of the Factory-Made House: Walter Gropius and Konrad Wachsmann* (Cambridge, Mass.: MIT Press, 1984), 318.

46. 'Mr. Churchill's Prefab', *The Architectural Forum*, vol. 80, no. 6 (June 1944), 90–95.

47. R. B. White, 'Post-War Non Traditional Houses?, in *Prefabrication. A History of its Development in Great Britain* (London: Her Majesty's Stationery Office, 1965), 122–65.

48. Brenda Vale, *Prefabs: A History of the U.K. Temporary Housing Programme* (London: Spon, 1995). Greg Stevenson, *Palaces for the People: Prefabs in Post-war Britain* (London: Batsford, 2003).

49. Max Bill provided an account of these processes: Max Bill, *Wiederaufbau. Dokumente über Zerstörungen, Planungen, Konstruktionen* (Erlenbach-Zurich: Verlag fur Architektur AG, 1945), 93–123.

50. For example, see 'Production of Prefabricated Aluminium Houses', *RIBA Journal*, vol. 53, no. 9 (July 1946), 402–05.

51. Andrew Saint, *Towards a Social Architecture: the Role of School Building in Post-War England* (New Haven: Yale University Press, 1987).

52. Peter Sulzer, *Jean Prouvé: Complete Works, vol. 2, 1934–1944* (Basel, Boston and Berlin: Birkhäuser), 238–39.

53. 'Préfabrication, industrialisation', *L'Architecture d'aujourd'hui*, vol. 16, no. 4 (November–December 1945).

54. Marcel Lods, 'Industrialisation et préfabrication; expériences américaines', *Techniques et architecture*, vol. 5, no. 5–6 (November 1945), 129.

55. 'The Design of Factories Today', *The Architectural Record*, vol. 98, no. 5 (November 1945), 136.

56. 'Building in One Package', *The Architectural Forum*, vol. 82, no. 1 (January 1945), 93.

57. Howard C. Crane, 'Planning of Industrial Buildings', in *The Architect's Year Book*, edited by Jane Drew (London: Paul Elek, 1945), 55–63.

58. 'Literally Mountains of Material Have Been Created by Industry Under the Pressures of War Conditions', *California Arts and Architecture*, vol. 61, no. 7 (July 1944), unpaginated.

59. B. K. Hardy and C. G. Watson, 'Aluminium Alloys and their Structural Use', *Structural Engineer*, vol. 24, no. 3 (March 1946), 65–112.

60. 'Materials for 194X', *The Architectural Forum*, vol. 80, no. 3 (March 1944), 12–14.

61. John Gloag, *Plastics and Industrial Design* (London: Allen & Unwin, 1945).

62. 'Test-Tube Marvels of Wartime Promise a New Era in Plastics', *Newsweek*, vol. 17 (May 1943), 42, quoted by Annmarie Brennan, 'Forecast', in *Cold War Hothouses. Inventing Postwar Culture, from Cockpit to Playboy*, edited by Beatriz Colomina, Annmarie Brennan and Jeannie Kim (New York: Princeton Architectural Press, 2004), 97.

63. For the radio set, see Robert Elwall, *Ernö Goldfinger* (London: Academy Editions, 1996), 60.

64. Edgar Kaufmann Jr., 'The Department of Industrial Design', *The Bulletin of the Museum of Modern Art*, vol. 14, no. 1 (1946), 6.

65. 'A Review of New Lamps', *The Architectural Forum*, vol. 81, no. 2 (July 1944), 12.

66. 'Home-Freezing', *The Architectural Forum*, vol. 80, no. 4 (April 1944), 12–14.

67. U.S. Department of Commerce, *Materials Survey*, II 3, quoted by Annmarie Brennan, 'Forecast', in Colomina, Brennan and Kim, op. cit. note 62, 65.

68. Marème Dione and André Guillerme, *Techniques et politiques économiques, les travaux publics en Afrique du Nord 1953–1962*, research report, Paris, Laboratoire Théorie des mutations urbaines, Plan urbain, 1986.

69. Alison and Peter Smithson, *The Charged Void - Architecture* (New York: The Monacelli Press, 2000), 55.

70. Alec Edward Davis, 'New Shapes on Wartime Roads', *The Architectural Review*, vol. 94, no. 560 (1943), 52.

71. 'Beauty Had to be Thrust Upon Us', *California Arts and Architecture*, vol. 60, no. 1 (January 1943), 29.

72. Douglas Haskell, 'What Does Military Design Offer to the Planning of Peace?', *The Architectural Record*, vol. 85, no. 1 (January 1939), 50–56, and no. 3 (March 1939), 68–75.

73. Council of Industrial Design, 'Proposed Summer Exhibition 1946; Draft Plan 2', typescript, n.d. [1945], V & A, AAD 4/12-1977.

74. Notes for the info . . . typescript, AAD 4/12-1977. Ibid.

75. 'Group YY. War to Peace', in *War to Peace*, catalogue supplement (London: Victoria and Albert Museum, 1946), 217–18.

76. *The Daily Telegraph*, 24 September 1946, 3.

77. 'Spitfires to Saucepans', in *Britain Can Make It*, supplement to the *Board of Trade Journal*, 28 September 1946, 4.

78. Noel Carrington, 'A Plea for Standardized Equipment', *The Architectural Review*, vol. 93, no. 553 (February 1943), 82.

79. 'What's an Airplane Exhaust Got To Do with Roof Drainage?', *The Architectural Forum*, vol. 79, no. 2 (July 1943), 33.

80. Council of Industrial Design, 'Proposed Summer Exhibition 1946, Suggested Theme', typescript, 17 August 1945, AAD 4/12-1977.

81. 'Britons Can't Buy It', *The Evening Standard*, 28 September 1946.

82. Becky E. Conekin, *'The Autobiography of a Nation': the 1951 Festival of Britain*, (Manchester and New York: Manchester University Press, 2003).

83. Nazionalsozialistischer Bund Deutscher Technik / Fachgruppe Bauwesen / Arbeitskreis Baugestaltung, *Soldatengräber und Gedenkstätten* (Munich: Kastner & Callwey, 1944).
84. Ekkehard Mai, 'Von 1930 bis 1945: Ehrenmäler und Totenburgen', in *Wilhelm Kreis. Architekt zwischen Kaiserreich und Demokratie*, edited by Ekkehard Mai and Winfried Nerdinger (Munich and Berlin: Klinkhardt & Biermann, 1994), 157–67. Wilhelm Kreis, *Soldatengräber und Gedenkstätten*, a publication of the Nazionalsozialistischer Bund Deutscher Technik / Fachgruppe Bauwesen / Arbeitskreis Baugestaltung (Munich: Kastner & Callwey, 1944).
85. George L. Mosse, *Fallen Soldiers: Reshaping the Memory of the World Wars* (New York and Oxford: Oxford University Press, 1990), 86.
86. Friedrich Tamms, 'Die Kriegerehrenmäler von Wilhelm Kreis', *Die Kunst im Deutschen Reich*, vol. 7, no. 3 (March 1943), 50ff.
87. Speer, op. cit. note 6, 56. See also Éric Michaud, *Un art de l'éternité. L'image et le temps du national-socialisme* (Paris: Gallimard, 1996).
88. Tatiana Malinina, ed., *Iz istorii sovetskoi arkhitektury 1941–1945 gg.: Dokumenty i materialy: Khronika voennykh let: Arkhitekturnaia pechat* (Moscow: Nauka, 1978), 66–68.
89. Olga I. Rzhekhina, R. N. Blachkevich and R. G. Burova, *A. K. Burov* (Moscow: Stroiizdat, 1984).
90. The projects were published in *Kenchiku zasshi*, vol. 56, no. 693 (December 1942). See Jonathan M. Reynolds, *Maekawa Kunio and the Emergence of Japanese Modernist Architecture* (Berkeley: University of California Press, 2001), 126–28 and Benoît Jacquet, *Les principes de monumentalité dans l'architecture moderne. Analyse du discours architectural dans les premières œuvres de Tange Kenzô (1936–1962)*, doctoral thesis, Université de Paris 8, 2007.
91. Kunio Maekawa, 'Shichi umi no shuto' (The capital of the Seven Seas), *Kenchiku zasshi*, op. cit. note 90, 976. See Jacquet, op. cit. note 90, 394–95.
92. José Luis Sert, Fernand Léger and Sigfried Giedion, 'Nine Points

on Monumentality', *Architecture, You and Me: The Diary of a Development* (Cambridge, Mass.: Harvard University Press, 1958), 48–52.
93. Robert F. Gatje, *Marcel Breuer: a Memoir* (New York: Monacelli Press, 2000), 27.
94. Ulrike Jehle-Shulte Strathaus and Bruno Reichlin, 'Parole di pietra – architettura di parole', in *BBPR Monumento ai caduti nei campi nazisti 1945–1995; Il segno della memoria* edited by Marco Pogacnik (Milan: Electa/Triennale di Milano, 1995), 11–53.
95. Alessandro Portelli, *L'ordine è già stato eseguito: Roma, le Fosse Ardeatine, la memoria*, (Rome: Donzelli, 2005).
96. Manfredo Tafuri, *History of Italian Architecture, 1944–1985*, translated by Jessica Levine (Cambridge, Mass.: MIT Press, 1989), 4–5.
97. André Bruyère, *Pourquoi des architectes?* (Paris: Jean-Jacques Pauvert, 1968), 190–93, 230–33, 236–37.
98. Niels Gutschow, *Ordnungswahn: Architekten planen im 'eingedeutschten Osten' 1939–1945* (Gütersloh: Bertelsmann; Basel, Boston and Berlin: Birkhäuser, 2001), 198–99.
99. Mai, op. cit. note 84, 157–58. Here Mai cites the memoirs of Wilhelm Kreis.
100. Danièle Voldmann, 'L'épuration des architectes', *Matériaux pour l'histoire de notre temps*, vol. 39, no. 39–40 (1995), 26–27.
101. Dominique Barjot, 'French Industry during the German Occupation, 1940–44: the Case of the Public Works Industry', in *World War II and the Transformation of Business Systems: the International Conference on Business History 20: Proceedings of the Fuji Conference*, edited by Jun Sakudo and Takao Shiba (Tokyo: University of Tokyo Press, 1994), 211–36.
102. Udo Kultermann, *Wassili und Hans Luckhardt. Bauten und Entwürfe* (Tübingen: Wasmuth, 1958), 74–77.
103. Herbert Rimpl, *Die geistigen Grundlagen der Baukunst unserer Zeit* (Munich: Verlag Georg D. W. Callwey, 1953), 96.
104. 'The Architect in Large-Scale Operations', *The Architectural Record*, vol. 84, no. 3 (March 1941), 89.
105. Henry-Russell Hitchcock, 'The Architecture of Bureaucracy and the Architecture of Genius',

The Architectural Review, vol. 101, no. 501 (January 1947), 3–6.
106. 'The Architect's Dilemma', *The Economist*, 25 July 1953, in Jeremy Melvin, *FRS Yorke and the Evolution of English Modernism* (Chichester and Hoboken, NJ: Wiley-Academy, 2003), 109.
107. My thanks to Roberta Grignolo for this suggestion.
108. Hugh Casson, 'The Aesthetics of Camouflage', *The Architectural Review*, vol. 96, no. 5723 (September 1944), 68.
109. David Medd, 'Stirrat Johnson-Marshall, a Personal Tribute', *Performancer*, April–May 1982, 67–70; cited by Saint, p. 21.
110. Werner Durth, *Deutsche Architekten: biographische Verflechtungen, 1900–1970*, (Brunswick: F. Vieweg & Sohn, 1988), 247–77.
111. Henrietta Gooden, *Camouflage and Art: Design for Deception in World War 2* (London: Unicorn Press, 2007), 8.
112. Gatje, op. cit. note 93, 29.
113. John Harwood and Janet Parks, *The Troubled Search: the Work of Max Abramowitz* (New York: Miriam and Ira D. Wallach Art Gallery, Columbia University, 2004).
114. Thus I found the copy that Guy Pison, a prisoner in East Prussia, had held on to of Walter Kratz's *Das Buch vom eigenen Haus* (Berlin: Bauwelt-Verlag, 1937).
115. I. I. Kostin, A. N. Popov and N. P. Remizov, 'Proektirovanie promyshlennykh predpriatii v SShA'. V. I. Bogomolov, 'Planirovka i zastroika zhilyh raionov', in *Amerikanskoe stroitelstvo*, edited by A. N. Popov (New York: Amtorg Trading Co., 1946), 11–45 and 127–75.
116. John Maynard Keynes, *The Economic Consequences of the Peace* (London: Macmillan, 1919).
117. For the German case, see for example *Verletztes Gedächtnis: Erinnerungskultur und Zeitgeschichte im Konflikt*, edited by Konrad H. Jarausch and Martin Sabrow (Frankfurt-am-Main: Campus, 2002).
118. Tony Judt, *Postwar: a History of Europe Since 1945* (London and New York: Penguin Books, 2005). Krzysztof Pomian, Élie Barnavi, *La Révolution européenne. 1945–2007* (Paris: Perrin, 2008). John Lukacs, *The Legacy of the Second World War* (New Haven and London: Yale University Press, 2010).

Index of people and institutions

Edward Davis, Alec 422

Eggerstedt, Heinrich 297

Eiermann, Egon 102, 130, 342, 385, 403

Einstein, Albert 263, 300

Eisenhower, General Dwight D. 223

Ellington, K. D. 130

Elman, Kimberly J. 214, 381

Elstub, J. H. 130

Elwall, Robert 178, 422

Ensor, Arthur *272*

Entenza, John 398, 407

Erichsen, Johannes 313

Erker, Paul 131

Ertl, Fritz 291, 293, *308*, 417

Esquillan, Nicolas 231, 242

Evans, John 228

Experimental Bridging Establishment (UK) 271

Fabbri, Paolo 187, 214

Facetti, Germano 31, *33*

Faulkner, Barry 189

Feder, Gottfried 102, 128, 130

Federal Housing Administration (US) 125

Federal Public Housing Authority (US) 111, 284

Fehl, Gerhardt *159*, 313

Fenzy, Fernand 32

Ferguson, Niall 12, 19

Fermi, Enrico 300

Ferriss, Hugh *104*, 228, *229*

Fick, Roderich *175*, *230*

Field, Hermann H. 131

Fieser, Louis F. 232, 242

Findeli, Alain 214, 215, 344

Finley, David E. 240, 243

Fiorentino, Mario 416, *416*

Fischer, Theodor 99

Fischer, Wilhelm 380

Fisher, David 215

Fletcher, Reginald T. H. 177

Flewelling, Ralph C. 113

Flinchum, Russell 344

Flouquet, Pierre-Louis 47

Focke-Wulff Flugzeugbau A.G. 100

Foedrowitz, Michael 179, 242, 421

Fontanon, Claudine 78

Föppl, August 261, 278

Forain, Jean-Louis 189

Forbes, Peter 214

Ford J. Twaits Co. 232, 236

Ford, John 322

Ford, Ruth 393, *393*

Foreman, Clark 122, 131

Forshaw, John Henry 371, *371*, 381

Förster, Stig 19

Forty, Adrian 354, 379

Foss, Brian 130

Foster Jr., Richard H. 131

Foulkes, Robert Arthur 279

Fox, Celina 78

Francis, Paul 278

Frank, Hans 362

Frank, Hartmut 8, 46, 313, 380, 421

Frankl, Paul 241

Frederick, Christine 70

Freiwald, Kurt 418

Freyssinet, Eugène 225

Friedel, Robert 78

Friedman, Samuel L. 177

Friedrich, Jörg 42, 47

Friedrich, Karl 149, 177

Fritzsche, Peter 177

Frunze, Mikhail 223

Fry, Maxwell 18, 19, 371, 381

Fry, Sherry H. 189

Fuller, R. Buckminster 254, 255, *255*, 257, *257*, 258, 259, *259*, 278, 322, 396, *396*, 397, *397*, 398, 421

Funck, Marcus 47, 177, 215, 380

Gadda, Carlo Emilio 62, 78

Garbisch, Edgar W. 283

Garcia Espuche, Albert *39*

Garde, Anne *247*, *275*

Gardner, James 203, 408

Gardner, Paul V. *73*

Garnier, Tony 371

Garratt, Geoffrey T. 177

GATCPAC (Grup d'Arquitectes i Tècnics Catalans per al Progrés de l'Arquitectura Contemporània) 24

Gatje, Robert F. 423

Gauthier, Maurice 129

Geddes, Norman Bel 152, *152*, 193, *194*, 214, 251, *252*, 278, 322, *326*, 327, *327*, 328, *329*, 340, 344, *347*, *349*, *351*

Geiler, H. F. 27, 46

General Electric Corporation 97, 99

General Panel Corporation 266

Génie civil (Le) (periodical) 143

Gérard, Philip 215

Germer, Edmund 99

Gervereau, Laurent 312

Gibb, Sir Alexander 85, 108

Gibberd, Frederick 335, 405

Gibrin, Commandant Charles 153, *153*, 154, 156, 158, 177, 178

Gibson, Donald 371

Giedion, Sigfried 241, 379, 416, 423

Giesler, Alfred 214

Giesler, Hermann 8, 18, 224, 242

Gilbert, Cass 281, 282, 312

Giovannoni, Gustavo 160, 178

Giral, Angela 214, 381

Giraudoux, Jean 25

Glasson, L. M. 190, 203

Gloag, John 422

Glover, Charles 162, *163*, *164*, *172*

Goff, Bruce 30, 46, 392, 393, *393*, *394*, 421

Gofman, V. D. 129

Goldberg, Alfred 312

Goldberg, Bertrand 267, *269*, 278, 279, 322, 391, *392*

Goldfinger, Ernö 158, 159, 173, 178, 179, 191, 267, *270*, 332, 335, 344, *403*, 405, 422

Goldsmith, Myron *11*, *259*, *260*, 273, *288*, 289, 312

Gollancz, Victor 178

Gollert, Friedrich 362

Golosov, Ilya *414*, 415

Goltz, Georgui *377*

Gonser, Karl 226

Gooden, Henrietta 214, 215, 423

Goodman, Paul 214, 372, 373, 381

Goodman, Percival 194, 214, 372, 373, 381

Göring, Hermann 42, 99, 127, *127*, 131

Gorio, Federico 369

Gorky, Arshile 195

Graf, Franz 129

Graffer, Giorgio 228, *228*

Granell, Enrique 46

Grasser, Kurt 242

Gray, Milner 334, 410

Grayling, A. C. 243

Graziosi, Andrea 12, 19

Great Lakes Steel Corporation 391

Greer, Guy 374, 381

Gregg, John 179

Grelon, André 78

Gremiachinskaia, Yulia P. 210

Gresleri, Giuliano 46

Gris, Juan 204

Groag, Jacques 75

Gröning, Gert 380

Gropius, Walter *16*, 100, 114, *116*, *117*, 130, 147, 148, *148*, 177, 261, 264, *265*, 266, 267, 278, 323, 354, 379, 390, 398, 399, 421, 422

Gropman, Alan 129, 312

Groß, Hubert 361

Grossman, Vasily 43, 47

Groves, Colonel Leslie R. 284, 301, 312

Gruenbaum, Victor 375

Grüning, Michael 278

Guderian, General Heinz 222

Guérard, Albert 144, 177

Guidi, Ignazio 24

Guidoni, Elsa 398

Guilhermy, G., de 177

Guilissen-Hoa, Simone 31, 47

Guillerme, André 422

Guirand de Scévola, Lucien-Victor 189

Gutheim, Frederick 401

Gutschow, Konstanty 176, 240

Gutschow, Niels 19, 47, *227*, 242, 243, 290, 312, *360*, *368*, 380, 381, 423

Haacke, Heinz 353

Hage, Koos 47

Hailey, Lord Malcolm 164

Haird, D. N. 130

Haldane, J. B. S. (John Burdon Sanderson) 163, 168, 171, 178, 179

Halévy, Élie 13, 19

Hamlin, Talbot Faulkner 47, 307, 313

Hansen, Alvin Harvey 374, 381

Harbers, Guido 242, 380

Harding, Valentine 30

Hardy, B. K. 422

Harlander, Tilman *159*, 313

Harpur, Brian 279

Harris, Air Marshall Arthur H. 176, 240

Bibliography

Works published before the end of 1945

Abercrombie, Patrick, and John H. Forshaw. *County of London Plan*. London: Macmillan, 1943.

Alabian, Karo S., ed. *Stroitelstvo voennogo vremeni*. Moscow: Soyuz sovetskih arkhitektorov, 1941.

Alabian, Karo S. , F. F. Kizelov and Iu. Savitskii. *Spravochnik maskirovshchika*. Moscow: Gosudarstvennoe arkhitekturnoe izdatelstvo Akademii arkhitektury SSSR, 1944.

Tecton Architects. *Planned A. R. P*. London: The Architectural Press, 1939.

Arup, Ove. *Design, cost, construction, and relative safety of trench, surface, bomb-proof and other air-raid shelters*. London: Concrete Publications Ltd, 1939.

Arup, Ove. *London Shelter Problem*. London: D. Gestetner Ltd, 1939.

Bahrmann, Henri. *L'Urbanisme et la défense du pays*. Paris: Institut d'urbanisme de l'Université de Paris, 1935.

Bill, Max. *Wiederaufbau; Dokumente über Zerstörungen, Planungen, Konstruktionen*. Erlenbach-Zurich: Verlag für Architektur AG, 1945.

Bobrov, Klavdii V. *Maskirovka, posoby dlia voenno-inzhenernykh uchilish krasnoi armii*. Moscow: Voennoe Izdatel'stvo, 1940.

Breckenridge, Major Robert P. *Modern Camouflage, The New Science of Protective Concealment*. New York: Farrar & Rinehart, Inc., 1942.

Calvo, Edmond-François, Victor Dancette and Jacques Zimmermann. *La Bête est morte! - La Guerre mondiale chez les animaux*. Paris: Gallimard, 1945.

Cambridge Scientists Anti-War Group. *The Protection of the Public from Aerial Attack*. London: Victor Gollancz, 1937.

Chesney, Lieut.-Colonel C. H. R., and J. Huddlestone. *The Art of Camouflage*. London: R. Hale Ltd, 1941.

Christaller, Walter. *Die zentralen Orte in den Ostgebieten und ihre Kultur- und Marktbereiche*. Leipzig: Koehler, 1941.

Darvillé, Jacques, and Simon Wichené. *Drancy la Juive ou la 2e inquisition*. Paris: A. Bréger, 1945.

Douhet, General Giulio. *The Command of the Air*. Edited by J. P. Harahan and R. H. Kohn. Translated by Dino Ferrari. New York: Coward-McCann, 1942.

Feder, Gottfried. *Die neue Stadt : Versuch der Begründung einer neuen Stadtplanungskunst aus der sozialen Struktur der Bevölkerung*. Berlin: Springer, 1939.

Fry, Maxwell. *Fine Building*. London: Faber & Faber, 1944.

Gibrin, Commandant, and Louis C. Heckly. *Défense passive organisée. Personnel et matériel*. Paris: Dunod, 1936.

Gloag, John. *Plastics and Industrial Design*. London: Allen & Unwin, 1945.

Glover, Charles. *Civil Defence*. London: Chapman & Hall, 1938. 2nd edition 1940, 3rd edition 1941.

Haldane, John Burdon Sanderson. *Air Raid Precautions*. London: Victor Gollancz, 1938.

Harrison, Tom, and Charles Madge, eds. *War Begins at Home*. London: Chatto & Windus, 1940.

Hilberseimer, Ludwig. *The New City. Principles of Planning*. Introduction by Ludwig Mies van der Rohe. Chicago: Paul Theobald, 1944.

Koppe, Richard, and Myron Kozman. *Protective Concealment Discipline*. Chicago: n.p., 1943.

Kreis, Wilhelm. *Soldatengräber und Gedenkstätten,* Munich: Kastner & Callwey, 1944.

Kühn, Karl F. *Fliegerschutz für Kunst- und Kulturdenkmale. Ein technischer Wegweiser*. Brno, Vienna and Leipzig: Rudolf M. Rohrer Verlag, 1938.

Le Corbusier. *La ville radieuse*. Boulogne-sur-Seine: Éditions de L'Architecture d'aujourd'hui, 1935.

Le Corbusier. *Aircraft*. London: The Studio, 1935.

Le Corbusier. *Des Canons ? Des munitions ? Merci... Des logis S.V.P.* Boulogne-Billancourt: Éditions de l'Architecture d'aujourd'hui, 1938.

Le Corbusier. *Les Constructions 'Murondins'*. Paris and Clermont-Ferrand: Etienne Chiron, 1942.

Lescaze, William. *On Being an Architect*. New York: G. P. Putnam's Sons, 1942.

Löfken, Alexander. *Baulicher Luftschutz zur Sicherung von Stadt und Land, Wirtschaft und Industrie gegen Luftangriffe*. Berlin: Schriftenreihe Baulicher Luftschutz, vol. 2, 1937.

Lougee, E. F. *Plastics from Farm and Forests*. New York: Plastics Institute, 1943.

Mäckler, Hermann. *Ein deutsches Flugzeugwerk: die Heinkel-Werke Oranienburg*. Berlin: Wiking-Verlag, 1939.

Meissner, Carl. *Wilhelm Kreis*. Essen: G. D. Baedeker, 1925.

Mendelsohn, Erich. *Three Lectures on Architecture Today*. Berkeley and Los Angeles: University of California Press, 1944.

Mock, Elizabeth. *Built in USA, 1932–1944*. New York: Museum of Modern Art, 1944.

Mumford, Lewis. *Technics and Civilization*. New York: Harcourt, Brace & World, 1934.

Neufert, Ernst. *Bauentwurfslehre*. Berlin: Bauwelt-Verlag, 1936.

Neufert, Ernst. *Bauordnungslehre*. Berlin: Volk und Reich Verlag, 1943.

Paetsch, Heinrich, and Ernst Baum. *Luftschutz*. Leipzig: Reclam, 1938.

Penrose, Roland. *Home Guard Manual of Camouflage*. London: George Routledge & Sons Ltd, 1941.

Prentiss, Augustin M. *Civil Air Defense*. New York: McGraw-Hill, 1941.

Samuely, Felix J. *Civil Protection: the Application of the Civil Defence Act and Other Government Requirements for Air Raid Shelters*. London: The Architectural Press, 1939.

Schoszberger, Hans. *Bautechnischer Luftschutz*. Berlin: Bauwelt-Verlag, 1934.

Sert, José Luis. *Can Our Cities Survive?* Cambridge, Mass.: Harvard University Press, 1942.

Solomon, Joseph. *Strategic Camouflage*. London: J. Murray, 1920.

Spaight, James Molony. *Air Power and the Cities*. London and New York: Longmans, Green, 1930.

Stellingwerff, Giuseppe. *La protezione dei fabbricati agli attachi aerei. L'applicazione del cemento armato nella protezione antiaerea*. Milan: Reggia Scuola d'Ingegneria, 1933.

Stellingwerff, Giuseppe. *La protezione antiaerea nel quadro del piano regolatore di Roma imperiale*. Rome: Istituto Nazionale di Studi Romani, 1939.

Tan, Pei-ying. *The Building of the Burma Road*. New York and London: Whittlesey House, McGraw-Hill, 1945.

Taylor, John P. *The Prefabricated Port of Arromanches*. London: Shipbuilding and Shipping Record, 1945.

Vauthier, Lieutenant-Colonel. *Le Danger aérien et l'avenir du pays*. Nancy, Paris and Strasbourg: éditions Berger-Levrault, 1930.

Vauthier, Lieutenant-Colonel. *La Doctrine de guerre du général Douhet*. Paris: Berger-Levrault, 1935.

Vollbehr, Ernst. *Mit der OT beim Westwall und Vormarsch*. Berlin: Elsner, 1941.

Wittmann, Konrad F. *Industrial Camouflage Manual, Prepared for the Industrial camouflage program at Pratt Institute, Brooklyn, New York*. New York: Reynold Publishing Co., 1942.

Works published since 1946

Addison, Paul, and Jeremy A. Crang, eds. *Firestorm. The Bombing of Dresden, 1945*. London: Pimlico, 2006.

Agamben, Giorgio. *État d'exception, Homo sacer*. Paris: Seuil, 2003.

Albrecht, Donald, ed. *World War II and the American Dream ; How Wartime Building Changed a Nation*. Washington, D.C., and Cambridge, Mass.: National Building Museum, MIT Press, 1995.

Allais, Lucia. *Will to War, Will to Art : Cultural Internationalism and the Modernist Aesthetics of Monuments, 1932–1964*. Ph.D. thesis, MIT, 2008.

Allan, John. *Berthold Lubetkin, Architecture and the Tradition of Progress*. London: RIBA Publications, 1992.

Aly, Götz, and Susanne Heim. *Vordenker der Vernichtung. Auschwitz und die deutsche Pläne für eine europäische Ordnung*. Hamburg: Hoffmann und Campe, 1990.

Attfield, Judy, ed. *Utility Reassessed: the Role of Ethics in the Practice of Design*. Manchester: Manchester University Press, 1999.

Baker, Lord John. *Enterprise versus Bureaucracy: The Development of Structural Air-Raid Precautions during the Second World War*. Oxford: Pergamon, 1978.

Bakhareva, Iu. Iu., T.V. Kovaleva and T.G. Shishkina. *Arkhitektory blokadnogo Leningrada*. Saint-Petersburg: Gosudarstvennyi Muzei Istorii Sankt-Peterburga, 2005.

Belgiojoso Barbiano di, Lodovico. *Notte, nebbia -Racconto di Gusen*. Milan: Guanda, 1996.

Behrens, Roy R. *Camoupedia: A Compendium of Research on Art, Architecture and Camouflage*. Dysart, Iowa: Bobolink Books, 2009.

Benton, Charlotte, ed. *A Different World: Emigré Architecture in Britain 1928–1938*. London: RIBA Publications, 1995.

Bergdoll, Barry, and Peter Christensen, eds. *Home Delivery. Fabricating the Modern Dwelling*. New York, Basel, Boston and Berlin: The Museum of Modern Art, Birkhäuser, 2008.

Beseler, Hartwig, Niels Gutschow and Frauke Kretschmer. *Kriegsschicksale deutscher Architektur: Verluste, Schäden, Wiederaufbau: eine Dokumentation für das Gebiet der Bundesrepublik Deutschland*. Neumünster: K. Wachholtz, 1988.

Bialer, Uri. *The Shadow of the Bomber: The Fear of Air Attack and British Politics, 1932–1939*. London: Royal Historical Society, 1980.

Bierut, Boleslaw. *The Six-Year Plan for the Reconstruction of Warsaw*. Warsaw: Ksiażka i Wiedza, 1951.

Black, Misha. *Exhibition Design*. London: The Architectural Press, 1950.

Bonifazio, Patrizia, and Sergio Pace, eds. *Tra guerra e pace, società, cultura e architettura nel secondo dopoguerra*. Milan: Franco Angeli, 1998.

Bode, Volkhard, and Gerhard Kaiser. *Raketenspuren. Peenemünde 1936–1994: eine historische Reportage*. Berlin: Ch. Links Verlag, 1995.

Bosma, Koos. *Schuilstad, Bescherming van de bevolking tegen luchtaanvallen*. Amsterdam: SUN, 2006.

Brinkley, David. *Washington Goes to War*. New York: Alfred A. Knopf, 1998.

Brown, Mike, and Carol Harris. *The Wartime House: Home Life in Wartime Britain 1939–1945*. Thrupp, Stroud, Gloucestershire: Sutton Publishing Ltd, 2001.

Brownlee, David B., and David G. De Long. *Louis I. Kahn: in the Realm of Architecture*. Los Angeles, New York: Museum of Contemporary Art, Rizzoli, 1991.

Brüggemeier, Franz-Josef, Mark Cioc and Thomas Zeller, eds. *How Green Were the Nazis?: Nature, Environment, and Nation in the Third Reich*. Athens, Ohio: Ohio University Press, 2005.

Bucci, Federico, *Albert Kahn: Architect of Ford*, New York, Princeton Architectural Press, 1993.

Bullock, Nicholas. *Building the Post-War World: Modern architecture and reconstruction in Britain*. London and New York: Routledge, 2002.

Cabanes, Bruno, and Edouard Husson, eds. *Les Sociétés en guerre 1911–1946*. Paris: Armand Colin, 2003.

Cairncross, Alec. *Planning in Wartime: Aircraft Production in Britain, Germany, and the USA*. New York: St. Martin's Press, 1991.

Calder, Angus. *The Myth of the Blitz*. London: Jonathan Cape, 1991.

Campbell, Duncan. *War Plan UK: the Truth about Civil Defence in Britain*. London: Burnett Books, 1982.

Carr, Lowell J., and James E. Stermer. *Willow Run: a Study of Industrialization and Cultural Inadequacy*. New York: Harper and Brothers, 1952.

Chalou, George C., ed. *The Secrets War: the Office of Strategic Services in World War*. Washington, D.C.: National Archives and Records Administration, 1992.

Chassaigne, Philippe, and Jean-Marc Largeaud, eds. *Villes en guerre*. Paris: Armand Colin, 2004.

Cherry, Gordon E., and Leith Penny. *Holford. A Study in Architecture, Planning and Civic Design*. London and New York: Mansell, 1986.

Chickering, Roger, and Stig Förster, eds. *Great War, Total War. Combat and Mobilization on the Western Front, 1914–1918*. Cambridge and New York: Cambridge University Press, 2000.

Ciucci, Giorgo, and Giorgio Muratore, eds. *Storia dell'architettura italiana. Il primo Novecento*. Milan: Electa, 2004.

Coates, Kenneth, ed. *The Alaska Highway. Papers of the 40th Anniversary Symposium*. Vancouver: University of British Columbia Press, 1992.

Coates, Kenneth, and Morrison, William R. *The Alaska Highway in World War II: The U.S. Army of Occupation in Canada's Northwest*. Norman: University of Oklahoma Press, 1992.

Cohen, Jean-Louis, and Hartmut Frank, eds. *Les relations franco-allemandes 1940–1950 et leurs effets sur l'architecture et la forme urbaine*. Paris and Hamburg: École d'Architecture Paris-Villemin, Hochschule für bildende Künste, 1989.

Colomina, Beatriz. *Domesticity at War*. Barcelona: Actar, 2006.

Colomina, Beatriz, Annemarie Brennan and Jeannie Kim, eds. *Cold War Hothouses. Inventing Postwar Culture, from Cockpit to Playboy*. New York: Princeton Architectural Press, 2004.

Cooke, Alistair. *The American Home Front, 1941–1942*. New York: Atlantic Monthly Press, 2006.

Cooke, Jeffrey. *The Architecture of Bruce Goff*. London: Granada, 1978.

Cruickshank, Charles. *Deception in World War II*. Oxford and New York: Oxford University Press, 1979.

Cuff, Dana. *The Provisional City. Los Angeles Stories of Architecture and Urbanism*. Cambridge, Mass.: MIT Press, 2000.

Davies, Jennifer. *The Wartime Kitchen and Garden*. London: BBC Books, 1993.

De Long, David G. *Bruce Goff. Toward Absolute Architecture*. Cambridge, Mass., and New York: MIT Press, The Architectural History Foundation, 1988.

De Magistris, Alessandro, ed. *URSS anni '30-50. Paesaggi dell'utopia staliniana*. Milan: Mazzotta, 1997.

Decker, Julie, and Chris Chiei, eds. *Quonset Hut: Metal Living for a Modern Age*. New York: Princeton Architectural Press, 2005.

Della Volpe, Nicola. *Difesa del territorio e protezione antiaerea (1915–1943)*. Rome: Marchese grafiche editoriali, 1986.

Diefendorf, Jeffry M. *In the Wake of War: The Reconstruction of German Cities after World War II*. New York and Oxford: Oxford University Press, 1993.

Diller, Liz, and Ricardo Scofidio, eds. *Visites aux armées: tourismes de guerre / Back to the Front: Tourism of War*. Caen and New York: FRAC Basse Normandie, Princeton Architectural Press, 1994.

Dover, H. *Home Front Furniture: British Utility Design 1941–1951*. Aldershot: Scolar Press, 1991.

Doxiadis, Constantinos. *The Sacrifices of Greece in the Second World War*. Athens: Ministry of Reconstruction, 1946.

Duis, Perry R., and Scott La France. *We've Got a Job to Do. Chicagoans and World War II*. Chicago: Chicago Historical Society, 1993.

Duménil, Anne, Nicolas Beaupré and Christian Ingrao, eds. *1914–1945, l'ère de la guerre: violence, mobilisation, deuil*. Paris: Agnès Viénot, 2004.

Durth, Werner. *Deutsche Architekten: biographische Verflechtungen, 1900–1970*. Braunschweig: F. Vieweg & Sohn, 1988.

Durth, Werner, and Niels Gutschow. *Träume in Trümmern: Planungen zum Wiederaufbau zerstörter Städte im Westen Deutschlands, 1940–1950*. Braunschweig: Friedr. Vieweg & Sohn, 1988.

Düwel, Jörn, and Niels Gutschow. *Fortgewischt sind alle überflüssigen Zutaten. Hamburg 1943: Zerstörung und Städtebau*. Berlin: Lukas Verlag, 2008.

Elwall, Robert. *Ernö Goldfinger*. London: Academy Editions, 1996.

Emmerson, Andrew, and Tony Beard. *London's Secret Tubes*, London: 2004.

Feldman, Gerald D. *Army, Industry, and Labor in Germany, 1914–1918*. Princeton, NJ: Princeton University Press, 1966.

Ferguson, Niall. *The War of the World: History's Age of Hatred*. London and New York: Allen Lane, 2006.

Fisher, David. *The War Magician*. New York: Coward-McCann, 1983.

Flinchum, Russell. *Henry Dreyfuss, Industrial Designer: the Man in* the Brown Suit. New York: Cooper-Hewitt National Design Museum, Rizzoli, 1997.

Foedrowitz, Michael. *Die Flaktürme in Berlin; Hamburg und Wien 1940–1950*. Wölfersheim-Berstadt: Podzun-Pallas, 1996.

Foedrowitz, Michael. *Bunkerwelten. Luftschutzanlagen in Norddeutschland*. Berlin: Ch. Links Verlag, 1998.

Foedrowitz, Michael. *Luftschutztürme und ihre Bauarten 1934–1945*. Eggolsheim: Nebel, 2003.

Forbes, Peter. *Dazzled and Deceived: Mimicry and Camouflage*. New Haven and London: Yale University Press, 2009.

Forty, George. *Fortress Europe: Hitler's Atlantic Wall*. Hersham, Surrey: Ian Allan, 2002.

Foss, Brian. *War Paint. Art, War, State and Identity in Britain 1939–1945*. New Haven: Yale University Press, 2007.

Fowle, Barry W., ed. *Builders and Fighters. US Army Engineers in World War II*. US Navy Corps of Engineers, 2005.

Francis, Paul. *British Military Airfield Architecture. From Airships to the Jet Age*. Sparkford, Somerset: Patrick Stephens Ltd, 1996.

Friedrich, Jörg. *The Fire: The bombing of Germany, 1940–1945*. New York: Columbia University Press, 2006.

Funck, Marcus, and Roger Chickering, eds. *Endangered Cities: Military Power and Urban Societies in the Era of the World Wars*. Boston: Brill Academic Publishers, 2004.

Fussell, Paul. *Wartime: Understanding and Behavior in the Second World War*. New York: Oxford University Press, 1989.

Gaffen, Fred. *The Road to Victory. A History of Canada in the Second World War. La route de la victoire. La participation du Canada à la Deuxième Guerre mondiale*. Ottawa: Canadian War Museum/Musée canadien de la guerre, 1995.

Garner, John S. *World War II Temporary Military Buildings. A Brief History of the Architecture and Planning of Cantonments and Training Stations in the United States*. Champaign, IL: US Army Corps of Engineers, Construction Engineering Research Laboratories, 1993.

Garnier, B., Jean Quellien, F. Passera and Odette Hardy-Hémery, eds. *La Main d'œuvre française exploitée par le IIIe Reich: actes du colloque international, Caen, 13–15 décembre 2001*. Caen: Centre de recherche d'histoire quantitative, 2003.

Gérard, Philip. *Secret Soldiers: How a Troupe of American Artists, Designers, and Sonic Wizards Won World War II's Battles of Deception Against the Germans*. New York: Dutton, 2002.

Giesler, Hermann. *Ein anderer Hitler: Bericht seines Architekten Hermann Giesler, Erlebnisse, Gespräche, Reflexionen*. Leoni am Starnberger See: Druffel, 1977.

Gluck, Sherna Berger. *Rosie the Riveter Revisited: Women, the War, and Social Change*. Boston: Twayne Publishers, 1987.

Goldberg, Alfred. *The Pentagon: The First Fifty Years*. Washington, D.C.: Historical Office, Office of the Secretary of Defense, 1992.

Goodden, Henrietta. *Camouflage and Art; Design and Deception in World War 2*. London: Unicorn Press, 2007.

Gorman, Michael John. *Buckminster Fuller: Designing for Mobility*. Milan: Skira, 2005.

Grasser, Kurt. *Westwall, Maginot-Linie, Atlantikwall: Bunker- und Festungsbau 1930–1945*. Leoni am Starnberger See: Druffel-Verlag, 1983.

Grayling, A. C. *Among the Dead Cities*. New York: Walker Publishing Company Inc., 2006.

Graziosi, Andrea. *Guerra e rivoluzione in Europa, 1905–1956*. Bologna: Il Mulino, 2001.

Gregg, John. *The Shelter of the Tubes*. London: Capital Transport Publishing, 2001.

Greif, Martin. *The New Industrial Landscape: the Story of The Austin Company*. Clinton, NJ: The Main Street Press, 1978.

Gröning, Gert, and Joachim Wolschke-Bulmahn. *Die Liebe zur Landschaft. Teil 3. Der Drang nach Osten. Zur Entwicklung der Landespflege im Nazionalsozialismus und in den 'eingegliederten Ostgebieten' während des Zweiten Weltkriegs*. Munich: Minerva, 1987.

Gropman, Alan, ed. *The Big 'L': American Logistics in World War II*. Washington: National Defense University Press, 1997.

Grüning, Michael. *Der Wachsmann-Report; Auskünfte eines Architekten*. Basel, Berlin and Boston: Birkhäuser, 2001.

Guidi, Guido. *Bunker: Along the Atlantic Wall*. Milan: Electa, 2006.

Gutman, Yisrael, and Michael Berenbaum, eds. *Anatomy of the Auschwitz Death Camp*. Bloomington, Indianapolis: Indiana University Press, 1994.

Gutschow, Niels. *Ordnungswahn: Architekten planen im 'eingedeutschten Osten' 1939–1945*. Gütersloh, Basel, Boston and Berlin: Bertelsmann Fachzeitschriften, Birkhäuser, 2001.

Gutschow, Niels, and Barbara Klain. *Vernichtung und Utopie : Stadtplanung Warschau 1939–1945*. Hamburg: Junius, 1994.

Hales, Peter Bacon. *Atomic Spaces: Living on the Manhattan Project*. Urbana: University of Illinois Press, 1997.

Harlander, Tilman, and Gerhardt Fehl, eds. *Hitlers Sozialer Wohnungsbau 1940–1945*. Hamburg: Christians, 1986.

Harpur, Brian. *A Bridge to Victory: the Untold Story of the Bailey Bridge*. London: HMSO, 1991.

Harris, Mark J., Franklin D. Mitchell and Steven Schecter. *The Homefront: America During World War II*. New York: G. P. Putnam's Sons, 1984.

Hartcup, Guy. *Code Name Mulberry. The Planning, Building and Operation of the Normandy Harbours*. Newton Abbott, London and Vancouver: David & Charles, 1977.

Hartcup, Guy. *Camouflage. A History of Concealment and Deception in War*. Newton Abbott, London and Vancouver: David & Charles, 1979.

Hartcup, Guy. *The Effect of Science on the Second World War*. London: Macmillan, 2000.

Hartmann, Susan M. *The Home Front and Beyond: American Women in the 1940s*. Boston: Twayne Publishers, 1982.

Hastings, Max. *Retribution. The Battle for Japan 1944–1945*. New York, Alfred A. Knopf, 2008.

Hauser, Kitty. *Shadow Sites: Photography, Archaeology, and the British Landscape, 1927–1955*. Oxford: Oxford University Press, 2007.

Hein, Carola, Jeffry M. Diefendorf and Ishida Yorifusa, eds. *Rebuilding Urban Japan After 1945*. Houndmills and New York: Palgrave Macmillan, 2003.

Helfrich, Kurt G. F., and William Whitaker, eds. *Crafting a Modern World: the Architecture and Design of Antonin and Noémi Raymond*. New York: Princeton Architectural Press, 2006.

Helphand, Kenneth I. *Defiant Gardens: Making Gardens in Wartime*. San Antonio: Trinity University Press, 2006.

Herbert, Gilbert. *The Dream of the Factory-Made House: Walter Gropius and Konrad Wachsmann*. Cambridge, Mass.: MIT Press, 1984.

Hilberseimer, Ludwig. *The New Regional Pattern. Industries and Gardens, Workshops and Farms*. Chicago: Paul Theobald, 1949.

Hildebrand, Grant. *Designing for Industry, the Architecture of Albert Kahn*. Cambridge, Mass.: MIT Press, 1974.

Hildebrand, Sonja. *Egon Eiermann. Die Berliner Zeit. Das architektonische Gesamtwerk bi 1945*. Braunschweig/Wiesbaden: Vieweg, 1999.

Hillier, Marlene P., Eberhard Jäckel and Jürgen Rohwer, eds. *Städte im Zweiten Weltkrieg, Ein internationaler Vergleich*. Essen: Klartext Verlag, 1991.

Hise, Greg. *Magnetic Los Angeles: Planning the Twentieth-Century Metropolis*. Baltimore: Johns Hopkins University Press, 1997.

Holden, C. H., and W. G. Holford. *The City of London. A Record of Destruction and Survival*. London: The Architectural Press, 1951.

Howard, Michael. *Strategic Deception in the Second World War*. New York and London: W. W. Norton & Co, 1990.

Hudemann, Rainer, and F. Walter, eds. *Villes et guerres mondiales en Europe au xxᵉ siècle*. Paris: L'Harmattan, 1997.

Hughes, Agatha C. , and Thomas P. Hughes, eds. *Systems, Experts, and Computers : the Systems Approach in Management and Engineering, World War II and After*. Cambridge, Mass.: MIT Press, 2000.

Irace, Fulvio, ed. *Carlo Mollino 1905–1973*. Milan: Electa, 1989.

Jarausch, Konrad H., and Martin Sabrow, eds. *Verletztes Gedächtnis: Erinnerungskultur und Zeitgeschichte im Konflikt*. Frankfurt am Main: Campus, 2002.

Jaskot, Paul. *The Architecture of Oppression: the SS, Forced Labor and the Nazi Monumental Building Economy*. London and New York: Routledge, 2000.

Jaskot, Paul, and Gavriel D. Rosenfeld, eds. *Twelve German Cities Confront The Nazi Past*. Ann Arbor: University of Michigan Press, 2008.

Johnson, Charles W., and Charles O. Johnson. *City Behind a Fence: Oak Ridge, Tennessee, 1942–1946*. Knoxville: University of Tennessee Press, 1981.

Jones, Peter. *Ove Arup. Masterbuilder of the Twentieth Century*. London and New Haven: Yale University Press, 2006.

Judt, Tony. *Postwar: a History of Europe Since 1945*. London and New York: Penguin Books, 2005.

Katz, Barry. *Foreign Intelligence: Research and Analysis in the Office of Strategic Services, 1942–1945*. Cambridge, Mass.: Harvard University Press, 1989.

Kaufmann, J. E., and Robert M. Jurga. *Fortress Europe. European Fortifications of World War II*. London: Greenhill Books, 1999.

Kaufmann, J. E., and H. W. Kaufmann. *Fortress France: the Maginot Line and French defenses in World War II*. Westport, CT: Praeger Security International, 2006.

Kelly, Burnham. *The Prefabrication of Houses*. Cambridge, Mass.: Technology Press/Wiley, 1951.

Kelly, Cynthia C., ed. *The Manhattan Project. The Birth of the Atomic Bomb in the Words of Its Creators, Eyewitnesses, and Historians*. New York: Black Dog & Leventhal Publishers, 2007.

Kemp, Anthony. *The Maginot Line. Myth and Reality*. London: Frederick Warne, 1981.

Kennett, Lee. *A History of Strategic Bombing. From the First Hot-Air Balloons to Hiroshima and Nagasaki*. New York: Scribner's, 1980.

Khristoforov, V. S., and V. S. Vinogradov. *Liubianka v dny bitvy za Moskvu*, Moscow: Zvonnitsa, 2002.

Kiley, Dan, and Jane Amidon. *Dan Kiley. The Complete Works of America's Master Landscape Architect*. Boston, New York and London: Bulfinch Press, 1999.

Kimpel, Harald, ed. *Innere Sicherheit: Bunker-Ästhetik*. Marburg: Jonas Verlag, 2006.

Kirkham, Pat, and David Thoms, eds. *War Culture: Social Change and Changing Experience in World War Two Britain*. London: Lawrence & Wishart, 1995.

Kleinmanns, Joachim, and Christiane Weber, eds. *Fritz Leonhardt 1909-1999. Die Kunst des Konstruierens*. Stuttgart and London: Edition Axel Menges, 2009.

Kyrtsis, Alexandros-Andreas. *Constantinos A. Doxiadis: Texts, Design Drawings, Settlements*. Athens: Ikaros, 2006.

Laar, Paul van de, and Koos Hage, eds. *Brandgrens Rotterdam 1930 / 2010*. Bussum: Uitgeverij Thoth, 2010.

Lamonaca, Marianne, and Sarah Schleuning. *Weapons of Mass Dissemination: the Propaganda of War.* Miami Beach: The Wolfsonian, Florida International University, 2004.

Lange, Thomas H. *Peenemünde. Analyse einer Technologie-entwicklung im Dritten Reich.* Düsseldorf: VDI Verlag 2006.

Le Cour Grandmaison, Olivier. *Coloniser, exterminer: sur la guerre et l'État colonial.* Paris: Fayard, 2005.

Lemke, Bernd. *Luftschutz in Großbritannien und Deutschland 1923 bis 1939.* Munich: R. Oldenbourg Verlag, 2005.

Leonhardt, Fritz. *Baumeister in einer umwälzenden Zeit. Erinnerungen.* Stuttgart: Deutsche Verlags-Anstalt, 1984.

Light, Jennifer, S. *From Warfare to Welfare: Defense Intellectuals and Urban Problems in Cold War America.* Baltimore: Johns Hopkins University Press, 2003.

Lindqvist, Sven. *A History of Bombing. Translated by Linda Haverty Rugg.* New York: W. W. Norton & Co, 2001.

Lotchin, Roger W. *The Bad City in the Good War. San Francisco, Oakland, and San Diego.* Bloomington, Indianapolis: Indiana University Press, 2003.

Lowe, Keith. *Inferno: The Devastation of Hamburg, 1943.* New York: Viking, 2007.

Lukacs, John. *The Legacy of the Second World War.* New Haven, London: Yale University Press, 2010.

MacIsaac, David. *Strategic Bombing in World War Two: the Story of the United States Strategic Bombing Survey.* New York: Garland, 1976.

Madajczyk, Czesław, ed. *Vom Generalplan Ost zum Generalsiedlungsplan.* Munich, New Providence, London and Paris: K. H. Saur, 1993.

Maguire, Patrick J., and Jonathan M. Woodham. *Design and Cultural Politics in Post-War Britain: the 'Britain Can Make it' Exhibition of 1946.* London and New York: Leicester University Press, 1997.

Malinina, Tatiana, ed. *Iz istorii sovetskoi arkhitektury 1941–1945*

gg.: Dokumenty i materialy. Moscow: Nauka, 1978.

Mallory, Keith, and Arvid Ottar. *The Architecture of War.* New York: Pantheon Books, 1973.

Marín, Fernando. *Engaños de guerra. La acciones de decepción en los conflictos belicos.* Barcelona: Inédita editores, 2004.

Marwick, Arthur. *Britain in the Century of Total War: War, Peace, and Social Change, 1900–1967.* Boston: Little, Brown and Co., 1968.

Mazower, Mark. *Inside Hitler's Greece: the Experience of Occupation, 1941–44.* New Haven: Yale University Press, 1993.

Mazower, Mark. *Hitler's Empire: How the Nazis Ruled Europe.* New York: The Penguin Press, 2008.

McLaine, Ian. *Ministry of Morale: Home Front Morale and the Ministry of Information in World War II.* London and Boston: Allen & Unwin, 1979.

Meilinger, Phillip S., ed. *The Paths of Heaven: The Evolution of Air Power Theory.* Maxwell Air Force Base, Alabama: Air University Press, 1997.

Melvin, Jeremy. *FRS Yorke and the Evolution of English Modernism.* Chichester and Hoboken, NJ: Wiley-Academy, 2003.

Mengeringhausen, Max. *Raumfachwerke aus Stäben und Knoten : Theorie, Planung, Ausführung.* Wiesbaden and Berlin: Bauverlag, 1975.

Mens, Noor *W. G. Witteveen en Rotterdam.* Rotterdam: Uigeverij 010, 2007.

Messenger, Charles. *The Century of Warfare. Worldwide Conflict from 1900 to the Present Day.* London: HarperCollins, 1995.

Michaud, Eric. *Un art de l'éternité. L'image et le temps du National-socialisme.* Paris: Gallimard, 1996.

Middleton, Drew. *Crossroads of Modern Warfare.* Garden City, NY: Doubleday, 1983.

Milleris, Algirdas, and Annie Périssel. *Bunker. Gegenbilder eines Mythos. L'envers du mythe. Beyond the Myth.* Neustadt an der Aisch: Ph. C. W. Schmidt, 1999.

Milward, Alan S. *War, Economy, and Society, 1939–1945.* Berkeley: University of California Press, 1977.

Monegal, Antonio, and Francesc Torres, eds. *At War.* Barcelona: Centre de Cultura Contemporània, 2004.

Mosse, George L. *Fallen Soldiers: Reshaping the Memory of the World Wars.* New York and Oxford: Oxford University Press, 1990.

Motte, Martin, and Frédéric Thébault, eds. *Guerre, idéologie, populations 1911–1946.* Paris: L'Harmattan, 2005.

Nash, Gerald D. *The American West Transformed: The Impact of the Second World War.* Lincoln and London: University of Nebraska Press, 1985.

Nash, Gerald D. *World War 2 and the West: Reshaping the Economy.* Lincoln: University of Nebraska Press, 1989.

Neder, Federico. *Fuller Houses. R. Buckminsger Fuller's Dymaxion Dwellings and Other Domestic Adventures.* Translated by Elsa Lam. Baden: Lars Müller, 2008.

Nelson, Donald Marr. *Arsenal of Democracy: the Story of American War Production.* New York: Harcourt, Brace and Co, 1946.

Nerdinger, Winfried, ed. *Bauhaus-Moderne im Nazionalsozialismus. Zwischen Anbiederung und Verfolgung.* Munich: Prestel, 1993.

Neufeld, Michael J. *The Rocket and the Reich. Peenemünde and the Coming of the Ballistic Missile Era.* New York: The Free Press, 1995.

Newark, Timothy. *Camouflage: Now You See Me, Now You Don't.* London: Thames & Hudson, 2007.

Nossack, Hans. *The End: Hamburg 1943.* Chicago: University of Chicago Press, 2004.

Nye, David E. *American Technological Sublime.* Cambridge, Mass.: MIT Press, 1994.

O'Brien, Terence H. *Civil Defence. History of the Second World War, United Kingdom Civil Series.* London: Her Majesty's Stationery Office, 1955.

Oberle, Clara Magdalena. *City in Transit: Ruins, Railways, and the Search for Order in Postwar Berlin (1945–1948)*. Ph.D thesis, University of Princeton, 2006.

Olmo, Carlo, ed. *Mirafiori 1936–1962*. Milan: Umberto Allemandi, 1997.

Olwell, Russell B. *At Work in the Atomic City: a Labor and Social History of Oak Ridge*. Knoxville: University of Tennessee Press, 2004.

Partridge, Colin. *Hitler's Atlantic Wall*. Guernesey: D. I. Publications, 1976.

Pelkonen, Eeva-Liisa. *Alvar Aalto: Architecture, Modernity, and Geopolitics*. New Haven: Yale University Press, 2009.

Pelt, Robert Jan van, and Deborah Dwork. *Auschwitz: 1270 to the present*. New Haven and London: Yale University Press, 1996.

Pevsner, Nikolaus. *Visual Planning and the Picturesque*. Edited by Mathew Aitchison, Los Angeles: Getty Research Institute, 2010.

Pfeiffer, Bruce Brooks, and Robert Wojtowitz, eds. *Frank Lloyd Wright + Lewis Mumford: Thirty Years of Correspondence*. New York: Princeton Architectural Press, 2001.

Pogačnik, Marco, ed. *Il segno della memoria; BBPR, Monumento ai caduti nei campi nazisti, 1945–1995*. Milan: Electa, 1995.

Popov, A. N. *Amerikanskoe stroitelstvo*. New York: Amtorg Trading Co, 1946.

Portelli, Alessandro. *L'ordine è già stato eseguito. Roma, le Fosse Ardeatine, la memoria*. Rome: Donzelli, 2005.

Pressac, Jean-Claude. *Les Crématoires d'Auschwitz, la machinerie du meurtre de masse*. Paris: CNRS Éditions, 1993.

Prigge, Walter, ed. *Ernst Neufert: normierte Baukultur im 20. Jahrhundert*. Frankfurt am Main: Campus, 1999.

Pujadó i Puigdomènech, Judit. *Oblits de reraguarda: els refugis antiaeris a Barcelona (1936–1939)*. Barcelona: Federació de l'edificació de Catalunya, 1998.

Pulos, Arthur J. *The American Design Adventure, 1940–1975*. Cambridge, Mass.: MIT Press, 1988.

Ratti, Marzia. *Non mi avrete : disegni da Mauthausen e Gusen: la testimonianza di Germano Facetti e Lodovico Belgiojoso*. La Spezia: Istituzione per i servizi culturali, 2006.

Raymond, Antonin. *An Autobiography*. Rutland, VT: C. E. Tuttle, 1973.

Recker, Marie-Luise. *Die Großstadt als Wohn- und Lebensbereich im Nationalsozialismus. Zur Gründung der 'Stadt des KdF-Wagens'*. Frankfurt am Main: Campus, 1981.

Reinhard, Oliver, Matthias Neutzner and Wolfgang Hesse, eds. *Das rote Leuchten. Dresden und der Bombenkrieg*. Dresden: Edition Sächsische Zeitung, 2005.

Reit, Seymour. *Masquerade. The Amazing Camouflage Deceptions of World War II*. New York: Hawthorn Books, Inc., 1978.

Reitsam, Charlotte. *Das Konzept der 'bodenständigen Gartenkunst' Alwin Seiferts: fachliche Hintergründe und Rezeption bis in die Nachkriegszeit*. Frankfurt am Main and New York: P. Lang, 2001.

Reynolds, Jonathan M. *Maekawa Kunio and the Emergence of Japanese Modernist Architecture*. Berkeley: University of California Press, 2001.

Richard, Lionel. *L'Art et la guerre: les artistes confrontés à la Seconde Guerre mondiale*. Paris: Flammarion, 1995.

Rimpl, Herbert. *Die geistigen Grundlagen der Baukunst unserer Zeit*. Munich: Verlag Georg D. W. Callwey, 1953.

Robert, Jean-Louis, and Jay Winter, eds. *Capital Cities at War*. Cambridge: Cambridge University Press, 1996.

Rolf, Rudi. *Der Atlantikwall, Perlenschnur aus Stahlbeton*. Beetsterzwaag: AMA-Verlag, 1983.

Rorimer, James J. *Survival. The Salvage and Protection of Art in War*. New York: Abelard Press, 1950.

Rössler, Mechthild, and Sabine Schleiermacher, eds. *Der 'Generalplan Ost'. Hauptlinien der nationalsozialistischen Planungs- und Vernichtungspolitik*. Berlin: Akademie Verlag, 1993.

Rzhekhina, Olga I., R.N. Blashkevich and R. G. Burova. *A. K. Burov*. Moscow: Stroiizdat, 1984.

Saint, Andrew. *Towards a Social Architecture: the Role of School Building in Post-War England*. New Haven: Yale University Press, 1987.

Sakudo, Jun, and Takao Shiba, eds. *World War II and the Transformation of Business Systems: the International Conference on Business History 20. Proceedings of the Fuji Conference*. Tokyo: University of Tokyo Press, 1994.

Schlicht, Sandra. *Krieg und Denkmalpflege: Deutschland und Frankreich im Zweiten Weltkrieg*. Schwerin: Helms, 2007.

Schmal, Helga, and Tobias Selke. *Bunker: Luftschutz und Luftschutzbau in Hamburg*. Hamburg: Christians, 2001.

Schneider, Christian. *Stadtgründungen im Dritten Reich: Wolfsburg und Salzgitter. Ideologie, Ressortpolitik, Repräsentation*. Munich: Heinz Moos Verlag, 1979.

Schütte-Lihotzky, Margarete. *Erinnerungen aus dem Widerstand 1938–1945*. Edited by Chup Friemert. Hamburg: Konkret Literatur Verlag, 1985.

Sebald, Winfried Georg. *On the Natural History of Destruction*. Translated by Anthea Bell. New York: Random House, 2004.

Sellier, André. *Histoire du camp de Dora*. Paris: La Découverte, 2010.

Sforza, Michele. *La città sotto il fuoco della guerra*. Turin: Allemandi, 1998.

Shale, Richard. *Donald Duck Joins Up: the Walt Disney Studio during World War II*. Ann Arbor: UMI Research Press, 1982.

Shanken, Andrew M. *194X. Architecture, Planning, and Consumer Culture on the American Home Front. Minneapolis: University of Minnesota Press, 2009.

Showell, Jak P. Mallmann. *Hitler's U-Boat Bases*. Annapolis: Naval Institute Press, 2002.

Simini, Massimo, ed. *Dal lager. Disegni di Lodovico Belgiojoso*. Milan: Edizioni delle Raccolte storiche del comune di Milano, 2008.

Sladen, C. *The Conscription of Fashion: Utility Cloth, Clothing and Footwear 1941–1952*. Scholar Press, 1995.

Smith, Harold J. *War and Social Change: British Society in the Second World War*. Manchester: Manchester University Press, 1986.

Speer, Albert. *Inside the Third Reich*. New York: Simon and Schuster, 1970.

Stanley II, R. M. *To Fool a Glass Eye: Camouflage Versus Photo Reconnaissance in World War II*. Washington, D.C.: Smithsonian Press, 1998.

Stevenson, Greg. *Palaces for the People: Prefabs in Post-war Britain*. London: Batsford, 2003.

Stewart, Richard. *Design and British Industry*. London: John Murray, 1987.

Stüwe, Botho. *Peenemünde-West. Die Erprobungsstelle der Luftwaffe für geheime Fernlenkwaffen und deren Entwicklungsgeschichte*. Esslingen and Munich: Bechtle, 1995.

Sulzer, Peter. *Jean Prouvé: Complete Works. Vol. 2, 1934–1944*. Basel, Boston and Berlin: Birkhäuser, 2000.

Tamms, Friedrich. *Von Menschen, Städten und Brücken*, Vienna and Düsseldorf: Econ Verlag, 1974.

Thoms, David. *War, Industry, and Society: the Midlands, 1939–45*. London and New York: Routledge, 1989.

Treib, Marc, ed. *An Everyday Modernism: the Houses of William Wurster*. Berkeley: University of California Press, 1995.

Twichell, Heath. *Northwest Epic: The Building of the Alaska Highway*. New York: Saint Martin's Press, 1992.

Vale, Brenda. *Prefabs: A History of the U.K. Temporary Housing Programme*. London: Spon, 1995.

Vanstiphout, Wouter. *Rotterdam en de architectuur van J. H. van den Broek*. Rotterdam: Uitgeverij 010, 2005.

Verge, Arthur C. *Paradise Transformed: Los Angeles During the Second World War*. Dubuque, Iowa: Kendall//Hunt Publishing Co, 1993.

Virilio, Paul. *Esthétique de la disparition*. Paris: Galilée, 1989.

Virilio, Paul. *Bunker Archeology*. New York: Princeton Architectural Press, 1994.

Virilio, Paul, and Marianne Brausch. *Voyage d'hiver, entretiens*. Marseille: Parenthèses, 1997.

Vogel, Steve. *The Pentagon, a History: the Untold Story of the Wartime Race to Build the Pentagon – and to Restore it Sixty Years Later*. New York: Random House, 2007.

Voigt, Wolfgang. *Planifier et construire dans les territoires annexés, architectes allemands en Alsace de 1940 à 1944*. Strasbourg: Publications de la société savante d'Alsace, 2008.

Volchok, Yuri, ed. *40 Let velikoi pobedy*. Moscow: Stroiizdat, 1985.

Voldman, Danièle. *La Reconstruction des villes françaises de 1940 à 1954: histoire d'une politique*. Paris: L'Harmattan, 1997.

Voldman, Danièle, and Frédérique Boucher. *Les Architectes sous l'Occupation*. Paris: Institut d'histoire du temps présent, 1992.

Wachsmann, Konrad. *The Turning Point of Building; Structure and Design*. New York: Reinhold Pub. Corp., 1961.

Wagenaar, Cor. *Welvaaarsstad in wording. De wederopbouw van Rotterdam 1940–1952*. Rotterdam: NAi Uitgevers, 1992.

Wagner, Jens Christian. *Produktion des Todes. Das KZ Mittelbau-Dora*. Göttingen: Wallstein, 2004.

Wallis, Allan D. *Wheel Estate: The Rise and Decline of Mobile Homes*. Baltimore: Johns Hopkins University Press, 1991.

Warburton, Nigel. *Ernö Goldfinger: the Life of an Architect*. London: Routledge, 2004.

Wasser, Bruno. *Himmlers Raumplanung im Osten. Der Generalplan Ost in Polen 1940-1944*. Basle, Berlin and Boston: Birkhäuser Verlag, 1993.

Welch, Philip B., ed. *Goff on Goff: Conversations and Lectures*. Norman: University of Oklahoma Press, 1996.

White, R. B. *Prefabrication. A History of its Development in Great Britain*. London: Her Majesty's Stationery Office, 1965.

Wiechmann, Günter. *Peenemünde-Karlshagen 1937–1943. Die geheime Siedlung der Wissenschaftler, Techniker und Arbeiter*. Frankfurt am Main: Peter Lang, 2006.

Wilburn, James Richard. *Social and Economic Aspects of the Aircraft Industry in Metropolitan Los Angeles During World War II*. Los Angeles: UCLA, 1971.

Williamson, Gordon. *U-Boat Bases and Bunkers 1941-45*. Oxford: Osprey Publishing, 2005.

Yenne, Bill. *The American Aircraft Industry in World War II*. St Paul, Minn.: MBI Publishing Co., 2006.

Zevi, Adachiara. *Fosse Ardeatine*. Rome and Turin: Testo e Immagine, 2000.

Zilbert, Edward R. *Albert Speer and the Nazi Ministry of Arms: Economic Institutions and Industrial Production in the German War Economy*. Rutherford, N.J., and London: Fairleigh Dickenson University Press, Associated University Presses, 1981.

Author's acknowledgements

I would like to thank all those who enabled me to progress from my initial intuitions of the mid-1990s as to the possibility of carrying out this project to actually being in a position to conceive an exhibition and publish a book some fifteen years later. Some names will appear more than once in this list, because the role of each individual over the course of this long gestation period has sometimes changed.

The collegial interlocutors, readers and sources of information and useful material include: Nico Gautier, who is familiar with the fortifications of The Hague; Thomas Hines, who provided me with a letter from Maxwell Fry to Richard Neutra; Niall Hobhouse, who referred me to the article on the 'Battle of the Railings'; Benoît Jacquet, who shared his knowledge of Japanese projects; Timo Keihänen, who directed me to Finnish buildings; Valentina Mulas, who explored Italian collections; Joan Ockman, who provided illuminating conclusive remarks at the 2009 New York symposium; Carlo Olmo, whose encouragement and careful reading of the manuscript were invaluable as always; Nicholas Olsberg, whose initial enthusiasm propelled the project forward and whose later suggestions were stimulating; Enrique Ramirez, whose research on Dugway was illuminating; Nina Rappaport, who revealed the secrets of the 'windowless' factories to me, and Michal Wisniewski, who elucidated a mystery about Kraków.

I would also like to thank the directors and staff of the libraries and archives and the curators of the various collections that my research led me to: at the Baukunstarchiv at the Akademie der Künste, Eva-Maria Barkhofen; at the Architekturmuseum der Technische Universität in Munich, Winfried Nerdinger and Anja Schmidt; at the École Nationale Supérieure des Beaux-Arts in Paris, Elisabeth Colas-Adler; at the Fondation Le Corbusier, Michel Richard and Arnaud Dercelles; at the Frances Loeb Library of the Harvard University Graduate School of Design, Mary Daniels and Inés Zalduendo; at the archives of the Illinois Institute of Technology, Ralph Pugh; at the Archives d'Architecture du XXᵉ Siècle of the Institut Français d'Architecture, David Peyceré and Alexandre Ragois; at the Shchusev State Museum of Architecture, the sadly deceased David Sarkisyan, Irina Korobina, Pavel Kuznetsov and Elizaveta Pashina; at the Auschwitz-Birkenau State Museum, Szymon Kowalski; at the Turin Politecnico, Elena Tamagno and Sergio Pace; at the Royal Institute of British Architects, Irena Murray and Charles Hind; at the Harry Ransom Center of the University of Texas at Austin, Rick Watson; at the Wolfsonian, Cathy Leff and Kim Bergen; as well as Niels Gutschow and Koos Bosma.

During my stay at the Getty Research Institute in spring 2009, the library team provided me with precious support: Jacob Stewart Halevy vigorously accelerated the pace of research, while Rachel Eisley was checking on and obtaining essential images from the National Archives and Record Administration in Washington. I am also grateful to Pierre-Édouard Latouche, whose deep knowledge of the collections of the Canadian Centre for Architecture enriched both this work and the exhibition it accompanies.

I also would like to thank the students who participated in seminars over the course of the five years on both coasts of North America and on both sides of the Atlantic, where a stimulating dialogue unfolded.

I would like to express my appreciation for the contributions at the Institute of Fine Arts, in spring 2005, of Richard Anderson, Helen Gyger, Maggie Hartnick, Karen Hung, Lauren Jacobi, Elsa Lam, Emanuele Lugli, Jamie Melin and Susan Schafer; I would also like to thank Deanna Sheward, Matico Josephson, Johanna Blokker and Kat Koh for their subsequent help.

At the Princeton University Graduate School of Architecture, I would like to thank the dean, Stan Allen and Joaquim Moreno, the teaching assistant, in a memorable seminar in spring 2008 that included Pep Aviles, Julia Chapman, Alexis Cohen, Craig Cook, Alicia Imperiale, Sarah Jazmine Fugate, Aris Kardasis, Thomas Kelley, Joy Knoblauch, Diana Kurkovsky, Tamicka Marcy, Masha Panteleyeva, Enrique Ramirez, Amie Shao, Dayun Shin, Molly Steenson, Sarah Stevens, Samuel Stewart Halevy, Andrea Wong and Yee Man Wong.

At the Department of Architecture and Urban Design of the University of California, Los Angeles, where I taught an intense seminar in spring 2009, made possible by Sylvia Lavin and Dana Cuff, I would like to thank Rebecca Lyn Cooper, Xárene Eskandar, Jonathan Frommer, Daniella Gohari, Matthew Gilio-Tenan, Kimberly Henry, Esra Kahveci – who was an efficient assistant – Sergio Lopez Figueiredo, Brigid McManama, Susan Nwankpa, Heiner Pflugfelder, Brian Sahotsky, Alexandra Schioldager, Cristina Toma, Pelin Yoncaci and Claudia Ziegler.

And finally at the Architecture School of the Université de Montréal, where a seminar and studio was held in autumn 2009, with the help of the Canadian Centre for Architecture, I would like to express my appreciation to the director, Anne Cormier, and to Stephan Kowal, who energetically organised the day-to-day work, as well as the students Maryse Barette, Elsa Brès, Josiane Crampé, Corinne Deleers, Marie-Véronique Dionne, Virginie Fortin-Dapozzo, Ivan Hon, Reza Kananian, Sarah Lavallière, David Merlin, Hélène Plamondon, Alex de Repentigny, Antoine Wang and, in particular, Maxime Leclerc and Victor Maréchal, who continued their work in the context of the exhibition.

This study was enriched by contributions from the audiences at academic conferences where I put forward and discussed various hypotheses, especially at the University of Texas at Austin, Cornell University, the Architectural Association, the Roma Tre University, the Universidade Federal do Porto Alegre, the Moscow Architecture Institute and the Hafen-City Universität of Hamburg.

The organisers, moderators and participants at the two events held in New York and Milan broadened the scope of my reflection by adding their specific contributions, and I would like to extend my warm appreciation to the organisers of the 'Front to Rear' symposium held in March 2009, with the support of the Institute of Fine Arts, Princeton University and the Canadian Centre for Architecture, in particular to Anna Jozefacka and Susan Schafer and to all the participants: Lucia Allais, Pep Aviles, Maristella Casciato, Jeffry Diefendorf, Maria Dimitrieva-Einhorn, Hartmut Frank, Carola Hein, Alicia Imperiale, Paul Jaskot, Benoît Jacquet, Joy Knoblauch, Roland May, Eeva-Liisa Pelkonen, Antoine Picon, Enrique Ramirez, Vladimir Šlapeta, Ioanna Theocharopoulou, Pieter Uyttenhove, Anna Vallye, Anthony Vidler and Roberto Zancan.

My warmest thanks also go to Patrizia Bonifazio, who organised the 'War Perspectives' conference at the Politecnico in Milan, in January 2010, in collaboration with the Canadian Centre for Architecture, and to all the participants: Pier Luigi Bassignana, Gaia Caramellino, Maristella Casciato, Eray Cayli, Alessandro De Magistris, Filippo De Pieri, Davide Deriu, Hartmut Frank, Oscar Gaspari, Roberta Grignolo, Chiara Ingrosso, Andrea Maglio, Javier Martínez, Luca Mocarelli, Luca Molinari, Carlo Olmo, Serena Pesenti, Antonio Pizza, Francesca Romana Castelli, Piero Ostilio Rossi, Ulla Salmela, Roze Tzalmona, Annalisa Viati Navone and Inés Zalduendo.

Everyone knows how many different skills must be mobilised to transform a manuscript into a published work, and I would like to express my profound gratitude to the team at the Canadian Centre for Architecture, which was unsparing in its efforts: its founder and president Phyllis Lambert, whose commitment made the project possible, its receptive and courageous director Mirko Zardini, Meredith Carruthers, Daria Der Kaloustian – the rigorous and realistic coordinator of the book – Theodora Doulamis, Laura Killam, Sébastien Larivière, Natasha Leeman, and Émilie Retailleau – the enthusiastic coordinator of the exhibition. Finally, I would like to thank Christian Hubert for his expertise in translating the work from French into English, as well as the Hazan team – Jean-François Barrielle, Anne-Isabelle Vannier and Laure Pétrissans, as well as the editor of the English version, Bernard Wooding.

Copyrights and photography credits

p. 10 (top left) Photograph: Charles Alexander
p. 10 (top right), p. 387 (top) Courtesy of the Frances Loeb Library, Harvard Graduate School of Design
p. 17 © Fondazione Adriano Olivetti
p. 20, p. 23, p.61, p. 62, p. 103, p. 145, p. 146–147, p. 254 © FLC / SODRAC (2011)
p. 25 www.louis-leygue.fr
p. 27, p. 57, p. 65 © Hanley Wood
p. 30, p. 126, p. 210, p. 376–377, p. 391, p. 412–413 (bottom), p. 414 © Shchusev State Museum of Architecture
p. 32, p. 337, p. 368 (top left) © Estate of Henry Bernard / SODRAC (2011)
p. 33 (bottom) © André Lurçat / SODRAC (2011)
p. 34 © Editoriale Domus S.p.A., Rozzano (Milano) All rights reserved.
p. 35, p. 56, p. 74, p. 110, p. 158, p. 191, p. 212, p. 240 (top), p. 333, p. 334, p. 335, p. 336, p. 369, p. 385 © The Architectural Review
p. 38–39 Mary Evans Picture Library
p. 40, p. 41 Smithsonian Institution
p. 42 © State Museum of the History of St. Petersburg
p. 44–45 NAi, Rotterdam BROX_635t1339
p. 48–49, p. 50, p. 51, p. 52, p. 53 © Estate of August Sander / SODRAC (2011)
p. 58, p. 320 IIT Archives (Chicago)
p. 59 © Eames Office, LLC (eamesoffice.com). Library of Congress, Prints & Photographs Division
p. 60 Photograph: © The Metropolitan Museum of Art / Art Resource, NY
p. 63, p. 83 © Casabella
p. 64, p. 67, p. 68, p. 142 (bottom), p. 155, p. 157, p. 401 © L'Architecture d'aujourd'hui
p. 70 © L'Illustration / www.pixplanete.com
p. 71, p. 77, p. 140, p. 151, p. 198, p. 343 (right) Photograph: Silvia Ros
p. 72, p. 115, p. 338, p. 339, p. 341, p. 396 © The Museum of Modern Art / Licensed by SCALA / Art Resource, NY
p. 73 Photograph: © Denis Farley
p. 84–85, p. 231 © Auguste Perret / UFSE / SAIF / 2011
p. 86, p. 86–87, p. 125, p. 285 (top) © Architectural Record
p. 88, p. 98, p. 132–133, p. 134, p. 135 (bottom), p. 136 (bottom), p. 137 (top) © Chicago History Museum, HB-06539, HB-07327-I, HB-07074-G, HB-07074-W, HB-07074-O, HB-07870-P, HB-07595-M, HB-06928-H, Hedrich-Blessing (Firm)
p. 90–91, p. 92–93, p. 135 (top), p. 136 (top), p. 137 (bottom), p. 138–139 © Albert Kahn Associates
p. 95, p. 109, p. 205 © Boeing
p. 101 (top), p. 276–277, p. 277, p. 309, p. 311, p. 314, p. 315, p. 316, p. 317, p. 318, p. 319 © Neufert-Stiftung, Germany
p. 101 (bottom) Photograph: Frédéric Harster © Région Alsace – Inventaire général
p. 102 © Otto Reich

444

Lenders

Anne Garde

Akademie der Künste,
Baukunstarchiv, Berlin

Architekturmuseum der
Technischen Universität München

Canadian War Museum

Cité de l'Architecture et
du Patrimoine / Archives
d'Architecture du xxᵉ Siècle

Jean-Louis Cohen

Department of Architecture and
Design, The Art Institute of Chicago

École Nationale Supérieure
des Beaux-Arts, Paris

Fondation Le Corbusier, Paris

Frances Loeb Library, Special
Collections Department, Harvard
University Graduate School of
Design

Guido Guidi

Harry Ransom Center,
The University of Texas at Austin

Sylvia Lavin & Greg Lynn

McGill Rare Books and Special
Collections, McGill University,
Montréal

MERO-TSK International GmbH
& Co. KG Exhibit Systems 97084
Würzburg

The Museum of Modern Art,
New York

National Film Board of Canada

RIBA Library Drawings and Archives
Collections

Shchusev State Museum of
Architecture

Elaine Stevens

The Liliane and David M. Stewart
Program for Modern Design

UCLA Library, Special Collections

Louis I. Kahn Collection,
The University of Pennsylvania
and the Pennsylvania Historical
and Museum Commission

Victoria and Albert Museum

The Wolfsonian – Florida
International University, Miami Beach,
Florida, The Mitchell Wolfson, Jr.
Collection

Credits

Guest Curator and Author
Jean-Louis Cohen

PUBLICATION

**Editorial Assistance
and Coordination**
Daria Der Kaloustian

Graphic Design (Hazan)
Sylvie Millet
Jean-Marc Barrier
(jacket's design)

**Editing
and coordination (Hazan)**
Bernard Wooding
Anne-Isabelle Vannier

Translation
Christian Hubert

Rights & Reproductions
Marc Pitre
Esther Ste-Croix

EXHIBITION

Exhibition Coordination
Emilie Retailleau

Administrative Coordination
Theodora Doulamis

Installation Design
WORK Architecture Company
(WORKac), New York

Graphic Design
Project Projects, New York

Design Development
Laura Killam
Sébastien Larivière

The exhibition catalogue
was prepared in part thanks
to the financial support of the
Graham Foundation for Advanced
Studies in the Fine Arts.
The CCA would also like to thank
the Ministère de la Culture,
des Communications et de la
Condition féminine, the Canada
Council for the Arts, and the
Conseil des arts de Montréal
for their continuous support.

Published by the Canadian
Centre for Architecture and
Éditions Hazan to accompany
the exhibition *Architecture in
Uniform: Designing and Building
for the Second World War*,
presented at the CCA from
12 April to 5 September 2011 and
the Nederlands Architectuurinstitut
from 10 December 2011 to
25 March 2012.

Library of Congress
Cataloging-in-Publication
Data Number: 2011006761
A catalogue record for this book is
available from The British Library

Legal depot: April 2011
Printed and bound by
Grafiche Flaminia, Foligno, Italy
First edition
Printed on acid-free paper
Arctic the volume white 130g
Typeset in DIN
Photoengraving: Sogec, Turin

978-0-920785-92-8
Canadian Centre for Architecture
1920 rue Baile
Montréal, Québec
Canada H3H 2S6
www.cca.qc.ca

978-2-7541-0530-9
Éditions Hazan
Hachette Livre
58, rue Jean Bleuzen
92178 Vanves Cedex
Tel 01 41 23 67 44
Fax 01 41 23 64 37

Bibliothèque et Archives
nationales du Québec and
Library and Archives Canada
cataloguing in publication

Cohen, Jean-Louis
*Architecture in Uniform:
Designing and Building
for the Second World War*

Catalogue of an exhibition held
at the Canadian Centre for
Architecture, Montréal, Québec,
12 April–5 September, 2011.
Issued also in French under title:
Architecture en uniforme
Co-published by Éditions Hazan
Includes bibliographical
references and index

ISBN 978-0-920785-92-8
(Canadian Centre for Architecture)
ISBN 978-2-7541-0530-9 (Hazan)

1. Architecture, Modern -
20th century - Exhibitions.
2. World War, 1939–1945 -
Art and the war - Exhibitions.
3. Reconstruction (1939–1951) -
Exhibitions.
I. Canadian Centre for Architecture.
II. Title.

NA680.C64 2011
724'.607471428
C2010-942762-9